Business in Action

Canadian Edition

Business in Action

Canadian Edition

Courtland L. Bovée Grossmont College
John V. Thill Communication Specialists of America
Barbara E. Schatzman Keller Graduate School of Management
George Dracopoulos Vanier College
Peter Mombourquette Mount Saint Vincent University

Toronto

Library and Archives Canada Cataloguing in Publication

Business in action / Courtland L. Bovée ... [et al.]. — Canadian ed.

Includes bibliographical references and index.

ISBN 0-13-039096-8

1. Business—Textbooks. 2. Commerce—Textbooks. 3. Industrial management—Textbooks. I. Bovée, Courtland L.

HF1008.B89 2006 650 C2005-906111-1

0-13-039096-8

Vice President, Editorial Director: Michael J. Young
Acquisitions Editor: Karen Elliott
Director of Marketing, Business and Economics: Bill Todd
Senior Developmental Editor: Paul Donnelly
Production Editor: Mary Ann McCutcheon
Copy Editor: Susan Broadhurst
Production Coordinator: Andrea Falkenberg
Page Layout: Carolyn E. Sebestyen
Photo and Permissions Research: Alene McNeill
Art Director: Julia Hall
Cover Design: Anthony Leung
Cover Image: Larry Williams & Associates/Zefa/Corbis

1 2 3 4 5 10 09 08 07 06

Printed and bound in the United States.

Brief Contents

Contents

Preface

A GUIDED TOUR of the text that lets students experience Business in Action!

Business in Action lets students experience business firsthand through a variety of highly involving activities and real-world examples that no other textbook can match. Students will appreciate the broad selection of featured companies along with the text's user-friendly layout, manageable length, eye-catching graphics, conversational tone, and tie-in with Business PlanPro software. From the global economy to the world of small business, *Business in Action* takes students on an engaging exploration of the fundamentals, strategies, and dynamics that make the business world work.

Business in Action is a compelling model of today's most effective instructional techniques. The text uses an extraordinary number of devices that simplify teaching, promote active learning, stimulate critical thinking, and develop career skills. This text is the most effective teaching and learning tool you'll find for an introductory business course. As you'll see on the pages that follow, *Business in Action* will make your classes livelier, more relevant, and more enjoyable.

LEARN ABOUT THE FEATURES OF THIS EXCITING TEXT

Behind the Scenes

Chapter-Opening Vignette

Each chapter begins with a slice-of-life vignette that attracts student interest by vividly portraying a challenge faced by a company or businessperson. These opening cases help the student understand the origins of the company's growth and success. Each vignette ends with thought-provoking questions that draw students into the chapter.

Behind the SCENES

Canadian Home Renovation Centres: Strategic Battleground

www.rona.ca
www.homehardware.ca

During the past decade, the most notable change in the home renovation retail industry has been the expansion of Home Depot into the Canadian marketplace. However, two Canadian companies have chartered their own plans for growth and an increased share in this consolidating industry. Both firms offer an interesting look at evolving business models in the face of an ever-changing environment. Both firms are characterized by striking similarities despite recent strategic differences.

Rona and Home Hardware possess a shared history; they were both created to protect small independent hardware retailers from the threat of large industry discounters. Rona was initially founded in 1939 as a loose coalition of Quebec hardware merchants; by the 1960s the group had emerged as a dealer-owned cooperative. Around the same time, Walter Hatchborn founded Home Hardware in Ontario as a privately held dealer-owned cooperative. The company has not changed much in the past four decades.

Home Hardware and Rona represent two different business models in the increasingly competitive home renovation industry.

Chapter-Ending Case

Each chapter ends with a case that expands on the chapter-opening vignette. The case includes critical-thinking questions that require students to apply the concepts covered in the text. Plus, students can find out more about the company featured in the case by completing the "Learn More Online" exercise.

The authors' commitment to the case method does not end with the published text; case updates will be available on the website every six months. Students will not need to wait for a new edition or be forced to conduct detailed web searches to have access to the latest articles on the highlighted companies.

Behind the SCENES

Recruiting the Independent Retailer

An estimated 4500 independent retailers still control nearly 50 percent of the home renovation industry. The race to recruit them is intensifying between Home Hardware and Rona. Meanwhile, Home Depot continues to build more big-box stores and has also created a new smaller neighbourhood format (small by Home Depot standards). The small independents will continue to feel pressure to pick sides between the two active recruiters: Home Hardware and Rona. The following examines the options available to retailers with an existing operational store.

COMPARING BUSINESS MODELS

Home Hardware's cooperative network consists of more than 1000 owner-operated retail outlets. The system is served by regional warehouses that are stocked by a single companywide buying arm. Home Hardware also provides a nationwide marketing campaign that emphasizes the diversity of these outlets. Home Hardware is positioned as anti–big box, preferring to focus on service instead. According to Paul Strauss, this non-imposing approach is a key selling point, especially in rural areas.

Rona has a unique approach: it is a publicly traded company with various business models. It consists of a combination of big-box, medium-sized, and neighbourhood outlets with both corporate- and dealer-owned franchise stores as well as affiliated independent dealers. This allows it to absorb independent retailers of all sizes. According to CEO Robert Dutton, "With three types of ownership options and three types of stores the firm now offers nine

COSTS AND COMMITMENT

Rona expects an initial investment of $96 000 in Rona stock over a four-year period. It also expects its retailers to sign a 10-year contract. Home Hardware does not require a time commitment and the initial investment amounts to just $1500 in member fees.

FINAL THOUGHTS

Paul Strauss, Home Hardware's CEO, is very secretive about the company's plans and he points to this as one of the advantages of running a privately held organization. According to Strauss, his dealers and not some analyst on Bay Street are his first priority. In addition to keeping members informed and placing reasonable investment demands, this model champions the little guy. On the other hand, Rona's CEO, Robert Dutton, can point out that although there is a substantial initial investment, Rona's original dealers each now own $3 to $4 million worth of Rona shares because of the appreciation of their corporate stock. Rona also offers the flexibility of a hybrid system that includes corporate, franchise, and affiliated stores. Critics argue that there is a danger that the small independent affiliated store is so low on the pecking order that it doesn't have much say despite its commitment.

Rona's goal to capture 25 percent of the market will not be easy to attain. But its determination is unquestionable. As 2005 began, it was digesting a recent purchase of the 14-store, Alberta-based Totem Building Supplies Inc. for $100 million in cash. By mid-year Rona was aggressively pursu-

Learning Objectives

In each chapter, clearly stated learning objectives signal important concepts to be mastered. The end-of-chapter Summary of Learning Objectives reinforces basic concepts by reviewing chapter highlights for students.

Special Feature Boxes

There are 37 special feature boxes in the text. Each chapter contains between two and four boxes that make the world of business come alive with current examples to further enhance student learning. Each box includes two critical-thinking questions that are ideal for developing team or individual problem-solving skills.

Chapter 3 Practising Ethical Behaviour and Social Responsibility 67

Airline Espionage: Air Canada and WestJet Face Off

Air Canada and WestJet have been fighting to control air travel in Canada. The battle has now found a new runway: the courtroom. Air Canada has accused WestJet of using corporate spying to illegally access company information.

The following information may sound like something out of a James Bond film, but is actually a saga that describes the latest battleground for Canada's two largest airlines. In early 2004, Air Canada hired a private investigator who digitally reconstructed a WestJet executive's trash. Air Canada suspected this particular executive of tapping into its computers and attaining confidential information and filed a $220 million lawsuit in Ontario Superior Court. The central figure in this case is WestJet co-founder Mark Hill, who effectively acknowledges that he went to great lengths to understand the competition. However, Air Canada is not accusing him of harmless ambition; rather, they are building a case around foul play. The specific allegations are that a former employee, who now works for WestJet, allowed his employee code to be used thousands of times to gain valuable information on Air Canada's routes, seats sold, and load factor (percentage of available seats filled). Air Canada has even tried to implicate Clive Beddoe, WestJet's CEO, directly. In response, WestJet has accused Air Canada of grandstanding and says that the lawsuit is nothing more than an opportunity to attack the company publicly. This case is casting light on important ethical and legal issues. How far can a company go to gain competitive intelligence? What will the court rule in this spectacular case? Will the punishment fit the crime?[2]

Questions for Critical Thinking

1. Do you think that "dumpster diving" is an acceptable form of gathering market intelligence? Explain your answer.
2. Companies will often pursue employees from the competition in order to access valuable knowledge. Is this any different than accessing information from a competitor's website by using an ex-employee's code?

Video Cases

There are two video cases at the end of each of the six parts of the text. These cases help students see how real-life businesses and the people who run them apply fundamental business principles on a daily basis.

Chapter 3 Practising Ethical Behaviour and Social Responsibility 89

LEARNING OBJECTIVES

The purpose of this video is to help you

1. Identify the methods that governments use to stimulate growth and protect industries.
2. Recognize uncontrollable macroeconomic threats and implement appropriate protection measures.
3. Understand the obstacles and opportunities that companies face in the global economy.

Schwarzenegger, the "Terminator" governor, began a campaign to bring film production back to California. In addition, "reality TV" reduced the need for conventional television productions. Finally, because of global competition, dollars continued to flow out of Hollywood, but much of them began to flow past Canada to other low-cost locations such as Romania and Timbuktu. What does the future hold? It is difficult to predict, as doing business in the global economy is a dynamic challenge. The playing field can change in the blink of an eye, or in this case, in a single movie frame.

90 Part 1 Conducting Business in the Global Economy

LEARNING OBJECTIVES

The purpose of this video is to help you

1. Recognize the strategic challenges faced by a growing company.
2. Understand how supply and demand considerations affect product decisions.
3. Discuss how and why a company may shift production operations to other countries and other companies.

SYNOPSIS

Riding the wave of public interest in water sports, Body Glove began manufacturing wetsuits in the 1950s. The company's founders, dedicated surfers and divers, came up with the idea of making the wetsuits from neoprene, offering more comfortable insulation than the rubber wetsuits of the time. The high costs of neoprene and labour were major considerations in Body Glove's eventual decision to have its wetsuits manufactured in Thailand. The company's constant drive for higher quality was also a factor. Now company management can focus on building Body Glove's image as a California-lifestyle brand without worrying about inventory range of goods and services—from cellphone cases to flotation devices, footwear, resorts, and more—Body Glove has created a network of partners around the world.

Discussion Questions

1. *For analysis:* Even though Body Glove makes its wetsuits in Thailand, why must its managers continually research how domestic customers use its products?
2. *For application:* When deciding whether to license its name for a new product, what issues might Body Glove's managers research in advance?
3. *For debate:* Should the products that Body Glove does not manufacture be labelled to alert buyers that they are produced under license? Support your chosen position.

ONLINE EXPLORATION

Visit the Body Glove website, www.bodyglove.com, and follow the links to read the Body Glove story and see the variety of products sold under the Body Glove brand. Also look at the electronics products, including the cellphone cases. Then browse the contacts listing to find out which companies have licensed the Body Glove brand for various products. How do the licensed products fit with the Body Glove brand image? What challenges might Body Glove face in coordinating its

Test Your Knowledge

Questions for Review

Five end-of-chapter questions reinforce learning and help students review the chapter material.

Questions for Analysis

Five end-of-chapter questions help students analyze chapter material. One of these questions is ethics-based and is labelled "Ethical Considerations."

Questions for Application

Five end-of-chapter questions give students the opportunity to apply principles presented in the chapter material. Selected questions labelled "Integrated" ask students to tie material learned in previous chapters to the topics in the chapter they're currently studying.

TEST YOUR KNOWLEDGE

Questions for Review

1. What are the four basic forms of business ownership?
2. What is the difference between a general and a limited partnership?
3. What is a closely held corporation, and why do some companies choose this form of ownership?
4. What is the role of a company's board of directors?
5. What is culture clash?

Questions for Analysis

6. Why is it advisable for partners to enter into a formal partnership agreement?
7. To what extent do shareholders control the activities of a corporation?
8. How might a company benefit from having a diverse board of directors that includes representatives of several industries, countries, and cultures?
9. Why do so many mergers fail?
10. **Ethical Considerations.** Your father sits on the board of directors of a large, well-admired, public company. Yesterday, while looking for an envelope in his home office, you stumbled on a confidential memorandum. Unable to resist the temptation to read the memo, you discovered that your father's company is talking with another publicly traded company about the possibility of a merger, with your father's company being the survivor. Dollar signs flashed in your mind. Should the merger occur, the value of the other company's stock is likely to soar. You're tempted to log on to your E*Trade Canada account in the morning and place an order for 1000 shares of that company's stock. Better still, maybe you'll give a hot tip to your best friend in exchange for the four Nickelback tickets that your friend has been flashing in your face all week. Would either of those actions be unethical? Explain your answer.

Questions for Application

11. Suppose you and some friends want to start a business to take tourists on wilderness backpacking expeditions. None of you has much extra money, so your plan is to start small. However, if you are successful, you would like to expand into other types of outdoor tours and perhaps even open up branches in other locations. What form of ownership should your new enterprise take, and why?
12. Selling antiques on the Internet has become more successful than you originally imagined. Overnight your website has grown into a full-fledged business—now generating some $200 000 in annual revenue. It's time to think about the future. Several competing online antique dealers have approached you with a proposal to merge their website with yours to create the premier online antique store. The money sounds good, but you have some concerns about joining forces. What might they be? What other growth options should you consider before joining forces with another business?
13. **Integrated.** In Chapter 2 we discussed international strategic alliances and joint ventures. Why might a Canadian company want to enter into those types of arrangements instead of merging with a foreign concern?
14. **Integrated.** Look back at Chapter 4. How might each of the following small business scenarios affect your selection of a form of business ownership?
    a. You have decided to purchase a franchise operation instead of starting a business from scratch.
    b. You can't tap into your personal financial resources or rely on friends or family for financial assistance.
    c. You are a hard worker, visionary, a risk-taker, highly disciplined, and very bright. But you lack managerial experience.

Practise Your Knowledge

Sharpening Your Communication Skills

These exercises call on students to practise a wide range of communication activities, including one-on-one and group discussions, personal interviews, panel sessions, oral and written papers, and letter- and memo-writing assignments.

Building Your Team Skills

These exercises teach students important team skills, such as brainstorming, collaborative decision making, developing a consensus, debating, role playing, and resolving conflict.

PRACTISE YOUR KNOWLEDGE

SHARPENING YOUR COMMUNICATION SKILLS

You have just been informed that your employer is going to merge with a firm in Germany. Because you know very little about the German culture and business practices, you think it might be a good idea to do some preliminary research—just in case you have to make a quick trip overseas. Using the Internet or library sources, find information on the German culture and customs and prepare a short report discussing such cultural differences as German social values, decision-making customs, concepts of time, use of body language, social behaviour and manners, and legal and ethical behaviour.

BUILDING YOUR TEAM SKILLS

Directors often have to ask tough questions and make difficult decisions, as you will see in this exercise. Imagine that the director general of your college or university has just announced plans to retire. Your team, playing the role of the school's board of directors, must decide how to choose a new director general to fill this vacancy next semester.

First, generate a list of the qualities and qualifications you think the school should seek in a new director general. What background and experience would prepare someone for this key position? What personal characteristics should this individual possess? What questions would you ask to find out how each candidate measures up against the list of credentials you have prepared? Now list all the stakeholders that your team, as directors, must consider before deciding on a replacement for the retiring director general. Of these stakeholders, whose opinions do you think are most important? Whose are least important? Who will be directly and indirectly affected by the choice? Of these stakeholders, which should be represented as participants in the decision-making process?

Select a spokesperson to deliver a brief presentation to the class summarizing your team's ideas and the reasoning behind your suggestions. After all the teams have completed their presentations, discuss the differences and similarities among credentials proposed by all the teams for evaluating candidates. Then compare the teams' conclusions about stakeholders. Do all teams agree on the stakeholders who should participate in the decision-making process? Lead a classroom discussion on a board's responsibility to its stakeholders.

Expand Your Knowledge

Exploring Career Opportunities

Students are given the opportunity to explore career resources on campus, observe businesspeople in their jobs, interview businesspeople, and perform self-evaluations to assess their own career skills and interests.

Developing Your Research Skills

These exercises familiarize students with the wide variety of business reference material that's available, and they give students practice in developing research skills.

See It on the Web

End-of-chapter "See It on the Web" exercises acquaint students with the wealth of information on the web that relates to the content of each chapter. Students explore websites and answer questions that reinforce and extend chapter learning.

138 **Part 2** Starting and Organizing a Small Business

EXPAND YOUR KNOWLEDGE

DISCOVERING CAREER OPPORTUNITIES

Are you best suited to working as a sole proprietor, as a partner in a business, or in a different role within a corporation? For this exercise, select three businesses with which you are familiar: one run by a single person, such as a dentist's practice or a local landscaping firm; one run by two or three partners, such as a small accounting firm; and one that operates as a corporation, such as Petro-Canada or Telus.

1. Write down what you think you would like about being the sole proprietor, one of the partners, and the corporate manager or an employee in the businesses you have selected. For example, would you like having full responsibility for the sole proprietorship? Would you like being able to consult with other partners in the partnership before making decisions? Would you like having limited responsibility when you work for other people in the corporation?
2. Now write down what you might dislike about each form of business. For example, would you dislike the risk of bearing all legal responsibility in a sole proprietorship? Would you dislike having to talk with your partners before spending the partnership's money? Would you dislike having to write reports for top managers and shareholders of the corporation?
3. Weigh the pluses and minuses you have identified in this exercise. In comparison, which form of business most appeals to you?

DEVELOPING YOUR RESEARCH SKILLS

Review recent issues of business newspapers or periodicals (print or online editions) to find an article or series of articles illustrating one of the following business developments: merger, acquisition, hostile takeover, or leveraged buyout.

1. Explain in your own words what steps or events led to this development.
2. What results do you expect this development to have on (a) the company itself, (b) consumers, and (c) the industry the company is part of? Write down and date your answers.
3. Follow your story in the business news over the next month (or longer, as your instructor requests). What problems, opportunities, or other results are reported? Were these developments anticipated at the time of the initial story, or did they seem to catch industry analysts by surprise? How well did your answers to question 2 predict the results?

See It on the **WEB**

URLs for all Internet exercises are provided at the website for this book, www.pearsoned.ca/bovee. When you log on to this text's website, select Chapter 5, select Destinations, then click on the name of the featured website, and review the website to complete the following exercises.

Explore the following chapter-related websites, review their content, and answer the following questions for each website you visit:

1. What is the purpose of this website?

CHOOSE A FORM OF OWNERSHIP

Which legal form of ownership is best suited for a new

Focusing on E-Business in Action

From the smallest dot-coms to lumbering global giants, e-business is influencing the way all companies do business today. While the Internet bubble has burst, Internet technology and e-commerce remain very much a part of the business environment. "E-Business in Action" is a dedicated section that appears at the end of each text part and will expand student learning by explaining, in depth, the important challenges companies are facing in the world of e-business.

E-Business **IN ACTION**

E-Business and the Global Economy

Name the world's most connected place. Did you guess the United States? If so, you are wrong. South Korea is the world's most connected high-speed Internet country. Approximately three of every four households have high-speed connections and 70 percent of its citizens are also equipped with cellphones. The U.S. lags behind in eleventh position. In fact, Japan and Canada occupy second and third place, respectively. With many Asian and European countries leapfrogging the U.S. in terms of infrastructure efficiency, the groundwork is being laid for even greater global e-business opportunities.

Historical Framework

Europe and Asia initially trailed North America in their use and enthusiasm for the Web; however, young firms around the globe are now taking their businesses to the Web and overcoming difficult obstacles such as cultural resistance, government regulations, and inefficient infrastructures.

Cultural Resistance

Because purchasing over the Internet does not involve an immediate exchange of goods or money, it generates feelings of

display of goods to be sold at auction and legislative mazes turn the simple act of registering a web address into a long and complex process. Such red tape curbs the growth of e-commerce.

Government support for e-commerce is minimal or nonexistent in some Asian countries. In Malaysia and parts of China, for instance, e-commerce is seen as a threat to government control. Dot-com companies highlight the central contradiction of China today—the drive to modernize without giving up one-party rule. The government wants the economic benefits of the Internet without the freedom it gives: the information revolution, minus the revolution. The question is not whether the Chinese government will pull the plug on the Internet, but whether it will regulate it in a way that will make it commercially viable.

Ineffective and Inefficient Infrastructures

In addition to cultural and governmental acceptance, the availability of Internet access is another prerequisite for e-commerce growth. Without a telecommunications infrastructure, it becomes impossible for large parts of the population to participate in the Internet economy. Scandinavians were early e-commerce adopters, thanks to the excellent mobile

Business PlanPro Exercises

The end-of-part "Business PlanPro Exercises" enable students to apply the knowledge they've gained from reading the chapters to the Business PlanPro software. Each exercise has two tasks: "Think Like a Pro" tasks require students to navigate the software, find and review information in sample business plans, and evaluate and critique some of the thinking that went into these plans. "Create Your Own Business Plan" tasks provide students with an opportunity to apply their skills to create their own winning business plan.

Business PlanPro **EXERCISES**

Conducting Business in the Global Economy

Review Appendix C, "Your Business Plan," to learn how to use Business PlanPro Software so you can complete these exercises.

Think Like a Pro

Objective: By completing these exercises you will become acquainted with the sections of a business plan that address forms of competition, company and product/service descriptions, and the economic outlook for the related industry. You will use the sample business plan for Adventure Excursions Unlimited (listed as Travel Agency–Adventure Sports in the Sample Plan Browser) in this exercise. Use the table of contents to move from section to section as you explore the plan and answer the following questions.

1. What products and services does Adventure Excursions provide? Will the company compete on the basis of price, speed, quality, service, or innovation to gain a competitive advantage?
2. What is the economic outlook for the travel industry? What competition does Adventure Excursions face?
3. How does Adventure Excursions plan to use the Internet?

Create Your Own Business Plan

Now start a new plan for your own business. Answering the following questions will help you think about different aspects of your business plan. Enter your answers in the appropriate sections of the new business plan.

What information should you include about your product or service when creating a business plan? Describe in detail the product or service your company will provide. Indicate whether you will compete on price, speed, quality, service, or innovation. What are some of the things you should discuss about your competition in a business plan? In what industry will you compete? What is the economic outlook for that industry? What kinds of competition do you expect to face?

Business Plan (Appendix C)

Instructors who want a more complete business-planning experience for their students will want to take advantage of this text's appendix. Using Business PlanPro software as a foundation, this appendix carefully takes students through each step toward creating a winning business plan. In addition, by completing the chapters in the text, and after studying numerous business plan examples, students will be able to build their own complete business plan by the end of the term.

Four-Way Approach to Vocabulary Development

This text's four-way method of vocabulary reinforcement helps students learn basic business vocabulary with ease. First, each term is printed in boldface within the text. Second, a definition appears in the margin adjacent to the term. Third, an alphabetical list of key terms appears at the end of each chapter, with convenient cross-references to the pages where the terms are defined. Fourth, all marginal definitions are assembled in an alphabetical glossary at the end of the book.

TEACH WITH AN UNPARALLELED SUPPLEMENTS PACKAGE

The instructional resource package accompanying this text is specially designed to simplify the task of teaching and learning.

Instructor's Resource Manual

This Manual contains a set of completely integrated support materials. It is designed to assist instructors in quickly finding and assembling the resources available for each chapter of the text and includes the following new material:

- Learning objectives
- Learning objectives summarized
- Brief chapter outline
- Detailed lecture outlines and notes with suggested classroom activities integrated throughout
- A list of the difficulties (for each chapter) that students often face with material presented and suggestions given for overcoming them
- Real-world cases with discussion questions
- Answers to all end-of-chapter questions, problems, and assignments
- A detailed video guide with answers to video exercise questions
- One 10- to 15-question pop quiz for each chapter
- Sample syllabus

Test Generator

The Test Generator contains 14 chapters of 100-125 questions per chapter, all of which have been carefully checked for accuracy and quality. It consists of multiple-choice, true/false, fill-in-the-blank, and essay questions. Each test question is ranked based on Bloom's Taxonomy and by level of difficulty (easy, moderate, or difficult) and contains page references to allow the instructor a quick and easy way to balance the level of exams or quizzes.

The user-friendly TestGen software allows you to generate random tests with our extensive bank of questions. You can also edit our questions/answers and even add some of your own. You can create an exam, administer it traditionally or online, and analyze your success with a simple click of the mouse.

Videos

Twelve videos are linked to end-of-part cases and exercises to help students see how real-life businesses and the people who run them apply fundamental business principles on a daily basis.

PowerPoint Presentation

Enhance your classroom presentations with this well-developed PowerPoint presentation set, which contains more than 250 text-specific slides that highlight fundamental concepts by integrating key graphs, figures, and illustrations from the text. Free to adopters, these PowerPoint slides are available on the Instructor's Resource CD-ROM or can be downloaded from the instructor's resource section of the Companion Website at www.pearsoned.ca/bovee.

Instructor's Resource CD-ROM

This CD includes the Instructor's Resource Manual, Test Generator, PowerPoint Presentations, Videos, and Digital Image Gallery.

New! Career Portfolio Supplement

This unique saleable supplement, written by James O'Rourke, University of Notre Dame, takes students through the process of building their individualized career portfolio. Students walk through the process of self-assessment, matching career opportunities, initiating the job search using the latest Internet-based search vehicles, preparing all job-search-related documents, and following up. Upon completion of the supplement, students will have a career portfolio they can use and build on as their career progresses.

New! *Business Ethics in Uncertain Times: A Special Supplement*

This special supplement covers key issues in contemporary business ethics, including the following:

- Management's responsibility for accountability; conflicts of interest, protection of employees, protection of stockholders, and compliance with legal and regulatory standards
- Corporate governance, including how and why it's supposed to work but doesn't always; outside directors versus insiders with conflicts of interest; and audit committees
- Accounting practices, including why and how public corporations hide debt and mischaracterize expenses, how previously accepted accounting practices are now being questioned, the role of CPA firms in auditing statements, and ways to manage conflicts of interest with consulting clients
- Stakeholder relations, including the importance of honest and complete financial statements to inform current and potential shareholders, ways to maintain employee trust, and relations with unions
- Ethical decisions and behaviour, including what can be done to encourage and support ethical actions, such as codes of conduct, ethical training, whistleblower and ombudsman structures, legal and regulatory oversight of auditors and managers, separation of consulting and auditing, and director accountability
- Chapter-ending pedagogy includes "Questions for Review", "Questions for Discussion and Analysis", "For Further Research", and "Ethics Resources Online". This new supplement can be packaged with the text for free. To order, contact your local Pearson Education representative (ISBN: 0-13-141422-4).

Business PlanPro Software

Business PlanPro

Business PlanPro software provides students with a step-by-step approach to creating a comprehensive business plan. Preformatted report templates, charts, and tables do the mechanics so students can focus on the thinking. Business PlanPro software can be packaged with the textbook for a nominal fee of $15.

Mastering Business Essentials CD

This innovative, interactive CD introduces students to the wide range of concerns facing businesses today. The CD contains 12 episodes that use a series of videos with enhanced interactive exercises that help students apply the lessons of the classroom to all the key areas of business at an e-business called CanGo. The Mastering Business Essentials CD can be shrinkwrapped with this text for under $10. The following topics are covered:

- The Goal of the Firm and Social Responsibility
- The Economic Way of Thinking
- Ethical Issues
- Concepts of Strategic Management
- Working in Groups and Teams
- Managerial Accounting and Cost Behaviour
- Raising Capital
- Work Motivation
- Leadership
- Marketing Concepts/Strategy
- Understanding Consumer Behaviour
- Strategy and Operations

PREVIEW THE COMPANION WEBSITE FOR *BUSINESS IN ACTION*, CANADIAN EDITION

The Companion Website (**www.pearsoned.ca/bovee**) is your personal tool to the free online resources for this book.

The website features one-click access to all of the resources created by an award-winning team of educators. Here is a preview of its exciting features.

For the Student

- Study Guide. Test your knowledge with this interactive study guide that offers a wide variety of self-assessment questions for each chapter. Results from the automatically graded questions for every chapter provide immediate feedback that can serve as practice or can be e-mailed to the instructor for extra credit.
- Case Updates. Just click on the link to find recent developments on companies featured in the book.
- Student Resources. Access the websites featured in this text by using the hotlinks, review chapter content by viewing the PowerPoint slides, or improve your understanding of key terms by using the flashcards/glossary.

For the Instructor

Online Faculty Support. In this password-protected area, get the most current and advanced support materials available, including downloadable supplements, such as the Instructor's Resource Manual, PowerPoints, Test Generator, Bi-Annual Case Updates, and videos.

ONLINE LEARNING SOLUTION

Pearson Education Canada supports instructors interested in using online course management systems. We provide text-related content in WebCT, Blackboard, and CourseCompass. To find out more about creating an online course using Pearson content in one of these platforms, contact your Pearson sales rep.

PERSONAL ACKNOWLEDGMENTS

Many individuals assisted in the development of this text; their comments, ideas and recommendations were vital elements in shaping the Canadian Edition of *Business in Action.*

John Chatzidakis, CIBC World Markets
Vic DeWitt, Red River College
Diane Gauvin, Dawson College
Cyndi Hornby, Fanshawe College
Suzanne Iskander, Humber College
Paul Myers, St. Clair College
David Parker, George Brown College
Andy Rezaei, Goldman Sachs
John Roumeliotis, ADM
Robert Soroka, Dawson College
Peter Turner, Vanier College

I would like to acknowledge all the staff at Pearson Canada for their various contributions to this project. In particular, I would like to recognize Karen Elliott, Acquisitions Editor, for her energy, enthusiasm and her creative approach; Paul Donnelly, Senior Developmental Editor, for his skillful input and for being the constant link throughout the process; Mary Ann McCutcheon, Production Editor, for her attention to detail and timely efforts.

I would like to thank Michael J. Young, Vice President and Editorial Director, for providing strong support for this project, and Allen Dykler, Senior Sales and Editorial Representative, for his instrumental role and advice at every stage. It has also been a great pleasure meeting and gaining insight from many individuals, including Bill Todd, Director of Marketing, Susan Erickson, Senior Sales Manager, and Michael Campbell, Vice President of Marketing & Innovative Solutions.

I would also like to recognize my colleagues at Vanier College, Dawson College, and Concordia University for providing important feedback. Finally, a special thank you goes to my collaborator, Peter Mombourquette, Mount Saint Vincent University, for his detailed adaptation of Chapters 13, 14, and Appendix B.

George Dracopoulos

A Great Way to Learn and Instruct Online

The Pearson Education Canada Companion Website is easy to navigate and is organized to correspond to the chapters in this textbook. Whether you are a student in the classroom or a distance learner you will discover helpful resources for in-depth study and research that empower you in your quest for greater knowledge and maximize your potential for success in the course.

[www.pearsoned.ca/bovee]

Home >

PH Companion Website

Business in Action, Canadian Edition, by Bovée, Thill, Schatzman, Dracopoulos, and Mombourquette

Student Resources

This online study guide provides students with tools for learning course material. Among other resources, each chapter will include:

- Chapter Objectives
- Chapter Overview
- Study Guide
- Case Updates
- Weblinks
- Flashcards/Glossary

In the quiz modules students can send answers to the grader and receive instant feedback on their progress through the Results Reporter. Coaching comments and references to the textbook may be available to ensure that students take advantage of all available resources to enhance their learning experience.

Instructor Resources

A link to this book on the Pearson Education Canada online catalogue (www.pearsoned.ca) provides instructors with additional teaching tools. Downloadable PowerPoint Presentations and an Instructor's Manual are just some of the materials that may be available. The catalogue is password protected. To get a password, simply contact your Pearson Education Canada Representative or call Faculty Sales and Services at 1-800-850-5813.

Chapter 1
Fundamentals of Business, Economics, and the New Role of E-Business

LEARNING OBJECTIVES

After studying this chapter, you will be able to

1. Define what a business is and identify four key social and economic roles that businesses serve
2. Differentiate between goods-producing and service businesses. List five factors for the rise in the number of service businesses
3. Differentiate between a free-market system and a planned system
4. Explain how supply and demand affect price
5. Explain how a free-market system monitors its economic performance
6. Explain the four major economic roles of the Canadian government
7. Identify five challenges that businesses are facing in the global economy
8. Learn how companies are using the Internet to improve efficiency
9. Distinguish between e-business and e-commerce

Behind the SCENES

Roots: A Canadian Success Story

Canadian Olympic athletes proudly walk into the stadium sporting their stylish Roots apparel. This association between the Canadian Olympic team and Roots has helped Roots increase its profile domestically and internationally.

www.roots.com

Michael Budman and Don Green opened their first store in Toronto with one main product: the Roots Negative Heel Shoe. From these humble beginnings, more than 30 years ago, armed with one fad product, these two American-born entrepreneurs managed to create a recognized Canadian lifestyle brand. Roots currently consists of 225 stores, with 140 outlets in Canada. It also has stores in the United States, Taiwan, and Korea, with announced intentions to expand into Europe and China. The current product line includes a wide range of items: shoes, jackets, bags, athletic sportswear, leather furniture, linens, towels, and accessories. The company also has licensing agreements for watches, perfume, and luggage.

Like most businesses, Roots has faced challenges and there have been bumps along the road. As ambitious entrepreneurs, Budman and Green have not shied away from risky ventures beyond the obvious scope of their fashion expertise. Some of the company's more notable offbeat adventures include Roots Air, Roots vitamin pills, and the purchase of a Colorado lodge. Roots Air was launched in 2000 with a lot of fanfare and public relations efforts. It was supposed to be a new take on air travel with well-dressed cabin attendants and cockpit crews. Even the mechanics were to be sportingly dressed in Roots apparel. The venture survived only a few days as an operating entity. Despite these setbacks the company continues to consider the offbeat track. There is word that Michael Budman is considering a Roots hotel in Vancouver, to be built to coincide with the 2010 Winter Olympic Games.

In recent years, Roots has earned tremendous accolades and exposure because of its association with the Olympic movement. It created a buzz by outfitting the 1998 Canadian Olympic team in Nagano, Japan, which gained attention for both the athletes and the company. This success was confirmed when the U.S. Olympic team contracted the Canadian retailer to furnish its official outfits. Roots's trademark berets were a huge success at the 2002 Winter Olympics in Salt Lake City. By the 2004 Summer Olympics in Athens, Greece, the Roots signature on the games was growing, with Britain, the U.S., and the Barbados signing deals with the retailer to provide their national uniforms. The Olympics were providing exposure and a short-term marketing buzz, but could Roots harness the positive word of mouth for lasting international retail sales?[1]

L.O. 1

WHY STUDY BUSINESS?

Business is everywhere. Whether you're logged on to a website, flying in an airplane, watching a movie, buying a CD over the Internet, enjoying your favourite coffee drink, or withdrawing money from an ATM, you're involved in someone else's business. In fact, you engage in business just about every day of your life. But like many college students, for most of your life you've been observing and enjoying the efforts of others. Now that you're taking an introduction to business course, however, your perspective is about to change.

In this course you'll learn what it takes to run a business. You will begin to look at things through the eyes of an employee or a manager instead of a consumer. You'll develop a fundamental business vocabulary that will help you keep up with the latest news and make more informed decisions. By participating in classroom discussions and completing the chapter exercises, you'll gain some valuable critical-thinking, problem-solving, team-building, and communication skills that you can use throughout your career.

This course will introduce you to a variety of jobs in fields such as accounting, economics, human resources, management, finance, marketing, and so on. You'll see how people who work in these business functions contribute to the success of a company as a whole. You'll gain insight into the types of skills and knowledge these jobs require. And most important, you'll discover that a career in business today is fascinating, challenging, and often quite rewarding.

WHAT IS A BUSINESS?

Like Michael Budman and Don Green, many people start a new **business**—a profit-seeking activity that provides goods and services that satisfy consumers' needs. Roots, for example, provides products that satisfy consumers' clothing and accessory needs with an emphasis on sportswear. In addition to providing a society with necessities such as housing, clothing, food, transportation, communication, health care, etc., businesses provide people with jobs and a means to prosper; they pay taxes that are used to build highways, fund education, and provide grants for scientific research; and they reinvest their profits in the economy, thereby creating a higher standard of living and quality of life for society as a whole.

business
Activity and enterprise that provide goods and services a society needs

The driving force behind most businesses is the prospect of earning a **profit**—what remains after all expenses have been deducted from business revenue. Such a prospect is commonly referred to as a *profit motive*. Businesses may keep and use their profits as they wish, within legal limits. Still, not every organization exists to earn a profit. **Non-profit organizations** such as museums, public schools and universities, symphonies, libraries, government agencies, and charities exist to provide society with a social or educational service. The Canadian Red Cross, for example, provides relief to victims of disasters and helps people prevent, prepare for, and respond to emergencies. The organization took in approximately $198 million in 2004 and spent almost all of that money on its programs and supporting services.[2] From domestic relief efforts for people affected by events such as forest fires in British Columbia to international crises such as the Asian tsunami relief effort, the Canadian Red Cross is there. Although non-profit organizations such as the Red Cross do not have a profit motive, they must operate efficiently and effectively to achieve their goals. Thus, the business opportunities, challenges, and activities discussed throughout this textbook apply to both profit-seeking and non-profit organizations. Moreover, to be successful, both profit-seeking and non-profit organizations must be socially responsible and ethical when dealing with investors, employees, customers, the community, and society (as Chapter 3 discusses).

profit
Money that remains after expenses and taxes have been deducted from revenue generated by selling goods and services

non-profit organizations
Firms whose primary objective is something other than returning a profit to their owners

Goods-Producing Businesses versus Service Businesses

L.O. 2

Most organizations can be classified into two broad categories (or industry sectors): goods-producing and service businesses. **Goods-producing businesses** produce tangible goods by engaging in activities such as manufacturing, construction, mining, and agriculture. Boeing, the world's largest manufacturer of commercial jetliners, military aircraft, and satellites, is a perfect example. The company has the largest building, by volume, in the world. Spanning 98 acres under one roof, the facility is big enough to handle construction of 20 wide-body jets at once.[3] Of course, most manufacturing operations do not require a facility as big as Boeing's. Nonetheless, it's diffi-

goods-producing businesses
Businesses that produce tangible products

Manufacturers of resistance-training machines have characteristics of both goods-producing and service-producing businesses. In addition to producing high-quality equipment, they must provide product training, technical support, warranties, and on-site repair and maintenance. Some manufacturers even offer seminars on resistance training and how to maintain a healthy lifestyle.

cult to start a goods-producing business without substantial investments in buildings, machinery, and equipment. For this reason, most goods-producing organizations are **capital-intensive**; they generally require large amounts of money or equipment to get started and to operate.

Service businesses produce intangible products (ones that cannot be held in your hand) and are created in fields such as finance, insurance, transportation, utilities, wholesale and retail trade, banking, entertainment, health care, repairs, and information. AOL Canada, Fairmont Hotels, The Canadian Imperial Bank of Commerce (CIBC), and eBay are examples of service businesses. Most service businesses are **labour-intensive**. That is, they rely more on human resources than on buildings, machinery, and equipment to prosper. A consulting firm is an example of a labour-intensive service business because its existence depends heavily on the knowledge and skills of its consultants. A group of consultants can go into business simply by purchasing some computers and telephones.

Keep in mind that some companies produce both goods and services. IBM, for example, is primarily a manufacturer of computers and other business machines, but at least one-third of the company's sales come from computer-related services such as systems design, consulting, and product support.[4] Similarly, Bombardier provides flight training, maintenance technician training, fleet and logistics support, and a number of aviation services to support sales of its commercial aircraft.[5] As more and more manufacturers such as Bombardier and IBM focus on servicing and supporting their products, it becomes increasingly difficult to classify a company as either a goods-producing business or a service business.

Growth of the Service Sector

Services have always played an important role in the Canadian economy. However, since the mid-1980s, services have become the engine of growth for the Canadian economy (see Exhibit 1.1).[6] In fact, most of the increase in Canadian employment in the last two decades has been generated by the service sector. Today about half of the 1000 largest North American companies are service based.[7] Economists project that the number of service-related jobs will continue to increase. In contrast, employment growth in the goods-producing sector is projected to remain relatively flat through 2006.[8]

capital-intensive businesses
Businesses that require large investments in capital assets

service businesses
Businesses that provide intangible products or perform useful labour on behalf of another business

labour-intensive businesses
Businesses in which labour costs are more significant than capital costs

Wal-Mart's rise to the top spot as the world's largest company underscores the changing face of the global economic system.[9] An increasing number of individuals are employed in the service sector. Growth in the service sector is attributable to five key factors:

- *Consumers have more disposable income.* The dominant baby boomer population (people born between 1947 and 1966) are in their peak earning years. These consumers find themselves with more disposable income and look for services to help them invest, travel, relax, and stay fit.[10]
- *Services target changing demographic patterns and lifestyle trends.* Canada has more elderly people, more single people living alone, more two-career households, and more single parents than ever before. These trends create opportunities for service companies that can help people with all the tasks they no longer have time for, including home maintenance, food service, and child care.[11]
- *Services are needed to support complex goods and new technology.* Computers, home entertainment centres, recreational vehicles, security systems, and automated production equipment are examples of products that require specialized installation, repair, user training, or extensive support services. As new technology is incorporated into more and more products, companies will need to provide more of these types of product-support services to remain competitive.
- *Companies are increasingly seeking professional advice.* To compete in the global economy, many firms turn to consultants and professional advisers for help as they

Exhibit 1.1 **Goods and Services: Employment Breakdown**

The service sector (finance, professional services, trade, transportation, education, etc.) accounts for 74.7 percent of Canadian employment while the goods-producing sector (manufacturing, construction, agriculture, etc.) accounts for the remaining 25.3 percent.[12]

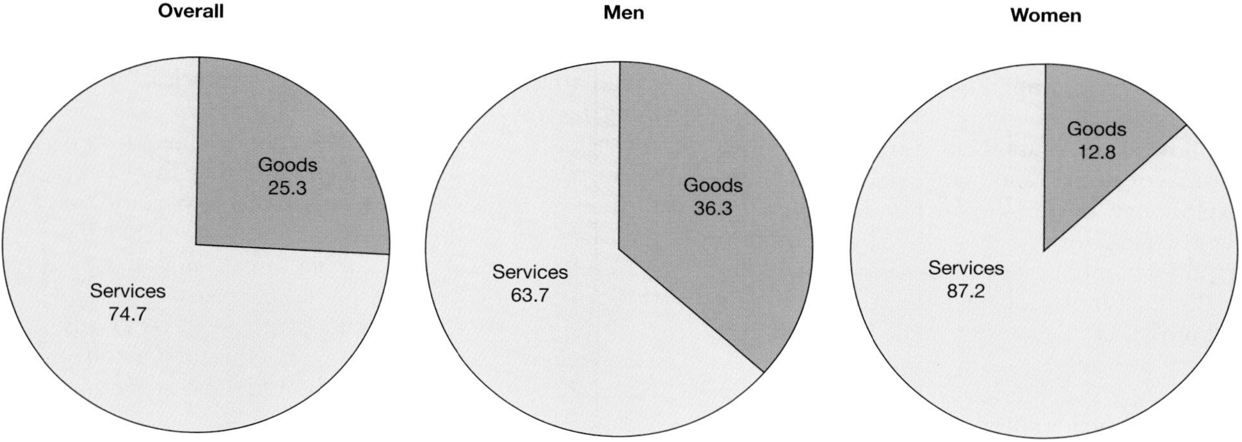

Source: Adapted from Statistics Canada CANSIM database http://cansim2statscan.ca, Table 282-0008.

seek ways to cut costs, refine their business processes, expand overseas, and engage in **electronic commerce (e-commerce)**—buying and selling over the Internet.

- *Barriers to entry are low for service businesses.* Capital-intensive manufacturing businesses generally have high **barriers to entry**, which means that conditions exist that make entry into these businesses extremely difficult. Such conditions include significant capital requirements, high learning curves, tightly controlled markets, strict licensing procedures, the need for highly skilled employees, and the use of specialized equipment or skills. By contrast, the barriers to entry for most service companies are low.

electronic commerce (e-commerce)
The general term for the buying and selling of goods and services on the Internet

barriers to entry
Factors that make it difficult to launch a business in a particular industry

Whether you're running a service or a goods-producing business, world economic situations affect all businesses that compete in the global economy. Thus, running a successful business today requires a firm understanding of basic economic principles, of the different economic systems operating in the world, and of how businesses compete in the global and electronic economy (see the box entitled "The Electronic Economy" on page 6).

WHAT IS AN ECONOMIC SYSTEM?

Economics is the study of how a society uses its scarce resources to produce and distribute goods and services. All societies must deal with the same basic questions: How should limited economic resources be used to satisfy society's needs? What goods and services should be produced? Who should produce them? How should these goods and services be divided among the population? In some countries these decisions are made by individuals (or households) when they decide how to spend or invest their income and by businesses when they decide what kinds of goods and services to produce; in other countries these decisions are made by governments.

Economists call the resources that societies use to produce goods and services *factors of production.* To maximize a company's profit, businesses use five **factors of production** in the most efficient way possible:

- **Natural resources**—things that are useful in their natural state, such as land, forests, minerals, and water

economics
The study of how society uses scarce resources to produce and distribute goods and services

factors of production
Basic inputs that a society uses to produce goods and services, including natural resources, labour, capital, entrepreneurship, and knowledge

natural resources
Land, forests, minerals, water, and other tangible assets usable in their natural state

The Electronic Economy

Without a doubt, the Internet is ushering in an era of sweeping change. It is tearing down geographic barriers, allowing businesses to reach markets anywhere in the world. It's spawning new businesses, transforming existing ones, saving companies money, and creating wealth. It's changing the way people shop for books, cars, vacations, advice—just about everything. It's forcing companies of all sizes and types to face new competition, explore new business opportunities, and adopt new ways of conducting business. In the span of just a few years, the Internet has touched every business and industry. But that's not good news for everyone.

Companies that take advantage of the Internet to revamp their businesses, build brand new ones, or expand their markets stand to reap the rewards; those that don't risk extinction. After all, tasks such as selling airline tickets, booking reservations, and selling all kinds of consumer and business goods can easily be accomplished on the Internet. This means that traditional companies must find new ways to add value to their services or products, or be left behind.

Even more frightful—or exciting (depending on which side of the casualty line you're on)—is the fact that e-commerce (the buying and selling of goods and services over a network) is only in its infancy, and by all measures it is expected to provide much of the fuel that will power the twenty-first century. Still, companies transacting e-commerce face many obstacles. For one thing, they must accept constant change as a reality. For another, they must redefine their relationships with suppliers, customers, and employees and they must transform every aspect of their operations to become true e-businesses.

Fresh opportunities and big threats aptly describe the Web. In subsequent chapters, we'll take a closer look at how e-commerce is revolutionizing all facets of business life. You'll see that becoming an e-business in today's electronic economy takes much more than launching a website.

Questions for Critical Thinking

1. How is the Internet changing the way companies do business?
2. Why must companies move at an accelerated pace in the Internet economy?

human resources
All of the people who work for an organization

capital
The physical, human-made elements used to produce goods and services, such as factories and computers; can also refer to the funds that finance the operations of a business

entrepreneurs
People who accept the risk of failure in the private enterprise system

knowledge
Expertise gained through experience or association

- **Human resources**—anyone (from company presidents to grocery clerks) who works to produce goods and services
- **Capital**—resources (such as money, computers, machines, tools, and buildings) that a business needs to produce goods and services
- **Entrepreneurs**—people such as Roots co-founders Michael Budman and Don Green who are innovative and willing to take risks to create and operate new businesses (see Exhibit 1.2)
- **Knowledge**—the collective intelligence of an organization

Traditionally, a business was considered to have an advantage if it was located in a country with a plentiful supply of natural resources, human resources, capital, and entrepreneurs. But in the global marketplace, intellectual assets are the key. Today companies can obtain capital from one part of the world, purchase supplies from another, and locate production facilities in still another. They can relocate their operations to wherever they find a steady supply of affordable workers. Thus, countries with the greatest supply of knowledge workers and ones with economic systems that give workers the freedom to pursue their own economic interests will have an advantage in the new economy (see Exhibit 1.3).

Types of Economic Systems

economic system
Means by which a society distributes its resources to satisfy its people's needs

The role that individuals and government play in allocating a society's resources depends on the society's **economic system**, the basic set of rules for allocating a society's resources to satisfy its citizens' needs. Two main economic systems exist in the world today: *free-market systems* and *planned systems.*

Exhibit 1.2 **Success Stories**

Few start-up companies are resource rich. Still, they become successful because an entrepreneur substitutes ingenuity for capital resources.

THE COMPANY	ITS START
Bombardier	In 1942, J.-Armand Bombardier founded a modest company to manufacture tracked vehicles for transportation on snow-covered terrain. Today Bombardier is a leading firm in aerospace and transportation with annual sales exceeding $21 billion.[13]
Coca-Cola	Pharmacist John Pemberton invented a soft drink in his backyard in 1886. Asa Chandler bought the company for US$2300 in 1891.
MEC	In 1971, after being inspired on a weekend camping trip, a group of University of British Columbia students decided to create Mountain Equipment Cooperative (MEC) to serve Canadians' outdoor sporting needs. What began with six founding members is now Canada's largest retail cooperative with 2 million members and counting.[14]
Nike	In the early 1960s, Philip Knight and his college track coach sold imported Japanese sneakers from the trunk of a station wagon. Start-up costs totalled US$1000.
United Parcel Service	In 1907, two teenagers pooled their cash, came up with US$100, and began a message and parcel delivery service for local merchants.
Cirque du Soleil	In the early 1980s, a group of young street performers began entertaining people in the Old Port of Montreal. Two decades later, these dreamers and unconventional entrepreneurs have turned Cirque du Soleil into an international success story. The company has unique shows playing across the world, including main shows in Las Vegas and touring shows in Asia, Europe, and North America.[15]
Amazon.com	In 1994, Jeff Bezos came across a report projecting annual Web growth at 2300 percent. He left his Wall Street job, headed to Seattle in an aging Chevy Blazer, and drafted his business plan en route. His e-business, Amazon.com, initially focused on selling books over the Internet, but Bezos later expanded his product offerings to include toys, consumer electronics, software, home improvement products, and more. Today Amazon.com is exploding in size. The company now generates more than US$2.7 billion in annual sales.
WestJet	WestJet was founded in 1996 by four Calgary entrepreneurs who saw an opportunity to provide low-rate airfare travel to western Canadians. They began operations with three 737 Boeing planes. Today WestJet has expanded across the country and has increased its fleet to 57 planes, with plans to add 74 more by 2008.[16]

Exhibit 1.3 **What's New about the New Economy?**

The new economy is different from the old economy in a number of key ways. Besides being faster and more volatile, it's highly dependent on the use of information technology to gain a competitive advantage.

OLD ECONOMY	NEW ECONOMY
General Characteristics	■ Competitive advantage based on physical assets ■ Profits maximized by controlling costs ■ Competitive advantage based on intellectual assets ■ Profits maximized by adding value to products and services
Technology	■ Mechanical technology is main influence on economic growth ■ Information technology is main influence on economic growth
Workforce	■ Job-specific skills ■ Transferable skills and lifelong learning
Geography	■ Firms locate near resource to reduce costs ■ Firms locate near collaborators and competitors to boost innovation
Capital	■ Debt financing ■ Venture capital

L.O. 3

free-market system
Economic system in which decisions about what to produce and in what quantities are decided by the market's buyers and sellers

capitalism
Economic system based on economic freedom and competition

Free-Market System

In a **free-market system**, individuals are free to decide what products to produce, how to produce them, whom to sell them to, and at what price to sell them. Thus, they have the chance to succeed—or to fail—based on their own efforts. **Capitalism** is the term most often used to describe the free-market system—one in which individuals own and operate the majority of businesses and where competition, supply, and demand determine which goods and services are produced. Capitalism owes its philosophical origins to eighteenth-century philosophers such as Adam Smith. According to Smith, in the ideal capitalist economy (pure capitalism) the *market* (an arrangement between buyer and seller to trade goods and services) serves as a self-correcting mechanism—an "invisible hand" to ensure the production of the goods that society wants in the quantities that society wants, without regulation of any kind.[17]

Because the market is its own regulator, Smith was opposed to government intervention. He believed that if anyone's prices or wages strayed from acceptable levels that the forces of competition would drive them back. In modern practice, however, governments sometimes interfere in free-market systems to influence prices and wages or to change the way resources are allocated. This practice of limited intervention is called *mixed capitalism*, which is the economic system of Canada. Other countries with variations of this economic system include the United States, Germany, and Japan. Under mixed capitalism, the pursuit of private gain is regarded as a worthwhile goal that ultimately benefits society as a whole. This is not the case in a planned system.

planned system
Economic system in which the government controls most of the factors of production and regulates their allocation

communism
Economic system in which all productive resources are owned and operated by the government, to the elimination of private property

socialism
Economic system characterized by public ownership and operation of key industries combined with private ownership and operation of less vital industries

Planned System

In a **planned system**, governments control all or part of the allocation of resources and limit the freedom of choice in order to accomplish government goals. Because social equality is a major goal of planned systems, private enterprise and the pursuit of private gain are generally regarded as wasteful and exploitive.

The planned system that allows individuals the least degree of economic freedom is **communism**, which still exists in such countries as North Korea and Cuba. (Keep in mind that even though communism and socialism are discussed here as economic systems, they can be political and social systems as well.) The degree to which communism is actually practised varies. In its purest form, almost all resources are under government control. Private ownership is restricted to personal and household items. Resource allocation is handled through centralized planning by a handful of government officials who decide what goods to produce, how to produce them, and to whom they should be distributed.[18] Although pure communism still has its supporters, the future of communism is not bright. As economists Lester Thurow and Robert Heilbroner put it, "It's a great deal easier to design and assemble the skeleton of a mighty economy than to run it."[19]

Socialism lies somewhere between capitalism and communism in the degree of economic freedom that it permits. Like communism, socialism involves a relatively high degree of government planning and some government ownership of land and capital resources (such as buildings and equipment). However, government involvement is limited to industries considered vital to the common welfare, such as transportation, utilities, medicine, steel, and communications. In these industries, the government owns or controls all of the facilities and determines what will be produced and how the output will be distributed. Private ownership is permitted in industries that are not considered vital, and in these areas both businesses and individuals are allowed to benefit from their own efforts. Taxes are high in socialist states because the government must cover public care costs. Canada falls under the category of a mixed capitalist economy because many programs such as medicare, subsidized education, and housing are borrowed from the socialist model. As such, Canada is more closely linked to this model than the United States, which provides fewer public services.

The Trend toward Privatization

Although varying degrees of socialism and communism are practised around the world today, several socialist and communist economies are moving toward free-market systems. Anxious to unload unprofitable businesses for badly needed cash and to experiment with free-market capitalism, countries such as Great Britain, Mexico, Argentina, Israel, France, Sweden, and China are **privatizing** some of their government-owned enterprises by selling them to privately held firms. Great Britain, for example, has sold the national phone company, the national steel company, the national sugar company, Heathrow Airport, water suppliers, and the company that makes Rover automobiles. Like Great Britain, China is also privatizing its major industries and planned to convert more than 60 percent of its state-owned industries by 2005.[20] The Canadian government went through a similar divestment process during the last two decades. Recently, the federal government sold its remaining shares in Petro-Canada.[21]

PETRO-CANADA *

Over the years the Canadian government has followed the trend toward privatization. The government recently sold its remaining 19% stake in Petro-Canada.

HOW DOES A FREE-MARKET ECONOMIC SYSTEM WORK? (A MICROECONOMIC VIEW)

Earlier in this chapter we noted that in a free-market system, the marketplace determines what goods and services get produced. In this section we will discuss three underlying elements that differentiate a free-market system from other economic systems: supply and demand, competition, and limited government intervention.

privatizing
The conversion of public ownership to private ownership

The Theory of Supply and Demand in a Free-Market System

L.O. 4

The theory of supply and demand is the driving force of the free-market system. It is the basic tool that economists use to describe how the market works in determining prices and the quantity of goods produced. **Demand** refers to the amount of a good or service that consumers will buy at a given time at various prices. **Supply** refers to the quantities of a good or service that producers will provide on a particular date at various prices. Simply put, *demand* refers to the behaviour of buyers, whereas *supply* refers to the behaviour of sellers. Both forces work together to create order in the free-market system.

demand
Buyers' willingness and ability to purchase products

supply
Specific quantity of a product that the seller is able and willing to provide

On the surface, the theory of supply and demand seems little more than common sense. Consumers should buy more when the price is low and buy less when the price is high. Producers would offer more when the price is high and offer less when the price is low. The quantity supplied and the quantity demanded continuously interact, and the balance between them at any given moment should be reflected by the current price on the open market. However, a quick look at any real-life market situation shows you that balancing supply with demand by adjusting price isn't quite that simple.

Consider the airline industry. Airline travel is a cyclical business; its revenues rise and fall with the economy. When the economy is strong, consumers and businesses are willing to spend more on discretionary travel. When the economy is weak, they cut back on such discretionary spending (see Exhibit 1.4). Airlines can respond by reducing ticket prices, by offering promotions, and by scaling back the number of flights. But airlines must plan their businesses years in advance, which means they must always be able to provide a base level of service regardless of how many people want to use it. Maintaining a fixed network of scheduled flights as traveller demand fluctuates is expensive. A new commercial jet costs from several million dollars (e.g., Bombardier's regional narrow-body jet) to several *hundred* million dollars (e.g., wide-body jets such as Boeing's 767s and 747s and Airbus's A340s and A330s). Further complicating the matter, new planes must be ordered years before they are needed. Air Canada has major fixed costs; it operated 230 narrow-body jets and 63 wide-body jets in 2005.[22] Add the costs of airport leases, landing fees, jet fuel, and employees such as pilots, flight attendants, and maintenance crews, and you can begin to see why airlines simply can't shrink their way back to profitability when demand falls. In recent years, Air Canada has served as a prominent case study of the industry's challenges.

Exhibit 1.4 **Effect of Faltering Economy on Demand for Business Travel**

During poor economic times, demand for business travel softens as companies take steps such as these to reduce their travel costs.

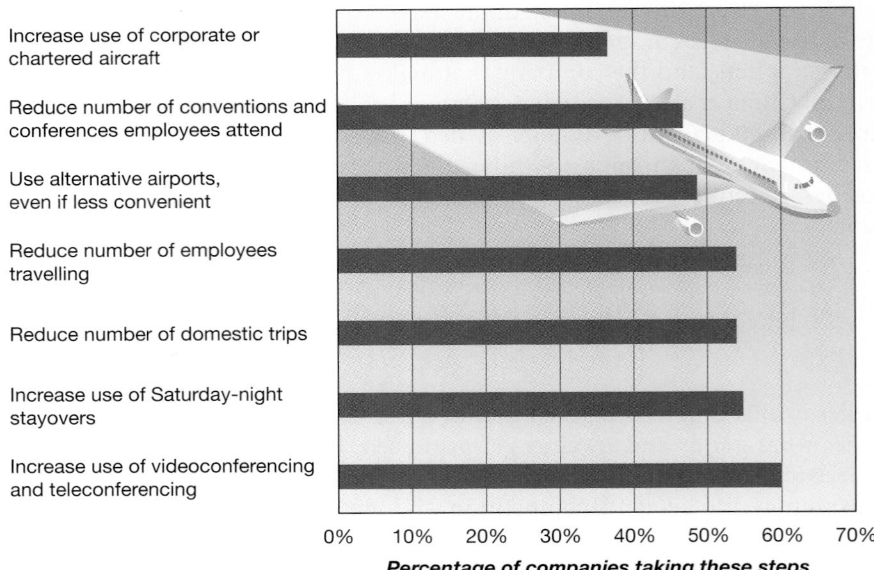

Nevertheless, in broad terms, the interaction of supply and demand regulates a free-market system by determining what is produced and in what amounts. For example, a movie studio might produce more comedies if ticket sales for similar films are brisk. On the other hand, it might decide to produce fewer comedies and more action-adventure movies if attendance at comedies lags. The result of such decisions—in theory, at least—is that consumers will get what they want and producers will earn a profit by keeping up with public demand.

By adjusting prices, airlines can influence demand for their services to a degree, but factors such as security threats and the health of the economy have a tremendous influence on consumer airline behaviour.

Buyer's Perspective (Simple Example)

The forces of supply and demand determine the market price for products and services. Say you're shopping for a hat, and the one you want is priced at $35. This is more than you can afford, so you don't make the purchase. When the store puts the hats on sale the following week for $18, you run right in and buy one.

But what if the store had to buy the hats from the manufacturer for $20? It would have made a profit selling them to you for $35, but it loses money selling them for $18. What if the store tries to buy more from the manufacturer at $10 or $15 but the manufacturer refuses? Is there a price that will make both the supplier and the customer happy? The answer is yes—the price at which the quantity of hats demanded equals the quantity supplied.

This relationship is shown in Exhibit 1.5. A range of possible prices is listed vertically at the left of the graph, with the lowest at the bottom and the highest at the top. Quantity of hats is represented along the horizontal axis. The points plotted on the curve labelled *D* indicate that on a given day the store would sell 10 hats if they were priced at $35, 15 hats if they were priced at $27, and so on. The curve that describes this relationship between price and quantity demanded is a *demand curve.* (Demand curves are not necessarily curved; they may be straight lines.)

Exhibit 1.5 The Relationship between Supply and Demand

In a free-market system, prices aren't set by the government; nor do producers alone have the final say. Instead, prices reflect the interaction of supply (S) and demand (D). The equilibrium price (E) is established when the amount of a product that producers are willing to sell at a given price equals the amount that consumers are willing to buy at that price.

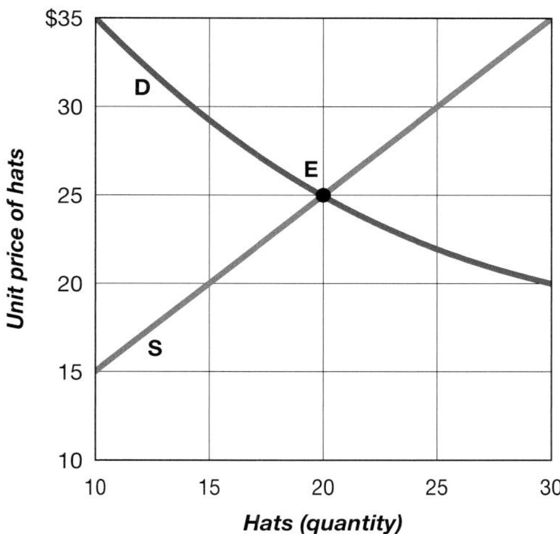

Seller's Perspective

Now think about the situation from the seller's point of view. The more profit the store can make on a particular item, the more of that item it will want to sell. Take a look at Exhibit 1.5. The line labelled *S* shows that the store would be willing to offer 30 hats at $35, 25 at $30, and so on. The store's willingness to carry the item increases as the price it can charge and its profit potential per item increase. In other words, as the price goes up, the quantity supplied goes up. The line tracing the relationship between price and quantity supplied is called a *supply curve.*

As much as the store would like to sell 30 hats at $35, you and your fellow consumers are likely to want only 10 at that price. If the store offered 30 hats, therefore, it would probably be stuck with some that it would have to mark down. How does the store avoid this problem? It looks for the point at which the demand curve and the supply curve intersect; the point at which the intentions of buyers and sellers coincide. The point marked *E* in Exhibit 1.5 shows that when hats are priced at $25, consumers are willing to buy 20 and the store is willing to sell 20. In other words, at the price of $25, the quantity supplied and the quantity demanded are in balance. The price at this point is known as the **equilibrium price.** Note that this intersection represents both a specific price—$25 in our example—and a specific quantity of goods—here, 20 hats. It is also tied to a specific point in time. Note also that it is the mutual interaction between quantity demanded and quantity supplied that determines the equilibrium price.

equilibrium price
Point at which quantity supplied equals quantity demanded

FREE-MARKET SYSTEM (A MACROECONOMIC VIEW)

Competition

In a free-market system, customers are free to buy whatever and wherever they please. Therefore, companies must compete with rivals for potential customers. Roots, for example, competes with other fashion apparel retail outlets. **Competition** is the situation in which two or more suppliers of a product are rivals in the pursuit of the same customers.

In theory, the ideal type of competition is **pure competition**, which is characterized by three conditions: a marketplace of multiple buyers and sellers, a product or service

competition
Rivalry among businesses for the same customer

pure competition
Situation in which so many buyers and sellers exist that no single buyer or seller can individually influence market prices

with nearly identical features such as wheat or cotton, and low barriers of entry (that is, the ability to easily enter and exit the marketplace). When these three conditions exist, no single firm or group of firms in an industry becomes large enough to influence prices and thereby distort the workings of the free-market system. By contrast, in a **monopoly** there is only one producer of a product in a given market, and thus the producer is able to determine the price. A situation in which an industry (such as commercial aircraft manufacturing) is dominated by only a few producers (wide-body jets: Boeing and Airbus; narrow-body regional jets: Bombardier and Embraer) is called an **oligopoly**.

monopoly
Market in which there are no direct competitors so that one company dominates

oligopoly
Market dominated by a few producers

Between pure competition and monopoly lie a number of firms with varying degrees of competitive power. Most of the competition in advanced free-market economic systems is **monopolistic competition**, in which a large number of sellers (none of which dominates the market) offer products that can be distinguished from competing products in at least some small way. Toothpaste, cosmetics, soft drinks, Internet search engines, and restaurants are examples of products that can vary in the features each offers.

monopolistic competition
Situation in which many sellers differentiate their products from those of competitors in at least some small way

When markets become filled with competitors and products start to look alike, companies use price, speed, quality, service, or innovation to gain a **competitive advantage**—something that sets one company apart from its rivals and makes its products more appealing to consumers (see the box entitled "LivePerson Puts a Pulse on the Web"). For example, WestJet built its reputation by offering low fares and good value. Fast-food outlets compete on speed and convenience. Harvey's locations further distinguish themselves by allowing customers to customize garnishes and view final preparation. Second Cup competes on quality by delivering a premium product to the masses of caffeine-craving individuals. Finally, Mountain Equipment Co-op (MEC) competes on customer service. Not only are MEC's customers allowed to return their online purchases to any physical MEC store, but those who live near an MEC retail outlet can arrange to pick up online sales at the store or receive them at home.

competitive advantage
Ability to perform in one or more ways that competitor cannot match

Product innovation is another way that companies compete in the free-market economy. For nearly a century, 3M's management has promoted innovation by giving employees the freedom to take risks and try new ideas. Beginning with the invention of sandpaper in 1904, 3M has produced such staples as masking tape, cellophane tape, magnetic tape, videotape, and Post-it Notes. Sometimes product innovation can revolutionize an entire industry, just as Rollerblades, AbFlex, Atomic hour-glass skis, and Burton and Sims snowboards did by creating new market opportunities for the sporting goods industry.[23]

L.O. 5

How a Free-Market System Monitors Its Economic Performance

Each day we are presented with complex statistical data that describe the current status and past performance of the economy. Sorting, understanding, and interpreting this information are difficult tasks even for professional economists. **Economic indicators** include statistics such as interest rates, unemployment rates, and housing data that are used to monitor and measure economic performance. Statistics that point to what may happen to the economy in the future are called *leading indicators;* statistics that signal a swing in the economy after the movement has begun are called *lagging indicators.*

economic indicators
Statistics that measure variables in the economy

Watching Economic Indicators

Economists monitor the performance of the economy by watching a variety of indicators. Unemployment statistics, for example, signal future changes in consumer spending. When unemployment rises, people have less money to spend, and the economy suffers. Housing starts, another leading indicator, show where several industries are headed. Housing is very sensitive to interest rate changes. If mortgage rates are high, fewer people can afford to build new homes. When housing starts drop, builders stop hiring, and may even lay off workers. Meanwhile, orders fall for plumbing fixtures, carpets, and appliances, so manufacturers decrease production and workers' hours. These cutbacks ripple through the economy and lead to slower income and job growth and

LivePerson Puts a Pulse on the Web

You're shopping online, but you'd like some more information. Does that sweater come in red? Will you get free shipping? Before you click and buy, sometimes you need the help of a real, live person. That's why Robert LoCascio developed LivePerson.com, a software company that puts the human touch into online shopping. Bell Canada is one of the many large corporations that use LivePerson's services.

LoCascio knows that many retail websites are ineffective. They confuse and frustrate shoppers and force them to sift through page after page of details to find the information they need. As a result, many consumers give up and abandon their electronic shopping carts. But LoCascio's LivePerson helps companies doing business on the Internet to maximize their customers' online shopping experience. Websites with LivePerson services invite online shoppers to chat with a real, live person. Shoppers simply click on the LivePerson icon and a pop-up window appears on the screen. Type in your name and you're instantly greeted by a customer service rep who asks, "What can I do for you?"

"Bell Canada uses LivePerson's online sales solution to engage customers as they browse its business solutions website . . . . This initiative targets small and medium enterprises (SME), and focuses on high-speed Internet and Web hosting services."[24]

The LivePerson reps can also help customers with unique product questions and selections. For instance, LivePerson reps can suggest alternatives to customers by clicking on different web pages to show similar products. They can also supply customers with valuable information about their past purchases and previous visits to the website. As LoCascio explains, the reps "embrace the customer and help them through the process of shopping."

All in all, LoCascio's LivePerson helps e-commerce companies compete by providing a high level of customer service. "If you walk into a store and there's no person there to help you, the experience is pretty bad," says LoCascio. "The same thing is true online."

Questions for Critical Thinking

1. How can a service like LivePerson help Internet retailers gain a competitive advantage?
2. A business is a profit-seeking activity that provides goods and services that satisfy consumers' needs. What consumer needs does LivePerson try to satisfy?

weaker consumer spending.[25] Another leading indicator is durable-goods orders, or orders for goods that typically last more than three years (which can mean everything from desk chairs to airplanes). A rise in durable-goods orders is a positive indicator that business spending is turning around. Besides unemployment data, housing starts, and durable-goods orders, economists closely monitor a nation's price changes and output.

Measuring Price Changes

Price changes, especially price increases, are another important economic indicator. **Inflation** refers to a steady rise in the prices of goods and services throughout the economy. In a period of rising prices, the purchasing power of a dollar declines, which means that you can purchase fewer things with today's dollar than you could in a prior period. Over time, price increases tend to lead to wage increases, which in turn add pressures for higher prices, setting a vicious cycle in motion. On the other hand, a sustained fall in the general price level for goods and services is known as **deflation**. In this case, purchasing power increases because a dollar held today will buy more tomorrow. In a deflationary period, investors postpone major purchases in anticipation of lower prices.

inflation
Economic condition in which prices rise steadily throughout the economy

deflation
Economic condition in which prices fall steadily throughout the economy

Keep in mind that although prices in the overall economy tend to increase year after year, not all industries and product categories necessarily follow this trend. In the electronics industry, for instance, prices tend to drop as technology advances and production becomes more efficient.

Consumer Price Index The **consumer price index (CPI)** measures the rate of inflation by comparing the change in prices of a representative basket of goods and services, such

consumer price index (CPI)
Monthly statistic that measures changes in the prices of about 400 goods and services that consumers buy

as clothing, food, housing, and utilities, over time. A numerical weight is assigned to each item in the representative basket to adjust for each item's relative importance in the marketplace. The CPI has always been a hot topic because it is used by the government to index programs, and it is widely used by businesses in private contracts to calculate cost-of-living increases. But, like most economic indicators, the CPI is far from perfect. For one thing, the representative basket of goods may not accurately represent the prices and consumption patterns of the area in which you live. For another, the mix in this basket may not include new innovations or capture the shift of consumer purchases to products with falling prices.

Measuring a Nation's Output

gross domestic product (GDP) Dollar value of all the final goods and services produced by businesses located within a nation's borders; excludes receipts from overseas operations of domestic companies

gross national product (GNP) Dollar value of all the final goods and services produced by domestic businesses that includes receipts from overseas operations and excludes receipts from foreign-owned businesses within a nation's borders

The broadest measure of an economy's health is the **gross domestic product (GDP)**. The GDP measures a country's output—its production, distribution, and use of goods and services—by computing the sum of all goods and services produced for *final* use in a market during a specified period (usually a year). Either domestic or foreign companies may produce the goods—as long as these companies are located within a nation's boundaries. Sales from a Honda assembly plant in Ontario would be included in the GDP.

A less popular measure of a country's output is the **gross national product (GNP)**. This measure excludes the value of production from foreign-owned businesses within a nation's boundaries (such as Honda Canada), but it includes receipts from the overseas operations of domestic companies—such as Canadian companies like Aldo shoes in the United States. Put another way, GNP considers *who* is responsible for the production; GDP considers *where* the production occurs. Although far from perfect, the GDP enables a nation to evaluate its economic policies and to compare its current performance with prior periods or with the performance of other nations.

L.O. 6

Government's Role in a Free-Market System

Although the free-market system generally works well, it's far from perfect. If left unchecked, the economic forces that make capitalism succeed may also create severe problems for some groups or individuals. To correct these types of problems, the government serves four major economic roles: It enacts laws and creates regulations to foster competition; it regulates and deregulates certain industries; it protects stakeholders' rights; and it intervenes to contribute to economic stability.

Fostering Competition

In Canada, the Competition Act is a key piece of legislation that regulates business practices. The purpose of this act is to maintain and encourage competition and efficiency of the Canadian economy. The Competition Act also serves to protect the rights of small and medium-sized businesses while ensuring that consumers have access to competitive prices and product choices. It clearly sets out the laws and consequences of unhealthy economic practices such as illegal trade practices, double-ticketing, bid-rigging, deceptive notice of a winning prize, false or misleading representations, deceptive telemarketing, and conspiracy.[26]

Because competition generally benefits the Canadian economy, the federal government as well as the provincial governments create laws and regulations every year to preserve competition and ensure that no single enterprise becomes too powerful. For instance, if a company has a monopoly, it can harm consumers by raising prices, cutting output, or stifling innovation. Furthermore, because most monopolies have total control over certain products and prices and the market share for those products, it's extremely difficult for competitors to enter markets where monopolies exist. For these reasons, over the last century or so, a number of laws and regulations have been established to help prevent individual companies or groups of companies from gaining control of markets in ways that restrain competition or harm consumers.

One of the highest profile cases in recent years involved the software giant Microsoft and the U.S. government. Microsoft makes the operating system software used by more than 90 percent of personal computers as well as a wide array of application software that runs on those operating systems. In the late 1990s, the U.S. Justice Department accused Microsoft of using its vast clout to give itself an unfair advantage in the application software business by bundling its popular Internet Explorer web browser with its Windows operating system. Competitors such as Netscape alleged that Microsoft was willing to use every tool at its disposal to damage competition by forcing or persuading companies to install Internet Explorer as a condition of licensing the Windows operating system. After a much-publicized two-year trial, on June 7, 2000, U.S. District Judge Thomas Jackson ordered that the company be split up after ruling that Microsoft was indeed a monopoly and that it had repeatedly and wilfully violated antitrust laws. However, in July 2001 the Court of Appeals reversed Judge Jackson's order to split Microsoft into smaller companies and sent the case back to district court to develop remedies to prevent Microsoft from using its Windows operating system monopoly in an anticompetitive manner.[27] The legal battles continue for Microsoft as the European Union placed a €497 million fine on the company in 2004 and is trying to force Microsoft to unbundle its multimedia software from Windows.[28]

It doesn't take long before innovative products such as scooters catch on. But just rolling out a "me-too" product in today's competitive marketplace will not guarantee success. Today's products must be exciting and create perceived consumer value to catch the savvy buyer's eye.

Mergers and Acquisitions To preserve competition, the government may also stipulate requirements that companies must meet to gain approval of a proposed merger or acquisition. This has been a hot area of debate in recent years since the Canadian government has repeatedly blocked or delayed the domestic chartered banks from merging. If left unchecked, the Canadian banking system would probably be dominated by three larger banks instead of the big six that reign today. In 1998, Paul Martin, then Canadian finance minister, rejected proposed mergers between the Royal Bank and the Bank of Montreal as well as a merger between the Canadian Imperial Bank of Commerce and the Toronto-Dominion Bank. According to the Competition Bureau the proposed bank mergers would lessen competition and result in many branches closing their doors. Thus Canadians would pay more for less.[29] A year later the government set up a framework for such cases by creating a merger review process for banks that have equity above $5 billion. The banks were informed that the process would include an application to the Competition Bureau, a Public Interest Impact Assessment filing as well as the need to jump through a few more hoops before awaiting a decision from the Minister of Finance.[30] Of course, the debate has continued and the opinions are mixed. A recent Bank of Canada study indicated that bank mergers would not necessarily lessen competition.[31]

Bill Gates, chairman of Microsoft, called Judge Jackson's ruling "unreasonable" and "clearly the most massive attempt at government regulation of the technology industry ever."

Regulating and Deregulating Industries

Sometimes the government imposes regulations on specific industries to ensure fair competition, ethical business practices, safe working conditions, or general public safety. The banking industry exemplifies the serious role of government in creating rules of conduct and outlining a framework for the system. In a *highly regulated industry,* close government control is substituted for free competition, and competition is either limited or eliminated. In extreme cases, regulators may even decide who can enter an industry, what customers they must serve, and how much they can charge. For years, the electric utility industries have fallen under strict government control.

Hydro-Québec is a closely run government-controlled entity. Other utilities such as Ontario Hydro and BC Hydro have begun to experiment with free-market approaches, with mixed results.[32] The trend in most industries over the past few decades has been to open up competition in regulated industries by removing or relaxing existing regulations. Hopes are that such *deregulation* will allow new industry competitors to enter the market, create more choices for consumers, and keep prices in check. But the debate is ongoing about whether deregulation achieves these goals.

Protecting Stakeholders

stakeholders
Individuals or groups to whom a business has a responsibility

In addition to fostering competition, another important role the government plays is to protect the stakeholders of a business. Businesses have many **stakeholders**—groups that are affected by (or that affect) a business's operations, including employees, investors, customers, suppliers, government, and society at large. In the course of serving one or more of these stakeholders, a business may sometimes neglect the interests of other stakeholders. For example, managers who are too narrowly focused on generating wealth for shareholders might not spend the funds necessary to create a safe work environment for employees or to reduce waste. Similarly, a public company that withholds information about its true financial performance may hamper the ability of investors to make solid decisions and may even harm the wealth of stakeholders. Nortel, once the pride of Canadian investors, has fallen on hard times. Originally it was hurt by a free-falling stock price as the stock market high-tech bubble burst. Further damaging its reputation was the firm's forced admission that the financial results for 2003, as well as earlier periods dating back to 2001, required restatement to reflect more accurately the financial position of the company.[33]

To protect consumers, employees, shareholders, and the environment from the potentially harmful actions of business, the government has established several regulatory agencies (see Exhibit 1.6). Many of these agencies have the power to pass and enforce rules and regulations within their specific area of authority. Such regulations are intended to encourage businesses to behave ethically and in a socially responsible manner. Chapter 3 takes a closer look at society's concerns for ethical and socially responsibly behaviour.

Contributing to Economic Stability

A nation's economy never stays exactly the same size. Instead, it grows and contracts in response to the combined effects of such factors as technological breakthroughs, changes in investment patterns, shifts in consumer attitudes, world events, and basic economic forces. *Economic expansion* occurs when the economy is growing and people are spending more money. Consumer purchases stimulate businesses to produce more goods and services, which in turn stimulates employment. *Economic contraction* occurs when such spending declines. Businesses cut back on production, employees are laid off, and the economy as a whole slows down. If the period of downward swing is severe, the nation may enter into a **recession**, traditionally defined as two consecutive quarters of decline in real gross domestic product.

recession
Period during which national income, employment, and production all fall

When a downward swing or recession is over, the economy enters into a period of *recovery:* Companies buy more, factories produce more, employment is high, and workers spend their earnings. These recurrent up-and-down swings are known as the **business cycle** (see Exhibit 1.7 on page 18). Despite the fact that economic swings are natural, and to some degree predictable, they cause hardship to individuals. In an attempt to avoid such hardship and to foster economic stability, the government can create new taxes or adjust the current tax rates, raise or lower interest rates, and regulate the total amount of money circulating in our economy. These government actions have two facets: monetary policy and fiscal policy.

business cycle
Fluctuations in the rate of growth that an economy experiences over a period of several years

monetary policy
Government policy and actions taken by the Bank of Canada to regulate the nation's money supply

Monetary Policy **Monetary policy** involves adjusting the nation's money supply by increasing or decreasing interest rates to help control inflation. In Canada, monetary

Exhibit 1.6 **Major Canadian Government Agencies and What They Do**

Government agencies protect stakeholders by developing and promoting standards, regulating and overseeing industries, and enforcing laws and regulations.[34]

GOVERNMENT AGENCY OR COMMISSION	MAJOR AREAS OF RESPONSIBILITY
Competition Bureau	Promote and maintain fair competition so that Canadians can benefit from lower prices, product choice, and quality services. Administration and enforcement of the Competition Act, the Consumer Packaging and Labelling Act, the Textile Labelling Act, and the Precious Metals Marking Act.
Environment Canada	Preserve and enhance the quality of the natural environment, including water, air and soil quality; conserve Canada's renewable resources; protect Canada's water resources; carry out meteorology.
Industry Canada	Help make Canadians more productive and competitive in the knowledge-based economy. Give consumers, investors, and businesses the confidence that the marketplace is fair, efficient, and competitive.
The Business Development Bank of Canada (BDC)	(BDC) provides small and medium-sized businesses with flexible financing, affordable consulting services, and venture capital.
Export Development Canada (EDC)	Devoted to providing trade finance services to support Canadian exporters and investors in some 200 markets, 130 of which are in developing markets.
Canadian Radio-television and Telecommunications Commission (CRTC)	Regulate and supervise all aspects of the Canadian broadcasting system, as well as telecommunications common carriers and service providers that fall under federal jurisdiction.
Transport Canada	Mandate to ensure that Canadians have the best transportation system by developing and administering policies, regulations, and programs for a safe, efficient, and environmentally friendly transportation system.
National Energy Board	Promote safety, environmental protection, and economic efficiency in the *Canadian public interest* within the mandate set by Parliament in the regulation of pipelines, energy development, and trade.
Fisheries and Oceans Canada	Responsible for developing and implementing policies in support of Canada's economic, ecological, and scientific interests in oceans and inland waters.
Health Canada	In partnership with provincial and territorial governments, Health Canada provides national leadership to develop health policy, enforce health regulations, promote disease prevention, and enhance healthy living for all Canadians.
Canadian Food Inspection Agency (CFIA)	Protects consumers by contributing to food safety, the protection of plants, and the health of animals in Canada. CFIA is responsible for the administration and enforcement of the numerous acts, including the Fish Inspection Act, the Meat Inspection Act, the Plant Protection Act, the Consumer Packaging and Labelling Act as it relates to food, and the enforcement of the Food and Drugs Act as it relates to food.
Canadian Wheat Board (CWB)	Farmer-controlled organization that markets wheat and barley grown by western Canadian producers. The CWB is the largest single seller of wheat and barley in the world, holding more than 20 percent of the international market.
Department of Human Resources & Skills Development (HRSD)	Responsible for providing Canadians with the tools they need to thrive and prosper in the workplace by supporting human capital development and labour market development and establishing a culture of lifelong learning for Canadians.
Canadian Centre for Occupational Health and Safety (CCOHS)	The CCOHS promotes a safe and healthy working environment and assists in the maintenance and development of policies and programs. The CCOHS reports to the Minister of Labour.

Exhibit 1.7 **The Business Cycle**

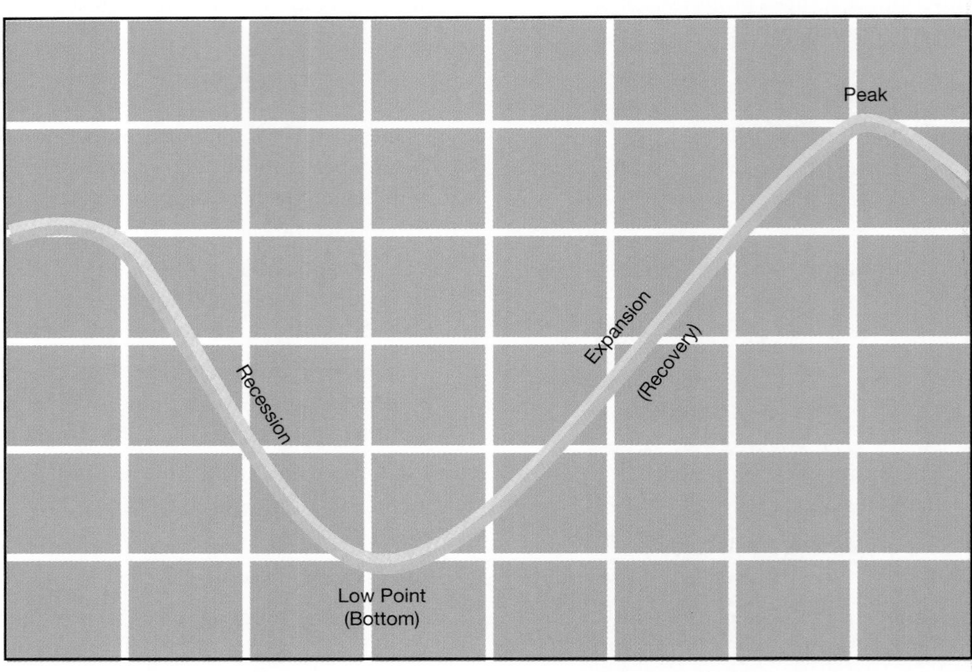

policy is controlled primarily by the Bank of Canada (BOC). It influences the money supply directly with policy decisions and indirectly with its implied vision for future decisions. The BOC must be certain that enough money and credit are available to fuel a healthy economy. However, it must act carefully, because altering the money supply affects interest rates, inflation, and the economy (see Exhibit 1.8). When the money supply is increased, more money is available for loans, so banks can charge lower interest rates to borrowers. On the other hand, an increased money supply can lead to greater consumer spending and can result in the demand for goods exceeding supply. When demand exceeds supply, sellers may raise their prices, leading to inflation. In turn, inflation can slow economic growth—a situation the BOC wants to avoid. Since so many companies now buy and sell across national borders, the BOC's changes may affect the interlinked economies of many countries and vice versa.[35]

target for the overnight rate
The midpoint rate the Bank of Canada wants to see in the marketplace for overnight loans

prime interest rate
Lowest interest rate banks offer on short-term loans to preferred borrowers

The BOC can change the **target for the overnight rate**, which represents the midpoint of the bank's operating band for overnight financing. This is the average rate the BOC wants to see in the marketplace for such short-term loans. The official rate was formerly the *bank rate*, which is at the upper level of the operating band and is set one-quarter percent above the target rate.[36] When the Bank of Canada raises the target for the overnight rate, banks generally raise the **prime interest rate**, the lowest interest rate on short-term loans offered to preferred borrowers. This discourages loans and tightens the money supply, which can slow down economic growth. In contrast, lowering the target for the overnight rate results in lower lending rates, which can encourage borrowing and stimulate economic growth.

The Bank of Canada can also conduct open market operations. It can influence the money supply by selling and buying government bonds. If the BOC is concerned about inflation, it can reduce the money supply by selling Canadian government bonds, which takes cash out of circulation. When the BOC wants to boost the economy, it can buy back government bonds, putting cash into circulation and increasing the money supply.

Keep in mind that money injected into the economy has a *multiplier effect* as it makes its way through the system. For example, if a company spends money to build a large office complex, thousands of construction workers will earn wages. If some of

Exhibit 1.8 **Influencing the Money Supply**

The Bank of Canada cautiously adjusts the money supply as it attempts to stimulate economic growth while keeping inflation and interest rates at acceptable levels.

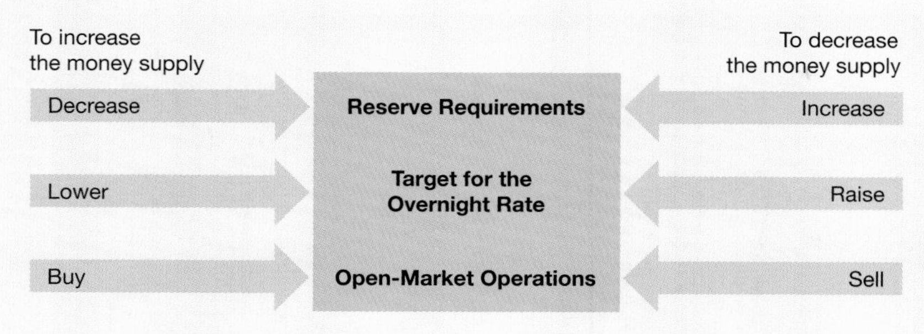

these workers decide to spend their extra income to buy new cars, car dealers will have more income. The car dealers might spend their income on new clothes, and the sales clerks (who earn commissions) might buy electronic products, and so on. This *circular flow* of money through the economic system links all elements of the Canadian economy by exchanging goods and services for money, which is then used to buy more goods and services, and so on.

Fiscal Policy **Fiscal policy** involves changes in the government's revenues and expenditures to stimulate or dampen the economy. Government spending is indeed an important factor in Canadian economic stability. For one thing, the Canadian federal, provincial, and municipal governments are responsible for supplying and maintaining such *public goods and services* as highways, military, public water works, fire and police protection, medicare, and so on. The Canadian government gets money to provide such public goods by collecting a variety of taxes, such as those listed in Exhibit 1.9.

fiscal policy
Use of government revenue collection and spending to influence the business cycle

When the Canadian government spends more money than it takes in, it creates annual budget deficits. Over the past 10 years the government has reversed the nega-

Exhibit 1.9 **Types of Taxes**

From road repair to regulation, running a government is an expensive affair. To fund government operations and projects, national governments, provinces, towns, and cities levy and collect a variety of revenue-raising taxes.

TYPE OF TAX	LEVIED ON
Income taxes	Income earned by individuals and businesses. Income taxes are the government's largest single source of revenue.
Property taxes	Assessed value of the land and structures owned by businesses and individuals.
Sales taxes (GST, PST)	Retail purchases made by customers. Sales taxes are collected by retail businesses at the time of the sale and then forwarded to the government.
Excise taxes	Selected items such as gasoline, tobacco, and alcohol. Often referred to as "sin" taxes, excise taxes are implemented to help control potentially harmful practices.
Payroll taxes	Earnings of individuals to help fund programs such as education, medicare, and employment insurance.

Exhibit 1.10 **Federal Debt-to-GDP Projections (Accumulated Deficit)**

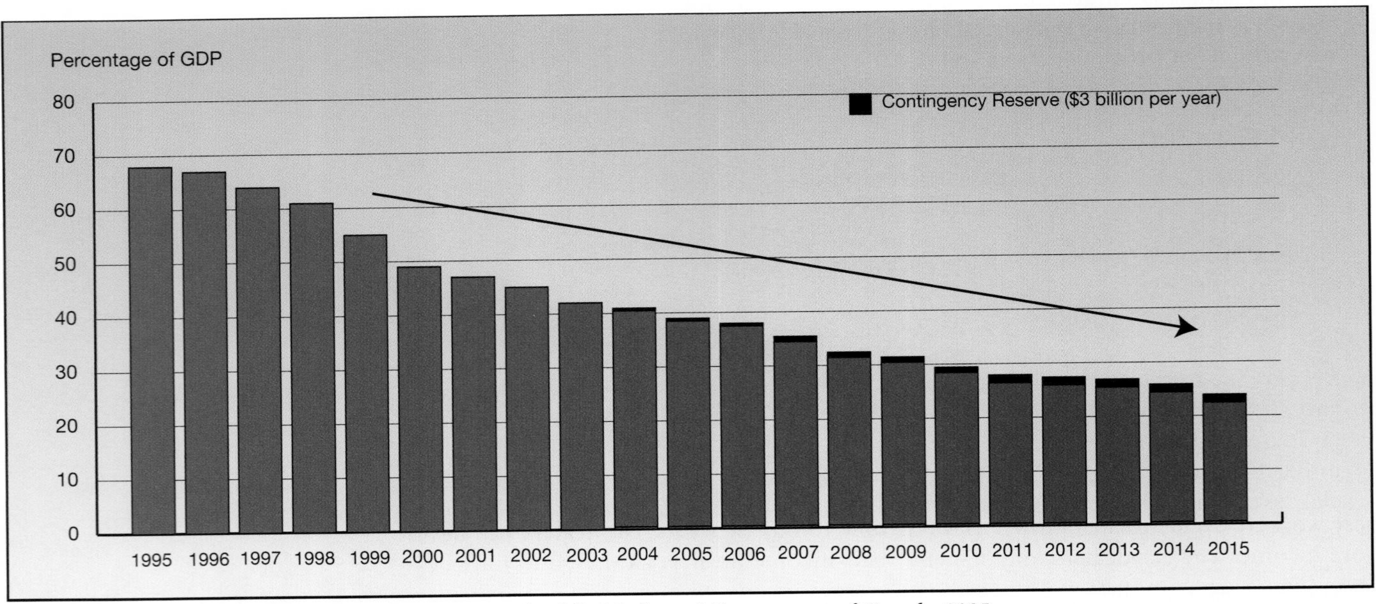

Source: Reproduced with permission of the Minister of Public Works and Government of Canada, 2005.

tive ritual of annual government deficits. In fact, since it achieved a surplus in 1997–1998, thus ending a nearly three-decade-old practice of deficits, the federal government has avoided the "D" word. Reducing the accumulated amount of annual budget deficits (the national debt) is a target on which the government has recently focused. Remember that the gross domestic product (GDP) represents the value of all final goods and services produced by businesses in the country. The Canadian government is determined to lower the debt-to-GDP ratio to 25 percent within 10 years by paying down the debt with a portion of the budget surpluses (see Exhibit 1.10). The debt-to-GDP ratio stood at 68.4 percent in 1995–1996 and had fallen to 42 percent by 2003–2004.[37]

L.O. 7

CHALLENGES OF A GLOBAL ECONOMY

globalization
Tendency of the world's economies to act as a single interdependent economy

Whether economic indicators suggest that the economy is in a period of contraction or expansion, businesses must be prepared to meet the many challenges of a global economy. **Globalization** refers to the increasing integration of the world's economies. This evolution can be credited to technological and human innovation that has forced independent markets to slowly evolve and embrace the new world market. With this transformation we have seen a move toward labour mobility and the freer flow of technology and knowledge across international borders. This has created new opportunities for a company's goods and services, but at the same time it has created tougher competition and new challenges for businesses:

- *Producing quality products and services that satisfy customers' changing needs.* Today's customer is well-informed and has many product choices. For businesses such as Waterloo, Ontario's, Research In Motion, maker of the BlackBerry wireless platform, competing in the global economy means competing on the basis of *speed* (getting products to market sooner), *quality* (doing a better job of meeting customer expectations), and *customer satisfaction* (making sure buyers are happy with every aspect of the purchase, from the shopping experience until they have finished using the product).

- *Starting and managing a small business in today's competitive environment.* Starting a new business or successfully managing a small company in today's global economy requires creativity and a willingness to exploit new opportunities. Small companies often lack the resources to buffer themselves from competition. Furthermore, once a new product or process is brought to the market, competitors need only a short time to get up and running with something similar. Thus, the biggest challenge for small businesses today is to make a product or provide a service that is hard to imitate.
- *Thinking globally and committing to a culturally diverse workforce.* Globalization opens new markets for a company's goods, increases competition, and changes the composition of the workforce into one that is more diverse in race, gender, age, language, physical and mental abilities, lifestyle, culture, education, ideas, and background. Thus, to be competitive in the global economy, companies must commit to a culturally diverse workforce, think globally, and adopt global standards of excellence.
- *Behaving in an ethically and socially responsible manner.* As businesses become more complex through global expansion and technological change, they must deal with an increasing number of ethical and social issues. These include the marketing of unhealthy products, the use of questionable accounting practices to compute financial results, and the pollution of the environment (as Chapter 3 discusses). In the future, businesses can expect continued pressure from environmental groups, consumers, employees, and government regulators to act ethically and responsibly.
- *Keeping pace with technology and electronic commerce.* Everywhere we look, technology is reshaping the world. The Internet and innovations in computerization, miniaturization, and telecommunication have made it possible for people anywhere in the world to exchange information and goods. Such technologies are collapsing boundaries and changing the way customers, suppliers, and companies interact.

How Is the Internet Changing the Way Companies Do Business?

L.O. 8

The Internet is revolutionizing all facets of business. It's changing the way customers, suppliers, and companies interact, creating huge opportunities as well as unforeseen competitive threats. Ford Canada credits its "build and price" site with driving up sales. About 750 000 people visit www.ford.ca each month, with 75 percent of buying customers indicating that they used the website prior to purchase.[38] Individuals are overcoming their reluctance to use the Internet for routine transactions as well. Approximately 45 percent of Canadians with Internet access pay at least some of their bills online.[39] The Internet is changing the way companies work internally—collapsing boundaries and redefining relationships among various functions, departments, and divisions. Despite the technology bubble, and the reality check it brought to over-enthusiastic speculators, the role of the Internet cannot be dismissed or ignored. According to Statistics Canada, total online sales in 2004 amounted to $28.3 billion. Approximately 93 percent of these sales came from the private sector, with the public sector accounting for the remaining 7 percent. Sales by retailers to consumers also grew to $2.9 billion, up from $1.9 billion in the previous year.[40]

Perhaps more importantly, the Internet is changing the way companies communicate.[41] The Internet offers businesses a wide variety of choices for online communication, including e-mail, discussion mailing lists, Usenet groups, Telnet, instant messaging, and Internet telephony. In addition to these communication choices, companies can use intranets and extranets—two types of websites specifically designed for internal and external communication.

Intranets

Companies that want to set up special employees-only websites can use an **intranet**—a private, internal network. Intranets use the same technologies as the Internet and the World Wide Web, but the information provided and the access allowed are restricted

intranet
A private network, set up within a corporation or organization, that operates over the Internet and may be used to link geographically remote sites

An intranet set up by his law firm enables attorney David Beckman to view documents and other legal resources whether he's in the office or in the courtroom.

to members of the organization (regardless of their actual location). Whereas employees can use a password to log on to the corporate intranet and then move to public areas of the Internet, unauthorized people cruising the Internet cannot enter the internal site.

According to one study, nearly 90 percent of North American companies are using some form of corporate intranet, with 25 percent using the portals for more than just publishing material. Three factors are fuelling this intranet boom: (1) the desire to share global knowledge, (2) the need for greater access to company information, and (3) the Web's ease of use and flexibility.[42] For example, Ford Motor Company uses its intranet to enable engineers and designers worldwide to collaborate in real time on the design of new car models. Every model has its own internal website to track design, production, quality control, and delivery processes. The site serves more than 175 000 employees who access the site about 500 000 times each day.[43] At IBM, employees can log on to the corporate intranet to check their health benefits more conveniently. The intranet is also used as a high-tech suggestion box, with more than 6000 IBM employees responding to a recent company question in the span of three days.[44]

Intranets can be used for numerous communication functions. In addition to sending e-mail, other uses include filing electronic forms and reports, gaining remote access to company information, and publishing electronic phone directories, company newsletters, and other company material such as:[45]

- *Policy manuals.* The most current version is always available to all employees without the need to reprint manuals when policies change.
- *Employee benefits information.* Employees can find out about benefits, reallocate the funds in their retirement and benefit plans, fill out electronic forms, view an electronic pay stub, and sign up for training programs.
- *Presentation materials used by marketing and sales departments.* Sales representatives can download marketing materials at customer sites all over the world. In addition, changes made by marketing representatives at company headquarters are immediately available to field salespeople.
- *Company records and information.* Company directories, customer information, employee skills inventories, project status reports, and company calendars and events can be stored on an intranet so that they're accessible from anywhere in the world.

Putting this material on an intranet allows employees to find information quickly and more easily than they would by digging through multiple filing cabinets or contacting different offices to find what they need.

Extranets

extranet
Similar to an intranet, but extending the network to select people outside the organization

Once a company has an intranet in place, the cost of adding external capabilities is minimal, but the benefits can be substantial. An **extranet** is an external intranet that allows people (business partners) to communicate and exchange data within a secured network.[46] Unlike intranets, which limit access to employees, extranets allow qualified people from outside the company—such as suppliers and customers—to enter the network using a password. Extranets can enhance communication with clients, suppliers, and colleagues, and they can save companies time and money. Consider Boeing. Every year the aerospace giant would ship a mountain of technical manuals, parts lists, and other maintenance documents to its 600 airline customers—enough papers to make a stack more than 43 000 metres tall—at an annual cost of millions of dollars. But now Boeing places all this information on an extranet so customers can review the data, obtain product updates, and discuss maintenance issues in chat areas.[47]

Extranets have many other uses. Some executive search firms and employment agencies are allowing clients to tap into their extranets to search for job prospects. More companies are inviting customers to use their extranets to check on the status of orders and shipping details. Doctors and hospitals are also using extranets to share best practices among their individual organizations. In the past they faxed this information to each other, but there was no guarantee that the right person would receive a fax or even know it existed before the information became obsolete.

In short, companies are using Internet, intranet, and extranet technology to

- Locate information from external sources
- Collaborate with local, national, and international business partners
- Find new business partners and attract new customers
- Communicate with customers about their orders
- Promote and sell goods and services to customers at any location
- Provide customers with service, technical support, and product information
- Search out and buy parts and materials from domestic and international suppliers
- Permit employees to **telecommute**, or work away from a conventional office, whether at home, on the road, or across the country
- Cost-effectively recruit and train employees
- Share text, photos, slides, videos, and other data within the organization
- Inform investors, industry analysts, government regulators, customers, and other stakeholders about business developments
- Conduct video conferences as an alternative to face-to-face meetings

telecommute
To work from home and communicate with the company's main office via computer and communication devices

All these uses of the Internet have one thing in common: They involve communication, the most important benefit of the Internet according to a recent survey by Booz-Allen & Hamilton and the Economist Intelligent Unit (see Exhibit 1.11).

Exhibit 1.11 **Greatest Internet Benefits**

More than 525 executives who responded to a survey by Booz-Allen & Hamilton and the Economist Intelligent Unit listed the following business benefits as the key contributions of the Internet.

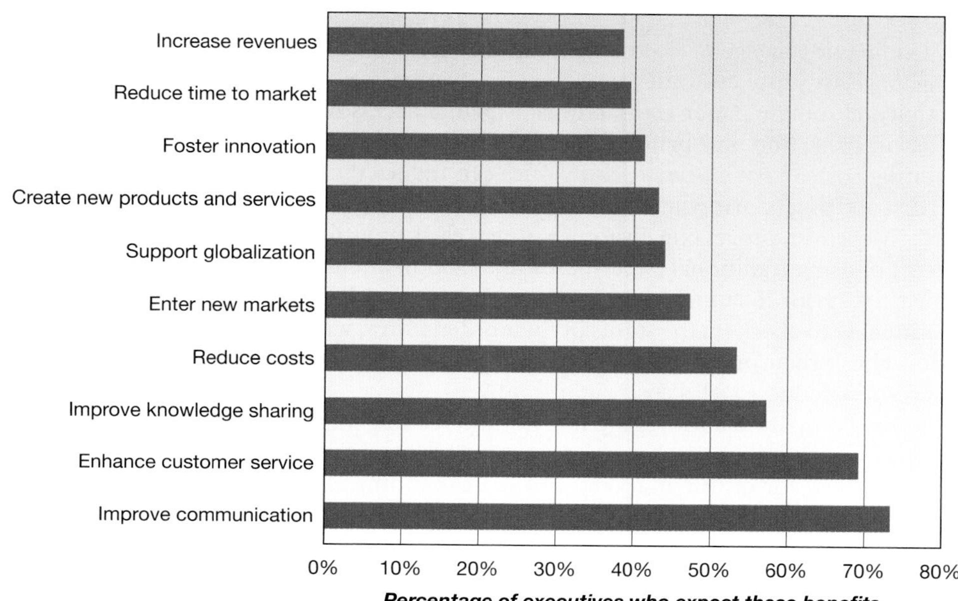

WHAT IS ELECTRONIC COMMERCE?

In addition to using the Internet for communication, businesses are using it to conduct electronic commerce. We defined electronic commerce (e-commerce) as the buying and selling of goods and services over an electronic network. Specifically, e-commerce is classified into four broad categories:

business-to-consumer e-commerce
Electronic commerce that involves transactions between businesses and the end user or consumer

- **Business-to-consumer e-commerce**. Referred to as B2C, e-tailing, or electronic retailing, this form of e-commerce involves interactions and transactions between a company and consumers, with a focus on selling goods and services and marketing to consumers. Typical B2C transactions include such functions as sales, marketing (advertising, coupons, catalogues), order processing and tracking, credit authorization, customer service, and electronic payments. The latter option is still in its early stages but companies such as Imperial Oil and Shell are leading the charge with their Speedpass payment systems. Organizations like Tim Hortons and Second Cup are slowly experimenting with such systems, most notably in Toronto's downtown office core.[48]

business-to-business e-commerce
Electronic commerce that involves transactions between companies and their suppliers, manufacturers, or other companies

- **Business-to-business e-commerce**. Known as B2B, this form of e-commerce uses the Internet to conduct transactions between businesses. Seventy-five percent of e-commerce sales can be traced to B2B deals. B2B typically involves a company and its suppliers, distributors, manufacturers, and retailers, but not consumers. In Canada, the wholesale trade business led the way with $6 billion worth of goods sold in 2004.[49] Generally, the types of goods sold in B2B transactions include office materials, manufacturing supplies, equipment, and other goods a company needs for operations. Companies from Honeywell to Sears and the Big Three automakers (Ford, GM, and DaimlerChrysler) have all started electronic marketplaces to purchase supplies and transact business. Industry experts anticipate that the B2B segment of e-commerce will continue to grow significantly.[50]

consumer-to-consumer e-commerce
Electronic commerce that involves transactions between consumers

- **Consumer-to-consumer e-commerce.** This category of e-commerce involves consumers who sell products directly to each other using the Internet as the intermediary. Auction sites such as eBay are C2C electronic channels. Sellers list their products with the auction site and buyers bid on listed sellers' products. Once a bid is accepted, the seller ships the product to the buyer.

mobile commerce
Transaction of electronic commerce using wireless devices and wireless Internet access instead of PC-based technology

- **Mobile commerce.** Also known as m-commerce, this category uses wireless Internet access and wireless handheld devices such as cellphones, Palm Pilots, and pagers to conduct business.

Companies engage in electronic commerce for a wide variety of reasons: to improve their image, improve customer service, simplify processes, compress time, increase productivity, eliminate paper transactions, expedite access to information, reduce transportation costs, find new benefits, increase flexibility, locate new customers, and reduce operating costs.[51] For instance, companies can reduce the costs of publishing, processing, distributing, storing, and retrieving information by engaging in electronic commerce. Moreover, processing customer orders electronically can be done at a fraction of the cost of using traditional paper-based and labour-intensive processes. Dell Computer reports that prior to launching its website, customers called an average of once or twice per purchase to check on the status of their orders. Now, with online order tracking, customers check their order status electronically instead of calling a customer service rep. This process reduces Dell's costs significantly.[52]

Many companies also engage in e-commerce to generate new revenue streams by (1) creating new online markets for existing products, (2) creating new products specifically designed for online markets, and (3) expanding existing or new products into international markets.[53]

Customers stand to gain as much if not more from e-commerce than companies do. Electronic commerce:[54]

- Enables customers to shop or conduct other transactions 24 hours a day, from almost any location

- Provides customers with more choices (many vendors, more products, and price competition)
- Allows for quick delivery of digitized products and information
- Allows customers to interact with other customers, exchange ideas, and compare experiences
- Facilitates competition, which can keep prices in line

For example, with a few clicks of a mouse, travellers can plan and price trips, purchase tickets, receive travel confirmations, review current reservations, and review the status of their rewards accounts. In short, today's customers can make buying decisions as if they had an army of intelligent helpers running to all the stores around the world to find the best products and prices. This ability is putting customers in a position of unprecedented control.

What Is the Difference Between E-Commerce and E-Business?

L.O. 9

As discussed earlier, e-commerce involves buying and selling over electronic networks. By contrast, an **electronic business (e-business)** uses Internet technology to do much more than set up a website to sell or deliver goods. E-commerce is indeed an important part of becoming an e-business, but it is only one step in the process. To become an e-business, companies must develop systems and structures that help the organization innovate constantly, react rapidly, and handle dynamic change. An e-business also integrates technology and the Internet into every phase of the business process—production, marketing, sales, customer support, advertising, public relations, and more—with one goal in mind: to meet customers' changing needs and priorities.[55]

electronic business (e-business) A company that has transformed its key business processes to incorporate Internet technology into every phase of the operation

However, successfully weaving technology into every part of an operation is a huge task. *Fortune* magazine reports that less than 10 percent of e-business strategies are effectively executed. Moreover, for a business to become a successful e-business, it must not only meet the needs and priorities of its customers but also anticipate and prepare for the unexpected.[56] See Exhibit 1.12.

Hot Topics and Issues in E-Commerce and E-Business

Electronic commerce may be a merchant's and consumer's dream, but once a website is up and running, companies must confront a variety of hot topics and issues. Among them are channel management, privacy, employee productivity, data security, and sab-

Exhibit 1.12 **E-Business Adoption in Canada by Size of Firm**[57]

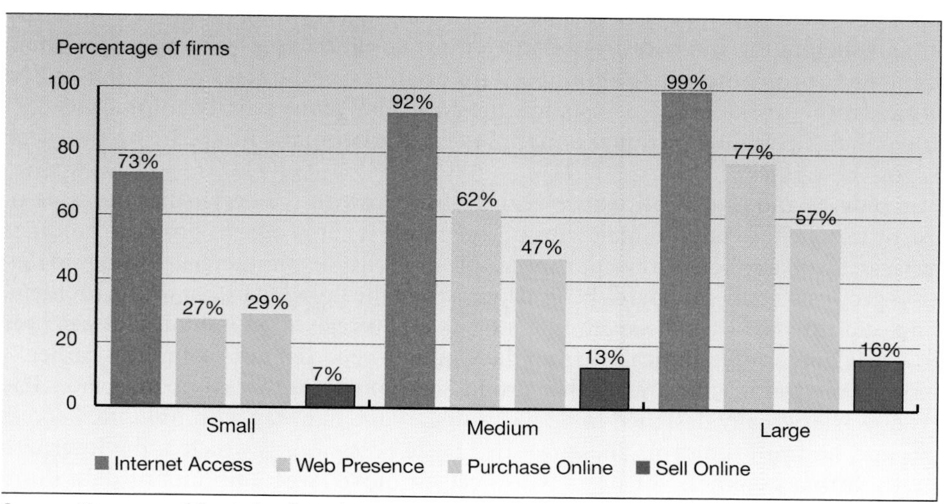

Source: Courtesy of Statistics Canada.

otage and theft. As you read through the text be sure to pay attention to the E-Business in Action cases that elaborate on these and other subjects. You can find them at the end of each Part of this text.

Channel Management

The Internet presents an opportunity for the producer to sell directly to the consumer. But the decision to modify the traditional channel structure is a critical one, with consequences unique to each situation. As Chapter 12 discusses in detail, some producers are using the Internet to eliminate the intermediary; others are using it to restructure their distribution channels to make them more cost-effective; still others are using the Internet to expand their reach. Additionally, barriers to entry can be reduced because the Internet provides opportunities that did not previously exist. Richard Strang of Erin, Ontario, grew his hobby of collecting old books into a business called Richard's Discount Books. He operates out of his basement with the help of a pretty efficient channel partner: eBay.[58]

Information Privacy

Information privacy in today's workplace is another hot issue. Employers must find the right balance between protecting valuable company information and respecting employees' privacy rights. For instance, many employees believe that their e-mail and voice mail messages are private, and are surprised when e-mail ends up in places they did not intend it to go. But employers have the legal right to monitor everything from employees' Web access to the content of their company e-mail or voice mail messages. Both e-mail and voice mail can be used as evidence in court cases. Therefore, a good rule of thumb is not to say anything in an e-mail or voice mail that you would not want to see published in a newspaper.[59] The $220 million corporate espionage lawsuit between Air Canada and WestJet is a prime example. Recently, an Ontario Superior Court judge cleared the way to allow H+A Computer Forensics Inc. to conduct sophisticated searches on WestJet hard drives. This investigation will include Chairman Clive Beddoe's own personal computer; the goal is to find e-mails and other electronic files that can be used as evidence in the case.[60] Other recent high-profile cases involving employees at CIBC and ATI reinforce the legal issues regarding e-mail.[61]

Employee Productivity

Maintaining a high level of employee productivity is another challenge companies are facing. E-mail, voice mail, conference calls, and faxes interrupt employees while they work. Chat or real-time conversation windows can pop up on computer screens and demand immediate conversation. Moreover, the percentage of employees who use company resources for personal business is astounding. Sending personal e-mail and faxes and surfing the Internet are the three most common employee abuses. To help prevent such problems, more employers are establishing policies governing online activities in the workplace. For instance, the *New York Times* strictly enforces its corporate policy forbidding personal e-mail. In fact, the company fired 23 employees for violating these rules.[62]

spam
Unsolicited "junk" e-mail sent to large numbers of people to promote products or services

Employees and organizations are also confronted with the ever-annoying issue of **spam**, or unsolicited "junk" e-mail sent to large numbers of people to promote products or services. Spam also refers to inappropriate promotional or commercial postings to discussion groups or bulletin boards.[63] To demonstrate the growing extent of the problem, Symnatec claims that its anti-spam filters block an average of 33 million messages per week. This figure is up significantly from the 9 million reported just six months earlier.[64]

Electronic traffic jams are another productivity problem that companies face. The Internet was originally designed to be like a single-lane highway with unlimited access points and no traffic control. These features make accessibility, which is the Internet's strength, into a weakness for users who need to move large amounts of data more quickly. When traffic gets heavy, the Internet slows down. To get around this problem, several universities have created an ultra-"high-speed" Internet2 with connections 400 times faster than standard high-speed lines. However, this service is available to only a limited number of users.[65]

Data Security

Before computers, companies typically conducted business mainly on paper, locking up sensitive documents and using security precautions when transporting important files. Furthermore, only a limited number of people had access to vital company data. But today's electronic data systems pose a real threat to corporate data security.[66] Global networks increase the possibility that crucial information on an intranet or sent over the Internet will be altered or destroyed. In fact, Internet attacks on businesses continue to rise, with the average organization experiencing 13.6 attacks per day. This figure is up from 10.6 attacks per day in the previous year.[67] These infiltration attempts include **hacking**—or breaking into a computer network such as an intranet to steal, delete, or change data—and **cracking**—or entering a computer network for non-destructive reasons, such as to play a prank or show off.

hacking
Breaking into a computer network to steal, delete, or change data

cracking
Entering a computer network for non-destructive reasons, such as to play a prank

For these reasons, most companies go beyond simple identification and password protection to prevent unauthorized computer access by installing a **firewall**, a type of gateway that controls access to the company's local network. The firewall allows access only to users who present the proper password and system identification. At Fairmont Hotels, superhighway cops monitor what guests bring into the "guest network" and also control the separate corporate network.[68] In addition to firewalls, companies protect their data by (1) determining which employees should receive passwords to vital networks, (2) providing ongoing security enforcement and education, (3) conducting background checks on all new employees, (4) adopting a security policy that requires employees to use passwords, turn computers off when not in use, encrypt sensitive e-mail, and apply stronger security measures to safeguard trade secrets, and (5) developing a plan for data recovery if disaster strikes.[69]

firewall
Computer hardware and software that protects part or all of a private computer network attached to the Internet by preventing public users from accessing it

Taking these measures will, of course, deter potential offenders, but doing so will not guarantee security of information or completely protect data from sabotage.

Sabotage

Today, criminals are using technology to disrupt website and computer operations and cause other problems for companies, governments, and individuals. Among the most common forms of sabotage are viruses and worms:

- **Viruses** are programs that can change or delete files or programs. They are embedded in legitimate software (without the manufacturer's knowledge) or in files passed from one computer to another.
- **Worms** are programs specifically designed to replicate over and over again. Spread by e-mail, they send more worms to everyone in the recipient's e-mail address book—taking up precious network space and snarling connections.

viruses
Form of computer sabotage embedded in software or passed from one computer to the next that changes or deletes computer files or programs

worms
Form of computer sabotage sent by e-mail that reproduces—taking up network space and snarling connections

Nearly every workplace has had one or more computers infected with a virus. In a recent study, 85 percent of the firms surveyed said they had been victims of viruses. Virus damage can be costly; cleaning up the wreckage and protecting against additional viruses has forced companies to spend more than US$12.1 billion annually on virus protection programs and other safeguards. The problem is increasing; Symantec documented 4500 new Windows viruses and worms in the first six months of 2004. This was four times the amount documented in the previous year.[70]

Cost is not the only concern. As worms and viruses spread, they can disrupt other interconnected government and company systems and slow Internet traffic. Even a relatively simple sabotage technique such as repeatedly trying to access an Internet address can tie up a site or crash its equipment, as eBay, E*Trade, Amazon.com, and other web-based businesses have learned.[71]

Moving Forward

As these challenges suggest, doing business in the twenty-first century means working in a world of increasing uncertainty where change is the norm, not the exception. In the coming chapters, we explore specific challenges that businesses are facing in the global economy and provide real-world examples of how companies are tackling and meeting these challenges. As you read through the text be sure to pay attention to the E-Business in Action cases, which appear at the end of each Part and show the relationship between the chapter material and e-business practices that companies are currently employing.

SUMMARY OF LEARNING OBJECTIVES

1 Define what a business is and identify four key social and economic roles that businesses serve.

A business is a profit-seeking activity that provides goods and services to satisfy consumers' needs. The driving force behind most businesses is the chance to earn a profit; however, non-profit organizations exist to provide society with a social or educational service. Businesses serve four key functions: they provide society with necessities; they provide people with jobs and a means to prosper; they pay taxes that are used by the government to provide services for its citizens; and they reinvest their profits in the economy, thereby increasing a nation's wealth.

2 Differentiate between goods-producing and service businesses. List five factors for the rise in the number of service businesses.

Goods-producing businesses produce tangible goods and tend to be capital-intensive, whereas service businesses produce intangible goods and tend to be labour-intensive. The number of service businesses is increasing because (1) consumers have more disposable income to spend on taking care of themselves, (2) many services target consumers' needs brought about by changing demographic patterns and lifestyle trends, (3) consumers need assistance with using and integrating new technology into their business operations and lifestyles, (4) companies are turning to consultants and other professionals for advice to remain competitive, and (5) in general, barriers to entry are lower for service companies than they are for goods-producing businesses.

3 Differentiate between a free-market system and a planned system.

In a free-market system, individuals have a high degree of freedom to decide what is produced, by whom, and for whom. Moreover, the pursuit of private gain is regarded as a worthwhile goal. In a planned system, governments limit the individual's freedom of choice in order to accomplish government goals, control the allocation of resources, and restrict private ownership to personal and household items. The pursuit of private gain is nonexistent under a planned system.

4 Explain how supply and demand affect price.

In the simplest sense, supply and demand affect price in the following manner: When the price goes up, the quantity demanded goes down but the supplier's incentive to produce more goes up. When the price goes down, the quantity demanded increases but the quantity supplied may (or may not) decline. When the interests of buyers and sellers are in balance, an equilibrium price is established. However, adjusting price or supply to meet or spur demand does not guarantee profitability, as the airline example illustrates. The important thing to remember is that in a free-market system, the interaction of supply and demand determines what is produced and in what amounts.

5 Explain how a free-market system monitors its economic performance.

Economists evaluate economic performance by monitoring a variety of economic indicators, such as unemployment statistics, housing starts, durable-goods orders, and inflation. They compute the consumer price index (CPI) to keep an eye on price changes—especially inflation. In addition, economists measure the productivity of a nation by computing the country's gross domestic product (GDP)—the sum of all goods and services produced by both domestic and foreign companies as long as they are located within a nation's boundaries.

6 Discuss the four major economic roles of the Canadian government.

The Canadian government fosters competition by enacting laws and regulations and by approving mergers and acquisitions, retaining the power to block those that might restrain competition. It regulates certain industries where competition would be wasteful or excessive. It protects stakeholders from potentially harmful actions of businesses. Finally, it contributes to economic stability by regulating the money supply and by spending for the public good.

Identify five challenges that businesses are facing in the global economy.

The five challenges identified in the chapter are (1) producing quality products and services that satisfy customers' changing needs, (2) starting and managing a small business in today's competitive environment, (3) thinking globally and committing to a culturally diverse workforce, (4) behaving in an ethically and socially responsible manner, and (5) keeping pace with technology and electronic commerce.

Learn how companies are using the Internet to improve their efficiency.

Nearly all aspects of business can be improved with the help of Internet technology. From improved communication in the supply chain to efficient 24-hour sales information to improved customer service and delivery, the Internet is a tool that, when properly employed, can be used as a weapon for competitive advantage.

Distinguish between e-business and e-commerce.

E-commerce involves buying and selling over electronic networks whereas e-business uses Internet technology to do much more than simply set up a website to sell or deliver goods. An e-business integrates technology and the Internet into every phase of the business process—production, marketing, sales, customer support, advertising, public relations, etc.—with one goal in mind: to meet customers' changing needs and priorities

Behind the SCENES

Establishing New Roots: Building an International Brand

Roots is a dynamic company that has grown from a small local venture to a large, diverse international enterprise. Despite the change the company retains its entrepreneurial spirit. Michael Budman and Don Green are always on the lookout for the next big opportunity to expand the firm. For example, in recent years licensing agreements for items ranging from watches to luggage, sold in stores like Sears and The Bay, have become a positive contributor to the bottom line. According to a recent interview, Budman's intentions are clear: "When I look at Puma, Adidas, and Nike, I aspire to get up there with Roots." Will these aspirations eventually lead to a true global brand?

Teaming up with the Canadian Olympic Committee was a great move that helped Roots attain both domestic and international recognition. Roots earned the highest brand awareness ratings of any sponsor among Canadian consumers, prior to and after the 2004 Summer Olympics in Athens. The sponsorship of the Canadian Olympic team, which began in 1998 in Nagano, Japan, led to positive word of mouth and to contracts with the U.S., Barbados, and British teams—good promotional tools for a company looking for expansion opportunities.

A major part of Roots's most recent expansion strategy is tied to this Olympic association. Major plans are being discussed for the 2010 Vancouver–Whistler games, including the possibility of a Roots hotel. The company is also planning to open 100 stores in China to coincide with the 2008 Olympics. Roots is also looking to re-enter Europe, with dozens of store openings planned for the next five to ten years. Goals are being established, but as this chapter emphasizes, the business world is dynamic and challenges are behind every turn.

Success leads to attention and imitation. This is a golden rule of business. At home, the success Roots achieved from its Olympic ties did not go unnoticed. With Roots still enjoying its post-Olympic buzz, Hudson's Bay Company (HBC) snuck in and signed a $100 million sponsorship and clothing deal with the Canadian Olympic Committee, securing an association until the 2012 Games. This all-important domestic tool is now out of Roots's control, and with it goes an important piece of the foundation of a successful strategy. Budman publicly questioned HBC's ability to use this tool effectively, but was forced to accept the decision. Roots still possesses the rights to serve the U.S. Olympic team until 2008, and will surely continue to pursue other such deals.

Roots is an interesting company to examine because it demonstrates many modern business contrasts. The owners want to create a true global brand (similar to Nike) yet they still produce some products in Canada, at a higher cost, to remain loyal to the home market. Roots was founded by two American-born entrepreneurs yet has become a symbol of Canadian pride. The company has created tremendous success stories (Olympic poor-boy hats) and major failures (Roots Air). Its leaders are constantly battling to achieve goals, deal with competitors, promote the brand, maintain a positive image, satisfy stakeholders, and expand the geographic base of the firm. What does the future hold for this privately held company? With Michael Budman and Don Green at the helm, it is hard to say; however, it will certainly continue to be an interesting journey.[72]

Critical Thinking Questions

1. Describe how Roots meets the four key social and economic roles that businesses serve, as described in the chapter.
2. What challenges and opportunities does Roots encounter in today's global economy?
3. Should Roots continue to manufacture some products in Canada, despite higher costs?
4. How will the loss of the Canadian Olympic team contract affect Roots's expansion plans?

Learn More Online

Find out the latest news about this company. Has Roots embarked on any new adventures? Has it secured any new Olympic sponsorship deals with foreign governments? Go to Chapter 1 of this text's website at www.pearsoned.ca/bovee, and click on the Roots hotlink to read the latest news releases about the company and its plans for expansion.

KEY TERMS

barriers to entry (5)
business (3)
business cycle (16)
business-to-business e-commerce (24)
business-to-consumer e-commerce (24)
capital (6)
capital-intensive businesses (4)
capitalism (8)
communism (8)
competition (11)
competitive advantage (12)
consumer price index (CPI) (13)
consumer-to-consumer e-commerce (24)
cracking (27)
deflation (13)
demand (9)
economic indicators (12)
economic system (6)
economics (5)
electronic business (e-business) (25)
electronic commerce (e-commerce) (5)
entrepreneurs (6)
equilibrium price (11)
extranet (22)
factors of production (5)
firewall (27)
fiscal policy (19)
free-market system (8)
globalization (20)
goods-producing businesses (3)
gross domestic product (GDP) (14)
gross national product (GNP) (14)
hacking (27)
human resources (6)
inflation (13)
intranet (21)
knowledge (6)
labour-intensive businesses (4)
mobile commerce (24)
monetary policy (16)
monopolistic competition (12)
monopoly (12)
natural resources (5)
non-profit organizations (3)
oligopoly (12)
planned system (8)
prime interest rate (18)
privatizing (9)
profit (3)
pure competition (11)
recession (16)
service businesses (4)
socialism (8)
spam (26)
stakeholders (16)
supply (9)
target for the overnight rate (18)
telecommute (23)
viruses (27)
worms (27)

TEST YOUR KNOWLEDGE

Questions for Review

1. Why do business people study economics?
2. Why are knowledge workers the key economic resource?
3. How is capitalism different from communism and socialism in the way it achieves key economic goals?
4. Why is government spending an important factor in economic stability?
5. Why might the government block a merger or acquisition?

Questions for Analysis

6. Why is it often easier to start a service business than a goods-producing business?
7. Why is competition an important element of the free-market system?
8. Why do governments intervene in a free-market system?
9. How do countries know whether their economic system is working?
10. **Ethical Considerations.** Because knowledge workers are in such high demand, John decides to enrol in an evening MBA program. His company has agreed to reimburse him for 80 percent of his tuition. He hasn't revealed, however, that once he earns his degree, he plans to apply for a management position at a different company. Is it ethical for John to accept his company's tuition reimbursement, given his intentions?

Questions for Application

11. Company sales are skyrocketing, and projections show that your computer consulting business will outgrow its current location by next year. What factors should you consider when selecting a new site for your business?
12. How would a decrease in government old age security (OAS) benefits affect the economy?
13. Think about the many ways in which technology has changed your life as a consumer. Record your thoughts on a sheet of paper. On that same sheet of paper, make a second list of how you envision technology will change your life in the near future. Compare your thoughts to those of your classmates.

PRACTISE YOUR KNOWLEDGE

SHARPENING YOUR COMMUNICATION SKILLS

Select a local service business you are familiar with. How does that business try to gain a competitive advantage in the marketplace? Write a brief summary, as directed by your instructor, describing whether the company competes on speed, quality, price, innovation, service, or a combination of these attributes. Be prepared to present your analysis to your classmates.

BUILDING YOUR TEAM SKILLS

Economic indicators help businesses and governments determine where the economy is headed. You may have noticed news headlines such as the following, each of which offers clues to the direction of the Canadian economy:

1. Housing Starts Lowest in Months
2. The Bank of Canada Lowers the Target for the Overnight Rate and Interest Rates Tumble
3. Retail Sales Up 4 Percent over Last Month
4. Business Debt Down from Last Year
5. Businesses Are Buying More Electronic Equipment
6. Industry Jobs Go Unfilled as Area Unemployment Rate Sinks to 6 Percent
7. Telephone Reports 30-Day Backlog in Installing Business Systems

Discuss each of these headlines with the students on your team. Is each item good news or bad news for the economy? Why? What does each item mean for large and small businesses? Report your team's findings to the class as a whole. Did all of the teams come to the same conclusions about each headline? Why or why not? Within your team, discuss how these different perspectives might influence the way you interpret economic news in the future.

EXPAND YOUR KNOWLEDGE

DISCOVERING CAREER OPPORTUNITIES

Thinking about a career in economics? Find out what economists do by reviewing the *Occupational Outlook Handbook* in your library or online at www.bls.gov/oco. This is an authoritative resource for information about all kinds of occupations. Click on Search and enter "economists."

1. Briefly describe what economists do, and their typical working conditions.
2. What is the job outlook for economists? What is the average salary for starting economists?
3. What training and qualifications are required for a career as an economist? Are the qualifications different for jobs in the private sector as opposed to those in government?

DEVELOPING YOUR RESEARCH SKILLS

Gaining a competitive advantage in today's marketplace is critical to a company's success. Look through recent copies of business journals and newspapers (online or in print) to find an article about a company whose practices have set it apart from its competitors. Use your favourite online search engine to find more information about that company online.

1. What products or services does the company manufacture or sell?
2. How does the company set its goods or services apart from its competitors? Does the company compete on price, quality, service, or innovation?
3. Does the company have a website, and if so, how does the company use it? What kinds of information does the company include on its website?

See It on the **WEB**

URLs for all Internet exercises are provided at the website for this book, www.pearsoned.ca/bovee. When you log on to the text website, select Chapter 1, then select Destinations, then click on the name of the featured website and review the website to complete these exercises.

Explore the following chapter-related websites, review their content, and answer the following questions for each website you visit:

1. What is the purpose of this website?
2. What kinds of information does this website contain? Please be specific.
3. How is the information provided at this website useful for business people? Consumers?
4. How did you expand your knowledge of economics by reviewing the material at this website? What new things did you learn about this topic?

FIND THE RIGHT STUFF

Getting information on a specific company can be a challenge, especially if you don't know where to begin. One of the best starting points is the SEDAR website, www.sedar.com. This website provides an incredible amount of information on public companies in Canada. Public disclosure documents are available, including brief profiles, financial data, history, annual reports, and current events. So log on and use the toolbox to browse company data. Another site that provides some valuable information is Hoover's online site, www.hoovers.com.

STEP INSIDE THE ECONOMIC STATISTICS BRIEFING ROOM

Want to know where the economy is headed? Visit the Statistics Canada website, www.statcan.ca, to find the latest economic indicators. Check out the statistics and graphs for new housing starts, unemployment, average hourly earnings, and more.

DISCOVER WHAT'S IN THE CPI

The consumer price index (CPI) is an important tool that allows analysts to track changes in prices over time. However, the CPI doesn't always match a given individual's inflation experience. Check out how the CPI measures homeowners' costs, how the CPI is used, what goods and services it covers, and whose buying habits it reflects. Explore the Statistics Canada site to discover the CPI figures for your province. Then click onto the Bank of Canada website, www.bankofcanada.ca/en/inflation/index.htm, and look up the definition of core CPI.

Appendix A
Internet Fundamentals and Tools for Effective Searches

As Chapter 1 demonstrates, it's pretty difficult to study business today without understanding the Internet and electronic commerce. This appendix reviews the Internet and e-commerce fundamentals you will need in order to complete the readings and assignments in this introduction to business course. More importantly, this appendix is designed to help you increase your knowledge of the Internet and help you maximize your research time. We begin by explaining some basics.

INTERNET FUNDAMENTALS 101

The Internet is the world's largest computer network; it is a voluntary, cooperative undertaking; no one individual, organization, or government owns it. The Internet is accessible to individuals, companies, universities and colleges, government agencies, and other institutions in countries all over the world. It links thousands of smaller computer networks and millions of individual computer users in homes, businesses, government offices, and schools worldwide.

To reach the Internet, you need a computer with a modem and an **Internet service provider (ISP)**—a company that provides access to the Internet. For a flat monthly fee or per-use fee, you can dial into one of the ISP's host computers, which will link you to one of the networked computers on the Internet. You can dial into an ISP in a variety of ways. Although many people use a standard telephone line, others are willing to pay a bit more for the speed and convenience of a cable connection or a **digital subscriber line (DSL)**, a high-speed phone line that carries both voice and data. In addition, you can connect on the go using either a handheld computer or a cellphone set up for wireless access.

The most widely used part of the Internet is the World Wide Web (WWW or Web) which enables users to search for, display, and save multimedia resources such as graphics, text, audio, and video files. This information is typically stored on a series of web pages, which are related files containing multimedia data that are made available on a website. You need a web browser—software such as Netscape Navigator or Microsoft's Internet Explorer—to read web pages.

The **homepage** of a website is the primary screen that users first access when visiting a site. Furthermore, each page in a website is identified by a unique address known as a **uniform resource locator (URL)**. Take http://www.yahoo.com, for example. The address begins with *http*, which is the abbreviation for **hypertext transfer protocol**, the communications protocol that allows you to navigate the Web. The address continues with *www*, indicating that the site is located on the World Wide Web. The next part of the address is the registered **domain name** (in this case *yahoo.com*), a name unique to that site. The abbreviation following the *period* is the top-level domain (TLD). The original seven TLDs identified businesses (com), educational institutions (edu), government agencies (gov), international sources (int), the military (mil), network resources (net), and non-profit organizations (org). To keep up with demand, additional TLDs (such as pro, biz, info, coop, museum, and name) are being introduced. There are also country code TLDs such as ca for Canada and uk for the United Kingdom.[1]

Just about every bit of information on the Web has a **hyperlink** or *hot link*, which means you can click on words in **hypertext mark-up language (HTML)**—coloured, underlined, or highlighted words—with your mouse and automatically jump to another web page or website. Once you get to your new destination, you can **bookmark** the site by using a browser feature that places the site's URL in a file on your computer for future use. Then, whenever you are online and you click on a bookmark, you automatically go to that site's address. Another handy browser feature is the ability to navigate your trail backwards or forward at any time by using the *back* and *forward* buttons on your browser software. See the glossary at the end of this appendix for more definitions of Internet-related terms.

Internet Communication

There are various methods that companies can employ to communicate with internal and external stakeholders, such as:

- *E-mail:* enables users to create, send, and read written messages entirely on the computer. An **e-mail** document may be a simple text message, or it might include complex files or programs.
- *Discussion mailing lists*: also known as a *listservs*, groups to which you subscribe by sending a message to the list's

e-mail address. From then on, copies of all messages posted by any other subscriber are sent to you via e-mail. It's like subscribing to an electronic newsletter to which everyone can contribute.

- *Newsgroups:* **Usenet newsgroups** consist of posted messages on a particular subject and responses to them. You can think of a newsgroup as a *place* you visit to read posted messages, whereas a discussion mailing list *delivers* posted messages to you.
- *Instant messaging and chat:* many companies encourage the use of **instant messaging (IM)** and chat to collaborate. Both allow online conversations in which any number of computer users can type in messages to each other and receive responses in real time.
- *Telnet.* A class of Internet application programs that allow you to communicate with other computers on a remote network even if your computer is not a permanent part of that network. For instance, you would use **Telnet** to access your local library's electronic card catalogue from your home computer.
- *Internet telephony:* users can converse vocally over the Internet using **Internet telephony**. Converting traditional voice calls to digital signals and sending them over the Internet is much less expensive than calling over standard phone lines. It can also be more efficient, allowing an organization to accommodate more users on a single line at once.
- *File transfers.* **File transfer protocol (FTP)** is an Internet service that enables you to download files or transfer data from a server to your computer and upload files or transfer data from your computer to another system. FTP also allows you to attach formatted documents to your e-mail messages and download formatted files. Sometimes users compress or zip large files—such as graphics files—to make them easier and faster to transfer. If you receive a zipped file, you must use special software (usually provided with your web browser) to decompress it before you can read it. The Internet also makes peer-to-peer file sharing possible. Using the Internet and software, people can exchange files directly (from user to user) without going through a central server.

How Do You Find Information on the Internet?

The Internet is rich in business information. It contains current news, business issues, industry trends, and company information such as financial performance, products, goals, and employment. In fact, the Web is so vast and changes so often that it's easy to get sidetracked. If you've ever been lost in cyberspace, take heart—it happens to everybody. Chances are good that you'll find information on the Internet about almost any research topic. However, locating that information can be frustrating if you don't know how to conduct an effective search.

One important thing to keep in mind when looking for business information on the Internet is that anyone can post anything on a website. No one filters it. No one checks it for accuracy. No one can be sure of who is producing the information or why they are placing it on the Internet. For that reason, it's best to refrain from seriously surfing the Web for business information until you've had a chance to learn a bit about your topic from journals, books, and other sources that are carefully edited for the accuracy of their content. That way you'll be able to detect skewed or erroneous information, and you can be more selective about the websites and documents you choose to use as a resource.

If you are looking for specific company **data** (recorded facts and statistics), your best source may be the company's own website (assuming it maintains one). Websites generally include detailed information about the company's products, services, history, mission, strategy, financial performance, and employment needs. Furthermore, many sites provide links to related company information, such as public records and financial statements, news releases, and more.

Keep in mind that a lot of the information that you may want simply isn't on the Web. If you're researching small organizations, for instance, you may find nothing or just an address and phone number. Furthermore, even if the information you're seeking does exist on the Web, you may not be able to locate it. The Internet contains hundreds of millions of web pages, with hundreds of pages being added every day. But even the best **search engines**—Internet tools that identify and screen resources—manage to index only about a third of the pages on the Web.[2] Some sites are better than others. For example, Google rates very highly in terms of customer awareness and it also rated highly on customer satisfaction ratings, with an 82 percent positive evaluation.[3]

When a search engine turns up what you're looking for, it will probably also turn up a mountain of stuff you won't need. Suppose you're looking for information about available jobs for writers. The search engine may turn up information on openings at an insurance company. Why? The insurance company may have described itself on the Web as one of the largest *writers* of insurance policies. Go to Google.ca. If you type in "Canadian actors" you will not be directed to a Keanu Reeves fan website or any other website related to a famous actor. Instead you will be directed to Canadian Actors Online, an educational website for aspiring actors. If you type in "Canadian tax law information," the Google response is www.taxpage.com, the website of Rotfleisch and Samulovitch, a tax consulting firm. How does a company get to be number one on a search engine? According to a recent article in *Backbone Magazine*, there are a few tips to follow: use defined keywords like the ones people use when they search, employ embedded keywords in the text, get stakeholders with related pages to link to your site, and register with all major search engines.[4] These tips are also important to understand from the researcher's perspective. You can produce more targeted search results by learning how to conduct an effective database search with the help of the following section.

How Do You Conduct an Effective Database Search?

A **database** is a collection of data stored in a computerized format. Whether you are using a library database or an Internet search engine such as the ones listed in Exhibit A.1, follow these search strategies and tips to conduct an effective database search:[5]

- *Select appropriate databases.* You'll want a good business database. However, journals on your topic may be in a database that also includes journals on psychology, computers, or medicine.
- *Use multiple search engines.* Don't limit yourself to a single search engine, especially if you are looking for less popular topics. Try your search on several engines by using meta-crawlers, special engines that search several search engines at once.
- *Translate concepts into key words and phrases.* For instance, if you want to determine the "effect of TQM on company profits," you should select the key words *TQM, total quality management, profits, sales, companies,* and *corporations.* Remember to use synonyms or word equivalents whenever possible, and use quotation marks around phrases to look for the entire phrase instead of separate words.
- *Use a short phrase or single term rather than a long phrase.* Search engines look for the words exactly as you key them in. If the words occur in a different order, you may miss relevant hits.
- *Do not use stop-words.* This refers to words that the computer disregards and will not search for. Database documentation will identify any stop-words in addition to the common ones: *a, an, the, of, by, with, for,* and *to.*
- *Do not use words contained in the name of the database.* Using words such as business or finance in the ABI Inform database will work, but they appear so often that searching for them slows the processing time and adds no precision to your results.
- *Use variations of your terms.* Use abbreviations (CEO, CPA), synonyms (man, male), related terms (child, adolescent, youth), different spellings (dialog, dialogue), singular and plural forms (man, men), nouns and adjectives (manager, management, managerial), and open and compound forms (online, on line, on-line).
- *Specify a logical relationship between the key words.* Must the documents contain both companies and corporations, or are either fine? Must it contain both profits and companies, or should it contain TQM or total quality management and profits or sales?
- *Use Boolean operators.* Narrow or broaden your search by including AND, OR, and NOT. As Exhibit A.2 shows, such Boolean operators can help you create complex, precise search strategies. For example you could create a search strategy such as "(marketing or advertising) AND (organizations or associations) AND NOT consultants." This means that qualifying documents or websites must have either the word *marketing* or the word *advertising* and must have either the word *organizations* or the word *associations,* but they can't have the word *consultants.* Many search engines automatically include Boolean operators in their strategies even though you can't see them on the screen. Either insert your own (which should override automatic operators) or review the instructions for your search engine.
- *Use proximity operators.* To specify how close one of your key words should be to another, use a proximity operator such as NEAR. For example, the search phrase "marketing NEAR/2 organizations" means that marketing must be within two words of organizations.
- *Use wildcards.* Wildcard characters help you find plurals and alternate spellings of your key words. For example, by using a question mark in the word organi?ations, you'll find documents with both *organisations* (British spelling) and *organizations.* Similarly, by using an asterisk at the end of the stem *chair**, you'll find *chairman, chairperson, chairs,* and *chairlift.*
- *Evaluate the precision and quality of your search results to refine your search if necessary.* If you end up with more than 60 to 100 links to sort through, refine your search. If your first page of results doesn't have something of interest, you've entered the wrong words or too few words. Also, pay attention to whether you are searching in the title, subject, or document field of the database. Each will return different results.

Exhibit A.1 Best of Internet Searching

Searchers can get the most dependable results from well-known, commercially backed search engines. These major search engines (and directories) are likely to be well maintained and upgraded when necessary to keep pace with the growing Web. Most have simple or advanced search features, plus extras such as interactive maps and weather, travel information, phone and e-mail directories, and company profiles. When researching Canadian content, for improved results use the Canadian version of a site such as google.ca.

MAJOR SEARCH ENGINES	
AllThe Web	www.alltheweb.com Consistently one of the largest indexes of the Web.
Alta Vista	www.altavista.com Indexes data from millions of web pages and articles from thousands of Usenet newsgroups.
Ask Jeeves	www.ask.com Finds answers to natural-language questions such as: "Who won the Stanley Cup in 2003–2004?"
Canada on the Web	www.canadaontheweb.ca A searchable directory of exclusively Canadian websites.
Google	www.google.ca A simple directory that is especially useful for finding homepages of companies and organizations.
HotBot	www.hotbot.com *Wired* magazine packs all kinds of searching possibilities into this site.
LookSmart	www.looksmart.com Closest rival to Yahoo! in terms of being a human-compiled directory. Choose "Your Town" for local directories.
Lycos	www.lycos.com One of the oldest of the major search engines; provides short abstracts for each match.
WebCrawler	www.webcrawler.com Allows you either to search the entire site or to browse any of the pre-selected categories.
Yahoo!	www.ca.yahoo.com The oldest major website directory.
Multiple Search Engine Sites—Meta-crawlers	
C4 Total	www.c4.com Search up to 20 search engines at the same time. Customized search options are available.
Dogpile	www.dogpile.com Despite the silly name, just enter one query and this hound sniffs through FTP files, Usenet message boards, and websites.
IXQuick	www.ixquick.com Search up to 14 search engines at the same time. Results are ranked by relevancy.
Mamma	www.mamma.com Claiming to be the "Mother of All Search Engines," this multi-legged spider queries the major search engines for fast results.
Vivisimo	www.vivisimo.com Results are organized with document clustering technology, which provides users with lists of documents in meaningful groups.
Zworks	www.zworks.com Results are ranked based on the cumulative score of all engines used in the search. Duplicate results are eliminated.

of overseas markets with the help of fax machines, overnight delivery services, e-mail, and the Internet.

Entire industries have been transformed by global accessibility. It was not long ago that Hollywood had a virtual monopoly over the North American filmmaking industry. Today, North American films are produced around the world in places like Ireland, the Czech Republic, Australia, and New Zealand. Of course, Canada has been a major winner in the globalization of the film industry. In particular, Vancouver, Toronto, and Montreal accounted for the majority of the $1.7 billion spent in Canada during one recent year. British Columbia alone accounted for $857 million, which represents more than the comparable number for foreign-produced films in the United Kingdom ($603 million).[2] In the last few years the task of attracting film production has become more difficult with the rise of the Canadian dollar and competition from locations around the world.

Russell Crowe starred in Cinderella Man, *which was based on the true story of a boxer from the 1930s named Jim Braddock; the movie was filmed in Toronto.*

Companies know that selling goods and services in foreign markets can generate increased sales, produce operational efficiencies, expose companies to new technologies, and provide greater consumer choices. But venturing abroad also exposes companies to many new challenges, as Whirlpool's David Whitwam discovered. For instance, each country has unique ways of doing business that must be learned: laws, customs, consumer preferences, ethical standards, labour skills, and political and economic stability. All of these factors can affect a firm's international prospects. Furthermore, volatile currencies, international trade relationships, and the threat of terrorism can make global expansion a risky proposition.

Still, in most cases the opportunities of the global marketplace greatly outweigh the risks. Consider UPS. When this company began its rapid global expansion program in the 1980s, it had to attain air rights into each country, unravel a patchwork of customs laws, learn how to deal with varying work ethics and employment policies, and so on. But the company's efforts paid off. Today UPS delivers more than 14.1 million documents and packages daily in more than 200 countries. The company receives more than 145 million hits per day on its website, with more than 10 million package tracking requests daily. Over 17 percent of the company's revenue now comes from international package deliveries.[3]

Cultural Differences in the Global Business Environment

L.O. 2

Cultural differences present a number of challenges in the global marketplace, as David Whitwam's experience shows. For one thing, companies must recognize and respect differences in language, social values, ideas of status, decision-making habits, attitudes toward time, use of space, body language, manners, and ethical standards. Otherwise, such differences can lead to misunderstandings in international business relationships, particularly if differences in business practices also exist (see Exhibit 2.1). Furthermore, companies that sell their products overseas must often adapt these products to meet the unique needs of international customers, as Whirlpool discovered.

The best way to prepare for doing business with people from another culture is to study that culture in advance. Learn everything you can about the culture's history, religion, politics, and customs—especially its business customs. Who makes decisions? How are negotiations usually conducted? Is gift giving expected? What is the proper attire for a business meeting? In addition to the suggestion that you learn about the culture, seasoned international business people offer the following tips for improving intercultural communication:

Exhibit 2.1 **Going Global Has Its Barriers**

Learning a country's business customs and cultural differences is the first step in going global.

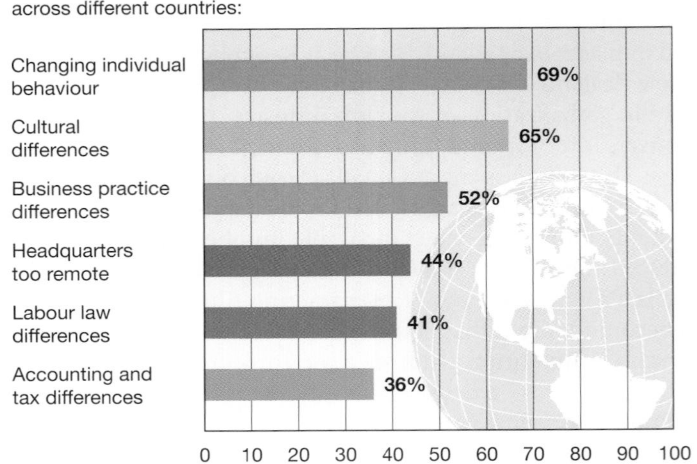

- *Be aware of the other person's customs.* Expect the other person to have values, beliefs, expectations, and mannerisms different from yours. For instance, don't be surprised when business people in Pakistan excuse themselves in the middle of a meeting to conduct prayers.
- *Deal with the individual.* Don't stereotype the other person or react with preconceived ideas. Regard the person as an individual first, not as a representative of another culture.
- *Clarify your intent and meaning.* The other person's body language may not mean what you think, and the person may read unintentional meanings into your message. Clarify your true intent by repetition and examples. Ask questions and listen carefully. The Japanese are generally appreciative when foreigners ask them about proper behaviour, because it shows respect for the Japanese way of doing things.[4]
- *Adapt your style to the other person's.* If the other person appears to be direct and straightforward, follow suit. If not, adjust your behaviour to match. In many African countries, people are suspicious of others who seem to be in a hurry. Therefore, you should allow plenty of time to get to know the people you are dealing with.
- *Show respect.* Learn how respect is communicated in various cultures—through gestures, eye contact, and so on. For example, in Spain, let a handshake last five to seven strokes; pulling away too soon may be interpreted as a rejection. In France, however, the preferred handshake is a single stroke.

These are just a few tips for doing business in the global marketplace. Exhibit 2.2 can guide you in your efforts to learn more about a country's culture before doing business abroad.

Legal Differences in the Global Business Environment

All Canadian companies that conduct business in other countries must be familiar with Canadian law, international law, and the laws of the specific countries where they plan to trade or do business. Corporate legal departments work to ensure that firms can take every advantage within the means of the law. However, oftentimes laws and norms across nations come into direct conflict with each other. Practices that are frowned upon in one nation are tolerated and even encouraged in others (see the box entitled "China: Reality Check" on page 44).What is a firm to do if it is trying to earn a deal with a foreign company or a foreign nation that sees bribery as a routine part of

Exhibit 2.2 **Checklist for Doing Business Abroad**

Use this checklist as a starting point when investigating a foreign culture.

UNDERSTAND SOCIAL CUSTOMS

- ✓ How do people react to strangers? Are they friendly? Hostile? Reserved?
- ✓ How do people greet each other? Should you bow? Nod? Shake hands?
- ✓ How are names used for introductions?
- ✓ What are the attitudes toward touching people?
- ✓ How do you express appreciation for an invitation to lunch or dinner, or to someone's home? Should you bring a gift? Send flowers? Write a thank-you note?
- ✓ How, when, or where are people expected to sit in social or business situations?
- ✓ Are any phrases, facial expressions, or hand gestures considered rude?
- ✓ How close do people stand when talking?
- ✓ How do you attract the attention of a waiter? Do you tip the waiter?
- ✓ When is it rude to refuse an invitation? How do you refuse politely?
- ✓ What are the acceptable patterns of eye contact?
- ✓ What gestures indicate agreement? Disagreement? Respect?
- ✓ What topics may or may not be discussed in a social setting? In a business setting?
- ✓ How is time perceived?
- ✓ What are the generally accepted working hours?
- ✓ How do people view scheduled appointments?

LEARN ABOUT CLOTHING AND FOOD PREFERENCES

- ✓ What occasions require special clothing? What colours are associated with mourning? Love? Joy?
- ✓ Are some types of clothing considered taboo for one sex or the other?
- ✓ What are the attitudes toward human body odours? Are deodorants or perfumes used?
- ✓ How many times a day do people eat?
- ✓ How are hands or utensils used when eating?
- ✓ What types of places, food, and drink are appropriate for business entertainment?
- ✓ Where is the seat of honour at a table?

ASSESS POLITICAL PATTERNS

- ✓ How stable is the political situation? Does it affect businesses in and out of the country?
- ✓ How is political power manifested? Military power? Economic strength?
- ✓ What are the traditional government institutions?

LEARN ABOUT ECONOMIC AND BUSINESS INSTITUTIONS

- ✓ Is the society homogeneous?
- ✓ What minority groups are represented?
- ✓ What languages are spoken?
- ✓ Do immigration patterns influence workforce composition?
- ✓ What are the primary resources and principal products?
- ✓ What vocational/technological training is offered?
- ✓ What are the attitudes toward education?
- ✓ Are businesses generally large? Family controlled? Government controlled?
- ✓ Is it appropriate to do business by telephone? By fax? By e-mail?
- ✓ Do managers make business decisions unilaterally, or do they involve employees?
- ✓ How are status and seniority shown in an organization? In a business meeting?
- ✓ Must people socialize before conducting business?

APPRAISE THE NATURE OF ETHICS, VALUES, AND LAWS

- ✓ Is money or a gift expected in exchange for arranging business transactions?
- ✓ What ethical or legal issues might affect business transactions?
- ✓ Do people value competitiveness or cooperation?
- ✓ What are the attitudes toward work? Toward money?
- ✓ Is politeness more important than factual honesty?
- ✓ What qualities are admired in a business associate?

China: Reality Check

Welcome to the People's Republic of China, where copies of well-known foreign products are as available as tea and rice at meals. China produces more fakes than any other nation—everything from automobiles to aircraft parts, beer to razor blades, soap to shampoo, TVs to toilets. Nearly half of the world's 14 billion batteries are produced in China, but most of them are fake versions of Panasonic, Gillette, and other big brands. Bikes with names like Yamaha zip along the roads from Beijing to Tibet, but Yamaha didn't make many of them. Procter & Gamble (P&G) claims that counterfeiters sell US$150 million of fake P&G products annually.

Counterfeiting has infiltrated nearly every sector of China's economy. Most counterfeiters work at small to mid-sized factories, but many stay at home, doing things like filling Head & Shoulders bottles with concoctions from large vats in their living rooms. Overall, the amount of China's manufacturing base that is dependent on illegal knockoffs is estimated to be 10 to 30 percent—and growing. The simple reason for the explosion in counterfeits is the big money and low risk involved. A Chinese counterfeiter knows he'll only get a slap on the wrist if caught.

Raids do occur daily, but even the government's efforts aren't deterring the number of counterfeiters. Local officials are hesitant to stop the pirates because they create millions of jobs. "Entire villages live off counterfeiting. If you suddenly throw these people out of work, you'll have riots," says one spokesperson for a leading private anti-counterfeiting agency. Shutting down the fakes at Yiwu—China's largest wholesale distribution centre, where it is estimated that 80 percent of the consumer goods sold are counterfeits—would cripple the city's economy, because many hotels, restaurants, and businesses cater to the trade.

Worse still, the fakes are exported everywhere—to Europe, Russia, the Middle East. Unilever says that fake Dove soap is making its way from China into Europe. Bose, a maker of high-end audio systems, is finding Chinese fakes in overseas markets. The pirates have indeed moved to a whole new level of sophistication. Ten years ago, China's knockoffs were below Western standards. Now, many fake Duracell batteries look so genuine that Gillette has to send them to a forensics lab to analyze them. Fake watches even contain full-sized Swiss movements and real gems. It's scary to think about what could wind up on the world's shelves.

So what are pirated brand owners to do? For the most part, companies are trying to boost government enforcement, a tough task. For example, although sunglasses maker Oakley has gotten Chinese authorities to close counterfeiters' factories, new ones pop up in their place. Many multinationals are shutting down or shrinking some product lines in China because these products are overrun by counterfeits. But China's market is so vast and promising, few companies are willing to pull out entirely. General Motors recently announced a US$3 billion additional investment based on the expectation that China will become the world's largest car market by 2025.[5]

When will China get real? Not in the near future. For one thing, China's legal system is full of loopholes. For another, counterfeiting is so ingrained in China's culture that many Chinese view it as harmless. Moreover, a real crackdown on counterfeiting could create serious social turmoil and costs to the central government, because counterfeiting is the livelihood of so many citizens. So while China's lawmakers search for a solution, endless raids are all China has to offer—for now.

Questions for Critical Thinking

1. Why don't more Chinese companies use their manufacturing skills to make their own branded products?
2. Honda recently set up a joint venture to make and sell motorcycles with a Chinese company that used to produce Honda knockoffs. Why would Honda do this?

doing business? Laws and policies have been put in place to deal with this problem. According to the Corruption of Foreign Public Officials Act, "every person commits an offence who, in order to obtain or retain an advantage in the course of business, directly or indirectly gives, offers or agrees to offer a loan, reward, advantage or benefit to a foreign public official."[6] These offences are punishable by imprisonment. Export Development Canada does not provide support to firms convicted of corruption unless the firm has instituted severe anti-corruption policies and implemented reforms.[7] Despite the policies and laws to deter business corruption, many firms will make attempts to subvert the law.

Do honest companies lose out to foreign competitors and domestic firms willing to operate in grey areas? The answer is yes. In order to even the playing field the

Organization for Economic Cooperation and Development (OECD) along with national governments and regulators are attempting to create an accepted international order.

Forms of International Business Activity

L.O. 3

Once a company decides to operate in the global marketplace, it must decide on the level of involvement it is willing to undertake and develop strategies for marketing its products internationally. Five common forms of international business activities are importing and exporting, licensing, franchising, strategic alliances and joint ventures, and foreign direct investment. Each has varying degrees of ownership, financial commitment, and risk.

Importing and Exporting

Importing, the buying of goods or services from a supplier in another country, and **exporting**, the selling of products outside the country in which they are produced, have existed for centuries. In the last few decades, however, the increased level of these activities has caused the economies of the world to become tightly linked.

importing
Purchasing goods or services from another country and bringing them into one's own country

exporting
Selling and shipping goods or services to another country

Exporting, one of the least risky forms of international business activity permits a firm to enter a foreign market gradually, assess local conditions, and then fine-tune its product to meet the needs of foreign consumers. In most cases, the firm's financial exposure is limited to market research costs, advertising costs, and the costs of either establishing a direct sales and distribution system or hiring intermediaries.

Such intermediaries include *export management companies,* which are domestic firms that specialize in performing international marketing services on a commission basis, and *export trading companies,* which are general trading firms that will buy a company's products for resale overseas as well as perform a variety of importing, exporting, and manufacturing functions. Still another alternative is to use foreign distributors. Working through a foreign distributor with connections in the target country is often helpful to both large and small companies because such intermediaries can provide the connections, expertise, and market knowledge needed to conduct business in a foreign country.[8] In addition, many countries now have foreign trade offices to help importers and exporters interested in doing business within their borders. Other helpful resources include professional agents, local business people, and agencies like Export Development Canada. This government organization offers a variety of services, including credit insurance, political risk insurance, direct loans, and lines of credit to encourage buyers to choose Canadian products.[9]

International Licensing

Licensing is another popular approach to international business. Licensing agreements entitle one company to use some or all of another firm's intellectual property (patents, trademarks, brand names, copyrights, or trade secrets) in return for a royalty payment. Underwear manufacturer Jockey licenses the rights to use the Jockey name to certain foreign manufacturers of women's activewear, sleepwear, and slippers. Jockey licenses its products in more than 120 countries but is careful that all such arrangements add value to the Jockey name.[10]

licensing
Agreement to produce and market another company's product in exchange for a royalty or fee

Many firms choose licensing as an approach to international markets because it involves little out-of-pocket cost. A firm has already incurred the costs of developing the intellectual property to be licensed. Pharmaceutical firms, for instance, routinely use licensing to enter foreign markets. Once a pharmaceutical firm has developed and patented a new drug, it is often more efficient to grant existing local firms the right to manufacture and distribute the patented drug in return for royalty payments. Israel's Teva Pharmaceutical Industries, for example, has a licence to manufacture and market Merck's pharmaceutical products in Israel. This arrangement saves Merck the expense of establishing its own Israeli sales force.[11] Of course, licensing agreements are not restricted to international business. A company can also license its products or technology to other companies in its domestic market.

In the past few years, China's major cities have sprouted Western franchises like McDonald's.

International Franchising

Some companies choose to expand into foreign markets by *franchising* their operation. International franchising is among the fastest-growing forms of international business activity today. Under this arrangement, a franchisor enters into an agreement whereby the franchisee obtains the rights to duplicate a specific product or service—perhaps a restaurant, photocopy shop, or video rental store—and the franchisor obtains a royalty fee in exchange. Holiday Inn Worldwide has used this approach to reach customers globally and now consists of nearly 1500 hotels. KFC, McDonald's, and scores of other companies have used this approach. Even some smaller companies have found that franchising is a good way for them to enter the global marketplace.[12] By franchising its operations, a firm can minimize the costs and risks of global expansion and bypass certain trade restrictions. (The advantages and disadvantages of franchising will be discussed in detail in Chapter 4.)

International Strategic Alliances and Joint Ventures

strategic alliance
Long-term relationship in which two or more companies share ideas, resources, and technologies in order to establish competitive advantages

joint venture
Cooperative partnership in which organizations share investment costs, risks, management, and profits in the development, production, or selling of products

A **strategic alliance** is a long-term partnership between two or more companies to jointly develop, produce, or sell products in the global marketplace. To reach their individual but complementary goals, the companies typically share ideas, expertise, resources, technologies, investment costs, risks, management, and profits.

Strategic alliances are a popular way to expand one's business globally. Starbucks uses this approach in venturing overseas by partnering with locals.[13] In Canada, Starbucks formed a strategic alliance with Indigo and Chapters bookstores to increase its presence. The benefits of this form of international growth include ease of market entry, shared risk, shared knowledge and expertise, and synergy. Companies that form a strategic alliance with a foreign partner can often compete more effectively than if they entered the foreign market alone. Consider the 15-member Star Alliance that includes notable airlines such as Air Canada, Air New Zealand, Lufthansa, United, and Singapore Airlines. The network provides various advantages. For example, Star Alliance travellers have access to more than 575 lounges in airports worldwide and the ability to earn and redeem frequent flier miles on any member airline.[14]

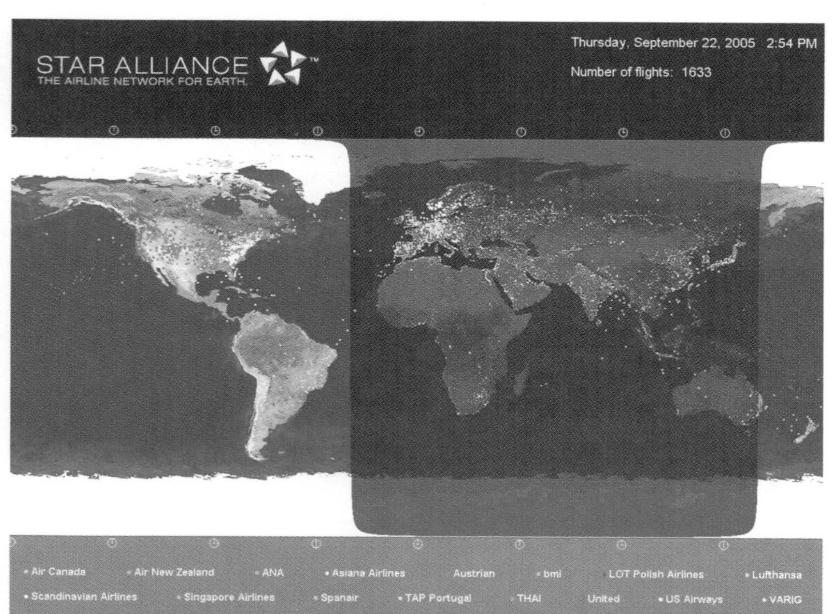

Air Canada passengers, along with clients of the other 14 members of the Star Alliance, enjoy the benefits of shared resources and operational cooperation.

A **joint venture** is a special type of strategic alliance in which two or more firms join together to create a new business entity that is legally separate and distinct from its parents. The CAMI automotive plant, located in Ingersoll, Ontario, is an example of a joint venture between General Motors and Suzuki. The vehicles produced in this plant include the Chevrolet Equinox and the Suzuki Grand Vitara.[15]

In some countries, foreign companies are prohibited from owning facilities outright or from investing in local business. Thus, establishing a joint venture with a local partner may be the only way to do business in that country. In other cases, foreign companies may be required to move some of their production facilities to the country to earn the right to sell their products there. For instance, the Chinese government would not allow Boeing to sell airplanes in China until the company agreed to move half of the tail-section production for its 737s to Xian.[16] Despite similar pressure, Bombardier has held off on making such an investment for its aerospace division. However, Bombardier has shown a tremendous commitment to China by creating three railway industry joint ventures: one for signalling equipment, one for subway cars, and one for mainline cars.[17]

The Chevrolet Equinox is built in the Suzuki/GM joint venture plant located in Ingersoll, Ontario.

Foreign Direct Investment

Exporting, licensing, franchising, and strategic alliances allow a firm to enter the global marketplace without investing in foreign factories or facilities. However, many firms prefer to enter international markets through ownership and control of assets in foreign countries.

The most comprehensive form of international business is a wholly owned operation run in another country, without the financial participation of a local partner. Many Canadian firms conduct business this way, as do companies based in other countries. These operations vary in form, size, and purpose. Some are started from scratch; others are acquired from local owners. The history of Whirlpool Canada is a prime example of this approach; in the 1970s Whirlpool Corporation purchased Inglis, which had been selling appliances as an independent Canadian entity since 1859. On the other hand, Couche-Tard, a leader in the Canadian convenience store industry, provides a countering example. The firm recently purchased Circle K, a southern U.S. convenience chain with 2290 stores, for $1.1 billion.[18]

Some operations are small sales offices; others are full-scale manufacturing facilities. Some are set up to exploit the availability of raw materials; others take advantage of low wage rates; still others minimize transportation costs by choosing locations that give them direct access to markets in other countries. In almost all cases, at least part of the workforce is drawn from the local population.

Companies with a physical presence in numerous countries are called **multinational corporations (MNCs)**. Since 1969, the number of multinational corporations in the world's 14 richest countries has more than tripled, from 7000 to 24 000.[19] Some multinational corporations increase their involvement in foreign countries by establishing **foreign direct investment (FDI)**. That is, they either establish production and marketing facilities in the countries where they operate or purchase existing foreign firms. Such foreign direct investment constitutes the highest level of international involvement. Moreover, it carries much greater economic and political risk and is more complex than any other form of entry in the global marketplace.[20]

multinational corporations (MNCs)
Companies with operations in more than one country

foreign direct investment (FDI)
Investment of money by foreign companies in domestic business enterprises

The ability to attract foreign direct investment is an important element of national economic competitiveness. Among developed countries, Canada, Italy, France, and Australia are no longer among the world's top 10 spots for foreign direct investment. Emerging markets such as China, India, Mexico, Poland, Russia, and Brazil have grown significantly in that area. In fact, China has overtaken the United States as the world's preferred location for FDI.[21]

Product Strategies for International Markets

Whether exporting, licensing, or franchising its products in a foreign country, a company must decide on an appropriate product strategy. For instance, it must decide whether to *standardize* the product, selling the same product everywhere in the world, or to *customize* the product to accommodate the lifestyles and habits of local target markets. Keep in mind that the degree of customization can vary. A company

China is becoming too big a PC market for anyone to ignore. Dell, which recently opened its fourth PC factory in the world on China's southeastern coast, can now deliver PCs to Chinese customers as fast as it does to North American ones.

may change only the product's name or packaging, or it can modify the product's components, size, and functions. Of course, understanding a country's culture and regulations helps a company make these important choices. But even the most successful companies have blundered (see the box entitled "How to Avoid Business Blunders Abroad").

After being slammed for its ignorance of European ways and losing US$1 billion in Euro Disney's first year of operation, Disney realized that Paris was not Anaheim or Orlando. Disney had insulted French employees with its required dress code and angered its European customers, who were not accustomed to standing in line for rides or eating fast food standing up. "When we first launched Euro Disney there was the belief that it was enough to be Disney," says Euro Disney CEO Jay Rasulo. "Now we realize that our guests need to be welcomed on the basis of their own culture and travel habits."[22] To cease alienating the Europeans, Disney switched from a standardized to a customized product strategy by modifying its theme park for the European culture. The company ditched its controversial dress code, authorized wine with meals, lowered admission prices, hired a French investor relations firm, and changed the name of the complex from Euro Disney to Disneyland Paris to lure French tourists. Today, Disneyland Paris is a strong tourist attraction.

Like Disney, many manufacturers have customized their products after learning that international customers are not all alike. For instance, KFC believes that business, like politics, is local. So it doesn't just open restaurants based on the North American model and expect success. It adapts KFC's product offerings to local tastes. In Japan KFC sells tempura crispy strips. In northern England KFC stresses gravy and potatoes, while in Thailand it offers fresh rice with soy or sweet chili sauce. In Holland the company makes a potato-and-onion croquette. In France it sells pastries alongside chicken, and in China the chicken gets spicier the farther inland you travel.[23]

On the other hand, Kellogg sells the same Corn Flakes in Europe that it sells in Canada. Only recently has Kellogg made significant inroads in European markets, however, thanks to television advertising and lifestyle changes that favour bigger breakfasts.[24] The latest twist is for companies to adapt products or brands from their foreign operations to their local markets. For example, well before the recent strategic merger with Coors, Molson launched the Marca Bavaria brand from their Brazilian operations into Canada.

FUNDAMENTALS OF INTERNATIONAL TRADE

The success of businesses such as Bombardier, RIM, Whirlpool, UPS, and others that operate in the global marketplace depends, in part, on the international economic relationships forged between nations. From a Canadian perspective it is important that the government devise policies that balance the interests of local firms, Canadian workers, foreign firms operating in Canada, and Canadian consumers. Other countries are trying to do the same thing. As you might expect, the many players in world trade sometimes have conflicting goals.

L.O. 4

Why Nations Trade

No single country has the resources to produce everything its citizens want or need. Businesses and countries specialize in the production of certain goods and engage in international trade to obtain raw materials and goods that are unavailable to them or too costly for them to produce. International trade has many benefits: it increases a

How to Avoid Business Blunders Abroad

Doing business in another country can be extremely tricky. Here are some issues to consider when you conduct business abroad.

THE IMPORTANCE OF PACKAGING

Numerous problems result from the failure to adapt packaging for other cultures. Sometimes only the colour of the package needs to be altered to enhance a product's sales. For instance, white symbolizes death in Japan and much of Asia; green represents danger or disease in Malaysia. Using the wrong colour in these countries might produce negative reactions.

THE LANGUAGE BARRIER

Some product names travel poorly. For instance, the gasoline company Esso found out that its name means "stalled car" in Japan. However, some company names have travelled well. Kodak may be the most famous example. A research team deliberately developed this name after searching for a word that was pronounceable everywhere but had no specific meaning anywhere. Canadians firms have an advantage over companies that operate in a unilingual country with a more homogeneous population; domestic companies are trained in cultural diversity just from dealing with the idiosyncrasies of cultural and linguistic adaptation. For example, before expanding into the Quebec market Medicine Hat, Alberta-based Spitz sunflower seeds sent personnel to the market to assess the competition, design packaging, and adapt its approach for the market.[25]

PROBLEMS WITH PROMOTIONS

In its promotion, one company had effectively used this sentence: "You can use no finer napkin at your dinner table." The company decided to use the same commercials in England because, after all, the British do speak English. To the British, however, the word *napkin* or *nappy* actually means "diaper." The ad could hardly be expected to boost sales of dinner napkins in England.

LOCAL CUSTOMS

Social norms vary greatly from country to country and it is difficult for any outsider to be knowledgeable about all of them, so local input is vital. For example, one firm promoted eyeglasses in Thailand with commercials featuring animals wearing glasses. However, in Thailand animals are considered a low form of life; humans would never wear anything worn by an animal.

TRANSLATION PROBLEMS

The best translation of an advertising message conveys the concept of the original but does not precisely duplicate it. PepsiCo learned this lesson when it discovered that its slogan "Come alive with Pepsi" was translated into German as "Come alive out of the grave with Pepsi." In Asia, the slogan was once translated as "Bring your ancestors back from the dead." This did not go over well in a region that reveres their elders and ancestors.

THE NEED FOR RESEARCH

Proper market research may reduce or eliminate most international business blunders. Market researchers can uncover needs for product adaptations, potential name problems, promotional requirements, and useful market strategies. Good research may even uncover potential translation problems.

As you can see, doing business in other cultures can be risky if a company is unprepared. However, awareness of differences, consultations with local people, and concern for host-country feelings can reduce problems and save money.

Questions for Critical Thinking

1. If you were thinking of selling a breakfast cereal in Japan, what issues might you want to consider?
2. What steps can companies take to avoid business blunders abroad?

---

country's total output, it offers lower prices and greater variety to consumers, it subjects domestic oligopolies and monopolies to competition, and it allows companies to expand their markets and achieve cost, production, and distribution efficiencies, known as **economies of scale**.[26]

How does a country know what to produce and what to trade for? In some cases, the answer is easy: A nation may have an **absolute advantage**, which means it can produce a particular item more efficiently than all other nations, or it is virtually the only country producing that product. Absolute advantages rarely last, however, unless they are based on the availability of natural resources. Saudi Arabia, for example, has an absolute

economies of scale
Savings from manufacturing, marketing, or buying in large quantities

absolute advantage
A nation's ability to produce a particular product with fewer resources per unit of output than any other nation

advantage in crude oil production because of its huge developed reserves. Thus, it makes sense for Saudi Arabia to specialize in providing the world with oil and to trade for other items it needs.

comparative advantage theory
Theory that states that a country should produce and sell to other countries those items it produces most efficiently

In most cases, a country can produce many of the same items that other countries do. The **comparative advantage theory** explains how a country chooses which items to produce and which items to trade for. The theory states that a country should produce and sell to other countries those items it produces more efficiently or at a lower cost, and it should trade for those it can't produce as economically. Canada has an abundance of natural resources. Canada's strengths include lumber, aluminium, and wheat export industries. Canada does not compete in the world marketplace for bananas. With enough money and technology, Canadians could make a valiant attempt to mass-produce bananas; government programs have sponsored such questionable projects in the past. However, in this case the cost cannot possibly match the pennies per kilogram that Canadian wholesalers pay Caribbean, South American, and Central American nations to keep supermarkets well stocked with bananas. This example is extreme and provides an obvious course to follow, but in other industries—despite a less efficient cost and resource structure—Canadian firms continue to produce less efficient products.

The basic argument behind the comparative advantage theory is that specialization and exchange will increase a country's total output and allow both trading partners to enjoy a higher standard of living. Like many theories, it is based on a solid foundation of logic but it is not always put into practice. Traditionally, some industries have been protected in Canada and elsewhere and have corrupted such comparisons. With trade barriers falling it would seem as though comparative advantage theory should be increasingly respected, but the global nature of business today makes these bilateral comparisons seem a bit simplistic in practice.

How International Trade Is Measured

In Chapter 1 we discussed how economists monitor certain key economic indicators to evaluate how well their country's economic system is performing. One trend that economists watch carefully is the level of a nation's imports and exports. For instance, at any given time a country may be importing more than it is exporting. Two key measurements of a nation's level of international trade are the *balance of trade* and the *balance of payments.*

balance of trade
Total value of the products a nation exports minus the total value of the products it imports, over some period of time

trade surplus
Favourable trade balance created when a country exports more than it imports

trade deficit
Unfavourable trade balance created when a country imports more than it exports

balance of payments
Sum of all payments one nation receives from other nations minus the sum of all payments it makes to other nations, over some specified period of time

The total value of a country's exports *minus* the total value of its imports, over some period of time, determines its **balance of trade**. When the value of goods and services exported by Canada exceeds the value of goods and services it imports, Canada's balance of trade is said to be positive: People in other countries buy more goods and services from Canada than Canadians buys from them, creating a **trade surplus** (see Exhibit 2.3). The trade surplus in 2004 amounted to more than $56 billion.[27] Conversely, if Canadians purchase more from foreign countries than the foreign countries buy from Canada, the balance of trade would be negative. That is, imports exceed exports, creating a **trade deficit**.

The **balance of payments** is the broadest indicator of international trade. It is the total flow of money into the country *minus* the total flow of money out of the country, over some period of time. The balance of payments includes the balance of trade plus the net dollars received and spent on foreign investment, military expenditures, tourism, foreign aid, and other international transactions. For example, when a Canadian-based company like Alcan buys all or part of a company like Pechiney, based in France, that investment is counted in the balance of payments but not in the balance of trade. Similarly, when a foreign-based company such as Best Buy purchases a Canadian company such as Future Shop or purchases Canadian stocks, bonds, or real estate, those transactions are part of the balance of payments. The Canadian government, like all governments, desires a favourable balance of payments, which means that more money is coming into the country than is flowing out of it.

In theory, the balance of payments is always zero. "If Canada buys more goods and services than it sells (i.e., if it has a current account deficit), it has to sell its assets to finance the spending (i.e., run a capital account surplus) or go into debt."[28]

Exhibit 2.3 **Canada's Trade Balance**

The Canadian trade balance is consistently in a surplus position mainly because of tremendous exports to the United States.

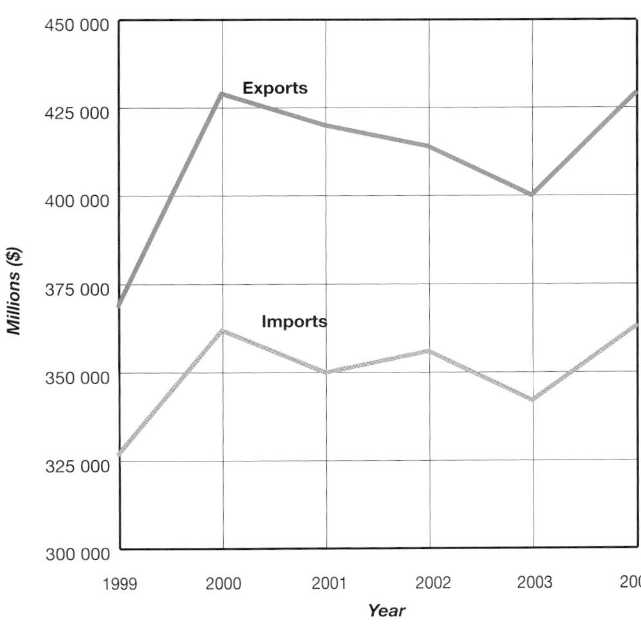

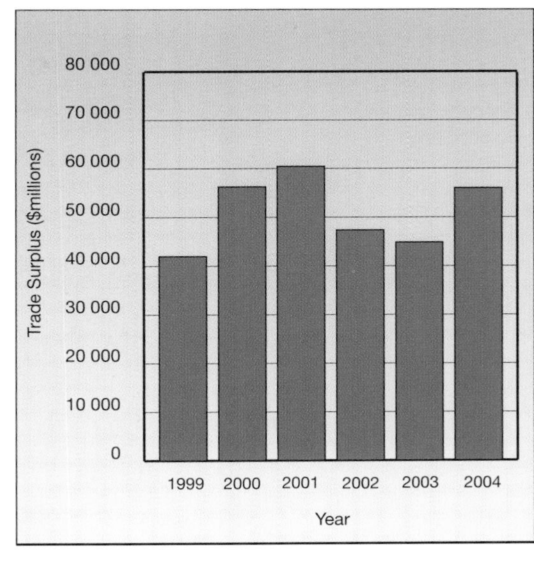

Source: Trade Balance (1999–2003) adapted from Statistics Canada website http://statscan/ca/trade/scripts/trade_search.cgi.

Trade Restrictions

L.O. 5

Even though international trade has many economic advantages, sometimes countries practise **protectionism**; that is, they restrict international trade for one reason or another. Sometimes they restrict trade to shield specific industries from foreign competition and the possible loss of jobs in these industries. Sometimes they try to protect certain industries that are key to their national defence and the health and safety of their citizens. At other times they engage in protectionist measures to give new or weak industries an opportunity to grow and strengthen.[29]

protectionism
Government policies aimed at shielding a country's industries from foreign competition

Despite its leadership position in the fight to reduce trade barriers, the United States uses protectionist tools with some regularity. From Canadian lumber to Chinese bras, the U.S. is often out of step with its official stance on free trade. In fact, the United States has been involved in more than 50 percent of the trade disputes brought to the World Trade Organization (WTO) since 1995 (see Exhibit 2.4).[30] Of course, the U.S. is also the economic leader in international trade and therefore is involved in a tremendous amount of transactions open to dispute. American officials argue that their tactics are appropriate but many in the world see a double standard, and the official rulings have often supported these claims. Is the United States acting like a child who goes home and takes her ball with her when things don't go her way on the playground?

L.O. 6

Are trade restrictions a good idea or a bad idea? Study after study has shown that in the long run, they hurt a country because they remove competition, stifle innovation, and allow domestic producers to charge more for their goods. The most commonly used forms of trade restrictions include:

- *Tariffs*. **Tariffs** are taxes, surcharges, or duties levied against imported goods. Sometimes tariffs are levied to generate revenue for the government, but more often they are imposed to restrict trade or to punish other countries for disobeying international trade laws.
- *Quotas*. **Quotas** limit the amount of a particular good that countries can import during a year. Limits may be set in quantities, such as kilograms of salt, or in values, such as total dollars' worth of peanuts.

tariffs
Taxes levied on imports

quotas
Fixed limits on the quantity of imports a nation will allow for a specific product

Exhibit 2.4 Fighting the United States

More than half of the trade disputes brought before the World Trade Organization (WTO) since its founding in 1995 involve the United States.

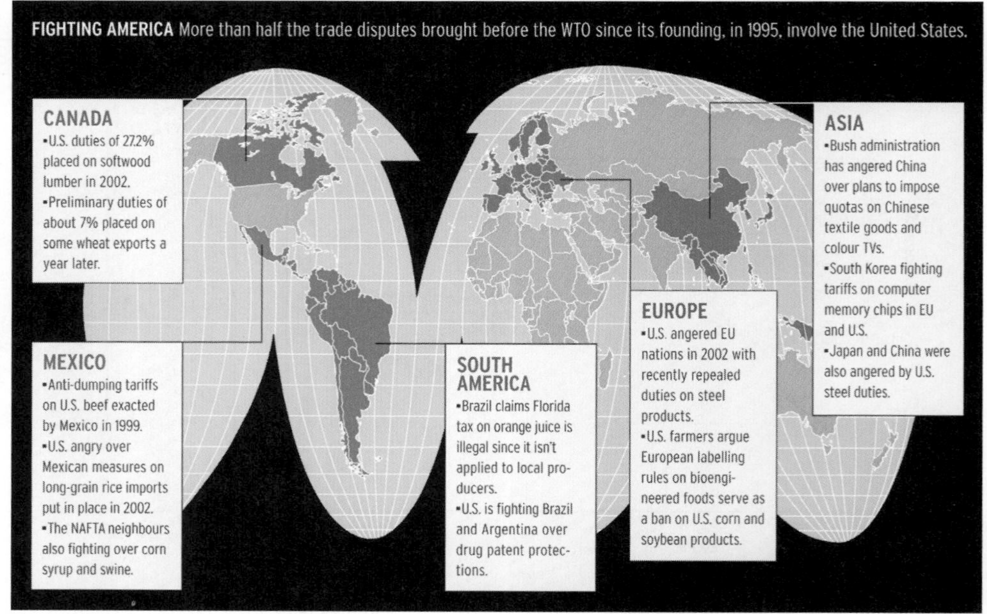

Source: Courtesy of *Canadian Business* magazine.

embargo
Total ban on trade with a particular nation (a sanction) or of a particular product

- *Embargoes.* In its most extreme form, a quota becomes an **embargo**, a complete ban on the import or export of certain products. The Canadian beef industry suffered after a single case of mad cow disease was discovered in 2003. Strict embargoes on Canadian beef set by the United States and other countries have translated into lost revenues and hardship for Canadians in this industry.[31]
- *Sanctions.* Sanctions are politically motivated embargoes that revoke a country's normal trade relations status; they are often used as forceful alternatives short of war. Sanctions can include arms embargoes, foreign-assistance reductions and cut-offs, trade limitations, tariff increases, import-quota decreases, visa denials, air-link cancellations, and more. Most governments use sanctions sparingly, because studies show that they are ineffective at getting countries to change.[32]

In addition to restricting foreign trade, governments sometimes give their domestic producers a competitive edge by using these protectionist tactics:

- *Restrictive import standards.* Countries can assist their domestic producers by establishing restrictive import standards, such as requiring special licences for doing certain kinds of business and then making it difficult for foreign companies to obtain such a licence. For example, Saudi Arabia restricts import licences for a variety of products, including chemicals, pasteurized milk, and information technology products.[33] At the provincial level, Quebec's Regulation Respecting Dairy Product Substitutes restricts the sale of yellow margarine in the province.[34] Trading blocs also impose standards that ensure local content. Toyota recently complained of unfair restrictions in the North American Free Trade Agreement (NAFTA), which requires vehicle manufactures to have 62.5 percent NAFTA content for products sold within the trading bloc. Canada, the United States, and Mexico are each re-evaluating the agreement more than a decade after the deal. Toyota would like to see this particular rate reduced to 50 percent.[35]

subsidies
Government support provided to businesses in the form of money, tax breaks, or low-rate/interest-free loans.

- *Subsidies.* Rather than restrict imports, some countries subsidize domestic producers so that their prices can compete favourably in the global marketplace.

Bombardier and Embraer have continuously accused each other of receiving unfair subsidies from their respective home governments, Canada and Brazil. The disputes have routinely ended up at the WTO.

- *Dumping.* The practice of selling large quantities of a product at a price lower than the cost of production or below what the company would charge in its home market is called **dumping.** The U.S. government accused the Canadian lumber industry of dumping and unilaterally imposed a 27.2 percent duty. The U.S. subsequently began to ease its stance and eventually announced plans to reduce the rate to 13.2 percent. However, Canada launched separate actions at the WTO and with the NAFTA panel, which ruled that the duties were not warranted.[36] Despite this judgment the dispute is still not completely settled. The Canadian government even enlisted the help of Paul Tellier, former CEO of Bombardier and Canadian National Railways, to serve as a negotiator. The goal is to reach agreements to help recover the more than $4 billion in tariffs paid by lumber companies and to establish a fair system to deal with future disputes.[37] The tone has become increasingly aggressive in recent months as Canadian officials have demanded that the U.S. honour its commitments.

dumping
Charging less than the actual cost or less than the home country's price for goods sold in other countries

Agreements and Organizations Promoting International Trade

To prevent trade disputes from escalating into full-blown trade wars, and to ensure that international business is conducted in a fair and orderly fashion, countries worldwide have created trade agreements and organizations. Philosophically, most of these agreements and organizations support the basic principles of **free trade.** The assumption is that each nation will ultimately benefit by freely exchanging the goods and services it produces most efficiently for the goods and services it produces less efficiently. The major trade agreements and organizations include GATT, WTO, the IMF, the World Bank, and APEC.

free trade
International trade without restrictive measures

The General Agreement on Tariffs and Trade (GATT)

The General Agreement on Tariffs and Trade (GATT) is a worldwide pact that was first established in the aftermath of the Second World War. The pact's guiding principle—most favoured nation (MFN)—is one of non-discrimination. Any trade advantage a GATT member gives to one country must be given to all GATT members, and no GATT nation can be singled out for punishment. In 1995 GATT established the World Trade Organization (WTO), which has replaced GATT as the world forum for trade negotiations.

The World Trade Organization (WTO)

The World Trade Organization (WTO) is a permanent forum for negotiating, implementing, and monitoring international trade procedures and for mediating trade disputes among its 144 member countries. The organization's goals include facilitating free trade, lowering the costs of doing business, enhancing the international investment environment, simplifying customs, and promoting technical and economic cooperation. The WTO builds upon the principles of GATT and in addition provides a formal legal structure for settling disputes.

Admission to the WTO is by application process and requires approval by two-thirds of the members. All WTO members enjoy "favoured" access to foreign markets in exchange for adhering to a long list of fair-trading rules and laws governing patents, copyrights, and trademarks. After 15 years of negotiations, China was finally admitted to the WTO in 2001. As a condition to its membership, China made extraordinary concessions. Over a five-year period, China must eliminate many tariffs and quotas on a wide range of products and open its market of 1.4 billion people to foreign goods.[38]

The U.S. duty of 27.2 percent on Canadian softwood lumber was accompanied by an unsubstantiated claim of dumping.

The International Monetary Fund (IMF)

The International Monetary Fund (IMF) is an international organization of 184 member countries.[39] Founded in 1945, its primary function is to provide short-

China's Trade Minister Shi Guangsheng claps as China joins the World Trade Organization. Among the many advantages of trading with China are its enormous population and good infrastructure.

term loans to countries that are unable to meet their budgetary expenses. As such, the IMF is often looked upon as a lender of last resort. For example, the IMF provided a combined total of more than US$150 billion in loans to South Korea, Indonesia, Brazil, Thailand, and other countries to help rescue them from a global financial crisis at the end of the twentieth century.[40]

The World Bank

The World Bank was initially founded to finance reconstruction after the Second World War. It now provides low-interest loans to developing nations for improvement of transportation, telecommunications, health, and education. Currently, the World Bank is focused on bringing the Internet to the less-developed regions of the world, such as Africa. World Bank officials and telecommunication executives hope that Internet connections will attract more companies to the region and lead to more rapid economic development.[41] Both the IMF and the World Bank are funded by deposits from its 184 member nations.

The Asia Pacific Economic Cooperation Council (APEC)

The Asia Pacific Economic Cooperation Council (APEC) is an organization of 21 countries that are making efforts to liberalize trade in the Pacific Rim (the land areas that surround the Pacific Ocean). Member nations include Canada, Japan, China, Thailand, Mexico, Australia, South Korea, and the United States. In 1994, the members established the "Bogor Goals." They agreed to work toward the elimination of all tariffs and trade barriers among industrialized countries of the Pacific Rim by 2010 and among developing countries by 2020.[42] The objectives are lofty; only time will tell if this agreement will live up to its enormous promise.

L.O. 7

trading blocs
Organizations of nations that remove barriers to trade among their members and that establish uniform barriers to trade with non-member nations

Trading Blocs

Trading blocs are another type of organization that promotes international trade. Generally comprising neighbouring countries, trading blocs promote free trade among regional members. Although specific rules vary from group to group, their primary objective is to ensure the economic growth and benefit of members. As such, trading blocs generally promote trade inside the region while creating uniform barriers against goods and services entering the region from non-member countries. Trading blocs are becoming a significant force in the global marketplace.[43]

Trading blocs can be advantageous or disadvantageous in promoting world trade, depending on one's perspective. Some economists are apprehensive about the growing importance of regional trading blocs. They fear that the world is splitting into three camps, revolving around the Americas, Europe, and Asia. Any nation that does not fall into one of these economic regions could suffer, they say, because members of the trading blocs could place severe restrictions on trade with non-member countries. The critics fear that overall world trade could decline as members become more protective of their own regions. As a result, consumers could find themselves with fewer choices, and many producers could lose sales in lucrative foreign markets.

Others claim that trading blocs could improve world trade. The growth of commerce and the availability of customers and suppliers within a trading bloc could be a boon to smaller or younger nations that are trying to build strong economies. The lack of trade barriers within the bloc could help member industries compete with producers in more-developed nations, and, in some cases, member countries could reach a wider market than before.[44] Furthermore, close ties to more stable economies could help shield emerging nations from fluctuations in the global economy and could promote a greater sharing of knowledge and technology; both outcomes could aid future economic development.

The four most powerful trading blocs today are the Association of Southeast Asian Nations (ASEAN), South America's Mercosur, the North American Free Trade Agreement (NAFTA), and the European Union (EU), with the latter two being the largest and most powerful (see Exhibit 2.5). Because many trading nations see Latin America as an area for large-scale economic growth in the future, they are eager to establish ties with Mercosur, which links Argentina, Brazil, Paraguay, and Uruguay (Bolvia and Chile are associate members) and encompasses a population of 210 million who produce more than US$1 trillion in goods and services.[45] Like other trading blocks, Mercosur's objectives include the free movement of goods and services across the borders of its members. Furthermore, the group seeks an economic integration that it hopes will make the four countries more competitive in the global marketplace.[46] Some NAFTA officials hope that Mercosur will eventually join NAFTA to form a Free Trade Area of the Americas (FTAA).[47]

The European Union

One of the largest trading blocs is the European Union (EU). It combines 25 countries, 10 of which joined in May 2004. Another two countries will possibly gain

Exhibit 2.5 **Members of Major Trade Blocs**

As the economies of the world become increasingly linked, many countries have formed powerful regional trade blocs that trade freely with one another and limit foreign competition.

European Union (EU)*	North American Free Trade Agreement (NAFTA)	Association of Southeast Asian Nations (ASEAN)	Mercosur
Austria	Canada	Brunei	Argentina
Belgium	Mexico	Cambodia	Bolivia†
Cyprus*	United States	Indonesia	Brazil
Czech Republic		Laos	Chile†
Denmark		Malaysia	Paraguay
Estonia		Myanmar	Uruguay
Germany		Philippines	
Greece		Singapore	
Finland		Thailand	
France		Vietnam	
Hungary			
Ireland			
Italy			
Latvia			
Lithuania			
Luxembourg			
Malta			
The Netherlands			
Poland			
Portugal			
Slovakia			
Slovenia			
Spain			
Sweden			
United Kingdom			

* Only the Southern part of Cyprus is a member; † Chile and Bolivia are associate members

membership by 2007 and increase its population to nearly half a billion people. The four candidate countries awaiting accession are Bulgaria, Croatia, Romania, and Turkey.[48] EU nations are working to eliminate hundreds of local regulations, variations in product standards, and protectionist measures that limit trade among member countries. Eliminating barriers enables the nations of the EU to function as a single market, with trade flowing among member countries as it does among regions within a country. This is no small feat considering the nationalistic feelings and a long history of war and conflict among member nations. The challenge of forming the EU and other such trading blocs is to deal with cultural resistance, respect fragile national identities, deal with inflation and conversion costs, integrate the national vehicles (such as central banks), and in effect give up some autonomy for a cooperative arrangement that will hopefully bring greater peace and economic prosperity to the region.

The EU's Impact on the Rules of Global Trade Increasingly, the rules governing the food we eat, the software we use, and the cars we drive are set in Brussels, the unofficial capital of the European Union. The European Union regulates frequently and rigorously when it comes to consumer protection and it has significantly affected global product standards. Twenty years ago if manufacturers designed something to North American standards, they could pretty much sell it around the world. Now items must conform to EU standards. When it comes to consumer or environmental protections, EU regulators believe it's better to be safe than sorry. That approach evolved partly from a series of food scares, such as mad cow disease, in Europe over the past 10 to 14 years. It also reflects the fact that Europeans are more inclined to expect governments to protect their citizens. Because of stricter EU rules, McDonald's has stopped serving soft-plastic toys with its Happy Meals and United Technologies has redesigned its Carrier air conditioners to comply with European recycling rules.[49]

The Euro In 1999, 11 of the 15 EU countries formed the economic and monetary union (EMU) and turned over control of their individual monetary policies to the newly created European Central Bank. Greece joined in January 2002. With a combined population of more than 300 million, these 12 countries account for about 20 percent of the world's gross domestic product (GDP), making them the world's second-largest economy.[50] One of the driving forces behind the decision to join the EMU was the anticipated advantages these countries would enjoy by creating a unified currency called the **euro**.

euro
The currency used by 12 European nations

The decision to move to the euro was a complicated issue for all member nations. For example, the Greek drachma was officially established in 1827 and traced its roots to the time of Alexander the Great. Despite historical and emotional reservations, the weakness of the Greek currency made the decision to move to the euro both logical and inevitable. Once the country met the criteria, the decision was made. Moving forward, all new members of the union will also need to meet the following criteria before being integrated into the euro family: curbing inflation, cutting interest rates, reducing budget deficits to a maximum of 3 percent of GDP, and limiting public borrowing to a maximum of 60 percent of GDP and stabilizing the currency's exchange rate.

On the other end of the spectrum, countries such as the United Kingdom and Denmark decided to maintain their currencies (the British pound and the Danish crown) in order to preserve more direct control over their economic policies.[51] Additionally, in Sweden, a referendum was held in late 2003 on the euro and integration was defeated by a 14 percent margin. More than 80 percent of registered voters went to the polls for this emotional issue. "The no supporters said joining the euro could damage the country's strong economic performance and generous welfare system, while the yes backers said trade and future growth would be enhanced by becoming a member."[52]

Officially launched in 1999 (with notes and coins available in 2002), the euro got off to a rocky start. But European leaders believed it would build a bond among Europe's cities and improve trade. Moreover, the euro could wipe out some US$65 billion annually in currency exchange costs among participants and cut the intermediary out of trillions of dollars' worth of foreign exchange transactions. The initial difficulties were resolved and the currency has flourished. With prices in member nations now visible in

Exhibit 2.6 **Exchange Rates: Recent History of the Canadian Dollar**

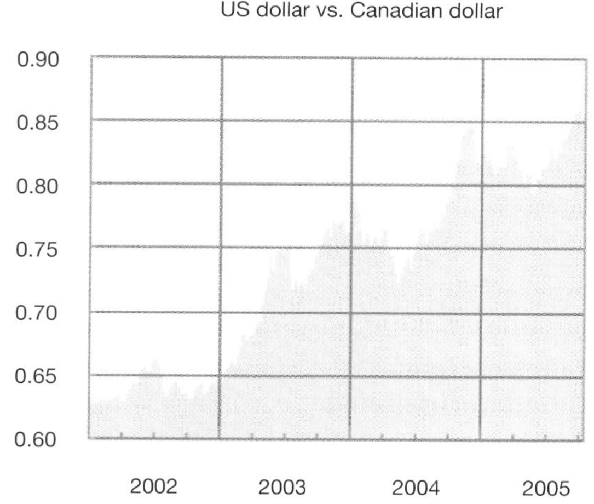

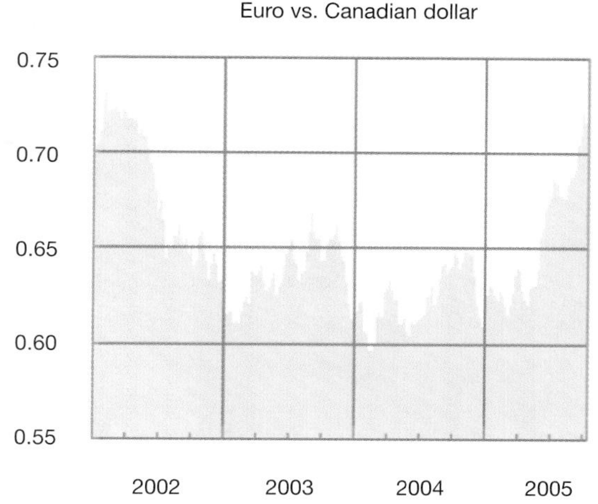

Source: Available at the Bank of Canada website at http://bankofcanada.ca/en/graphs/currencies.html

one currency, consumers can compare prices on similar items whether they are sold in Lisbon, Paris, Athens, Milan, Vienna, or Berlin.[53]

Despite this strength in numbers, the euro, like older established currencies such as the U.S. dollar, is subject to severe price variations. For instance, in the summer of 2005, the currency took a hit when French and Dutch voters decided to reject the new EU constitution. Joining forces can lead to more economic power and stability; however, balancing opinions can also lead to political and economic instability, which tends to put downward pressure on currency values (see Exhibit 2.6).[54]

NAFTA

In 1994, Canada, the United States, and Mexico formed a powerful trading bloc, the North American Free Trade Agreement (NAFTA). The agreement paves the way for the free flow of goods, services, and capital within the bloc by eliminating all tariffs and quotas on trades among the three nations.[55] So far the scorecard for NAFTA seems positive. It has been a huge success in promoting trade between Canada and its Mexican and American partners. Canada and Mexico now send more than 85 percent of their exports to the United States and get a similar percentage of their imports from the United States.[56] Fears that NAFTA would move Canadian jobs to Mexico have for the most part proved unfounded. Ultimately, NAFTA's supporters would like to see the agreement expanded to include all of Central and South America—making it the largest free-trade zone on the planet.[57]

Foreign Exchange Rates and Currency Valuations

When companies buy and sell goods and services in the global marketplace, they complete the transaction by exchanging currencies. For instance, if a Japanese company borrows money from a Canadian bank to build a manufacturing plant in Japan, it must repay the loan in Canadian dollars. Or if a South Korean car manufacturer imports engine parts from Japan, it must pay for them in yen (Japan's currency). To do so, companies exchange their currency at any international bank that handles *foreign exchange,* the conversion of one currency into an equivalent amount of another currency. The number of yen, zloty, or pounds that must be exchanged for every dollar, koruna, or won is known as the **exchange rate** between currencies.

exchange rate Rate at which the money of one country is traded for the money of another

Argentines gathered in front of a Buenos Aires currency exchange as the government lifted restrictions against citizens' trading pesos at a free-floating rate against the dollar.

Most international currencies operate under a *floating exchange rate system*; thus, a currency's value or price fluctuates in response to the forces of global supply and demand (as we discussed in Chapter 1). The supply and demand of a country's currency are determined in part by what is happening in the country's own economy. Moreover, because supply and demand for a currency are always changing, the rate at which it is exchanged for other currencies may change a little each day. Japanese currency might be trading at 82.26 yen to the Canadian dollar on one day and 81.77 on the next.

Even though most governments allow the value of their currency to respond to the forces of supply and demand, sometimes a government will intervene and adjust the exchange rate of its country's currency. Why would a government do this? One reason is to keep the price of a nation's goods and services more affordable in the global marketplace and to protect the nation's economy against trade imbalances. Another is to boost or slow down the country's economy.

Devaluation, or the drop in the value of a nation's currency relative to the value of other currencies, can at times boost a country's economy because it makes the country's products and services more affordable in foreign markets while it increases the price of imports. Because fewer units of foreign currency are required to purchase the devalued currency, such situations tend to raise a country's exports and lower its imports. Conversely, a strong currency boosts imports and dampens exports.

Some countries fix, or peg, the value of their currencies to the value of more stable currencies, such as the U.S. dollar, the euro, or the yen, instead of letting it float freely. Hong Kong, for example, pegs its currency to the U.S. dollar. If a currency is pegged, its value fluctuates proportionately with the value of the foreign currency to which it is linked. So if the U.S. dollar declines, so will the Japanese yen and other currencies that are pegged to it. This system works well as long as the proportionate relationship between the two currencies remains valid. But if one partner suffers economic hardship, demand for its currency will decline significantly and the exchange rate at which the two are pegged will become unrealistic. Such was the case with Thailand's currency (the baht), Indonesia's currency (the rupiah), and Argentina's currency (the peso). When these countries unpegged their currencies from the U.S. dollar to let them gradually seek their true value, the currencies went into a free fall.

L.O. 8

DEALING WITH ECONOMIC SHOCKS IN A GLOBAL BUSINESS ENVIRONMENT

Canadians felt the pain and fear of the SARS epidemic. Toronto residents were the primary combatants against the spread of the disease; however, the economic and human impact was felt by all residents of Canada and the global community at large. The effects on travel and trade were not restricted to various Asian locations experiencing the outbreak. More recently, Hurricane Katrina's devastation sent shock waves through the global economy as gas prices skyrocketed. A few years earlier, the world experienced the Asian economic flu, which did not create the medical problems of the SARS outbreak but still managed to cause pain and hardship as markets, firms, and investors suffered worldwide. In the global marketplace, the problems of one country can greatly affect world economics. The September 11, 2001, terrorist attacks on the World Trade Center in New York City and the Pentagon in Washington D.C. were aimed at the American people and the free-market system, but emotionally and economically the attacks knew no borders. There is an old joke that says when the United States sneezes, Canada catches a cold.

In today's global environment we are susceptible to ailments from around the world. The terrorist bombings in Spain and, more recently, in London had an immediate impact on European markets and stimulated old fears that were felt around the world.[58] What does this new global reality translate into? The airline industry has been bolstered by security and safety moves that lead to some annoying yet worthwhile time delays. The mad cow disease discoveries have led to old protectionist measures. The rules have been slightly altered; however, organizations will not shy away from their global pursuits.

KFC, for example, is one firm that doesn't plan on hitting the brakes. KFC has approximately 13 000 restaurants worldwide. It has more than 200 franchises in Indonesia, which has the world's largest Muslim population. It has a restaurant in the holy city of Mecca, Saudi Arabia. In all, KFC has restaurants in more than 90 countries, including Japan, Australia, Egypt, Mexico, Malaysia, and Swaziland. In China, where KFC has more than 1200 restaurants, it is opening about 10 new stores a month and not about to slow down. KFC plans to open more than 1000 stores a year overseas for the foreseeable future.[59]

SUMMARY OF LEARNING OBJECTIVES

1 Highlight the opportunities and challenges of conducting business in other countries.

Conducting business in other countries can provide such opportunities as increased sales, operational efficiencies, exposure to new technologies, and consumer choices. At the same time, it poses challenges such as the need to learn unique laws, customs, and ethical standards. Furthermore, it exposes companies to the risks of political and economic instabilities, volatile currencies, international trade relationships, and the threat of global terrorism.

2 List five ways to improve communication in an international business relationship.

To improve international communication, learn as much as you can about the culture and customs of the people you are working with, keep an open mind and avoid stereotyping, anticipate misunderstandings and guard against them by clarifying your intent, adapt your style to match the style of others, and learn how to show respect in other cultures.

3 Identify five forms of international business activity.

Importing and exporting, licensing, franchising, strategic alliances and joint ventures, and foreign direct investment are five of the most common forms of international business activity. Each provides a company with varying degrees of control and entails different levels of risk and financial commitment.

4 Explain why nations trade.

Nations trade to obtain raw materials and goods that are unavailable to them or too costly to produce. International trade benefits nations by increasing a country's total output, offering lower prices and greater variety to its consumers, subjecting domestic oligopolies and monopolies to competition, and allowing companies to expand their markets and achieve production and distribution efficiencies.

5 Explain why nations restrict international trade and list four forms of trade restrictions.

Nations restrict international trade to boost local economies, to shield domestic industries from head-to-head competition with overseas rivals, to save specific jobs, to give weak or new industries a chance to grow strong, and to protect a nation's security. The four most commonly used forms of trade restrictions are tariffs (taxes, surcharges, or duties levied against imported goods), quotas (limitations on the amount of a particular good that can be imported), embargoes (the banning of imports and exports of certain goods), and sanctions (politically motivated embargoes).

6 Highlight three protectionist tactics nations use to give their domestic industries a competitive edge.

From time to time countries give their domestic producers a competitive edge by imposing restrictive import standards, such as requiring special licences or unusually high product standards; by subsidizing certain domestic producers so they can compete more favourably in the global marketplace; and by dumping or selling large quantities of a product at a lower price than it costs to produce the good or at a lower price than the good is sold for in its home market.

7 Explain how trading blocs affect trade.

Trading blocs are regional groupings of countries in which trade barriers have been removed. These alliances ease trade among bloc members and strengthen barriers for nonmembers. Critics of trading blocs fear that as members become more protective of their regions, those not in the bloc could suffer. Proponents see them as a way to help smaller or younger nations compete with producers in more-developed nations. The four most powerful trading blocs today are the Association of Southeast Asian Nations (ASEAN), the Mercosur, the North American Free Trade Agreement (NAFTA), and the European Union (EU).

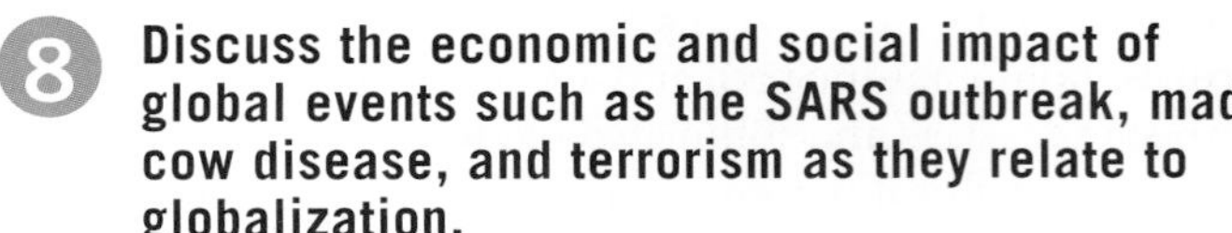

8 Discuss the economic and social impact of global events such as the SARS outbreak, mad cow disease, and terrorism as they relate to globalization.

The growing mutual dependence and interrelation in the business environment is inevitable. This fact leaves multinational firms vulnerable to events across the globe but at the same time protects them from facing financial ruin when a devastating event occurs in any one region. Whether it is mad cow disease, SARS, or terrorism, companies and governments will handle each event and then legislate and create protection measures to deal with these new threats.

Behind the SCENES

Doing Everybody's Wash—Whirlpool's Global Lesson

David Whitwam's timing couldn't have been worse. Just as the company was planting its feet in international markets, economic turmoil hit Asia and Europe. Wildly fluctuating foreign exchange rates created chaos in Asia, where Whirlpool had participated in several joint ventures. Fortunately, less than 5 percent of Whirlpool's sales came from Asia, so the company was not seriously hurt. Still, ongoing global economic troubles contributed to Whirlpool's multimillion-dollar losses overseas.

David Whitwam's global strategy, however, was not widely copied by rivals. As Whirlpool continued to expand in Europe, Latin America, and Asia, the company's major competitor, Maytag, was selling its European and Australian businesses to refocus on the lucrative North American market. Nevertheless, Whitwam was willing to ride out the storm, even as global economic troubles dragged on.

He expedited Whirlpool's entry into foreign markets by focusing less on manufacturing its own products overseas and more on developing licensing arrangements and strategic alliances with other companies. For example, Whirlpool formed strategic alliances with Tupperware to work jointly on marketing, branding, and product development in Europe, Africa, and the Middle East.

Whirlpool also kept things simple by developing basic appliance models that used about 70 percent of the same parts. For instance, feature-rich German appliances were combined with efficient, low-cost Italian technologies to produce a "world washer." Then Whirlpool modified the machines for local preferences. Front-loading washing machines were scaled down for European homes, as were refrigerators for India. Despite their widely different exteriors and sizes, the appliances had plenty of common parts.

The global economic crisis forced Whitwam to fine-tune his expansion plans. Whirlpool dropped one joint venture in China (costing the company US$350 million) and rearranged others as weak economic conditions and intense competition drove appliance prices down and sapped profits. "The thing we misjudged was how rapidly Chinese manufacturers could improve their quality," notes Whitwam.

In Brazil, where Whirlpool had long been profitable, a currency crisis coupled with inflation worries slowed appliance sales to a trickle. Still, Whitwam remained committed to the market. Anticipating future growth opportunities in this emerging market, Whirlpool invested hundreds of millions of dollars to modernize operations, cut costs, and solidify its position as the country's market leader in refrigerators, room air conditioners, and washers.

In less than a decade, Whitwam transformed Whirlpool into the world's leading manufacturer of major home appliances. With various brands sold in 170 countries, international sales now account for about 45 percent of the company's US$12 billion annual revenue. The company has created a network of 50 manufacturing and technology centres around the world. Moreover, the outlook for growth in the global appliance industry looks promising. With the recent US$1.4 billion acquisition of Maytag, its main competitor, the company is on a roll. Still, Whitwam understands that doing business in the global marketplace is full of risk; conditions can change at the drop of a baht, ruble, euro, or dollar.[60]

Critical Thinking Questions

1. What did Whirlpool find to be the advantages and disadvantages of doing business around the world?
2. How did global expansion affect Whirlpool's products?
3. Should Whirlpool be concerned about currency devaluation in a country in which it sells few appliances?

Learn More Online

Find out how Whirlpool is faring with its global strategy. Go to Chapter 2 of this text's website at www.pearsoned.ca/bovee, and click on the Whirlpool hotlink to read the latest news releases about Whirlpool's financial performance, international operations, and plans for expansion. How do Whirlpool's international sales figures look? Where is the company strongest? Where is it struggling? What changes, if any, is the company making to its global strategy?

KEY TERMS

absolute advantage (49)
balance of payments (50)
balance of trade (50)
comparative advantage theory (50)
dumping (53)
economies of scale (49)
embargo (52)
euro (56)
exchange rate (57)
exporting (45)
foreign direct investment (FDI) (47)
free trade (53)
importing (45)
joint venture (46)
licensing (45)
multinational corporations (MNCs) (47)
protectionism (51)
quotas (51)
strategic alliance (46)
tariffs (51)
trade deficit (50)
trade surplus (50)
trading blocs (54)

TEST YOUR KNOWLEDGE

Questions for Review

1. How can a company use a licensing agreement to enter world markets?
2. What two fundamental product strategies do companies choose between when selling their products in the global marketplace?
3. What is the balance of trade, and how is it related to the balance of payments?
4. What is dumping, and how does Canada respond to this practice?
5. What is a floating exchange rate?

Questions for Analysis

6. Why would a company choose to work through intermediaries when selling products in a foreign country?
7. How do companies benefit from forming international joint ventures and strategic alliances?
8. What types of situations might cause the Canadian government to implement protectionist measures?
9. How do tariffs and quotas protect a country's own industries?
10. **Ethical Considerations.** Should the Canadian government more closely regulate the practice of giving trips and other incentives to foreign managers to win their business? Is this bribery?

Questions for Application

11. Suppose you own a small company that manufactures hockey equipment. You are aware that Russia is a large market, and you are considering exporting your products there. What steps should you take? Who might be able to give you assistance?
12. Because your Brazilian restaurant caters to Western business people and tourists, much of the food you buy is imported from North American sources. Lately, the value of the real (Brazil's currency) has been falling relative to the U.S. dollar. This change makes your food imports much more costly, and it negatively affects your profitability. You have three options; which one will you choose? (a) Raise menu prices across the board. (b) Accept only U.S. dollars from customers. (c) Try to purchase more of your food items locally. Please explain your selection.
13. **Integrated.** Review the theory of supply and demand discussed in Chapter 1. Using this theory, explain how a country's currency is valued and why governments sometimes adjust the values of their currency.
14. **Integrated.** You just received notice that a large shipment of manufacturing supplies you have been waiting for has been held up in customs for two weeks. A local business associate tells you that you are expected to give customs agents some "incentive money" to see that everything clears easily. How will you handle this situation?

PRACTISE YOUR KNOWLEDGE

SHARPENING YOUR COMMUNICATION SKILLS

Languages never translate on a word-for-word basis. When doing business in the global marketplace, choose words that convey only their most specific denotative meaning. Avoid using slang or idioms (words that can have meanings far different from their individual components when translated literally). For example, if a Canadian executive tells an Egyptian executive that a certain product "doesn't cut the mustard," chances are that communication will fail.

Team up with two other students and list 10 examples of slang (in your own language) that would probably be misinterpreted or misunderstood during a business conversation with someone from another culture. Next to each example, suggest other words you might use to convey the same message. Make sure the alternatives mean exactly the same as the original slang or idiom. Compare your list with those of your classmates.

BUILDING YOUR TEAM SKILLS

Although the steel industry has experienced a recent renaissance in the marketplace, the cycle has ebbed and flowed in both favourable and unfavourable directions over the years. In today's interdependent global economy, fluctuations in a country's currency can have a profound effect on the flow of products across borders. The North American steel industry, for example, at times has felt intense competition from an influx of Korean, Brazilian, and Russian steel imports. After the currencies of those countries plummeted in value, the price of steel products exported to Canada dropped as well, making Canadian and U.S. steel much more expensive by comparison.

Fuelled by low prices, steel flooded into North America, hurting sales of Canadian and U.S. steel. Over the course of several months, the volume of steel imports soared. To protect the industry the Canadian government imposed duties to protect domestic firms, such as Stelco, against foreign steel invasion. Recently, the Canadian international trade tribunal ruled that the tariffs are unnecessary and lifted duties on steel coming from four nations: France, Russia, Romania, and the Slovak republic.[61] With your team, brainstorm a list of at least three ways Canada might handle this situation. Once you have your list, consider the probable effect of each option on the following stakeholders:

- Canadian businesses that buy steel
- Canadian steel manufacturers
- Canadian businesses that export to Korea, Brazil, or Russia
- Employees of Canadian steel manufacturers

On the basis of your analysis and discussion, which option will your team recommend? Select a spokesperson to explain your selection and your team's reasoning to the other teams. Compare your recommendation with those of your classmates.

EXPAND YOUR KNOWLEDGE

DISCOVERING CAREER OPPORTUNITIES

If global business interests you, consider working for a Canadian government agency that supports or regulates international trade. For example, Export Development Canada (EDC) offers a Student Summer Employment Program. The EDC provides trade finance services to support Canadian exporters and investors in more than 200 markets. Visit its website at www.edc.ca, go to the Student Summer Employment Program section, and then answer these questions: Who can apply for these positions? Where are the work terms located? What positions are available for this upcoming summer?

DEVELOPING YOUR RESEARCH SKILLS

Companies involved in international trade have to watch the foreign exchange rates of the countries in which they do business. Use your research skills to locate and analyze information about the value of the Canadian dollar relative to the U.S. dollar. As you complete this exercise, make a note of the sources and search strategies you used.

1. How many Canadian dollars do you need to purchase one U.S. dollar? Find yesterday's foreign exchange rate for the U.S. dollar in the *Globe and Mail* or on the Internet.
2. Investigate this foreign exchange rate over the past month. Is the Canadian dollar growing stronger (buying more U.S. dollars) or growing weaker (buying fewer U.S. dollars)?
3. If you were a Canadian exporter selling to the United States, how would a stronger dollar be likely to affect demand for your products? How would a weaker dollar be likely to affect demand?

See It on the **WEB**

URLs for all Internet exercises are provided at the website for this book, www.pearsoned.ca/bovee. When you log on to the text website, select Chapter 2, select Destinations, click on the name of the featured website, and review the website to complete these exercises.

Explore the following chapter-related websites, review their content, and answer the following questions for each website you visit:

1. What is the purpose of this website?
2. What kinds of information does this website contain? Please be specific.
3. How is the information provided at this website useful for business people? Consumers?
4. How did you expand your knowledge of conducting business in the global environment by reviewing the material at this website? What new things did you learn about this topic?

NAVIGATING GLOBAL BUSINESS DIFFERENCES

In today's global marketplace, knowing as much as possible about your international customers' business practices and customs could give you a strategic advantage. To help you successfully conduct business around the globe, navigate the resources at www.edc.ca/corpinfo/careers/eye/eye_e.htm. Specifically, take a look at the following sections: Export Wise, Case Studies, Project Finance, Diversity, Social Responsibility, and Research Tools.

BANKING ON THE WORLD BANK

The World Bank plays an important role in today's fast-changing, closely meshed global economy. Do you know what this organization of five closely associated institutions does? Do you know who runs the bank, where the bank gets its money, and where the money goes? Learn how this organization's programs and financial assistance help poorer nations as well as affluent ones. Log on to the World Bank website and find out why global development is everyone's challenge. www.worldbank.org

Chapter 3
Practising Ethical Behaviour and Social Responsibility

LEARNING OBJECTIVES

After studying this chapter, you will be able to

1. Discuss what it means to practise good business ethics and highlight three factors that influence ethical behaviour
2. Identify three steps that businesses are taking to encourage ethical behaviour and explain the advantages and disadvantages of whistle-blowing
3. List four questions you might ask yourself when trying to make an ethical decision
4. Explain the difference between an ethical dilemma and an ethical lapse
5. Discuss the relationship between corporate social responsibility and profits
6. Explain how businesses can become more socially responsible
7. Outline activities that the government and businesses are undertaking to improve the environment

Behind the SCENES

Telus Corporation: Profit and Sustainability

www.telusmobility.com

As modern, tech-savvy Canadian students, you are no doubt aware of the Telus brand name. Many of you have a Telus-served phone in your bag, purse, or pocket as you sit through your lectures (reminder: turn it off during class!). So it should be no surprise that Telus is the largest telecommunications company in western Canada and second in the country with more than 3.9 million wireless subscribers. Telus is a relative newcomer on the national scene; the entity as it is known today was officially formed in February 1999 with the merger of Alberta-based Telus Corporation and British Columbia-based BC Telecom. Despite the relatively recent merger, the company can draw from the knowledge and experience of generations, as both founding companies have more than 100 years of service.

Behind the expansion and the success of the company is a strong commitment to social responsibility and ethical conduct. Telus has become a standard example cited by *Corporate Knights*, the magazine of Canadian corporate social responsibility. Telus was recently named Best Environmental Corporate Citizen. According to Patricia Mackenzie, assistant vice-president of environmental health and safety, "Telus envisions a day when telecommunications will allow them to move ideas and information instead of goods, services, and people." Telus has begun to deliver on this goal by enabling 299 265 teleconferences and avoiding carbon dioxide emissions of more than 128 tonnes in one calendar year alone. Additionally, the green agenda was pushed forward through a recovery and recycling program that allowed Telus to recycle 7183 metric tonnes of material that would otherwise have ended up in landfills. For these and other achievements, Telus is listed on the Dow Jones Sustainability Index. How do they deliver consistently? The *Corporate Knights* assessment identified three key factors:

1. *The environmental agenda is not isolated in a corner collecting dust.* Telus does not simply leave it to the public relations department to look after its environmental image. Instead it has empowered the finance department and created a system in which environmental performance reports are provided to the audit committee on a quarterly basis. Telus also pushes the agenda forward by continuously training its workforce. In each of the past three years more than 6000 courses were completed by Telus employees.
2. *Telus sets hard targets.* If a company wants to reach a goal, it must be specific in setting a target. Telus has established targets for many environmental goals, including water use, paper use, air emissions, reclamation activity, energy use, fuel consumption, and training.
3. *Telus is willing to take the lead.* The firm was a key player in the development of the Communications Environmental Excellence Initiative, a North American telecommunications commitment to improve environmental accountability.

Were you aware of Telus's environmentally friendly track record? As you read this chapter, consider the following issues: How does Telus balance the basic profit-seeking motive with its environmental agenda? Does this factor influence customer loyalty? Does it influence your purchase decisions?[1]

Telus has earned a reputation as a firm that embraces socially responsible practices.

L.O. 1

ETHICS AND SOCIAL RESPONSIBILITY IN THE WORKPLACE

Telus works hard to make sure that the company behaves in an ethical and socially responsible manner; businesses can't control each action or individual decision, but they can set expectations and enforce policies and codes. From the CEO to the newest entry-level clerk, every individual in an organization makes choices and decisions that have moral implications. These choices and decisions affect the company and its stakeholders. Moreover, they ultimately determine whether the company is recognized as a responsible corporate citizen.

This chapter explains what it means to conduct business in an ethically and socially responsible manner and discusses the importance of doing so. Many people use the terms *social responsibility* and *ethics* interchangeably, but the two are not the same. **Social responsibility** is the idea that business has certain obligations to society beyond the pursuit of profits. **Ethics**, by contrast, is defined as the principles and standards of moral behaviour that are accepted by society as right versus wrong. To make the "right choice" individuals must think through the consequences of their actions. *Business ethics* is the application of moral standards to business situations.

social responsibility
The concern of businesses for the welfare of society as a whole

ethics
The rules or standards governing the conduct of a person or group

We begin our discussion of ethics by explaining what it means to behave ethically. Next we highlight factors that influence ethical behaviour and provide examples of what some companies are doing to improve their ethical behaviour. We continue by showing how a business's behaviour affects its many stakeholders. In the second part of the chapter, we discuss what it means to be a socially responsible business and explore business's efforts to become more socially responsible.

What Is Ethical Behaviour?

Wanting to be an ethical corporate citizen isn't enough; people in business must actively practise ethical behaviour. In business, besides obeying all laws and regulations, practising good ethics means competing fairly and honestly, communicating truthfully, and not causing harm to others.

Competing Fairly and Honestly

Businesses are expected to compete fairly and honestly and not knowingly deceive, intimidate, or misrepresent customers, competitors, suppliers, clients, or employees. While most companies compete within the boundaries of the law, some knowingly break laws or take questionable steps in their zeal to maximize profits and gain a competitive advantage. For example, to get ahead of the competition, some companies have engaged in corporate spying, stealing patents, hiring employees from competitors to gain trade secrets, and eavesdropping electronically. Although businesses need to gather as much strategic information as they can, ethical companies steer clear of such practices.

In some cases, the line between legal and ethical behaviour is blurred. For instance, breaking into an office to gather sensitive information or crucial documents from the trash is illegal, but once the trash makes its way to a dumpster on public property, it's fair game. Still, rifling through a competitor's trash bins—a practice commonly referred to as *dumpster diving*—is unethical. Companies that practise good ethical behaviour frown on dumpster diving and even take corrective steps to make sure their employees compete fairly and honestly in the workplace. The box entitled "Airline Espionage: Air Canada and WestJet Face Off" provides a current example of this topic.

Communicating Truthfully

Companies that practise good ethical behaviour refrain from issuing false or misleading communications. Publishers Clearing House recently learned this ethical lesson. The company paid more than US$34 million to settle lawsuits that claimed it deceived consumers by mailing "you are a winner" notices that looked like cheques for large amounts. The company was also charged with accompanying such notices with decep-

Airline Espionage: Air Canada and WestJet Face Off

Air Canada and WestJet have been fighting to control air travel in Canada. The battle has now found a new runway: the courtroom. Air Canada has accused WestJet of using corporate spying to illegally access company information.

The following information may sound like something out of a James Bond film, but is actually a saga that describes the latest battleground for Canada's two largest airlines. In early 2004, Air Canada hired a private investigator who digitally reconstructed a WestJet executive's trash. Air Canada suspected this particular executive of tapping into its computers and attaining confidential information and filed a $220 million lawsuit in Ontario Superior Court. The central figure in this case is WestJet co-founder Mark Hill, who effectively acknowledges that he went to great lengths to understand the competition. However, Air Canada is not accusing him of harmless ambition; rather, they are building a case around foul play. The specific allegations are that a former employee, who now works for WestJet, allowed his employee code to be used thousands of times to gain valuable information on Air Canada's routes, seats sold, and load factor (percentage of available seats filled). Air Canada has even tried to implicate Clive Beddoe, WestJet's CEO, directly. In response, WestJet has accused Air Canada of grandstanding and says that the lawsuit is nothing more than an opportunity to attack the company publicly. This case is casting light on important ethical and legal issues. How far can a company go to gain competitive intelligence? What will the court rule in this spectacular case? Will the punishment fit the crime?[2]

Questions for Critical Thinking

1. Do you think that "dumpster diving" is an acceptable form of gathering market intelligence? Explain your answer.
2. Companies will often pursue employees from the competition in order to access valuable knowledge. Is this any different than accessing information from a competitor's website by using an ex-employee's code?

tive communications that led consumers to believe they could increase their chances of winning a grand prize by purchasing magazine subscriptions. As part of the settlement agreement, Publishers Clearing House promised it would stop mailing simulated cheques and sending consumers misleading information. It also promised that future mailings would disclose the odds of winning and inform the public that buying subscriptions would not increase the chances of winning.[3]

Not Causing Harm to Others

According to a recent *Business Week* poll, some 79 percent of the general population believe that corporate executives put their own personal interests ahead of workers' and shareholders' interests.[4] Placing one's personal welfare above the welfare of the organization can cause harm to others. For instance, every year tens of thousands of people are the victims of investment scams. Lured by promises of high returns, people sink more than a billion dollars annually into nonexistent oil wells, gold mines, and other fraudulent operations touted by complete strangers over the telephone and the Internet.[5] Does anyone remember Bre-X? In the late 1990s, many Canadian and international investors bought this stock based on false information about a remarkable gold discovery in Busang, Indonesia. The reports were fabricated and investors lost fortunes.[6]

Shady companies use other types of scams to take people's money. For example, con artists can fool investors by offering shares in start-up companies that don't exist. They also can misrepresent the potential of an investment while staying within the boundaries of the law. For example, with a little "creative accounting," a business that is in financial trouble can be made to look reasonably good to all but the most educated investors. In recent years, investors have discovered that such practices are sometimes committed by even the most respected firms, such as Nortel.

One major source of fraud is the often-criticized world of telemarketing. According to the National Fraud Information Center, the most popular scams include credit card offers, advance fee loans, lotteries (false claims that require an upfront tax fee), and telephone slamming (switching consumers' phone service without consent). The average individual loss accounted for about $1504. Lottery scams, which often prey on seniors, only accounted for about 2 percent of cases; however, the average loss was the largest at $5376 per victim. In terms of regional breakdown, Ontario and Quebec both made the North American top 10 list with 7 percent and 3 percent, respectively, of North American cases.[7]

Some business executives take advantage of the investor by using the company's earnings or resources for personal gain. Perhaps the most common approach is to cheat on expense accounts. Padding invoices and then splitting the overcharge with the supplier is another common ploy. Other tactics include selling company secrets to competitors and using confidential, non-public information gained from one's position in a company to benefit from the purchase and sale of stocks. Such **insider trading** is illegal and is closely checked by the appropriate governing body (Ontario Securities Commission, British Columbia Securities Commission, etc.).

insider trading
The use of unpublicized information that an individual gains from the course of his or her job to benefit from fluctuations in the stock market

Another way that business people can harm others is by getting involved in a **conflict of interest** situation. A conflict of interest exists when choosing a course of action will benefit one person's interests at the expense of another or when an individual chooses a course of action that advances his or her personal interests over those of the employer. For example, a lawyer would find himself in a conflict of interest situation if he represented both the plaintiff and the defendant in a lawsuit. Similarly, independent auditors could be in a conflict of interest situation if their firm also served as the client's consultants, as Chapter 13 discusses in detail.

conflict of interest
Situation in which a business decision may be influenced by the potential for personal gain

L.O. 2

Factors Influencing Ethical Behaviour

Although a number of factors influence the ethical behaviour of business people, three in particular appear to have the greatest impact: cultural differences, knowledge, and organizational behaviour.

Cultural Differences

Globalization exposes business people to a variety of different cultures and business practices. What does it mean for a business to do the right thing in Thailand? In Africa? In Norway? What may be considered unethical in Canada may be an accepted practice in another culture. Consider bribes, for example. In Canada, bribing officials is illegal, but to get something done in Mexico it's common to pay officials *una mordida* ("a small bite"). In China businesses pay *huilu,* and in Russia they pay *vzyatka.*

To crack down on illegal payoffs, industrialized nations have now signed a treaty that makes bribes to foreign officials a criminal offence. Still, bribery won't end just because a treaty has been signed or because it is illegal.

Knowledge

In most cases, a well-informed person is in a position to make better decisions and avoid ethical problems. Making decisions without all of the facts or a clear understanding of the consequences could harm employees, customers, the company, and other stakeholders. As an employee or manager, you are held accountable for your decisions and actions. So be sure to ask questions and gather enough information before making a decision or choosing a course of action. For instance, if a business superior tells you to shred a drawer full of documents, you might want to ask why and inquire whether doing so would be in violation of the law.

Organizational Behaviour

The foundation of an ethical business climate is ethical awareness. Organizations that strongly enforce company codes of conduct and provide ethics training help employees recognize and reason through ethical problems. Similarly, companies with strong ethical practices set a good example for employees to follow. On the other hand, companies that commit unethical acts in the course of doing business open the door for employees to follow suit.

To avoid such situations, many companies proactively develop programs designed to improve their ethical conduct. Additionally, more than 80 percent of large companies have adopted a written **code of ethics**, which defines the values and principles that should be used to guide decisions (see Exhibit 3.1 for an example). By itself, however, a code of ethics cannot accomplish much. "You can have grand motives, but if your employees don't see them, they aren't going to mean anything," says one ethics manager.[8] To be effective, a code must be supported by employee communications efforts, a formal training program, employee commitment to follow it, and a system through which employees can get help with ethically difficult situations.[9]

code of ethics
Written statement setting forth the principles that guide an organization's decisions

Like most firms, Petro-Canada has created a code of business conduct for all employees. In addition, Petro-Canada has created a specific code of ethics for senior financial officers to promote honest and ethical conduct, proper disclosure of financial information, and compliance with appropriate laws and rules. After the Enron scandal, energy firms are being scrutinized and have responded with increased attention to the ethical questions facing their firms. To guide employees in their day-to-day activities, Petro-Canada has even set up an anonymous ethics telephone hotline available to employees through the company intranet.[10] This practice has swept across the business landscape. Exhibit 3.1 shows a copy of Bell Canada's code.

Codes of ethics are an important starting point that can be used as a reference. As one ethics expert explains, "If you have an active ethics program in place ahead of time, then bad things shouldn't happen; but if they do happen, it won't hurt you as badly."[11] Perhaps inspired by these guidelines, some companies have created an official position—the ethics officer—to guard morality. Originally hired to oversee corporate conduct—from stealing company pens to endangering the environment to selling company secrets—many ethics officers today function as corporate coaches for ethical decision making. Keep in mind, however, that ethical behaviour starts at the top. The CEO and other senior managers must set the tone for people throughout the company (see the box entitled "Actions Speak Louder Than Codes").

Exhibit 3.1 **Bell Canada Code of Business Conduct**[12]

Bell Canada has set the following principles of business conduct for its employees, officers, and directors:

1. To comply with applicable laws, regulations, and company policies and procedures;
2. to carry out work duties and conduct business relationships with integrity, honesty and fairness;
3. to avoid all conflicts of interest;
4. to foster a work environment based on trust and respect for all stakeholders of the Bell Canada Enterprises community;
5. to foster a work environment which encourages open communication;
6. to maintain a safe and secure workplace and protect the environment;
7. to sustain a culture in which ethical conduct is recognized, valued and exemplified by us all.

As the Petro-Canada example demonstrates, companies that support ethical behaviour can establish a system for reporting unethical or illegal actions at work with an ethics hotline. Companies that value ethics will try to correct reported problems. If a serious problem persists, or in cases where management may be involved in the act, an employee may choose to speak up. *Whistle-blowing* is an employee's disclosure to the media or government authorities of illegal, unethical, or harmful practices by the company. But whistle-blowing can bring with it high costs: Public accusation of wrongdoing hurts the business's reputation, requires attention from managers who must investigate the accusations, and damages employee morale. Moreover, whistle-blowers risk being fired or demoted, and they often suffer career setbacks, financial strain, and emotional stress. The fear of such negative repercussions may allow unethical or illegal practices to go unreported. Still, all things considered, many employees do the right thing, as Exhibit 3.2 suggests.

According to a recent poll of more than 2000 Canadians conducted by the Environics Research Group, an overwhelming majority—89 percent—want the government to create new laws to improve protection for whistle-blowers.[13] Many firms today have incorporated a whistle-blowing aspect in their code of conduct. At the Bank of Montreal, employees are instructed that they can file such reports at the FirstPrinciples website and are protected under the Whistle-Blower Protection and Prohibition against Retaliation clause.[14] Despite such policies, individual behaviour is usually guided by the individual's perception of the firm's true commitment to upholding rules of conduct.

Actions Speak Louder Than Codes

Once you write a code of ethics and establish an ethics hotline, what more does your business need to do? A lot more, according to experts. Some companies develop detailed codes of behaviour and establish ethics hotlines only to pay them lip service. Perhaps that's why 81 percent of top managers believe they use ethics in day-to-day decision making, whereas 43 percent of employees believe managers routinely overlook ethics. When leaders make decisions that clearly show profits winning out over ethics, employees become skeptical and mistrustful—attitudes that lead to unethical behaviour.

To avoid the lip-service trap, support your ethics programs with a dose of reality:

- *Inspire concretely.* Tell employees how they will personally benefit from participating in ethics initiatives. People respond better to personal benefits than to company benefits.
- *Acknowledge reality.* Admit errors. Discuss what went right and what went wrong. Solicit employee opinion: What do you think? What's your view? Act on those opinions.
- *Incorporate reality into your solutions.* Use practical strategies that can be accomplished in the time available. Obtain real feedback by asking employees to name three realities the company isn't facing, three reasons the company won't meet its goals, and three competitive weaknesses the company exhibits in the marketplace.
- *Be honest.* Tell employees what you know as well as what you don't know. Talk openly about real results, not about what you'd like them to be. Accept criticism—and listen to it.

Make personal benefits, company errors, and tactical solutions more concrete by being straightforward and specific. By acknowledging the realities in every situation, you turn your words into action and build trust with your employees.

Questions for Critical Thinking

1. How does building trust encourage employees to be more ethical?
2. Some companies ask job candidates to take pre-employment tests such as drug tests or lie detector tests. Does such testing build trust with potential employees? Explain.

Exhibit 3.2 Doing the Right Thing

According to a recent survey of 1002 randomly selected adults, when it comes to ethics in the workplace, most employees try to do the right thing.

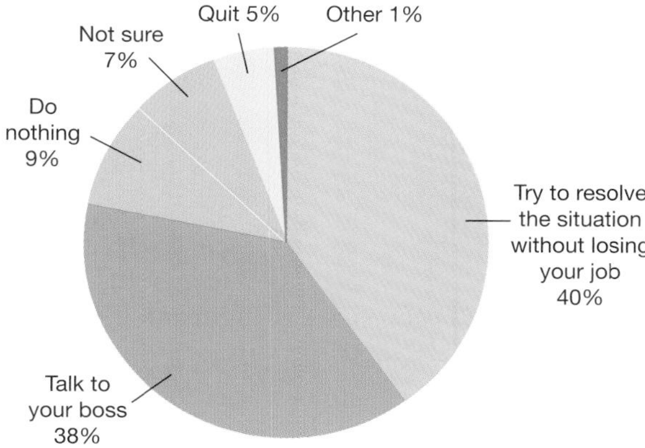

How Do You Make Ethical Decisions?

L.O. 3

Determining what's ethically acceptable in any given situation can be difficult. One approach is to measure each act against certain absolute standards. In Canada, these standards are often grounded in teachings such as "Do not lie" and "Do not steal." Another place to look for ethical guidance is the law. If saying, writing, or doing something is clearly illegal, you have no decision to make; you obey the law.

Even though legal considerations will resolve some ethical questions, you'll often have to rely on your own judgment and principles. When trying to decide the most ethical course of action, you might apply the Golden Rule: Do unto others as you would have them do unto you. Or you might examine your motives: If your intent is honest, the decision is ethical; however, if your intent is to mislead or manipulate, the decision is unethical. You might also consider asking yourself a series of questions:

L.O. 4

1. Is the decision legal? (Does it break any laws?)
2. Is it balanced? (Is it fair to all concerned?)
3. Can you live with it? (Does it make you feel good about yourself?)
4. Is it feasible? (Will it actually work in the real world?)

When you need to determine the ethics of any situation, these questions will get you started. You may also want to consider the needs of stakeholders, and you may want to investigate one or more philosophical approaches such as those mentioned in the third column of Exhibit 3.3. These approaches are not mutually exclusive alternatives. On the contrary, most business people combine them to reach decisions that will satisfy as many stakeholders as possible without violating anyone's rights or treating anyone unjustly.

When making ethical decisions, keep in mind that most ethical situations can be classified into two general types: ethical dilemmas and ethical lapses. An **ethical dilemma** is a situation in which one must choose between two conflicting but arguably valid sides.

ethical dilemma
Situation in which both sides of an issue can be supported with valid arguments

ethical lapse
Situation in which an individual makes a decision that is morally wrong, illegal, or unethical

All ethical dilemmas have a common theme: the conflict between the rights of two or more important groups of people. The second type of situation is an **ethical lapse**, in which an individual makes a decision that is clearly wrong, such as divulging trade secrets to a competitor. Be careful not to confuse ethical dilemmas with ethical lapses. A company faces an ethical dilemma when it must decide whether to continue operating a

Exhibit 3.3 Itemized Lists for Making Ethical Decisions

Companies with the most success in establishing an ethical structure are those that balance their approach to making decisions.

IS THE DECISION ETHICAL?	DOES IT RESPECT STAKEHOLDERS?	DOES IT FOLLOW A PHILOSOPHICAL APPROACH?
IS IT LEGAL? Does it violate civil law? Does it violate company policy? **IS IT BALANCED?** Is it fair to all concerned, in both the short and the long term? **CAN YOU LIVE WITH IT?** Does it make you feel good about yourself? Would you feel good reading about it in a newspaper? **IS IT FEASIBLE?** Does it work in the real world? Will it improve your competitive position? Is it affordable? Can it be accomplished in the time available?	**WILL OUTSIDERS APPROVE?** Does it benefit customers, suppliers, investors, public officials, media representatives, and community members? **WILL SUPERVISORS APPROVE?** Did you provide management with information that is honest and accurate? **WILL EMPLOYEES APPROVE?** Will it affect employees in a positive way? Does it handle personal information about employees discreetly? Did you give proper credit for work performed by others?	**IS IT A UTILITARIAN DECISION?** Does it produce the greatest good for the greatest number of people? **DOES IT UPHOLD INDIVIDUAL, LEGAL, AND HUMAN RIGHTS?** Does it protect people's own interests? Does it respect the privacy of others and their right to express their opinion? Does it allow people to act in a way that conforms to their religious or moral beliefs? **DOES IT UPHOLD THE PRINCIPLES OF JUSTICE?** Does it treat people fairly and impartially? Does it apply rules consistently? Does it ensure that people who harm others are held responsible and make restitution?

production facility that is suspected, but not proven, to be unsafe. A company makes an ethical lapse when it continues to operate the facility even after the site has been proven unsafe. Other examples of ethical lapses include inflating prices for certain customers, hiring employees from competitors to gain trade secrets, selling technological secrets to unfriendly foreign governments, switching someone's long-distance service without their consent (a practice known as *slamming*), slipping unauthorized charges into phone bills (a practice known as *cramming*), and using insider information to profit on the sale of company securities—something Enron executives were accused of doing (see the box entitled "Enron: A Case Study in Unethical Behaviour").

SOCIAL RESPONSIBILITY IN BUSINESS

In addition to practising ethics in the workplace, companies such as Telus strive to create organizations that encourage social responsibility in their policies and among their employees. Social responsibility is a concept with decades-old roots. In the nineteenth and early twentieth centuries, the prevailing view among industrialists was that business had only one responsibility: to make a profit. "The public be damned," said railroad tycoon William Vanderbilt, "I'm working for the shareholders."[15] *Caveat emptor*—"Let the buyer beware"—was the rule of the day. If you bought a product, you paid the price and took the consequences. No consumer groups or government agencies would help you if the product was defective or caused harm.

In the mid-twentieth century, Milton Friedman's view of a company's responsibility toward society was representative and remained influential for many years: "There is

Enron: A Case Study in Unethical Behaviour

Formed in 1985, Enron began as a transmitter of natural gas through pipelines. The company later evolved into the leading market maker in electricity and natural gas by buying power from generators and selling it to customers. The company also traded in coal, fibre optics, bandwidth, plastic, and other energy-related goods. From 1998 to 2000, Enron's revenue rose from US$31 billion to more than US$100 billion, making it the seventh-largest company on the *Fortune* 500 list.

In 1999 Enron was cited by *Fortune* magazine as one of the "100 best companies to work for." Enron's former chairman, Kenneth Lay, boasted to the press that "Our corporate culture and our world-class employees make Enron a great place to work." He added that "We are proud to receive recognition as a top workplace; it's a reflection of our commitment to our employees and their key role in our company's success." Less than two years later, the company's empire unravelled, exposing one of the biggest business scandals in history.

WHO'S ACCOUNTABLE?

Although the indictments have begun, it could take years to untangle the Enron mess, as investigators and regulatory agencies try to piece together clues that could explain how a company that reported revenues exceeding US$100 billion and profits of US$979 million became worthless overnight. Several acts of unethical behaviour have been uncovered during hearings and reviews of company documents: Enron's accountants used wildly creative accounting practices to grossly overestimate company profits and hide losses through a web of partnerships; financial analysts, who also served as Enron's investment bankers, continued to urge investors to buy Enron stock even as the company headed toward bankruptcy; and several top Enron executives allegedly used insider information and withheld information from the public as they cashed out more than US$1 billion of company stock when it was at its peak.

Although these acts contributed to Enron's failure and subsequent bankruptcy filing in December 2001, the company's fate was sealed by the negligence of its managers and auditors, who were either unaware of the company's lurking financial problems or who chose to look the other way—even as warning lights began to flash. Enron's managers kept its company's employees and stakeholders in the dark. They continued to paint a rosy picture of the company's financial health, even as the giant energy conglomerate was sliding toward financial ruin. "The continued excellent prospects in Enron's market position make us very confident in our strong earnings outlook," Kenneth Lay told Wall Street executives, after he was allegedly advised of questionable accounting practices by Enron's vice-president Sherron Watkins.

ENRON OFFICIAL SOUNDED ALARM

Watkins had sent a seven-page letter to Lay informing him, among other things, that Enron executives "consistently and constantly" questioned the company's accounting methods to senior officials. "I am incredibly nervous that we will implode in a wave of accounting scandals," wrote Watkins. Upon receiving the letter, Lay asked Watkins not to blow the whistle while he tried to deal with the situation. But Lay did nothing, and Watkins, believing that he would investigate as promised, did not inform outside authorities.

ONE COZY BUNCH

Unethical behaviour by Enron's auditors, Arthur Andersen Company, also contributed to the company's demise. Andersen entered into a conflict of interest situation by acting as both Enron's independent auditor and management adviser. The accounting firm was paid fees of US$1 million per week and maintained unusually close ties with Enron executives, compromising the firm's independence. Long before Enron's collapse, Arthur Andersen accountants knew of the company's growing losses. But they continued to bend to the wishes of Enron executives, who didn't want to recognize the losses or make them public. Once the losses were disclosed, Andersen managers began a massive shredding campaign of Enron documents—which they claimed was standard company procedure. On June 15, 2002, a jury convicted Arthur Andersen on a single felony count of obstruction of justice for interfering with a federal investigation of its failed client Enron. Although the accounting firm was originally indicted for shredding Enron-related documents, it was convicted because an Andersen lawyer ordered critical deletions to an internal memo for the purpose of impeding an official proceeding. The conviction will forever stain the legacy of this once-revered institution. In August 2002, the 89-year-old, 85 000-employee firm ceased auditing public companies—the core of its worldwide business.

CANADIAN COMPLICITY?

You might be tempted to look at this case as an example of American greed in its most extreme form. However, with Nortel's financial statements being restated regularly and accounting practices in question worldwide, it would be foolish to do so. Furthermore, the Enron case has a direct tie to one of Canada's great financial institutions: the Canadian Imperial Bank of Commerce (CIBC). Such a huge debacle does not occur without some aid from important sources both at home and abroad. Names such as J.P Morgan Chase and Merrill Lynch along with CIBC and others have paid more than US$400 million to settle Enron-related cases. The CIBC has agreed to pay $80 million in penalties due to their involvement with Enron. That figure includes $37.5 million for proceeds stemming from illegal activities, a $37.5 million fine, and a $5 million payment of interest. The bank also agreed to abandon large portions of its structured finance business for three years.[16]

THE RIPPLE EFFECT

In short, Enron serves as an example of how negligent conduct by a company's managers and advisers and the failure to communicate truthfully to stakeholders can severely harm a company's employees, investors, customers, and other innocent stakeholders. Enron's 21 000 employees lost their jobs and saw their retirement savings wiped out. Tens of thousands of shareholders—including some of the nation's biggest institutional investors—lost billions of dollars when Enron's stock value plummeted from US$80 to pennies a share.

Questions for Critical Thinking

1. What unethical acts did Enron's managers and auditors commit?
2. How did such acts affect the company's stakeholders?

only one social responsibility of business," said Friedman. "To use its resources and engage in activities designed to increase its profits so long as it stays within the rules of the game, which is to say, engages in open and free competition without deception or fraud." Friedman argued that only real people, not corporations, could have responsibilities and that dividends and profit maximization would allow the shareholders to contribute to the charities and causes of their choice.[17] As he saw it, the only social responsibility of business was to provide jobs and pay taxes.

L.O. 5

Social Responsibility and Profits

Of course, the ideal relationship between business and society is a matter of debate. Historically, investors have been primarily interested in a company's financial performance. But a recent *Business Week* poll found that 95 percent of adults reject the notion that a corporation's only role is to make money.[18]

Many investors and managers now support a broader view of social responsibility. They argue that a company has an obligation to society beyond the pursuit of profits, and that becoming more socially responsible can actually improve a company's profits. This line of thinking is best captured by a newspaper headline: "Do Good? Do Business? No, Do Both!" The Ethical Funds Company is an example of a firm that has merged these two goals into an indistinguishable entity. The firm was launched in 1986 as the first socially responsible mutual fund company in Canada. The goal was quite clear: help

investors earn a good return on investment without sacrificing ethical or socially responsible duties.

In addition to examining financial criteria in their investment decision making, the Ethical Funds Company assesses a company's social and environmental performance using the criteria set out in their Core Values. Shareholder action strategies are employed to improve performance in these areas (see Exhibit 3.4). The firm continues to exclude companies who are primarily involved in weapons manufacturing, tobacco, and nuclear power.

Companies that support this line of thinking link the pursuit of socially responsible goals with their overall strategic planning. Such socially responsible companies are just as dedicated to building a viable, profitable business as they are to adhering to a mission—and they think strategically to make both happen. Increasingly, companies and employees are caring about their communities and want to be a part of the greater cause (see Exhibit 3.5). They want to be good corporate citizens and satisfy shareholders' needs for a return on their investment. Still, finding the right balance can be challenging.

Exactly how much can businesses contribute to social concerns? This is a difficult decision for most companies because they have limited resources. They must allocate their resources to a number of goals, such as upgrading facilities and equipment, developing new products, marketing existing products, and rewarding employee efforts, in addition to contributing to social causes. This juggling act is a challenge that every business faces. For example, if a company consistently ignores its stakeholders, it will suffer and eventually fold. If the company disregards society's needs (such as environmental concerns), voters will clamour for laws to limit the offensive business activities, consumers who feel their needs and values are being ignored will spend their money on a competitor's products, investors who are unhappy with the company's performance will invest elsewhere, and employees whose needs are not met will become unproductive or will quit and find other jobs. As Exhibit 3.6 on page 77 shows, stakeholders' needs sometimes conflict. In such cases, which stakeholders should be served first—society, consumers, suppliers, government, investors, or employees?

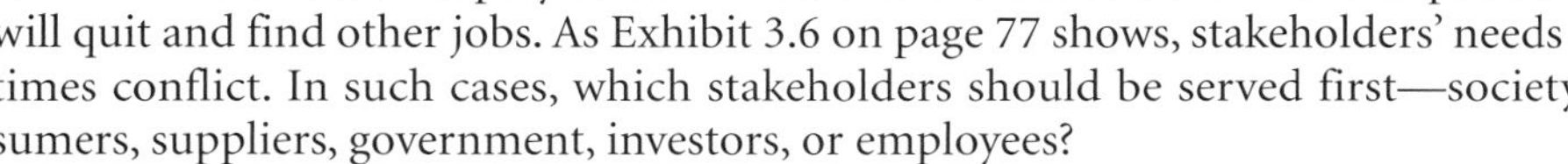

Exhibit 3.4 **Ethical Funds: Core Values of Their Sustainable Investing Program**

Respect for the environment	Ecosystems have intrinsic value to all of us, and are essential to human well being and growth. We encourage companies to reduce adverse impacts, adopt a precautionary approach to the environment, and help restore ecological health.
Respect for stakeholders	Shareholders, employees, customers, and communities all share in the successes and failures of an organization's business endeavours. It's important that companies offer solid financial performance while also contributing positively to the local economy, demonstrating good ethics, governance, and accountability.
Respect for human rights	We want companies to acknowledge their responsibility to protect and promote human and labour rights within their spheres of influence. This includes avoiding complicity in human rights abuses, helping to reduce poverty, improving health and safety for workers, contributing to civil society, and encouraging the peaceful resolution of conflict.

Source: Courtesy of Ethical Funds.

Exhibit 3.5 **Civic Responsibilities**

Executives generally support the notion that companies should serve their communities and be socially responsible citizens in a number of ways.

PERCENTAGE OF EXECUTIVES WHO "STRONGLY AGREE" OR "AGREE" THAT COMPANIES SHOULD:	PERCENTAGE
Be environmentally responsible	100
Be ethical in operations	100
Earn profits	96
Employ local residents	94
Pay taxes	94
Encourage and support employee volunteering	89
Contribute money and leadership to charities	85
Be involved in economic development	75
Be involved in public education	73
Involve community representatives in business decisions that affect community	62
Target a proportion of purchasing toward local vendors	61
Help improve quality of life for low-income populations	54

L.O. 6

BUSINESS'S EFFORTS TO INCREASE SOCIAL RESPONSIBILITY

As the Ethical Funds Company and Telus show, socially responsible businesses can indeed make a difference in the world. Some work to curb child abuse or domestic violence. Others provide generous benefits packages for employees. Still others have strong recycling programs to keep the environment clean. In the past five years, General Mills has provided some US$155 million in donations and contributions to help combat hunger, to provide education to students, and to ensure the safety of the neighbourhoods where the company operates.[19] Those that give back to society are finding that their efforts can lead to a more favourable public image and stronger employee morale. Thus, more and more organizations are attempting to be socially responsible citizens by conducting a *social audit,* by engaging in *cause-related marketing,* or by being *philanthropic.*

social audit
Assessment of a company's performance in the area of social responsibility

A **social audit** is a systematic evaluation and reporting of the company's social performance. The report typically includes objective information about how the company's activities affect its various stakeholders. Companies can also engage in *cause-related marketing,* in which a portion of product sales helps support worthy causes. For example, Johnson & Johnson gives the World Wildlife Fund a cut from sales of a special line of children's toiletries. Similarly, Peaceworks encourages joint business ventures among people of different backgrounds who live in volatile regions of the world. One of the company's product lines is *sprat́é,* uniquely flavoured spreads produced in Israel by a Jewish-owned company that buys all of its ingredients from Israeli Arabs and Palestinians. When consumers buy a jar of spraté, they not only get a tasty spread but also support the peace process in the Middle East.[20]

philanthropic
Descriptive term for altruistic actions such as donating money, time, goods, or services to charitable, humanitarian, or educational institutions

Some companies choose to be socially responsible corporate citizens by being **philanthropic**; that is, they donate money, time, goods, or services to charitable, humanitarian, or educational institutions. In accordance with Canada's Imagine program, Alcan sets aside a minimum of 1 percent of pre-tax profits for charitable donations. Corporations such as Alcan, Telus, and General Electric donate millions of dollars in cash and products to charity each year.

Exhibit 3.6 **Balancing Business and Stakeholders' Rights**

Balancing the individual needs and interests of a company's stakeholders is one of management's most difficult tasks.

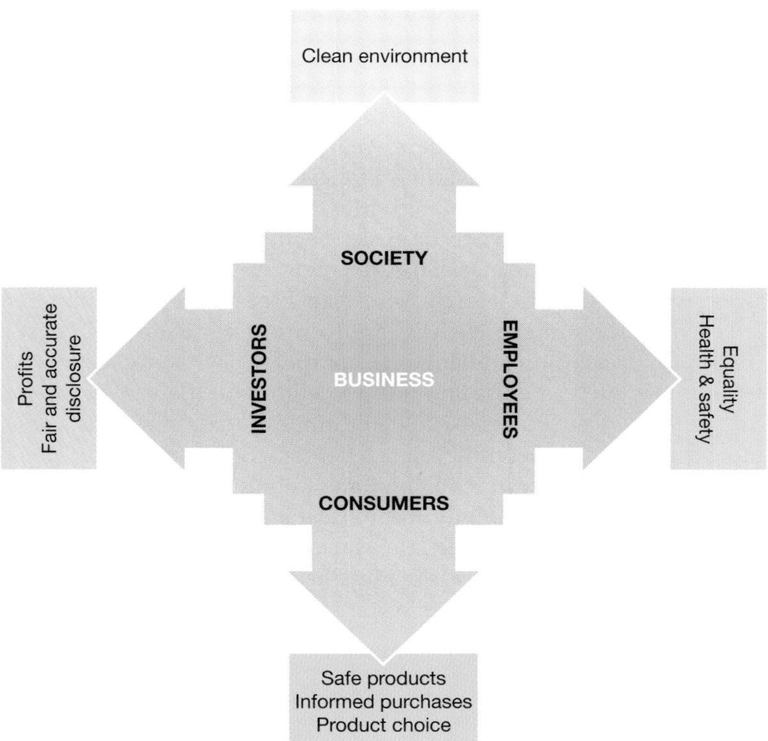

Responsibility toward Society and the Environment

Mountain Equipment Cooperative (MEC) sends a portion of sales to environmental concerns. The cooperative serves outdoor enthusiasts who appreciate nature and have a vested interest in the environment. But for many firms, environmental issues exemplify the difficulty that businesses encounter when they try to reconcile conflicting interests: Society needs as little pollution as possible from businesses. But producing quality products to satisfy customers' needs can cause pollution to some degree. Business executives try to strike a balance by making environmental management a formal part of their business strategy—along with quality, profit, safety, and other daily business operations.[21]

Merging industrialism with environmentalism is not an easy task, but some companies have stepped up to the plate. For example, Canadian Tire launched an annual Community Environmental Award program to support projects that improve the environment in local communities served by the retailer. In recent years, these programs have included tree planting in Cochrane, Alberta; a beach cleanup initiative in Saint John, New Brunswick; a lake cleanup in Rouyn-Noranda, Quebec; a schoolyard naturalization program in Corner Brook, Newfoundland; and a River Shore cleanup and naturalization in Windsor, Ontario.

The Pervasiveness of Pollution

For decades, environmentalists have warned businesses and the general public about the dangers of **pollution** (the contamination of the natural environment by the discharge of harmful substances). Our air, water, and land can easily be tainted by industrial discharges, aircraft and motor vehicle emissions, and a number of chemicals that spill into the environment as industrial waste products. Moreover, the pollution in any

pollution
Damage to or destruction of the natural environment caused by the discharge of harmful substances

one element can easily taint the others. For instance, when emissions from coal-burning factories and electric utility plants react with air, they can cause acid rain, which damages lakes and forests.

L.O. 7

ecology
Study of the relationships among living things in the water, air, and soil, their environments, and the nutrients that support them

The Government Effort to Reduce Pollution

Widespread concern for the environment has been growing since the 1960s with the popularization of **ecology**, or the study of the balance of nature. The new Canadian Environmental Protection Act (CEPA) entitles companies, individuals, and government agencies to request independent reviews of Environmental Protection Compliance Orders (EPCOs). Since 1999, EPCOs allow enforcement officers to act immediately to stop suspected illegal activities, as well as to prevent or remedy an action.[22] International treaties have recognized the importance of environmental concerns. For example, the North American Agreement on Environmental Cooperation (NAAEC) was signed when the North American Free Trade Agreement came into effect. "The key objectives of the NAAEC are to promote sustainable development, encourage pollution prevention and enhance compliance with environmental laws."[23] Agreements and laws such as these should help eliminate the risk of environmental disasters like the Sydney Tar Ponds—700 000 tonnes of toxic sludge as a result of 100 years of runoff from a local steel mill.[24]

Progress has also been made in reducing water pollution. Both government and private business have made major expenditures to treat and reuse waste water, as well as to upgrade sewage systems. Unfortunately, the war on toxic waste has not been quite as successful. Government attempts to force businesses to clean up certain sites have yielded more disappointing results. At some sites, the groundwater may never be restored to drinking-water purity.

The Kyoto Protocol

In December 1997, 160 countries met in Kyoto, Japan, to discuss the reduction of greenhouse gas (GHG) emissions and agree on specific reduction targets. In December 2002, when former Prime Minister Jean Chretien signed Canada's ratification of the Kyoto Protocol, it marked another step in a very long road. Under the Kyoto Protocol, Canada agrees to reduce GHG emissions to 6 percent below 1990 levels by 2012. The protocol took effect on February 16, 2005, after it met key conditions and was ratified by a minimum of 55 countries, covering at least 55 percent of the emissions addressed by the protocol. The second condition proved the greatest obstacle to overcome because the United States, which alone represents 36.1 percent of GHG emissions, decided to bow out of the deal and continues to downplay the importance of the treaty.[25] It was only after Russia agreed to endorse the deal that the second condition could be met. The countdown now truly begins as the committed countries plan environmental programs to meet their targets by 2012.

The move toward these overall goals will be facilitated by the Kyoto Mechanisms that allow countries to earn and buy credits outside their borders:

- *Clean Development Mechanism (CDM)*—countries can earn credits by investing in emission-reducing projects in developing countries.
- *Joint Implementation (JI)*—allows countries to earn credits from developed countries that have introduced Kyoto targets.
- *International Emissions Trading (IET)*—allows developed countries to buy and sell credits among themselves.[26]

The debate over the Kyoto Protocol has been and continues to be intense. Before the 2004 national election campaign Stephen Harper vowed that, if elected, he would scrap Kyoto and implement a clean-air bill instead. Despite opposition, Kyoto has become an important treaty that will have a widespread impact as it gradually takes effect. The focus has now shifted toward negotiating fair and reasonable emission caps. Progress has been reported in many industries, including the oil and gas sector.[27]

Ottawa also avoided a messy fight and reached a voluntary deal with the auto sector, which has agreed to cut GHG emissions from vehicles by 5.3 million tonnes by the year 2010. This goal will be achieved through more fuel-efficient technologies, more hybrid vehicles, improved technology in areas such as vehicle air conditioning, and joint advertising deals with Ottawa to encourage people to switch to more fuel-efficient cars.[28]

The Business Effort to Reduce Pollution

While some companies must be pressured by the federal government or private citizens to stop polluting the environment, others do a good job of regulating themselves. For example, Cascades is showing some leadership. It has the lowest water consumption of any Canadian pulp and paper company. It also has gradually abandoned coal and heavy oil in favour of less polluting energy sources. Furthermore, Cascades recently worked with Greenpeace in changing several aspects of its manufacturing process for bathroom tissue. In so doing, Greenpeace has included this product in its "green products" category.[29] Another example is 3M's decision to discontinue Scotchguard fabric protector, a noteworthy example of company self-regulation. 3M was under no government mandate to stop manufacturing products with perfluorooctane sulfonate (PFO). Moreover, evidence that PFO harms humans does not exist. But when traces of the chemical showed up in humans, 3M decided to pull the plug on the product rather than wait until scientific evidence might someday link PFO to a disease. This decision cost 3M US$500 million in annual sales because the company did not have a substitute product to fill Scotchguard's void. Like Cascades and 3M, many companies are addressing environmental concerns by taking the following actions:[30]

- Considering environmental issues a part of everyday business and operating decisions
- Accepting environmental staff members as full-fledged partners in improving the company's competitiveness
- Measuring environmental performance
- Tying compensation to environmental performance
- Determining the long-term environmental costs *before* such costs occur
- Considering environmental impact in the product development process
- Challenging suppliers to improve environmental performance
- Conducting environmental training and awareness programs

In addition to these actions, companies are reducing the amount of solid waste they send to landfills by implementing companywide recycling programs. Companies and individuals alike generate enormous amounts of solid waste, much of which is electronic waste (computer monitors, circuit boards, and so on).[31] Companies are also cleaning up land pollution that was created years ago by carelessly—but legally—disposing of substances (now known to be unhealthy) in landfills.

Hundreds of thousands of tonnes of waste have also been eliminated through conservation and more efficient production.[32] Some companies are using high-temperature incineration to destroy hazardous wastes or are giving their wastes to other companies that can use them in their manufacturing processes. Some even neutralize wastes biologically or have redesigned their manufacturing processes so that they don't produce these wastes in the first place.

Businesses that recognize the link between environmental performance and financial well-being are discovering that spending now to prevent pollution can end up saving more money down the road (by reducing cleanup costs, litigation expense, and production costs). From building eco-industrial parks to improving production efficiency, these activities are a part of the *green marketing* movement, in which companies distinguish themselves by using fewer packaging materials, recycling more

Electronics recycling centres like this one near the Lianjiang River in China are releasing toxic pollutants, environmental groups say.

waste, and developing new products that are easier on the environment.

Responsibility toward Consumers

The 1960s activism that awakened business to its environmental responsibilities also gave rise to **consumerism**, a movement that put pressure on businesses to consider consumer needs and interests. Consumerism prompted many businesses to create consumer affairs departments to handle customer complaints. It also prompted federal and provincial agencies to set up bureaus to offer consumer information, assistance, and protection and an outlet to file complaints. In Canada, the Competition Bureau is an agency that gives consumers an avenue of complaint when a company policy or action violates the Competition Act, Consumer Packaging and Labelling Act, Textile Labelling Act, or Precious Metals Marking Act. South of the border, a key moment for the consumerism movement can be traced to President John F. Kennedy, who announced a "bill of rights" for consumers, laying the foundation for a wave of consumer-oriented legislation. These rights include the right to safe products, the right to be informed, the right to choose, and the right to be heard. This movement also led to the creation of non-profit organizations such as the Automobile Protection Association (APA), which offers an annual Canadian used car guide to its members along with the very popular Lemon-Aid review of the industry's worst cars.

consumerism
Movement that pressures businesses to consider consumer needs and interests

The Right to Safe Products

The Canadian Standards Association (CSA) is a membership-based non-profit organization that serves government, industry, and consumers. The CSA develops standards and codes that help ensure reasonable safety requirements, and its seal is recognized as a comforting symbol.[33] The federal government along with the various provincial governments impose many safety standards that range from food inspection to drug approval to emission controls. Theoretically, companies that do not comply with these rules are forced to take corrective action. Moreover, the threat of product liability suits and declining sales motivates many companies to meet safety standards. After all, a poor safety record can damage a company's reputation. But with or without government action, many consumer advocates complain that some unsafe products still slip through the cracks.

The Right to Be Informed

Consumers have a right to know what is in a product and how to use it. They also have a right to know the sales price of goods or services and the details of any purchase contracts. For example, the Consumer Packaging and Labelling Act contains provisions that regulate everything from units of measurement to the representation of the number of servings to pictorial representations on food labels.[34] If a product is sufficiently dangerous, a warning label is required by law, as in the case of cigarettes. However, warning labels can be a mixed blessing for consumers. To some extent, the presence of a warning protects the manufacturer from product liability suits, but the label may not deter people from using the product or from using it incorrectly. The billions of dollars a year still spent on cigarettes illustrate this point.

The Canadian government, through the Competition Bureau, also works to ensure that consumers are accurately informed through transparent information. For example, the Forzani group agreed to pay a record $1.7 million to settle a federal Competition Bureau investigation of their Sport Chek and Sport Mart stores. The Bureau accused

Forzani of significantly inflating regular prices to make sales appear larger. Forzani is threatening to sue the Bureau for its handling of the case; the company has agreed to pay the fine but admits no wrongdoing in the process. The previous record for such a case in Canada was imposed on Suzy Sheer—$1 million.[35] The Bureau also pursued Sears Canada for pitching exaggerated savings on automobile tires in its advertisements. Sears is examining its options after the tribunal ruled against it. While the penalty has not been decided on, it is expected to be in the area of $500 000.[36]

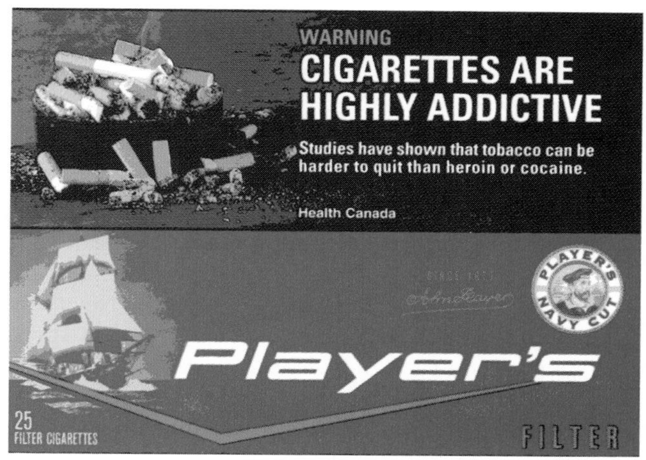

Canadians have become accustomed to the strong warning labels on cigarette packages.

The Right to Choose Which Products to Buy

The number of products available to consumers is truly amazing. But how far should the right to choose extend? Are we entitled to choose products that are potentially harmful, such as cigarettes, liquor, or guns? To what extent are we entitled to learn about these products? Consumer groups and businesses are concerned about these questions, but no clear answers have emerged. Moreover, some consumer groups say that government does not do enough. For example, when a product has been proven to be dangerous, does the fact that it is legal justify its sale? Should the government take measures to make the product illegal, or should consumers be allowed to decide for themselves what they buy?

Consider cigarettes, for example. Scientists determined long ago that the tar and nicotine in tobacco are both harmful and addictive. Cigarette legislation has become increasingly aggressive over the years. Anti-tobacco legislation restricts tobacco advertising and has now removed the traditional domain of event sponsorship from the hands of tobacco manufacturers. Furthermore, the graphic warning labels that became law in June 2000 ushered in a new age, as Canada became the first nation to implement such strong labelling and reporting measures. You are no doubt familiar with the warning labels that Health Canada forces tobacco manufacturers to include on their packages, such as: "Cigarettes hurt babies," "Idle but deadly," "Cigarettes cause strokes," and "Tobacco use makes you impotent."[37] Even so, consumers can still purchase cigarettes in the marketplace.

The Right to Be Heard

Many companies have established toll-free numbers for consumer information and feedback, and print these numbers on product packages. In addition, more and more companies are establishing websites to provide product information and as a vehicle for customer feedback. Companies use such feedback to improve their products and services and to make informed decisions about offering new ones. However, the right to be heard extends beyond simple customer product feedback; smart firms are aware of the importance of their various stakeholders (see the box entitled "Voisey's Bay: Native Canadians Exercise Right to Be Heard").

Responsibility toward Investors

Today, a growing number of investors are concerned about the ethics and social responsibility of the companies in which they invest. Allegations range from executives dumping stock ahead of bad news to companies using dirty accounting tricks to misrepresenting the investment.

The job of looking out for a company's investors falls to its board of directors. Lately, more investors are turning up the heat on the individuals who sit on those boards. Concerned investors are targeting board members who fail to attend meetings, who sit on the boards of too many companies, who are underinvested (own very little stock in the companies they direct), and who sit on boards of companies with which their own firms do business.

Voisey's Bay: Native Canadians Exercise Right to Be Heard

When Inco purchased the rights to the Voisey's Bay property in 1996 for $4.3 billion, they could not have imagined that obstacles would delay this potential site from reaching operational status for nearly a decade. Unfortunately, Inco spent the next few years negotiating the terms of the project with the Newfoundland-Labrador government and stakeholders such as the local Innu and Inuit. The early years of the project were characterized by a drop in the price of nickel and costly, time-consuming environmental reviews.

The right to be heard is a concept that extends beyond consumer rights. Various stakeholders can play pivotal roles in the project approval and development stages, in influencing opinions of corporate image, and in pressuring governments to respond to local needs. In the Voisey's Bay case, the Innu and Inuit population had a tremendous stake in the potential development of this project. Inco was spending its time considering estimated reserves, annual production capacity, and expected daily activity and workforce requirements. Meanwhile, locals were considering how the increased ship traffic would affect hunting season, which is dictated largely by ice in Labrador. What did these miners know about the way in which local communities use the waterways and land? Did they care? According to some locals, the company saw ice as something that needed to be broken whereas the native population sees it as a way to get around. Needless to say, the education process was lengthy.

In 2002, after years of negotiating and many lessons, Inco struck a deal with the Innu nation and the Labrador Inuit Association (LIA). The agreement addresses issues ranging from employment targets to supplying traditional food on-site to plans that nurture aboriginal joint ventures. Furthermore, Inco managed to agree that shipping would be suspended twice a year, when ice is forming and when it is melting, to minimize impact on wildlife and hunting patterns.

Since this agreement was reached, Inco has made attempts to solidify the relationship with various programs. For example, it sponsored the Nunatsiavut Drum Dancers and brought them to Toronto to participate in the First Night festival. Inco began production in 2005; the company will need to maintain a good relationship with the native population and hear its voice loud and clear.[38]

Questions for Critical Thinking

1. What were three key factors behind the Voisey's Bay project delays?
2. What lesson(s) can other companies learn from Inco's experience at Voisey's Bay?

Aggrieved investors are filing lawsuits not just against the management of companies that admit to "accounting irregularities" but also against their boards of directors and audit committees. The audit committee signs off on all financial statements and is supposed to protect shareholders, acting as a check on management's corporate reporting methods and asking tough questions about accounting practices. Looking out for investors is no easy task, but investors are finding that holding individual directors more accountable improves overall performance.[39] Of course, any action that cheats the investors out of their rightful profits is also unethical. An Ontario Superior Court judge recently awarded damages worth as much as $10 million to unhappy investors of Danier Leather because of claims that management withheld critical information.[40]

Alliance Atlantis Communications Inc., producer of the popular *CSI: Crime Scene Investigation* television programs, has made a concerted effort to deal with internal control issues. Admitting that its corporate governance was not up to par, the company made numerous changes to improve its board and address the problems. The company's reforms include annual reviews of director performance, expensing stock options, and requiring directors to own stock. It has also reduced the size of its board by half to 10.[41]

Responsibility toward Employees

For some companies, the past 30 years have brought dramatic changes in the attitudes and composition of the workforce. These changes have forced businesses to modify their recruiting, training, and promotion practices, as well as their overall corporate values and behaviours. (Consult Chapter 10 for an in-depth discussion of the staffing and demographic challenges employers face in today's workplace.) According to the *Corporate Knights* review, Dofasco laid claim to Best Employer in Canada for 2004.

The Push for Equality in Employment

Canadians have always supported economic freedom and the individual's right to pursue opportunity. Unfortunately, until the past few decades many people were targets of economic **discrimination**, relegated to low-paying, menial jobs and prevented from taking advantage of many opportunities solely on the basis of their gender, disability, ethnic background, or religion.

discrimination
In a social and economic sense, denial of opportunities to individuals on the basis of some characteristic that has no bearing on their ability to perform in a job

Employment Equity Act The Employment Equity Act has been featured often in newspaper headlines over the past few years. Since it was first introduced in 1995, the act has been the catalyst in the fight to eliminate perceived injustices, especially as they apply to professions deemed to be female dominated that traditionally and systematically earned lower wages. The other three key groups addressed are aboriginals, visible minorities, and the disabled. The Canadian government, the source of this legislation, along with other branches of government have faced challenges as they moved to eliminate their own systematic injustices.

The stated goal of the Employment Equity Act is as follows:

> to achieve equality in the workplace so that no person shall be denied employment opportunities or benefits for reasons unrelated to ability and, in fulfillment of that goal, to correct the conditions of disadvantage in employment experienced by women, aboriginal peoples, persons with disabilities and members of visible minorities, by giving effect to the principle that employment equity means more than treating persons in the same way but also requires special measures and the accommodation of differences.[42]

The Employment Equity Act directly applies to federally regulated companies and those doing business with the government under the federal contractors program, which accounts for about 1425 organizations. With Canadian baby boomers set to vacate the workforce in the coming years and the birth rate at low levels, this legislation grows in importance. If the Canadian economy is to reach its full potential and continue to grow, it must not shut out key groups. Each year 220 000 newcomers arrive; 70 to 80 percent are visible minorities. The aboriginal population is quite small in western Canada; however, aboriginals will play a major role in the next 10 to 20 years. For example, by 2015 aboriginals are expected to account for 20 percent of the population of Saskatchewan. Based on such trends, it is not surprising that many firms are creating their own workforce **diversity initiatives.**[43] These initiatives include increasing minority employment and promotion, contracting with more minority vendors, adding more minorities to boards of directors, and targeting a more diverse customer base. Many companies also offer employees diversity training to promote understanding of the unique cultures, customs, and talents of all employees.

diversity initiatives
Company policies designed to enhance opportunities for minorities and to promote understanding of diverse cultures, customs, and talents

Occupational Safety and Health

Each day 15 workers lose their lives on the job while another 15 500 are injured in the private workplace (see Exhibit 3.7). The problem exists in varying degrees around the world. In Canada, the Canadian Centre for Occupational Health and Safety was established in 1978 as a federal departmental corporation that reports to the Parliament of Canada through the Minister of Labour. The department's mandate is to promote health and safety in the workplace; facilitate cooperation among federal, provincial, and territorial jurisdictions; to assist in the development of policies and programs; and to serve as a national information centre.[44]

Enbridge Inc., a leading energy transportation and distribution company, earned top marks in health and safety in the *Corporate Knights* ranking. Most firms have implemented strict policies and procedures to reduce risks.[45] However, concerns for employee safety have been raised by the international expansion of businesses. Many Canadian

Exhibit 3.7 **Workplace Killers**

Transportation accidents are the leading workplace killer.

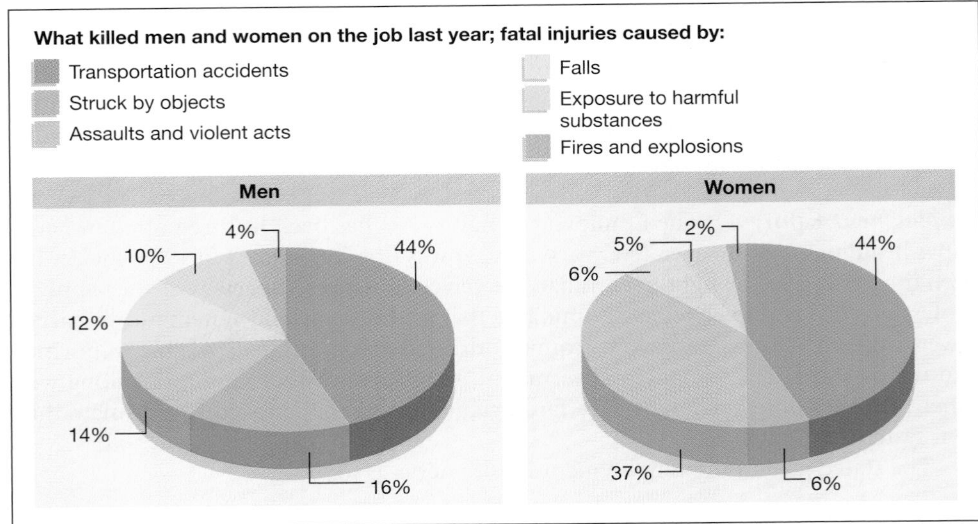

companies subcontract production to companies in foreign countries, making it even more difficult to maintain proper standards of safety and compensation for workers.

ETHICS AND SOCIAL RESPONSIBILITY AROUND THE WORLD

As complicated as ethics and social responsibility can be for Canadian businesses, these issues grow even more complex when cultural influences are applied in the global business environment. As discussed in Chapter 2, countries' ethical codes of conduct, laws, and cultural differences vary greatly. Corporate executives may face simple questions regarding the appropriate amount of money to spend on a business gift or the legitimacy of a payment to "expedite" business. Or they may encounter out-and-out bribery, environmental abuse, and other unscrupulous business practices.

SUMMARY OF LEARNING OBJECTIVES

1 Discuss what it means to practise good business ethics and highlight three factors that influence ethical behaviour.

Business people who practise good business ethics obey all laws and regulations, compete fairly and honestly, communicate truthfully, and do not cause harm to others by putting themselves ahead of others or by placing themselves in a conflict of interest situation. Of the many factors that influence ethical behaviour, the three most common are cultural differences, knowledge of the facts and consequences involving a decision or action, and the ethical practices and commitment to ethical behaviour at a place of work.

Identify three steps that businesses are taking to encourage ethical behaviour and explain the advantages and disadvantages of whistle-blowing.

Businesses are adopting codes of ethics, appointing ethics officers, and establishing ethics hotlines. In spite of these efforts, if illegal, unethical, or harmful practices persist, an employee may need to blow the whistle or disclose such problems to outsiders. Doing so may force the company to stop the problematic practices. But bringing these issues into the public eye has consequences. It can hurt the company's reputation, take managers' time, damage employee morale, and affect the informant's job with the company.

3 List four questions you might ask yourself when trying to make an ethical decision.

When making ethical decisions, ask yourself: (1) Is the decision legal? (Does it break any law?), (2) Is it balanced? (Is it fair to all concerned?), (3) Can you live with it? (Does it make you feel good about yourself?), (4) Is it feasible? (Will it work in the real world?).

4 Explain the difference between an ethical dilemma and an ethical lapse.

An ethical dilemma is an issue with two conflicting but arguably valid sides, whereas an ethical lapse occurs when an individual makes a decision that is illegal, immoral, or unethical.

5 Discuss the relationship between corporate social responsibility and profits.

For years, many companies believed that the only role of a company was to make money and that social problems were the concern of the state. It was believed that socially responsible companies could not be profitable. But supporters of social responsibility now argue that a company has an obligation to society beyond the pursuit of profits and that companies can be both socially responsible and profitable. In fact, being a socially responsible company can help improve profits and being profitable can help companies stick to their social mission.

6 Explain how businesses can become more socially responsible.

Companies can conduct social audits to assess whether their performance is socially responsible, they can engage in cause-related marketing by using a portion of product sales to help support worthy causes, and they can become philanthropic by donating their money, time, goods, or services to charitable, humanitarian, or educational institutions. Companies can also protect and improve the environment by taking a variety of actions to reduce pollution. They can become good citizens by considering consumers' needs and respecting their four basic rights: the right to safe products; the right to be informed—which includes the right to know a product's contents, use, price, and dangers; the right to choose which products to buy; and the right to be heard, such as the right to voice a complaint or concern. They can look out for a company's investors and protect the value of their interests and they can foster good employee relationships by treating employees fairly and equally and by providing a safe working environment.

7 Outline activities that the government and businesses are undertaking to improve the environment.

The federal government improved upon the Canadian Environmental Protection Act (CEPA) in 1999, going much further than the previous act. The Canadian government is actively working with the international community and ratified the Kyoto Protocol in 2002. The federal government also signed the North American Agreement on Environmental Cooperation (NAAEC) as part of the North American Free Trade Agreement. Companies are taking the following steps to improve the environment: (1) considering it a part of everyday business and operating decisions, (2) making environmental staff members full-fledged partners in improving competitiveness, (3) measuring environmental performance, (4) tying compensation to environmental performance, (5) determining environmental costs before they occur, (6) considering the environmental impact of the product development process, (7) helping suppliers improve their environmental performance, and (8) conducting training and awareness programs.

Behind the SCENES

Telus: Green Leadership

Many firms are willing to make a token verbal commitment to socially responsible and ethical behaviour; however, few take a leadership position in this particular area. Telus is not afraid to declare, implement, and influence other firms in this pursuit. It begins with the company's commitment to triple bottom-line reporting, which addresses economic, environmental, and social aspects of the firm's performance. It continues with lobbying efforts; Telus has urged the government to make triple bottom-line reporting a requirement for corporate accounting in Canada, to create a website that evaluates corporate social responsibility performance, and to educate investors on the merits of investing in such socially responsible firms.

Leadership is characterized by an ability to initiate change in others. Telus has leveraged its large purchasing power through its Environmentally Responsible Procurement Policy to force its suppliers to be more environmentally friendly. The company prefers to purchase products that contain the maximum level of post-consumer waste and/or recycled content. The company has also managed to save 9792 kilograms of paper per year by employing paperless invoices for its top 100 clients.

Although Telus operates in an industry that is fairly environmentally friendly, the company has made additional efforts to increase its positive impact on Mother Nature. They have adopted an Environmental Management System (EMS) that includes the elements of the ISO 14000 model. Working with stakeholders is a key part of this tool. Telus gathers and analyzes both internal and external information and collaborates with various groups, including the Canadian Chamber of Commerce and the Conference Board of Canada.

A true test of a company's dedication is its reaction to a system failure. Despite all good intentions and attention to environmental detail, Telus was guilty of releasing waste (diesel) into the environment as a result of a fuel system failure at Strathcona Mountain, British Columbia, in 2000. The firm paid $50 000 to the Habitat Conservation Trust Fund to atone for the failure. It also spent considerable time and effort to clean up the site and improve its fuel systems to avoid possible future recurrence.

Telus employees are faced with obstacles and decisions in performing their day-to-day duties. However, extensive systems are in place to guide them. From the EMS to the ethics hotline to training programs to triple bottom-line reporting and external lobbying, Telus demonstrates leadership in the area of socially responsible ethical management.[46]

Critical Thinking Questions

1. Which of Telus's stakeholders are most affected by the company's environmentalism?
2. What is meant by triple bottom-line accounting? Should this practice be implemented as a standard accounting practice in Canada?
3. Telus's system failure at Strathcona Mountain, B.C., was a test of the company's green image. If you were the public relations officer at that time, what elements would you include in a press release to deal with the problem? Would you deny the allegations?

Learn More Online

Go to Chapter 3 of this text's website at www.pearsoned.ca/bovee, and click on Telus to read about the company.

KEY TERMS

code of ethics (69)
conflict of interest (68)
consumerism (80)
discrimination (83)
diversity initiatives (83)
ecology (78)
ethical dilemma (71)
ethical lapse (72)
ethics (66)
insider trading (68)
philanthropic (76)
pollution (77)
social audit (76)
social responsibility (66)

TEST YOUR KNOWLEDGE

Questions for Review

1. Who shapes a company's ethics?
2. What is a conflict of interest situation?
3. How do companies support ethical behaviour?
4. How are businesses responding to the environmental issues facing society?
5. What can a company do to assure customers that its products are safe?

Questions for Analysis

6. Why can't legal considerations resolve every ethical question?
7. How do individuals employ philosophical principles in making ethical business decisions?
8. Why does a company need more than a code of ethics to be ethical?
9. Why is it important for a company to balance its social responsibility efforts with its need to generate profits?
10. **Ethical Considerations.** How did the Enron debacle affect all businesses?

Questions for Application

11. You sell musical gifts on the Web and in quarterly catalogues. Your two-person partnership has quickly grown into a 27-person company, and you spend all of your time on quality matters. You're losing control of important environmental choices about materials suppliers, product packaging, and even the paper used in your catalogues. What steps can you take to be sure your employees continue making choices that protect the environment?

12. At quitting time, you see your new colleague filling a briefcase with expensive software programs that aren't supposed to leave the premises. What do you do? Explain your answer.
13. **Integrated.** In Chapter 1 we identified knowledge workers as the key economic resource of the twenty-first century. If an employee leaves a company to work for a competitor, what types of knowledge would it be ethical for the employee to share with the new employer and what types of knowledge would it be unethical to share?
14. **Integrated.** Is it ethical for provincial and municipal governments to entice businesses to relocate their operations to that province or city by offering them special tax breaks that are not extended to other businesses operating in that area?

PRACTISE YOUR KNOWLEDGE

SHARPENING YOUR COMMUNICATION SKILLS

All organizations, not just corporations, can benefit from having a code of ethics to guide decision making. But whom should a code of ethics protect, and what should it cover? In this exercise, you and your team are going to draft a code of ethics for your school.

Start by thinking about who will be protected by this code of ethics. What stakeholders should the school consider when making decisions? What negative effects might decisions have on these stakeholders? Then think about the kinds of situations you want your school's code of ethics to cover. One example might be employment decisions; another might be disclosure of confidential student information.

Next, using Exhibit 3.1 as a model, draft your school's code of ethics. Write a general introduction explaining the purpose of the code and who is being protected. Then write a positive statement to guide ethical decisions in each situation you identified earlier in this exercise. Your statement about promotion decisions, for example, might read: "School officials will encourage equal access to job promotions for all qualified candidates, with every applicant receiving fair consideration."

Compare your code of ethics with the codes drafted by your classmates. Did all of the codes seek to protect the same stakeholders? What differences and similarities do you see in the statements guiding ethical decisions?

BUILDING YOUR TEAM SKILLS

Choosing to blow the whistle on your employees or co-workers can create all kinds of legal, ethical, and career complications. Here are five common workplace scenarios that might cause you to search your soul about whether to go public with potentially damaging charges. Read them carefully and discuss them with your teammates. Then decide what your team would do in each situation.

1. You believe your company is overcharging or otherwise defrauding a customer or client.
2. With all of the headlines generated by sexual harassment cases lately, you'd think employees wouldn't dare break the law, but it's happening right under your company's nose.
3. You discover that your company, or one of its divisions, products, or processes, presents a physical danger to workers or to the public.
4. An employee is padding overtime statements, taking home some of the company's inventory, or stealing equipment.
5. You smell alcohol on a co-worker's breath and notice that individual's work hasn't been up to standard lately.

EXPAND YOUR KNOWLEDGE

DISCOVERING CAREER OPPORTUNITIES

Businesses, government agencies, and non-profit organizations offer numerous career opportunities related to ethics and social responsibility. How can you learn more about these careers?

1. Search through Appendix D to identify jobs related to ethics and social responsibility. One example is Occupational Health and Safety Manager, a job concerned with a company's responsibility toward its employees. What are the duties and qualifications of the jobs you have identified? Are the salaries and future outlooks attractive for all of these jobs?
2. Select one job for further consideration. Following the suggestions in Appendix D, what sources of employment information might provide more details about this job? Which of these sources are available in your school or public library? What additional sources can you consult for more information about the daily activities of this job and for ideas about locating potential employers?

3. What skills, educational background, and work experience do you think employers are seeking in applicants for the specific job you are researching? What key words do you think employers would search for when scanning electronic resumés submitted for this position?

DEVELOPING YOUR RESEARCH SKILLS

Articles on corporate ethics and social responsibility regularly appear in business journals and newspapers. Look in recent issues (print or online editions) to find one or more articles discussing one of the following ethics or social responsibility challenges faced by a business:

- Environmental issues, such as pollution, acid rain, and hazardous waste disposal
- Employee or consumer safety measures
- Consumer information or education
- Employment discrimination or diversity initiatives
- Investment ethics
- Industrial spying and theft of trade secrets
- Fraud, bribery, and overcharging
- Company codes of ethics

1. What was the nature of the ethical challenge or social responsibility issue presented in the article? Does the article report any wrongdoing by a company or agency official? Was the action illegal, unethical, or questionable? What course of action would you recommend the company or agency take to correct or improve matters now?
2. What stakeholder group(s) is affected? What lasting effects will be felt by (a) the company and (b) this stakeholder group(s)?
3. Writing a letter to the editor is one way consumers can speak their mind. Review some of the letters to the editor in newspapers or journals. Why are letters to the editor an important feature for that publication?

See It on the **WEB**

URLs for all Internet exercises are provided at the website for this book, www.pearsoned.ca/bovee. When you log on to the text website, select Chapter 3, then select Destinations, click on the name of the featured website, and review the website to complete these exercises.

Explore the following chapter-related websites, review their content, and answer the following questions for each website you visit:

1. What is the purpose of this website?
2. What kinds of information does this website contain? Please be specific.
3. How is the information provided at this website useful for business people? Consumers?
4. How did you expand your knowledge of ethics and social responsibility in business by reviewing the material at this website? What new things did you learn about this topic?

BUILD A BETTER BUSINESS

One way to distinguish a business as an ethical organization is to join the Better Business Bureau (BBB). Members of this private, non-profit business group agree to maintain specific standards for operating ethically and addressing customer complaints. The BBB website is packed with information about the organization, member businesses, and programs that benefit businesses and consumers alike. You can find reports on companies, register complaints, get help with consumer problems, and access publications on all kinds of consumer issues, such as avoiding business scams and investigating charitable organizations. www.bbb.org

PROTECT THE ENVIRONMENT

The Canadian Environmental Protection Act (CEPA) has ushered in a more stringent approach to environmental protection. The goal is a cleaner, healthier environment for Canadians. Visit the following website, www.ec.gc.ca/CEPARegistry/the _act/, to learn more about the act, including the codes of practice; policies, enforcement and compliance; substance lists; and orders.

Hollywood North: The Big Chill

LEARNING OBJECTIVES

The purpose of this video is to help you

1. Identify the methods that governments use to stimulate growth and protect industries.
2. Recognize uncontrollable macroeconomic threats and implement appropriate protection measures.
3. Understand the obstacles and opportunities that companies face in the global economy.

SYNOPSIS

Select the word that does not fit: *stars, movies, glamour, Hollywood, Canada.* A couple of decades ago the choice would have been obvious. At that time, Canadian film production was primarily limited to creating content for the CBC and CTV. But with the Canadian dollar declining and local costs rising, Hollywood looked north. The weak Canadian dollar enabled U.S. film producers to create films and TV programs at bargain discount prices. Production in Vancouver and across the nation spread quickly and a prosperous domestic industry, worth more than $5 billion, soon developed.

Today, Canadians have become accustomed to film production trailers, movie stars, and blocked streets in their cities. The cheap Canadian currency fuelled the industry's growth, but currency rates vary and can take a turn with little notice. When the Canadian dollar climbed more than 20 percent in one recent year, it posed a direct threat to film production in the nation. At the time, Arnold Schwarzenegger, the "Terminator" governor, began a campaign to bring film production back to California. In addition, "reality TV" reduced the need for conventional television productions. Finally, because of global competition, dollars continued to flow out of Hollywood, but much of them began to flow past Canada to other low-cost locations such as Romania and Timbuktu. What does the future hold? It is difficult to predict, as doing business in the global economy is a dynamic challenge. The playing field can change in the blink of an eye, or in this case, in a single movie frame.

Discussion Questions

1. *For analysis:* Why did Hollywood film producers set up shop in Canada?
2. *For analysis:* How does pressure from politicians like Arnold Schwarzenegger affect company decisions?
3. *For application:* How can Canadian film production companies protect their investment and help ensure that facilities are running despite the new economic pressures?
4. *For application:* Look up the current exchange rate between the U.S. and Canadian dollars. A film production company is considering two production locations for a new movie: one in the U.S. and one in Canada. Assume that the film will cost US$40 million to produce south of the border. How much money would the company save by moving production to Canada (assuming equal costs, paid in Canadian dollars)?
5. *For debate:* Should governments provide subsidies and tax breaks to lure film production to their country, province, or city?

On Location VIDEO CASE

Managing Production around the World: Body Glove

LEARNING OBJECTIVES

The purpose of this video is to help you

1. Recognize the strategic challenges faced by a growing company.
2. Understand how supply and demand considerations affect product decisions.
3. Discuss how and why a company may shift production operations to other countries and other companies.

SYNOPSIS

Riding the wave of public interest in water sports, Body Glove began manufacturing wetsuits in the 1950s. The company's founders, dedicated surfers and divers, came up with the idea of making the wetsuits from neoprene, offering more comfortable insulation than the rubber wetsuits of the time. The high costs of neoprene and labour were major considerations in Body Glove's eventual decision to have its wetsuits manufactured in Thailand. The company's constant drive for higher quality was also a factor. Now company management can focus on building Body Glove's image as a California-lifestyle brand without worrying about inventory and other production issues. In licensing its brand for a wide range of goods and services—from cellphone cases to flotation devices, footwear, resorts, and more—Body Glove has created a network of partners around the world.

Discussion Questions

1. *For analysis*: Even though Body Glove makes its wetsuits in Thailand, why must its managers continually research how domestic customers use its products?
2. *For application*: When deciding whether to license its name for a new product, what issues might Body Glove's managers research in advance?
3. *For debate*: Should the products that Body Glove does not manufacture be labelled to alert buyers that they are produced under license? Support your chosen position.

ONLINE EXPLORATION

Visit the Body Glove website, www.bodyglove.com, and follow the links to read the Body Glove story and see the variety of products sold under the Body Glove brand. Also look at the electronics products, including the cellphone cases. Then browse the contacts listing to find out which companies have licensed the Body Glove brand for various products. How do the licensed products fit with the Body Glove brand image? What challenges might Body Glove face in coordinating its work with so many different companies?

E-Business IN ACTION

E-Business and the Global Economy

Name the world's most connected place. Did you guess the United States? If so, you are wrong. South Korea is the world's most connected high-speed Internet country. Approximately three of every four households have high-speed connections and 70 percent of its citizens are also equipped with cellphones. The U.S. lags behind in eleventh position. In fact, Japan and Canada occupy second and third place, respectively. With many Asian and European countries leapfrogging the U.S. in terms of infrastructure efficiency, the groundwork is being laid for even greater global e-business opportunities.

Historical Framework

Europe and Asia initially trailed North America in their use and enthusiasm for the Web; however, young firms around the globe are now taking their businesses to the Web and overcoming difficult obstacles such as cultural resistance, government regulations, and inefficient infrastructures.

Cultural Resistance

Because purchasing over the Internet does not involve an immediate exchange of goods or money, it generates feelings of uncertainty and loss of control over the buying process. As a result, many Europeans were reluctant to adopt online shopping. They used the Internet for communication such as e-mail and information services, but they resisted online purchases. Additionally, employee resistance to change delayed many European businesses from dabbling in e-commerce. Resistance to shopping on the Internet also exists in many Asian countries. Most commercial transactions in Asia still require cash and written receipts. A lack of comprehensive credit services also means that each e-marketplace buyer and seller must be painstakingly screened, which can take weeks. "It's difficult enough in the real world, but on the Internet, it can be even harder," says one Asian e-business owner.

Government Regulations

European leaders openly support the rise of the Internet economy. Nonetheless, many governments burden e-commerce with a maze of rules, regulations, and tax laws from another era. For instance, to protect neighbourhood stores, Germany developed rules to prohibit most price-discounting on consumer goods. The same laws keep airlines from dumping unsold seats at the last minute with fire-sale fares. Online auctions run into legal tangles because laws require the physical display of goods to be sold at auction and legislative mazes turn the simple act of registering a web address into a long and complex process. Such red tape curbs the growth of e-commerce.

Government support for e-commerce is minimal or nonexistent in some Asian countries. In Malaysia and parts of China, for instance, e-commerce is seen as a threat to government control. Dot-com companies highlight the central contradiction of China today—the drive to modernize without giving up one-party rule. The government wants the economic benefits of the Internet without the freedom it gives: the information revolution, minus the revolution. The question is not whether the Chinese government will pull the plug on the Internet, but whether it will regulate it in a way that will make it commercially viable.

Ineffective and Inefficient Infrastructures

In addition to cultural and governmental acceptance, the availability of Internet access is another prerequisite for e-commerce growth. Without a telecommunications infrastructure, it becomes impossible for large parts of the population to participate in the Internet economy. Scandinavians were early e-commerce adopters, thanks to the excellent mobile telecommunications infrastructure. But an overall lack of solid infrastructure throughout portions of Europe delayed the growth of electronic commerce on that continent.

Lack of access to investment capital and expensive, uneven telecommunications service are two reasons for the Internet's lag in some areas of Asia. Getting a decent phone connection, let alone an Internet connection, is a challenge in many parts of Asia. This is not the case for fast-growing, ambitious Asian countries such as Taiwan or South Korea, where government support of infrastructure improvements is strong. However, those who do make online purchases in Asia face delivery problems. Local ground delivery equivalents to Canpar and FedEx do not exist in some parts of Asia, or they are ineffective. Qualified shippers, warehouses, insurers, credit agencies, and finance companies are in great demand to move goods.

The Future of Global E-Commerce

We are still in the infant stages of the e-commerce revolution. For example, in Canada many of the obstacles listed above are nearly nonexistent. Connectivity is strong and improving, government interference is not a major issue, and consumers are slowly being socialized into a brave new e-commerce world. Yet e-sales still account for only about 1 percent of the Canadian economy. What does this mean? Major evolutions take time; the optimism of the late twentieth century was unrealistic. The benefits will evolve, but they won't materialize overnight. The advantages of traditional global trade have been evident for generations, but the rules of the game are still being negotiated on a daily basis with countries jockeying for position in the business domain and in the courts. As all the pieces come into place, expect to see more companies hang out global signs. In the meantime, individual companies must build systems, achieve growing domestic e-commerce goals, and position themselves for developing global e-opportunities.[47]

Questions for Critical Thinking

1. What are some of the challenges European and Asian countries face as they attempt to expand their presence in the e-commerce domain?
2. Why is a country's infrastructure an important factor in e-commerce development and success?
3. Why aren't more North American companies global e-commerce players?

Business PlanPro **EXERCISES**

Conducting Business in the Global Economy

Review Appendix C, "Your Business Plan," to learn how to use Business PlanPro Software so you can complete these exercises.

Think Like a Pro

Objective: By completing these exercises you will become acquainted with the sections of a business plan that address forms of competition, company and product/service descriptions, and the economic outlook for the related industry. You will use the sample business plan for Adventure Excursions Unlimited (listed as Travel Agency–Adventure Sports in the Sample Plan Browser) in this exercise. Use the table of contents to move from section to section as you explore the plan and answer the following questions.

1. What products and services does Adventure Excursions provide? Will the company compete on the basis of price, speed, quality, service, or innovation to gain a competitive advantage?
2. What is the economic outlook for the travel industry? What competition does Adventure Excursions face?
3. How does Adventure Excursions plan to use the Internet?

Create Your Own Business Plan

Now start a new plan for your own business. Answering the following questions will help you think about different aspects of your business plan. Enter your answers in the appropriate sections of the new business plan.

What information should you include about your product or service when creating a business plan? Describe in detail the product or service your company will provide. Indicate whether you will compete on price, speed, quality, service, or innovation. What are some of the things you should discuss about your competition in a business plan? In what industry will you compete? What is the economic outlook for that industry? What kinds of competition do you expect to face?

Chapter 4
Starting and Financing a Small Business

LEARNING OBJECTIVES

After studying this chapter, you will be able to

1. Highlight the major contributions small businesses make to the Canadian economy
2. Identify the key characteristics that differentiate small businesses from larger ones
3. Discuss three factors contributing to the increase in the number of small businesses
4. Cite the key characteristics common to most entrepreneurs
5. List three ways of going into business for yourself
6. Identify three sources of small business assistance
7. Highlight several factors you should consider when evaluating financing options, and discuss the principal sources of small business private financing

Behind the SCENES

Itech: An Entrepreneur's Clear Vision

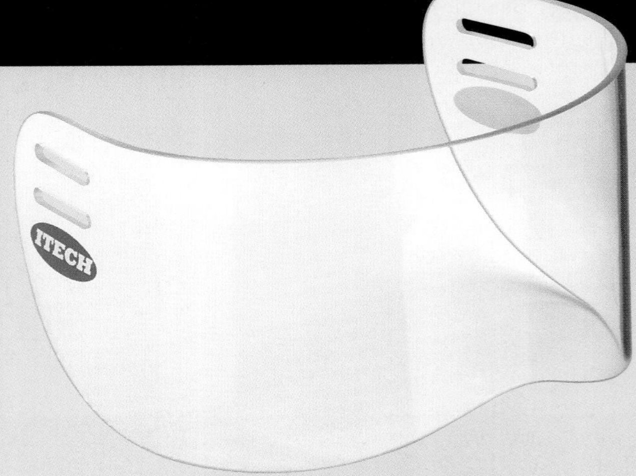

Itech is the pioneer of clear full-face hockey visors. The company was founded on this product but soon expanded its product line.

www.itech.com

Like many Canadians, Robin Burns grew up on an outdoor rink playing ice hockey with passion and pride. Frozen purple toes along with bumps and bruises were accepted and expected. Unlike most, in 1967 his dream led him to the NHL and an opportunity to play with the Montreal Canadiens. His career also brought him to the Pittsburgh Penguins, the Colorado Rockies, and the Kansas City Scouts. As a child of his generation, it never occurred to him to wear a helmet, mask, or mouth guard. According to Burns, "losing your four front teeth was a badge of honour." Yet the business of protective hockey gear was to hold the key to his post-NHL future.

After a decade in the NHL, Burns returned to Montreal and joined the start-up of Micron, a company that produced a unique and controversial skate in the early 1980s. Throughout his playing years, Mr. Burns had been involved with the development, marketing, and sales of hockey equipment. However, this entrepreneur's moment of clarity would soon take him on a new venture. Like many players before and after him, Burns was hit in the eye by an errant stick during an old-timers' match. This moment triggered the idea for Itech's clear hockey visor. Burns quit his job at Micron and began developing the prototype for the initial product in his basement. The risky move did not come without its trials and tribulations. As with most innovations, the bar for successful commercialization was set high. According to Randy Burns, vice-president of marketing, "one of the biggest obstacles was achieving official certification with the CSA (Canadian Standards Association) in Canada and the HECC (Hockey Equipment Certification Council) in the U.S." But, of course, jumping through hoops comes with the territory when creating a new segment in the market. People naturally doubt the unknown.

From these humble origins, Itech emerged as a pioneer that changed the face of hockey by developing the first clear full-face shield. The company grew to a stage where they had more than 200 employees and an extensive product line comprising shoulder pads, elbow pads, sticks, shin protectors, neck protectors, gloves, jocks, and goalie pads. That list includes just some of the company's extensive hockey equipment. Itech also boasts a growing baseball product line that was solidified by the purchase of the Cooper Baseball brand and resources. Cooper's North American sales network is extensive and Itech can also count on an established network of global distributors. It has also paid attention to the key industry players and has formed alliances with organizations like Hockey Canada, USA Hockey, and the Central Hockey League (CHL).

The Itech story is a classic Canadian tale that most of us can identify with. This business's success is an inspiring example of innovation fuelled by market knowledge and an entrepreneur's clear vision in an evolving market. Growth and evolution inevitably lead to change. Like most industries, the hockey equipment segment is consolidating. As Itech entered its twentieth year of operation in 2004, it needed to examine all possible avenues to continue its growth and maintain its industry standing. Many questions remained. How else could it diversify its product line? Should it consider a merger with another industry player?[1]

UNDERSTANDING THE WORLD OF SMALL BUSINESS

Many small businesses start out like Itech: with an entrepreneur, an idea, and a drive to succeed. In fact, Canada was originally built by people involved in small businesses—the family farmer, the shopkeeper, the craftsperson. Successive waves of immigrants carried on this tradition, launching restaurants and laundries, providing repair and delivery services, and opening newsstands and bakeries. This trend continued for decades, until improvements in transportation and communication enabled large producers to manufacture goods at low costs and pass the savings on to consumers. Many smaller businesses could not compete with larger retailers on price, so scores of them closed their doors and big business emerged as the primary economic force. The trend toward bigness continued for several decades, and then it reversed.

The 1990s were a golden decade for entrepreneurship in Canada. Entrepreneurs launched small companies in droves to fill new consumer needs. Many took advantage of Internet technologies to gain a competitive edge. Some succeeded; others failed. But the resurgence of small businesses helped power the Canadian economy forward.

There are approximately 2.3 million business establishments in Canada.[2] But defining what constitutes a small business is surprisingly tricky, because *small* is a relative term. For example, a manufacturing firm with 500 employees might be considered small if it competes against much larger companies, but a retail establishment with 500 employees might be classified as big when compared with its competitors.

One reliable source of information for small businesses is Industry Canada. This government agency serves as a resource and advocate for small firms, by promoting investment and trade, by promoting scientific research, and through other supportive initiatives.[3] A **small business** can be defined as a firm that (a) is independently owned and operated, (b) is not dominant in its field, (c) is relatively small in terms of annual sales, and (d) has fewer than 500 employees.[4]

small business
Company that is independently owned and operated, is not dominant in its field, and meets certain criteria for the number of employees and annual sales revenue

L.O. 1

Economic Roles of Small Businesses

Small businesses are the cornerstone of the Canadian economy. They bring new ideas, processes, and vigour to the marketplace and fill a niche market that generally is not served by large businesses. Here are just some of the important roles small businesses play in the economy:

- *They provide jobs.* In Canada, small businesses and the self-employed are an engine for economic growth. Small and medium-sized businesses (SMEs) account for about 60 percent of private sector employment and around 43 percent of private sector output.[5]
- *They introduce new products.* According to a recent study, Canadian SMEs accounted for 41 percent of world or Canadian firsts.[6] Small firms tend to develop a high percentage of "radical" new products.
- *They supply the needs of large corporations.* Many small businesses act as distributors, servicing agents, and suppliers to large corporations. Consider Terpac Plastic Inc., a niche player that identified and filled a need in the market; this Montreal-based hanger manufacturer seized an opportunity to service the retail market in a city with an established needle trade in the early 1980s. At the time, no local company was churning out this basic but vital product in the clothing business cluster. Today, Terpac serves the needle trade with this product and has an impressive client list that

While recuperating from a broken ankle, Perry Klebahn decided to try out a pair of snowshoes he found in his friend's closet. Today, his company, Atlas Showshoe, sells products across North America in more than 1000 stores, including retailers like Mountain Equipment Cooperative, Sport Mart, Hiker's Haven, Bernard Trottier, and Baron Sport.

includes Wal-Mart, The Bay, Zellers, Federated Department Stores, Costco, as well as high-end boutiques across North America.[7]

- *They provide specialized goods and services.* When Mike Woods tried to teach his son how to read, he couldn't find any toys that helped teach phonics. So he left his job as a partner in a big law firm and started LeapFrog. The company's initial product was the Phonics Disk, a US$50 toy that teaches children shapes, sounds, and pronunciation of letters and words. Since 1995 LeapFrog, a division of Knowledge Universe, has created more than 50 interactive learning products and 40 interactive books.[8]

Today, people are experiencing more pressure to balance personal demands with work responsibilities. Many small businesses have been created to deal with this problem (see the box entitled "Filling a Void in the Health Care Sector").

L.O. 2

Characteristics of Small Businesses

Small businesses are of two distinct types: lifestyle businesses and high-growth ventures. Roughly 80 to 90 percent are modest operations with little growth potential (although some have attractive income potential for the solo business person). The self-employed consultant working part-time from a home office, the corner florist,

Filling a Void in the Health Care Sector

www.rthealth.ca

Entrepreneurship has much to do with recognizing evolving trends and applying good old-fashioned marketing strategy to create a plan that responds to the needs of a desired segment. This principle led to the creation of Royal Treatment Health Care Services Inc., which specializes in providing medical services to patients that are hospitalized, institutionalized, or at home. The company provides nurses, nurses' aides, companions, sitters, and housekeepers to care for patients on both a short-term and a long-term basis. The company also offers counselling services for families experiencing grief.

The Canadian health care industry will grow significantly in the next few years. The number of senior citizens has grown by 62 percent since 1981, and it is estimated that within 10 years this segment will represent more than 19 percent of the country's population. By 2041, that number will soar to 25 percent. Public and private home care expenditures increased by 204 percent from 1991 to 2001. In 2000, total home care expenditures exceeded $3 billion. Over the last 20 years the industry has seen an average growth rate of 17.3 percent per annum. As there are more than 275 000 people aged 65 and over living on the island of Montreal, the market conditions were favourable for a new entrant.

Royal Treatment started out the right way: a marketing plan was created. The plan focused on the analysis of market conditions, the competitive level of the industry, and the existence of a sufficiently attractive market segment. It was concluded that although home care services were currently offered by both public and private organizations, there was still significant opportunity for a market that shows no signs of slowing down. The next step was to secure human resources. Since the company deals with patients' lives, getting the right people was critical. The company sought experienced, trained staff. Even "sitters," or those employees whose role it was to monitor a patient and call a medical professional in case of any trouble, were required to possess a degree from an accredited program before being considered for employment.

Royal Treatment continues to offer a wide range of patient services to families in Montreal.[9]

Questions for Critical Thinking

1. What are some of the initial challenges faced by a start-up service business such as Royal Treatment?
2. What key factors determine the long-term success of service-based companies such as Royal Treatment?

Adapted by: Robert Soroka

and the neighbourhood pizza parlour fall into the category of *lifestyle businesses*—firms built around the personal and financial needs of an individual or a family.[10] Lifestyle businesses aren't designed to grow into large enterprises.

In contrast to lifestyle businesses, some firms are small simply because they are new. Many companies—such as Magna International, Microsoft, and Bombardier—start out as small entrepreneurial firms but quickly outgrow their small business status. Magna International started off as a one-man Toronto-based tool and die shop in 1957, with sales of $13 000. Today Frank Stronach's company employs more than 81 000 people in 223 manufacturing divisions in 22 countries. Annual sales have increased from $13 000 to $20.7 billion.[11] *High-growth ventures* are usually run by a team rather than by one individual, and they expand rapidly by obtaining a sizable supply of investment capital and introducing new products or services to a large market. But expanding from a small firm into a large enterprise is no easy task; there's a world of difference between the two.

The typical small business has few products or services, focuses on a narrow group of customers, and remains in close contact with its markets. In addition, most small business owners work with limited resources and tend to be more innovative.

Limited Resources

Small companies tend to have limited resources, so owners and employees must perform a variety of job functions to get the work done. Being a jack-of-all-trades is not for everyone, however (see Exhibit 4.1); many executives who leave the corporate world to start a small business have trouble adjusting to the daily grind of entrepreneurship. They miss the support services, conveniences, and fringe benefits they enjoyed in large corporations.[12]

Innovation

Small businesses also tend to be more open-minded and willing to try new things than big businesses. Case studies show that being small can stimulate innovation: (1) small businesses can make decisions faster, (2) the owners are more accessible, and (3) employees have a greater opportunity for individual expression.

Putting an idea into action in big companies often means filing formal proposals, preparing research reports, and attending many meetings. This process could kill an idea before it has a chance to take off. Consider Microsoft, for example. One manager quit out of frustration with the company's snail's pace for decision making. It took 10 meetings

Exhibit 4.1 **How Entrepreneurs Spend Their Time**

The men and women who start their own companies are jacks-of-all-trades, but they devote the lion's share of their time to selling and producing the product.

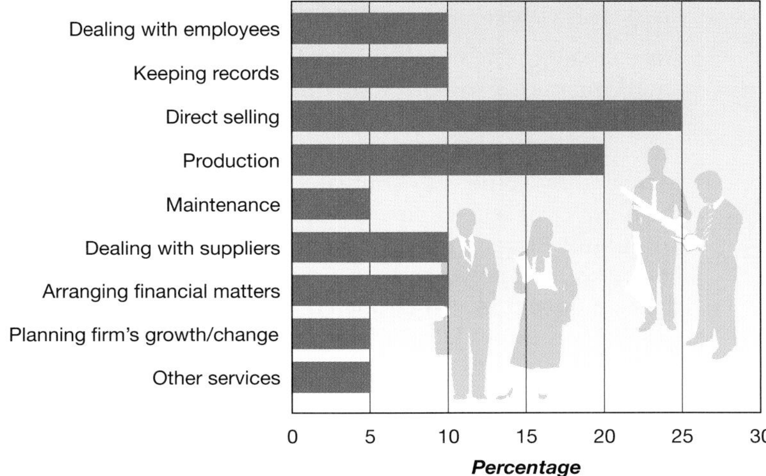

and three months to act on his suggestion to add a feature to Hotmail (the company's free Internet e-mail service) that would quickly take 40 million users to Microsoft's MSN website. In contrast, it took only 30 minutes to write the code for this feature.[13]

To compete with small companies, many big companies now divide their organizations into smaller work units. Xerox, Motorola, and others have launched their own small enterprises to keep new ideas from falling through the cracks. Run by *intrapreneurs*—people who create innovation of any kind *within* an organization (not to be confused with *entrepreneurs,* risk takers in the private enterprise system)—these ventures get funding and support from the parent organization. Nevertheless, some intrapreneurial ventures continue to face giant obstacles because the parent corporation burdens them with strict reporting requirements and formal procedures.[14]

L.O. 3

Factors Contributing to the Increase in the Number of Small Businesses

Three factors are contributing to the increase in the number of small businesses today: technological advances, an increase in the number of female business owners, and corporate downsizing and outsourcing.

Technology and the Internet

The Internet, together with e-commerce, has spawned thousands of new business ventures. Retiredworker.ca is one such firm. Linda Welstead, a former teacher, along with her daughter, Sarah Welstead, founded this small business in order to serve the needs of retired workers looking for part-time or occasional work. Linda saw an opportunity when she noticed that the main job sites like Monster.ca and Workopolis.com were mainly serving the needs of workers at the beginning of their careers. She then set out to create a site geared toward the specific needs of older workers; larger fonts and easy-to-read pages forego flashy options and present information in a clear, concise manner. With the baby boomers aging and increasingly fighting the stereotypical Florida retirement, Retiredworker.ca is on to something. It now serves customers from coast to coast.[15]

The Internet makes it possible for small companies to compete on a level playing field with larger ones. Small businesses can use the Internet to communicate with customers and suppliers all over the world—any time of the day—and to access the types of resources and information that were previously available only to larger firms. The Internet also makes it easier to start a small home-based business. With the Internet and online resources, accountants, writers, lawyers, and consultants can set up shop at home—or on the Web (see the box entitled "Create a Winning Website"). Some predict that as much as half the workforce soon may be involved in full- or part-time home-based businesses.[16]

Retiredworker.ca addresses a particular niche for older workers who are not adequately serviced by the main job websites like Monster.ca. Linda Welstead is its spokeperson.

Rise in Number of Female Small-Business Owners

An increase in the number of women entrepreneurs is also fuelling small business growth. According to Statistics Canada there are approximately 826 000 self-employed women in the country. In fact, over the last ten years, the number of self-employed women has increased by 26 percent compared to 16 percent for men. By 2010, the number of self-employed women in Canada is expected to reach 1 million.[17] Some of these women would not classify themselves as entrepreneurs; however, they are an important growing element in the economy. It is also estimated that 45 percent of SMEs or about 647 000 businesses have at least some degree of female ownership.[18] Although men still account for about 60 percent of new start-ups the statistics indicate that women tend to stick to a business over the long haul; in other words, the survival rate for female-run start-ups is higher.[19]

Create a Winning Website

These days anyone can learn to design and construct web pages. All you need is the right web-authoring software and a reasonably good computer to create pages with text, photos, and animated graphics. An estimated 75 percent of small Canadian businesses are on the Web.[20] But if you want to create a winning website, here are a few tips to consider:

- *Present a professional corporate image.* Be sure to provide a corporate profile that tells people a little bit about your company. Include news releases or articles about your business so that customers can see how well known or dynamic you are in the industry. Make sure your material is accurate, interesting, and related to your products. Identify the key benefits of your product (include product details on a second page). Check out other websites for inspiration—especially your competitors' sites—and decide what you like or dislike about their appearance. Think of ways to distinguish your site.
- *Don't forget the basics.* Always give visitors a person to call and a place to send for information. Be sure to list your postal and e-mail addresses and phone and fax numbers. Remember that the Internet is international, so list the nation where your company or its dealers are located.
- *Make your website easy to use.* Web surfers have a short attention span, so keep large graphics (which take forever to load) to a minimum. If you must include any large, embedded graphics or photos, provide an option for users to select a text-only interface, or provide small images of photos (called thumbnails) for users to click on if they want to view larger, more detailed versions. Always provide hyperlinks at the bottom of each page to allow users to move backwards and forward through a multi-page site.
- *Anticipate your customers' needs.* Plan ahead. By including answers to frequently asked questions, chances are you'll cover about 90 percent of your customers' concerns. Remember, users tend to provide both frank and useful input, but only if you ask them for it. So be sure to include an active customer feedback mechanism such as e-mail, open feedback forms, or structured survey forms. Don't require users to register before they can see your site. You may drive them away.
- *Promote your website.* Be sure to list with numerous search engines—giant indexes that allow web users to find information by entering key words. Most of these listings are free. Maximize the number of times your site will be listed by jamming in as many words as you can that best describe your site. Take out an ad in the newspaper and list your company in the Internet yellow pages. Finally, don't just sit back and expect your website to perform magic. Use it to find out as much as possible about your customers. Ask yourself: How can I benefit from all this customer information?

Questions for Critical Thinking

1. Why do web surfers have a short attention span?
2. List some of the ways companies can benefit from having a website on the Internet.

As Exhibit 4.2 shows, women are starting small businesses for a number of reasons. Some choose to run their own companies so they can enjoy a more flexible work arrangement; others start their own business because of barriers to corporate advancement, known as the *glass ceiling.* Christine Nicholls chose to leave a successful career in a high-tech company where she worked as a consultant in the health-care field. After earning her MBA and starting a family, she decided to look into operating a home-based business that she could run while raising her children. She came up with the idea to sell children's mail-order crafts and now sells them primarily online at www.creativekidsathome.com.[21]

Downsizing and Outsourcing

Contrary to popular wisdom, business start-ups soar when the economy sours. During hard times, many companies downsize or lay off talented employees, who then have little to lose by pursuing self-employment. In fact, several well-known companies were started during recessions. For example, Bill Gates started Microsoft during the 1975 recession.

Exhibit 4.2 **Women Starting Businesses**

More than half of all women business owners started their own businesses because they had an entrepreneurial idea or wished to further advance their careers.

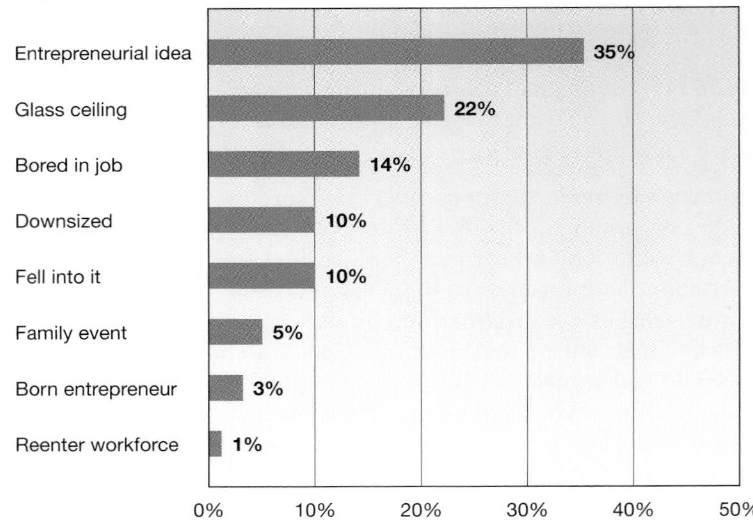

outsource
Subcontract work to outside companies (often in other countries)

To make up for layoffs of permanent staff, some companies **outsource** or subcontract special projects and secondary business functions to experts outside the organization. Others turn to outsourcing as a way to permanently eliminate entire company departments. Regardless of the reason, the increased use of outsourcing provides opportunities for smaller businesses to service the needs of larger enterprises.

L.O. 4

STARTING A SMALL BUSINESS

According to a recent CIBC survey, as many as 100 000 new small businesses will be started over the next five years.[22] Could you or should you join the thousands of entrepreneurs who start new businesses every year? What qualities would you need? What tasks would you have to perform to get started?

Characteristics of Entrepreneurs

Contrary to what you might expect, most entrepreneurs are not glamorous adventurers; instead, they are often ordinary people who have a good idea. But it takes more than a good idea to launch a successful business. Most entrepreneurs have these qualities in common:

- They are highly disciplined.
- They like to control their destiny.
- They listen to their intuitive sense.
- They relate well to others.
- They are eager to learn whatever skills are necessary to reach their goal.
- They learn from their mistakes.
- They stay abreast of market changes.
- They are willing to exploit new opportunities.
- They are driven by ambition.

- They think positively.
- They prefer the excitement and potential rewards of risk taking over security.[23]

While most entrepreneurs are anxious to become their own boss, surprisingly they cite making money as the secondary reason for starting their own business.[24]

John Stanton, founder of Alberta-based Running Room, operates 66 outlets across Canada and the U.S. The company has made great strides since its humble beginnings two decades ago. The original store was located in a renovated living room of an old Edmonton home. The goal was to create a retail outlet that serviced the needs of its client base. The retailer distinguishes itself with a simple philosophy: Running Room is a store for runners by runners. This statement must be qualified because Running Room is not an exclusive, elitist club; the firm has a tradition of creating runners and holds regular clinics that cost about $69 for 10 to 18 lessons. These lessons include instruction on fitness, walking, running, sports medicine, and nutrition. The goal is to ease the individual into the world of running. Stanton initially got the idea for this business based on the poor service he received in a retail outlet when he decided to transform himself from an overweight executive who smoked two and a half packs a day into a healthy, avid runner. On the twentieth anniversary of the firm's inception, Stanton celebrated, along with 20 000 runners across Canada, with a special 20-minute run. The firm is involved in many events and promotes the sport by example. Healthy living has meshed effectively with entrepreneurial pursuits.[25]

Entrepreneurs such as Itech's Robin Burns start with relatively small sums of money and operate informally from their homes, at least for a while. Most have diverse backgrounds in terms of education and business experience. Some come from companies unlike the ones they start; others use their prior knowledge and skills—such as editing, telemarketing, public relations, or selling—to start their own businesses. Still others have less experience but an innovative idea or a better way of doing something. Like John Stanton and Robin Burns, they find an overlooked corner of the market, exploit a demographic trend unnoticed by others, or meet an unsatisfied consumer need through better service or a higher-quality product. Moreover, they often plan and develop their product quickly, while the rest of the business world ponders whether a market for the product exists.

Importance of Preparing a Business Plan

Getting started in a new business requires a lot of work (see Exhibit 4.3), not the least of which is planning. Although many successful entrepreneurs claim to have done little formal planning, even the most intuitive of them have *some* idea of what they're trying to accomplish and how they hope to do it. Jeff Bezos, founder of Amazon.com, planned the world's first online bookstore in the backseat of his car as his wife drove them from New York to Seattle. As Bezos and other entrepreneurs know, planning is essential for success. No amount of hard work can turn a bad idea into a profitable one: The health food store in a meat-and-potatoes neighbourhood and the child-care centre in a retirement community are probably doomed from the beginning.

Planning forces you to think ahead. Before you rush in to supply a product, you need to be sure that a market exists. You must also try to predict some of the problems that might arise and figure out how you will deal with them. For instance, what will you do if one of your suppliers suddenly goes out of business? Can you locate another supplier quickly? What if the neighbourhood starts to change—even for the better? An influx of wealthier neighbours may cause such a large increase in rent that your business must move. Also, tough competition may move into the neighbourhood along with the fatter pocketbooks. Do you have an alternative location staked out? What if styles suddenly change? Can you switch quickly from, say, hand-painted crafts to some other kind of artwork?

One of the first steps you should take toward starting a new business is to develop a **business plan**, a written document that summarizes an entrepreneur's proposed business venture, communicates the company's goals, highlights how management intends to achieve those goals, and shows how consumers will benefit from the company's products or services.

business plan
A written document that provides an orderly statement of a company's goals and how it intends to achieve those goals

Exhibit 4.3 Business Start-up Checklist

You have many tasks to perform before you start your business. Here are just a few.

- ✓ Choose a business name, verify the right to use it, and register it.
- ✓ Reserve a corporate name if you will be incorporating.
- ✓ Register or reserve trademarks.
- ✓ Apply for a patent if you will be marketing an invention.
- ✓ Write a business plan.
- ✓ Choose a location for the business.
- ✓ File partnership or corporate papers.
- ✓ Get any required business licences or permits.
- ✓ Have business phone lines installed.
- ✓ Check into business insurance needs.
- ✓ Apply for a sales tax number.
- ✓ Apply for an employee identification number if you will have employees.
- ✓ Open business bank account(s).
- ✓ Have business cards and stationery printed.
- ✓ Purchase equipment and supplies.
- ✓ Order inventory.
- ✓ Order signage.
- ✓ Order fixtures.
- ✓ Print brochures and other sales literature.
- ✓ Send out publicity releases.
- ✓ Call everyone you know and tell them you are in business.

Preparing a business plan serves two important functions: First, it guides the company operations and outlines a strategy for turning an idea into reality; second, it helps persuade lenders and investors to finance your business. In fact, without a business plan, many investors won't even grant you an interview. According to Jacques Lemoine, senior vice-president of Ontario Operations for the Business Development Bank of Canada, writing an effective plan is often the difference between getting financing and walking out empty handed.[26] Keep in mind that sometimes the greatest service a business plan can provide an entrepreneur is the realization that "the concept just won't work." Discovering this on paper can save you considerable time and money (see the box entitled "Blueprint for a Comprehensive Business Plan").

L.O. 5

Small Business Ownership Options

start-up companies New ventures

Once you've done your research and planning, if you decide to take the risk you can get into business for yourself in three ways: start from scratch, buy an existing business, or obtain a franchise. Roughly two-thirds of business founders begin **start-up companies**; that is, they start from scratch rather than buy an existing operation or inherit a family business. Starting a business from scratch has many advantages and disadvantages, as Exhibit 4.4 points out. Of the three options for going into business for yourself, starting a new business is the most common route and, in many cases, the most difficult.

Exhibit 4.4 Weighing the Advantages and Disadvantages of Starting a New Business

Owning a business has many advantages, but you must also consider the potential drawbacks.

Blueprint for a Comprehensive Business Plan

Although the business plan has a simple, straightforward purpose, it still requires a great deal of thought. For example, before you open your doors, you have to make important decisions about personnel, marketing, facilities, suppliers, and distribution. A written business plan forces you to think about those issues and develop programs that will help you succeed. If you are starting out on a small scale and using your own money, your business plan may be relatively informal. But at a minimum, you should describe the basic concept of the business and outline its specific goals, objectives, and resource requirements. A formal plan, suitable for use with banks or investors, should cover the following points:

- *Summary.* In one or two pages, summarize your business concept. Describe your product or service and its market potential. Highlight some things about your company and its owners that will distinguish your firm from the competition. Summarize your financial projections and the amount of money investors can expect to make on their investment. Be sure to indicate how much money you will need and for what purpose.
- *Mission and objectives.* Explain the purpose of your business and what you hope to accomplish.
- *Company and industry.* Give full background information on the origins and structure of your venture and the characteristics of its industry.
- *Products or services.* Give a complete but concise description of your product or service, focusing on its unique attributes. Explain how customers will benefit from using your product or service instead of those of your competitors.
- *Market and competition.* Provide data that will persuade the investor that you understand your target market and can achieve your sales goals. Be sure to identify the strengths and weaknesses of your competitors.
- *Management.* Summarize the background and qualifications of the principals, directors, and key management personnel in your company. Include resumés in the appendix.
- *Marketing strategy.* Provide projections of sales and market share, and outline a strategy for identifying and contacting customers, setting prices, providing customer services, advertising, and so forth. Whenever possible, include evidence of customer acceptance, such as advance product orders.
- *Design and development plans.* If your product requires design or development, describe the nature and extent of what needs to be done, including costs and possible problems.
- *Operations plan.* Provide information on the facilities, equipment, and labour needed.
- *Overall schedule.* Forecast development of the company in terms of completion dates for major aspects of the business plan.
- *Critical risks and problems.* Identify all negative factors and discuss them honestly.
- *Financial projections and requirements.* Include a detailed budget of start-up and operating costs, as well as projections for income, expenses, and cash flow for the first three years of business. Identify the company's financing needs and potential sources.
- *Exit strategy.* Explain how investors will be able to cash out or sell their investment, such as through a public stock offering, sale of the company, or a buyback of the investors' interest. When covering these points, keep in mind that your audience wants short, concise information—not lengthy volumes—and realistic projections for growth.

Questions for Critical Thinking

1. What details should you know about your business before writing a business plan?
2. Why is it important to identify critical risks and problems in a business plan?

Another way to go into business for yourself is to buy an existing business. This approach tends to reduce the risks—provided, of course, that you check out the company carefully. When you buy a business, you generally purchase an established customer base, functioning business systems, a proven product or service, and a known location. You don't have to go through the painful period of building a reputation, establishing a clientele, finding suppliers, and hiring and training employees. In addition, financing an existing business is often much easier than financing a new one; lenders are reassured by the company's history and existing assets and customer base.

Danvin, a recent start-up company, obtains the distribution rights to sell branded foods products in the Canadian market. The company sells to supermarkets, like Sobeys, Metro and Loblaws, as well as to restaurants and hotels. Danvin owns the rights to Sweet Baby Ray's Barbecue Sauce, Simply Potatoes, My Grandma's of New England Coffee Cakes and Arriba Salsa.

With these major details already settled, you can concentrate on making improvements.

Still, buying an existing business is not without disadvantages. For one thing, the business may be overpriced. For another, inventories and equipment may be obsolete. Furthermore, the location may no longer be satisfactory, the previous owner may have created ill will, your personality may clash with those of existing managers and employees, and outstanding bills owed by customers may be difficult to collect. Keep in mind that no matter how fast you learn and how much investigating you do, you're likely to find that the challenges of running an existing business are far greater than you anticipated. [27]

The Franchise Alternative

An alternative to buying an existing business is to buy a **franchise** in somebody else's business. This approach enables the buyer to use a larger company's trade name and sell its products or services in a specific territory. In exchange for this right, the **franchisee** (the small business owner who contracts to sell the goods or services) pays the **franchisor** (the supplier) an initial fee (and often monthly royalties as well). Franchises are a factor of rising importance in the Canadian economy. The Canadian Franchise Association (CFA) is a trade association that represents firms in a wide variety of industries that use the franchise format. Information can be obtained from their website at www.cfa.ca, by phone, or in person at their annual franchising show in Toronto. The show offers a variety of seminars, discussion panels, and workshops in important aspects of the process, such as financing, marketing, buying contracts, and obligations. The CFA also publishes *Franchise Canada Magazine*, a bimonthly magazine geared toward entrepreneurs interested in buying a franchise.[28] According to the International Franchise Association, there are approximately 1327 franchisors and 63 642 franchisees with annual sales in excess of US$90 billion in Canada.[29]

franchise
Business arrangement in which a small business obtains the rights to sell the goods or services of the supplier (franchisor)

franchisee
Small business owner who contracts for the right to sell goods or services of the supplier (franchisor) in exchange for some payment

franchisor
Supplier that grants a franchise to an individual or group (franchisee) in exchange for payments

Types of Franchises

Franchises are of three basic types. A *product franchise* gives you the right to sell trademarked goods, which are purchased from the franchisor and resold. Car dealers and gasoline stations fall into this category. A *manufacturing franchise*, such as a soft-drink bottling plant, gives you the right to produce and distribute the manufacturer's products, using supplies purchased from the franchisor. A *business-format franchise* gives you the right to open a business using a franchisor's name and format for doing business. Chains such as Harvey's, Second Cup, Tim Hortons, and Pizza Hut typify this form of franchising.

How to Evaluate a Franchise

How do you protect yourself from a poor franchise investment? The best way is to study the opportunity carefully before you commit. Speak to knowledgeable and experienced individuals, attend the CFA trade show, and do your homework before signing an agreement. By studying this information, you can determine the financial condition of the franchisor and discover whether the company has been involved in lawsuits with franchisees. Before signing a franchise agreement, it's also wise to consult an attorney. Exhibit 4.5 suggests some points to consider as you study the package of information on the franchise.

Nevertheless, some people find out too late that franchising isn't the best choice for them. They make a mistake common among prospective franchisees—buying without really understanding the day-to-day business. Often, prospects simply don't get beyond the allure of the successful name or concept—or the mistaken notion that a franchise brings instant success. "People go into a sub shop at the noon hour and see the cash register opening and closing," says the president of Franchise Solutions. "What they don't

Exhibit 4.5 **Ten Questions to Ask Before Signing a Franchise Agreement**

A franchise agreement is a legally binding contract that defines the relationship between the franchisee and the franchisor. Because the agreement is drawn up by the franchisor, the terms and conditions generally favour the franchisor. Before signing the franchise agreement, be sure to consult an attorney.

1. What does the initial franchise fee cover? Does it include a starting inventory of supplies and products?
2. How are the periodic royalties calculated and when are they paid?
3. Are all trademarks and names legally protected?
4. Who provides and pays for advertising and promotional items?
5. Who selects the location of the business?
6. Is the franchise assigned an exclusive territory?
7. If the territory is not exclusive, does the franchisee have the right of first refusal on additional franchises established in nearby locations?
8. Is the franchisee required to purchase equipment and supplies from the franchisor or other suppliers?
9. Under what conditions can the franchisor and/or the franchisee terminate the franchise agreement?
10. Can the franchise be assigned to heirs?

see is having to get there at 4 a.m. to bake the bread." Buying a franchise is much like buying any other business: It requires analyzing the market, finding capital, choosing a site, hiring employees, and buying equipment. The process also includes an element not found in other businesses—evaluating the franchisor.[30]

One of the best ways to evaluate a prospective franchisor is by talking to other franchisees. At a minimum, you should find out what other franchisees think of the opportunity. If they had it to do over again, would they still invest? You might even want to spend a few months working for someone who already owns a franchise you're interested in.

Nevertheless, as Jim and Laura White discovered, evaluating a franchise means more than assessing the current operation. What the market will be like tomorrow is just as important an issue to address. For example, when the Whites opened their Body Shop franchise, they expected to earn a comfortable living on their $300 000 investment. Instead, the outlet lost money every year. What they hadn't taken into account was that less than a year after the Whites' Body Shop opened, other retail stores opened to compete directly with their outlet.[31]

Advantages of Franchising

Why is franchising so popular? For one thing, when you invest in a franchise, you know you are getting a viable business, one that has "worked" many times before. If the franchise is well established, you get the added benefit of instant name recognition, national advertising programs, standardized quality of goods and services, and a proven formula for success. Buying a franchise also gives you instant access to a support network, and in many cases a ready-made blueprint for building a business. For an initial investment (from a few thousand dollars to upward of a million, depending on the franchise), you get services such as site-location studies, market research, training, and technical assistance, as well as assistance with building or leasing your structure, decorating the building, purchasing supplies, and operating the business for 6 to 12 months. Because few franchisees are able to write a cheque for the amount of the total investment, some franchisors also provide financial assistance.

Prospective Subway franchisees must attend company training classes and pass a final exam before they can own a Subway sandwich shop.

Disadvantages of Franchising

Although franchising offers many advantages, it is not the ideal vehicle for everyone. First, owning a franchise is no guarantee of wealth. Even though it may be a relatively easy way to get into business, not all franchises are hugely profitable. Some franchisees barely survive. One of the biggest disadvantages of franchising is the monthly payment, or royalty, that must be turned over to the franchisor. Royalties are not necessarily bad as long as the franchisee receives ongoing assistance in return. Royalty fees vary from nothing at all to 20 percent of sales. Harvey's restaurants, for example, charge a monthly royalty fee of 5 percent.[32] The Harvey's restaurant concept is owned by Cara along with the following franchises: Swiss Chalet, Kelsey's, Montana's, Outback Steakhouse, Milestone Grill and Bar, and Second Cup.[33]

Another drawback of franchises is that many allow individual operators little independence. Franchisors can prescribe virtually every aspect of the business, down to the details of employee uniforms and the colour of the walls. Furthermore, when a chain loses its cutting edge in the marketplace, being stuck with a franchise can be painful. By contrast, if independent retailers run into trouble with their product lines, they can change suppliers or perhaps switch rapidly to a whole new line of business. Franchisees can't. They're usually bound by contracts to sell only authorized goods, often supplied by the franchisor itself at whatever price the franchisor wants to charge.

Although franchisors can make important decisions without consulting franchisees, the days of franchisors exercising such control are ending. In many cases the relationship between franchisor and franchisee is becoming more of a joint venture. Some franchisors are rewriting contracts to become less dictatorial. Newer contracts offer stock options, automatic contract renewals, and empowerment through franchise advisory boards.[34] Some franchisors are giving franchisees a voice in how advertising funds are used.

Why New Businesses Fail

Even if you carefully evaluate a prospective franchisor or write a winning business plan, you have no guarantee of success. In fact, you may have heard some depressing statistics about the number of new businesses that fail. Some reports say your chances of succeeding are only one in three; others claim that the odds are even worse, stating that 85 percent of all new business ventures fail within 10 years. Actual statistics, however, show otherwise. Among all companies that close their doors, only about one in seven actually fails—that is, goes out of business leaving behind unpaid debts. Moreover, the true failure rate is much lower if you remove those operations that Dun & Bradstreet (D&B) business analysts say aren't "genuine businesses." For instance, a freelancer who writes one article for a magazine and then stops writing would be counted as a failed business under the traditional measurement (which is based on tax returns).[35]

Most new businesses fail for a number of reasons, as Exhibit 4.6 suggests. Lack of management skills, experience, and proper financing are among the top 10 reasons for failure. So is uncontrolled growth. Growth forces changes throughout the organization that affect every aspect of the business operation. In general, growing companies need to install more sophisticated systems and processes. They must staff positions that never existed and learn how to delegate responsibilities and control. They must hire experienced managers and stay focused.

When growth is too rapid, it can force so much change that things spin out of control. And nothing can kill a successful business faster than chaos. Oftentimes, once the firm starts to expand, it takes the entrepreneur a while to realize she is not running a mom-and-pop operation. The tendency to avoid delegating work and attempting to do it all are common; however, at a certain stage the firm must put key people in place to serve the needs of the operation.

Besides growing too rapidly, another mistake entrepreneurs make is to stray too far from the original product or market. As the Chapter 1's opening case mentioned, Roots, despite its success as a retailer, made an ambitious move into the airline industry. While it had partnered with an industry player, Skyservice Airlines Inc., the operation was quickly terminated after just 40 days.[36]

Exhibit 4.6 **Why New Businesses Fail**

Experts have identified the following 10 reasons as the most likely causes of new business failure.

1. Management incompetence
2. Lack of industry experience
3. Inadequate financing
4. Poor business planning
5. Unclear or unrealistic goals
6. Failure to attract and keep target customers
7. Uncontrolled growth
8. Inappropriate location
9. Poor inventory and financial controls
10. Inability to make the entrepreneurial transition

Even when signs of failure begin to surface, some entrepreneurs don't pull the plug fast enough. Jeff Schwarz worked three years without drawing a salary and used up $100 000 of his personal savings before closing his photography business, Remarkable Moments.[37] Keep in mind that failure isn't always the end of the world. Many presidents of big, successful companies, including Fred Smith of FedEx, can spin long tales about how failure got them where they are today or how failure was a valuable learning experience.[38] Moreover, many sources of small business assistance exist to help you plan your new business and overcome these obstacles.

Sources of Small Business Assistance

L.O. 6

Many local business professionals are willing to serve as mentors and can help you avoid the pitfalls of business. As a small business owner, you may turn to small business resources such as the Business Development Bank of Canada (BDC), the Canadian Youth Business Foundation (CYBF), incubators, and the Internet. These resources can help you evaluate your business idea, develop a business plan, locate start-up funding sources, and show you how to package your business image professionally.

Business Development Bank of Canada

The Business Development Bank of Canada (BDC) is a financial institution wholly owned by the Government of Canada. BDC has been servicing Canadian business needs for over 60 years. BDC offers a variety of financial products designed to help Canadian businesses grow, such as term loans, subordinate financing and venture capital. BDC is also a major player in helping businesses improve their management techniques by providing tailored consulting services through a national network of consultants. BDC's financing and consulting solutions are readily accessible from 85 locations nationwide or by calling 1-877-BDC-BANKS.

BDC

Incubators

Incubators are centres that provide "newborn" businesses with just about everything a company needs to get started—office space, expert advice, legal and accounting services, clerical services, marketing support, contacts, and more.[39] Some incubators are open to businesses of all types; others specialize in a specific industry or product. For example, AgriTECH Park, in Nova Scotia, caters to developing technology companies; the Toronto Fashion Incubator nurtures young fashion designers; and the Centre d'Entreprises et d'Innovation de Montreal (CEIM) offers support to various sectors from e-commerce to manufacturing.[40] Regardless, the goal is to convert "tenant" firms into "graduates," so most incubators set limits—from 18 months to 5 years—on how long a company can stay in the nest.[41]

incubators
Facilities that house small businesses during their early growth phase

Studies show that firms that start out in incubators typically increase sales by more than 400 percent from the time they enter until the time they leave.[42] Furthermore, 8 out of 10 businesses nurtured in incubators succeed beyond 5 years. Incubators, of course, are not a new idea. Thousands of them hatch successful businesses each year.

The Internet

The Internet is another source of small business assistance. Sonja Edmond, owner of Heavenly Bounty Giftbaskets, a handcrafted gift basket business, had to look no further than her computer screen when she needed help. Although she enjoyed making gift baskets as a hobby, she wasn't sure whether a viable market existed to support a home-based business. So she posted a price-setting question on CompuServe's Working from Home and Handcrafts forum. Within 24 hours, her e-mail box was flooded with answers from forum members, who "convinced me I could do this," she says. Edmond struck a resource gold mine: Not only did she find the encouragement she needed to plunge into entrepreneurship; she also got valuable business leads and advice on licensing her product.[43]

For pertinent information on Canadian business visit www.businessgateway.ca. This federal government website provides a variety of sources and information on taxes and regulations, start-ups, importing and exporting, research and development tax credits, human resources, etc. The site also has convenient links to information divided by province.

L.O. 7

FINANCING A NEW BUSINESS

Once you've decided to go into business for yourself, you will probably need some money to get started. Start-up companies must pay employees, purchase inventory, and acquire assets such as land, production facilities, and equipment before they can generate revenue.

Where can firms obtain the money they need to launch and operate a new business? Most new businesses turn to private financing sources, such as family, friends, and loans from banks, finance companies, or other commercial lenders. As the start-up grows, owners can raise additional funds by selling shares of stock to the public. For instance, The Brick was founded in 1971 as a prototypical small business with only four employees. William Comrie, founder and CEO, preferred to retain tight control of the firm over the years. In 2004, more than 30 years after founding the company, and after the former small business had been transformed into the top Canadian furniture appliance and electronics chain, the company raised $272 million by tendering an initial public offering (IPO) in the income trust market.[44] Conversely, other firms embrace major external financing in their infant years as a means to growth and/or survival.

As you can imagine, financing an enterprise is a complex undertaking. The process begins by assessing the firm's financing needs and determining whether funds are needed for the short or the long term. You must also assess the cost of obtaining financing, and you must weigh the advantages and disadvantages of financing through debt or equity, taking into consideration the firm's special needs and circumstances. In short, choosing the right sources of financing can be just as important as choosing the right location. Your decision will affect your company's *capital structure*—the mix of debt and equity—forever.

Length of Term

Financing can be either short-term or long-term. *Short-term financing* is any financing that will be repaid within one year, whereas *long-term financing* is any financing that will be repaid in a period longer than one year. The primary purpose of short-term debt financing is to ensure that a company maintains its liquidity, or its ability to meet financial obligations (such as inventory payments) as they become due. By contrast, long-term financing is used to acquire long-term assets such as buildings and equipment or to fund a start-up and expansion via any number of growth options.

Cost of Capital

In general, a company wants to obtain money at the lowest cost and least amount of risk. However, lenders and investors want to receive the highest possible return on their investment, also at the lowest risk. A company's *cost of capital,* the average rate of interest it must pay on its financing, depends on three main factors: the risk associated with the company, the prevailing level of interest rates, and management's selection of funding vehicles. Obviously, the more financially solid a company is, the less risk investors face. However, time also plays a vital role. Because a dollar will be worth less tomorrow than it is today, lenders need to be compensated for waiting to be repaid. As a result, long-term financing generally costs a company more than short-term financing.

Regardless of how financially solid a company is, the cost of money will vary over time because interest rates fluctuate. Companies must take such interest rate fluctuations into account when making financing decisions. For instance, a company planning to finance a short-term project when interest rates are 8.5 percent would want to re-evaluate the project if interest rates rose to, say, 10 percent a few months later. Even though companies try to time their borrowing to take advantage of drops in interest rates, this option is not always possible. A firm's need for money doesn't always coincide with a period of favourable rates. At times, a company may be forced to borrow when rates are high and then renegotiate the loan when rates drop. Sometimes projects must be put on hold until interest rates become more affordable.

Debt versus Equity Financing

Debt financing refers to what we normally think of as a loan. A creditor agrees to lend money to a debtor in exchange for repayment, with accumulated interest, at some future date. Loans can be secured or unsecured. **Secured loans** are those backed by something of value, known as *collateral,* which may be seized by the lender in the event that the borrower fails to repay the loan.

The most common types of collateral are accounts receivable, inventories, and property such as marketable securities, buildings, and other assets. **Unsecured loans** are ones that require no collateral. Instead, the lender relies on the general credit record and the earning power of the borrower.

Equity financing is achieved by selling shares of a company's stock. Whenever a corporation offers its shares of ownership, or **stock**, to the public for the first time, the company is said to be *going public.* The initial shares offered for sale are the company's **initial public offering (IPO)**. Going public is an effective method of raising needed capital, but it can be an expensive and time-consuming process. Public companies must file a variety of statements, pay costly fees, and prepare audited financial statements.

When choosing between debt and equity financing, you should weigh the advantages and disadvantages of each (see Exhibit 4.7). In addition to considering whether the financing is for the short or the long term and assessing the cost of the financing, such as interest, fees, and other charges, you must also evaluate your desire for ownership control. Two of the biggest benefits of debt financing are (1) the lender does not gain an ownership interest in the business, and (2) a firm's obligations are limited to repaying the loan. By contrast, equity financing involves an exchange of money for a share of business ownership: It allows firms to obtain funds without pledging to repay a specific amount of money at a particular time, but in exchange for this benefit the firm must give up some ownership control.

secured loans
Loans backed up with something of value that the lender can claim in case of default, such as a piece of property

unsecured loans
Loans requiring no collateral but a good credit rating

stock
Shares of ownership in a corporation

initial public offering (IPO)
Corporation's first offering of stock to the public

Private Financing Sources

Most new companies obtain start-up capital from personal assets, family and friends, or strategic partners or customers. Another source of private financing is big business. Companies such as Coca-Cola and Procter & Gamble fund young companies in exchange for stock or exclusive rights to future products. By working with start-ups, larger companies hope to hasten product development and infuse their own operations with more of the entrepreneurial spirit.[45]

Bank loans are another source of private financing, but obtaining such financing can be difficult for most start-ups. For one thing, banks consider start-ups risky so they shy away from lending money to new businesses. For another, the risk inherent in some

Exhibit 4.7 Debt versus Equity

When choosing between debt and equity financing, companies evaluate the characteristics of both types of funding.

CHARACTERISTIC	DEBT	EQUITY
Maturity	**Specific:** Specifies a date by which it must be repaid.	**Nonspecific:** Specifies no maturity date.
Claim on income	**Fixed cost:** Company must pay interest on debt held by bondholders and lenders before paying any dividends to shareholders. Interest payments must be met regardless of operating results.	**Discretionary cost:** Shareholders may receive dividends after creditors have received interest payments; however, company is not required to pay dividends.
Claim on assets	**Priority:** Lenders have prior claims on assets.	**Residual:** Shareholders have claims only after the firm satisfies claims of lenders.
Influence over management	**Little:** Lenders are creditors, not owners. They can impose limits on management only if interest payments are not received.	**Varies:** As owners of the company, shareholders can vote on some aspects of corporate operations. Shareholder influence varies, depending on whether stock is widely distributed or closely held.

start-ups justifies higher interest rates than banks are allowed to charge by law. Thus, most banks will finance a start-up only if they can obtain payment guarantees from other financially sound parties or to the extent that the business has marketable collateral, such as buildings and equipment, to back the loan.[46] The Canadian Small Business Financing Program (CSFB) helps some businesses access such loans by having the federal government guarantee up to 85 percent of the lender's losses in case of default. Of course, each business must meet certain criteria to be considered for the program.

In addition to friends, corporate financing, and bank loans, other sources of private financing assistance include venture capitalists, angel investors, credit cards, and government programs.

Venture Capitalists

venture capitalists
Investment specialists who provide money to finance new businesses or turnarounds in exchange for a portion of the ownership, with the objective of making a considerable profit on the investment; also called VCs

Venture capitalists are investment specialists who raise pools of capital from large private and institutional sources (such as pension funds) to fund ventures that have a high, rapid growth potential and a need for large amounts of capital. Venture capitalists, or VCs as they're called in entrepreneurial circles, do not simply lend money to a small business as a bank would. Instead, they provide money and management expertise in return for a sizable ownership interest in the business. Once the business becomes profitable, venture capitalists reap the reward by selling their interest to other long-term investors for a sizable profit.

Burned by the dot-com fallout at the end of the millennium, many VCs have become more selective in whom they lend money to. In 2004, VC investments rose by 6 percent over the previous year (see Exhibit 4.8) but fewer firms received funding; dollars invested have not approached the enthusiastic levels found at the turn of the century.[47] In addition to being more selective, venture capitalists are also becoming more aggressive in their oversight and management of firms they've already funded. For instance, they are shutting down firms that show little promise and pumping extra cash into those they think can survive. VCs are also scrutinizing business plans of capital seekers more skeptically. Applicants must now show real revenue, real customers, and a clear path to profits.[48] Still, most Canadian venture capitalist firms will finance only companies that

Exhibit 4.8 Venture Capital in Canada

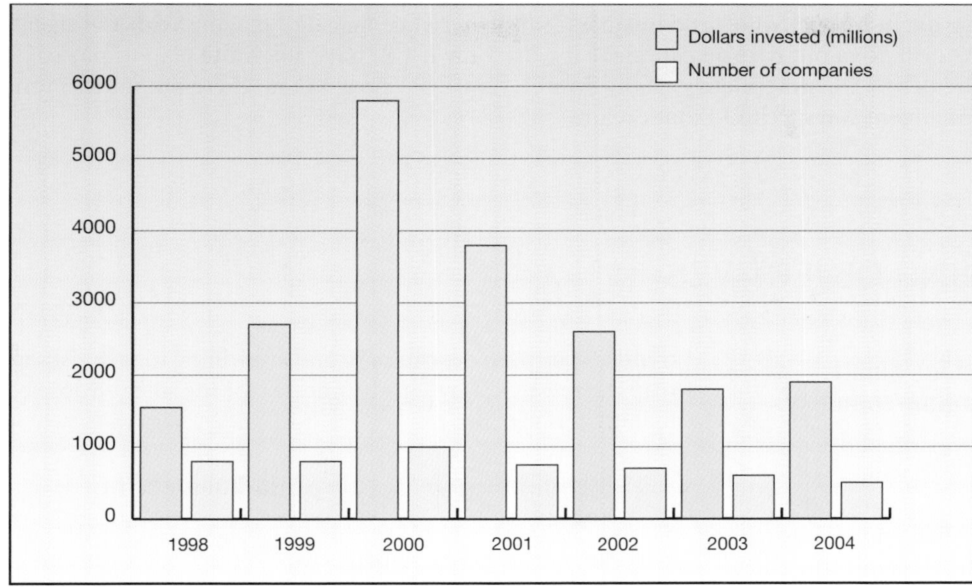

Source: Reprinted with permission of the *Globe and Mail.*

need $1 million or more.[49] Thus, if you're looking for a more modest amount of financing, you might want to find an angel instead.

Angel Investors

Comfortable with risks that scare off many banks, *angel investors* put their own money into start-ups with the goal of eventually selling their interest for a large profit. These wealthy individuals are willing to loan smaller amounts of money than are VCs and to stay involved with the company for a longer period of time.

Start-ups that seek out angels typically have spent their first $50 000 to $100 000 and are now looking for the next $250 000 to grow their business. In addition to providing financing; angels can be a great source of business expertise and credibility. High-profile angels range from individuals like Bill Gates to Dave Chilton. For example, when Greta and Janet Podleski decided to write their own corny and creative cookbook called *LooneySpoons,* they had a great idea but lacked financing. Many of their early initiatives were financed by credit cards and their limited personal funds. But when push came to shove, the sisters recruited Dave Chilton, author of the all-time Canadian bestseller *The Wealthy Barber.* He ended up taking a much more active role in the company than he had initially planned, since the book quickly entered the bestsellers list and a production cash crunch followed. The relationship has been successful and the follow-up cookbook, *Crazy Plates,* also earned bestseller status.[50]

Burdened with debt and struggling to cope with their project, Greta and Janet Podleski turned to an angel investor for help. In Dave Chilton, they found the financing and the experience they needed.

Credit Cards

According to one recent study, one-third of businesses with 19 or fewer employees use credit cards to finance their new business ventures.[51] Many people turn to credit cards because credit card companies don't care how borrowers spend the money just as long as they pay the bill. Others use credit cards because they are the only source of funding available to them. But with high interest rates, credit cards are a risky way to finance a business, as Jorge de la Riva discovered. He used personal credit cards to start up his industrial wholesale business—an experience he calls "playing with the tiger." As de la Riva put it, "You can make it work only if you have a definite plan to pay back the debt."[52] Unfortunately, many do not. As we have examined, there are much more intelligent ways to build that dream.

SUMMARY OF LEARNING OBJECTIVES

1 Highlight the major contributions small businesses make to the Canadian economy.

Small businesses bring new ideas, processes, and vigour to the marketplace. According to Statistics Canada's Survey of Employment Payroll and Hours (SEPH), 49 percent of the private labour force was employed by small enterprises with fewer than 100 employees.[53] Small businesses introduce new goods and services, provide specialized products, and supply the needs of large corporations. Additionally, they spend almost as much as big businesses in the economy each year.

2 Identify the key characteristics that differentiate small businesses from larger ones.

In general, small businesses tend to sell fewer products and services to a more targeted group of customers. They have closer contact with their customers and tend to be more open-minded and innovative because they have less to lose than established companies. Small business owners generally make decisions faster and give employees more opportunities for individual expression and authority. Because they have limited resources, however, small business owners must work harder and perform a variety of job functions.

3 Discuss three factors contributing to the increase in the number of small businesses.

One factor is the advancement of technology and the Internet, which makes it easier to start a small business, compete with larger firms, or work from home. A second factor is the increase in the number of women and minority entrepreneurs entering the workforce. Finally, corporate downsizing and outsourcing have made self-employment or small business ownership an attractive and viable option.

4 Cite the key characteristics common to most entrepreneurs.

Entrepreneurs are highly disciplined, intuitive, innovative, ambitious individuals who are eager to learn and like to set trends. They prefer excitement and are willing to take risks to reap the rewards. Few start businesses for the sole purpose of making money.

5 List three ways of going into business for yourself.

You can start a new company from scratch, you can buy a going concern, or you can invest in a franchise. Each option has advantages and disadvantages when it comes to cost, control, certainty, support, and independence.

6 Identify three sources of small business assistance.

One source for small business assistance is the Business Development Bank of Canada (BDC), a federally owned organization that provides financial and consulting services to a select group of firms. Incubators are another source. They provide facilities, business resources, and all types of start-up support. Finally, the Internet is an excellent resource for product and market research, business leads, advice, and contacts.

7 Highlight several factors you should consider when evaluating financing options, and discuss the principal sources of small business private financing.

When assessing financing options, you should consider the cost and risk of capital and the firm's special needs and circumstances. You should also weigh the term for which financing is needed and the advantages and disadvantages of debt versus equity financing, including impact on ownership control. Bank loans are a principal source of private financing. Family and friends are another. Other alternatives include big businesses, venture capitalists, angel investors, and credit cards. Finally, the Canadian Small Business Financing (CSBF) program can assist entrepreneurs by guaranteeing small bank loans up to 85 percent of the amount borrowed.

Behind the SCENES

Mission-Itech: Growing, Diversifying, and Competing

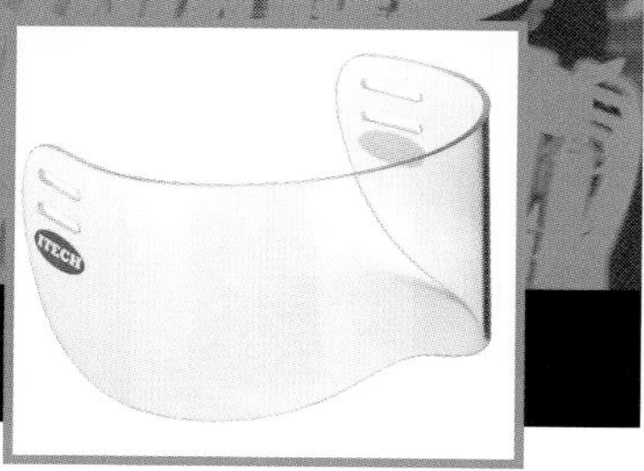

As Itech celebrated its twentieth year of operation, the company was thriving under a diversified product umbrella. Competition for its core visor product was coming from conventional sources like Bauer, Nike, and Easton, as well as from new industry players like Oakley. Despite these challengers, Itech could still proudly lay claim to about two-thirds of the full-face guard visor market. However, the hockey gear industry was transforming itself from a collection of independent firms into a select group of powerful, consolidated companies. Bauer had been acquired by Nike a decade earlier and, more recently, the Hockey Company, which markets the CCM, Koho, Jofa, and Heaton brands, was acquired by Reebok. Itech had previously gone its own way and resisted the merger temptation. However, in May 2004, Itech, the market leader in hockey facial protection, announced that it was merging with Mission Hockey, the California-based market leader in roller hockey equipment and a strong marketer of sticks, skates, and gloves. Each company possessed a diversified but largely complimentary product mix with growing brands.

The new consolidated entity was named Mission-Itech. The combined power of these organizations makes the new company one of the top four players in the market along with the Hockey Company, Bauer/Nike, and Easton. According to Itech's founder, "The merger is a dream come true. It's rare when you find individuals that share your personal faith, love of product and passion for hockey. With the strengths of the brands, and the commitment of this ownership team to winning, the future of Mission-Itech is limitless."

The two brands have maintained their grass roots and build on each others strengths. Mission-Itech continues to be a generous contributor to Canadian minor hockey associations, providing $150 000 worth of equipment annually. It also continues to build on and secure agreements with various leagues. It recently signed a deal with the British Columbia Hockey League (BCHL) to become the league's exclusive helmet and facial protection provider. A similar deal was struck with the Saskatchewan Junior Hockey League (SJHL).

Mission-Itech's future is exciting. The company has established itself as a full-service hockey organization with a proven track record of success. It will be interesting to see how this marriage evolves.[54]

Critical Thinking Questions

1. Do you believe that the merger with Mission was a good fit for Itech? Why? Why not?
2. How will this agreement allow the new firm to compete more effectively in the industry?

Learn More Online

Go to Chapter 4 of this text's website at www.pearsoned.ca/bovee, and click on Mission-Itech to read more about the company. Has the company secured any additional contracts with another hockey league? Is there any news about the integration of the Mission and Itech operations? Are any new products being launched?

KEY TERMS

business plan (101)
franchise (104)
franchisee (104)
franchisor (104)
incubators (107)
initial public offering (IPO) (109)
outsource (100)
secured loans (109)
small business (95)
start-up companies (102)
stock (109)
unsecured loans (109)
venture capitalists (110)

TEST YOUR KNOWLEDGE

Questions for Review

1. What are two essential functions of a business plan?
2. What are the advantages of buying a business rather than starting one from scratch?
3. What are the advantages and disadvantages of owning a franchise?
4. What are the key reasons for most small business failures?
5. What is a business incubator?

Questions for Analysis

6. Why is writing a business plan an important step in starting a new business?
7. Why is it important to establish a time limit for a new business to generate a profit?
8. What things should you consider when evaluating a franchise agreement?
9. What factors should you consider before selecting financing alternatives for a new business?
10. **Ethical Considerations.** You're thinking about starting your own hot dog and burger stand. You have the perfect site in mind, and you've analyzed the industry and all of the important statistics. It looks as if all systems are go. Uncle Daniel is even going to back you on this one. You really understand the fast-food market. In fact, you've become a regular at a competitor's operation (down the road) for over a month. The owner thinks you're his best customer. He even wants to name a sandwich creation after you. But you're not there because you love Heather's fancy fries. No, you're actually spying. You're learning everything you can about the competition so you can outsmart it. Is this behaviour ethical? Explain your answer.

Questions for Application

11. Briefly describe an incident in your life pertaining to a particular failure. What was it and what did you learn from this experience?
12. Take the Entrepreneur Test at www.wd.gc.ca/tools/xindex_e.asp to assess your entrepreneurial skills. What did you learn about yourself from this test? How can tests like these help you fine-tune your business skills?
13. **Integrated.** Entrepreneurs are one of the five factors of production, as discussed in Chapter 1. Review that material plus Exhibit 1.2 (Success Stories; see page 7) and explain why entrepreneurs are an important factor for economic success.
14. **Integrated.** Pick a local small business or franchise that you visit frequently and discuss whether that business competes on price, speed, innovation, convenience, quality, or any combination of those factors. Be sure to provide some examples.

PRACTISE YOUR KNOWLEDGE

SHARPENING YOUR COMMUNICATION SKILLS

Effective communication begins with identifying your primary audience and adapting your message to your audience's needs. This is true even for business plans. One of the primary reasons for writing a business plan is to obtain financing. With that in mind, what do you think are the most important things investors will want to know? How can you convince them that the information you are providing is accurate? What should you assume investors know about your specific business or industry?

BUILDING YOUR TEAM SKILLS

The 10 questions shown in Exhibit 4.5 on page 105 cover major legal issues you should explore before putting down money for a franchise. In addition, however, there are many more questions you should ask when deciding whether to buy a particular franchise.

With your team, think about how to investigate the possibility of buying a Harvey's franchise. First, brainstorm with your team to draw up a list of sources (such as printed sources, Internet sources, and any other suitable sources) where you can locate basic background information about the franchisor. Also list at least two sources you might consult for detailed information about buying and operating a Harvey's franchise. Next, generate a list of at least 10 questions any interested buyer should ask about this potential business opportunity.

Choose a spokesperson to present your team's ideas to the class. After all the teams have reported, hold a class discussion to analyze the lists of questions generated by all teams. Which questions were on most teams' lists? Why do you think those questions are so important? Can your class think of any additional questions that were not on any team's lists but seem important?

EXPAND YOUR KNOWLEDGE

DISCOVERING CAREER OPPORTUNITIES

Would you like to own and operate your own business? Whether you plan to start a new business from scratch or buy an existing business or a franchise, you will need certain qualities to be successful. Start your journey to entrepreneurship by reviewing this chapter's section on entrepreneurs and by studying Exhibit 4.3. Now you are ready to delve deeper into the career opportunities of owning and running a small business.

1. Which of the entrepreneurial characteristics mentioned in the chapter and in Exhibit 4.3 describe you? Which of those characteristics can you develop more fully in advance of running your own business?
2. Using library sources, find a self-test on entrepreneurial qualities. Analyze the test's questions. Which of the characteristics discussed in this chapter are mentioned or suggested by the questions included in the test?
3. Answer all of the questions in the self-test you have selected. Which questions seem most critical for entrepreneurial success? How did you score on this self-test and on the questions you think are most critical? Before you go into business for yourself, which characteristics will you need to work on?

DEVELOPING YOUR RESEARCH SKILLS

Scan issues of print or online editions of business journals or newspapers for articles describing problems or successes faced by small businesses in Canada. Clip or copy three or more articles that interest you and then answer the following questions.

1. What problem or opportunity does each article present? Is it an issue faced by many businesses, or is it specific to one industry or region?
2. What could a potential small business owner learn about the risks and rewards of business ownership from reading these articles?
3. How might these articles affect someone who is thinking about starting a small business?

See It on the **WEB**

URLs for all Internet exercises are provided at the website for this book, www.peasoned.ca/bovee. When you log on to the text website, select Chapter 4, select Destinations, then click on the name of the featured website, and review the website to complete these exercises.

Explore the following chapter-related websites, review their content, and answer the following questions for each website you visit:

1. What is the purpose of this website?
2. What kinds of information does this website contain? Please be specific.
3. How is the information provided at this website useful for business people? Consumers?
4. How did you expand your knowledge of starting and financing a small business by reviewing the material at this website? What new things did you learn about this topic?

GUIDE YOUR WAY TO SMALL-BUSINESS SUCCESS

Canadaone.com has an outstanding selection of articles and advice on buying, owning, and running a small business that you won't want to miss. If you're considering a franchise, the tools and tips at this site will help you find your ideal business. From marketing plans to exporting guides, this site has it covered. Concerned about financing? Check out the articles on raising start-up capital, finding an angel, or attracting venture capital. You can also find information on how to create or spruce up a website, set up your first office, develop entrepreneurial savvy, and overcome burnout. Running a small business is no easy feat, so get a head start by visiting www.canadaone.com.

START A SMALL BUSINESS

Thinking about starting your own business? The Canada Business Services Centres (CBSC) website puts you in touch with a wealth of resources to assist you in your start-up. Perhaps you would like some professional business counselling, financial assistance, or advice on developing a business plan. Starting a new business or buying an existing one can be an overwhelming process. But you can increase your chances of success by taking your first steps with the CBSC Business Start-up Assistant. So log on to find out if entrepreneurship is for you. Then do your research and discover some of the secrets of success. www.cbsc.org/english

LEARN THE ABCS OF IPOS

Taking a company public is not for the faint of heart. But like a Broadway opening, a successful debut can launch a relatively unknown company into stardom—or allow it to quietly disappear from the public eye. Even today's largest corporations were at some point small start-ups looking for public financing. Which company is the next AOL, RIM, or Microsoft? How do IPOs work? How does a young company play the IPO game? You can find the answer to these questions and more by checking out the Beginners Guide to IPOs at Hoover's IPO Central, www.hoovers.com/ipo. Then visit www.baystreet.ca and learn about the latest Canadian listings.

Chapter 5
Selecting the Proper Form of Business Ownership and Exploring Business Combinations

LEARNING OBJECTIVES

After studying this chapter, you will be able to

1. List five advantages and four disadvantages of sole proprietorships
2. List five advantages and two disadvantages of partnerships
3. Explain the differences between common and preferred stock
4. Highlight the advantages and disadvantages of public stock ownership
5. Cite four advantages and three disadvantages of corporations
6. Delineate the three groups that govern a corporation and describe the role of each
7. List advantages and disadvantages offered by the cooperative business format
8. Identify some of the synergies companies hope to achieve by combining their operations
9. Identify how a public company can fight a hostile takeover.

Behind the SCENES

Canadian Home Renovation Centres: Strategic Battleground

www.rona.ca
www.homehardware.ca

Home Hardware and Rona represent two different business models in the increasingly competitive home renovation industry.

During the past decade, the most notable change in the home renovation retail industry has been the expansion of Home Depot into the Canadian marketplace. However, two Canadian companies have chartered their own plans for growth and an increased share in this consolidating industry. Both firms offer an interesting look at evolving business models in the face of an ever-changing environment. Both firms are characterized by striking similarities despite recent strategic differences.

Rona and Home Hardware possess a shared history; they were both created to protect small independent hardware retailers from the threat of large industry discounters. Rona was initially founded in 1939 as a loose coalition of Quebec hardware merchants; by the 1960s the group had emerged as a dealer-owned cooperative. Around the same time, Walter Hatchborn founded Home Hardware in Ontario as a privately held dealer-owned cooperative. The company has not changed much in the past four decades. According to Hatchborn, Home Hardware's philosophy has remained the same: "Maybe I'm stubborn, and I hope that the rest of our dealers are stubborn as well, but I feel that we have to protect the independent from the invasion of large corporations." While Home Hardware hasn't varied from its original strategy, even years after Hatchborn's retirement in 1988, Rona has definitely changed its course. It now represents one of those large publicly traded, growth-oriented corporations that Hatchborn warns against. But Home Hardware is not a helpless victim; it is now a powerful cooperative with revenues of $4 billion and is more than capable of fighting the competition.

The links between Home Hardware and Rona do not end with their initial founding missions. Home Hardware and Rona actually joined forces to create a national wholesaler called United Hardware Wholesalers in 1964. Along with this mutually beneficial partnership came a gentleman's agreement that neither firm would invade the other's territory. Neither firm actively tried to recruit across provincial boundaries and the relationship remained intact for decades.

External pressure from indirect competitors like Canadian Tire, the market entry of retailers like Home Depot Canada, and the threat of other potential entrants like U.S.-based Lowe's led to a new era of relations that would redefine the map. In 2000, Rona bought the Cashway Building Centres in Ontario for $50 million. In 2001, it purchased 51 Revy, Revelstoke, and Lansing stores located in western Canada and Ontario. In 2003, it purchased Quebec-based Reno-Depot along with that company's Ontario brand, The Building Box. This last move effectively blocked Lowe's from its planned entry into the Canadian market. (Lowe's recently announced renewed plans to expand into Canada in 2007. Some analysts have talked about a possible but unlikely merger of Lowe's and Rona.). For its part, Home Hardware doubled its sales with the 1999 acquisition of Beaver Lumber at a cost of $68 million. The gentleman's agreement was over and former allies had become bitter rivals. Both began actively seeking customers in their adversary's home market and across the nation.

Rona and Home Depot each held approximately 14 to 15 percent of the market at the beginning of 2005. At that time, Home Hardware and Canadian Tire claimed about 13 percent each. Rona has boldly set a goal to capture 25 percent of the market by 2007. Home Hardware is out to defend its territory. The true battleground in the next few years is the fight for independent proprietors that still own about 50 percent of the market. Will they be put out of business by the big-box outlets like Home Depot? Will they join with Home Hardware and defend themselves within a cooperative system? Will they opt for the growth machine that Rona represents? How many will resist these forces and fight on as independent proprietors?[1]

CHOOSING A FORM OF BUSINESS OWNERSHIP

One of the most fundamental decisions you must make when starting a business is selecting a form of business ownership. This decision can be complex and have far-reaching consequences for your business. Picking the right ownership structure involves knowing your long-term goals and how you plan to achieve them. Your choice also depends on your desire for ownership and your tolerance for risk. Furthermore, as your business grows, chances are you may change the original form you selected.

The four common forms of business ownership are sole proprietorships, partnerships, corporations, and cooperatives. Each form has its own characteristic internal structure, legal status, size, and fields to which it is best suited (see Exhibit 5.1). Each has key advantages and disadvantages for the owners.

Exhibit 5.1 **Characteristics of the Forms of Business Ownership**

The "best" form of ownership depends on the objectives of the people involved in the business.

STRUCTURE	OWNERSHIP RULES AND CONTROL	TAX CONSIDERATIONS	LIABILITY EXPOSURE	EASE OF ESTABLISHMENT AND TERMINATION
Sole Proprietorship	One owner has complete control.	Profits and losses flow directly to the owners and are taxed at individual rates.	Owner has unlimited personal liability for business debts.	Easy to set up but leaves owner's personal finances at risk. Owner must generally sell the business to get his or her investment out.
Partnership	Two or more owners; each partner is entitled to equal control unless the agreement specifies otherwise. In a limited partnership the general partner controls the business; limited partners don't participate in the day-to-day management.	Profits and losses flow directly to the partners and are taxed at individual rates. Partners share income and losses equally unless the partnership agreement specifies otherwise.	Personal assets of operating partners are at risk from business creditors. In a limited partnership the limited partners are only liable for the amount of their investment.	Easy to set up. Partnership agreement recommended but not required. Partners must generally sell their share in the business to recoup their investment.
Corporation	Unlimited number of shareholders; no limits on stock classes or voting arrangements. Ownership and management of the business are separate. Shareholders in public corporations are not involved in daily management decisions; in private or closely held corporations, owners are more likely to participate in managing the business.	Profits and losses are taxed at corporate rates. Profits are taxed again at individual rates when they are distributed to investors as dividends. The dividend tax credit was created to offset the effects of this double taxation.	Investor's liability is limited to the amount of his or her investment.	Expense and complexity of incorporation varies depending on the jurisdiction; it can be costly. In a public corporation, shareholders may trade their shares on the open market; in a private corporation shareholders must find a buyer for their shares to recoup their investment.

L.O. 1

Sole Proprietorships

sole proprietorship
Business owned by a single individual

A **sole proprietorship** is a business owned by one person (although it may have many employees), and it is the easiest and least expensive form of business to start. Many farms, retail establishments, and small service businesses are sole proprietorships, as are many home-based businesses (such as caterers, consultants, and computer programmers).

Advantages of Sole Proprietorships

A sole proprietorship has many advantages. One is ease of establishment. All you have to do to launch a sole proprietorship is obtain necessary licences, start a chequing account for the business, register a name with the provincial government, and open your doors. Another advantage is the satisfaction of working for yourself. As a sole proprietor, you can make your own decisions, such as which hours to work, whom to hire, what prices to charge, whether to expand, and whether to shut down. Best of all, you can keep all after-tax profits.

As a sole proprietor, you also have the advantage of privacy; you do not have to reveal your performance or plans to anyone. Although you may need to provide financial information to a banker if you need a loan, and you must provide certain financial information when you file tax returns, you do not have to prepare any reports for outsiders as you would if the company were a public corporation.

Disadvantages of Sole Proprietorships

unlimited liability
Legal condition under which any damages or debts attributable to the business can also be attached to the owner because the two have no separate legal existence

One major drawback of a sole proprietorship is the proprietor's **unlimited liability**. From a legal standpoint, the owner and the business are one and the same. Any legal damages or debts of the business are the owner's responsibility. As a sole proprietor, you might have to sell personal assets, such as your home, to satisfy a business debt. If someone sues you over a business matter, you might lose many of your personal possessions if you do not have the proper types and amount of business insurance.

In some cases, the sole proprietor's independence can also be a drawback, because it means that the business depends on the talents and managerial skills of one person. If problems crop up, the sole proprietor may not recognize them or may be too proud to seek help, especially given the high cost of hiring experienced managers and professional consultants. Other disadvantages include the difficulty of a single-person operation obtaining large sums of capital and the limited life of a sole proprietorship. Although some sole proprietors pass their business on to their heirs as part of their estate, the owner's death may mean the demise of the business. Even if the business does transfer to an heir, the founder's unique skills may have been crucial to the successful operation of the business.

L.O. 2

Partnerships

partnership
Unincorporated business owned and operated by two or more people under a voluntary legal association

general partnership
Partnership in which all partners have the right to participate as co-owners and are individually liable for the business's debts

limited partnership
Partnership composed of one or more general partners and one or more partners whose liability is usually limited to the amount of their capital investment

If starting a business on your own seems a little intimidating, you might decide to share the risks and rewards of going into business with a partner. In that case, you would form a **partnership**—a legal association of two or more people as co-owners of a business for profit. You and your partners would share the profits and losses of the business and perhaps the management responsibilities. Your partnership might remain a small, two-person operation or it might have multiple partners.

Partnerships are of two basic types. In a **general partnership**, all partners are considered equal by law, and all are liable for the business's debts. To guard against personal liability exposure, some organizations choose to form a **limited partnership**. Under this type of partnership one or more persons act as *general partners* who run the business, while the remaining partners are passive investors (that is, they are not involved in managing the business). These partners are called *limited partners* because their liability (the amount of money they can lose) is limited to the amount of their capital contribution.

Some North American jurisdictions now recognize *limited liability partnerships* (LLPs). Under this form, all partners in the business are limited partners and have limited liability for the debts and obligations of the partnership. The LLP was created to protect members from being wiped out by claims against their firms. Under this format the limited partners are only liable if they are personally negligent. Most jurisdictions restrict LLPs to professionals such as attorneys, physicians, dentists, and accountants.[2] This form originated in the United States in 1991 and is slowly gaining popularity in Canada, with Alberta, Ontario, Quebec, Saskatchewan, Manitoba, and Nova Scotia enacting various forms of LLPs in recent years.[3]

Advantages of Partnerships

Proprietorships and partnerships have some of the same advantages. Like proprietorships, partnerships are easy to form. Partnerships also provide the same tax advantages as proprietorships, because profits are taxed at individual tax rates rather than at corporate rates. This can lead to savings while the company is in its infancy and profits are fairly modest.

However, in a couple of respects, partnerships are superior to sole proprietorships, largely because there's strength in numbers. When you have several people putting up their money, you can start a more ambitious enterprise. In addition, the diversity of skills that good partners bring to an organization leads to innovation in products, services, and processes, which improves your chances of success.[4] The partnership form of ownership also broadens the pool of capital available to the business. Not only do the partners' personal assets support a larger borrowing capacity but the ability to obtain financing increases because general partners are legally responsible for paying off the debts of the group. Finally, by forming a partnership you increase the chances that the organization will endure, because new partners can be drawn into the business to replace those who die or retire. For example, even though the original partners of the accounting firm KPMG Peat Marwick (founded in 1897) died many years ago, the company has maintained the operations and expanded into a worldwide entity.

Disadvantages of Partnerships

All general partners have unlimited liability. Thus, if one of the firm's partners makes a serious business or professional mistake and is sued by a disgruntled client, all general partners are financially accountable. At the same time, general partners are responsible for any debts incurred by the partnership.

Another disadvantage of partnerships is the potential for interpersonal problems. Difficulties often arise because each partner wants to be responsible for managing the organization. Electing a managing partner to lead the organization may diminish the conflicts, but disagreements are still likely to arise. Moreover, the partnership may have to face the question of what to do with unproductive partners. Additionally, if a partner wants to leave the firm, conflicts can arise over claims on the firm's profits and on capital the partner invested. Provisions for handling the departure and addition of partners are usually covered in the partnership agreement.

Partnership Agreement

A *partnership agreement* is a written document that states the terms of operating the partnership by spelling out the partners' rights and responsibilities. Although the law does not require a written partnership agreement, it is wise to work with a lawyer to develop one. One of the most important features of such an agreement is to address sources of conflict that could result in battles between partners. The agreement spells out such details as the division of profits, decision-making authority, expected contributions, and dispute resolution. Moreover, a key element of this document is the buy/sell agreement, which defines the steps a partner must take to sell his or her partnership interest or what will happen if one of the partners dies.

Corporations

A **corporation** is a legal entity with the power to own property and conduct business. The modern corporation evolved in the nineteenth century when large sums of

corporation
Legally chartered enterprise having most of the legal rights of a person, including the right to conduct business, to own and sell property, to borrow money, and to sue or be sued; owners of the corporation enjoy limited liability

Chairman of the Board Eric Molson led the fight to merge Molson with Adolph Coors to create the fifth-largest brewery in the world.

capital were needed to build railroads, steel mills, and manufacturing plants. Such endeavours required so much money that no single individual or group of partners could hope to raise it all. The solution was to sell shares in the business to numerous investors, who would get a cut of the profits in exchange for their money. These investors got a chance to vote on certain issues that might affect the value of their investment, but they were not involved in managing day-to-day operations. The investors were protected from the risks associated with such large undertakings by having their liability limited to the amount of their investment.

It was a good solution, and the corporation quickly became a vital force in the economy. As rules and regulations developed to define what corporations could and could not do, corporations acquired the legal attributes of people. Like you, a corporation can receive, own, and transfer property; make contracts; sue; and be sued. Unlike the case with sole proprietorships and partnerships, a corporation's legal status and obligations exist independently of its owners.

L.O. 3

shareholders
Proportionate owners of a corporation; based on the number of shares held

stock certificate
Document that proves stock ownership

common stock
Shares whose owners have voting rights and have the last claim on distributed profits and assets

Ownership

The corporation is owned by its **shareholders**, who are issued shares of stock in return for their investments. These shares are represented by a **stock certificate**, and they may be bequeathed or sold to someone else. As a result, the company's ownership may change drastically over time while the company and its management remain intact (as long as the company is economically sound). The corporation's unlimited life span, combined with its ability to raise capital, gives it the potential for significant growth.

Common Stock Most stock issued by corporations is **common stock**. Owners of common stock have voting rights and get one vote for each share of stock they own. They can elect the company's board of directors in addition to voting on major policies that will affect ownership—such as mergers, acquisitions, and takeovers. For example, the fight that emerged after Montreal-based Molson announced that it planned to merge with Colorado-based Coors turned into a battle for shareholder votes. On one side of the Molson fight stood Chairman Eric Molson and his supporters pushing for the deal that would make the merged company the world's fifth-largest brewer. On the other side of the battle stood former deputy chairman Ian Molson, who was opposed to the deal and trying to create a rival bid with Toronto-based Onex and London-based SABMiller PLC. After a hard fight, the deal was finalized with two clear and decisive votes of confidence. The deal was approved by 80 percent of Molson voters and 90 percent of Coors voters.[5]

Besides conferring voting privileges, common stock frequently pays **dividends**, payments to shareholders from the company's profits. Dividends can be paid in cash or stock (called *stock dividends*). They are declared by the board of directors but their payment is not mandatory. For example, some companies, especially young or rapidly growing ones, pay no dividends. Instead, they reinvest their profits in new product research and development, equipment, buildings, and other assets so they can grow and earn future profits. For example, Research In Motion (RIM), the Waterloo, Ontario–based designer, manufacturer, and marketer of wireless communications tools such as the BlackBerry devices, does not pay cash dividends. RIM chooses to focus on a long-term growth strategy.[6]

In addition to dividends, common shareholders can earn a return on their investment. If shareholders sell their stock in good times for more than they paid for it, they stand to pocket a handsome gain. Since the value or price of a company's common stock is subject to many economic variables besides the company's own performance, common stock investments are risky and shareholders may not get any profit at all (see the box entitled "From Rags to Riches to Rags to . . . ").

Avis has never paid cash dividends to shareholders. The company believes that shareholders are best served by reinvesting profits into the company to foster long-term growth.

Preferred Stock In contrast to common stock, **preferred stock** does not usually carry voting rights. It does, however, give preferred shareholders the right of first claim on the corporation's assets (in the form of dividends) after all of the company's debts have been paid. This right is especially important if the company ever goes out of business. Moreover, preferred shareholders get their dividends before common shareholders do. The amount of preferred dividend is usually set (or fixed) at the time the preferred stock is issued and can provide investors with a source of steady income. Like common stock, however, dividends on preferred stock may be omitted in times of financial hardship. Still, most preferred stock is *cumulative preferred stock,* which means that any unpaid dividends must be paid before dividends are paid to common shareholders.

dividends
Distributions of corporate assets to shareholders in the form of cash or other assets

preferred stock
Shares that give their owners first claim on a company's dividends and assets after paying all debts

L.O. 4

Public versus Private Ownership The stock of a **private corporation** such as Cirque du Soleil is held by only a few individuals or companies and is *not publicly traded.* By withholding their stock from public sale, the owners retain complete control over their operations and ownership. Other companies like McCain Foods, The Jim Pattison Group, Kruger, and Hyatt Hotels have opted to remain private corporations (also referred to as *closed corporations* or *closely held companies*). These companies finance their operating costs and growth from either company earnings or other sources, such as bank loans. In contrast, the stock of a **public corporation** is held by and available for sale to the general public; thus the company is said to be *publicly traded.*

private corporation
Company owned by private individuals or companies

public corporation
Corporation that actively sells stock on the open market

In an interview conducted by *60 Minutes*, Guy Laliberte, founder of Cirque du Soleil, was asked why he had not taken his company public. He began to laugh and assured the interviewer that the firm was content as a private corporation. He pointed to his organization's need for creativity that investors, shareholders, and accountants should not be part of. As a private corporation, Cirque does not have to jump through hoops to please investors.[7]

In Chapter 4 we discussed the concept of going public in the context of financing the enterprise. Bear in mind that in addition to providing a ready supply of capital, public ownership has other advantages and disadvantages. Among the advantages are increased liquidity, enhanced visibility, and the establishment of an independent market value for the company. Moreover, having a publicly traded stock gives companies flexibility to use such stock to acquire other firms. This was one of the main reasons UPS decided to sell 10 percent of its stock to the public in 1999, after nearly a century of

From Rags to Riches to Rags to . . .

There is no doubt that great fortunes can be made from common stock investments. However, despite analytical tools and expert opinions, making the right choices can be a difficult proposition. Investors have seen fortunes created and evaporate within years, months, and even days. For a few years during the technology boom of the late 1990s, Nortel was the golden child of the Canadian investment industry. Expert and amateur investors pointed to this firm as a great opportunity with limitless potential. Those who heard the message early were handsomely rewarded as the stock increased tremendously and peaked at $120 in September 2000. Those who made their money and took out their profits were pleased with their capital gains. However, when the technology bubble burst, the stock plummeted from $120 per share into a penny stock valued at $0.67 as of October 2002. Years later, the formerly golden company remains under a cloud of mystery as it issues and reissues financial statements that correct previous misinformation. Will Nortel ever fully recover? Will the company become the pride of Canadian investors again? These questions remain to be answered but Nortel's recent history is a sure reminder that when it comes to stocks, anything is possible.

Questions for Critical Thinking

1. Why did so many investors continue to put good money into Nortel stock as the share price steadily slid from above $120 to below $1?
2. What is the stock worth today? What was it worth 52 weeks ago? Do you believe that Nortel stock is currently a worthwhile investment?

According to founder Guy Laliberte, Cirque du Soleil's business model is not really suited to investor constraints. Creativity is its key to success, and the systems involved in running a public company could dampen creativity. How could you justify a new risky acrobatic act to an accountant?

remaining a privately held organization.[8] Rona first issued stock in 2002, an important step in its plan to expand and become a true national retailer. That stock issue raised $150 million and was followed up by a second issue of stock, in 2003, which raised an additional $150 million. These moves were vital to the firm's various acquisitions, including the purchase of Reno-Depot.[9] Nevertheless, selling stock to the public has distinct disadvantages: (1) the cost of going public is high, (2) filing requirements are burdensome, (3) some ownership control is lost, (4) management must be ready to handle the administrative and legal demands of heightened public exposure, and (5) the value of the company's stock becomes subject to external forces beyond the company's control.

L.O. 5

Advantages of Corporations

No other form of business ownership can match the success of the corporation in bringing together money, resources, and talent; in accumulating assets; and in creating wealth. (Exhibit 5.2 lists the top 20 Canadian companies as ranked by market capitalization). As the corporation grows it capitalizes on a diverse labour pool, greater financing options, and expanded research and development capabilities. The corporation has certain inherent qualities that make it the best vehicle for reaching those objectives. One such quality is limited liability. Although a corporate entity can assume tremendous liabilities, it is the corporation that is liable and not the private shareholders. For example, Johannes Schwartlander ran his marble and granite business as a sole proprietorship for seven years. When the company began to grow, Schwartlander decided to incorporate to protect himself. According to Schwartlander, "When they added so many employees and started installing marble panels ten stories up, he realized that if five years later something fell down, he would be responsible." Incorporation also protects him from personal liability should his business go bankrupt.[10]

Exhibit 5.2 **Top 20 Canadian Corporations Ranked by Market Cap**[11]

RANK	COMPANY	MARKET CAP ($MILLION)	RANK	COMPANY	MARKET CAP ($MILLION)
1	Royal Bank of Canada	47 691	11	Great-West Lifeco Inc.	23 645
2	Manulife Financial Corp.	46 085	12	Sun Life Financial Inc.	22 552
3	Bank of Nova Scotia	39 288	13	Power Financial Corp.	22 462
4	Toronto-Dominion Bank	35 408	14	Shell Canada Ltd.	22 353
5	EnCana Corp.	35 340	15	Newmont Mining Corp. of Canada Ltd.	21 539
6	Imperial Oil Ltd.	31 565	16	Loblaw Cos. Ltd.	20 487
7	Bank of Montreal	28 110	17	Suncor Energy Inc.	20 257
8	BCE Inc.	27 731	18	Canadian National Railway Co.	20 103
9	Thomson Corp.	25 787	19	Brascan Corp.	18 364
10	Canadian Imperial Bank of Commerce	24 818	20	Petro-Canada	17 498

Source: Courtesy of *Canadian Business* Magazine.

In addition to limited liability, corporations that sell stock to the general public have the advantage of **liquidity**, which means that investors can easily convert their stock into cash by selling it on the open market. This option makes buying stock in a corporation attractive to many investors. In contrast, liquidating the assets of a sole proprietorship or a partnership can be difficult. Moreover, shareholders of public corporations can easily transfer their ownership by selling their shares to someone else. Thus, corporations tend to be in a better position than proprietorships and partnerships to make long-term plans, with their unlimited life span and funding available through the sale of stock. As they grow, corporations can benefit from the diverse talents and experience of a large pool of employees and managers. Moreover, large corporations are often able to finance projects internally.

liquidity
The level of ease with which an asset can be converted to cash

Keep in mind that a company need not be large to incorporate. Most corporations, like most businesses, are relatively small, and most small corporations are privately held. The big ones, however, are *really* big. Wal-Mart employs more than 1.3 million people. To put that figure into perspective, only three Canadian cities have a population that surpasses Wal-Mart's employee roster: Vancouver, Toronto, and Montreal.[12]

Hyatt's owners, the Pritzker family, have opted to retain control of their enterprise because they appreciate the long-term value of doing so. That status also has a profound effect on the way Hyatt runs its 213 hotels and resorts worldwide. Public companies, which have an eye trained on the stock price, tend to overlook the long-term effects of decisions in favour of short-term gains. But Hyatt general managers have freedom from concern about quarterly earning reports and stock prices. This gives them a certain entrepreneurial attitude that other hotel managers might not enjoy.

Disadvantages of Corporations

Corporations are not without some disadvantages. The paperwork and costs associated with incorporation can be burdensome, particularly if you plan to sell stock. The complexity varies by jurisdiction, but regardless of where you live, it is wise to consult an attorney and an accountant before incorporating. In addition, corporations are taxed twice. They must pay corporate income tax on the company's profits, and individual shareholders must pay income taxes on their share of the company's profits received as dividends.

Another drawback pertains to publicly owned corporations. As mentioned earlier, such corporations are required by the government to publish information about their finances and operations. Disclosing financial information increases the company's vulnerability to competitors and to those who might want to take over control of the company against the wishes of the existing management. It also increases the pressure on corporate managers to achieve short-term growth and earnings targets in order to satisfy shareholders and to attract potential investors. Some cite such earnings pressure as the driving force behind the aggressive accounting practices recently adopted by some corporations, as Chapter 13 discusses.

subsidiary corporations
Corporations whose stock is owned entirely or almost entirely by another corporation

parent company
Company that owns most, if not all, of another company's stock and takes an active part in managing that other company

Some corporations are not independent but actually owned by a single entity. For example, **subsidiary corporations** are partially or wholly owned by another corporation known as a **parent company**, which supervises the operations of the subsidiary. For example, Mac's Convenience Stores LLC is a subsidiary of Quebec-based Alimentation Couche Tarde. Many of Canada's largest corporations are subsidiaries of foreign companies. For example, Home Depot Canada and General Motors of Canada are subsidiaries of their American parent companies.

L.O. 6

Corporate Governance

Although a corporation's common shareholders own the business, they are rarely involved in managing it, particularly if the corporation is publicly traded. Instead, the common shareholders elect a board of directors to represent them, and the directors select the corporation's top officers, who actually run the company (see Exhibit 5.3).

chief executive officer (CEO)
Person appointed by a corporation's board of directors to carry out the board's policies and supervise the activities of the corporation

The centre of power in a corporation usually lies with the **chief executive officer**, or **CEO**. Together with the chief financial officer (CFO) and the chief operating officer (COO), the CEO is responsible for establishing company policies, managing corporate direction, and making the big decisions that will affect the company's growth and competitive position, as Chapter 6 discusses in detail. Keep in mind that the CEO may also be the chairman of the board, the president of the corporation, or both. Moreover, because corporate ownership and management are separate, the owners may get rid of the managers (in theory, at least) if the owners vote to do so.

proxy
Document authorizing another person to vote on behalf of a shareholder in a corporation

Shareholders Shareholders of a corporation can be individuals, other companies, nonprofit organizations, pension funds, and mutual funds. All shareholders who own voting shares are invited to an annual meeting to choose directors, select an independent accountant to audit the company's financial statements, and attend to other business. Those who cannot attend the annual meeting in person vote by **proxy**, signing and returning a slip of paper that authorizes management to vote on their behalf. Since shareholders elect the directors, in theory they are the ultimate governing body of the corporation. In practice, however, most individual shareholders in large corporations—where the shareholders may number in the millions—accept the recommendations of management. For example, the Bank of Nova Scotia has 1 008 181 000 shares outstanding.[13] An individual investor, with a few hundred shares, will not make an impact on the major policy decisions.

Typically, the more shareholders a company has, the less tangible the influence each shareholder has on the corporation. However, some shareholders have more influence than others. In recent years, *institutional investors* such as pension funds (e.g., Ontario Teacher's Pension Plan, Caisse de Depot), insurance companies, and mutual funds have accumulated an increasing number of shares in Canadian corporations. As

Exhibit 5.3 **Corporate Governance**

In theory the shareholders of a corporation own the business, but in practice they elect others to run it.

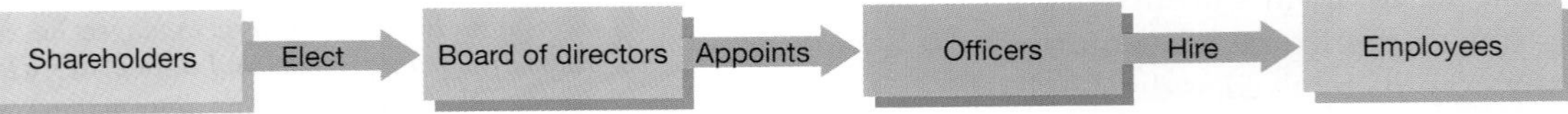

a result, these large institutional investors are playing a more powerful role in governing the corporations in which they own substantial shares, especially with regard to the election of a company's board of directors.[14] Furthermore, at companies such as Avis and Bombardier, employees are major shareholders and so they have a voice in how the company is run.

Board of Directors Representing the shareholders, the **board of directors** is responsible for declaring dividends, guiding corporate affairs, reviewing long-term strategic plans, selecting corporate officers, and overseeing financial performance. Depending on the size of the company, the board might have anywhere from 3 to 35 directors, although 15 to 25 is the typical range for traditional corporations, with a smaller number for e-businesses. The board has the power to vote on major management decisions, such as building a new factory, hiring a new president, or buying a new subsidiary. The board's actual involvement in running a corporation varies from one company to another. Some boards are strong and independent and serve as a check on the company's management. Others act as a "rubber stamp," simply approving management's recommendations. The level of board independence has been steadily improving. According to a recent *Report on Business* review, only 7 percent of companies in Canada's benchmark S&P/TSX index do not have a majority of independent directors on their boards.[15]

board of directors
Group of people, elected by the shareholders, who have the ultimate authority in guiding the affairs of a corporation

Retired CEOs are popular choices to serve on boards. Peter Godsoe, former chairman and CEO of the Bank of Nova Scotia serves on several boards. According to Godsoe, the recruitment process began early: he was courted by companies five years before he actually retired. Former CEOs are popular choices because they possess a wide range of knowledge and invaluable business experience.[16] Former politicians are also attractive candidates for such posts. For example, former prime minister Brian Mulroney sits on the following boards: Barrick Gold, Archer Daniels Midland, Quebecor, Trizec Properties, Forbes Global, and America Online Latin America.[17] Politicians such as Brian Mulroney possess connections at the highest levels of political and business circles. Mulroney is not alone; Brian Tobin and John Manley are recent examples of this selection pattern.

At most large corporations, boards are composed exclusively of directors from outside the company, with only the CEO and a senior executive or two from inside the organization. This arrangement helps ensure that the board provides diligent and independent oversight.[18] But the debate over the optimal number of inside versus outside directors continues. On the one hand, too many insiders can give management too much power over a group whose function is to protect shareholders' rights and investments. On the other hand, outside directors are at a serious information disadvantage. Thus, they must rely largely on the CEO's portrayal of the firm's condition and prospects. Moreover, many outside directors are selected for their accomplishments and stature and are often exceedingly busy. Most are top executives at other companies and typically work 50 to 70 hours per week, travel extensively, and incur a lot of stress in their jobs. Many also serve on the boards of several large companies. Beyond his various boardroom duties, Brian Mulroney is a senior partner in the Montreal-based law firm Ogilvy Renault.

To compensate directors for their time and contributions, most large companies pay their directors a sizable fee and issue them stock options—the right to purchase a set number of shares of stock at a specific price (see Chapter 9). Some think compensation in the form of company stock aligns the directors' interests with those of other stockholders and is the most effective way to get outside directors to vigorously represent the shareholder. Evidence shows that companies in which directors own large amounts of stock and take an active role in guiding the company usually outperform those with more passive boards. Nonetheless, critics of this practice claim that directors with excessive stockholdings could compromise their independent decision making by placing too much focus on a company's short-term stock performance.

Former Prime Minister Brian Mulroney serves on the board of directors of various companies, such as Archer Daniels Midland and Forbes Global.

Recent debacles involving unethical behaviour by corporate directors are shedding new light on the importance of director independence, integrity, and

Every Home Depot director must make formal visits to at least 20 stores each year to gain hands-on knowledge of the company's operation.

compensation. When directors profit from consulting fees or other forms of business transactions as a result of their company board position, they enter into in a conflict of interest situation. Such was the case at Enron, where one outside director received hundreds of thousands of dollars in consulting fees and another director headed a cancer institute that received more than US$1 million in Enron donations.[19] Expect to see more discussion of this topic as the business community re-examines the composition, operations, and roles of company directors in the future.

According to a recent *Report on Business* review, the other end of the spectrum is occupied by firms like Manulife Financial, which has earned the distinction of possessing the top ranked board in both 2002 and 2004. The other members of the distinguished top 10 are the Bank of Montreal, Finning International, Suncor Energy, the Bank of Nova Scotia, CN Railway, Canfor Corp., Enbridge Inc., the Royal Bank of Canada, and Sun Life Financial.[20]

L.O. 7

Cooperatives

Cooperatives are organized and controlled by their members, who pool their resources in order to create benefits for themselves and their clients. The cooperative form is characterized by open voluntary membership and a democratic control mechanism that provides each member with one decision-making vote. Unlike public corporations, which can be controlled by individuals who possess the majority of shares, cooperatives are designed to give each member an equal say.[21] As we saw in the opening feature, Home Hardware operates as a retail cooperative. Membership in this group permits retailers to enjoy the benefits of bulk buying power and centralized advertising, which enables them to compete. There are various forms of cooperatives ranging from financial to housing to retail and beyond. Among the top financial cooperatives are recognizable names such as Desjardins Group, Vancouver City Savings, Coast Capital Savings, Co-Operators Group, Credit Union Central of Saskatchewan, and Credit Union Central of Ontario.[22]

Advantages of Cooperatives

The primary advantage of the cooperative form is the strength provided by being affiliated with a group. When a cooperative negotiates with a manufacturer, on behalf of its members, it possesses the buying power that each individual member would not possess if it negotiated alone. The cooperative form champions the little guy because each member possesses one equal vote; all voices are heard. Furthermore, at the end of the year surplus earnings are distributed to members based on their level of service usage. Finally, members of a cooperative enjoy the protection of limited liability.[23]

Disadvantages of Cooperatives

Of course the cooperative form has its share of drawbacks. The cooperative structure tends to lead to a longer decision-making process and it also demands extensive record keeping. There is also less incentive to invest in additional capital as members may choose short-term surplus dividends over long-term investments. As with all collections of opinions, cooperatives can lead to disagreements and or conflicts among members.[24]

L.O. 8

UNDERSTANDING BUSINESS COMBINATIONS

Companies have been combining in various configurations since the early days of business. Joining two companies is a complex process because it involves every aspect of both companies. For instance, executives have to agree on how the combination will be financed and how the power will be transferred and shared. Marketing departments need to figure out how to blend advertising campaigns and sales forces. Data processing and information systems, which seldom mesh, must be joined together seamlessly. Companies must deal with layoffs, transfers, and changes in job titles and work assignments. Reebok acquired the Hockey Company (CCM, Jofa, Koho) in early 2004. At the time, former Hockey Company CEO Matt O'Toole said that it would be business as usual for the employees. Only time will tell. A decade earlier the acquisition of Canstar Sports (manufacturer of Bauer equipment) was consummated by Nike with similar predictions. A decade later approximately 1400 of the 2200 Canadian employees had lost their jobs.[25]

Mergers and Acquisitions

Two of the most popular forms of business combinations are mergers and acquisitions. In a **merger**, two companies combine forces to create a new entity. Two famous hockey apparel companies, Itech and Mission, recently merged. In May 2004, the two companies ceased to exist as independent companies and a new entity called Mission-Itech was created.[26] Sometimes a merger is referred to as a consolidation; there is a minor technical difference between the two but they are used interchangeably.

merger
Form of business combination in which two companies combine forces to create a new single entity

A company can acquire another firm by purchasing that firm's voting stock. This transaction is generally referred to as an **acquisition** and is completed when the shareholders of the acquired firm tender their stock for either cash or shares of stock in the acquiring company. Recently, Reebok paid CAN$21.25 per outstanding share of the Hockey Company's stock. The total transaction was worth US$204 million.[27] A **leveraged buyout (LBO)** occurs when one or more individuals purchase a company's publicly traded stock by using borrowed funds. The debt is expected to be repaid with funds generated by the company's operations and, often, by the sale of some of its assets. For an LBO to be successful, a company must have a reasonably priced stock and easy access to borrowed funds. Unfortunately, in many cases, the acquiring company must make huge interest and principal payments on the debt, which then depletes the amount of cash that the company has for operations and growth.

acquisition
Form of business combination in which one company buys another company's voting stock

leveraged buyout (LBO)
Situation in which individuals or a group of investors purchase a company primarily with debt secured by the company's assets

Keep in mind that the purpose and outcome of mergers and acquisitions are basically the same, which is why you will often hear these terms used interchangeably.

Advantages of Mergers and Acquisitions

Business combinations provide several financial and operational advantages. Combined companies hope to eliminate expenses for redundant resources, increase their buying power as a result of their larger size, increase revenue by cross-selling products to each other's customers, increase market share by combining product lines to provide more comprehensive offerings, eliminate manufacturing overcapacity, and gain access to new expertise, systems, and teams of employees who already know how to work together. Often these advantages are grouped under umbrella terms such as *economies of scale, efficiencies,* or *synergies,* which generally mean that the benefits of working together will be greater than if each company continued to operate independently.

Disadvantages of Mergers and Acquisitions

Despite the promise of economies of scale, studies of merged companies show that 65 to 85 percent of these deals fail to actually achieve promised efficiencies.[28] One such study even found that the profitability of acquired companies on average declined.[29] Keep in mind that "bigger" does not always equate to "better." Honda is only a fraction of GM's size, yet it has consistently outperformed GM for the past 20 years. As one expert put it, if you combine two lumbering companies, you get one that runs worse, not better.[30]

Part of the problem with mergers is that companies often borrow immense amounts of money to acquire a firm, and the loan payments on this corporate debt gobble up cash needed to run the business. Moreover, managers must help combine the operations of the two entities, pulling them away from their normal day-to-day responsibilities. Another obstacle that companies face when combining forces is that they tend to underestimate the difficulties of merging two cultures.

In Chapter 6, we discuss organizational culture in detail. A company's culture is the way people in the organization do things. Culture includes not only management style and practices but also the way people dress, how they communicate, and whether they punch a time clock. *Culture clash* occurs when two joining companies have different beliefs about what is really important, how to make decisions, how to supervise people, how to communicate, and so on (see the box entitled "Merger of Equals"). Experts note that in too many deals the acquiring company imposes its values and management systems on the acquired company without any regard to what worked well there.

Current Trends in Mergers and Acquisitions

The pace of mergers and acquisitions has increased in recent years as firms have come face to face with global competition. No longer able to hide behind government-imposed barriers, many firms are looking for targets to acquire and/or partners to remain competitive. We have already seen how this trend has had an impact in the

Merger of Equals?

SOUNDS FAMILIAR

When Molson and Coors began negotiating a deal to merge the two companies into one single entity, it was hailed as a merger of equals, as an opportunity to consolidate strengths, create synergies, and move forward united to challenge the competition. Time will tell if this marriage succeeds. Will it be a merger of equals? In order to predict the future, you need to understand the past. This is not the first or the last deal of its kind. Below we will examine the initial announcement and the actual execution of the deal that united Mercedes and Chrysler.

GLOBAL FENDER BENDER

The champagne was on ice when Chrysler and Daimler-Benz announced a stunning US$36 billion merger in May 1998. Headquartered in Germany, DaimlerChrysler would be the world's third-largest automaker. On paper, the companies were a perfect fit—one was strong where the other was weak. Daimler's engineering was legendary, and it was strong in technology. Chrysler excelled at new product design and development. Complementary products and geographical mix would allow them to challenge rivals around the world. Moreover, expected synergies would save the new company US$3 billion annually.

Charged with excitement and curious about each other's cars and culture, the two companies began the integration process. But fundamental differences in management, operational, and decision-making styles made the transition difficult. For example, a German decision would work its way through the bureaucracy for final approval at the top. Then it was set in stone. By contrast, the Americans valued consensus building and shared decision making. Moreover, they allowed mid-level employees to proceed on their own initiative, sometimes without waiting for executive-level approval.

Turf battles also bogged down the combination process. Managers from both sides spent more time defending their way of doing things than promoting the integration of systems. Issues that should have been resolved by managers were bumped up to the company's board of directors. Differences in salary levels and management perks fuelled an undercurrent of tension. The Americans earned two, three, and in some cases four times as much as their German counterparts. But the expenses of U.S. workers were tightly controlled compared with those of the German system. Daimler-Benz employees thought nothing of flying to Paris or New York for a half-day meeting, then capping the visit with a fancy dinner and a night in an expensive hotel.

Friction led to the departure of talented Chrysler mid-level managers and several top Chrysler executives. Chrysler's president, Thomas Stallkamp, who had played a key role in orchestrating the merger, was one of those departing executives. Soon the management board was scaled down from 17 members to 13 (8 Germans and 5 Americans), and the reality became clear: Daimler executives were indeed running the show. DaimlerChrysler wasn't a merger of equals. Instead, Daimler-Benz had acquired Chrysler.

Critical Thinking Questions

1. What prevented DaimlerChrysler from achieving the promised synergies?
2. Which of these stakeholders benefited the most from the merger: the original Chrysler shareholders or the new DaimlerChrysler shareholders? Explain your answer.

home renovation and hardware business as Rona and Home Hardware scramble to meet the new competitive challenges brought by Home Depot Canada. In the insurance industry, Toronto-based Manulife Financial Corp. is no stranger to merger and acquisition practices. In the past decade, it has absorbed Zurich Canada, Commercial Life Insurance Company of Canada, and Daihyaku Mutual Life Insurance Co. of Japan. In 2003, Manulife merged with U.S.-based John Hancock Financial Services in a deal worth US$11 billion.[31] In 2004, Bain Capital LLC of Boston acquired Montreal-based discounter Dollarama in a deal worth about $1.05 billion. This 360-store discounter, formerly owned by the Rossy Group, has outlets in Quebec, Ontario, and the Maritimes.[32] Best Buy purchased Future Shop in 2001 for $580 million in cash; Best Buy/Future Shop is number one in the Canadian computer and consumer electronics retail market.[33] Canadian banks have been waiting for an opportunity to merge; the only reason that they have not done so is because of government regulations in the industry.[34] In 2004, the Jean Coutu Group made a major acquisition in the retail pharmacy business when it acquired the U.S.-based Eckerd Drug Chain for US$2.4 billion.[35] These are just a few examples from a long list.

This trend is not strictly a Canadian one, but evident in business of various sizes, including some of the biggest players in the world. Consider, for instance, the US$160 billion merger of America Online (the world's biggest Internet provider) and Time Warner (the world's biggest media company). This mega-deal, announced only 10 days into the new millennium, linked AOL's 20 million subscribers and unmatched e-commerce capabilities with Time Warner's extensive collection of world-class media, entertainment, news brands, and broadband delivery systems to produce the world's first fully integrated media and communications company.[36] The US$81 billion marriage of Exxon and Mobil created the world's largest oil company, while the US$36 billion combination of Daimler-Benz and Chrysler was the biggest acquisition of any U.S. company by a foreign buyer. In early 2005, the US$57 billion deal between Proctor and Gamble and Gillette enabled P&G to become the number one consumer products company in the world, overtaking Unilever.[37] From telecommunications to banking to oil to automobiles, mass consolidation among industry competitors is one strategy for competing in the global marketplace. As one economist put it, "If you don't play the game as a global company, you're going to wind up a niche player."[38]

Still, after a decade of unprecedented mega-mergers, some of the largest companies are shedding some unprofitable acquisitions and focusing on generating internal growth from their core businesses. Well before the Coors merger, Molson sold off various assets, including the Montreal Canadians hockey club, to focus on its core business of selling beer. Factors contributing to this trend reversal include an economic slowdown, increased political uncertainty, global market saturation, and pressure from shareholders to generate profits. (See the box entitled "Do Mergers Fulfill Management's Responsibility to Shareholders?")

Merger and Acquisition Defences

L.O. 9

Although 95 percent of all business combinations are friendly deals, some 5 percent are **hostile takeovers**, in which one party fights to gain control of a company against the wishes of the existing management.[39] Telus made a hostile bid to purchase Microcell Telecommunications Inc., which sells its wireless phone services under the Fido brand name. That move caught many by surprise, but it was quickly matched and exceeded by Rogers Wireless Communications Inc., which successfully bid $1.4 billion for the firm.[40] Alcan Inc., the Canadian aluminium giant, launched a successful $5 billion hostile bid to acquire French competitor Pechiney SA.[41]

hostile takeovers
Situations in which an outside party buys enough stock in a corporation to take control against the wishes of the board of directors and corporate officers

As mentioned earlier, every corporation that sells stock to the general public is potentially vulnerable to takeover by any individual or company that buys enough shares to gain a controlling interest. Basically, a hostile takeover can be launched in one of two ways: by tender offer or by proxy fight. In a *tender offer,* the raider offers to buy a certain number of shares of stock in the corporation at a specific price. The price offered is generally more than the current stock price so that shareholders are motivated to sell.

Do Mergers Fulfill Management's Responsibility to Shareholders?

For more than a century, mergers and acquisitions have continually changed the face of business. Corporations claim that mergers make them more competitive organizations and thus increase shareholder value. But do shareholders really benefit from mergers? Strong evidence suggests that often they do not.

A study by accounting and consulting firm KPMG showed that 83 percent of mergers failed to produce any benefits for shareholders—supposedly the key beneficiaries. Over half actually diminished shareholder value. Many promises of hefty shareholder returns through cross-selling products and achieving economies of scale by eliminating duplicate operations have failed to materialize. In fact, in many mergers, the only winners appear to be the shareholders of the acquired firm who sell their company stock for more than it was really worth.

Why do such a high percentage of mergers and acquisitions fail? Although no one answer applies to every situation, experts cite these common mistakes:

- *Companies often rush into deals in search of synergies but then fail to develop them.* Once the merger is done, management simply assumes that the computer programmers, sales managers, and engineers will cut costs and boost revenues according to plan.
- *Companies pay excessively high premiums for the companies they acquire.* According to one expert, any time an acquiring company pays a premium of 25 percent or more over the trading price of the acquired company's stock, the acquiring company is exposing itself and its shareholders to substantial risk. Canada 3000 was a growing airline with a good track record. It did not survive the crisis that followed after the September 11, 2001, terrorist attacks. A major reason for this failure was the fact that Canada 3000 overpaid when it acquired Royal Airlines.[42] This example should serve as a warning to WestJet as it seeks growth opportunities after Jetsgo ceased operations in March 2005.
- *Companies are unable to reconcile differences in corporate cultures.* A successful merger requires more than respecting each partner's differences. Procedures must be established to settle disputes and to integrate workforces and product lines strategically.

Without question, some mergers and acquisitions are beneficial to companies and shareholders in both the short term and the long term. Synergies can be realized. However, managers need to approach mergers and acquisitions with caution by answering the following questions: Will the regulatory environment change? How will competitors respond? Do the expected gains justify the up-front costs? Will the cultures of the two companies blend well? Without seeking honest answers to these questions, management may find it difficult to fulfill its obligation to the company's shareholders.

Critical Thinking Questions

1. If you were on the board of directors at a company and the CEO announced plans to merge with a competitor, what types of questions would you want answered before you gave your approval?
2. If a CEO has the opportunity to merge with or acquire another company and is reasonably certain that the transaction will benefit shareholders, is the CEO obligated to pursue the deal? Why or why not?

The raider hopes to get enough shares to take control of the corporation and to replace the existing board of directors and management. In a *proxy fight,* the raider launches a public relations battle for shareholder votes, hoping to enlist enough votes to oust the board and management.

Proxy fights sound easy enough, but they are tough to win. The insiders have certain advantages: They can get in touch with shareholders, and they can use money from the corporate treasury in their campaign. Walter Hewlett, son of Hewlett-Packard's (H-P's) co-founder, faced this uphill battle when he launched a five-month proxy fight against H-P's proposed US$19.4 billion acquisition of Compaq. Hewlett, whose family foundation and trusts owned 5.7 percent of H-P's shares, hoped to kill the largest technology merger in history, arguing that it was too expensive and too risky. Following a narrow victory margin for H-P, dissident Hewlett refused to concede. He sued H-P, alleging that the company had engaged in "improper means" to secure votes that resulted in a "slim but sufficient" majority vote.

Corporate boards and executives have devised a number of schemes to defend themselves against unwanted takeovers:

- *The poison pill.* This plan, triggered by a takeover attempt, makes the company less valuable to the potential raider; the idea is to discourage the takeover from actually happening. A good example is a special sale of newly issued stock to current stockholders at prices below the market value of the company's existing stock. Such action increases the number of shares the raider has to buy, making the takeover more expensive. Many shareholders believe that poison pills are bad for a company, because they can protect weak management and discourage takeover attempts that would improve company value.[44]
- *The golden parachute.* This method is designed to benefit a company's top executives by guaranteeing them generous compensation packages if they ever leave or are forced out after a takeover. These packages often total millions of dollars for each executive and therefore make the takeover much more expensive for the acquiring company. Thus, a golden parachute has an effect similar to that of a poison pill.
- *The shark repellent.* This tactic is more direct; it is simply a requirement that stockholders representing a large majority of shares approve of any takeover attempt. Of course, such a plan is viable only if the management team has the support of the majority of shareholders.
- *The white knight.* This tactic uses a friendly buyer to take over the company before a raider can. White knights usually agree to leave the current management team in place and to let the company continue to operate in an independent fashion.

Hewlett-Packard's former CEO Carly Fiorina claimed victory in the proxy fight over its merger with Compaq Computer Corp. However, a major challenge remained. She had to merge two struggling companies with divergent corporate cultures, restore the confidence of investors, and win over the many employees who opposed the deal. The challenge eventually led to her dismissal in early 2005.[43]

Sometimes a group of investors is able to take a publicly traded company off the open market by purchasing all of the company's stock. This tactic is known as "taking the company private." Descendants of Levi Strauss, for example, borrowed US$3 billion to buy back all the shares of Levi's stock so that the family could maintain control of the company.[45]

Although companies such as Levi Strauss may go private to thwart unwanted takeovers, this is a radical action. First, stockholders must be willing to sell, and second, buyers must have enough cash on hand to repurchase all of the company's stock. Moreover, going private eliminates the firm's ability to raise future capital by selling authorized shares to the public, so it's not a move that many corporations make.

Strategic Alliances and Joint Ventures

In Chapter 2 we discussed strategic alliances and joint ventures from the perspective of international expansion. We defined a strategic alliance as a long-term partnership between companies to jointly develop, produce, or sell products, and we defined a joint venture as a special type of strategic alliance in which two or more firms jointly create a new business entity that is legally separate and distinct from its parents. In this chapter we look at these forms of business combinations as an alternative to a merger or acquisition.

Many strategic alliances are driven by the realization that no single company can offer customers everything they need. Strategic alliances can accomplish many of the same goals as a merger or acquisition without requiring a painstaking process of integration.[46] They can help a company gain credibility in a new field, expand its market presence, gain access to technology, diversify offerings, and share best practices without forcing the partners to become fast friends for life. If the arrangement does not work out or its usefulness expires, the partners can simply go their separate ways.

Companies can also form joint ventures to accomplish the same benefits enjoyed by strategic alliances. Joint ventures are similar to partnerships except that they are formed for a specific, limited purpose. They allow companies to use each other's complementary strengths that might otherwise take too long to develop on their own, and they allow companies to share what may be the substantial cost and risk of starting a new operation.[47] This was the motivation behind the creation of Virgin Mobile Canada, a joint venture between Bell Mobility and Richard Branson's Virgin Group. Neither company needed the other to launch a new cellphone service but the venture made sense to both parties because the deal enabled them to share expertise, knowledge, and networks. Virgin provides specific expertise and brand equity in the youth market whereas Bell provides the best cellphone infrastructure network in Canada.[48]

SUMMARY OF LEARNING OBJECTIVES

1 List five advantages and four disadvantages of sole proprietorships.

Sole proprietorships have five advantages: (1) They are easy to establish, (2) they provide the owner with control and independence, (3) the owner reaps all the profits, (4) profits are taxed at individual rates, and (5) the company's plans and financial performance remain private. The four main disadvantages of a sole proprietorship are (1) the company's financial resources are usually limited, (2) management talent may be thin, (3) the owner is liable for the debts and damages incurred by the business, and (4) the business may cease when the owner dies.

2 List five advantages and two disadvantages of partnerships.

In addition to being easy to establish and having profits taxed at individual rates, partnerships offer a greater ability to obtain financing, longevity, and a broader base of skills. The two main disadvantages of partnerships are unlimited liability for general partners and the potential for personality and authority conflicts.

3 Explain the differences between common and preferred stock from a shareholder's perspective.

Common shareholders can vote and can share in the company's profits through discretionary dividends and adjustments in the market value of their stock. In other words, they can profit from their investment if the value of the stock rises above the price they paid for it, or they can lose money if the value of the stock falls below the price they paid for it. In contrast, preferred shareholders cannot vote, but they can get a fixed return (dividend) on their investment and a priority claim on assets after creditors.

4 Highlight the advantages and disadvantages of public stock ownership.

Public stock ownership offers a company increased liquidity, enhanced visibility, financial flexibility, and an independently established market value for the stock. The disadvantages of public stock ownership are high costs, burdensome filing requirements, loss of ownership control, heightened public exposure, and loss of direct control over the market value of the company's stock.

5 Cite four advantages and three disadvantages of corporations.

Because corporations are a separate legal entity, they have the power to raise large sums of capital, they offer shareholders protection from liability, they provide liquidity for investors, and they have an unlimited life span. In exchange for these advantages, businesses pay large fees to incorporate, and they are subject to double taxation. Finally, if publicly owned, corporations must adhere to strict government reporting requirements.

6 Delineate the three groups that govern a corporation and describe the role of each.

Shareholders are the basis of the corporate structure. They elect the board of directors, who in turn elect the officers of the corporation. The corporate officers carry out the policies and decisions of the board. In practice, the shareholders and board members have often followed the lead of the chief executive officer. However, some board members are more active than others. This is especially true of young dot-com corporations that appoint directors for their management expertise and industry connections.

7 List advantages and disadvantages offered by the cooperative business format.

Cooperatives provide the following advantages: strength in numbers, buying power, a democratic system, and year-end surplus earnings. Cooperatives have the following disadvantages: a long decision-making process, extensive record keeping, less incentive to invest in additional capital and conflicts among members.

8 Identify six main synergies companies hope to achieve by combining their operations.

By combining their operations, companies hope to eliminate redundant costs, increase their buying power, increase their revenue, improve their market share, eliminate manufacturing overcapacity, and gain access to new expertise and personnel.

Identify the defence mechanisms that a public company can employ to combat a hostile takeover.

Corporate boards and executives have come up with a number of techniques (poison pill, golden parachute, shark repellent, white knight) to defend public companies against unwanted takeovers. These approaches can devalue a company in the eyes of potential investors and transform an attractive opportunity into something far less desirable.

Behind the SCENES

Recruiting the Independent Retailer

An estimated 4500 independent retailers still control nearly 50 percent of the home renovation industry. The race to recruit them is intensifying between Home Hardware and Rona. Meanwhile, Home Depot continues to build more big-box stores and has also created a new smaller neighbourhood format (small by Home Depot standards). The small independents will continue to feel pressure to pick sides between the two active recruiters: Home Hardware and Rona. The following examines the options available to retailers with an existing operational store.

COMPARING BUSINESS MODELS

Home Hardware's cooperative network consists of more than 1000 owner-operated retail outlets. The system is served by regional warehouses that are stocked by a single companywide buying arm. Home Hardware also provides a nationwide marketing campaign that emphasizes the diversity of these outlets. Home Hardware is positioned as anti–big box, preferring to focus on service instead. According to Paul Strauss, this non-imposing approach is a key selling point, especially in rural areas.

Rona has a unique approach: it is a publicly traded company with various business models. It consists of a combination of big-box, medium-sized, and neighbourhood outlets with both corporate- and dealer-owned franchise stores as well as affiliated independent dealers. This allows it to absorb independent retailers of all sizes. According to CEO Robert Dutton, "With three types of ownership options and three types of stores the firm now offers nine possible combinations to suit retailers and ensure Rona's growth." Additionally, Rona has raised its profile nationwide by sponsoring Debbie Travis's *Facelift* on HGTV and *Rona Dream Home* on Global. This hybrid system offers something for everyone.

COSTS AND COMMITMENT

Rona expects an initial investment of $96 000 in Rona stock over a four-year period. It also expects its retailers to sign a 10-year contract. Home Hardware does not require a time commitment and the initial investment amounts to just $1500 in member fees.

FINAL THOUGHTS

Paul Strauss, Home Hardware's CEO, is very secretive about the company's plans and he points to this as one of the advantages of running a privately held organization. According to Strauss, his dealers and not some analyst on Bay Street are his first priority. In addition to keeping members informed and placing reasonable investment demands, this model champions the little guy. On the other hand, Rona's CEO, Robert Dutton, can point out that although there is a substantial initial investment, Rona's original dealers each now own $3 to $4 million worth of Rona shares because of the appreciation of their corporate stock. Rona also offers the flexibility of a hybrid system that includes corporate, franchise, and affiliated stores. Critics argue that there is a danger that the small independent affiliated store is so low on the pecking order that it doesn't have much say despite its commitment.

Rona's goal to capture 25 percent of the market will not be easy to attain. But its determination is unquestionable. As 2005 began, it was digesting a recent purchase of the 14-store, Alberta-based Totem Building Supplies Inc. for $100 million in cash. By mid-year Rona was aggressively pursuing the Pro Hardware banner and its 500 Pro-affiliated stores. (Rumours also indicated the company was looking south of the border at Ace, True Value, and Do-It-Best, three dealer-owned co-ops that account for 14 000 stores.)

As it moves forward each additional share of the market will be tougher to earn than the previous one. Home Hardware has its own plans, and so do the other competitors. These remaining independent retailers are standing in the centre of this intensifying market share battlefield.[49]

Critical Thinking Questions

1. Rona's decision to become a publicly traded company was an important element of their expansion plan. How has this decision helped Rona in realizing additional growth?
2. Home Hardware has maintained its strategy as a privately held cooperative. What is the primary goal of such a cooperative?
3. Evaluate the business decision being faced by independent Canadian retailers. Make a list of pros and cons for each option.
   a. Join Rona's corporate growth machine
   b. Join Home Hardware's cooperative business model
   c. Continue operating as an independent
4. If you owned an independent home renovation retail outlet, which model would you opt for? Explain your answer.

Learn More Online

Go to Chapter 5 of this text's website at www.pearsoned.ca/bovee, and click on Rona's hotlink to learn about the company's latest financial results. What were Rona's revenues in the most recent fiscal year? How many stores do they possess? Have they made any major acquisitions in the past 12 months?

KEY TERMS

acquisition (129)
board of directors (127)
chief executive officer (CEO) (126)
common stock (122)
corporation (121)
dividends (123)
general partnership (120)
hostile takeovers (131)
leveraged buyout (LBO) (129)
limited partnership (120)
liquidity (125)
merger (129)
parent company (126)
partnership (120)
preferred stock (123)
private corporation (123)
proxy (126)
public corporation (123)
shareholders (122)
sole proprietorship (120)
stock certificate (122)
subsidiary corporations (126)
unlimited liability (120)

TEST YOUR KNOWLEDGE

Questions for Review

1. What are the four basic forms of business ownership?
2. What is the difference between a general and a limited partnership?
3. What is a closely held corporation, and why do some companies choose this form of ownership?
4. What is the role of a company's board of directors?
5. What is culture clash?

Questions for Analysis

6. Why is it advisable for partners to enter into a formal partnership agreement?
7. To what extent do shareholders control the activities of a corporation?
8. How might a company benefit from having a diverse board of directors that includes representatives of several industries, countries, and cultures?
9. Why do so many mergers fail?
10. **Ethical Considerations.** Your father sits on the board of directors of a large, well-admired, public company. Yesterday, while looking for an envelope in his home office, you stumbled on a confidential memorandum. Unable to resist the temptation to read the memo, you discovered that your father's company is talking with another publicly traded company about the possibility of a merger, with your father's company being the survivor. Dollar signs flashed in your mind. Should the merger occur, the value of the other company's stock is likely to soar. You're tempted to log on to your E*Trade Canada account in the morning and place an order for 1000 shares of that company's stock. Better still, maybe you'll give a hot tip to your best friend in exchange for the four Nickelback tickets that your friend has been flashing in your face all week. Would either of those actions be unethical? Explain your answer.

Questions for Application

11. Suppose you and some friends want to start a business to take tourists on wilderness backpacking expeditions. None of you has much extra money, so your plan is to start small. However, if you are successful, you would like to expand into other types of outdoor tours and perhaps even open up branches in other locations. What form of ownership should your new enterprise take, and why?
12. Selling antiques on the Internet has become more successful than you originally imagined. Overnight your website has grown into a full-fledged business—now generating some $200 000 in annual revenue. It's time to think about the future. Several competing online antique dealers have approached you with a proposal to merge their website with yours to create the premier online antique store. The money sounds good, but you have some concerns about joining forces. What might they be? What other growth options should you consider before joining forces with another business?
13. **Integrated.** In Chapter 2 we discussed international strategic alliances and joint ventures. Why might a Canadian company want to enter into those types of arrangements instead of merging with a foreign concern?
14. **Integrated.** Look back at Chapter 4. How might each of the following small business scenarios affect your selection of a form of business ownership?
    a. You have decided to purchase a franchise operation instead of starting a business from scratch.
    b. You can't tap into your personal financial resources or rely on friends or family for financial assistance.
    c. You are a hard worker, visionary, a risk-taker, highly disciplined, and very bright. But you lack managerial experience.

PRACTISE YOUR KNOWLEDGE

SHARPENING YOUR COMMUNICATION SKILLS

You have just been informed that your employer is going to merge with a firm in Germany. Because you know very little about the German culture and business practices, you think it might be a good idea to do some preliminary research—just in case you have to make a quick trip overseas. Using the Internet or library sources, find information on the German culture and customs and prepare a short report discussing such cultural differences as German social values, decision-making customs, concepts of time, use of body language, social behaviour and manners, and legal and ethical behaviour.

BUILDING YOUR TEAM SKILLS

Directors often have to ask tough questions and make difficult decisions, as you will see in this exercise. Imagine that the director general of your college or university has just announced plans to retire. Your team, playing the role of the school's board of directors, must decide how to choose a new director general to fill this vacancy next semester.

First, generate a list of the qualities and qualifications you think the school should seek in a new director general. What background and experience would prepare someone for this key position? What personal characteristics should this individual possess? What questions would you ask to find out how each candidate measures up against the list of credentials you have prepared? Now list all the stakeholders that your team, as directors, must consider before deciding on a replacement for the retiring director general. Of these stakeholders, whose opinions do you think are most important? Whose are least important? Who will be directly and indirectly affected by the choice? Of these stakeholders, which should be represented as participants in the decision-making process?

Select a spokesperson to deliver a brief presentation to the class summarizing your team's ideas and the reasoning behind your suggestions. After all the teams have completed their presentations, discuss the differences and similarities among credentials proposed by all the teams for evaluating candidates. Then compare the teams' conclusions about stakeholders. Do all teams agree on the stakeholders who should participate in the decision-making process? Lead a classroom discussion on a board's responsibility to its stakeholders.

EXPAND YOUR KNOWLEDGE

DISCOVERING CAREER OPPORTUNITIES

Are you best suited to working as a sole proprietor, as a partner in a business, or in a different role within a corporation? For this exercise, select three businesses with which you are familiar: one run by a single person, such as a dentist's practice or a local landscaping firm; one run by two or three partners, such as a small accounting firm; and one that operates as a corporation, such as Petro-Canada or Telus.

1. Write down what you think you would like about being the sole proprietor, one of the partners, and the corporate manager or an employee in the businesses you have selected. For example, would you like having full responsibility for the sole proprietorship? Would you like being able to consult with other partners in the partnership before making decisions? Would you like having limited responsibility when you work for other people in the corporation?

2. Now write down what you might dislike about each form of business. For example, would you dislike the risk of bearing all legal responsibility in a sole proprietorship? Would you dislike having to talk with your partners before spending the partnership's money? Would you dislike having to write reports for top managers and shareholders of the corporation?

3. Weigh the pluses and minuses you have identified in this exercise. In comparison, which form of business most appeals to you?

DEVELOPING YOUR RESEARCH SKILLS

Review recent issues of business newspapers or periodicals (print or online editions) to find an article or series of articles illustrating one of the following business developments: merger, acquisition, hostile takeover, or leveraged buyout.

1. Explain in your own words what steps or events led to this development.

2. What results do you expect this development to have on (a) the company itself, (b) consumers, and (c) the industry the company is part of? Write down and date your answers.

3. Follow your story in the business news over the next month (or longer, as your instructor requests). What problems, opportunities, or other results are reported? Were these developments anticipated at the time of the initial story, or did they seem to catch industry analysts by surprise? How well did your answers to question 2 predict the results?

See It on the **WEB**

URLs for all Internet exercises are provided at the website for this book, www.pearsoned.ca/bovee. When you log on to this text's website, select Chapter 5, select Destinations, then click on the name of the featured website, and review the website to complete the following exercises.

Explore the following chapter-related websites, review their content, and answer the following questions for each website you visit:

1. What is the purpose of this website?

2. What kinds of information does this website contain? Please be specific.

3. How is the information provided at this website useful for business people? Consumers?

4. How did you expand your knowledge of forms of business ownerships and business combinations by reviewing the material at this website? What new things did you learn about this topic?

CHOOSE A FORM OF OWNERSHIP

Which legal form of ownership is best suited for a new business? Answering this question can be a challenge—especially if you're not familiar with the attributes of sole proprietorships, partnerships, and corporations. That's where Industry Canada's Strategis website, http://strategis.ic.gc.ca, can help. Because there's no right or wrong choice, your job is to understand how each legal structure works and then pick the one that best meets your needs. Start your research by browsing the "Starting a Business" link on the Strategis site. From there be sure to check out the award-winning business start-up assistant site.

FOLLOW THE FORTUNES OF THE FORTUNE 500

Quick! Name the largest corporation in the world, as measured by annual revenues. Give up? Check *Fortune* magazine's yearly ranking of the 500 largest companies. For years, General Motors has topped the list with its US$170 billion-plus in annual revenues, but now Wal-Mart has taken over with more than US$200 billion in annual revenues. The Fortune 500 not only ranks corporations by size but also offers brief company descriptions along with industry statistics and additional measures of corporate performance. You can search the list by ranking, by industry, by company name, or by CEO. www.fortune.com

REPORT ON BUSINESS MAGAZINE'S TOP 1000 CANADIAN COMPANIES

Report on Business Magazine lists the top 1000 publicly traded companies as measured by assets. Visit its site, www.globeinvestor.com/series/top1000/tables/companies/2004/, to view this listing.

BUILD A GREAT BOARD

Want a great board of directors? This inc.com guide contains the best resources for entrepreneurs who are ready to recruit outside directors for their boards. Find out how to recruit board members and how to persuade top-notch people to come on board. Once you've selected your members, learn how to maximize your board's impact and resolve conflicts among board members. Check out one expert's five practical tips for good nuts-and-bolts boardsmanship. www.inc.com/guides/growth/20672.html

Funny Business: Creating a Comedy Club

LEARNING OBJECTIVES

The purpose of this video is to help you

1. Understand the various challenges entrepreneurs face when starting a business from scratch.
2. Identify the advantages and disadvantages of dealing with partners.
3. Examine the importance of leadership vision and energy in small business endeavours.

SYNOPSIS

After years of living out of a suitcase and running from city to city, playing gigs in sites across North America, Rick Bronson seized an opportunity to build his own business. He found this opportunity when Yuk Yuk's moved out of the West Edmonton Mall. But how could someone who makes people laugh for a living handle the stages of stress involved in setting up a business from scratch? Like all aspiring entrepreneurs, Bronson soon realized that plans can be drawn up but they must constantly be adapted to deal with complications. Some of his problems were standard issues that young entrepreneurs face. His construction deadlines were threatened because of delays and he spent much of his time dealing with contractors. He had trouble getting food and beverage licenses, which is a typical problem when dealing with a government bureaucracy. Bronson also began to feel the squeeze of competition when Yuk Yuk's cancelled one of his shows in Ottawa citing conflict of interest. However, all of these problems were minor. Like most start ups, there were plenty of additional issues that Bronson had not counted on. He soon discovered that turning a good idea into reality required total commitment and tireless energy on his part.

Discussion Questions

1. *For analysis:* Based on the definition in the text, does Rick Bronson possess the traits of an entrepreneur?
2. *For analysis:* Did he possess a clear vision of his ultimate goal?
3. *For analysis:* What impact (positive or negative) did Bronson's partners have on the process of transforming his vision into reality?
4. *For application:* Launching a new business is very difficult, but sustaining one and growing it is where entrepreneurs earn their stripes. What should Bronson do to attract more customers and ensure the long-term success of the business?
5. *For debate:* In order for an entrepreneur to be successful, he or she must have an intimate knowledge of the industry with direct applicable experience.

ONLINE EXPLORATION

Visit the Comedy Strip website at www.thecomicstrip.ca and follow the links to read more about Rick Bronson and his comedy club. Has he opened a new location?

On Location VIDEO CASE

Doing Business Privately: Amy's Ice Creams

LEARNING OBJECTIVES

The purpose of this video is to help you

1. Consider the advantages and disadvantages of incorporation.
2. Understand the role that shareholders play in a privately held corporation.
3. Examine the various challenges of entrepreneurship.

SYNOPSIS

Amy's Ice Creams, based in Texas, is a privately held corporation formed in 1984 by Amy Miller and is owned by Miller and a group of family members and friends. At the outset, one of the most important decisions Miller faced was choosing an appropriate legal ownership structure for the new business. Fuelled by the founder's dedication to creating happy ice cream memories for customers, Amy's has continued to evolve and grow. The company now operates 11 stores and rings up close to US$4 million in annual sales. Applying for a job is an adventure in creativity, and Miller welcomes employees' suggestions for new flavours and new promotions to keep sales growing.

Discussion Questions

1. *For analysis:* How does Amy's Ice Creams differ from a publicly held company?
2. *For analysis:* What are some of the particular advantages for a firm such as Amy's Ice Creams?
3. *For application:* How well do you think Amy Miller is working to ensure continued survival and success? Looking ahead to future growth, what marketing, financial, or other suggestions would you make?
4. *For application:* What are some of the issues that Miller may have to confront because her 22 investors are family members?
5. *For debate:* Should Amy's Ice Creams become a publicly held corporation? Support your chosen position.

ONLINE EXPLORATION

Find out what is required to incorporate a business in your province. Begin by searching this Industry Canada webpage: http://strategis.ic.gc.ca/epic/internet/incd-dgc.nsf/en/cs01134e.html for "provincial registrars." The site provides links on incorporating in the various provinces as well as incorporating federally. If you were going to start a small business would you choose to incorporate, or would you choose a different form of legal organization? List the pros and cons of incorporation for the type of business you have chosen.

E-Business IN ACTION

Why Did the Dot-Coms Fall to Earth?

On April 8, 1999, Craig Winn, founder of Value America, became a dot-com billionaire. Investors flocked to his idea of a "Wal-Mart" of the Internet, where shoppers could order jars of caviar along with gas barbecues or desktop computers. The company served as a go-between: It transmitted customer orders immediately to manufacturers, who would ship the merchandise directly to buyers. The company's IPO was a success; its stock closed the first day at US$55 a share, valuing the three-year-old profitless company at US$2.4 billion.

Running on Empty

Twelve months later, Value America filed for bankruptcy protection, and the price of the company's stock fell to 72 cents. The cyber store was supposed to take advantage of every efficiency promised by the Internet: no inventory, no shipping costs, no warehouse, no physical store. But like many Internet entrepreneurs, Winn tried to do too much too soon. Company computers crashed, customers waited to get their orders filled, returned merchandise piled up in the halls of the company's offices, and discounting and advertising drained the company's cash, wiping out any chance of profitability.

Instant Paper Millions

The mid to late 1990s was an era of unbridled optimism; investors displayed an appetite for risk that would have been considered reckless just a few years earlier. A raging bull market, free-flowing capital, and technological advances created so many opportunities at the turn of the millennium that it was difficult to separate a calculated risk from a wild grab at the brass ring. Thus, just about any dot-com company that wanted to sell over the Internet found plenty of eager investors hoping to earn huge profits from the dot-com craze. The Web was like a vast, underdeveloped prairie. The new economy boom led many entrepreneurs to believe that the rules of business had changed. Young entrepreneurs with a good idea and a half-baked business plan could make a couple of phone calls to venture capitalists (VCs) and raise millions. Enthusiastic investors raced to claim a stake in the new frontier at Internet speed. Most went in with their eyes wide shut.

The Party's Over

Amid the popping of champagne corks, troubles soon began to brew. Entrepreneurs learned the hard way that successfully launching a public company is much different than successfully running one. Cyberspace got crowded. New dot-coms went unnoticed. Desperate to get consumers' attention and business, e-tailers spent large amounts on advertising. Some pumped out discount offers and free-shipping promises—hemorrhaging cash and piling up losses. This turn of events prompted investors to take a second look and change their minds—overnight. Profits, it seemed, mattered after all. Many investors watched in shock as dot-com stock prices fell through the floor.

Some, of course, had predicted the dot-com fallout. History, they said, would repeat itself. After all, from 1855 to 1861, the number of start-up telegraph companies in the U.S. alone shrank by 87 percent—from 50 to 6. The Internet, they predicted, would not escape a shakeout of its own. Why did the dot-coms run out of steam? Experts now cite the following reasons for the dot-com shakeout:

- *Poor management.* Many dot-coms were founded by people with cool ideas but no business sense. Some entrepreneurs were in such a rush to go public they forgot one small detail: a sound business plan. They were more attracted by the potential to get rich than by the need to create a company "built to last." Craig Winn's business background, for instance, consisted mainly of leading another public company into bankruptcy. His technology experience? None. Only during such an aggressive period of shallow optimism could someone with Winn's background amass the funds to launch such a risky venture.
- *Unrealistic goals.* Many dot-com start-ups were dedicated to achieving the impossible—launching companies in weeks and attracting millions of customers in months. But the evolution of consumers was far slower than most people predicted. Companies like Kanetix have now emerged and appear to be gaining acceptance in today's market. But at the time people were not ready to buy mortgages and new cars in volume over the Internet. In fact, most Internet firms found that hoped-for volume simply wasn't there. Take online grocers, for example. Buying groceries online requires consumers to make a big change in the way they shop for basic household goods. Online grocers soon discovered that going to the grocery store wasn't as terrible as e-companies had hoped. Moreover, to build a base of customers from scratch, the newcomers had to spend heavily on advertising and other types of marketing. Webvan, for instance, spent 25 to 35 percent of its revenue on advertising, compared with an average of about 1 percent spent by traditional grocers.

- *Going public too soon.* Venture capitalists (VCs), eager to back the next AOL or Amazon, tossed huge sums of money at companies that had barely a prayer of prospering. In many cases, the VCs took the dot-coms public way too soon. Instead of waiting the customary four to five years, dot-coms were taken public in two years or less—long before the company or its management could prove consistent performance to the public. Meanwhile, investors overlooked business fundamentals and threw money at these businesses—driving their stock prices ridiculously high.
- *Fighting the laws of supply and demand.* Demand-driven start-ups such as Cisco are born to fulfill existing needs of consumers or businesses. By contrast, supply-driven start-ups are born in the mind of the entrepreneur with little more than a gut feeling that someone will eventually need or want the company's product or service. Thus, supply-driven start-ups leave the company with the enormous task of establishing a market rather than participating in one. Moreover, with relatively low barriers to entry, other dot-coms could easily copy a good idea. At the turn of the twenty-first century, the supply of start-ups greatly exceeded their demand.
- *Extravagant spending.* Companies spent recklessly to lure customers with special promotions and silly marketing campaigns—no matter the cost. For instance, drkoop.com, an online health site, burned through three-quarters of the US$84 million it raised in an IPO in less than one year. Losses, of course, were excused as a necessary evil in the pursuit of new customers. Some dot-coms even began to act like conventional retailers—building costly warehouses and adding staff—to compete. Webvan officials argued in the company's early stages that the centres, which could handle up to 8000 orders a day—many times more than a traditional warehouse—would give it a big cost advantage over its traditional competitors. But it never gained the sales volume to take full advantage of the efficiencies, and so its gross margins trailed those of large traditional grocers. After spending US$830 million in start-up and IPO funds, Webvan sought bankruptcy protection and began liquidating its assets.
- *Locked out of cash.* Most dot-coms were started with venture capital. When they burned through that money, they had to find new funding or go public. For many, neither happened. Once more and more dot-coms began to fail, investors forced companies to cut costs vigorously, look for merger candidates, postpone or scrap their plans to go public, find a buyer at any price, or close up shop.

As a result of the shakeout, some dot-coms changed their plans to go public; the market was forced to come to its senses and the overnight money grabs of the dot-com bubble were part of history.

Return to Yesteryear

Although the dot-com world has slowly risen to its feet; today's entrepreneur has more reasonable expectations about the time and effort required to build a business, a resistance to get-rich-quick schemes, and an appetite for risk moderated by a sense of responsibility. In short, they're grown-ups. Today, not only must entrepreneurs work harder to make a convincing case before going public, but they must prove their ability to manage costs and show a clear sign of profitability (old-economy rules) before venture capitalists will consider them. Of course, there's always room for new killer ideas, but the IPO window of opportunity has closed for many. Meanwhile, Internet tycoons who scoffed at traditional business models have found out why they're traditional: They work.

Despite the long list of failed attempts there are real-life examples of companies properly employing new technologies. For example, Quebec-based Mediagrif Interactive Technologies is a publicly traded company with 410 employees and 12 e-business networks. The company links buyers and sellers in diverse industries: automotive parts, medical supplies, and heavy equipment. Its Wine Traders Club serves a specific niche and traffics in hard-to-find bottles. Even more shocking, in comparison to the early pioneers of e-commerce exchanges, the company announced profits of $3.2 million in the first quarter of 2005.[50]

Critical Thinking Questions

1. Why did many dot-com businesses fail at the beginning of the twenty-first century?
2. How did the attitude of dot-com investors change? Why did it change?
3. Why is it more difficult for entrepreneurs to start a dot-com business in today's environment?

Business PlanPro **EXERCISES**

Starting and Organizing a Small Business

Review Appendix C, "Your Business Plan" (see pages 397–398), to learn how to use Business PlanPro Software so you can complete these exercises.

Think Like a Pro

Objective: By completing these exercises you will become acquainted with the sections of a business plan that address forms of ownership, financing the enterprise, and the franchising alternative. You will use the sample business plan for Pegasus Sports (listed as Inline Skating Products in the Sample Plan Browser) in this exercise.

1. What form of ownership does Pegasus currently use? What are the advantages of selecting that form of ownership? What change in ownership form is Pegasus planning to make?
2. How is Pegasus financing its start-up operations? Has the company gone public (or does the plan indicate it wants to go public)?
3. Would you recommend that Pegasus use franchising to grow its business? Explain your answer.

Create Your Own Business Plan

Think about your own business. What form of ownership will you choose? Why? How much start-up money will you need? How will you finance your start-up costs? Where will you obtain the money you will need to grow your business? Enter your answers in the appropriate sections of your business plan.

Part 3
Managing a Business

Chapter 6
Understanding the Functions and Roles of Management

LEARNING OBJECTIVES

After studying this chapter, you will be able to

1. Define the four basic management functions
2. Outline the tasks involved in the strategic planning process
3. Explain the purpose of a mission statement
4. List the benefits of setting long-term goals and objectives
5. Cite three leadership styles and explain why no single style is superior to the others in every situation
6. Clarify how total quality management (TQM) is changing the way organizations are managed
7. Identify and explain the three types of managerial skills

Behind the SCENES

Nokia: A Finnish Fable

www.nokia.com

Many of you swear by your Nokia phone, but did you know that Nokia first entered the Canadian marketplace, nearly thirty years ago, selling tires and footwear? For more than a century Nokia, the Finnish-based corporation, produced everything from diapers and toilet paper to tires and rubber boots. All that changed during the early 1990s when a global recession threw the company into a tailspin. More than 125 years of profitable operations came to a sudden standstill when Nokia's customers stopped buying its products. The collapse of the Soviet Union, Finland's chief trading partner, made matters worse. Moreover, Nokia's struggling mobile phone division couldn't keep up with the mass production techniques used by competitors. By the time Jorma Ollila was appointed CEO in 1992, the company was losing US$80 million a year.

Ever since Jorma Ollila took charge of Nokia, the company has reported one success story after another.

Challenged to come up with a survival plan, Ollila took a gigantic gamble. He believed that people have a tendency to get complacent and that it takes a push to tap into their strongest instincts—those that guide success. Ollila and several colleagues concluded that mobile phones were about to move from business markets to consumer markets. So he ditched Nokia's multiple interests and gave the company a single, new focus: wireless telecommunications. He beefed up research and development, and soon the company developed a line of phones with stylish features to meet the mood of the market.

While rivals stumbled, Nokia came up with the best products, the best manufacturing logistics, and the best brand name in telecom. Still, Ollila knew that transforming a manufacturer of pulp, paper, chemicals, and rubber into a mobile-phone leader would require much more than just shedding its old skin and developing innovative products. If you were in Jorma Ollila's position, what management skills would you use to lead Nokia into a promising but different future? Would you assume an autocratic leadership style, or would you opt for a more hands-off approach? How would you transform your vision into reality? What goals would you establish to transform the stodgy Finnish conglomerate into a mobile phone industry leader?[1]

L.O. 1

THE FOUR BASIC FUNCTIONS OF MANAGEMENT

management
Process of coordinating resources to meet organizational goals

roles
Behavioural patterns associated with or expected of certain positions

Jorma Ollila knows that when managers possess the right combination of vision, skill, experience, and determination, they can lead an organization to success. Ollila also knows that not everyone is equipped to be an effective manager. So he focuses on finding the right managers to help him turn his vision into reality. In this chapter we explore the four basic functions that **management** entails: planning, organizing, leading, and controlling resources (land, labour, capital, and information) to efficiently reach a company's goals (see Exhibit 6.1).[2] We also highlight and examine the skills required for effective management.

In the course of performing the four management functions, managers play a number of **roles** that fall into three main categories:

- *Interpersonal roles.* Managers perform ceremonial obligations; provide leadership to employees; build a network of relationships with bosses, peers, and employees; and act as a liaison to groups and individuals both inside and outside the company (such as suppliers, competitors, government agencies, consumers, special-interest groups, and interrelated work groups).

Exhibit 6.1 The Four Basic Functions of Management

Although these functions tend to occur in a somewhat progressive order, sometimes they occur simultaneously, and often the process is ongoing.

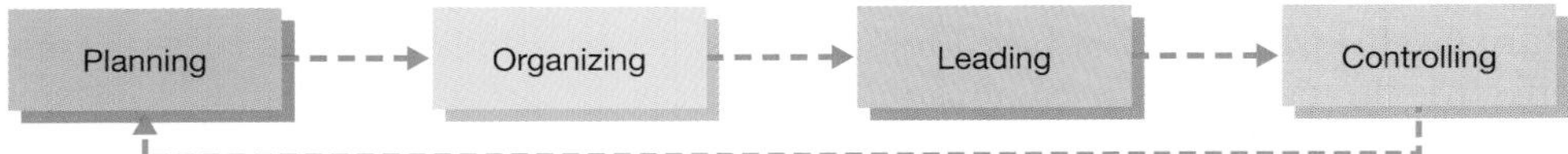

- *Informational roles.* Managers spend a fair amount of time gathering information by questioning people both inside and outside the organization. They also distribute information to employees, their managers, and outsiders.
- *Decisional roles.* Managers use the information they gather to encourage innovation, to resolve unexpected problems that threaten organizational goals (such as reacting to an economic crisis), and to decide how organizational resources will be used to meet planned objectives. They also negotiate with many individuals and groups, including suppliers, employees, and unions.[3]

Being able to move among these roles while performing the four basic management functions is just one of the many skills that managers must possess. But these functions are not discrete; they overlap and influence one another. Let's examine them in detail.

planning
Establishing objectives and goals for an organization and determining the best ways to accomplish them

strategic plans
Plans that establish the actions and the resource allocation required to accomplish goals; usually defined for periods of two to five years and developed by top managers

vision
A viable view of the future that is rooted in but improves on the present

The Planning Function

Planning is the primary management function, the one on which all others depend. Managers engaged in **planning** develop strategies for success, establish goals and objectives for the organization, and translate their strategies and goals into action plans. To develop long-term strategies and goals, managers must be well informed on a number of key issues and topics that could influence their decisions. A closer look at the strategic planning process will give you a clearer idea of the types of information managers need to help them plan for the company's future.

L.O. 2

Understanding the Strategic Planning Process

Strategic plans outline the firm's long-range (two to five years) organizational goals and set a course of action the firm will pursue. These long-term goals encompass eight major areas of concern: market standing, innovation, human resources, financial resources, physical resources, productivity, social responsibility, and financial performance.[4] A good strategic plan answers: Where are we going? What is the environment? How do we get there?

To answer these questions and establish effective long-term goals, managers require extensive amounts of information. For instance, managers must study budgets, production schedules, industry and economic data, customer preferences, internal and external data, competition, and so on. Managers use this information to set a firm's long-term course of direction during a process called *strategic planning*, which consists of six steps: developing a clear vision, creating a mission statement, developing forecasts, analyzing the competition, establishing goals and objectives, and developing action plans.

When John Lederer took over as head of Loblaws he had a tough act to follow. Within a few years he has made his mark and was identified as an all-star executive by Canadian Business. *His predecessor, Richard Currie, gets a lot of the credit for turning Loblaws into an industry powerhouse, but John Lederer and his team had their own unique challenges to address. For example, to deal with the Wal-Mart challenge, the grocer cut costs and prices and improved non-food offerings. It also launched the highly successful Real Canadian Superstores chain in the west, with plans to bring these megastores east.*

Develop a Clear Vision Most organizations are formed in order to realize a **vision**—a realistic, credible, and attainable view of the future that grows out of and improves on the present.[5] Fred Smith (founder of FedEx) envisioned making FedEx an information company (besides being a transportation company). Bill Gates (chairman of Microsoft) envisioned empowering people through great software, anytime, anyplace, and on any device. Nokia's Jorma Ollila was able to see, before others, that mobile phones would fill an important need in the consumer market. Henry Ford envisioned making affordable transportation available to every person. If Ballard Power, the Burnaby, British Columbia-based fuel cell maker, successfully commercializes a truly effective alternative to the combustion engine it will represent an equally important achievement. Without such visionaries, who knows how the world would be different? Thus, developing a clear vision is a critical task in the strategic planning process. But having a vision alone is no guarantee of success; it must also be communicated to others, executed, and modified as conditions change.

L.O. 3

mission statement
A statement of the organization's purpose, basic goals, and philosophies

Translate the Vision into a Meaningful Mission Statement To transform vision into reality, managers must define specific organizational goals, objectives, and philosophies. A starting point is to write a company **mission statement**, a brief document that defines why the organization exists, what it seeks to accomplish, and the principles that the company will adhere to as it tries to reach its goals (see Exhibit 6.2). Put differently, a mission statement communicates what the company is, what it does, and where it's headed. Typical components of a mission statement include the company's product or service; primary market; fundamental concern for survival, growth, and profitability; managerial philosophy; and commitment to quality and social responsibility.

Another important function of a mission statement is to bring clarity of focus to members of the organization. A mission statement helps employees understand how their role is tied to the organization's greater purpose. Thus, it should inspire and guide employees and managers in such a way that they can understand the firm's vision and

Exhibit 6.2 Mission Statement

The mission statement for Dell Computer embodies the firm's high standards for quality and customer service.

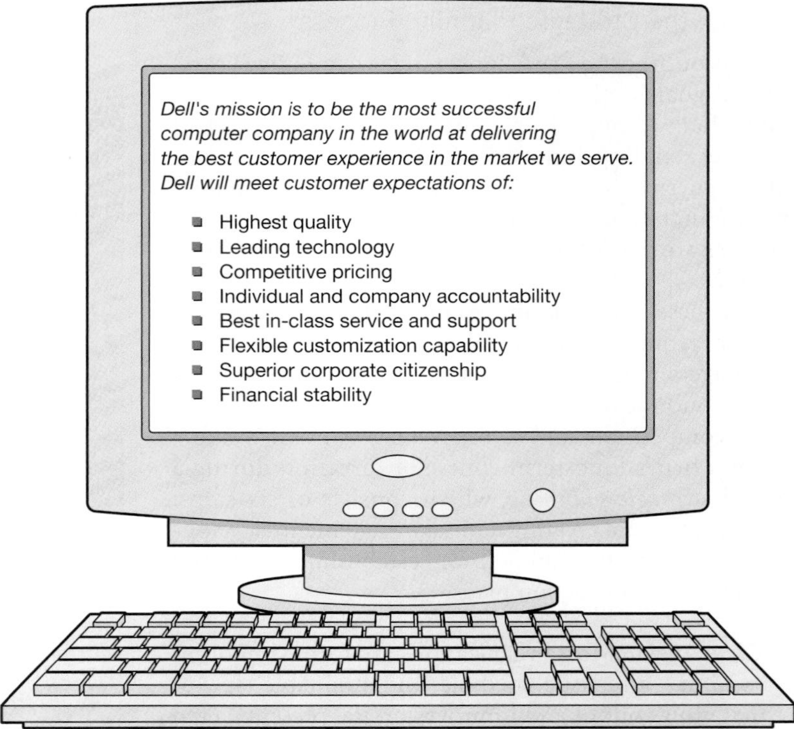

identify with it. Furthermore, the statement must be congruent with the organization's core values. Managers should use it to assess whether new project proposals are within the scope of the company's mission.[6]

Develop Forecasts To develop forecasts, managers must make a number of educated assumptions about future trends and events and modify those assumptions once new information becomes available. Some managers rely on expert forecasts such as those found in *Industry Week*'s "Trends and Forecasts," *Business Week*'s "Survey of Corporate Performance," and Standard & Poor's *Earnings Forecast* as a foundation for their projections. However, these sources may not always include key variables specific to an individual company or industry. Therefore, managers must also develop their own forecasts.

Managerial forecasts fall under two broad categories: *quantitative forecasts,* which are typically based on historical data or tests and which involve complex statistical computations, and *qualitative forecasts,* which are based on intuitive judgments or consumer research. Statistically analyzing the cycles of economic growth and recession over several decades to predict when the economy will take a downward turn is an example of quantitative forecasting. Making predictions about sales of a new product on the basis of experience and consumer responses to a survey is an example of qualitative forecasting. Neither method is foolproof, but both are valuable tools, enabling managers to fill in the unknown variables that inevitably crop up in the planning process.

Analyze the Competition "Business is like any battlefield. If you want to win the war, you have to know who you're up against," says one management consultant.[7] Thus, sizing up the competition is another important task in planning for a company's future. It gives management a realistic view of the market, the company's position in it, and its ability to attain certain goals (see the box entitled "Shoppers Drug Mart: Setting a Direction in Competitive Times"). Managers begin the competitive analysis process by identifying existing and potential competitors. Next they determine the competencies, strengths, and weaknesses of their major competitors. Armed with competitive information, they look for ways to capitalize on a competitor's weaknesses or match or surpass its strengths to gain a competitive edge.

A company can gain a competitive edge through at least one of three strategies:

- *Differentiation.* A company using differentiation develops a level of service, a product image, unique product features (including quality), or new technologies that distinguish its products from the competition. Volvo, for instance, stresses the safety of its cars. Caterpillar Tractor emphasizes product durability.
- *Cost leadership.* Businesses that pursue this strategy aim to become the low-cost leader in an industry by producing or selling products more efficiently and economically than competitors. Cost leaders have a competitive advantage by reaching buyers whose primary purchase criterion is price. Wal-Mart is a typical industry cost leader; its suppliers must justify all aspects of price in order to earn Wal-Mart's business.
- *Focus.* When using a focus strategy, companies concentrate on a specific regional market or consumer group, such as the Maritime provinces or drivers of economy cars. This type of strategy enables organizations to develop a better understanding of their customers and to tailor their products specifically to customer needs.[8] For example, Holt Renfrew retail outlets tailor their offerings to meet the needs of an upscale, sophisticated, brand-conscious clientele.

L.O. 4

Establish Company Goals and Objectives As mentioned earlier, establishing goals and objectives is the key task in the planning process. Although these terms are often used interchangeably, a **goal** is a broad, long-range accomplishment that the organization wishes to attain in typically five or more years, whereas an **objective** is a specific, short-range target designed to help reach that goal. For Nokia Canada, a goal might be to increase market share of mobile phone sales in Canada by 25 percent over the next five

goal
Broad, long-range target or aim

objective
Specific, short-range target or aim

Shoppers Drug Mart: Setting a Direction in Competitive Times

Shoppers Drug Mart (Pharmaprix in Quebec) was founded in 1962 by Murray Koffler. He had a vision to build a national chain that could provide the personalized service available at independent local pharmacies. That initial vision was the cornerstone of an expansion that led to the eventual emergence of 915 Shoppers Drug Mart outlets and 49 Shoppers Home Health Care centres.

Today Shoppers Drug Mart faces very distinct competitive challenges that will test it to the core. Loblaws and Wal-Mart have increased their pharmacy businesses and are offering clients the ability to fill prescriptions while shopping for groceries. The company is also feeling the heat from more traditional competitors like the Edmonton-based Katz Group that has 1800 stores under such banners as IDA and PharmaPlus. Additionally, Jean Coutu possesses 316 stores in Quebec, Ontario, and New Brunswick. Jean Coutu has a dominant share of the Quebec market and has already made a major expansion into the United States by acquiring the Brooks Pharmacy chain and more recently acquiring the 1549 Eckerd pharmacies. The competitors each have their own strategies that will likely result in more intense competition ahead.

Glenn Murphy has been the CEO of Shoppers Drug Mart since 2000. At that time, the competitive landscape demanded a re-evaluation and Murphy was just the man to provide a new perspective. He had a range of experience earned as CEO of Chapters as well as from various high-level posts he held during his 14 years at Loblaws, one of Shopper Drug Mart's new indirect challengers. He has earned the reputation of being a hands-on leader. While many of his peers are out on the golf greens, Glenn Murphy usually spends his Saturday afternoons visiting various stores and talking to employees (from cashiers to managers) on their home turf. He has turned this information into an updated vision for the company.

In order to compete in this new environment Shoppers Drug Mart is making important changes. First, new products have been added to the shelves and the chain is carrying more convenience goods. Second, the stores have been given a face lift. New central locations are also getting bigger; the average size of new outlets is now 15 000 square feet, doubling the size of old locations. Third, Shoppers is increasing private label brand presence in its stores (on average private labels provides 15 percent more profit per unit than national brands). Murphy understands private label issues, having spent 14 years at Loblaws during the emergence of the President's Choice brand. Fourth, Shoppers is trying to increase its cosmetics presence by adding higher-end lines. The cosmetics industry is worth $1.6 billion in Canada. Shoppers Drug Mart has a significant portion of the $1 billion market of moderately priced cosmetics, selling brands like Revlon and Maybelline. However, it only has a single-digit market share in the $600 million high-end cosmetics business. If Murphy has anything to say about it, that will soon change as the company pursues brands like Christian Dior and Chanel. It will not be easy.

The chain now generates more than $6.5 billion in annual revenue and growing. It remains to be seen whether the strategy pays off in the long term, but initial returns are promising.[9]

Questions for Critical Thinking

1. What do you think of the changes at Shoppers Drug Mart? Can the company fend off direct and indirect competitors with its updated approach?
2. Visit the Shoppers Drug Mart website at www.shoppersdrugmart.ca and find the company's most recent financial results (i.e., last year and last quarter). Analyze and discuss the results.

years, and an objective might be to sell 100 000 mobile phones to Canadian customers by year-end. To be effective, organizational goals and objectives should be specific, measurable, relevant, challenging, attainable, and time limited. For example it is better to state "increase our sales by 25 percent over the next five years" than "substantially increase our sales."

Setting appropriate goals has many benefits: It increases employee motivation, establishes standards for measuring individual and group performance, guides employee activity, and clarifies management's expectations. By establishing organizational goals, managers set the stage for the actions needed to achieve those goals. If actions aren't planned, the chances of reaching company goals are slim.

Develop Action Plans Once managers have established a firm's long-term strategic goals and objectives, they must then develop a plan of execution. **Tactical plans** lay out the actions and the allocation of resources necessary to achieve specific, short-term objectives that support the company's broader strategic plan. Tactical plans typically focus on departmental goals and cover a period of one to three years. Their limited scope permits them to be changed more easily than strategic plans. **Operational plans** designate the actions and resources required to achieve the objectives of tactical plans. Operational plans usually define actions for less than one year and focus on accomplishing a firm's specific objectives, such as developing a strategic partnership with another company.

Keep in mind that many highly admired CEOs have stumbled not because they didn't have strategies for success, but because they didn't execute their strategies or deliver on their commitments. That's because developing a strategy or vision is less than half the battle. It's executing it that counts. In today's information age, strategies quickly become public property. Everyone knows Dell's direct business model, for example, yet few companies, if any, have successfully copied its execution.

tactical plans
Plans that define the actions and the resource allocation necessary to achieve tactical objectives and to support strategic plans; usually defined for a period of one to three years and developed by middle managers

operational plans
Plans that lay out the actions and the resource allocation needed to achieve operational objectives and to support tactical plans; usually defined for less than one year and developed by first-line managers

crisis management
System for minimizing the harm that might result from some unusually threatening situations

Planning for a Crisis

No matter how well a company plans for its future, any number of problems can arise to threaten its existence. An ugly fight for control of a company, a product failure, a breakdown in routine operations (as a result of fire, for example), or an environmental accident could develop into a serious and crippling crisis. Managers can help a company survive these setbacks through **crisis management**, a plan for handling such unusual and serious problems.

The goal of crisis management is to keep the company functioning smoothly both during and after a crisis. Successful crisis management requires comprehensive contingency plans in addition to speedy, open communication with all who are affected by the crisis. Experts suggest setting up a crisis communications team with a knowledgeable spokesperson to handle the many requests for information that arise during a crisis. The individuals selected should be able to remain honest and calm when a crisis hits. Moreover, top managers should be visible in the hours immediately following the crisis to demonstrate that the company will do whatever is necessary to control the situation as best it can, find the cause, and prevent a future occurrence.[10]

Even the most efficient systems can go down and create chaos. In 2004, when the Royal Bank (RBC) experienced a major computer glitch, company executives and public relations people scrambled to calm their clients and fix the problem. The computer glitch occurred during a routine software upgrade; the end result was that millions of transactions were not processed over a two-day period. In the following hours and days, RBC addressed all aspects of the problem: it fixed the technical malfunction, extended its business hours and opened more locations on Saturdays to temporarily service concerned customers, and finally addressed its stakeholders with statements like the following from Rod Pennycook, an executive vice-president at the bank: "We recognize this has caused not only our own clients but also clients of some other institutions considerable inconvenience and for this we sincerely apologize." Many firms spent countless

Quick action and contingency planning enabled RBC to recover quickly after a routine computer upgrade triggered a processing disruption that led to millions of unprocessed transactions. The bank addressed all stakeholders, temporarily adjusted operational procedures, and reassured the general public.

hours and dollars preparing for the Y2K crisis at the end of the twentieth century but the problem never materialized. However, all of that preparation and crisis planning helped RBC deal with this unexpected event.[11]

The Organizing Function

organizing
Process of arranging resources to carry out the organization's plans

Organizing, the process of arranging resources to carry out the organization's plans, is the second major function of managers. During the organizing stage, managers think through all activities that employees carry out (from programming the organization's computers to mailing its letters), as well as all facilities and equipment employees need in order to complete those activities. They also give people the ability to work toward organizational goals by determining who will have the authority to make decisions, to perform or supervise activities, and to distribute resources.

The organizing function is particularly challenging because most organizations undergo constant change. Long-time employees leave, and new employees arrive. Equipment breaks down or becomes obsolete, and replacements are needed. The public's tastes and interests change, and the organization has to re-evaluate its plans and activities. Shifting political and economic trends can lead to employee cutbacks—or perhaps expansion. Long-time competitors take unexpected actions, and new competitors enter the market. Every week the organization faces new situations, so management's organizing tasks are never finished. Consider Microsoft. The company continually challenges itself by asking: "Are we making what customers want and working on products and technologies they'll want in the future? Are we staying ahead of all our competitors? What don't our customers like about what we do? What are we doing about it? Are we organized most effectively to achieve our goals?"[12]

management pyramid
Organizational structure comprising top, middle, and lower management

top managers
Those at the highest level of the organization's management hierarchy; they are responsible for setting strategic goals, and they have the most power and responsibility in the organization

middle managers
Those in the middle of the management hierarchy; they develop plans to implement the goals of top managers and coordinate the work of first-line managers

The organizing function will be discussed in detail in Chapter 7. In this chapter, however, we will discuss the three levels of a corporate hierarchy—top, middle, bottom—commonly known as the **management pyramid** (see Exhibit 6.3). In general, **top managers** are the upper-level managers who have the most power and who take overall responsibility for the organization. An example is the chief executive officer (CEO). Top managers establish the structure for the organization as a whole, and they select the people who fill the upper-level positions. Top managers also make long-range plans, establish major policies, and represent the company to the outside world at official functions and fundraisers.

Middle managers have similar responsibilities, but usually for just one division or unit. They develop plans for implementing the broad goals set by top managers, and they coordinate the work of first-line managers. In traditional organizations, managers

Exhibit 6.3 **The Management Pyramid**

Separate job titles are used to designate the three basic levels in the management pyramid.

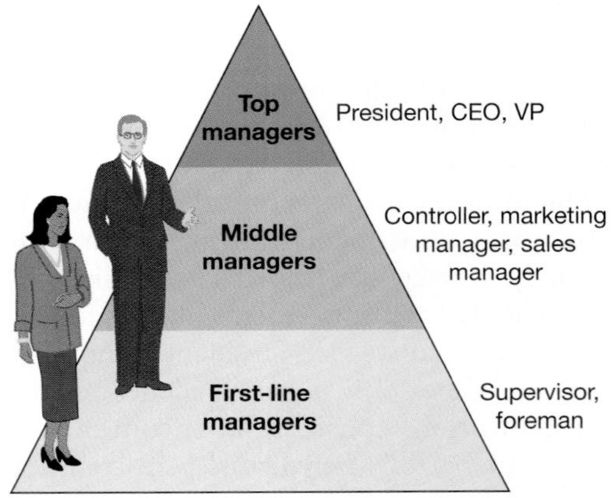

at the middle level are plant managers, division managers, branch managers, and other similar positions, all reporting to top-level managers. But in more innovative management structures, middle managers often function as team leaders who are expected to supervise and lead small groups of employees in a variety of job functions. Similar to consultants, they must understand every department's function, not just their own area of expertise. Furthermore, they are granted decision-making authority previously reserved for only high-ranking executives.[13]

At the bottom of the management pyramid are **first-line managers** (or *supervisory managers*). They oversee the work of operating employees, and they put into action the plans developed at higher levels. Positions at this level include supervisor, department head, and office manager.[14] Even though more managers are at the bottom level than at the top, as illustrated in Exhibit 6.3, today's leaner companies tend to have fewer levels, flattening the organizational structure, as Chapter 7 points out.

first-line managers
Those at the lowest level of the management hierarchy; they supervise the operating employees and implement the plans set at the higher management levels; also called supervisory managers

The Leading Function

Leading, the process of influencing and motivating people to work effectively and willingly toward company goals, is the third basic function of management. Leading becomes even more challenging in today's business environment, where individuals who have different backgrounds and unique interests, ambitions, and personal goals are melded into a productive work team. Managers with good leadership skills have greater success in influencing the attitudes and actions of others, both through the demonstration of specific tasks and through the manager's own behaviour and spirit. Furthermore, effective leaders are good at *motivating*, or giving employees a reason to do the job and to put forth their best performance (see Chapter 9).

leading
Process of guiding and motivating people to work toward organizational goals

What makes a good leader? When early researchers studied leadership, they looked for specific characteristics, or *traits*, common to all good leaders. At the time, they were unable to prove any link between particular traits and leadership ability. However, researchers found that leaders who have specific traits, such as decisiveness and self-confidence, are likely to be more effective.[15] Additional studies have shown that managers with strong interpersonal skills and high emotional quotients (EQs) tend to be more effective leaders. The characteristics of a high EQ include:[16]

- *Self-awareness.* Self-aware managers have the ability to recognize their own feelings and how they, their job performance, and other people are affected by those feelings. Moreover, managers who are highly self-aware know where they are headed and why.
- *Self-regulation.* Self-regulated managers have the ability to control or reduce disruptive impulses and moods. They can suspend judgment and think before acting. Moreover, they know how to use the appropriate emotion at the right time and in the right amount.
- *Motivation.* Motivated managers are driven to achieve beyond expectations—their own and everyone else's. They can capture people's attention and guide them to reach goals. (Chapter 9 takes a comprehensive look at motivating employees.)
- *Empathy.* Empathetic managers thoughtfully consider employees' feelings, along with other factors, in the process of making intelligent decisions.
- *Social skill.* Socially skilled managers tend to have a wide circle of acquaintances, and they have a knack for finding common ground with people of all kinds. They assume that nothing important gets done by one person alone and have a network in place when the time for action comes.

Keep in mind that these traits alone do not define a leader. Different leadership traits are appropriate under different leadership situations.[17]

Adopting an Effective Leadership Style

L.O. 5

Leadership style is the way a manager uses authority to lead others. Every manager, from the baseball coach to the university chancellor, has a definite style. The three broad categories of leadership style are *autocratic*, *democratic*, and *laissez-faire*.

Meg Whitman, CEO of eBay, is a perfect example of a democratic leader. She attributes much of eBay's success to involvement of employees and managers in decision making. "I'm really proud of what we've created at eBay, but I haven't done it alone," says Whitman. "It really has been our management team and the people that come to eBay and build our community. It's a partnership." Fortune recently named Meg Whitman the most powerful businesswoman.[18]

Autocratic leaders make decisions without consulting others. "My way or the highway" summarizes this style, which tends to go with traditional, hierarchical organizational structures. Although autocratic leadership can be highly effective when quick decisions are necessary, it does little to empower employees or encourage innovation. Al Dunlap, former CEO of Sunbeam, used an autocratic leadership style to try to turn the failing household appliance maker around. True to his word, Dunlap turned Sunbeam inside out and upside down—and nearly destroyed the company with his "chainsaw" management style—crushing employee morale and creating unbearable stress by exerting excruciating pressure on his staff. As Dunlap liked to brag, "I don't get heart attacks, I give them."[19]

In contrast, **democratic leaders** delegate authority and involve employees in decision making. Even though their approach can lead to slower decisions, soliciting input from people familiar with particular situations or issues may result in better decisions. An effective democratic leader also builds a work environment in which employees are not afraid to make a mistake and are encouraged to step out and make suggestions. This breeds organizational growth and creativity.[20] As more companies adopt the principles of teamwork, democratic leadership continues to gain in popularity.

autocratic leaders
Leaders who do not involve others in decision making

democratic leaders
Leaders who delegate authority and involve employees in decision making

laissez-faire leaders
Leaders who leave the actual decision making up to employees

The third leadership style, laissez faire, is sometimes referred to as free-rein leadership. The French term *laissez faire* can be translated as "leave it alone," or more roughly as "hands off." **Laissez-faire leaders** take the role of consultant, encouraging employees' ideas and offering insights or opinions when asked. The laissez-faire style may fail if workers pursue goals that do not match the organization's goals. However, the style has proven effective in some situations. Managers at Hewlett-Packard's North American distribution organization adopted a laissez-faire style when they were given nine months to reorganize their order-fulfillment process. The managers eliminated all titles, supervision, job descriptions, and plans, and they made employees entirely responsible for the project. At first there was chaos. However, employees soon began to try new things, make mistakes, and learn as they went. In the end, the team finished the reorganization ahead of schedule, reduced product delivery times from 26 days to 8 days, and cut inventory by 20 percent. Moreover, the employees experienced a renewed sense of challenge, commitment, and enjoyment in their work.[21]

More and more businesses are adopting democratic and laissez-faire leadership as they reduce the number of management layers in their corporate hierarchies and increase the use of teamwork. However, experienced managers know that no one leadership style works every time. In fact, new research shows that leaders with the best results do not rely on only one leadership style; instead they adapt their approach to match the requirements of the particular situation.[22] Adapting leadership style to current business circumstances is called **contingency leadership**. You can think of leadership styles as existing along a continuum of possible leadership behaviours, as suggested by Exhibit 6.4.

contingency leadership
Adapting the leadership style to what is most appropriate, given current business conditions

Coaching and Mentoring

Managers can provide effective leadership by coaching and mentoring their employees. On a winning sports team, the coach focuses on helping all team members perform at their highest potential. In a similar way, *coaching* managers strive to bring out the best in their employees.

Coaching involves taking the time to meet with employees, discussing any problems that may hinder their ability to work effectively, and offering suggestions and encouragement to help them find their own solutions to work-related challenges.

coaching
Helping employees reach their highest potential by meeting with them, discussing problems that hinder their ability to work effectively, and offering suggestions and encouragement to overcome these problems

Exhibit 6.4 **Continuum of Leadership Behaviour**

Leadership style occurs along a continuum, ranging from boss-centred to employee-centred. Situations that require managers to exercise greater authority fall toward the boss-centred end of the continuum. Other situations call for a manager to give workers leeway to function more independently.

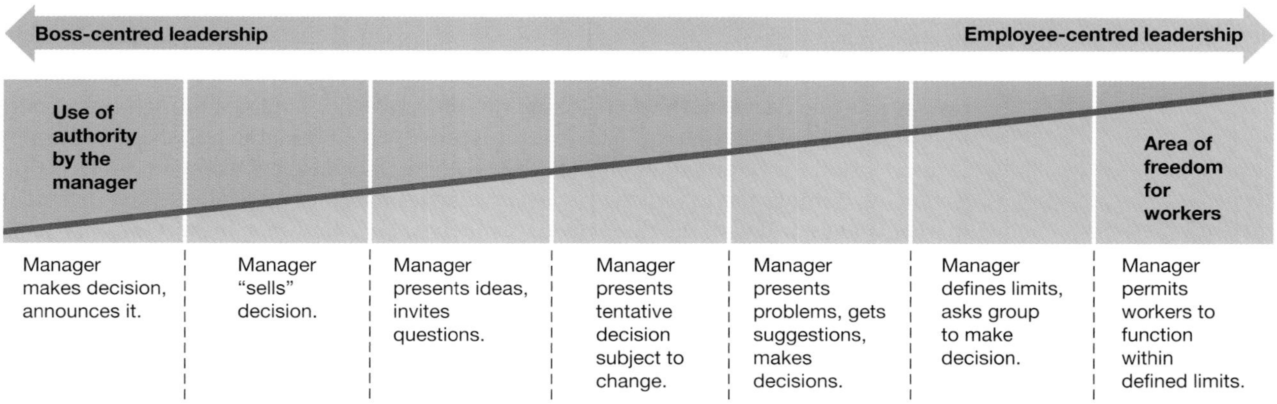

This process requires keen powers of observation, sensible judgment, and both a willingness and an ability to take appropriate action. However, just as a sports coach cannot play the game for team members, a coaching manager must step back and let employees perform when it's "game time." Coaching managers develop a solid game plan and empower their team to carry it out. If the team gets behind, the manager offers encouragement to boost morale. When team members are victorious, the manager recognizes and praises their outstanding achievement.[23]

Acting as a mentor is similar to coaching, but mentoring also emphasizes helping employees understand how the organization works. A **mentor** is usually an experienced manager or employee who can help guide other employees through the corporate maze. Mentors have a deep knowledge of the business and a useful network of industry colleagues. In addition, they can explain office politics, serve as a role model for appropriate business behaviour, and provide valuable advice about how to succeed within the organization. Your mentor won't necessarily be your boss. Relationships with mentors often develop informally between the individuals involved. However, some companies have established formal mentoring programs. In the program at Xerox, women employees can spend a few hours every month discussing work or career issues with any of the participating women executives.[24] Mentoring offers benefits for both parties: the less-experienced employee gains from the mentor's advice and ideas, and the mentor gains new networking contacts in addition to personal satisfaction.

mentor
Experienced manager or employee with a wide network of industry colleagues who can explain office politics, serve as a role model for appropriate business behaviour, and help other employees negotiate the corporate structure

Managing Change

Another important function of leaders is to manage the process of change. As competitive pressures get worse, the pace of change accelerates while companies search for even higher levels of quality, service, and overall speed. Sometimes managers initiate change; other times change is imposed from outside the company. Nonetheless, effective leaders refrain from launching new initiatives until current ones are embedded in the company's DNA. Take GE's former CEO Jack Welch as an example. He introduced only five major initiatives in his 18 years as CEO.[25] Leaders such as Welch provide a powerful vision to pull people in a desired direction.[26] Then they work with employees to ensure that the change process goes smoothly.

Managing change is a difficult process; even previous experience does not guarantee success. For example, Paul Tellier is a highly respected CEO who has received numerous awards for his leadership. He was largely credited with turning Canadian National Railway "from a bloated turkey into one of the continent's biggest and most profitable transportation players." More recently the change initiatives at his former post, as CEO of

Bombardier, did not achieve the same level of success. For instance, the sale of Bombardier's recreational division (which makes all-terrain vehicles and Ski-Doo and Sea-Doo vehicles) was criticized because many believed that the division was sold at a bargain basement price. The initial sales price was announced as $1.22 billion but according to the annual report, after adjustments, the sale netted Bombardier $740 million. This figure was just four times division earnings; at the time Bombardier's stock was trading at 12 times earnings. To make matters worse, the financial results at the Bombardier recreational entity have been very promising since the sale. The future of Bombardier does not rest on this one decision; the recreational division was only a small although historically important part of the company. However, this move was an initial step in shaping the new focused vision for Bombardier. In today's challenging business environment every action is vital. As Bombardier makes the necessary changes to retool, to deal with the turbulent market, and to deal with the threat from competitors like Embraer, important stakeholders like the firm's employees and investors will be watching. Bombardier has a major challenge over the next few years, and the firm has decided to tackle it without Tellier.[27]

According to one recent study, about 70 percent of all change initiatives fail.[28] Resistance to change often arises because people don't understand how it will affect them. Mention change and most people automatically feel victimized. Some worry that they may have to master new skills—ones that might be difficult. Others fear that their jobs will be in jeopardy. Experts advise that if managers want less resistance to change, they should build trust with employees long before the change arrives and, when it does, explain to them how it will affect their jobs. Moreover, cultivating constant change on a small scale can prepare employees for even larger changes; it's the difference between asking someone to run a race who has never even practised before versus asking someone to run a race who jogs every day.[29]

Building a Strong Organizational Culture

Strong leadership is a key element in establishing a productive *organizational culture*—the set of underlying values, norms, and practices shared by members of an organization. When you visit an organization, observe how the employees work, dress, communicate, address each other, and conduct business. Each organization has a special way of doing things. In corporations, this force is often referred to as **corporate culture**.

corporate culture
A set of shared values and norms that support the management system and that guide management and employee behaviour

A company's culture influences the way people treat and react to each other. It shapes the way employees feel about the company and the work they do; the way they interpret and perceive the actions taken by others; the expectations they have regarding changes in their work or in the business; and their ability to lead, be productive, and choose the best course of action (see the box entitled "How Much Do You Know about the Company's Culture").

Enron, once the world's leading market maker in electricity and natural gas, didn't fail just because of improper accounting or alleged corruption at the top. It also failed because of its culture—one that emphasized earnings growth and rewarded aggressive behaviour to such an extent that it fostered unethical corner cutting. Top performers were rewarded with huge cash bonuses and stock-option grants—a system that encouraged "every man for himself" instead of teamwork. Moreover, monetary and stock rewards were granted by a performance review committee. This system bred a culture in which people were afraid to go against anyone who could influence their review, and the whole culture at the vice-president level and above turned into a "yes-man" culture.

Things weren't much better in the lower ranks. Young people—many just out of undergraduate or MBA programs with little experience and perspective—were handed extraordinary authority and decision-making power. Some were even swiftly advanced to senior-level positions. It was like a bunch of kids running loose without adult supervision. So if senior managers were fudging earnings, the inexperienced managers assumed that this was the way it was done at most businesses.[30]

Of course, Enron is not the first or the last example of corruption and corporate culture gone bad. Even seasoned veterans have been known to push the limits into the domain of the illegal. For example, allegations surrounding the Woodbridge,

How Much Do You Know about the Company's Culture?

Before you accept a job at a new company, it's a good idea to learn as much as possible about the company's culture. Use this list of questions to guide you in your investigation.

COMPANY VALUES

- Is there a compelling vision for the company?
- Is there a mission statement supporting the vision that employees understand and can implement?
- Do employees know how their work relates to this vision?
- Is there a common set of values that binds the organization together?
- Do officers/owners follow these values, or is there a gap between what they say and what they do?

PEOPLE

- How are people treated?
- Is there an atmosphere of civility and respect?
- Is teamwork valued and encouraged, with all ideas welcomed?
- Are employee ideas acknowledged, encouraged, and acted upon?
- Are employees given credit for their ideas?
- Is there a positive commitment to a balance between work and life?
- Is there a commitment from top management to support working parents?

COMMUNITY INVOLVEMENT

- Is the company involved in the community?
- Is there a corporate culture of service?
- Is there a stated policy of community involvement by the company and its employees?

COMMUNICATION

- Is there open communication?
- Do officers/owners regularly communicate with all levels?
- Are the customer service and financial results widely distributed?
- Is there meaningful two-way communication throughout the organization?
- Are employee surveys on workplace issues conducted and published? Are employees asked for input on solutions?
- Is there an open-door policy for access to management?

EMPLOYEE PERFORMANCE

- How are personnel issues handled?
- Is employee feedback given regularly?
- Are employee evaluations based on agreed-upon objectives that have been clearly communicated?
- Are employees asked to provide a summary of their accomplishments for placement into their evaluations?

Questions for Critical Thinking

1. How might a job candidate find the answers to these questions?
2. Why is it important to learn about the company's culture before accepting a job?

Ontario-based Royal Group emerged and seemed eerily familiar. The company's senior executives were accused of "systematically deceiving and defrauding shareholders in a scheme to transfer money to a luxury Caribbean resort development owned by Chairman Victor De Zen."[31]

The Controlling Function

Controlling is the fourth basic managerial function. In management, **controlling** means monitoring a firm's progress toward meeting its organizational goals and objectives, resetting the course if goals or objectives change in response to shifting conditions, and correcting deviations if goals or objectives are not being attained.

controlling
Process of measuring progress against goals and objectives and correcting deviations if results are not as expected

Exhibit 6.5 **The Control Cycle**

The control cycle has four basic steps: (1) On the basis of strategic goals, top managers set the standards by which the organization's overall performance will be measured. (2) Managers at all levels measure performance. (3) Actual performance is compared with the standards. (4) Appropriate corrective action is taken (if performance meets standards, nothing other than encouragement is needed; if performance falls below standards, corrective action may include improving performance, establishing new standards, changing plans, reorganizing, or redirecting efforts).

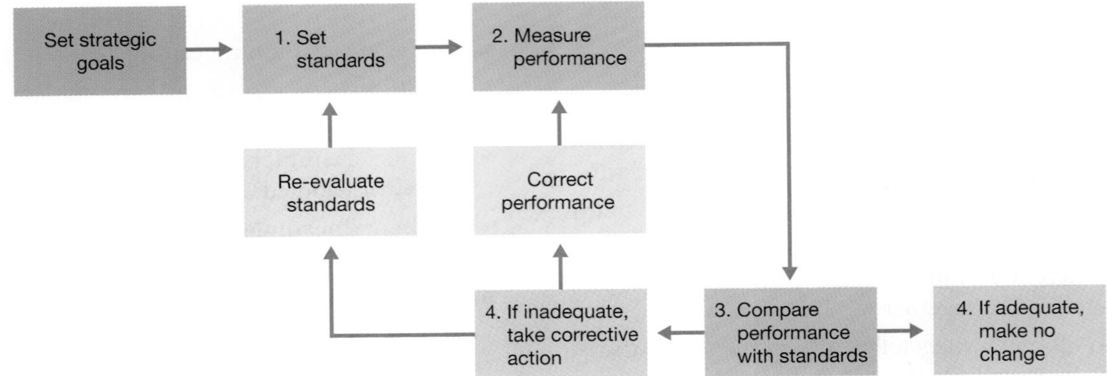

The Control Cycle

quality
A measure of how closely a product conforms to predetermined standards and customer expectations

standards
Criteria against which performance is measured

Managers strive to maintain a high level of **quality**—a measure of how closely goods or services conform to predetermined standards and customer expectations. Many firms control for quality through a four-step cycle that involves all levels of management and all employees (see Exhibit 6.5). In the first step, top managers set **standards**, or criteria for measuring the performance of the organization as a whole. At the same time, middle and first-line managers set departmental quality standards so they can meet or exceed company standards. Establishing control standards is closely tied to the planning function and depends on information supplied by employees, customers, and other external sources. Examples of specific standards might be "Produce 1500 circuit boards monthly with less than 1 percent failures."

In the second step of the control cycle, managers assess performance, using both quantitative (specific, numerical) and qualitative (subjective) performance measures. In the third step, managers compare performance with the established standards and search for the cause of any discrepancies. If the performance falls short of standards, the fourth step is to take corrective action, which may be done by either adjusting performance or re-evaluating the standards. If performance meets or exceeds standards, no corrective action is taken. As Exhibit 6.5 shows, if everything is operating smoothly, controls permit managers to repeat acceptable performance. If results are below expectations, controls help managers take any necessary action.

Take Nokia Canada. Suppose the company does not reach its objective of selling 100 000 Nokia mobile phones to Canadian customers by year-end. With proper control systems in place, managers will evaluate why this objective was not reached. Perhaps they will find that a shortage of parts created manufacturing delays. Or perhaps the market where sales were targeted became saturated with cellphones made by competitors. Regardless, management will search for the cause of the discrepancies before modifying the company's objectives or trying a different approach to achieve the company's long-term goals. Control methods are examined in greater detail in Chapter 8.

L.O. 6

Total Quality Management

The controlling function is an important part of total quality management, which is sometimes referred to as *total quality control.* In the past, *control* often meant those little sticky tags attached to new items that say "inspected by #47." Companies would inspect finished products and rework or discard items that didn't meet quality standards. Today, this inspection step is only one small part of the total control process.

total quality management (TQM) Comprehensive, strategic management approach that builds quality into every organizational process as a way of improving customer satisfaction

Total quality management (TQM) is both a management philosophy and a strategic management process that focuses on delivering the optimum level of quality to customers by building quality into every organizational activity (see Exhibit 6.6). Total quality management draws its ideas, principles, and tools from psychology, sociology, statistics, management, and marketing. The goal of TQM is to create an environment that encourages people to grow as individuals and to learn to bring about continuous and breakthrough improvements. Companies that adopt TQM create a value for all stakeholders—customers, employees, owners, suppliers, and the community.[32] Additionally, many companies seek out and attain ISO 9000 certification, which is a global standard set by the International Organization for Standardization that establishes a minimum level of quality management. This will be discussed in greater detail in Chapter 8.

The four key elements of TQM are employee involvement, customer focus, benchmarking, and continuous improvement.

participative management Sharing information with employees and involving them in decision making

- *Employee involvement.* Total quality management involves every employee in quality assurance. Workers are trained in quality methods and are empowered to stop a work process if they feel that products or services are not meeting quality standards. Managers also encourage employees to speak up when they think of better ways of doing things. This approach exemplifies a **participative management** style—the sharing of information at all levels of the organization (also known as *open-book management*). By directly involving employees in decision making, companies increase employees' power in an organization and improve the flow of information between employees and managers. Borg-Warner Automotive (BWA) is a global player in the auto industry with facilities in 14 countries, including a plant in Simcoe, Ontario. BWA is a manufacturer of highly engineered components and systems for vehicle engines and transmissions, and participatory management is ingrained in the company's culture. The product emphasis there is high tech and the workforce emphasis is high involvement. Management understands that people are the true drivers of improvement.[33]
- *Customer focus.* Focusing on the customer simply means finding out what customers really want and then providing it. This approach requires casting aside assumptions about customers and relying instead on accurate research. It also requires developing long-term relationships with customers. Harry Rosen's retail outlets have earned a reputation for excellent customer service with their core clients. The company's approach goes far beyond the sales experience. Harry Rosen spends a lot of time getting in tune with the consumer, conducting market research, organizing special parties for its clients, and using its database to meet the needs of the consumer.
- *Benchmarking.* This element of TQM involves comparing your company's processes and products against the standards of the world's best companies and then working to match or exceed those standards. This process involves rating the manufacturing process, product development, distribution, and other key functions against those of acknowledged leaders; analyzing how those role models achieve their outstanding results; and then applying that knowledge to make quality improvements. Among the world-class organizations frequently cited as benchmarks for production are Toyota, IBM, and Hewlett-Packard; for distribution, FedEx; and for customer service, American Express.[34]
- *Continuous improvement.* This key feature of TQM requires an ongoing effort to reduce defects, cut costs, slash production and delivery times, and offer customers innovative products. Improvements are often small, incremental changes that add up to greater competitiveness over the long run. Because responsibility for such improvement often falls on employees, it becomes management's job to provide employee incentives that will motivate them to want to improve.

Harry Rosen retail outlets have been serving Canadians for more than 50 years. The company has been recognized as one of the top 50 managed companies three years in a row.

Exhibit 6.6 **Total Quality Management**

These 14 points, based on the work of W. Edwards Deming, can help managers improve their goods and services through total quality management.

1. **Create constancy of purpose for the improvement of goods and services.** The organization should constantly strive to improve quality, productivity, and consumer satisfaction to improve performance today and tomorrow.
2. **Adopt a new philosophy to reject mistakes and negativism.** Customers, managers, and employees all need to change their attitudes toward unacceptable work quality and sullen service.
3. **Cease dependence on mass inspection.** Instead of inspecting products after production to weed out bad quality, improve the process to build in good quality.
4. **End the practice of awarding business on price alone.** Create long-term relationships with suppliers who can deliver the best quality.
5. **Improve constantly and forever the system of production and service.** Improvement is not a one-time effort; managers must lead the way to continuous improvement of quality, productivity, and customer satisfaction.
6. **Institute training.** Train all organization members to do their jobs consistently well.
7. **Institute leadership.** Managers must provide the leadership to help employees do a better job.
8. **Drive out fear.** Create an atmosphere in which employees are not afraid to ask questions or to point out problems.
9. **Break down barriers between units.** Ensure that people in organizational departments or units do not have conflicting goals and are able to work as a team to achieve overall goals.
10. **Eliminate slogans, exhortations, and targets for the workforce.** These alone cannot help anyone do a better job, and they imply that employees could do better if they tried harder; rather, management should provide methods for improvement.
11. **Eliminate numerical quotas.** Quotas count only finished units, not quality or methods, and they generally lead to defective goods, wasted resources, and demoralized employees.
12. **Remove barriers to pride in work.** Most people want to do a good job but are prevented from doing so by misguided management, poor communication, faulty equipment, defective materials, and other barriers that managers must remove to improve quality.
13. **Institute a vigorous program of education and retraining.** Both managers and employees have to be educated in the new quality methods.
14. **Take action to accomplish the transformation.** With top-management commitment, have the courage to make the changes throughout the organization that will improve quality.

Although many companies are enjoying greater success as a result of total quality initiatives, a recent study of the largest companies indicates that such initiatives have fallen short of expectations in a large number of companies. However, the fact that total quality principles played a significant role in propelling Japanese businesses from postwar ruins to pillars of innovation and productivity suggests that much can be gained from the process. What may be lacking in North America is a firm commitment to TQM. Many companies have jumped on the TQM bandwagon hoping for a quick boost in performance without really thinking about how to make total quality a part of their long-term strategy. Such companies often fail to provide the necessary managerial and financial support for the programs. In about half of the firms studied, less than 40 percent of workers and less than 80 percent of management teams were sufficiently knowledgeable about TQM philosophy, concepts, and tools.[35] Experts agree that the entire organization—from the bottom all the way up to the CEO—must be actively and visibly involved for TQM to work. Companies that make a half-hearted commitment should not expect dramatic improvements.[36]

At the same time, pursuing TQM is not necessarily a prerequisite for success. Many successful companies do not have TQM programs.[37] However, no business that operates in a competitive environment can expect long-term success unless managers strive to meet customers' needs, improve processes, lower costs, and empower employees in one way or another.

MANAGEMENT SKILLS

L.O. 7

Managers rely on a number of skills to perform their functions and maintain a high level of quality in their organizations. These skills can be classified into three basic categories: *interpersonal, technical,* and *conceptual.* As managers rise through the organization's hierarchy, they may need to strengthen their abilities in one or more of these skills; fortunately, managerial skills can usually be learned.[38]

Interpersonal Skills

The skills required to communicate with other people, work effectively with them, motivate them, and lead them are called **interpersonal skills**. Because managers mainly get things done through people at all levels of the organization, they use good interpersonal skills in countless situations. Encouraging employees to work together toward common goals, interacting with employees and other managers, negotiating with partners and suppliers, developing employee trust and loyalty, and fostering innovation—all these activities require interpersonal skills.

interpersonal skills
Skills required to understand other people and to interact effectively with them

Communication, or exchanging information, is the most important and pervasive interpersonal skill that managers use. Effective communication not only increases the manager's and the organization's productivity but also shapes the impressions made on colleagues, employees, supervisors, investors, and customers. Communication allows you to perceive the needs of these stakeholders (your first step toward satisfying them), and it helps you respond to those needs.[39] Moreover, as the workforce becomes more and more diverse, managers will need to adjust their interactions with others, communicating in a way that considers the different needs, backgrounds, and experiences of people.

technical skills
Ability and knowledge to perform the mechanics of a particular job

administrative skills
Technical skills in information gathering, data analysis, planning, organizing, and other aspects of managerial work

conceptual skills
Ability to understand the relationship of parts to the whole

Technical Skills

A person who knows how to operate a machine, prepare a financial statement, program a computer, or pass a football has **technical skills**; that is, the individual has the knowledge and ability to perform the mechanics of a particular job. Technical skills are most important at lower organizational levels because managers at these levels work directly with employees who are using the tools and techniques of a particular specialty, such as automotive assembly or computer programming. Still, twenty-first-century managers must have a strong technology background. They must find new computer applications that can complete daily work routines faster or provide more accurate information sooner.

Managers at all levels use **administrative skills**, which are the technical skills necessary to manage an organization. Administrative skills include the abilities to make schedules, gather information, analyze data, plan, and organize. Managers often develop such skills through education and then improve them by working in one or more functional areas of an organization, such as accounting or marketing.[40] Project-management skills are becoming an increasingly important administrative skill. Managers must know how to start a project or work assignment from scratch, map out each step in the process to its successful completion, develop project costs and timelines, and establish checkpoints at key project intervals.

Jenny J. Ming, president of Old Navy, oversees everything from store operations to marketing and advertising for the 850 stores in the U.S. and Canada. Her passion for fashion has helped drive the company's record growth. So has her ability to communicate effectively with others. Ming recognizes that people's needs change as quickly as the latest fashion trend. So when communicating with others, she takes extra care to focus on her audience's special needs and differing backgrounds.

Conceptual Skills

Managers need **conceptual skills** to see the organization as a whole, in the context of its environment, and to understand how its various parts interrelate. Conceptual skills are espe-

Exhibit 6.7 **Monumental Management Decisions**

Great decisions change things. Here are a few of the management decisions that made the greatest impact in the twentieth century.

Coca-Cola	During the Second World War, Robert Woodruff, president of Coca-Cola, committed to selling bottles of Coke to members of the armed services for a nickel per bottle. Customer loyalty never came cheaper.
Holiday Inn	When the Wilson family went on a motoring vacation, they discovered it was not much fun staying in motels that were either too expensive or too slovenly. Kemmons Wilson decided to build his own hotels; the first Holiday Inn opened in 1952.
Honda	When Honda arrived in North America in 1959 to launch its big motorbikes, customers weren't keen on their problematic performance. However, they did admire the little Supercub bikes that Honda's managers used. So Honda bravely changed direction and transformed the motorbike business overnight.
CNN	Ignoring market research, Ted Turner launched the Cable News Network in 1980. No one thought a 24-hour news network would work.
Dell	In 1984 Michael Dell decided to sell personal computers direct and built to order. Now everybody in the industry is trying to imitate Dell Computer's strategy.

cially important to top managers. These managers are the strategists who develop the plans that guide the organization toward its goals. Managers such as Jorma Ollila use their conceptual skills to acquire and analyze information, identify both problems and opportunities, understand the competitive environment in which their companies operate, develop strategies, and make decisions.

decision making
Process of identifying a decision situation, analyzing the problem, weighing the alternatives, choosing an alternative and implementing it, and evaluating the results

A key managerial activity requiring conceptual skills is **decision making**, a process that has five distinct steps: (1) recognizing the need for a decision; (2) identifying, analyzing, and defining the problem or opportunity; (3) generating alternatives; (4) selecting an alternative and implementing it; and (5) evaluating the results. Managers monitor the results of decisions over time to see whether the chosen alternative works, whether any new problem or opportunity arises because of the decision, and whether a new decision must be made (see Exhibit 6.7).[41]

Keep in mind that a company's managerial structure defines the way decisions are made. Today's flatter organizations, for example, allow information to flow more freely among all levels of the organization, and they push decision making down to lower organizational levels. As Chapter 7 discusses in detail, more and more organizations are empowering their employees and teams by giving them increasing discretion over work-related issues.[42]

SUMMARY OF LEARNING OBJECTIVES

Define the four basic management functions.

The four basic management functions are (1) planning—establishing objectives and goals for the organization and translating them into action plans; (2) organizing—arranging resources to carry out the organization's plans; (3) leading—influencing and motivating people to work effectively and willingly toward company goals; and (4) controlling—monitoring progress toward organizational goals, resetting the course if goals or objectives change in response to shifting conditions, and correcting deviations if goals or objectives are not being attained.

Outline the tasks involved in the strategic planning process.

The strategic planning process begins with a clear vision for the company's future. This vision is then translated into a mission statement so it can be shared with all members of the organization. Next, managers develop forecasts about future trends that affect their industry and products; then they analyze the competition—paying close attention to their strengths and weaknesses so they can use this information to gain a competitive edge. With an eye on the company's vision and mission as well as on competition, managers establish company goals and objectives. Finally, they translate these goals and objectives into action plans.

3 Explain the purpose of a mission statement.

A mission statement defines why the organization exists, what it does, what it hopes to achieve, and the principles it will follow to meet its goals. It is used to bring clarity of focus to members of the organization and to provide guidelines for the adoption of future projects.

4 List the benefits of setting long-term goals and objectives.

Goals and objectives establish long- and short-range targets that help managers fulfill the company's mission. Setting appropriate goals increases employee motivation, establishes standards by which individual and group performance can be measured, guides employee activity, and clarifies management's expectations.

5 Cite three leadership styles and explain why no single style is superior to the others in every situation.

Three leadership styles are autocratic, democratic, and laissez faire (also called free-rein). Each may work best in a different situation: autocratic when quick decisions are needed, democratic when employee participation in decision making is desirable, and laissez faire when fostering creativity is a priority. Good leaders are flexible enough to respond with the best approach for the situation.

6 Clarify how total quality management (TQM) is changing the way organizations are managed.

Total quality management is both a management philosophy and a management process that focuses on delivering quality to customers. TQM redirects management to focus on four key elements: (1) Employee involvement includes team building and soliciting employee input on decisions. (2) Customer focus involves gathering customer feedback and then acting on that feedback to better serve customers. (3) Benchmarking involves measuring the company's standards against the standards of industry leaders. (4) Continuous improvement requires an ongoing commitment to reducing defects, cutting costs, slashing production and delivery times, and offering customers innovative products.

7 Identify and explain the three types of managerial skills.

Managers use (1) interpersonal skills to communicate with other people, work effectively with them, and lead them; (2) technical skills to perform the mechanics of a particular job; and (3) conceptual skills (including decision making) to see the organization as a whole, to see it in the context of its environment, and to understand how the various parts interrelate.

Behind the SCENES

Nokia's Secret

Nokia's Jorma Ollila was on a mission. From the time Ollila was appointed CEO in 1992, he wanted to transform a company that once made toilet paper, tires, and rubber boots into a world-class mobile telecommunications company. He wanted the company to produce wireless phones that shaped new markets. But how?

Ollila created a culture that encouraged innovation and, above all, one in which employees were not afraid to make mistakes. He used a democratic, hands-off leadership style to empower employees. He demolished hierarchies that prevented the company from listening to customers and employees and reorganized the company into decision-making teams. Then he challenged employees to learn and to speak their minds. He even hosted a series of annual meetings known as the "Nokia Way" to give employees the opportunity to determine Nokia's priorities. Finally, he relied on management to translate these priorities into a strategic plan for the company.

Nokia shipped its first new stylish phones in 1993. Management had hoped to sell 400 000 phones; instead, the company sold 20 million. The competition was caught flat-footed. What was Nokia's secret? To begin with, Nokia stayed in touch with consumers' needs. It produced a constant stream of different models that appealed to specific market segments, encouraging consumers to upgrade their existing phones to take advantage of new technologies and cool designs. Nokia also engineered its phones so that the same models could be adapted to the varying frequencies and mobile phone standards around the world. Innovation became Nokia's lifeblood. The company created the first digital phone for global system mobile communications networks, the first mobile phone specially designed for Asian customers (with a large full-graphics display and Asian language interfaces), the first mobile phones with user-changeable covers and changeable ringing tones, and the first mobile phones with a unique short-message chat function. Bottom line: Nokia made cellphones that worked well and looked great. By late 1998, Nokia was pumping out a new model every 35 days. Such innovations helped Nokia capture 30 percent of the global mobile phone market, rolling over rivals Motorola and Ericsson to become the biggest mobile phone supplier in the world.

To keep the company on track, Nokia continually monitored its goals. For example, if annual growth of a specific mobile phone fell below 25 percent, the company shifted its focus to other product lines with more growth potential. Still, management was careful not to analyze data to death. "We're pretty determined about timeliness and about getting things done," says Ollila. "Somebody has to take responsibility and say, 'Okay, this is it. This is what we are going to do.' Otherwise you just have a lot of fun in discussing things and nobody takes the ball and carries it."

Of course, nobody does a better job of carrying the ball than Jorma Ollila. Over the years, he has received various acknowledgements for his approach, including recognition as *Industry Week*'s CEO of the year. Ollila helped transform Nokia into the leading maker of mobile phones. But with more than 55 000 employees and global sales of approximately 30 billion euros, his company now faces different challenges. Mobile phone sales account for 62 percent of the company's revenues and demand is shrinking. In Europe, just about everybody who wants an ordinary cellphone has one. Moreover, competition is intensifying as rivals like Motorola and Ericsson aggressively roll out cool phones to match Nokia's. That leaves Ollila and Nokia with a new problem: how to keep growing as the industry matures.

Although it managed to increase overall sales, Nokia actually lost global market share in the cellphone industry in 2004, dropping to 28.9 percent from 34.6 percent in 2003. Despite this setback the company maintained huge command of the market: Motorola had 16.4 percent of the market and Samsung had 12.5 percent. Part of the problem can be linked to the company's uncharacteristically late move into the lucrative flip phone sector. Despite this setback the company is still targeting a 40 percent share of the market going forward.

"This isn't a business where you do one big strategic thing right and you're set for the next five years," says Ollila. "It's a big orchestration task." If any cellphone maker can thrive, it's Nokia. In fact, Jorma Ollila is a man with a mission. While other high-tech industry executives are obsessed with wiring the planet, he is intent on creating the mobile information society—bringing people, words, data, and the Internet together anywhere and anytime without wires.

But big question marks loom. What will it take to convince more consumers to surf the Web via their mobile phones? When will technological improvements make such wireless communications more efficient? Will new products such as phones embedded with digital cameras continue to boom? Can Nokia continue to move faster than rivals? Ollila claims Nokia is ready to lead the industry with the next generation of wireless phones. Only time will tell whether this company can repeat its stunning performance.[43]

Critical Thinking Questions

1. Why did Jorma Ollila transform Nokia, and how did he do it? (Hint: In your discussion be sure to mention organizational culture, leadership style, mission, and vision.)
2. How does Nokia stay ahead of its competitors?
3. What new challenges does Nokia face today?

Learn More Online

Go to Chapter 6 of this text's website at www.pearsoned.ca/bovee, and click on the hotlink to Nokia's website. Review the company's website to answer these questions: How has Nokia achieved global success? What are Nokia's future goals?

KEY TERMS

administrative skills (161)
autocratic leaders (154)
coaching (154)
conceptual skills (161)
contingency leadership (154)
controlling (157)
corporate culture (156)
crisis management (151)
decision making (162)
democratic leaders (154)
first-line managers (153)
goal (149)
interpersonal skills (161)
laissez-faire leaders (154)
leading (153)
management (146)
management pyramid (152)
mentor (155)
middle managers (152)
mission statement (148)
objective (149)
operational plans (151)
organizing (152)
participative management (159)
planning (147)
quality (158)
roles (146)
standards (158)
strategic plans (147)
tactical plans (151)
technical skills (161)
top managers (152)
total quality management (TQM) (159)
vision (147)

TEST YOUR KNOWLEDGE

Questions for Review

1. What is management? Why is it so important?
2. What is forecasting, and how is it related to the planning function?
3. What is the goal of crisis management?
4. What are some common characteristics of effective leaders?
5. Why are interpersonal skills important to managers at all levels?

Questions for Analysis

6. Is the following statement an example of a strategic goal or an objective? "To become the number-one retailer of computers and computer accessories in terms of revenue, growth, and customer satisfaction." Explain your answer.
7. How do the three levels of management differ?
8. Why are coaching and mentoring effective leadership techniques?
9. How are the four main elements of total quality management related to the goal of delivering quality to customers?
10. **Ethical Considerations.** When an organization learns about a threat that could place the safety of its workers or its customers at risk, is management obligated to immediately inform these parties of the threat? Explain your answer.

Questions for Application

11. What are your long-term goals? Develop a set of long-term career goals for yourself and several short-term objectives that will help you reach those goals. Make sure your goals are specific, measurable, and time limited.
12. Do you have the skills it takes to be an effective manager? Find out by taking the Keirsey Temperment Sorter II personality test at www.keirsey.com.
13. **Integrated.** Using Dell Computer's mission statement in Exhibit 6.2 as a model and the material you learned in Chapter 3, develop a mission statement for a socially responsible company such as Telus or Ben & Jerry's.
14. **Integrated.** What is the principal difference between a business plan (as discussed in Chapter 4) and a strategic plan?

PRACTISE YOUR KNOWLEDGE

SHARPENING YOUR COMMUNICATION SKILLS

As the manager of Martin's Restaurant Supply, you see a huge potential for selling company products on the Internet to customers around the world. Your company already has a website but it's geared to Canadian sales only. Before you propose your ideas to senior management, however, you're going to do your homework. Studies have shown that companies selling products in the global marketplace benefit by modifying their websites to accommodate cultural differences. For instance, a mailbox with a raised flag has no meaning in many foreign countries.

Your task is to review the websites of several leading global companies and take notes on how they adapt their websites for global audiences. Once you've gathered your notes, write a short memo to management highlighting (via bullet points) some of the ways these leaders make their websites effective for a global audience.

BUILDING YOUR TEAM SKILLS

A good mission statement should define the organization's purpose and ultimate goals and outline the principles that are to guide managers and employees in working toward those goals. Using library sources such as annual reports or Internet sources such as organizational websites, locate mission statements from one non-profit organization, such as a school or a charity, and one company with which you are familiar.

Bring these statements to class and, with your team, select four mission statements to evaluate. How many of the mission statements contain all five of the typical components (product or service; primary market; concern for survival, growth, and profitability; managerial philosophy; commitment to quality and social responsibility)? Which components are most often absent from the mission statements you are evaluating? Which components are most often included? Of the mission statements your team is analyzing, which is the most inspiring? Why?

Now assume that you and your teammates are the top management team at each organization or company. How would you improve these mission statements? Rewrite the four mission statements so that they cover the five typical components, show all organization members how their roles are related to the vision, and inspire commitment among employees and managers.

Summarize your team's work in a written or oral report to the class. Compare the mission statement that your team found most inspiring with the statements that other teams found most inspiring. What do these mission statements have in common? How do they differ? Of all the inspiring mission statements reported to the class, which do you think is the best? Why? Does this mission statement inspire you to consider working for or doing business with this organization?

EXPAND YOUR KNOWLEDGE

DISCOVERING CAREER OPPORTUNITIES

If you become a manager, how much of your day will be spent performing each of the four basic functions of management? This is your opportunity to find out. Arrange to shadow a manager (such as a department head, a store manager, or a shift supervisor) for a few hours. As you observe, categorize the manager's activities in terms of the four management functions and note how much time each activity takes. If observation is not possible, interview a manager in order to complete this exercise.

1. How much of the manager's time is spent on each of the four management functions? Is this the allocation you expected?
2. Ask whether this is a typical workday for this manager. If it isn't, what does the manager usually do differently? During a typical day, does this manager tend to spend most of the time on one particular function?
3. Of the four management functions, which does the manager believe is most important for good organizational performance? Do you agree?

DEVELOPING YOUR RESEARCH SKILLS

Find two articles in business journals or newspapers (print or online editions) that profile two senior managers who lead a business or a non-profit organization.

1. What experience, skills, and business background do the two leaders have? Do you see any striking similarities or differences in their backgrounds?
2. What kinds of business challenges have these two leaders faced? What actions did they take to deal with those challenges? Did they establish any long-term goals or objectives for their company? Did the articles mention a new change initiative?
3. Describe the leadership strengths of each person as they are presented in the articles you selected. Is either leader known as a team builder? Long-term strategist? Shrewd negotiator? What are each leader's greatest areas of strength?

See It on the **WEB**

URLs for all Internet exercises are provided at the website for this book, www.pearsoned.ca/bovee. When you log on to the text website, select Chapter 6, select Destinations, then click on the name of the featured website, and review the website to complete the following exercises.

Explore the following chapter-related websites, review their content, and answer the following questions for each website you visit:

1. What is the purpose of this website?
2. What kinds of information does this website contain? Please be specific.
3. How is the information provided at this website useful for business people? Consumers?
4. How did you expand your knowledge of management by reviewing the material at this website? What new things did you learn about this topic?

BECOME A BETTER MANAGER

ManagementFirst.com can help you become a better manager. Focused on management theory and practice, this website is a management portal that explores in-depth management issues including leadership, time management, training, strategy, knowledge management, personal development, customer relationship management, and more. Each channel provides lengthy articles, advice, and a collection of carefully annotated links. Log on today and join ManagementFirst.com to become information rich and well organized. Learn why knowledge management is important. Discover what emotional intelligence is all about and find out why companies form strategic alliances. www.managementfirst.com

LINKING TO ORGANIZATIONAL CHANGE

Looking for more information on every aspect of organizational change management? You'll find a comprehensive collection of links on the website of the Management Assistance Program for Nonprofits. This is the place to access articles, discussion groups, and other resources related to organizational change in businesses and in non-profit organizations. Start with the overview, which sets the stage for browsing the many links devoted to exploring management and employee perspectives on the challenges and goals of managing change. www.managementhelp.org/org_chng/org_chng.htm

Chapter 7
Organizing and Working in Teams

LEARNING OBJECTIVES

After studying this chapter, you will be able to

1. Discuss the function of a company's organization structure
2. Explain the concepts of accountability, authority, and delegation
3. Define four types of departmentalization
4. Describe the five most common forms of teams
5. Highlight the advantages and disadvantages of working in teams
6. List the characteristics of effective teams
7. Review the five stages of team development
8. Highlight six causes of team conflict and three styles of conflict resolution

Behind the SCENES

Valuing Employee Input at Wainwright Industries

Embracing a people-first strategy has paid off for Wainwright Industries. Winner of the coveted Malcolm Baldrige National Quality Award, Wainwright impressed examiners by the extent to which employees assumed responsibility for making improvements.

www.wainwrightindustries.com

Wainwright Industries is a family-run manufacturer of components for the automotive and aerospace industries; its metal stamping and assembly division serves companies throughout the United States, Canada, and Mexico. After decades of successful operations, an important question began making the rounds in the company. Did the owners and managers sincerely trust and believe in their employees? CEO Arthur D. Wainwright first faced the question of trust in the early 1990s. He and several other managers were listening to a presentation by a winner of the Malcolm Baldrige National Quality Award, which honours the quality achievements of American companies. When the speaker mentioned "trust and belief," a Wainwright plant manager became intrigued. He wrote the phrase down and passed it to the other managers with the notation, "What is that?" Another manager scribbled, "I don't know. Do we have it at Wainwright?" The plant manager wrote back, "If we don't know what it is, we probably don't have it."

That exchange, captured on a napkin, changed Wainwright Industries forever. "We had a lot of discussions after that day," the CEO said later, "and we realized that no matter what we said about our commitment to involve employees, managers were still running the show." Prior to that day, CEO Wainwright had already taken some basic steps to improve participation, communication, and teamwork. Managers were trained in world-class operations; everyone, from assembly workers to senior managers, wore uniforms with "Team Wainwright" embroidered above the pocket; and employees had been renamed "associates" as part of a companywide team-building effort. Still, something wasn't right. Even though the business was growing, profits weren't keeping pace. Furthermore, frustration was building up and down the organizational hierarchy because, despite Wainwright's efforts, decision-making power was still firmly concentrated at the very top.

So Wainwright decided to make a daring, public break from the past. He and the other owners began with a confession: "We stood up in front of all the associates and told them we knew they were committed to us but that we were still trying to make decisions for them." From now on, he told them, the company would have "sincere trust and belief" in its employees, treating them like "responsible, adult human beings" who, with proper training, could do an even better job of applying their talents and energies.

With promises such as these, Wainwright certainly had his work cut out for him. What could he do to foster more effective teamwork and employee participation in the company's decisions, plans, and operations? How could he show employees that the company genuinely valued their ideas and involvement? How could he encourage more open communication within the organization?[1]

L.O. 1

DESIGNING AN EFFECTIVE ORGANIZATION STRUCTURE

organization structure
Framework enabling managers to divide responsibilities, ensure employee accountability, and distribute decision-making authority

The decision-making authority of employees and managers is supported by the company's **organization structure**. This structure helps the company achieve its goals by providing a framework for managers to divide responsibilities, effectively distribute the authority to make decisions, coordinate and control the organization's work, and hold employees accountable for their work. In some organizations, this structure is a relatively rigid, vertical hierarchy like the management organization structure pyramid described in Chapter 6. In other organizations, teams of employees and managers from various levels and functions work together to make decisions and achieve the organization's goals.[2]

When managers design the organization's structure, they use an **organization chart** to provide a visual representation of how employees and tasks are grouped and how the lines of communication and authority flow. Exhibit 7.1 shows the organization chart for a grocery store chain. An organization chart depicts the official design for accomplishing tasks that lead to achieving the organization's goals, a framework known as the **formal organization**. Every company also has an **informal organization**—the network of interactions that develop on a personal level among workers. Sometimes the interactions among people in the informal organization parallel their relationships in the formal organization, but often interactions transcend formal boundaries. An employee who is lower on the organizational chart may actually have more power to influence opinion than an individual higher up on the chart because of his or her informal influence. Crossing formal boundaries can help establish a more pleasant work environment, but it can also undermine formal work processes and hurt a company's ability to get things done.[3]

organization chart
Diagram showing how employees and tasks are grouped and where the lines of communication and authority flow

formal organization
A framework officially established by managers for accomplishing tasks that lead to achieving the organization's goals

informal organization
Network of informal employee interactions that are not defined by the formal structure

How do companies design an organization structure, and which organization structure is the most effective? In the past, organizations were designed around management's desire to control workers, with everything set up in a hierarchy. Today, however, more and more companies are designing organization structures around the customers' needs for fast decisions. As this chapter will discuss later, companies are eliminating layers of management, or flattening their organization structures, to give more decision-making authority to employees who deal directly with customers. In fact, as management guru Peter Drucker sees it, "There is no such thing as one right organization. Each has distinct strengths, distinct limitations, and specific applications." In other words, today's managers require a toolbox full of organization structures so they can select the right tool for each specific task.[4] Regardless, four factors must be taken into consideration when

Exhibit 7.1 **Organization Chart for a Grocery Store Chain**

Many organization charts look like this one. The traditional model of an organization is a pyramid in which numerous boxes form the base and lead up to fewer and fewer boxes on higher levels, ultimately arriving at one box at the top. A glance at this grocery store chain's organization chart reveals who has authority over whom, who is responsible for whose work, and who is accountable to whom.

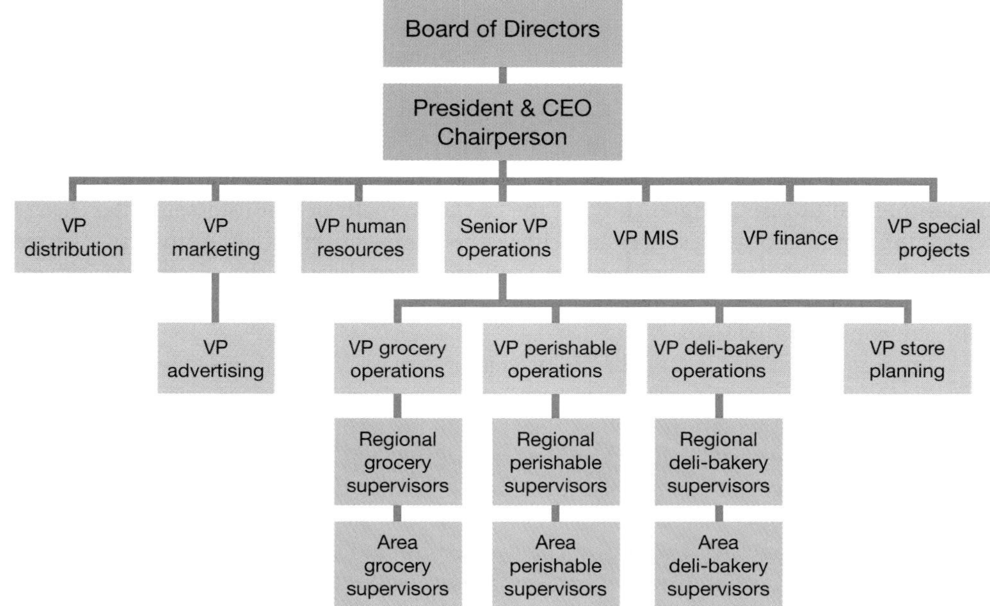

The photo shows a Bombardier factory assembly shop where employees perform specialized work tasks in order to create a unified product. Each employee is an expert in one area of the process.

designing an effective organization structure: work specialization, chain of command, vertical organization, and horizontal organization and coordination.

Work Specialization

Before designing an organizational structure, management must first decide on the optimal level of **work specialization**—the degree to which organizational tasks are broken down into separate jobs.[5] Few employees have the skills to perform every task a company needs. Therefore, work specialization can improve organizational efficiency by enabling each worker to perform tasks that are well defined and that require specific skills. For example, in 1776 Scottish economist Adam Smith found that if each of 10 workers went through every step needed to make a pin, the entire group could make 200 pins a day. However, if each worker performed only a few steps and no one made a pin from start to finish, the same 10 workers could make 48 000 pins a day. When employees concentrate on the same specialized tasks, they can perfect their skills and perform their tasks more quickly. A classic example of work specialization is the automobile assembly line.

However, organizations can overdo specialization. If a task is defined too narrowly, employees may become bored with performing the same tiny, repetitious job over and over. They may also feel unchallenged and alienated. Managers must think carefully about how specialized or how broad each task should be. In fact, a growing number of companies are balancing specialization and employee motivation through teamwork. This approach enables group members to decide how to break down a complex task, and it allows employees to rotate among the jobs that the team is collectively responsible for. The team then shares credit for the results, and workers feel that they have created something of value. The team approach to organization is discussed in more depth later in this chapter.

work specialization
Specialization in or responsibility for some portion of an organization's overall work tasks; also called division of labour

chain of command
Pathway for the flow of authority from one management level to the next

L.O. 2

Chain of Command

Besides incorporating work specialization into an organizational structure, companies must also establish a **chain of command**, the unbroken line of authority that connects each level of management with the next level. The chain of command helps organizations function smoothly by making two things clear: who is responsible for each task, and who has the authority to make official decisions.

All employees have a certain amount of **responsibility**—the obligation to perform the duties and achieve the goals and objectives associated with their jobs. As they work toward the organization's goals, employees must also maintain their **accountability**, their obligation to report the results of their work to supervisors or team members and to justify any outcomes that fall below expectations. Managers ensure that tasks are accomplished by exercising **authority**, the power to make decisions, issue orders, carry out actions, and allocate resources to achieve the organization's goals. Authority is vested in the positions that managers hold, and it flows down through the management pyramid. **Delegation** is the assignment of work and the transfer of authority and responsibility to complete that work.[6]

Look again at Exhibit 7.1. The senior vice-president of operations delegates responsibilities to the vice-presidents of grocery operations, perishable operations, deli-bakery operations, and store planning. These department heads have the authority to make certain decisions necessary to fulfill their roles, and they are accountable to the senior VP for the performance of their respective divisions. In turn, the senior VP is accountable to the company CEO.

The simplest and most common chain-of-command system is known as **line organization** because it establishes a clear line of authority flowing from the top down, as

responsibility
Obligation to perform the duties and achieve the goals and objectives associated with a particular position

accountability
Obligation to report results to supervisors or team members and to justify outcomes that fall below expectations

authority
Power granted by the organization to make decisions, take actions, and allocate resources to accomplish goals

delegation
Assignment of work and the authority and responsibility required to complete it

line organization
Chain-of-command system that establishes a clear line of authority flowing from the top down

Exhibit 7.1 depicts. Everyone knows who is accountable to whom, as well as which tasks and decisions each is responsible for. However, line organization sometimes falls short because the technical complexity of a firm's activities may require specialized knowledge that individual managers don't have and can't easily acquire. A more elaborate system called **line-and-staff organization** was developed out of the need to combine specialization with management control. In such an organization, managers in the chain of command are supplemented by functional groupings of people known as *staff,* who provide advice and specialized services but who are not in the line organization's chain of command (see Exhibit 7.2).

line-and-staff organization
Organization system that has a clear chain of command but that also includes functional groups of people who provide advice and specialized services

Span of Management

The number of people a manager directly supervises is called the **span of management** or *span of control.* When a large number of people report directly to one person, that person has a wide span of management. This situation is common in **flat organizations** with relatively few levels in the management hierarchy. Sun Microsystems, Visa, and Oticon (a hearing aid manufacturer in Denmark) are all companies that have flat organizations. British Petroleum (BP) is also amazingly flat and lean for an organization with $233 billion in revenues and 103 700 employees. At BP there is no level between the general managers of the business units and the group of nine operating executives who oversee the businesses.[7] The shift toward a larger span of control has been the trend in recent years as downsizing, restructuring, and empowerment have swept through organizations and altered the employment landscape.

span of management
Number of people under one manager's control; also known as span of control

flat organizations
Organizations with a wide span of management and few hierarchical levels

In contrast, **tall organizations** have many hierarchical levels, usually with only a few people reporting to each manager. In such cases, the span of management is narrow (see Exhibit 7.3 on page 172). General Motors traditionally had a tall organization structure with as many as 22 layers of management. Under tall organization structures, employees who want to institute a change must ask a supervisor, who in turn must ask a manager, who in turn must ask another manager at the next level up, and so on. To reduce the time it takes to make decisions, many companies are flattening their organization structures by removing layers of management and by delegating increased responsibilities and authority to middle managers, work teams, and individual employees.[8]

tall organizations
Organizations with a narrow span of management and many hierarchical levels

No formula exists for determining the ideal span of management. How well people work together is more important than the number of people reporting to one person.

Exhibit 7.2 **Simplified Line-and-Staff Structure**

A line-and-staff organization divides employees into those who are in the direct line of command (from the top level of the hierarchy to the bottom) and those who provide staff (or support) services to line managers at various levels. Staff report directly to top management.

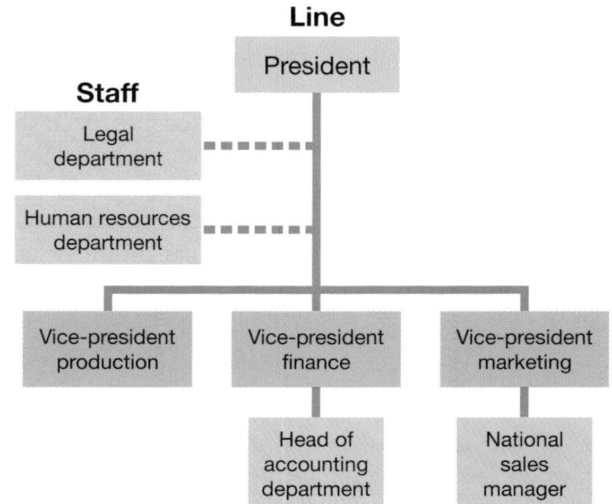

Exhibit 7.3 Tall versus Flat Organizations

A tall organization, like a national army, has many levels with a narrow span of management at each level so that relatively few people report to each manager on the level above them. In contrast, a flat organization, such as the Catholic Church, has relatively few levels with a wide span of management so that more people report to each manager.

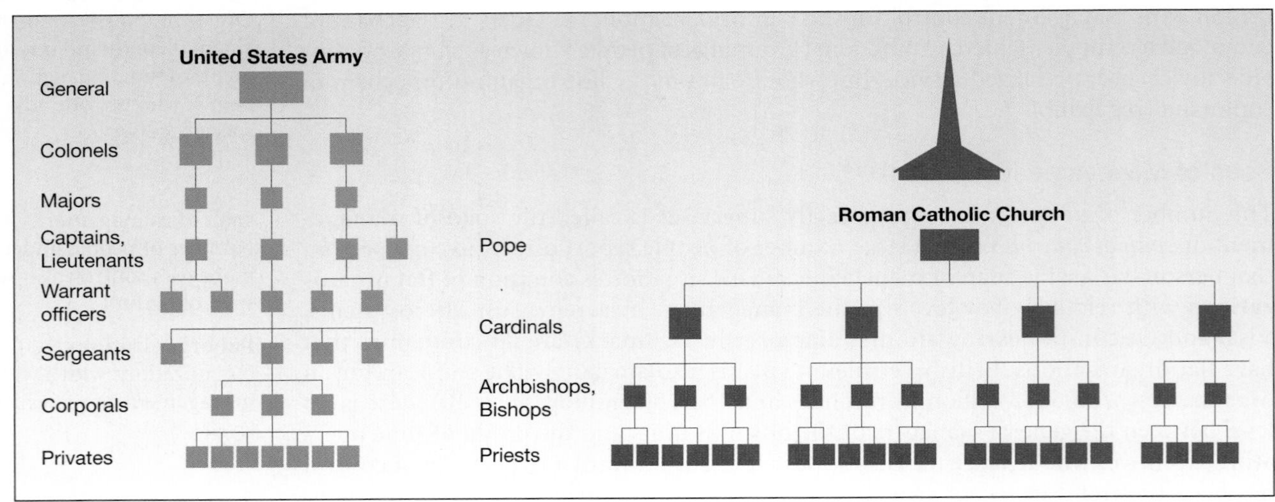

Still, several factors affect the number of people a manager can effectively supervise, including the manager's personal skill and leadership ability, the skill of the workers, the motivation of the workers, and the nature or complexity of the job. In general, employees who are highly skilled or who are trained in many work tasks don't require as much supervision as employees who are less skilled.

Centralization versus Decentralization

centralization
Concentration of decision-making authority at the top of the organization

decentralization
Delegation of decision-making authority to employees in lower-level positions

Organizations that focus decision-making authority near the top of the chain of command are said to be centralized. **Centralization** benefits a company by using top management's rich experience and broad view of organizational goals. Both line organizations and line-and-staff organizations tend to be centralized.

The trend in business today is moving in a different direction. **Decentralization** pushes decision-making authority down to lower organizational levels—such as department heads—while control over essential companywide matters remains with top management. Implemented properly, decentralization can stimulate responsiveness because decisions don't have to be referred up the hierarchy.[9] Consider General Electric. Managers at each of GE's 11 independent businesses have US$25 million they can spend as they see fit without having to get the approval of the board of directors or the CEO. Giving each core business more decision-making authority has helped GE achieve tremendous growth in sales and profits.[10] Magna's automotive manufacturing divisions operate as independent profit centres. The decentralized approach discourages bureaucratic mentality and makes the divisions more customer oriented.[11]

However, decentralization does not work in every situation or in every company. At times, strong authority from the top of the chain of command may be needed to keep the organization focused on immediate goals. Managers should select the level of decision making that will most effectively serve the organization's needs given the individual circumstances.[12]

Vertical Organization

Choosing between a vertical and a horizontal model is one of the most critical decisions a company can make. Many organizations use a traditional vertical structure to define formal relationships and the division of tasks among employees and managers.

Vertical organization links the activities at the top of the organization with those at the middle and lower levels.[13] This structure also helps managers delegate authority to positions throughout the organization's hierarchy. Besides authority, the structure defines specific jobs and activities across vertical levels. In a vertical organization, companies define jobs and activities by using **departmentalization**—the arrangement of activities into logical groups that are then clustered into larger departments and units that form the total organization.[14] Four common ways of departmentalizing are by function, division, matrix, and network. An organization may use more than one method of departmentalization, depending on its particular needs.

vertical organization
Structure linking activities at the top of the organization with those at the middle and lower levels

departmentalization
Grouping people within an organization according to function, division, matrix, or network

Departmentalization by Function

L.O. 3

Departmentalization by function groups employees according to their skills, resource use, and expertise. Common functional departments include marketing, human resources, operations, finance, research and development, and accounting, with each department working independently of the others.[15] As depicted in Exhibit 7.1, functional departmentalization is highly centralized.

departmentalization by function
Grouping workers according to their similar skills, resource use, and expertise

Splitting the organization into separate functional departments offers several advantages: (1) grouping employees by specialization allows for the efficient use of resources and encourages the development of in-depth skills, (2) centralized decision making enables unified direction by top management, and (3) centralized operations enhance communication and the coordination of activities within departments. Despite these advantages, functional departmentalization can create communication barriers between departments, thereby slowing response to change, hindering effective planning for products and markets, and overemphasizing work specialization, which alienates employees.[16] Moreover, employees may become too narrowly focused on departmental goals and lose sight of larger company goals. For these reasons, many large companies have abandoned the functional structure in the past decade or so.

Departmentalization by Division

Departmentalization by division establishes self-contained departments that encompass all major functional resources required to achieve their goals—such as research and design, manufacturing, finance, and marketing. These departments are typically formed according to similarities in product, process, customer, or geography.

departmentalization by division
Grouping departments according to similarities in product, process, customer, or geography

- *Product divisions.* Many organizations use a structure based on **product divisions**—grouping around each of the company's products or family of products. The logic behind this organizational structure is that each department can manage all the activities needed to develop, manufacture, and sell a particular product or product line. For example, Rogers is divided into three entities: Rogers Wireless, Rogers Cable, and Rogers Media. Rogers Media is further divided to reflect the various aspects of the business: publishing, television, radio, and shopping channel.[17]

product divisions
Divisional structure based on the products that are produced by the firm

- *Process divisions.* **Process divisions**, also called *process-complete* departments, are based on the major steps of a production process. For example, a table manufacturing company might have three divisions, one for each phase of manufacturing a table. A pharmaceutical company can be organized around process divisions such as drug development and distribution.

process divisions
Divisional structure based on the major steps of a production process

- *Customer divisions.* **Customer divisions** are organized based on satisfying specific groups of customers. For example, Acer, a computer equipment manufacturer, restructured into six customer-centric divisions: reseller, education, government, family PC, factory direct, and e-commerce. This was done to facilitate the fulfillment of the company's mission—to provide customers with the highest level of quality, reliability, and support (see Exhibit 7.4).[18]

customer divisions
Divisional structure that focuses on customers or clients

- *Geographic divisions.* **Geographic divisions** enable companies spread over a national or an international area to respond more easily to local customs, styles, and product preferences. For example, Nova Scotia-based Sobeys operates 1300 locations, with stores in all 10 provinces, and employs more than 75 000 people. Its stores operate under various

geographic divisions
Divisional structure based on location of operations

Exhibit 7.4 **Departmentalization by Customer Divisions**

Acer's organizational structure supports the company's mission to be more customer focused.

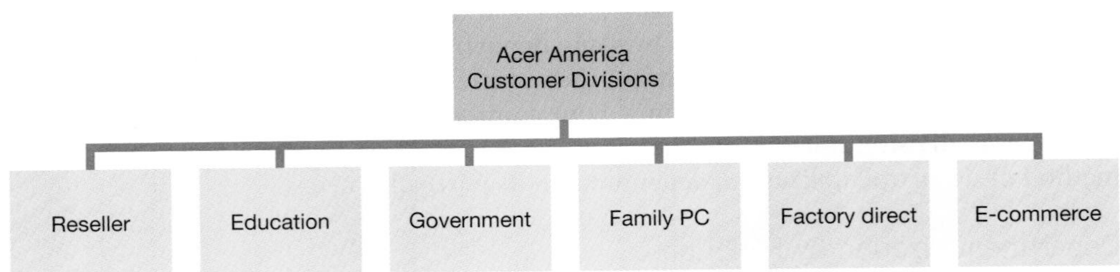

retail names: Sobeys, IGA, IGA Extra, and Price Chopper. The company structure is divided into four geographic divisions: Atlantic, Quebec, Ontario, and West.[19]

Divisional departmentalization offers both advantages and disadvantages. First, because divisions are self-contained, they can react quickly to change, thus making the organization more flexible. In addition, because each division focuses on a limited number of products, processes, customers, or locations, divisions can offer better service to customers. Moreover, top managers can focus on problem areas more easily, and managers can gain valuable experience by dealing with the various functions in their divisions. However, divisional departmentalization can also increase costs by duplicating the use of resources such as facilities and personnel. Furthermore, poor coordination between divisions may cause them to focus too narrowly on divisional goals and neglect the organization's overall goals. Finally, divisions may compete with one another for employees, money, and other resources, causing rivalries that hurt the organization as a whole.[20]

Departmentalization by Matrix

departmentalization by matrix Assigning employees to both a functional group and a project team (thus using functional and divisional patterns simultaneously)

Departmentalization by matrix is a structural design in which employees from functional departments form teams to combine their specialized skills (see Exhibit 7.5). This structure allows the company to pool and share resources across divisions and functional groups. The matrix may be a permanent feature of the organization's design, or it may be established to complete a specific project. Consider Black & Decker, which formed a matrix organization more than a decade ago. Departments such as mechanical design, electrical engineering, and model shop assigned employees with specific technical skills to work on product development projects in such categories as saws, cordless appliances, and woodworking.[21]

Matrix departmentalization can help big companies function like smaller ones by allowing teams to devote their attention to specific projects or customers without permanently reorganizing the company's structure. But matrix structures are not without drawbacks. One problem of a matrix structure is that team members usually continue to report to their functional department heads as well as to a project team leader. Another drawback is that authority tends to be more ambiguous and up for grabs, creating power struggles and other interpersonal conflicts. Black & Decker realized this problem soon after implementing its matrix organization. The manager with the most authority was always the functional department head, and the project team did not really hold any control. The company later redesigned its organization structure, which is now based on product divisions that employ teams of people from many functional areas.[22]

In a matrix organization, excellent communication and coordination are necessary to avoid conflicts. In addition, companies may find it difficult to coordinate the tasks of diverse functional specialists so that projects are completed efficiently. If poorly executed, the matrix can lead to confusion, lost time, and excessive overhead.[23] However, because it facilitates the pooling of resources across departments, a matrix organization can also enable a company to respond better to changes in the business environment.

Exhibit 7.5 **Departmentalization by Matrix**

In a matrix structure, each employee is assigned to both a functional group (with a defined set of basic functions, such as production manager) and a project team (which consists of members of various functional groups working together on a project, such as bringing out a new consumer product).

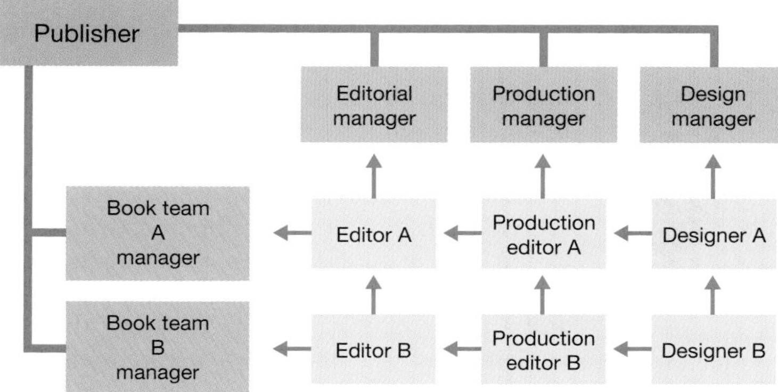

Departmentalization by Network

Departmentalization by network is a method of electronically connecting separate companies that perform selected tasks for a headquarters organization. Also called a *virtual organization,* the network organization *outsources* engineering, marketing, research, accounting, production, distribution, or other functions. That is, the organization hires other organizations under contracts to handle one or more of those functions. In fact, companies such as Nike and Dell Computers sell hundreds of millions of dollars' worth of products even though they outsource most of their manufacturing. As these companies have learned, the network approach is especially appropriate for international operations, allowing every part of the business to draw on resources no matter where in the world they may be.[24]

departmentalization by network
Electronically connecting separate companies that perform selected tasks for a small headquarters organization

The biggest advantage of the network structure is its flexibility. Companies hire whatever services are needed and then change them once they are no longer needed. The limited hierarchy required to manage a network organization also permits the company to make decisions and react to change quickly. Additional advantages are that the organization can continually redefine itself, and a lean structure usually means employees have greater job variety and satisfaction. However, the network approach lacks hands-on control, because the functions are not in one location or company. Also, if one company in the network fails to deliver, the headquarters organization could suffer or even go out of business. Finally, strong employee loyalty and team spirit are less likely to develop, because the emotional connection between the employee and the organization is weak.[25]

Horizontal Organization

More and more businesses are transforming their traditional bureaucratic and hierarchical vertical structure into a horizontal organization.[26] The horizontal organization uses the team concept to flatten hierarchies and integrate the many tasks of a business into a few smooth-flowing operations. The biggest benefit of horizontal organization is that everyone works together. Employees from various departments or functions are grouped around a few organization-wide, cross-functional core processes, and they are responsible for an entire core process from beginning to end. Employees who create new product designs, for instance, work with engineers and marketing personnel to make sure the designs can be manufactured and marketed.

A typical core process group might include staff from finance, research and development, manufacturing, and customer service. All core processes lead to one objective: creating and delivering something of value to the customer.

While some companies completely dismantle their vertical structure to create horizontal organizations, others prefer a hybrid organization—one that combines vertical

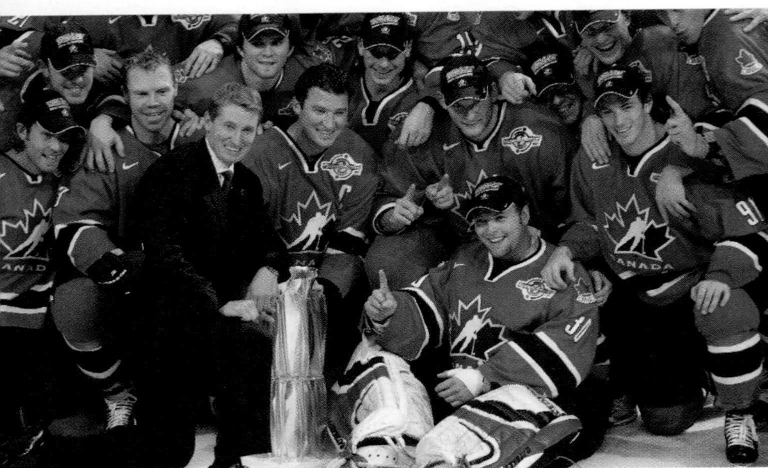

Wayne Gretzky, Team Canada's general manager and inspirational leader, poses with his victorious squad. This group of players truly exemplifies the concept of team. They represented a good mix of young and old players, and the team was created with individuals who fit roles rather than just the best scorers. Team Canada drew from the country's various regions. Rising star Brad Richards represented the Maritimes proudly; from Quebec, Martin Brodeur made it look easy in goal and Mario Lemieux inspired the young players; gritty Ontario defenceman Adam Foote stood tall and western Canadian sniper Joe Sakic led the charge. Despite talent and egos they all worked together, accepted roles, and succeeded in reaching their ultimate goal.

and horizontal functions. In these firms, core processes are supported by organization-wide functional departments such as human resources and finance. The Xerox Corporation, for example, organized its business operations around five core processes based on five types of products. The core processes are supported by two companywide vertical operations: technology management and customer service. This way, researchers are not constrained by specific markets, and customers face only one customer service representative even if they buy different product types.[27]

By now you can see that whether it uses a traditional vertical or an innovative horizontal organization structure, every organization must coordinate activities and communication among its employees. Without such coordination, functional departments would be isolated from one another, and they would be unable to align their objectives.[28] Designing an organization structure that facilitates teamwork and communication is an important first step.

WORKING IN TEAMS

While the vertical chain of command is a tried-and-true method of organizing for business, it is limited by the fact that decision-making authority is often located high up the management hierarchy. Companies that organize vertically may become slow to react to change, and high-level managers may overlook many great ideas for improvement that originate in the lower levels of the organization. As this section will show, the value of involving employees from all levels and functions of the organization in the decision-making process cannot be overstated. As a result, most companies now use a variety of team formats in day-to-day operations.

Even though the team approach has many advantages, shifting to a team structure often requires a fundamental shift in the organization's culture. Management must show strong support for team concepts by empowering teams to make important decisions about the work they do. Teams must also have clear goals that are tied to the company's strategic goals, and their outcomes need to be measured and compared with benchmarks. Moreover, employees must be motivated to work together in teams. Such motivation requires extensive training and a compensation system that is based, at least in part, on team performance. This last objective is sometimes accomplished by using stock options, profit sharing, performance bonuses, and other employee incentives.

What Is a Team?

team
A unit of two or more people who share a mission and collective responsibility as they work together to achieve a goal

A **team** is a unit of two or more people who work together to achieve a goal. Teams differ from work groups in that work groups interact primarily to share information and to make decisions to help one another perform within each member's area of responsibility. In other words, the performance of a work group is merely the summation of all group members' individual contributions.[29] By contrast, the members of a team have a shared mission and are collectively accountable for their work. By coordinating their efforts, team members generate a positive synergy and achieve a level of performance that exceeds what would have been accomplished if members had worked individually.[30]

The concept of the business work team has gained popularity in recent years. However, many companies still pay lip service to the idea of teamwork but fail to properly implement a team environment. A recent survey released by Ipsos-Reid and Microsoft Canada revealed that 86 percent of Canadian executives believe that teamwork is a critical element of business success. However, only 31 percent believed that their firms were meeting the standards of "effective teamwork." According to David Saffran, senior vice-president, Ipsos-Reid, "Business expectations have evolved faster than organizations have been able to keep pace. There appears to be a big gap between what a CEO expects and what an information worker is able to fulfill based on the toolset their employer provides." Not surprisingly, the findings pointed to the need for companies to use solutions like Microsoft-based Office Systems to improve communications and help companies in their quest.[31]

In Microsoft's defence, the company practises what it preaches. At corporate headquarters and beyond, almost all work is completed in teams. Two factors that have made Microsoft teams so successful are clear goals and strong leadership. This atmosphere has created a positive reputation for the firm that draws many new recruits to apply and to rate Microsoft at the top of their job wish list.[32]

Although the team's goals may be set by either the team or upper management, it is the job of the team leader to make sure the team stays on track to achieve those goals. Team leaders are often appointed by senior managers, but sometimes they emerge naturally as the team develops. To foster teamwork and to train employees to understand the techniques and the value of teamwork, many managers and executives are turning to experiential exercises like the ones offered by Outward Bound Canada (see the box entitled "Team Building Activities").

Types of Teams

L.O. 4

The type, structure, and composition of individual teams within an organization all depend on the organization's strategic goals and the objective for forming the team. The five most common forms of teams are *problem-solving teams, self-managed teams, functional teams, cross-functional teams,* and *virtual teams.* Such classifications are not exclusive. For example, a problem-solving team may also be self-managed and cross-functional. Similarly, some teams are established on an informal basis. That is, they are designed to encourage employee participation but do not become part of the formal organization structure.

Problem-Solving Teams

The most common type of informal team is the **problem-solving team**. Also referred to as *quality circles,* problem-solving teams usually consist of 5 to 12 employees from the same department who meet voluntarily to find ways of improving quality, efficiency, and the work environment. Any recommendations they come up with are then submitted to management for approval.[33] Land Rover, a manufacturer of luxury sport-utility vehicles, was able to save millions of dollars, improve productivity, and sell more vehicles by using problem-solving teams.[34] If such teams are able to successfully contribute to the organization, they may evolve into formal teams, a change that represents a fundamental shift in the way the organization is structured.

problem-solving team
Informal team of 5 to 12 employees from the same department who meet voluntarily to find ways of improving quality, efficiency, and the work environment

Self-Managed Teams

Self-managed teams take problem-solving teams to the next level. As the name implies, **self-managed teams** manage their own activities and require minimum supervision. Typically, they control the pace of work and determination of work assignments. Fully self-managed teams select their own members. As you might imagine, many managers are reluctant to embrace self-managed teams because it requires them to give up significant control.

self-managed teams
Teams in which members are responsible for an entire process or operation

SEI Investments administers more than $275 billion in mutual fund and pooled assets, and manages more than $109 billion in assets. SEI operates 22 offices in 12 countries including Canada; its defining unit of operation is the self-managed team. Finding itself indistinguishable from the competition, SEI took a wrecking ball to the traditional corporate pyramid. It formed 140 self-managed teams at its head office to speed up reaction time, innovate more quickly, and get closer to the customer. Some SEI teams are permanent, designed to serve big customers or important markets; others are tempo-

Team Building Activities

Creating an effective work team is not an easy task. For the most part, we were all taught at a young age that individuals excel. From elementary school we learned that good boys and girls earn stars for their performance. As adults we often find the same reward systems in place. Based on these simple individualistic socialization factors it should not be surprising that companies often struggle to transform work groups into highly functioning work teams. In order to improve the transition process, many firms are using experiential group activities. These activities are designed to force groups to work effectively and transform into teams. Companies can spend between $5000 and $15 000 for a session. Some major firms are spending as much as $50 000 per session to have employees learn valuable teamwork skills through diverse activities like mountain climbing, cooking, rowing, and improv theatre.

Outward Bound Canada offers a wide variety of activities and experiences that many high profile companies use for leadership training and team building.

Outward Bound Canada is an organization that offers a wide variety of outdoor experiences such as canoeing and mountaineering. They organize activities across the country, including expeditions in the Yukon, the Rockies, and the east coast. Outward Bound's client list includes companies like Sobeys, HSBC Bank Canada, and Purolator Courier. www.outwardbound.ca/default.asp

At Niagara-based Good Eats Cooking, teamwork essentials are taught in the kitchen. The chefs assign groups the task of cooking a four- or five-course meal that forces team members to work together. The setting is less threatening than an obstacle course and yet the same group dynamics need to be employed in order to achieve success. www.goodearthcooking.com/corporate_events.htm

Fort Angrignon, in Montreal, offers obstacle courses and brain-teasing activities that pit groups of individuals against each other in team competitions. The groups are awarded points for each activity. The competition concludes with a ceremony identifying the most effective teams and leads naturally to a discussion on effective strategies for success. www.fortangrignon.com

Alberta-based Mountain Quest offers a hands-on program that costs companies about $150 per person and forces individuals to work together to accomplish tasks such as conquering the "Electric Fence". www.mountainquest.ca

Regardless of the approach, these activities share certain common results: They force employees to break down imaginary walls and move away from the routine. They help nurture bonds among employees and open lines of communication in a team setting. Each of these programs offers a different approach, but the goals are essentially the same.[35]

Questions for Critical Thinking

1. What are the advantages and disadvantages of holding team building activity days?
2. If you were in charge of organizing a corporate group activity, which option would you choose? Explain your answer.

rary—they come together to solve a problem and disband when their work is done. This flexible team structure is supported by having all office furniture on wheels so that teams can easily create their own work areas. In fact, employees move their desks so often that SEI has created software to map every employee's location.[36]

functional teams
Teams whose members come from a single functional department and that are based on the organization's vertical structure

Functional Teams

Functional teams, or *command teams*, are organized along the lines of the organization's vertical structure and thus may be referred to as *vertical teams*. They are composed of managers and employees within a single functional department. For example, look again at Exhibit 7.1. Functional teams could be formed in the grocery chain's marketing, human resources, and finance departments. The structure of a vertical team typically follows the formal chain of command. In some cases, the team may include several levels of the organizational hierarchy within the same functional department.[37]

Cross-Functional Teams

In contrast to functional teams, **cross-functional teams**, or *horizontal teams*, draw together employees from various functional areas and expertise. In many cross-functional teams, employees are cross-trained to perform a variety of tasks. Cross-functional teams have many benefits: (1) they facilitate the exchange of information between employees, (2) they generate ideas for how to best coordinate the organizational units that are represented, (3) they encourage new solutions for organizational problems, and (4) they aid the development of new organizational policies and procedures.[38]

cross-functional teams
Teams that draw together employees from different functional areas

To develop its 777 airplane, Boeing used hundreds of "design-build" teams that integrated design engineers and production workers.[39] Cross-functional teams have also become a way of life at Harley-Davidson. At the heart of Harley's organization structure are three cross-functional teams or circles—the Create Demand Circle, the Produce Product Circle, and the Provide Support Circle. Each circle includes design engineers, purchasing professionals, manufacturing personnel, marketing personnel, and others. The cross-functional circles are responsible for every motorcycle produced by Harley—from product conception to final design. Within each circle, the leadership role moves from person to person, depending on the issue being addressed.[40]

Besides permanent circles such as the ones used at Harley-Davidson, cross-functional teams can take on a number of formats:

- *Task forces.* A **task force** is a type of cross-functional team formed to work on a specific activity with a completion point. Several departments are usually involved so that all parties who have a stake in the outcome of the task are able to provide input. However, once the goal has been accomplished, the task force is disbanded.[41] Organizations may establish a task force to find ways to reduce the cost of supplies, reduce operational inefficiencies, or solve a systematic problem. For example, the largest blackout in North American history knocked out service in Ontario as well as eight U.S. states and affected 50 million households. Months later in April 2004, a joint Canadian-U.S. task force, formed by Natural Resources Canada and the U.S. Secretary of Energy, rendered its analysis of the problem. They looked at the sequence of events, the responses, and the system failures and concluded by recommending necessary preventive actions to their respective government agencies.[42]

task force
Team of people from several departments who are temporarily brought together to address a specific issue

- *Special-purpose teams.* Like task forces, **special-purpose teams** are created as temporary entities to achieve specific goals. However, special-purpose teams are different because they exist outside the formal organization hierarchy. Such teams remain a part of the organization but have their own reporting structures, and members view themselves as separate from the normal functions of the organization. A special-purpose team might be used to develop a new product when complete creative freedom is needed. By operating outside the formal organization, the team would be able to test new ideas and new ways of accomplishing tasks.[43]

special-purpose teams
Temporary teams that exist outside the formal organization hierarchy and are created to achieve a specific goal

- *Committees.* In contrast to a task force, a **committee** usually has a long life span and may become a permanent part of the organization structure. Committees typically deal with regularly recurring tasks. For example, a grievance committee may be formed as a permanent resource for handling employee complaints and concerns. Because many committees require official representation in order to achieve their goals, committee members are usually selected on the basis of their titles or positions rather than their personal expertise.

committee
Team that may become a permanent part of the organization and is designed to deal with regularly recurring tasks

Virtual Teams

virtual team
Team that uses communication technology to bring geographically distant employees together to achieve goals

Virtual teams are groups of physically dispersed members who work together to achieve a common goal. Virtual team members communicate using a variety of technological formats and devices such as company intranets, e-mail, electronic meeting software, and telephones. Occasionally, they may meet face to face. The biggest advantage of virtual teams is that members are able to work together even if they are thousands of miles and several time zones apart. At Texas Instruments, for instance, microchip engineers in India, Texas, and Japan are able to pool ideas, design new chips, and collaboratively debug them—even though they're separated by more than 12 000 kilometres and 12 time zones.[44]

The three primary factors that differentiate virtual teams from face-to-face teams are the absence of nonverbal cues, a limited social context, and the ability to overcome time and space constraints. Since virtual teams must function with less direct interaction, team members require certain competencies: project-management skills, time management skills, the ability to use electronic communication and collaboration technologies, the ability to work across cultures, as well as a heightened interpersonal awareness. [45] (See the box entitled "Don't Leave Home to Go to Work: American Express Company's Virtual Environment.")

In many cases, virtual teams are as effective as teams that function under a single roof. At the Bank of Montreal a manager was able to retain her position even though she left Toronto to join her husband, who was retiring in Dorset, England. Since the bank wanted to keep a key employee it arranged for her to manage the group using teleconferencing, e-mail, and voice mail. Most of her team was in a glass building in downtown Toronto while she was in an old-fashioned British cottage. Worlds apart, the manger and employees were able to function in this new virtual reality.[46] At British Petroleum, virtual teams link workers in the Gulf of Mexico with those working in the eastern Atlantic and around the globe. By using a virtual team network, the company has decreased the number of helicopter trips to offshore oil platforms, avoided refinery shutdowns because technical experts at other locations were able to handle problems remotely, and experienced a significant reduction in construction rework, among other benefits.[47]

brainstorming
A preliminary technique often used in group situations to generate and develop ideas in a non-threatening environment

L.O. 5

Advantages and Disadvantages of Working in Teams

Even though teams can play a vital role in helping an organization reach its goals, they are not appropriate for every situation. Managers must weigh both the advantages and the disadvantages of teams when deciding whether to use them.[48]

One of the biggest advantages of teams is that the interaction of the participants leads to higher-quality decisions based on the combined intelligence of the group. Moreover, teams lead to increased acceptance of a solution. Team members who participate in making a decision are more likely to enthusiastically support the decision and encourage others to accept it.[49] Another big advantage is that teams have the potential to unleash vast amounts of creativity and energy in workers. Techniques such as **brainstorming** can be used to access the thoughts of various employees in a non-threatening environment. Motivation and performance are often increased as workers share a sense of purpose and mutual accountability. Teams can also fill the individual worker's need to belong to a group. Furthermore, they can reduce boredom, increase feelings of dignity and self-worth, and reduce stress and tension between workers. Finally, teams empower employees to bring more knowledge and skill to the tasks they perform and thereby often lead to greater efficiency and cost reduction.

A creative director at the TBWA/Chiat/Day ad agency attempts to stimulate this team of advertising people to think creatively by walking on the conference room table.

Don't Leave Home to Go to Work: American Express Company's Virtual Environment

"Don't leave home without it!" sends a powerful message about the dangers of travelling without an American Express card tucked into your pocket. Millions of customers listen to that advice each day, making American Express the world's largest travel agency and a leading provider of financial services. But providing a seamless network of services for customers around the globe requires effective teamwork from all employees, whether they're working from the New York headquarters or Canadian locations in Edmonton, Halifax, and Ottawa or telecommuting from home in Los Angeles. Employees have everything they need to work together and contribute to the company's success—even if they don't leave home to go to work.

As president of American Express Global Network and Establishment Services, the division that recruits new American Express merchants, David House encourages his staff members to work together to achieve their goals. But uniting employees in sales offices across long distances demands more than a few rousing pep talks. To build a successful team, House uses technology to promote communication within his division. He provides every employee with access to the company's highly efficient computer network. He offers employees the opportunity to work from home, eliminating the time, expense, and stress of daily commutes to the office. He even provides employees with computer training, software and hardware setup, and selection and delivery of office furniture to complete their virtual office environment.

Nevertheless, House knows that effective teams need more than equipment to produce quality work. They need to communicate. House's telecommuters conduct virtual meetings with colleagues around the world, taking advantage of e-mail and videoconferencing to brainstorm and collaborate on projects. Several units in House's division use a buddy system that requires remote workers to chat with on-site colleagues by phone every morning, covering topics from new customers to office politics. Other telecommuters report to a local or regional office several times each week, meeting with coworkers for specific purposes.

House's knack for developing and using virtual teams at American Express has indeed paid off. Not only do virtual teams save the company time and travel costs, but they have increased employee productivity and improved customer satisfaction rates. Moreover, by using virtual teams, House initially reduced the number of field offices from 85 to 7, resulting in large cost savings for the company.

Questions for Critical Thinking

1. How does American Express support virtual teams?
2. How do American Express telecommuters stay in touch with the company and with each other?

Organizational flexibility is another key benefit of using teams in the workplace. Such flexibility means employees are able to exchange jobs, workers can be reallocated as needed, managers can delegate more authority and responsibility to lower-level employees, and the company can meet changing customer needs more effectively.

In short, using teams can add up to more satisfied employees performing higher-quality work that helps the organization achieve its goals. Studies of individual industries show that companies using teamwork to organize, plan, and control activities enjoy greater productivity, increased profits, fewer defects, lower employee turnover, less waste, and even increased market value.[50] Consider the results these companies achieved by using employee teams: Kodak has halved the amount of time it takes to move a new product from the drawing board to store shelves, Texas Instruments increased revenues per employee by more than 50 percent, and Ritz-Carlton Hotels jumped to the top of the J. D. Power and Associates consumer survey of luxury hotels.[51]

Although teamwork has many advantages, it also has a number of potential disadvantages. For one thing, power within the organization sometimes becomes realigned with teams. Successful teams mean that fewer supervisors are needed, and usually fewer middle and front-line managers. Adjusting to changing job roles, or even to the loss of their jobs, is understandably difficult for many people. Another potential disadvantage is the emergence of **free riders**—team members who don't contribute their fair share to the group's activities because they aren't being held individually accountable for their work. The free-ride attitude can lead to the non-fulfillment of certain tasks. Still another drawback to teamwork is the high cost of coordinating group activities. Aligning schedules, arranging meetings, and coordinating individual parts of a project can eat up a lot

free riders
Team members who do not contribute sufficiently to the group's activities because members are not being held individually accountable for their work

Exhibit 7.6 **Team Member Roles**

Team members assume one of these four roles. Members who assume a dual role often make effective team leaders.

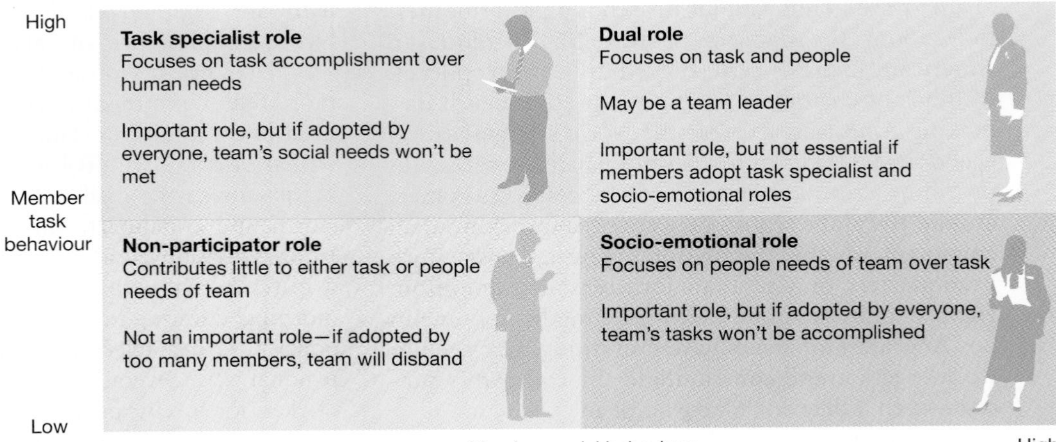

of time and money. A team may develop *groupthink*, a situation in which pressures to conform to the norms of the group cause members to withhold contrary or unpopular opinions. Groupthink can hinder effective decision making because some possibilities will be overlooked.[52]

Most people look at groups from the perspective that two heads are better than one and believe that teamwork works as follows: one plus one equals two. Some would argue that the equation is more closely related to multiplication. In a team full of halfwits the following calculations would apply: halfwit × halfwit = a quarter-wit. This of course represents a cynical look at teams, but at the very least it sarcastically emphasizes the importance of building effective teams rather than just loosely throwing individuals together.[53]

L.O. 6

Characteristics of Effective Teams

Size is one factor that contributes to a team's overall effectiveness. The optimal size for teams is generally thought to be between 5 and 12 members. Teams that contain fewer than five members may be lacking in skill diversity and may be less effective at solving problems. Teams of more than 12 people may be too large for group members to bond properly and may discourage some individuals from sharing their ideas. Larger groups are also prone to disagreements and factionalism because so many opinions must be considered, thus making the team leader's job more difficult. Moreover, studies have shown that turnover and absenteeism are higher in larger teams because members tend to feel that their presence makes less of a difference.

For a team to be successful over time, it must also be structured to accomplish its task and to satisfy its members' needs for social well-being. Effective teams usually fulfill both requirements with a combination of members who assume one of four roles: task specialist, socio-emotional role, dual role, or non-participator. People who assume the *task-specialist role* focus on helping the team reach its goals. In contrast, members who take on the *socio-emotional role* focus on supporting the team's emotional needs and strengthening the team's social unity. Some team members are able to assume *dual roles,* contributing to the task and still meeting members' emotional needs. These members often make effective team leaders. At the other end of the spectrum are members who are *non-participators,* contributing little to reaching the team's goals or to meeting members' emotional needs. Exhibit 7.6 outlines the behaviour patterns associated with each of these roles.

Other characteristics of effective teams include the following:[54]

- *Clear sense of purpose.* Team members clearly understand the task at hand, what is expected of them, and their role on the team.

- *Open and honest communication.* The team culture encourages discussion and debate. Team members speak openly and honestly, without the threat of anger, resentment, or retribution. They listen to and value feedback from others. As a result, all team members participate.
- *Creative thinking.* Effective teams encourage original thinking, considering options beyond the usual.
- *Focused.* Team members get to the core issues of the problem and stay focused on key issues.
- *Decision by consensus.* All decisions are arrived at by consensus. No easy, quick votes are taken.

Of course, learning effective team skills takes time and practice, so many companies now offer employees training in building their team skills. At Saturn, for example, every team member goes through a minimum of 92 hours of training in problem solving and people skills. Saturn teaches team members how to reach a consensus point they call "70 percent comfortable but 100 percent supportive." At that level of consensus, everybody supports the solution.[55] For a brief review of characteristics of effective teams, see Exhibit 7.7.

Five Stages of Team Development

L.O. 7

Developing an effective team is an ongoing process. Like the members who form them, teams grow and change as time goes by. You may think that each team evolves in its own way. However, research shows that teams typically go through five definitive stages of development: forming, storming, norming, performing, and adjourning.[56]

- *Forming.* The forming stage is a period of orientation and breaking the ice. Members get to know each other, determine what types of behaviours are appropriate within the group, identify what is expected of them, and become acquainted with each other's task orientation.

Exhibit 7.7 Characteristics of Effective Teams

Effective teams practise these good habits.

Build a sense of fairness in decision making

- ✓ Encourage debate and disagreement without fear of reprisal
- ✓ Allow members to communicate openly and honestly
- ✓ Consider all proposals
- ✓ Build consensus by allowing team members to examine, compare, and reconcile differences
- ✓ Avoid quick votes
- ✓ Keep everyone informed
- ✓ Present all the facts

Select team members wisely

- ✓ Involve stakeholders
- ✓ Limit size to no more than 12 members
- ✓ Select members with a diversity of views
- ✓ Select creative thinkers

Make working in teams a top management priority

- ✓ Recognize and reward individual and group performance
- ✓ Provide ample training opportunities for employees to develop interpersonal, decision-making, and problem-solving skills
- ✓ Allow enough time for the team to develop and learn how to work together

Manage conflict constructively

- ✓ Share leadership
- ✓ Encourage equal participation
- ✓ Discuss disagreements
- ✓ Focus on the issues, not the people
- ✓ Keep things under control

Stay on track

- ✓ Make sure everyone understands the team's purpose
- ✓ Communicate what is expected of team members
- ✓ Stay focused on the core assignment
- ✓ Develop and adhere to a schedule
- ✓ Develop rules and obey norms

- *Storming.* In the storming stage, members show more of their personalities and become more assertive in establishing their roles. Conflict and disagreement often arise during the storming stage as members jockey for position or form coalitions to promote their own perceptions of the group's mission.
- *Norming.* During the norming stage, these conflicts are resolved, and team harmony develops. Members come to understand and accept one another, reach a consensus on who the leader is, and reach an agreement on each member's role.
- *Performing.* In the performing stage, members are really committed to the team's goals. Problems are solved, and disagreements are handled with maturity in the interest of task accomplishment.
- *Adjourning.* Finally, if the team has a limited task to perform, it goes through the adjourning stage after the task has been completed. In this stage, issues are wrapped up and the team is dissolved.

cohesiveness
A measure of how committed the team members are to their team's goals

As the team moves through the various stages of development, two things happen. First, the team develops a certain level of **cohesiveness**, a measure of how committed the members are to the team's goals. The team's cohesiveness is reflected in meeting attendance, team interaction, work quality, and goal achievement. Cohesiveness is influenced by many factors. Two primary factors are competition and evaluation. If a team is in competition with other teams, cohesiveness increases as the team strives to win. In addition, if a team's efforts and accomplishments are recognized by the organization, members tend to be more committed to the team's goals. Strong team cohesiveness generally results in high morale. Moreover, when cohesiveness is coupled with strong management support for team objectives, teams tend to be more productive.

norms
Informal standards of conduct that guide team behaviour

The second thing that happens as teams develop is the emergence of **norms**—informal standards of conduct that members share and that guide their behaviour. Norms define acceptable behaviour, set limits, identify values, clarify what is expected of members, and facilitate team survival. Norms can be established in various ways: early behaviours that set precedents for future actions, significant events in the team's history, behaviours that come to the team through outside influences, and a leader's or member's explicit statements that have an impact on other members.[57]

Team Conflict

By now you can see that being an effective team member requires many skills. However, none is more important than the ability to handle *conflict*—the antagonistic interactions resulting from differences in ideas, opinions, goals, or ways of doing things. Conflict can be both constructive and destructive to a team's effectiveness. Conflict is constructive if it increases the involvement of team members and results in the solution to a problem. Conflict is destructive if it diverts energy from more important issues, destroys the morale of teams or individual team members, or polarizes or divides the team.[58]

L.O. 8

Causes of Team Conflict

Team conflicts can arise for a number of reasons. First, teams and individuals may feel they are in competition for scarce or declining resources, such as money, information, and supplies. Second, team members may disagree about who is responsible for a specific task; this type of disagreement is usually the result of poorly defined responsibilities and job boundaries. Third, poor communication can lead to misunderstandings and misperceptions about other team members or other teams. In addition, intentionally withholding information can undermine trust among members. Fourth, basic differences in values, attitudes, and personalities may lead to clashes. Fifth, power struggles may result when one party questions the authority of another or when people or teams with limited authority attempt to increase their power or exert more influence. Sixth, conflicts can arise because individuals or teams are pursuing different goals.[59]

For example, a British cardboard manufacturing company switched from a hierarchical, functionally oriented organization to a team-based structure with the hope of empowering employees and reducing scrap. However, once they got started, the teams realized that the company had many problems to solve. Conflicts resulted when team members couldn't agree on which problems to tackle first.[60] Some team conflicts intensify and transform into issues that can lead to workplace bullying and intimidation. This issue has become more visible in recent years and has led to the creation of websites like Vancouver-based No Bully for Me, www.nobullyforme.ca, which is trying to draw attention to the problem of worker intimidation.[61]

The important thing to remember about resolving conflict is that people can usually get what they want if they are willing to work together. In many cases, the resolution process is an exchange of opinions and information that gradually leads to a mutually acceptable solution

How to Resolve Team Conflict

Each team member has a unique style of dealing with conflict, but the members' styles are primarily based on how competitive or cooperative team members are when a conflict arises. Depending on the particular situation, the same individual may use one of several styles, which include avoidance, defusion, and confrontation.[62] *Avoidance* may involve ignoring the conflict in the hope that it will subside on its own, or it may even involve physically separating the conflicting parties. *Defusion* may involve several actions, including downplaying differences and focusing on similarities between team members or teams, compromising on the disputed issue, taking a vote, appealing to a neutral party or higher authority, or redesigning the team. *Confrontation* is an attempt to work through the conflict by getting it out in the open, which may be accomplished by organizing a meeting between the conflicting parties.

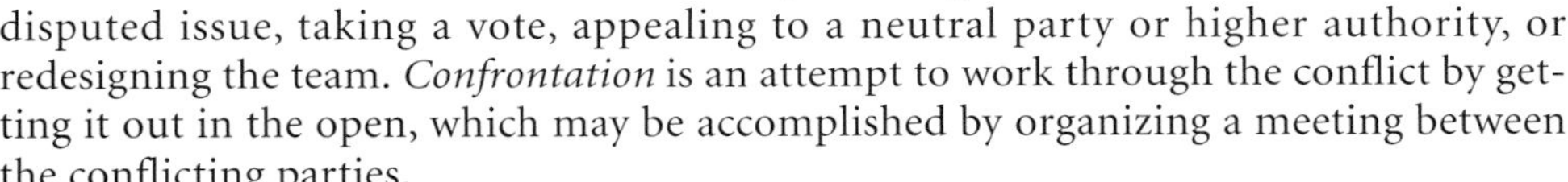

These three styles of conflict resolution come into play after a conflict has developed, but team members and team leaders can take several steps to prevent conflicts. First, by establishing clear goals that require the efforts of every member, the team reduces the chance that members will battle over their objectives or roles. Second, by developing well-defined tasks for each member, the team leader ensures that all parties are aware of their responsibilities and the limits of their authority. Finally, by facilitating open communication, the team leader can ensure that all members understand their own tasks and objectives as well as those of their teammates. Keep in mind that communication builds respect and tolerance, and provides a forum for bringing misunderstandings into the open before they turn into full-blown conflicts.

SUMMARY OF LEARNING OBJECTIVES

1 Discuss the function of a company's organization structure.

An organization structure provides a framework through which a company can coordinate and control the work, divide responsibilities, distribute authority, and hold employees accountable. An organization chart provides a visual representation of this framework.

2 Explain the concepts of accountability, authority, and delegation.

Accountability is the obligation to report work results to supervisors or team members and to justify any outcomes that fall below expectations. Authority is the power to make decisions, issue orders, carry out actions, and allocate resources to achieve the organization's goals. Delegation refers to the assignment of work and the transfer of authority and responsibility to complete that work.

3 Define four types of departmentalization.

Companies may departmentalize in any combination of four ways: (1) by function, which groups employees according to their skills, resource use, and expertise; (2) by division, which establishes self-contained departments formed according to similarities in product, process, customer, or geography; (3)

by matrix, which assigns employees from functional departments to interdisciplinary project teams and requires them to report to both a department head and a team leader; and (4) by network, which connects separate companies that perform selected tasks for a headquarters organization.

Describe the five most common forms of teams.

The five most common forms of teams are (1) problem-solving teams, which seek ways to improve a situation and then submit their recommendation to management; (2) self-managed teams, which manage their own activities and seldom require supervision; (3) functional teams, which are composed of employees within a single functional department; (4) cross-functional teams, which draw together employees from various departments and expertise in a number of formats such as task forces, special-purpose teams, and committees; and (5) virtual teams, which bring together employees from distant locations.

Highlight the advantages and disadvantages of working in teams.

Teamwork has the potential to increase creativity, motivation, performance, and satisfaction of workers and thereby can lead to greater company efficiency, flexibility, and cost savings. The potential disadvantages of working in teams include the difficulties of managing employees' changing roles, the possibilities of free riders and groupthink, and the costs and time needed to coordinate members' schedules and project parts.

List the characteristics of effective teams.

Effective teams have a clear sense of purpose, communicate openly and honestly, build a sense of fairness in decision making, think creatively, stay focused on key issues, manage conflict constructively, and select team members wisely by involving stakeholders, creative thinkers, and members with a diversity of views. Moreover, effective teams have an optimal size of between 5 and 12 members.

Review the five stages of team development.

Teams typically go through five stages of development. In the forming stage, team members become acquainted with each other and with the group's purpose. In the storming stage, conflict often arises as coalitions and power struggles develop. In the norming stage, conflicts are resolved and harmony develops. In the performing stage, members focus on achieving the team's goals. In the adjourning stage, the team dissolves upon completion of its task.

Highlight six causes of team conflict and three styles of conflict resolution.

Conflict can arise from competition for scarce resources; confusion over task responsibility; poor communication and misinformation; differences in values, attitudes, and personalities; power struggles; and goal incongruity. Conflict can be resolved by avoiding it and hoping that it will go away, by defusing it—downplaying team member differences or focusing on member similarities—or by confronting it and working hard to resolve the issues at hand.

Behind the SCENES

Wainwright Industries Turns Teamwork into Award-Winning Quality

In the early 1990s, Wainwright Industries was growing, but its employees and middle managers were frustrated because top managers controlled all decisions. After hearing a Baldrige Award winner talk about trust and belief in employees, Wainwright's owners and senior managers realized that they were not acting as if they trusted and believed in their own workforce. CEO Arthur Wainwright announced that the company was going to change. Now he had to follow through.

First, he designated worker safety and skills as a top priority. This was a tangible way for the company to demonstrate its commitment to its employees. Wainwright set aside 6 to 7 percent of the yearly payroll budget for training on safety, interpersonal skills, math, reading, and writing. New employees received a daylong orientation on the company and its safety procedures, followed by two weeks of on-the-job training with a trainer and one or more experienced employees.

Next, with training in place and ongoing management reinforcement, the company was able to implement a more effective team structure. Instead of following managers' orders, employees would participate in making and implementing decisions through a new team structure, with leaders serving as trainers and coaches to six members. This shift was initially unsettling to both managers and employees, but employees soon developed confidence in their abilities. "I can't imagine going back to the old way of doing things now," commented one employee. "If I say something isn't safe, nobody second-guesses me or tells me to go back to work."

Arthur Wainwright also implemented a new communication philosophy, which he summed up in two words: no secrets. "If you try to hide vital information," said the CEO, "you're wasting your money on training, because people can't make sound decisions. Furthermore, they won't trust that you are committed to equipping them with what they need to do a good job." The company jump-started the formal communication process by asking employees what was important to their performance. In addition, the CEO met with each new employee to explain company priorities and discuss any concerns. The result: Safety, involvement, customer satisfaction, quality, and financial performance were incorporated into Wainwright's goals and plans, and these new policies reduced the number of accidents, the amount of lost time, and the amount spent on workers' compensation.

Once all these changes were in place, the company went through the arduous process of applying for a Baldrige Award. Winning that award put Wainwright in the major leagues, alongside such award-winning giants as IBM. It also showed that trust, open communication, and participative teamwork can really make a difference.[63]

Critical Thinking Questions

1. What effect do you think the "no secrets" policy had on internal communication at Wainwright?
2. How was the company's new team structure likely to affect accountability and authority?
3. Is Wainwright's drive for more employee involvement in decision making an example of centralization or decentralization?

Learn More Online

Effective teamwork and communication have helped Wainwright and many other companies win the prestigious Baldrige Award. Visit the "winner's showcase" page of the Baldrige Award website by going to Chapter 7 of this text's website at www.pearsoned.ca/bovee and clicking on the Baldridge Award hotlink. Read through the profiles of recent winners. How have the winners improved quality through better teamwork? How have they boosted quality by paying closer attention to internal and external communication?

KEY TERMS

accountability (170)
authority (170)
brainstorming (180)
centralization (172)
chain of command (170)
cohesiveness (184)
committee (179)
cross-functional teams (179)
customer divisions (173)
decentralization (172)
delegation (170)
departmentalization (173)
departmentalization by division (173)
departmentalization by function (173)
departmentalization by matrix (174)
departmentalization by network (175)
flat organizations (171)
formal organization (169)
free riders (181)
functional teams (178)
geographic divisions (173)
informal organization (169)
line organization (170)
line-and-staff organization (171)
norms (184)
organization chart (169)
organization structure (168)
problem-solving team (177)
process divisions (173)
product divisions (173)
responsibility (170)
self-managed teams (177)
span of management (171)
special-purpose teams (179)
tall organizations (171)
task force (179)
team (176)
vertical organization (173)
virtual team (180)
work specialization (170)

TEST YOUR KNOWLEDGE

Questions for Review

1. Why is organizational structure important?
2. What are the characteristics of tall organizations and flat organizations?
3. What are the advantages and disadvantages of work specialization?
4. What are the advantages and disadvantages of functional departmentalization?
5. What are the advantages and disadvantages of working in teams?

Questions for Analysis

6. Why would you expect a manager of a group of nuclear physicists to have a wide span of management?

7. How does horizontal organization promote innovation?
8. What can managers do to help teams work more effectively?
9. How can companies benefit from using virtual teams?
10. **Ethical Considerations.** You were honoured that you were selected to serve on the salary committee of the employee negotiations task force. As a member of that committee, you reviewed confidential company documents listing the salaries of all department managers. You discovered that managers at your level are earning $5000 more than you, even though you've been at the company the same amount of time. You feel that a raise is justified on the basis of this confidential information. How will you handle this situation?

Questions for Application

11. You are the leader of a cross-functional work team whose goal is to find ways of lowering production costs. Your team of eight employees has become mired in the storming stage. They disagree on how to approach the task, and they are starting to splinter into factions. What can you do to help the team move forward?
12. Your warehouse operation is currently functioning at capacity. To accommodate anticipated new business, your company must either build a major addition to your current warehouse operation or build a new warehouse that would be located at a distant site. As director of warehouse operations, you would like several people to participate in this decision. Should you form a task force, a committee, or a special-purpose team? Explain your choice.
13. **Integrated.** One of your competitors has approached you with an intriguing proposition. The company would like to merge with your company. The economies of scale are terrific. So are the growth possibilities. There's just one issue to be resolved. Your competitor is organized under a horizontal structure and uses a lot of cross-functional teams. Your company is organized under a traditional vertical structure that is departmentalized by function. Using your knowledge about culture clash, what are the likely issues you will encounter if these two organizations are merged?
14. **Integrated.** In Chapter 6 we discussed three styles of leadership: autocratic, democratic, and laissez faire. Using your knowledge about the differences in these leadership styles, which style would you expect to find under the following organization structures: (a) vertical organization—departmentalization by function; (b) vertical organization—departmentalization by matrix; (c) horizontal organization; (d) self-directed teams?

PRACTISE YOUR KNOWLEDGE

SHARPENING YOUR COMMUNICATION SKILLS

Write a brief memo to your instructor describing a recent conflict you had with a peer at work or at school. Be sure to highlight the cause of the conflict and steps you took to resolve it. Which of the three conflict-resolution styles discussed in this chapter did you use? Did you find a solution that both of you could accept?

BUILDING YOUR TEAM SKILLS

What's the most effective organization structure for your college or university? With your team, obtain a copy of your school's organization chart. If this chart is not readily available, gather information by talking with people in administration, and then draw your own chart of the organization structure.

Analyze the chart in terms of span of management. Is your school a flat or a tall organization? Is this organization structure appropriate for your school? Does decision making tend to be centralized or decentralized in your school? Do you agree with this approach to decision making?

Finally, investigate the use of formal and informal teams in your school. Are there any problem-solving teams, task forces, or committees at work in your school? Are any teams self-directed or virtual? How much authority do these teams have to make decisions? What is the purpose of teamwork in your school? What kinds of goals do these teams have?

Share your team's findings during a brief classroom presentation, and then compare the findings of all teams. Is there agreement on the appropriate organization structure for your school?

EXPAND YOUR KNOWLEDGE

DISCOVERING CAREER OPPORTUNITIES

Whether you're a top manager, first-line manager (supervisor), or middle manager, your efforts will affect the success of your organization. To get a closer look at what the responsibilities of a manager are, log on to the Prentice Hall Student Success SuperSite at www.prenhall.com/success. Click on Majors Exploration, and select "Business" then "management" in the drop-down box. Then scroll down and read about careers in management.

1. What can you do with a degree in management?
2. What is the future outlook for careers in management?
3. Go to the American Management Association website and click on Research. Then scroll down and click on Administrative Professionals Current Concerns Survey. According to the survey, what has affected administrative professionals most recently? On which five tasks do managers spend most of their time?

DEVELOPING YOUR RESEARCH SKILLS

Although teamwork can benefit many organizations, introducing and managing team structures can be a real challenge. Search past issues of business journals or newspapers (print or online editions) to locate articles about how an organization has overcome problems with teams.

1. Why did the organization originally introduce teams? What types of teams are being used?
2. What problems did each organization encounter in trying to implement teams? How did the organization deal with these problems?
3. Have the teams been successful from management's perspective? From the employees' perspective? What effect has teamwork had on the company, its customers, and its products?

See It on the **WEB**

URLs for all Internet exercises are provided at the website for this book, www.pearsoned.ca/bovee. When you log on to the text website, select Chapter 7, then Destinations, then click on the name of the featured website, and review the website to complete the following exercises.

Explore these chapter-related websites, review their content, and answer the following questions for each website you visit:

1. What is the purpose of this website?
2. What kinds of information does this website contain? Please be specific.
3. How is the information provided at this website useful for business people? Consumers?
4. How did you expand your knowledge of organizing and working in teams by reviewing the material at this website? What new things did you learn about these topics?

BUILD TEAMS IN THE CYBER AGE

Let Teamworks, the Virtual Team Assistant, help you build a more effective team, resolve team conflict, manage projects, solve team problems, be a team leader, encourage team feedback, and teach with teams. Each of the site's nine information modules contains background information, self-assessment vehicles, skill development exercises, and links to helpful resources. Log on now and increase your effectiveness as a team member by learning more about how teams work, the stages of team development, tips for communicating with team members during a project, and some creative problem-solving techniques. www.vta.spcomm.uiuc.edu

BE DIRECT

If you want to learn more about building effective teams, you can read many excellent books on the subject. But you might be surprised by just how much information on team building you can find on the Internet. One good starting point is the Self-Directed and Self-Managed Work Teams page. This site's designers are passionate about teamwork, and they want to make it easier for people to work effectively in teams. Read the Frequently Asked Question (FAQs) about self-managed teams. Then explore some of the links to discover more about teams and teamwork. www.mapnp.org/library/grp_skll/slf_drct/slf_drct.htm

RESOLVE CONFLICT LIKE A PRO

The field of conflict resolution has been growing very quickly and includes practices such as negotiation, mediation, arbitration, international peace building, and more. Learn more about each of these topics along with basic information about conflict resolution by visiting CR Info. Be sure to check out the web resources, where you'll find links to communication and facilitation skills, consensus building, and more. Find out why BATNA is important. Discover what a mediator does. Learn how to conduct effective meetings. And don't leave without testing your knowledge of common negotiation terms. www.crinfo.org

Chapter 8 Producing Quality Goods and Services

LEARNING OBJECTIVES

After studying this chapter, you will be able to

1. Explain what production and operations managers do
2. Identify key tasks involved in designing a production process
3. Discuss the role of computers and automation technology in production
4. Explain the strategic importance of managing inventory
5. Distinguish among JIT, MRP, and MRP II inventory management systems
6. Highlight the differences between quality control and quality assurance
7. Describe the supply chain and explain how companies today are managing their supply chains

Behind the SCENES

Harley-Davidson Goes Full Throttle

Former chairman and chief executive officer Jeffrey Bleustein led Harley-Davidson during a period of tremendous growth from 1997 to 2005.

www.harley-davidson.com

Harley-Davidson had long enjoyed an unprecedented level of customer loyalty. Its reputation as the outstanding maker of heavy-weight motorcycles was legendary—until it hit a deep pothole in the 1970s. Cutting costs to battle stiff competition from imports, the company let production quality slip. Harley was also behind the curve on product design and development. Its big-iron cruisers and long-distance touring bikes were heavy, chrome laden, and expensive. They leaked oil and vibrated excessively. Some customers even joked that they should buy two Harleys—one to ride and one for parts. Motorcycle buyers tired of tolerating frequent breakdowns and turned to the smooth-riding imports. Harley's market share tumbled.

Over the next two decades, Harley rebuilt its production processes from the ground up, putting more emphasis on quality than on quantity. By the early 1990s, the company had quality firmly under control. With its reputation mended, demand rebounded so strongly that dealers reported long waiting lists of riders eager to climb back on a Harley. Some fiercely loyal customers even tattooed the company's logo on their chests. Management responded to the surge of orders by carefully increasing annual motorcycle production while maintaining quality. But products were snapped up as quickly as they could be cranked out.

By 1995, annual production had reached the 100 000 milestone and projections indicated a strong increase in demand for the coming years. So with every reason to celebrate, why were Harley-Davidson's top managers planning a major retooling of the motorcycle manufacturing production processes?

Harley's managers wanted to boost output and expand sales in Europe, Scandinavia, Australia, Japan, and other global markets without cutting back on North American distribution. They set an ambitious company-wide goal: to be able to produce 200 000 motorcycles annually by 2003, the company's centennial. But meeting this goal would require a top-to-bottom revamping of the entire production process. Not only was Harley's 84-year-old distribution warehouse cramped and outdated, but its equipment was decades old.

Facing a self-imposed deadline for boosting production output, what could chairman and CEO Jeff Bleustein and his top managers do to increase efficiency of the production process without sacrificing quality? How could they apply technology to improve the company's production process? How could the company work hand in hand with its suppliers to meet Harley's centennial goal?[1]

UNDERSTANDING PRODUCTION AND OPERATIONS MANAGEMENT

L.O. 1

As managers of Harley-Davidson know, the extremely competitive nature of the global business environment requires companies to produce high-quality goods and services in the most efficient way possible. Few defects, fast production, low costs, excellent customer service, broad market reach, innovative products and processes, less waste, and high flexibility are all objectives that improve quality by adding value to the good or service being produced. Companies pursue these objectives to maintain a competitive advantage.[2] Moreover, managers understand that the level of quality that a company aspires to in the production of goods and services affects its long-term ability to address the needs of its customers.

What Is Production?

production
Transformation of resources into goods or services that people need or want

production and operations management (POM)
Coordination of an organization's resources in manufacturing goods or delivering services

What exactly is production, and what does it involve? To most people, the term *production* suggests images of factories, machines, and assembly lines staffed with employees making automobiles, computers, furniture, motorcycles, or other tangible goods. That's because in the past people used the terms *production* and *manufacturing* interchangeably. With the growth in the number of service-based businesses and their increasing importance to the economy, however, the term **production** is now used to describe the transformation of resources into goods and services that people need or want. The broader term **production and operations management (POM)**, or simply *operations management,* refers to all of the activities involved in producing a firm's goods and services.

Like other types of management, POM involves the basic functions of planning, organizing, leading, and controlling. It also requires careful consideration of a company's goals, the strategies for attaining those goals, and the standards against which results will be measured. In both manufacturing and service organizations, the production and operations manager is the person responsible for performing these functions. One of the principal responsibilities of the production and operations manager is to design and oversee an efficient conversion process—one that lowers costs by optimizing output from each resource used in the process. These resources include money, materials, inventories, people, buildings, and time.

What Is the Conversion Process?

At the core of production is the *conversion process,* the sequence of events that converts resources (or inputs) into products and services. This process applies to both intangible services and tangible goods. An airline, like CanJet, uses such processes as booking flights, flying airplanes, maintaining equipment, and training crews to transform tangible and intangible inputs such as the plane, the pilot's skill, fuel, time, and passengers into the delivery of customers to their destinations. For a clothing manufacturer to produce a jacket, inputs such as cloth, thread, and buttons are transformed by the seamstress into the finished product (see Exhibit 8.1).

analytic system
Production process that breaks incoming materials into various component products and divisional patterns simultaneously

Conversion is of two basic types. An **analytic system** breaks raw materials into one or more distinct products, which may or may not resemble the original material in form and function. In meatpacking, for example, a steer is divided into hide, bone, steaks, and

Exhibit 8.1 **The Conversion Process**

Production of goods or services is basically a process of conversion. Inputs (the basic ingredients) are transformed (by the application of labour, equipment, and capital) into outputs (the desired product or service).

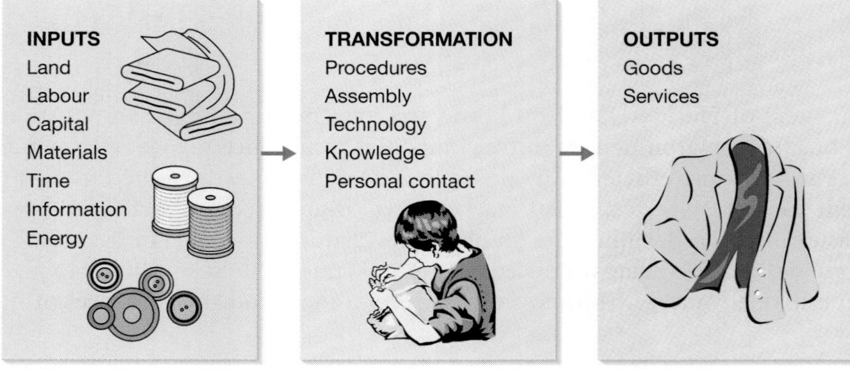

so on. A **synthetic system** combines two or more materials to form a single product. For example, in steel manufacturing, iron is combined with small quantities of other minerals at high temperatures to make steel.

Another thing to keep in mind is that the conversion process for a service operation and goods production operation is similar in terms of *what* is done—that is, inputs are transformed into outputs. However, the two differ in how the processes are performed (see Exhibit 8.2). That's because the production of goods results in a tangible output—something you can see or touch, such as a jacket, motorcycle, desk, or bicycle—while the production of a service results in an intangible act. As such, the production of services involves a much higher degree of customer contact, is subject to greater variability, is more labour intensive, and results in a lower uniformity of output than the production of goods.

A manufacturer, such as Vantage Furniture, must compile inputs (wood and fabric) and transformation components like tools, specialized machinery, and workers. The transformation process is the actual fabrication and assembly of the sofa; the desired output is a flawless piece of furniture ready for consumer purchase. Vantage Furniture sells their finished products in locations across Canada such as The Brick, Leons, Tanguay, and Brault & Martineau.

Mass Production versus Mass Customization

Mass production—manufacturing goods in large quantities—means little or no customization. Because of the high volume of similar goods produced, this process reduces production costs per unit and makes products available to more people. Even though mass production has economic advantages, the competitive pressures of the global economy often require production techniques that are flexible, customer focused, and quality oriented.

Consider Andersen Windows. Throughout most of its long history, Andersen mass-produced a range of standard windows in large batches. However, in the early 1990s customer demands and an increasing error rate caused Andersen to rethink the way it built windows. To better meet customer needs, the company developed an interactive computer catalogue that allows customers to add, change, and remove features of Andersen's standard windows until they've designed the exact windows they want. Once the customers select their design, the computer automatically generates a price quote and sends the order to the factory, where standardized parts are tailored to customer specifications. Today, the company offers close to 200 000 different products that are virtually error-

synthetic system
Production process that combines two or more materials or components to create finished products; the reverse of an analytic system

mass production
Manufacturing uniform products in great quantities

Exhibit 8.2 **Input-Transformation-Output Relationships for Typical Systems**

Both goods and services undergo a conversion process, but the components of the process vary to accommodate the differences between tangible and intangible outputs.

SYSTEM	INPUTS	TRANSFORMATION COMPONENTS	TRANSFORMATION FUNCTION	TYPICAL DESIRED OUTPUT
Hospital	Patients, medical supplies	Physicians, nurses, equipment	Health care	Healthy individuals
Restaurant	Hungry customers, food	Chef, waitress, environment	Well-prepared and well-served food	Satisfied customers
Automobile factory	Sheet steel, engine parts	Tools, equipment, workers	Fabrication and assembly of cars	High-quality cars
College or university	High school graduates, books	Teachers, classrooms	Impart knowledge and skills	Educated individuals
Department store	Shoppers, stock of goods	Displays, salesclerks	Attract shoppers, promote products, fill orders	Sales to satisfied customers

mass customization
Producing customized goods and services through mass production techniques

free. Andersen's current production system is known as **mass customization**—using mass production techniques to produce customized goods. The company also uses *batch-of-one manufacturing,* in which every product is made to order from scratch.[3] The basic idea behind mass customization is that consumers have individual needs and are best served by products that can be easily customized for them.

Like Andersen Windows, many companies are adopting manufacturing techniques that let them tailor goods to individuals on a large scale. The key to customizing on a mass scale is digital technology—a combination of hardware, software, and new machines that fine-tune the production process. Levi Strauss & Company is among those offering machine-customized clothing, thanks to new technologies that handle single items on the assembly line or take body measurements that are then zapped to a manufacturing plant through the Web. Nike created Nike ID, which allows customers to alter the colour, design, and even the construction of their shoes.[4]

L.O. 2

DESIGNING THE PRODUCTION PROCESS

When Jeff Bleustein and his management team at Harley-Davidson set out to return Harley to a competitive position, they learned that the way an organization designs its operations can dramatically affect a company's ability to deliver quality products. Designing an effective production process is one of the key responsibilities of production and operations managers. It involves five important tasks: forecasting demand, planning for capacity, choosing a facility location, designing a facility layout, and scheduling work.

Forecasting Demand

production forecasts
Estimates of how much of a company's goods and services must be produced in order to meet future demand

The first step in designing an effective production process for a manufacturing operation is to determine how much the company will need to produce in a certain time span. Using customer feedback, market research, past sales figures, industry analyses, and educated guesses about the future behaviour of the economy and competitors, operations managers prepare **production forecasts**, estimates of future demand for the company's products. These estimates are then used to plan, budget, and schedule the use of resources. Of course, many factors in the business environment cannot be predicted or controlled with certainty. For this reason, managers must regularly review and adjust their forecasts to account for these uncertainties.

Service companies must also forecast demand. For example, dentists must be able to project approximately how many patients they will treat in a given time period so they can staff their offices properly and have enough dental supplies on hand. Without such forecasts, dentists can't run their production process (treating patients) efficiently. Similarly, cruise ship operators must forecast exactly how much food and supplies to stock for one week's journey, because once the ship sets sail, there are no last-minute deliveries. On the basis of years of experience, operation managers for Carnival's Elation Cruise Line can now forecast that a one-week Caribbean cruise will require some 4500 kilograms of meat, 10 080 bananas, and 41 600 eggs.[5]

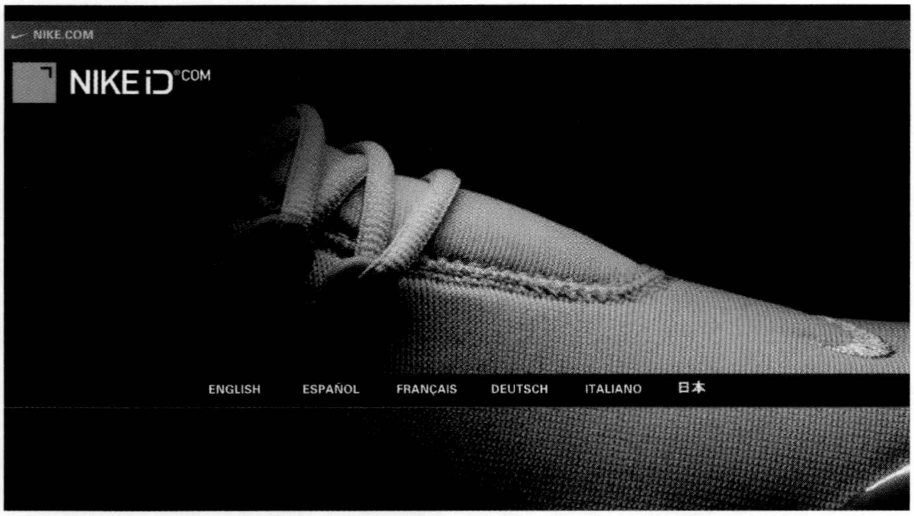

You may not have known the meaning of mass customization until now, but many of you have been served by the practice. The Nike ID website is user-friendly, allows consumers to custom-design features for their shoes, and enables them to place their own personalized ID on the end product. *http://nikeid.nike.com/*

Planning for Capacity

Many of the newer, larger cruise ships have elegant restaurants, boutiques, luxury spas, high-tech fitness rooms, conference and meeting rooms, theatres, playrooms, ice-skating rinks, and even rock-climbing walls. With passenger counts of 3000 and upward, forecasting customer demand for food, supplies, and entertainment is no easy task.

Once product demand has been estimated, management must determine the company's capacity to produce the goods or services. The term *capacity* refers to the volume of manufacturing or service capability that an organization can handle. For example, a doctor's office with only one examining room limits the number of patients the doctor can see each day. A cruise ship with 750 staterooms limits the number of passengers the ship can accommodate in any given week. Similarly, a beverage bottling plant with only one conveyor belt and one local warehouse limits the company's ability to manufacture beverage products.

Capacity planning is a long-term strategic decision that establishes the overall level of resources needed to meet customer demand. The neighbourhood convenience store needs to consider traffic volume throughout the day and night in order to plan staffing levels appropriately. At the other extreme of complexity, when managers at Bombardier plan for the production of a new plane, like the projected C-Series, they have to consider not only the staffing of thousands of people but also factory floor space, material flows from hundreds of suppliers, internal deliveries, cash flow, tools and equipment, and dozens of other factors. Because of the potential impact on finances, customers, and employees, capacity planning involves some of the most difficult decisions that managers have to make.

Top management uses long-term capacity planning to make significant decisions about an organization's ability to produce goods and services, such as expanding existing facilities, constructing new facilities, or phasing out unneeded ones. Such decisions entail a great deal of risk, for two reasons: (1) Large shifts in demand are difficult to predict accurately, and (2) long-term capacity decisions can be difficult to undo. For example, if a new facility is built to produce a new product that then fails, or if demand for a popular product suddenly declines, the company will find itself with expensive excess capacity. Managers must decide what they should do with this excess capacity. If they keep it, they might try to find an alternate use for this space. If they eliminate it and demand picks up again, the company will have to forgo profits because it is unable to meet customer demand.[6] Service companies face similar problems. Airlines provide transportation, which is a service, but they need facilitating products: airplanes. Purchasing planes to meet demand 3, 5, or 10 years down the line is difficult. For example, Air Canada recently announced that it was going to spend $6 billion on 32 airplanes from Boeing. This announcement was made just seven months after the company emerged from bankruptcy protection. The move was described as a key strategic decision to lower fuel costs and meet specific demand criteria.[7]

capacity planning
A long-term strategic decision that determines the level of resources available to an organization to meet customer demand

Choosing a Facility Location

One long-term issue that management must resolve early when designing the production process for goods and services is the location of production facilities. The goal is to choose a location that minimizes costs while increasing operational efficiencies and product quality. To accomplish this goal, management must consider such regional costs as land, construction, labour, local taxes, energy, and local living standards. In addition, management must consider whether the local labour pool has the skills that the firm needs. For example, firms that need highly trained accountants, engineers, or computer scientists often locate in areas near university communities. On the other hand, if most of the jobs can be filled by unskilled or semiskilled employees, firms can choose locations where such labour is available at a relatively low cost. The search for low-cost labour has led many companies to locate their manufacturing operations in countries such as Mexico, Taiwan, India, and China, where wages are relatively low.

Also affecting location decisions are transportation costs, which cover the shipping of supplies and finished goods. Almost every company needs easy, low-cost access to ground transportation such as highways and rail lines. Moreover, companies that sell a lot of products overseas must be able to arrange for efficient air or water transportation. Finally, companies must consider raw materials costs. For example, the location of a coal-based power plant must be chosen to minimize the cost of distributing electrical power to customers and to minimize the cost and *lead time* of shipping coal to the plant.

Gildan Activewear, has become a global powerhouse in the T-shirt business. This Montreal-based manufacturer has captured about 30 percent of the U.S. imprinted T-shirt business. To remain competitive the company operates manufacturing facilities in the Dominican Republic, Haiti, and Honduras. These locations offer both low-cost labour and shipping.[8]

Location considerations may be different for some service organizations. Although they may also take regional costs into consideration, the main objective for many service firms is to locate where profit potential is greatest. Unlike manufacturing operations, in which low production costs are an important consideration, services tend to focus on more customer-driven factors.[9] Because they often require one-on-one contact with customers, service organizations such as gas stations, restaurants, department stores, and charities must locate where their target market is large and sustainable. Therefore, market research often plays a central role in site selection. However, for service companies that reach customers primarily by telephone, mail, or the Internet, proximity to customers is less of a consideration.

Designing a Facility Layout

Once a site has been selected, managers must turn their attention to *facility layout,* the arrangement of production work centres and other elements (such as materials, equipment, and support departments) needed to process goods and services. Layout includes the efforts involved in selecting specific locations for each department, process, machine, support function, and other activity required for the operation or service. The need for a new layout design can occur for a number of reasons besides new construction; for instance, a new process or method might become available, the volume of business might change, a new product or service may be offered, an outdated facility may be remodelled, the mix of goods or services offered may change, or an existing product or service may be redesigned.[10]

Facility layout affects the amount of on-hand inventory, the efficiency of materials handling, the use of equipment, and the productivity and morale of employees. In goods manufacturing, the primary concern is the efficient movement of resources and inventory. In the production of services, facility layout controls the flow of customers through the system and influences the customer's satisfaction with the service.[11] In both services and goods operations, the major goals of a good layout design are to minimize materials-handling costs, reduce bottlenecks in moving material or people, provide flexibility, provide ease of supervision, use available space effectively and efficiently, reduce hazards, and facilitate coordination and communications wherever appropriate.[12] (See the box entitled "A Bike That Really Travels.") Four typical facility layouts are *process layout, product layout, cellular layout,* and *fixed-position layout* (see Exhibit 8.3 on page 198).[13]

process layout
Method of arranging a facility so that production tasks are carried out in separate departments containing specialized equipment and personnel

product layout
Method of arranging a facility so that production proceeds along a line of workstations

A **process layout** is also called a *functional layout* because it concentrates everything needed to complete one phase of the production process in one place. Specific functions, such as drilling or welding, are performed in one location for different products or customers (see Exhibit 8.3A). The process layout is often used in machine shops as well as in service industries. For example, a medical clinic might dedicate one room to X-rays, another room to routine examinations, and still another to outpatient surgery.

An alternative to the process layout is the **product layout**, also called the *assembly-line layout,* in which the main production process occurs along a line, and products in progress move from one workstation to the next. Materials and subassemblies of component parts may feed into the main line at several points, but the flow of production is continuous. Electronics and personal computer manufacturers are just two of many industries that typically use this layout (see Exhibit 8.3B).

Some production of services is also organized by product. For example, when you go to get a driver's licence, you usually go through a series of steps administered by sev-

A Bike That Really Travels

When bike industry veteran Hanz Scholz decided to pedal across Europe in 1987, his vision of packing a folding bike in a suitcase, when it was time to board a plane or train, soon began to fade. Scholz was disappointed by the quality of folding bikes available. So he set out to build his own: one compact enough to fit into a large suitcase but high quality enough to tackle steep hills and long, rugged stretches.

Five years later, the first commercial orders for Scholz's Bike Friday were rolling in. Unlike its fold-up predecessors—often one-size-fits-all models available in retail stores—all Bike Fridays are custom made by manufacturer Green Gear Cycling to meet the rider's size and component/colour preference. The bike fits into a car trunk, a tight storage space, or an optional suitcase to travel on a plane like regular baggage.

Green Gear's operations are as distinctive as its product. The relatively small company (US$3 million in sales, 30 employees, and 17 000 square feet of production space) uses advanced manufacturing principles adopted from Toyota Motor and other large manufacturers. Built individually, each Bike Friday begins its life as a bundle of tubes, components, and other structures. These elements are processed through a build-to-order, flow-manufacturing configuration organized in a series of cells. The cells are designed so that any one cell can do some of the work of the previous or next cell if production runs behind or ahead.

Once work on a bike has begun, it flows through the process without hesitation at any point. "It works like a track relay with a transition area," says Scholz. "We've set up everything with single-process-specific tools so there is no process changeover time. The flow motto is "touch it once, do it now." When a quality problem is discovered, the operator switches on a red light and all procedures stop until the production cell is adjusted to eliminate the problem.

Operating in a one-at-a-time flow system rather than in batches maximizes the chances for continuous improvement. "For us, every bike is a batch, so we have 150 to 200 chances per month to make process improvements," says Scholz. "A small manufacturer operating in a large-batch mode can be put out of business if he ruins just one. If you can make improvements as you find them, you can survive as a small manufacturer."

Today, Green Gear Cycling builds about 2000 bikes annually. At an average selling price of US$1700, Bike Friday commands a premium price primarily to North American customers. "We give people what they want, when they want it," says Scholz. "If you do that, people are willing to pay you for it."

Questions for Critical Thinking

1. What are the advantages of using a cellular layout to manufacture Bike Friday?
2. Does Green Gear Cycling mass-produce or mass-customize folding bikes? Explain your answer.

---

eral people: registering, taking a written or computerized test, having an eye exam, paying a cashier, and getting your picture taken. You emerge from this system a licensed driver (unless, of course, you fail one of the tests).

A **cellular layout** groups dissimilar machines into work centres (or cells) to process parts that have similar shapes and processing requirements (see Exhibit 8.3C). Arranging work flow by cells can improve the efficiency of a process layout while maintaining its flexibility. At the same time, grouping smaller numbers of workers in cells facilitates teamwork and joint problem solving. Employees are also able to work on a product from start to finish, and they can move between machines within their cells, thus increasing the flexibility of the team. Cellular layouts are commonly used in computer chip manufacturing and metal fabricating.[14]

cellular layout
Method of arranging a facility so that parts with similar shapes or processing requirements are processed together in work centres

Finally, the **fixed-position layout** is a facility layout in which labour, materials, and equipment are brought to the location where the good is being produced or the customer is being served. Buildings, roads, bridges, airplanes, and ships are examples of the types of large products that are typically constructed using a fixed-position layout (see Exhibit 8.3D). Service companies also use fixed-position layouts; for example, a plumber goes to a job site bringing the tools, material, and expertise needed to repair a broken pipe.

fixed-position layout
Method of arranging a facility so that the product is stationary and equipment and personnel come to it

Routing is the task of specifying the sequence of operations and the path through the facility that the work will take. The way production is routed depends on the type of product and the layout of the plant. A table-manufacturing company, for instance, uses a process layout because it has three departments, each handling a different phase of the table's manufacturing process and each equipped with specialized tools, machines, and

routing
Specifying the sequence of operations and the path the work will take through the production facility

Exhibit 8.3 Types of Facility Layouts

Facility layout is often determined by the type of product an organization is producing.

(A) Process layout: Typically, a process layout is used for an organization producing made-to-order products. A process layout is arranged according to the specialized employees and materials involved in various phases of the production process.

(B) Product layout: A product layout is used when an organization is producing large quantities of just a few products. In a product or assembly-line layout, the developing product moves in a continuous sequence from one workstation to the next.

(C) Cellular layout: A cellular layout works well in organizations that practise mass customization. In a cellular layout, parts with similar shapes or processing requirements are processed together in work centres, an arrangement that facilitates teamwork and flexibility.

(D) Fixed-position layout: A fixed-position layout requires employees and materials to be brought to the product and is used when the product is too large to move.

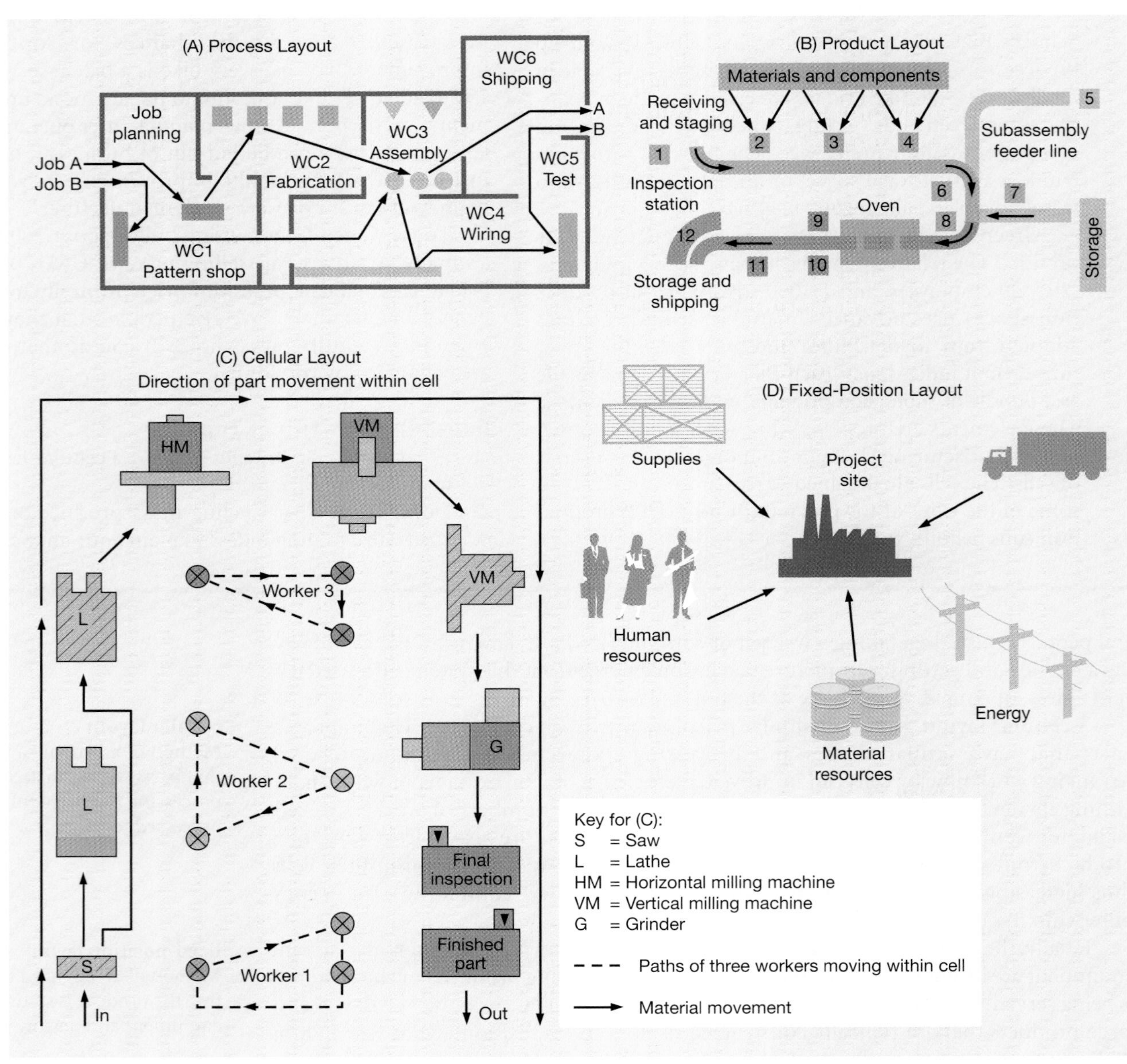

employees. Department 1 cuts wood into tabletops and legs. These pieces are then sent to department 2, where holes are drilled and rough finishing is done. Finally, the individual pieces are routed to department 3, where the tables are assembled and painted.

Scheduling Work

In any production process, managers must use **scheduling**—determining how long each operation takes and setting a starting and ending time for each. A master schedule, often called a *master production schedule (MPS),* lists the planned completion order of items. For example, in a health service setting, such as a doctor's office, the appointment book serves as the master schedule.

When a job has relatively few activities and relationships, many production managers keep the process on schedule with a **Gantt chart**. Developed by Henry L. Gantt in the early 1900s, the Gantt chart is a bar chart showing the amount of time required to accomplish each part of a process. It allows managers to see at a glance whether the process is in line with the schedule they had planned (see Exhibit 8.4).

For more complex jobs, the **program evaluation and review technique (PERT)** is helpful. PERT is a planning tool that helps managers identify the optimal sequencing of activities, the expected time for project completion, and the best use of resources within a complex project. To use PERT, the manager must (1) identify the activities to be performed, (2) determine the sequence of activities, (3) establish the time needed to complete each activity, (4) diagram the network of activities, (5) calculate the longest path through the network that leads to project completion, and (6) refine the network's timing or use of resources as activities are completed. The longest path through the network is known as the **critical path** because it represents the minimum amount of time needed to complete the project.

In place of a single time projection for each task, PERT uses four figures: an *optimistic* estimate (if things go well), a *pessimistic* estimate (if they don't go well), a *most likely* estimate (how long the task usually takes), and an *expected* time estimate—an average of the other three estimates.[15] The expected time is used to diagram the network of activities and determine the length of the critical path.

Consider the manufacturer of shoes in Exhibit 8.5. At the beginning of the process, three paths deal with heels, soles, and tops. All three processes must be finished before the next phase (sewing tops to soles and heels) can be started. However, one of the three paths—the tops—takes 33 days, whereas the other two take only 18 and 12 days. The shoe tops, then, are on the critical path because they will delay the entire operation if they fall behind schedule. In contrast, soles can be started up to 21 days after starting the tops without slowing down production. This free time in the soles schedule is called

scheduling
Process of determining how long each production operation takes and then setting a starting and ending time for each

Gantt chart
Bar chart used to control schedules by showing how long each part of a production process should take and when it should take place

program evaluation and review technique (PERT)
A planning tool that managers of complex projects use to determine the optimal order of activities, the expected time for project completion, and the best use of resources

critical path
In a PERT network diagram, the sequence of operations that requires the longest time to complete

Exhibit 8.4 A Gantt Chart

A chart like this one enables a production manager to see immediately the dates on which production steps must be started and completed if goods are to be delivered on schedule. Some steps may overlap to save time. For instance, after three weeks of cutting table legs, cutting tabletops begins. This overlap ensures that the necessary legs and tops are completed at the same time and can move on together to the next stage in the manufacturing process.

ID	Task Name	Start Date	End Date	Duration	2006
1	Make legs	8/1/06	8/28/06	20d	
2	Cut tops	8/22/06	8/28/06	5d	
3	Drill	8/29/06	9/4/06	5d	
4	Sand	9/5/06	9/11/06	5d	
5	Assemble	9/12/06	9/25/06	10d	
6	Paint	9/19/06	9/25/06	5d	

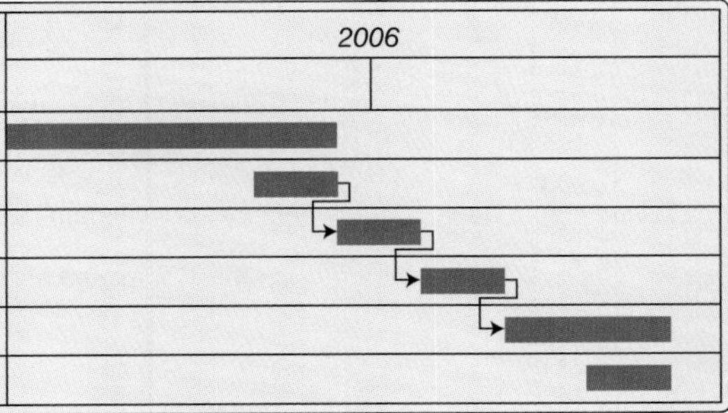

slack time because managers can choose to produce the soles any time during the 33-day period required by the tops.

dispatching
Issuing work orders and schedules to department heads and supervisors

Included in the scheduling process is the **dispatching** function, or the issuing of work orders to department supervisors. These orders specify the work to be done and the schedule for its completion. Work orders also inform department supervisors of their operational priorities and the schedule they must maintain.

Of course, once the schedule has been set and the orders dispatched, a production manager cannot just sit back and assume that the work will get done correctly and on time. Even the best scheduler may misjudge the time needed to complete an operation, and production may be delayed by accidents, mechanical breakdowns, or supplier problems. Therefore, the production manager needs a system for handling delays and preventing a minor disruption from growing into chaos. A successful system is based on good communication between the employees and the production manager.

Suppose a machine breakdown causes department 2 of a manufacturing company to lose half a day of drilling time. If the schedule is not altered to direct other work to department 3 (the next department), the employees and equipment in department 3 will sit idle for some time. However, if department 2 informs the production manager of its machine problem right away, the production manager can immediately reschedule some fill-in work for department 3.

L.O. 3

IMPROVING PRODUCTION THROUGH TECHNOLOGY

robots
Programmable machines that can complete a variety of tasks by working with tools and materials

Today, more and more companies are taking advantage of new production technologies to improve their efficiency and productivity. Two of the most visible advances in production technology are computers and **robots**—programmable machines that work with tools and materials to perform various tasks. Although industrial robots may seem exotic, like some science fiction creation, they are quite common and are really nothing more than smart tools. Industrial robots can easily perform precision functions as well as repetitive, strenuous, or hazardous tasks.[16] When equipped with machine vision, or electronic eyes, robots can place doors on cars in precise locations, identify blemished vegetables from frozen-food processing lines, check the wings of aircraft for dangerous ice build-up, make sure that drug capsules of the right colour go into the correct packages before they are shipped to pharmacies, and even assist with surgery.[17]

Exhibit 8.5 PERT Diagram for Manufacturing Shoes

In manufacturing these shoes, the critical path involves receiving, cutting the pattern, dyeing the leather, sewing the tops, sewing the tops to soles and heels, finishing, packaging, and shipping—a total of 61 days.

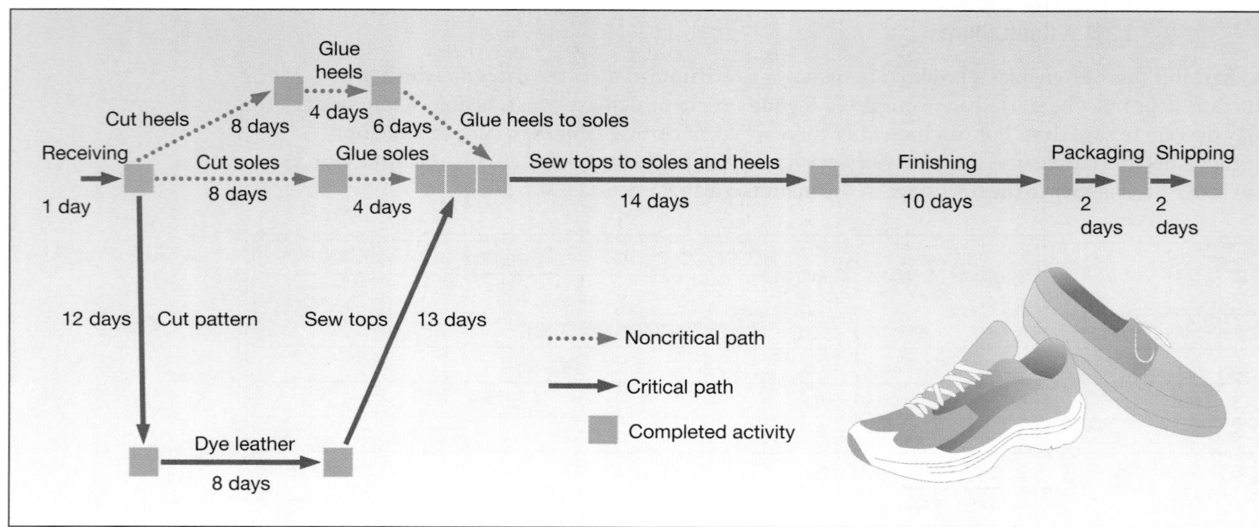

In addition to robots, other major developments in manufacturing automation include computer-aided design and engineering, computer-aided manufacturing, computer-integrated manufacturing, flexible manufacturing systems, and electronic information systems. Let's look a little closer at each of these.

Computer-Aided Design and Computer-Aided Engineering

Widely used today is **computer-aided design (CAD)**, the application of computer graphics and mathematical modelling to the design of products. A related process is **computer-aided engineering (CAE)**, in which engineers use computer-generated three-dimensional images and computerized calculations to test products. With CAE, engineers can subject proposed products to changing temperatures, various stresses, and even simulated accidents without ever building preliminary models. Moreover, the *virtual reality* capability of today's computers allows designers to see how finished products will look and operate before physical prototypes are built.

computer-aided design (CAD) Use of computer graphics and mathematical modelling in the development of products

computer-aided engineering (CAE) Use of computers to test products without building an actual model

Using computers to aid design and engineering saves time and money because revising computer designs is much faster than revising hand-drafted designs and building physical models. In fact, computer technology allows companies to perfect a product or abandon a bad idea before production even begins. The result is better overall product quality. For example, when Boeing engineers designed the 777 airplane, they corrected problems and tried out new ideas entirely on their computer screens. Digitally preassembling the 3 million parts of the 777 allowed Boeing to exceed its goals for reducing errors, changes, and rework.[18]

Computer-Aided Manufacturing and Computer-Integrated Manufacturing

The use of computers to control production equipment is called **computer-aided manufacturing (CAM)**. In a CAD/CAM system, computer-aided design data are converted automatically into processing instructions for production equipment to manufacture the part or product. This integration of design and production can increase the output, speed, and precision of assembly lines, as well as make customized production much easier.[19] In addition, the latest CAD/CAM software allows company departments to share designs and data over intranets and the Internet, enabling geographically dispersed departments to work together on complex projects.[20] For example, Ford uses a CAD/CAM/CAE system it calls C3P to develop new vehicle prototypes. Whereas it once took two to three months to build, assemble, and test a car chassis prototype, with C3P the entire process can now be completed in less than two weeks. Ford uses C3P to improve engineering efficiency and reduce prototype costs by up to 40 percent. In developing the new Ford F-150 trucks, engineers made extensive use of virtual prototypes thus saving time and money.[21]

computer-aided manufacturing (CAM) Use of computers to control production equipment

computer-integrated manufacturing (CIM) Computer-based systems, including CAD and CAM, that coordinate and control all elements of design and production

The highest level of computerization in operations management is **computer-integrated manufacturing (CIM)**, in which all elements of production—design, engineering, testing, production, inspection, and materials handling—are integrated into one automated system. Computer-integrated manufacturing is not a specific technology but rather a strategy that uses technology for organizing and controlling a factory. Its role is to link the people, machines, databases, and decisions involved in each step of producing a good.[22]

Robots don't do everything these days. At this Chrysler plant, polishing a limited-edition Viper GTS-R is still done by human hands.

Flexible Manufacturing Systems

Advances in design technology have been accompanied by changes in the way the production process is organized. Traditional automated manufacturing equipment is *fixed* or *hard-wired*, meaning it is capable of handling only one specific task. Although fixed automation is efficient when one type or model of good is mass produced, a change in product design requires extensive equipment changes. Such adjustments may involve high **setup costs**, the expenses incurred each time a manufacturer begins a production run of a different type of item. In addition, the initial investment for fixed automation equipment is high because specialized equipment is required for each of the operations involved in making a single item. Only after much production on a massive scale can a company recoup the cost of that specialized equipment. For example, Harley-Davidson invested US$4.8 million in fixed manufacturing equipment to make a particular motorcycle—only to dismantle the operation when the product faded.[23]

setup costs
Expenses incurred each time a producer organizes resources to begin producing goods or services

An alternative to a fixed manufacturing system is a **flexible manufacturing system (FMS)**. Such systems link numerous programmable machine tools by an automated materials-handling system of conveyors known as automatic guided vehicles (AGVs). These driverless computer-controlled vehicles move materials from any location on the factory floor to any other location. Changing from one product design to another requires only a few signals from a central computer. Each machine changes tools automatically, making appropriate selections from built-in storage carousels that can hold more than 100 tools. In addition, the sequence of events involved in building an item can be completely rearranged.[24] This flexibility saves both time and setup costs. Moreover, producers can outmanoeuvre less agile competitors by moving swiftly into profitable new fields. Flexible manufacturing also allows producers to adapt their products quickly to changing customer needs.[25] For instance, a flexible manufacturing system at Porsche allows 12 different versions of the Porsche 911 to be assembled on the same line.[26] Flexible manufacturing systems are also particularly suited for *job shops,* such as small machine shops, which make dissimilar items or produce at so irregular a rate that repetitive operations won't help.

flexible manufacturing system (FMS)
Production system using computer-controlled machines that can adapt to various versions of the same operation

electronic data interchange (EDI)
Information systems that transmit documents such as invoices and purchase orders between computers, thereby lowering ordering costs and paperwork

Ford is moving to a flexible manufacturing system. Even its oldest existing plant, which dates to 1924 and assembled the historic Model T automobile, is part of the revolution. How can a plant that once defined pure mass production make such a move? The simple answer is survival. Ford, GM, and Chrysler are playing catch up in order to maintain their profitability. Ford also plans to convert its Canadian operations in Oakville, Ontario, and recently secured $100 million in aid from the Ontario government. It is negotiating with the federal government for a matching $100 million to help build the $1.2 billion plant. This facility will replace an existing plant in which the company strictly produces minivans. At the new flexible plant, the company will be able to build several models off one, two, or three different platforms.[27]

Johnathan W. Ayers, president of Carrier Corp., the world's largest manufacturer of air conditioners, runs an extremely web-savvy operation. By purchasing more than 50 percent of its components and services through a web-based procurement system, Carrier saved an estimated US$100 million in one year.

Electronic Information Systems

Of course, none of the production technologies mentioned so far will increase profits unless the company designs products to fit customer needs. Today, many companies recognized for their quality link themselves with their customers through information systems. These systems enable companies to respond immediately to customer issues, support rapid changes in customer needs, and offer "made-to-order" products. Moreover, information technology allows customers to track their products and obtain status reports throughout the production cycle. It can also promote better communication within the company, thereby increasing the efficiency of employees and machines alike. In fact, many companies now rely on information systems to help establish a competitive advantage. For example, Siemens, a global producer of goods and services in industries ranging from communications to health care, cites its use of information technology as the key to its rapid growth in productivity.[28]

One important type of information technology is **electronic data interchange (EDI)**. Electronic data interchange systems transmit specially formatted documents (such as invoices and purchase orders) from one company's computers to another's. This process can greatly reduce the time, paperwork, and costs associated with placing and processing orders, thereby making it easier and more profitable for a customer to do business with the company. Nevertheless, EDI systems are expensive and complex to establish, which is why many companies are now moving their EDI transactions to the Internet, as the E-Business in Action feature "What's All the Buzz about B2B?" discusses (see page 218).

MANAGING AND CONTROLLING THE PRODUCTION PROCESS

During the production design phase, operations managers forecast demand, plan for capacity, choose facility locations, design facility layouts and configurations, and develop production schedules and sequences. Once the design of the production process has been completed, operations managers are responsible for managing and controlling these processes and systems. In this section, we will discuss two important management and control concepts: inventory management and quality assurance.

Inventory Management

L.O. 4

Forward-thinking companies have realized that maintaining a competitive advantage requires continuously seeking ways to reduce costs, increase manufacturing efficiency, and improve customer value. They know how wasteful it is to tie up large sums of money in **inventory**—the goods and materials kept in stock for production or sale. On the other hand, not having an adequate supply of inventory can delay production and result in unhappy customers. That's why more and more companies are changing the way they purchase and handle the materials they use to produce goods and services.

inventory
Goods kept in stock for the production process or for sales to final customers

Purchasing is the acquisition of the raw materials, parts, components, supplies, and finished products required to produce goods and services. The goal of purchasing is to make sure that the company has all of the materials it needs, when it needs them, at the lowest possible cost. To accomplish this goal, a company must always have enough supplies on hand to cover a product's **lead time**—the period that elapses between placing the supply order and receiving materials.

purchasing
Acquiring the raw materials, parts, components, supplies, and finished products needed to produce goods and services

lead time
Period that elapses between the ordering of materials and their arrival from the supplier

In the past, companies would buy supply inventories large enough to make sure they would not run out of parts during peak production times. As soon as inventory levels dropped to a predetermined level, the purchasing department would order new parts. Many companies continue to operate this way, which does offer certain benefits. For example, companies typically get a better price when they buy inventory in bulk, and having a large supply on hand enables them to meet customer demand quickly. Unfortunately, carrying a large inventory also ties up the company's money and increases the risk that products will become obsolete.

To minimize this risk and cost, and to increase manufacturing efficiency, many companies establish a system of **inventory control**—some way of (1) determining the right quantities of supplies and products to have on hand and (2) tracking where those items are. Three methods that companies use to control inventory and manage the production process are *just-in-time systems, material requirements planning,* and *manufacturing resource planning.*

inventory control
System for determining the right quantity of various items to have on hand and keeping track of their location, use, and condition

Just-in-Time Systems

L.O. 5

An increasingly popular method of managing operations, including inventory control and production planning, is the **just-in-time (JIT) system**. The goal of just-in-time systems is to have only the right amounts of materials arrive at precisely the times they are needed. Because supplies arrive just as they are needed, and no sooner, inventories are eliminated and waste is reduced.

just-in-time (JIT) system
Continuous system that pulls materials through the production process, making sure that all materials arrive just when they are needed with minimal inventory and waste

The maintenance of a "zero inventory" under JIT does have some indirect benefits. For instance, reducing stocks of parts to practically nothing encourages factories to keep production flowing smoothly, from beginning to end, without any hold-ups. A constant production flow requires good teamwork. On the other hand, JIT exposes a company to greater risks, as a disruption in the flow of raw materials from suppliers can slow or stop the production process. Shortly after the September 11, 2001, terrorist attacks, for instance, Toyota Motor Corp. came within 15 hours of halting production of its Sequoia sport-utility vehicle. One of its suppliers was waiting for steering sensors normally imported by plane from Germany, but the planes weren't flying.[29]

A JIT system also places a heavy burden on suppliers because they must be able to meet the production schedules of their customers. For instance, an increasingly strong demand for electronic and computer components at the beginning of the twenty-first century left many electronic equipment manufacturers battling one another for computer chips and other components. "Just-in-time has become just-in-trouble," says the chief financial officer of one electronics company.[30]

Thus, to be effective, JIT systems must be designed to include multifunctional teamwork, flexible manufacturing, small-batch production, strict production control, quick setups, consistent production levels, preventive maintenance, and reliable supplier networks. Furthermore, poor quality simply cannot be tolerated in a stockless manufacturing environment because one defective part can bring production to a grinding halt. In other words, JIT cannot be implemented without a commitment to total quality control.[31] When all of these factors work in sync, the manufacturer achieves *lean production;* that is, it can do more with less.[32]

Mississauga-based Russel Metals is geared to manage the greatest amount of customers with the least amount of inventory. According to CEO Bud Seigel, inventory decisions have been pushed down the chain to managers. The company's annual compensation package is linked to its return on assets, which makes it very conscious of inventory levels. According to John Novak of CIBC World Markets, "The company is lean, efficient and well run."[33] Keep in mind that JIT concepts can also be used to reduce inventory and cycle time for service organizations.

In those cases where it is difficult for manufacturers and suppliers to coordinate their schedules, JIT may not work. For example, shoemaker Allen-Edmonds cannot get its principal raw material whenever it wants because calfskin hides come on the market only at certain times each year.[34] Additional product factors can also affect JIT: seasonality (popularity during specific seasons such as winter), perishability, and unusual handling characteristics such as size or weight.

Material Requirements Planning (MRP)

material requirements planning (MRP)
Method of getting the correct materials where they are needed, on time, and without carrying unnecessary inventory

Material requirements planning (MRP) is another inventory control technique that helps a manufacturer get the correct materials where they are needed, when they are needed, and without unnecessary stockpiling. Managers use computer programs to calculate when certain materials will be required, when they should be ordered, and when they should be delivered so that storage costs will be minimal. These systems are so effective at reducing inventory levels that they are used almost universally in both large and small manufacturing firms.

perpetual inventory
System that uses computers to monitor inventory levels and automatically generate purchase orders when supplies are needed

A more automated form of material requirements planning is the **perpetual inventory** system, in which computers monitor inventory levels and automatically generate purchase orders when supplies fall below a certain level. The price scanners found at the checkout counters of many stores are part of perpetual inventory systems. Every time a product is purchased, the scanner deletes that particular item from the computer system's inventory data. When inventory of the product reaches a predetermined level, the system generates an order for more. Often, the store's system is linked to the supplier's own computer system, which enables the order to be placed with virtually no human involvement.

Manufacturing Resource Planning (MRP II)

The MRP systems on the market today are made up of various modules, including inventory control, purchasing, customer order entry, production planning, shop-floor control, and accounting. With the addition of more and more modules that focus on capacity planning, marketing, and finance, an MRP system evolves into a **manufacturing resource planning (MRP II)** system.

An MRP II system produces a companywide game plan; it draws together all departments and allows everyone to work with the same numbers (see Exhibit 8.6). Employees can draw on data such as inventory levels, back orders, and unpaid bills. In the past this information was reserved for top executives. The system can track each step of production, allowing managers throughout the company to consult other managers' inventories, schedules, and plans. In addition, MRP II systems are capable of running simulations (models of possible operations systems) that enable managers to plan and test alternative strategies.[35] An extension of MRP II is **enterprise resource planning (ERP)**, which expands the scope of the production planning process to include customer and supplier information. ERP is based on software developed by SAP AG, a German software company. Using this software and ERP, manufacturers can tap into huge databases of company information to improve production processes.

manufacturing resource planning (MRP II)
Computer-based system that integrates data from all departments to manage inventory and production planning and control

enterprise resource planning (ERP)
A comprehensive database system that includes information about the firm's suppliers and customers as well as data generated internally

Quality Assurance

L.O. 6

Besides maintaining optimal inventory levels, companies today must produce high-quality goods as efficiently as possible. In almost every industry you can name, this global challenge has caused companies to re-examine their definition of quality and re-engineer their production processes. Just as Harley-Davidson was able to re-establish itself as the worldwide leader, many other companies are following in Harley's footsteps by setting new standards for quality.

Still, adopting high quality standards is not an easy task, because the manufacture of complex goods is not simply a matter of adding part A to part B to part C and so forth until a product emerges ready to ship. For example, the Mercedes M-Class sport-utility vehicle is assembled from subunits built by 65 major suppliers and many other smaller ones.[36] Making sure that all the pieces are put together in the proper sequence and at the proper time requires large-scale planning and scheduling. The same is true for the production of complex services.

The traditional means of maintaining quality is called **quality control**—measuring quality against established standards after the good or service has been produced and weeding out any defects. A more comprehensive approach is **quality assurance**, a system of companywide policies, practices, and procedures to ensure that every product meets preset quality standards. Quality assurance includes quality control as well as doing the job right the first time by designing tools and machinery properly, demanding quality parts from suppliers, encouraging customer feedback, training employees, empowering them, and encouraging them to take pride in their work (see the box entitled

quality control
Routine checking and testing of a finished product for quality against an established standard

quality assurance
System of policies, practices, and procedures implemented throughout a company to create and produce quality goods and services

Exhibit 8.6 MRP II

An MRP II computer system gives managers and workers in every department easy access to data from all other departments, which in turn makes it easier to generate—and adhere to—the organization's overall plans, forecasts, and schedules.

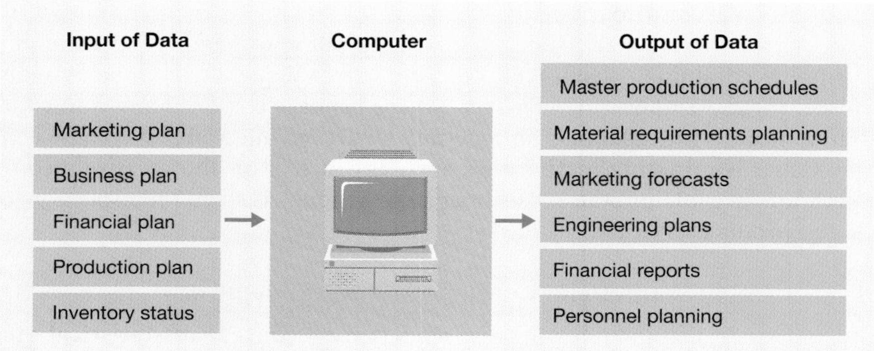

Chek Lap Kok's Turbulent Takeoff

Opening day at Chek Lap Kok, Hong Kong's new airport, was a monumental disaster. The state-of-the-art facility, designed to handle 80 million passengers annually, was promoted as a symbol of Swiss-watch efficiency. But on the airport's first day of operations, everything broke down—or so it seemed.

The airport lurched from crisis to crisis. Planes were stranded on the tarmac with no directions to parking gates. Passengers missed flights because of malfunctions in the flight information display system. Some planes left without food for their passengers; others went without passengers altogether. Arriving passengers were imprisoned in the aircraft while mechanics repaired broken jetway doors. Baggage systems (designed to handle 13 700 pieces of luggage an hour) crashed, leaving passengers without luggage and luggage loading on planes without passengers—a serious security breach.

Then, just as the chaos in the passenger terminal seemed under control, computer glitches all but paralyzed air-cargo operations. A software bug disabled the computer system running the new US$1.2 billion on-site automated cargo-handling facilities—one of the largest in the world. Thousands of air freight containers were strewn across the tarmac. Perishable goods rotted in state-of-the-art warehouses while new shipments were rerouted.

Poor communications, overconfidence, and lack of system testing and contingency planning are just a few of the reasons that the debut of Hong Kong's international airport at Chek Lap Kok turned into a nightmare. For example, communications systems and software on which the modern airport depended had not been thoroughly tested. Sample tests of 10 000 transactions had produced some minor problems, but when 70 000 actual transactions hit the systems on opening day, the systems were pushed to the breaking point. As well, political pressure forced officials to open the airport months before it should have been. Chek Lap Kok is a good example of what can happen without sufficient quality control. Besides inflicting serious short-term damage on Hong Kong's image, the airport's poor opening cost all parties involved more than US$5 billion—one-fifth of the airport's US$25 billion construction cost. The government wanted Chek Lap Kok to be world famous, and it was—but for all the wrong reasons.

Computer failures at Hong Kong's huge new airport, Chek Lap Kok, left cargo, including perishables, sitting on the tarmac for days.

Questions for Critical Thinking

1. What steps might airport managers have taken to prevent Chek Lap Kok's disastrous opening?
2. Why did statistical quality control tests fail to produce the serious problems that occurred on opening day?

"Chek Lap Kok's Turbulent Takeoff"). As discussed in Chapter 6, total quality management takes things to even a higher level by building quality into every activity within an organization.

Companies approach quality assurance in various ways. As a builder of sheet-metal components and electromechanical assemblies, Trident Precision Manufacturing empowers workers to make decisions on the shop floor and spends 4.7 percent of payroll on employee training.[37] High-end computer maker Sequent Computer Systems has a "customer process engineering manager" whose primary responsibility is to continually communicate with customers and identify any recurring problems. These companies know that eliminating inefficiency, such as a defect or an excessively complex process, can reduce total product costs because less money is spent on inspection, complaints, and product service.[38]

statistical quality control (SQC) Monitoring all aspects of the production process to see whether the process is operating as it should

Statistical Quality Control and Continuous Improvement

Quality assurance also includes the now widely used concept of **statistical quality control (SQC)**, in which all aspects of the production process are monitored so that managers can see whether the process is operating as it should. The primary tool of SQC is **statistical process control (SPC)**, which involves taking samples from the process periodically and plotting observations of the samples on a *control chart.* A large enough sample provides a reasonable estimate of the entire process. By observing the random fluctuations graphed on the chart, managers and workers can identify whether such changes are normal or whether they indicate that some corrective action is required in the process. In this way, SPC can prevent poor quality.[39]

Statistical quality control is not limited to goods-producing industries. For example, financial services provider GE Capital uses statistical control methods to make sure the bills it sends to customers are correct. The company's use of SQC lowers the cost of making adjustments while improving customer satisfaction.[40]

In addition to using SQC, companies can empower each employee to continuously improve the quality of goods production or service delivery. The Japanese word for continuous improvement is *kaizen.* Japanese manufacturers learned long before many North American manufacturers that continuous improvement is not something that can be delegated to one or a few people. Instead, it requires the full participation of every employee. This means encouraging all workers to spot quality problems, halt production when necessary, generate ideas for improvement, and adjust work routines as needed.[41]

It takes more than a quality mix to produce Krispy Kreme doughnuts all the time. To ensure consistent quality, Krispy Kreme supplies its stores with everything they need to produce premium doughnuts—including the production machinery and equipment.

Global Quality Standards

Many manufacturers and service providers in North America, Europe, and around the world require that suppliers comply with standards set by the International Organization for Standardization (ISO), a non-government entity based in Geneva, Switzerland. Recently revised into a family of quality-management-system standards and guidelines known as **ISO 9000**, ISO 9001, and ISO 9004, such standards are voluntary by definition. Companies may choose to comply with these standards and, if met, promote their certification to gain recognition for their quality achievements.

In the past, ISO 9000 standards applied mostly to products that had health and safety-related features. However, the newer 9001 and 9004 standards maintain a greater focus on customer satisfaction, user needs, and continuous improvement.[42] The standards are recognized in more than 152 countries, by approximately 634 000 companies. About one-quarter of the world's corporations insist that all their suppliers be ISO certified.[43]

ISO standards help companies become *world-class manufacturers,* a term used to describe the level of quality and operational effectiveness that puts a company among the top performers in the world. Some companies view ISO standards as a starting point to achieving other national quality awards such as Japan's Deming Prize, the Canada Award for Excellence (CAE; see Exhibit 8.7A), or the U.S. Malcolm Baldrige National Quality Award (see Exhibit 8.7B). Of course, even if an organization doesn't want to apply for an award, it can improve quality by measuring its performance against an award's standards and working to overcome any problems uncovered by this process.

statistical process control (SPC)
Use of random sampling and control charts to monitor the production process

ISO 9000
Global standards set by the International Organization for Standardization establishing a minimum level of acceptable quality

MANAGING THE SUPPLY CHAIN

L.O. 7

A company's ability to deliver quality products and services is often tied to the dynamics of its suppliers. One faulty part, one late shipment, can send ripple effects through the production system and can even bring operations to a grinding halt. When a surge of orders for new Boeing 747s stepped up demand for parts, for instance, Boeing's suppliers were caught flat-footed. "We had $25 000 engine mounts that couldn't be finished because we were waiting for $40 nuts and bolts," noted one Boeing supplier. As a result, promised aircraft delivery dates were delayed and Boeing suffered huge losses. To avoid such problems in the future, Boeing now works hand in hand with its suppliers to refine products and delivery schedules.[44]

The group of firms that provides all of the various processes required to make a finished product is called the *supply chain.* The chain begins with the provider of raw materials and ends with the company that produces the finished product that is delivered to the final customer. The members of the supply chain vary according to the nature of the operation and type of product but typically include suppliers, manufacturers, distribu-

Exhibit 8.7A **Canada Award for Excellence (CAE) Quality Award Framework**

More than 300 CAE Quality Awards have been handed out to model companies since 1984. They are awarded to small, medium, and large organizations in both the private and the public sectors. Awards are distributed in the areas of quality, healthy workplace, and education. Recent recipients include DaimlerChrysler Canada and the Canadian Auto Workers, Polywheels Manufacturing Ltd., M&M Meat Shops, and Delta Hotels. The following diagram illustrates the framework for the awards.

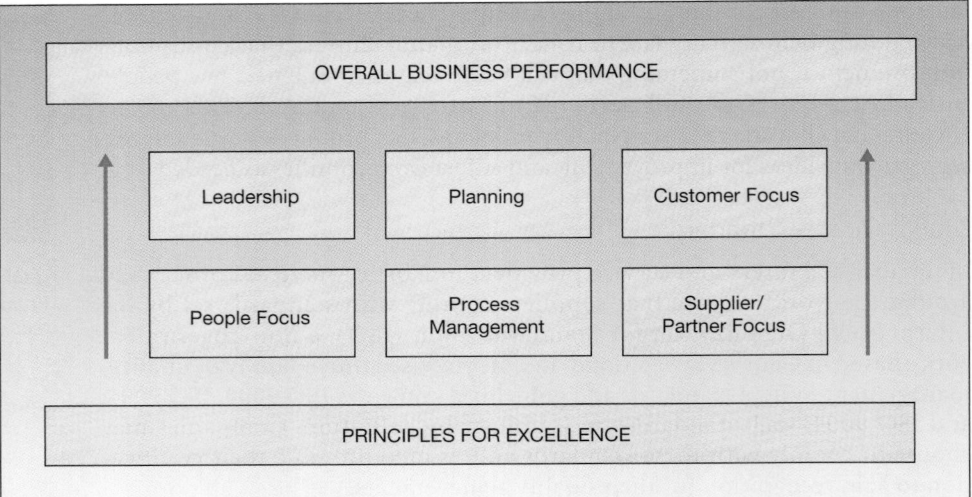

Source: Courtesy of CAE, taken from www.nqi.ca/caeawards/categories.aspx

Exhibit 8.7B **Criteria for the Malcolm Baldrige National Quality Award**

The Malcolm Baldrige National Quality Award is given annually to companies that demonstrate an outstanding commitment to quality. The awards are given to companies in each of four categories: manufacturing, services, small businesses, and universities and hospitals. This chart lists the criteria on which companies are judged for the award.

Leadership. Have senior leaders clearly defined the company's values, goals, and ways to achieve the goals? Is the company a model "corporate citizen"?

Information and analysis. Does the company effectively use data and information to support customer-driven performance excellence and marketplace success?

Strategic planning. How does the company develop strategies and business plans to strengthen its performance and competitive position?

Human resources development and management. How does the company develop the full potential of its workforce? How are its human resource capabilities and work systems aligned with its strategic and business plans?

Process management. How does the company design, manage, and improve key processes, such as customer-focused design and product and service delivery?

Business results. How does the company address performance and improvement in key business areas—product and service quality, productivity and operational effectiveness, supply quality, and financial performance indicators linked to these areas?

Customer focus and satisfaction. How does the company determine requirements, expectations, and preferences of customers? What are its customer satisfaction results?

tors, and retailers. For example, if the finished product is a wood table, the supply chain going backwards would include the retail store where it was sold, the shipping company that delivered it to the retail store, the furniture manufacturer, the hardware manufacturer, and the lumber company that acquired the wood from the forest.[45]

Through a process known as **supply-chain management**, many companies now integrate all of the facilities, functions, and activities involved in the production of goods and services going from suppliers to customers.[46] The process is based on the belief that because one company's output is another company's (or consumer's) input, all companies involved will benefit from working together more closely.[47] Building high-trust relationships was once thought possible only with internal suppliers. But today more and more companies are reducing the number of outside suppliers they use, working collaboratively with them, sharing information with them, and even involving them in the production and design processes.

supply-chain management Integrating all of the facilities, functions, and processes associated with the production of goods and services, from suppliers to customers

Honda, for example, has developed a process called Design In, which focuses directly on early supplier involvement. Honda will invite suppliers to work side by side with Honda's engineers, designers, and technologists in the very early stages of a new project. In addition, Honda believes in maintaining a frank, open, and collaborative relationship with its suppliers and even extends this philosophy to sharing cost data. "We show our suppliers our logic in coming up with the cost, and they show us theirs," notes Honda's senior purchasing manager.[48] This sharing of information with members of the supply chain has many benefits, including increased sales, cost savings, inventory reductions, improved quality, accelerated delivery time, and improved customer service.[49]

OUTSOURCING THE MANUFACTURING FUNCTION

As companies strive to find better ways to produce goods, some are turning to outsourcing the manufacturing function. Outsourcing the manufacturing function has several advantages. For one thing, it allows companies to redirect the capital and resources spent on manufacturing to new product research and development, marketing, and customer service. For another, many contract manufacturers are industry specialists with state-of-the art facilities and production efficiencies that would be costly to duplicate on an individual scale.

Magna International not only builds major car components for automobiles like the Smart car (see the box entitled "Smart Enough for Canada?"), but also actually produces entire vehicles that have been outsourced from major brands like BMW, Mercedes, Audi, Jeep, and Volkswagen. For example, BMW outsourced the production of its X3 SUV to Magna Steyr, a subsidiary of Magna International. With the help of some 500 engineers, Magna Steyr was able to bring the project from concept to production in only 28 months. This process was actually better than the average figure BMW produces in-house.[50]

Solectron is a contract electronic manufacturer (CEM) that assembles everything from pagers to printers to computers to television decoding boxes for some of the biggest brand names in electronics. It is the only company that has twice won the Malcolm Baldrige Award for manufacturing excellence.[51] Outsourced electronic products manufactured by Solectron still bear the original equipment manufacturer's (OEM's) brand name—such as Hewlett-Packard, Cisco, IBM, and Lucent. In some cases, the CEM provides additional services beyond the manufacturing function, including inventory management, delivery, and after-sales service.[52]

Besides outsourcing, another trend sweeping manufacturing organizations is the involvement of suppliers in the manufacturing process. For example, at Volkswagen's factory in Resende, Brazil, seven main suppliers build components and assemble them onto vehicles inside the Volkswagen factory, using the suppliers' own equipment and workers. Volkswagen figures that integrating the suppliers so closely into the production process is a strong incentive for the suppliers to deliver high-quality components in unprecedented time.[53]

Smart Enough for Canada?

In late 2004, gas prices skyrocketed to highs of 99.9 cents per litre for regular gasoline, thus shocking SUV-loving Canadians from coast to coast. Gas companies scrambled to replace outdated price signs that could not register an extra digit; the era of the $1+ gas price had arrived. Simultaneously, DaimlerChrysler introduced its famous smart car in the Canadian market. With about 120 000 of these cars sold annually in Europe, Asia, and Australia, Canada—traditionally a good market for small cars—was a logical choice to become the thirty-second "smart nation." A major question remained: Would Canadians warm up to these tiny vehicles? The answer came fairly quickly. Before the company could make a marketing push and begin an ad campaign, the vehicles were sold out. All 800 vehicles originally allocated to the market were sold, as well as an additional 200 cars, to reach an initial total of 1000 vehicles. Waiting lists grew quickly, with many customers waiting months to snatch up the hot product. Of course, at that point, the focus was on increasing Canadian supply rather than on marketing.

The smart car provides us with more than just an example of a unique product that has been successfully commercialized. The vehicle is a glowing example of outsourcing in today's global economy. In some companies, in-house manufacturing operations consist of nothing more than bolting together fabricated chunks that have been manufactured by suppliers. DaimlerChrysler's smart car is a good example of this process. Just about everything in Smartville, the production centre in France where the smart car is assembled, is relegated to suppliers—from inventorying nuts and bolts on the assembly line to delivering cars to dealers in Europe and Japan. More than half of the 2000 people working in Smartville aren't even on the manufacturer's payroll. The biggest suppliers are on site, building most of the car in the form of large modules—body, doors, rear section with engine, and so on. Conveyors link major suppliers' plants directly to the assembly building where the cars are bolted together. Suppliers carry much of the cost of work-in-progress inventory, since they aren't paid until the car comes off the line and is accepted for sale by inspectors—about every 90 seconds, which is quick for the auto industry. Meanwhile, DaimlerChrysler hopes to incorporate what it has learned about suppliers, modules, pay-on-build, and new technologies into its global operation. "We are getting more and more into learning from others," says one smart plant manager. "We take good things in other places and install them at our plant."[54]

Questions for Critical Thinking

1. What are the advantages and disadvantages of creating such powerful ties with suppliers?
2. Do you believe that the initial success of the smart car in Canada is a short-term trend or the beginning of a successful run in this market?

In automotive manufacturing circles, the way the smart car is built has attracted as much attention as the vehicle itself. Outsourcing the manufacturing function integrates the smart car supply chain to the maximum.

SUMMARY OF LEARNING OBJECTIVES

Explain what production and operations managers do.

Production and operations managers design and oversee an efficient conversion process—the sequence of events that convert resources into goods and services. To do this, they must coordinate a firm's resources and optimize output from each resource. Additionally, production and operations managers perform the four basic functions of planning, organizing, leading, and controlling, but the focus of these activities is the production of a company's goods and services.

Identify key tasks involved in designing a production process.

Managers must first prepare production forecasts, or estimates of future demand for the company's products. Next they must consider capacity, which is a business's volume of manufacturing or service delivery. The next step is to find a facility location that minimizes regional costs (land, construction, labour, local taxes, leasing, energy), transportation costs, and raw materials costs. Once a location has been selected, managers need to consider facility layout—the arrangement of production work centres and other facilities (such as material, equipment, and support departments) needed for the processing of goods and services. Finally, managers must develop a master production schedule.

Discuss the role of computers and automation technology in production.

Computers and automation technology improve the production process in several ways: (1) Robots perform repetitive or mundane tasks quickly and with great precision; (2) CAD and CAE systems allow engineers to design and test virtual models of products; (3) CAM systems easily translate CAD data into production instructions; (4) CIM systems link the people, machines, databases, and decisions involved in each step of producing a good; and (5) flexible manufacturing systems (FMSs) reduce setup costs and time by linking programmable, multifunctional machine tools through a computer network and an automated materials-handling system.

Explain the strategic importance of managing inventory.

The goods and materials kept in stock for production or sale make up inventory, which must be managed to minimize costs and ensure that the right supplies are in the right place at the right time. Having too much inventory is costly and increases the risk that products will become obsolete. Having too little inventory can result in production delays and unfilled orders.

Distinguish among JIT, MRP, and MRP II inventory management systems.

Just-in-time (JIT) systems reduce waste and improve quality by producing only enough to fill orders when they are due, thus eliminating finished-goods inventory. Furthermore, under the JIT system, parts or materials are ordered only when they are needed, thus eliminating supplies inventories. Material requirements planning (MRP) and perpetual inventory systems are used to determine when materials are needed, when they should be ordered, and when they should be delivered. A more advanced system is manufacturing resource planning (MRP II), which brings together data from all parts of a company (including financial, design, and engineering departments) to better manage inventory and production planning and control.

Highlight the differences between quality control and quality assurance.

Quality control focuses on measuring finished products against a preset standard and weeding out any defects. On the other hand, quality assurance is a system of company-wide policies, practices, and procedures that build quality into a product and ensure that each product meets quality standards.

Describe the supply chain and explain how companies today are managing their supply chains.

The supply chain consists of all companies involved in making a finished product. The members of the chain vary according to the nature of the operation and the type of product but typically include suppliers, manufacturers, distributors, and retail outlets. Today, more and more companies are managing their supply chains to be more responsive to the changing needs of their customers. To do this, companies are reducing the number of firms in their supply chain, developing long-term relationships with remaining members, and sharing information with them. Some companies are even involving members of their supply chain in the design and production processes.

Behind the SCENES

Harley-Davidson Revs Its Engines toward Higher Output and Productivity

During the 1970s, when attractive new imports were roaring into the North American motorcycle market, Harley-Davidson suffered a serious quality crisis. It took the company almost two decades to figure out how to maintain high quality standards while boosting output. But incorporating continuous improvement methods into the company's manufacturing processes eventually paid off. By the mid-1990s, Harley had won back market share and was selling US$2 billion in motorcycles, parts, and accessories to loyal fans all over the world. Still, CEO Jeff Bleustein was anything but complacent. Eyeing the projected increase in domestic demand and the huge sales potential of markets outside North America, he was determined to overhaul the production process for higher output and productivity.

One key target was the company's inefficient supply chain. Nearly 1000 suppliers provided Harley with raw materials, parts, and components. The head of purchasing soon narrowed the supplier list to just 425 and streamlined purchasing through a web-based system. These steps strengthened supplier commitment and helped purchasing get more mileage out of the company's US$1 billion yearly supply budget. The company also centralized purchasing and inventory into a single supply management department and in doing so improved Harley's buying power. Next, all purchasing agents were required to complete a training course in structured materials planning and buying, capped by testing and formal certification.

The distribution warehouse was another key target. Crowded, old, and inefficient, the warehouse was simply inadequate. After some analysis, the company decided to build a gigantic new distribution centre with state-of-the-art technology to track and control the inbound and outbound movement of items. This new distribution centre doubled productivity and sliced fulfillment time for orders from 12 days to 2.

In the race to boost output and productivity, Harley invested US$650 million in new production facilities and manufacturing equipment. One new plant, equipped with a sophisticated materials management system, could produce motorcycles 30 percent more efficiently than the older plant. Advanced technology was integrated throughout the production process, including a computer-aided design (CAD) system accessible to employees in many departments. Harley also allowed selected suppliers to access the CAD system so they could collaborate on product development.

Although Bleustein was investing heavily to expand capacity and update facilities and systems, the improvements were expected to shave US$40 million from overall production and inventory costs. Output and productivity soared, as did sales around the world. By 2001, Harley was selling 243 000 bikes a year and had surpassed its production goal. What proved to be disastrous economic times for hundreds of companies didn't faze Harley. At a time when automakers were struggling with their profit margins, Harley sold every bike it made, and dealers often charged US$2000 to US$4000 above the sticker price. By 2003 the company was selling more than 290 000 bikes, nearly double the output reached just five years earlier. In 2004 the company broke another barrier with more than 317 000 bikes sold. Revenues stood at just over US$5 billion. These impressive sales figure were expected to rise as the firm expected volume to increase to 339 000 bikes by the time sales were tallied in 2005 with a new goal of reaching 400 000 bikes by 2007.

Despite its success and ambitious goals, Harley might be heading for a nasty spill if it doesn't navigate its generational speed bump. The median age of a Harley buyer is 46, and the company has previously failed to attract younger riders who prefer the speedy, more technically advanced machines from Honda, Yamaha, and BMW. To address the problem and attract younger buyers Bleustein is pushing his company into places it has never gone. In 2002, Harley unveiled the V-Rod, its first small, cheap bike in more than 20 years. In 2005, the introduction of exciting new models for the Softail Deluxe, the Sportster 883 Low, and the Softail Springer Classic were elements to keep the momentum going. Furthermore, the company was revving up demand by teaching young people—especially women—how to ride a motorcycle through an instructional program called Rider's Edge.

While bikers continued to gawk at their Harleys, Bleustein and his staff were going hog wild to make sure the company thrived for another century. "We don't need new customers today, we don't need them tomorrow. But we may ten years from now," says Bleustein. So he constantly warns employees against his twin fears, complacency and arrogance: "We have to pretend 10 fiery demons are chasing us all the time," says Bleustein—a mighty task, even for a company that caters to Hells Angels.

In May 2005 Jeff Bluestein stepped down as CEO of Harley-Davidson. After years of tremendous double-digit growth the company reduced its growth projections to a respectable 5 to 8 percent range. Investors who had profited from all the momentum and made fortunes were noticeably concerned. The company was heading into an area where demand could exceed supply as many baby boomers might stop riding and cease buying. The company's new CEO, Jim Zeimer, has to deal with these issues and continue to implement new ideas to take advantage of opportunities and keep this icon in high-speed mode.[55]

Critical Thinking Questions

1. Why would Harley-Davidson allow employees in the purchasing department as well as selected suppliers access to information in the CAD system used for new product design and development?
2. How do you think reducing the time needed to fulfill parts orders would affect Harley's inventory costs?
3. What new challenges does Harley-Davidson face?

Learn More Online

Visit the Harley-Davidson website by clicking on the hotlink at Chapter 8 of this text's website at www.pearsoned.ca/bovee. Locate the section with company and investor information and read the company's latest annual report. Then look at the current and historical production and sales statistics posted on the site. How many motorcycles did Harley produce in the most recent quarter? In the most recent year? What is the output trend? Now review the demographic profile of a Harley-Davidson customer. How is the company's typical customer changing?

KEY TERMS

analytic system (192)
capacity planning (195)
cellular layout (197)
computer-aided design (CAD) (201)
computer-aided engineering (CAE) (201)
computer-aided manufacturing (CAM) (201)
computer-integrated manufacturing (CIM) (201)
critical path (199)
dispatching (200)
electronic data interchange (EDI) (202)
enterprise resource planning (ERP) (205)
fixed-position layout (197)
flexible manufacturing system (FMS) (202)
Gantt chart (199)
inventory (203)
inventory control (203)
ISO 9000 (207)
just-in-time (JIT) system (203)
lead time (203)
manufacturing resource planning (MRP II) (205)
mass customization (194)
mass production (193)
material requirements planning (MRP) (204)
perpetual inventory (204)
process layout (196)
product layout (196)
production (192)
production and operations management (POM) (192)
production forecasts (194)
program evaluation and review technique (PERT) (199)
purchasing (203)
quality assurance (205)
quality control (205)
robots (200)
routing (197)
scheduling (199)
setup costs (202)
statistical process control (SPC) (207)
statistical quality control (SQC) (206)
supply-chain management (209)
synthetic system (193)

TEST YOUR KNOWLEDGE

Questions for Review

1. What is the conversion process?
2. What is mass customization?
3. What factors need to be considered when selecting a site for a production facility?
4. Why is an effective system of inventory control important to every manufacturer?
5. Why might a company want to outsource its manufacturing function?

Questions for Analysis

6. Why is capacity planning an important part of designing operations?
7. How do JIT systems go beyond simply controlling inventory?
8. Why have companies moved beyond quality control to quality assurance?
9. How can supply-chain management help a company establish a competitive advantage?
10. **Ethical Considerations.** How does society's concern for the environment affect a company's decisions about facility location and layout?

Questions for Application

11. Assume you are the production manager for a small machine shop that manufactures precision parts for industrial equipment. How can you use CAD, CAE, CAM, CIM, and FMS to manufacture better parts more easily?
12. If your final product requires several unique subunits that are all produced with different machinery

and in differing lengths of time, what facility layout will you choose and why?

13. **Integrated.** Review the discussion of franchises in Chapter 4. From an operational perspective, why is purchasing a franchise such as Tim Hortons an attractive alternative for starting a business?

14. **Integrated.** Review the discussion of corporate cultures in Chapter 6. What things could you learn about a company's culture by observing the layout and design of its production facility? Discuss both goods and services operations.

PRACTISE YOUR KNOWLEDGE

SHARPENING YOUR COMMUNICATION SKILLS

As the newly hired manager of Campus Athletics, a shop featuring athletic wear bearing logos of colleges and universities, you are responsible for selecting the store's suppliers. Merchandise with team logos and brands can be very trendy. When a college team is hot, you've got to have merchandise. You know that selecting the right supplier is a task that requires careful consideration, so you have decided to host a series of selection interviews. Think about all of the qualities you would want in a supplier, and develop a list of interview questions that will help you assess whether that supplier possesses those qualities.

BUILDING YOUR TEAM SKILLS

Facility layout is one of the most critical decisions production managers must make. In this exercise, you and your team are playing the role of production managers for the following companies, some producing a specific good and some producing a specific service:

- Cott—soft drinks
- H&R Block—tax consultation
- Bob Mackie—custom-made clothing
- Burger King—fast food
- Bombardier—commercial jets
- Halifax General Hospital—medical services
- Brother—fax machines
- GM—sport-utility vehicles

For each company on the list, discuss and recommend a specific facility layout, referring to Exhibit 8.3 for an overview of the four layouts. Why does your team believe the recommended layout is best suited to the product or service each company produces? How would the recommended layouts affect the movement of resources and inventory for the manufacturers on the list? How would the layouts affect customer interaction for the service providers on the list?

EXPAND YOUR KNOWLEDGE

DISCOVERING CAREER OPPORTUNITIES

Whether you prefer to work with products or services, many possible careers await you in production and operations. From input to transformation to output, companies are looking for resourceful, results-oriented employees able to meet the demands of ever-changing schedules and specifications. Start your research by scanning the help-wanted classified and display ads in your local newspaper and in the *Globe and Mail;* also check help-wanted ads in business magazines such as *Industry Week.* Access, Monster.ca and search for production and manufacturing jobs. www.monster.ca

1. As you read through these want ads, note all the production-related job titles you find. How many of these jobs include quality or technology (or both) among the duties and responsibilities?
2. Select two job openings that interest you. Reread the ads for those jobs to find out what kind of work experience and educational background are required. What further preparation will you need to qualify for these jobs?
3. Assume you have the qualifications for the two jobs you have selected. What key words should you include on your electronic resumé to show the employers that you are a good job candidate?

DEVELOPING YOUR RESEARCH SKILLS

Seeking increased efficiency and productivity, a growing number of producers of goods and services are applying technology to improve the production process. Find an article in business journals or newspapers (print or online edition) that discusses how one company used CAD, CAE, robots, electronic information systems, or other technological innovations to refit or reorganize its production operations.

1. What problems led the company to rethink its production process? What kind of technology did it choose to address these problems? What goals did the company set for applying technology in this way?

2. Before adding the new technology, what did the company do to analyze its existing production process? What changes, if any, were made as a result of this analysis?
3. How did technology-enhanced production help the company achieve its goals for financial performance? For customer service? For growth or expansion?

See It on the **WEB**

URLs for all Internet exercises are provided at the website for this book, www.pearsoned.ca/bovee. When you log on to the text website, select Chapter 8, then Destinations, then click on the name of the featured website, and review the website to complete the following exercises.

Explore the following chapter-related websites, review their content, and answer the following questions for each website you visit:

1. What is the purpose of this website?
2. What kinds of information does this website contain? Please be specific.
3. How is this information provided at this website useful for business people? Consumers?
4. How did you expand your knowledge of operations management by reviewing the material at this website? What new things did you learn about this topic?

MAKE QUALITY COUNT

In today's competitive business environment, companies have to be concerned about the quality of their goods and services. For information and advice, many turn to the National Quality Institute (NQI), an independent, non-profit organization that focuses on workplace excellence based on quality systems and the elements of a healthy workplace environment. The organization is headed by individuals drawn from both the public and private sectors. Each year the NQI announces the annual Canada Awards for Excellence (CAE). Discover how winning companies are selected, which companies have won the award, and what distinguishes these firms. www.nqi.ca/caeawards/default.aspx

FOLLOW THIS PATH TO CONTINUOUS IMPROVEMENT

The business of manufacturing is more complex than ever before. Today's operations managers must address the conflicting needs of customers, suppliers, employees, and shareholders. Discover why many operations managers turn to *Industry Week* magazine to stay on top of trends, technologies, and strategies to help drive continuous improvement throughout their organization. Log on to this magazine's website and read about the world's best-managed companies. Find out which manufacturing plants have won awards. Check out the surveys and special industry reports. Take a peek at the factories of the future. Don't leave without browsing the current articles or reviewing the glossary of manufacturing terms. www.industryweek.com

STEP INSIDE ISO ONLINE

The International Organization for Standardization (ISO) is a worldwide federation of national standards bodies from some 146 countries, one from each country. Established in 1947, ISO is a nongovernmental organization with the following mission: to promote the development of standardization and related activities in the world with a view to facilitating the international exchange of goods and services and to developing cooperation in the spheres of intellectual, scientific, technological, and economic activity. Step inside ISO Online and take a closer look at how ISO standards are developed, why international standardization is needed, and what fields are covered by ISO standards. www.iso.org/iso/en/ISOOnline.frontpage

Trouble in Toyland

LEARNING OBJECTIVES

The purpose of this video is to help you

1. Understand the competitive challenges in the toy industry.
2. Consider how social trends are directly affecting the bottom line for toy companies.
3. Identify possible courses of action to deal with competitive threats.

SYNOPSIS

The holiday season has always been a happy and profitable period for the $1.4 billion per year Canadian toy industry. However, new trends and evolving social patterns are threatening this blissful time. Children are growing up faster than ever before, and "age compression" is a major factor that is leading to reduced toy sales. In this new social order children are trading in traditional toys such as Barbie and LEGO blocks for MP3s, cellphones, and trendy clothes. Simultaneously, the toy industry is facing increased pressure from foreign competition and from price-cutting retailers such as Wal-Mart. Small and large toy retailers have felt the pain, and many have disappeared in the past decade. Even major retailers like Toys "R" Us are being forced to re-evaluate their business models and are in the process of restructuring. Manufacturers are also feeling the heat to cut the bottom line. So what can a company do to meet these undeniable forces of change? The video highlights two opposing strategies being implemented by Spin Master (a major toy manufacturer) and Mrs. Tiggy Winkles (Ottawa retail outlets).

Discussion Questions

1. *For analysis:* How do social trends affect the toy industry in the short term? In the long term?
2. *For application:* What sort of products can Spin Master sell to take advantage of "age compression" in the marketplace?
3. *For application:* How can the owners of the Mrs. Tiggy Winkles outlets compete with industry bullies like Wal-Mart and Toys "R" Us?
4. *For debate:* Toy manufacturers are unable to advertise their products to children in Quebec. This law was created to protect impressionable minds. Should all provinces adopt this position? Support your answer.

ONLINE EXPLORATION

Visit the Spin Master website at www.spinmaster.com and browse through the interactive site. Visit the Toys "R" Us website at www.toysrus.ca. Can you identify any specific products that are geared to satisfy the needs of children who wish to be considered mature young adults?

LEARNING OBJECTIVES

The purpose of this video is to help you

1. Understand the importance of motivating employees.
2. Consider how financial and nonfinancial rewards can motivate employees.
3. Explain how high morale can affect organizational performance.

SYNOPSIS

Kingston Technology, based in California, is the world's largest independent manufacturer of computer memory products. Founded by John Tu and David Sun, Kingston employs more than 2400 people but makes each employee feel like part of the family. The company returns 10 percent of its company profits to employees every year through a profit-sharing program. Just as important, it fosters mutual trust and respect between employees and management. Senior managers stay in touch with employees at all levels and conduct surveys to obtain employee feedback. For their part, employees report high job satisfaction and develop both personal and professional connections with their colleagues—boosting morale and motivation.

Discussion Questions

1. *For analysis:* After the sale to Softbank, employees learned from news reports that Kingston's US$100 million profit-sharing distribution was one of the largest in history. What was the likely effect of this publicity on employee morale?
2. *For application:* What kinds of questions should Kingston ask to measure satisfaction and morale through employee surveys?
3. *For debate:* Do you agree with Kingston's policy of giving new employees profit-sharing bonuses even when they join the company just one week before profits are distributed? Support your position.

ONLINE EXPLORATION

Visit Kingston Technology's website at www.kingston.com and follow the link to browse company information and read about its awards. From the company information page, follow the link to learn about the organization's values. How do these values support the founders' intention to create a family feeling within the company? How do they support employees' achievement of higher-level needs? Why would Kingston post this listing of milestones on its website, starting with the company's founding and continuing with honours bestowed by *Fortune* and others?

E-Business IN ACTION

What's All the Buzz about B2B?

Thanks to the Internet and e-commerce, many industries have established huge online trading hubs where purchasing, selling, and other supply chain transactions for the entire industry can take place under one virtual roof. Despite the failures of many of the pioneers of the B2B hub experiment, there are many advantages that the established survivors provide to their participants.

B2B Basics

Called B2B for short, business-to-business e-commerce exchanges are easier and more cost-effective to implement than traditional electronic data interchange (EDI) systems. Companies can link electronically via the Internet without installing costly private networks. Moreover, the common platform of the Internet makes it possible for all users to hook up regardless of the company's computer operating system.

B2B exchanges can be run by an independent third party or by existing industry players who join forces to form a new venture. They can be as basic as a manufacturer putting up a bare-bones website to let distributors securely order a handful of products, or they can be as complex as a public marketplace where buyers, sellers, creditors, distributors, and shippers share all kinds of information about inventory, prices, markets, purchase orders, invoices, payments, credit approvals, and so on.

The two most common types of B2B exchanges are *buyer exchanges* and *supplier exchanges. Buyer exchanges* are marketplaces formed by large groups of buyers (even competitors) who purchase similar items. By joining forces and aggregating demand for a product, they can achieve economies of scale that are not possible individually. *Supplier exchanges* are formed by suppliers who band together to create marketplaces to sell their goods online. These groups of suppliers typically sell complementary products, offering buyers one-stop shopping for most of their needs.

Promises Promises

Arriving at the turn of the twenty-first century, amid overblown hype, B2B exchanges promised to save members billions of dollars annually in reduced supply chain costs and to transform the way companies did business overnight. But the revolution never came. Expectations as to what the electronic marketplaces would do and how quickly they would be up and running were highly inflated. The Internet's availability and ease led many to believe that establishing a B2B network could be done quickly. Proposals for B2B electronic marketplaces sounded intriguing on paper. But many of the online marketplaces that started with fanfare at the turn of the century have since dried up and blown away. Among the casualties were many small exchanges and some big exchanges such as PetroCosm, an online buying site formed by Chevron and Texaco for the petroleum industry, and Zoho.com, a B2B marketplace formed by Starwood Hotels for the hotel industry. These start-ups learned that launching an online exchange involved much more than designing a cool website, and that the path to B2B prosperity was full of unanticipated roadblocks:

Estimated Savings from B2B E-Commerce	
Aerospace machining	11%
Chemicals	10%
Communications	5–15%
Computing	11–20%
Electronic components	29–39%
Food ingredients	3–5%
Forest products	15–25%
Freight transport	15–20%
Health care	5%
Life sciences	12–19%
Machining (metals)	22%
Media and advertising	10–15%
Oil and gas	5–15%
Paper	10%
Steel	11%

- *Member rivalry.* For large, public B2B exchanges to work effectively, competitors must be willing to expose business processes that give them a competitive advantage. Some companies were concerned that participation in public exchanges would put sales information and other critical data in the hands of customers and competitors. For instance, using a public exchange to purchase goods could tip a company's hand to competitors interested in buying patterns, giving them valuable information.
- *Supplier resistance.* It was easy to see how buyers would benefit by joining forces, but suppliers worried that online marketplaces, auction-like pricing, and easy access to cheaper goods would drive down the prices of their goods. So many refused to join.

- *Customer resistance.* Many companies were unwilling to dump the network of suppliers they'd built over the years and make all their purchases through a new, unfamiliar exchange. Larger companies such as Dell, Intel, and Wal-Mart, for example, already get the best prices possible from suppliers and have no plans to join public marketplaces that operate in their industry. Moreover, many manufacturers have long-term buying contracts and didn't see how the exchanges would get them lower prices or offer additional benefits. As a result, the anticipated droves of customers never showed up.
- *Incompatible systems.* One of the biggest challenges facing B2B exchanges was the need to seamlessly blend the operating systems used by exchange members. This included dozens of software packages, accounting systems, data-management systems, and manufacturing schedules. Different customs, languages, and laws further complicated the endeavours.

B2B... To Be?

Despite these roadblocks, some public B2B exchanges are making progress. Among them are exchanges for chemicals (CheMatch.com), shipping (LevelSeas.com), health care supplies (Broadlane.com), investment banking (The Markets.com), and automobile manufactures (Covisint.com). Although these exchanges are years away from reaching their goals—where fully integrated supply chains will shorten production cycles and dramatically improve their profit margins—they are making progress.

Covisint, the auto industry's public exchange, is the most notable. The exchange was created in February 2000 by the Big Three automakers—DaimlerChrysler, Ford Motor Company, and General Motors Corp—and later joined by other automakers such as Nissan, Renault, and Mitsubishi to move parts purchasing online, save costs, and speed up buying cycles. In the first year of business, the exchange handled more than 84 000 catalogue transactions and US$50 billion in auto-parts orders. Among the kinds of items that automakers and suppliers purchase via the exchange are paint, gearshift knobs, seat leather, interior mirrors, liftgates, footwear, fuses, and accelerator-pedal modules. There were 76 000 members by the end of 2003. By using the automotive industry exchange, DaimlerChrysler saved 40 percent of the cost of stamping dies for a future vehicle program. Moreover, when DaimlerChrysler needed to buy 10 000 personal computers and 10 000 laptops for employees on four continents, it turned to Covisint. The US$27 million package was wrapped up in a matter of hours instead of several weeks. The Covisint exchange boldly moved into 2005 as a model electronic marketplace that has a strong chance of proving that B2B will be.[56]

Questions for Critical Thinking

1. Why would a company want to participate in a B2B exchange?
2. Why have B2B exchanges been slow to take off?
3. How might B2B exchanges affect the supply chain? (Give both positive and negative examples.)

Business PlanPro **EXERCISES**

Managing a Business

Review Appendix C, Your Business Plan (on pages 397–398), to learn how to use Business PlanPro Software so you can complete these exercises.

Think Like a Pro

Objective: By completing these exercises you will become acquainted with the sections of a business plan that address a company's mission, goals and objectives, and management team. You will use the sample business plan for JavaNet (listed as Internet cafe in the Sample Plan Browser) in this exercise.

1. Evaluate JavaNet's mission statement. Does it summarize why the organization exists, what it seeks to accomplish, and the principles that the company will adhere to as it tries to reach its goals? How might you improve this mission statement?
2. Evaluate JavaNet's objectives. Are they clearly stated? Are they measurable? Do they seem realistic? Which objectives might need some refining?
3. Assess the risks facing JavaNet. How do you expect these threats to affect the company's ability to compete?
4. Read about the company's management structure and personnel plan. What challenges might JavaNet face as a result of its chosen structure and personnel plan?

Create Your Own Business Plan

Return to the plan you are creating for your own business. List your company's goals and objectives, and be sure they are clearly stated and measurable. How will you reach these goals and objectives? What might prevent you from achieving them? What information should you include about your management team? Should you mention the team's weaknesses in addition to its strengths? Why?

Chapter 9
Motivating Today's Workforce and Handling Employee-Management Relations

LEARNING OBJECTIVES

After studying this chapter, you will be able to

1. Identify and explain four important theories of employee motivation
2. Discuss three staffing challenges employers are facing in today's workplace
3. Highlight two trends contributing to the diversity of the Canadian workforce
4. Discuss three popular alternative work arrangements companies are offering their employees
5. Understand the role of unions and the challenges of reaching a collective bargaining agreement in the modern era
6. Cite three options unions can exercise when negotiations with management break down
7. Cite three options management can exercise when negotiations with a union break down

Behind the SCENES

Bombardier's Rise and...

Bombardier has come a long way from its humble origins as a manufacturer of Ski-Doos. It is now a powerful global transportation company that produces planes and trains for customers around the world.

In 1942, J. Armand Bombardier founded a modest company to manufacture tracked transportation vehicles for snow-covered terrain. From these humble beginnings the seeds were planted to create one of the world's largest and most respected transportation companies. Following an initial period of growth that saw the company develop and consolidate its business in the snowmobile industry, Bombardier took a major step forward in 1974, when it expanded its scope of operations. The firm landed a contract to build subway cars for the Montreal metro system. In 1986 the bold move to purchase Canadair launched the firm into the glamorous but tricky world of the aerospace industry. The rise of a Canadian legend was only beginning. The maker of planes, trains, and recreational products enjoyed massive growth from 1985 to 2000 as revenues and profits soared. For example, an investor who bought 1000 shares of Bombardier in 1982 at $10.25 each ($10 250 total) owned 128 000 shares by the end of 2000 after all stock splits were accounted for. When the shares peaked in the $26 range, that initial investment was worth approximately $3.3 million.

Employee Benefits and Demands

Employees were direct beneficiaries of the rise in stock since they were also encouraged to participate in generous share ownership plans. Additionally, many assembly workers benefited with systematic overtime pay that allowed shop workers to supplement their income to help the company deal with a huge backlog of aircraft orders. Employees shared in the success of the firm as massive hiring campaigns saw the global employee roster increase to 75 000 by 2003. This was also achieved through several acquisitions, particularly that of Adtienz. Despite these perks and because of the rapid growth of the firm, unions began to flex their muscles eager to earn a larger piece of a growing pie. When times are prosperous, employees, such as the one representing Bombardier's machinists, are able to put pressure on and succeed in earning concessions from an employer that has precious time-sensitive orders to fill. However, one question remained: Could wages continue to rise when Bombardier's main rival Embraer was able to maintain a much lower cost structure and with foreign low-cost locations like China battling for a piece of the aerospace assembly business.

Undeniable Forces of Change

The tremendous optimism began to wear off in 2000, as financial analysts and investors started to question whether the company could continue to grow at the same rate. Within a year the September 11, 2001, terrorist attacks occurred and the airline industry fell into a state of depression. This was later compounded by the SARS outbreak. Many airlines faced severe cash problems, leading some to bankruptcy. Bombardier, which derives the majority of its profits from airplane sales, saw its share price fall into a tailspin, dropping from $26 to less than $5 in a few short years. Chairman of the board Laurent Beaudoin felt compelled to act and replaced his friend and CEO of the company, Robert Brown, with Paul Tellier in January 2003.

Paul Tellier is a bit of a folk hero among CEOs in Canada; he took over the troubled Canadian National Railway (CN) in 1992. He performed what many consider to be a management miracle by transforming a government-owned company, with serious financial difficulties, into a private money-making corporation. Tellier performed this task through massive layoffs, cost cutting, and by acquiring two railways in the United States. He also advocated strong accounting and corporate governance practices. Tellier immediately started to change Bombardier's focus from growth to stability. He made it clear that he wasn't interested in growing revenue as much as he was in increasing profits and lowering costs.

The stage was set for a new era; this move would serve as a warning for employees and union leaders that had made considerable gains in membership and benefits during the previous years. Upon his arrival at Bombardier, Tellier immersed himself in the company and implemented an action plan to return Bombardier to its previous lofty heights. The firm raised capital by issuing an equity offering of $1.2 billion, sold the recreational product division, reduced the workforce by thousands (from 75 000 to 59 000), and tried to ensure that financial practices were simple and transparent. Unfortunately Bombardier's problems were growing. Most of its airplane customers were the financially strapped U.S. airline firms; the train division continued to generate low returns; the company's debt rating was cut to "junk bond" status by Moody's Investor Services, thus limiting its ability to borrow money. All this created a mood that the former darling of the Canadian investor world had fallen from grace; the company's share price plummeted below $3.

New Challenges

As the firm entered 2005, Paul Tellier was abruptly replaced by Laurent Beaudoin. The Bombardier family decided to take back control from the external professional management it had installed. Investors were baffled and concerned. With some of the company's biggest decisions and competitive challenges on the horizon they had changed course once again. Management, employees, and union leadership were faced with a new challenge that would have major repercussions on staff, investors, suppliers, and government officials. The company was at the point of a decision that could make or break it. Should it build the new 110- to 135-seat C Series planes that would cost an estimated $2 billion to create and an additional $1 billion to fully launch? If so, where should the planes be built? Could it compete with Embraer without this plane? Was it risking a fight with Boeing and Airbus if it began building larger airplanes?[1]

UNDERSTANDING HUMAN RELATIONS

Employees are a company's most valuable asset. But when it comes to attracting and keeping talented people, money alone won't do it. Although compensation and employee benefits are indeed important, research shows that every employee, by human nature, needs to feel valued, challenged, and respected.

morale
Attitude an individual has toward his or her job and employer

Employees who maintain a high **morale** or a positive attitude toward both their job and organization perform better.[2] But cultivating high workplace morale is especially challenging in a depressed economy. Declining stock values, plummeting sales, and workforce cutbacks, such as the ones described in the opening case on Bombardier, can result in employee turnover, unscheduled absenteeism, and poor morale—all of which can negatively affect a company's productivity and bottom line.[3]

human relations
Interaction among people within an organization for the purpose of achieving organizational and personal goals

In organizations, the goal of **human relations**—interactions among people within the organization—is to balance the diverse needs of employees with those of management. For instance, employers must motivate employees and keep them satisfied. But they must also remain competitive in the marketplace to ensure the organization's long-term success. Bombardier's decision to layoff about 30 percent of its aerospace workforce was directly related to the near collapse of the airline industry. Achieving this balance becomes increasingly difficult as companies face many staffing and demographic challenges. In this chapter we'll explore these issues. Then, in Chapter 10 we'll take a close look at what human resources managers do, as we explain the details of the hiring process, employee compensation, and specific employee benefits.

MOTIVATING EMPLOYEES

Studies show that all employees want and expect their employers to treat them fairly. They want more than a good paycheque and satisfying work. They want to balance their careers and their family lives. "There's an increasing interest in people finding meaning in their lives and in their work," notes Don Kuhn, the executive director of the International University Consortium for Executive Education. "People are no longer content with income alone. They are looking for personal satisfaction."[4] They want to be part of something they can believe in, something that confers meaning on their work and on their lives. They want to be motivated.[5]

What Is Motivation?

Motivation is an inner force that moves individuals to take action. Some companies motivate their employees by providing a culture that makes it enjoyable to come to work. Cirque du Soleil is a professionally run organization that has a unique culture stemming from the company's origins. The firm was founded by street performers who have evolved their company into an entertainment empire. Needless to say, based on these roots the culture of the firm is more laid back than a company like IBM. Other firms try to motivate employees by controlling or changing their actions through **behaviour modification**. They systematically encourage those actions that are desirable by providing pleasant consequences and discourage those that are undesirable by providing unpleasant consequences.

motivation
Inner force that moves someone to take action

behaviour modification
Systematic use of rewards and punishments to change human behaviour

Positive reinforcement offers pleasant consequences (such as a gift, praise, certificate, medal, dinner, or trip) for completing or repeating a desired action. Experts recommend the use of positive reinforcement because it emphasizes the desired behaviour rather than the unwanted behaviour. By contrast, *negative reinforcement* allows people to avoid unpleasant consequences by behaving in the desired way. For example, fear of losing a job (unpleasant consequences) may move an employee to finish a project on time (desired behaviour). Such negative motivation, however, is much less effective than encouraging an individual's own sense of direction, creativity, and pride in doing a good job.

Another proven motivation technique used by many organizations is **management by objectives (MBO)**, a companywide process that empowers employees and involves them in goal setting and decision making. This process consists of four steps: setting goals, planning actions, implementing plans, and reviewing performance (see Exhibit 9.1). Because employees at all levels are involved in all four steps, they learn more about company objectives and feel that they are an important part of the companywide team. Furthermore, they understand how even their small job function contributes to the organization's long-term success.

management by objectives (MBO)
A motivational tool whereby managers and employees work together to structure personal goals and objectives for every individual, department, and project to mesh with the organization's goals

One of the key elements of MBO is a collaborative goal-setting process. Together, a manager and employee define the employee's goals, the responsibilities for achieving those goals, and the means of evaluating individual and group performance so that the employee's activities are directly linked to achieving the organization's long-term goals. Jointly setting clear and challenging—but achievable—goals can encourage employees to reach higher levels of performance. MBO and behaviour modification are two ways companies motivate employees to perform. As you can imagine, people are motivated by many factors. Thus, the challenge for managers is to select motivators that will inspire employees to achieve organizational objectives. But which ones are the most effective? Several theories of motivation have attempted to answer that question.

Theories of Motivation

L.O. 1

Motivation has been a topic of interest to managers for more than a hundred years. Frederick W. Taylor was a machinist and engineer who became interested in employee efficiency and motivation late in the nineteenth century. Taylor developed **scientific management**, an approach that sought to improve employee efficiency through the scientific study of work. In Taylor's view, people were motivated almost exclusively by money, so he set up pay systems that rewarded employees when they were productive. Under Taylor's piecework system, for example, employees who just met or fell short of the quota were paid a certain amount for each unit produced. Those who produced more were paid a higher rate for *all* units produced, not just for those that exceeded the quota; this pay system gave employees a strong incentive to boost productivity.

scientific management
Management approach designed to improve employees' efficiency by scientifically studying their work

Exhibit 9.1 Management by Objectives (MBO)

The MBO process has four steps. This cycle is refined and repeated as managers and employees at all levels work toward establishing goals and objectives, thereby accomplishing the organization's strategic goals.

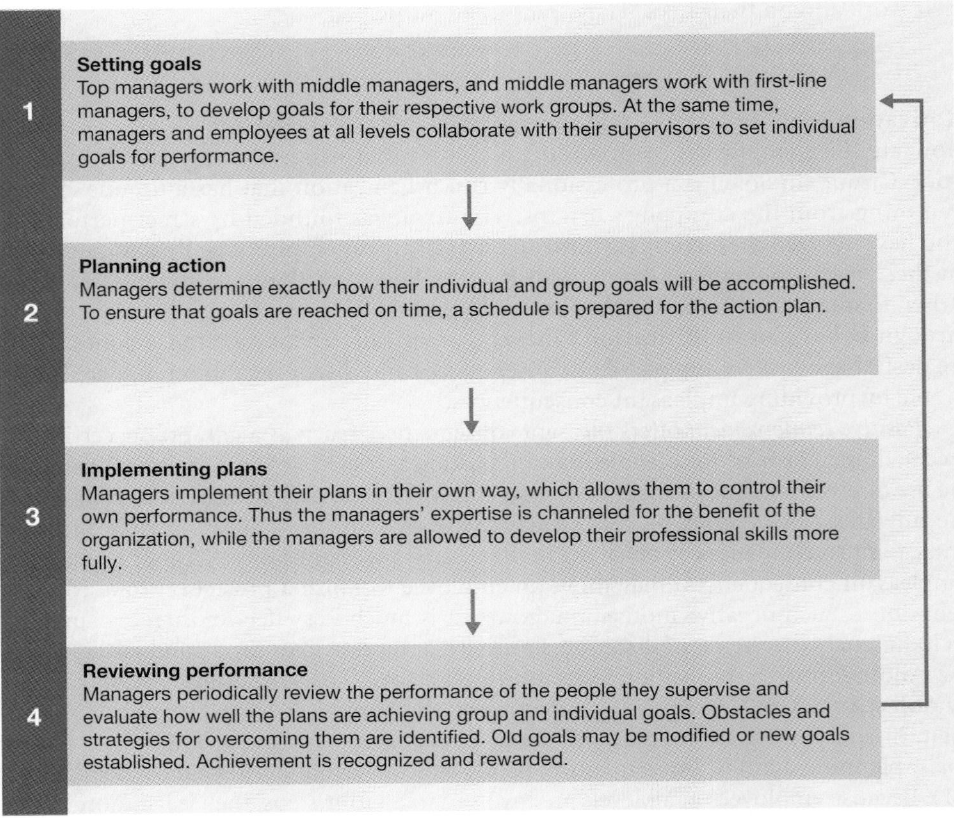

Although money has always been a powerful motivator, scientific management fails to take into account other motivational elements, such as opportunities for personal satisfaction or individual initiative. Thus, scientific management can't explain why someone still wants to work even though that person's spouse already makes a good living or why a Wall Street lawyer or a Bay Street executive will take a hefty pay cut to serve in government. For example, John McCallum, a member of Paul Martin's cabinet, held the position of chief economist and senior vice-president at the Royal Bank of Canada before entering the political arena.[6] Belinda Stronach, formerly a member of the Conservative party but now a member of the Liberal party, entered politics and left her post as president and CEO of Magna Corporation.[7] Money was not the driving force behind these decisions. Therefore, researchers have looked beyond money to discover what else motivates people.

The Hawthorne Effect

A major discovery on human motivation was uncovered in a study initiated in 1924 by Elton Mayo and his colleagues. This famous experiment attempted to measure worker performance at the Hawthorne Western Electric Plant, located near Chicago. The initial goal of the study was to examine the effects of lighting, ventilation, and fatigue on employee productivity in the plant.

In one part of the study the researchers selected two groups of employees that were doing similar work under similar conditions and tracked their productivity. After a while they began to increase the lighting in the work environment of one group while keeping the lighting constant for the other group. Each time they increased the level of lighting, worker productivity improved. To determine whether brighter lighting levels led to increased productivity, they began to lower the lighting to measure the reverse effect. *Much to their surprise, the employee productivity continued to rise as the lighting levels were lowered.* The study concluded that the workers were not responding to the lighting variations; instead, they were motivated by the attention they were getting. Test conditions made them feel special and also gave them more freedom from supervisor control. The group was inspired to improve performance by an internal feeling of importance and the feedback and interactions associated with the experiment.[8]

Belinda Stronach left her position as president and CEO of Magna Corporation, the company her father founded, to enter politics. She ran for the leadership of the Conservative party in 2004 and lost. She crossed the floor and joined the Liberal party in 2005 before a key vote. Before the unexpected move, she was a rising star in the Conservative party and had been described as a strong candidate to become the second female prime minister in Canadian history. Time will tell whether she still aspires to the post and whether the bold move will help or hinder her chances.

Maslow's Hierarchy of Needs

In 1943 psychologist Abraham Maslow proposed the theory that behaviour is determined by a variety of needs. He organized these needs into five categories and then arranged the categories in a hierarchy. As Exhibit 9.2 shows, the most basic needs are at the bottom of this hierarchy and the more advanced needs are toward the top. In Maslow's hierarchy, all of the requirements for basic survival—food, clothing, shelter, and the like—fall into the category of *physiological needs.* These basic needs must be satisfied before the person can consider higher-level needs such as *safety needs, social needs* (the need to give and receive love and to feel a sense of belonging), and *esteem needs* (the need for a sense of self-worth and integrity).

At the top of Maslow's hierarchy is *self-actualization*—the need to achieve one's ultimate potential. This need is also the most difficult to fulfill. Employees who reach this point work not only to make money or to impress others but also because they feel their work is worthwhile and satisfying in itself. Self-actualization needs partially explain why some people make radical career changes or strike out on their own as entrepreneurs.

Although Maslow's hierarchy is a convenient way to classify human needs, it would be a mistake to view it as a rigid sequence. A person need not completely satisfy each level of needs before being motivated by a higher need. Indeed, at any one time, most people are motivated by a combination of needs.

Herzberg's Two-Factor Theory

In the 1960s Frederick Herzberg and his associates undertook their own study of human needs. They asked accountants and engineers to describe specific aspects of their jobs that made them feel satisfied or dissatisfied. Upon analyzing the results, they found that two entirely different sets of factors were associated with satisfying and dissatisfying work experiences: *hygiene factors* and *motivators* (see Exhibit 9.3).

Exhibit 9.2 Maslow's Hierarchy of Needs

According to Maslow, needs on the lower levels of the hierarchy must be satisfied before higher-level needs can be addressed.

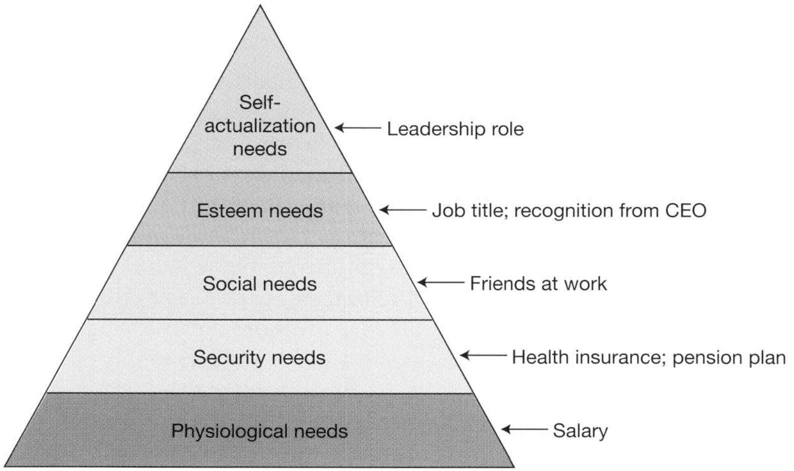

Exhibit 9.3 **Two-Factor Theory**

Hygiene factors such as working conditions and company policies can influence employee dissatisfaction. On the other hand, motivators such as opportunities for achievement and recognition can influence employee satisfaction.

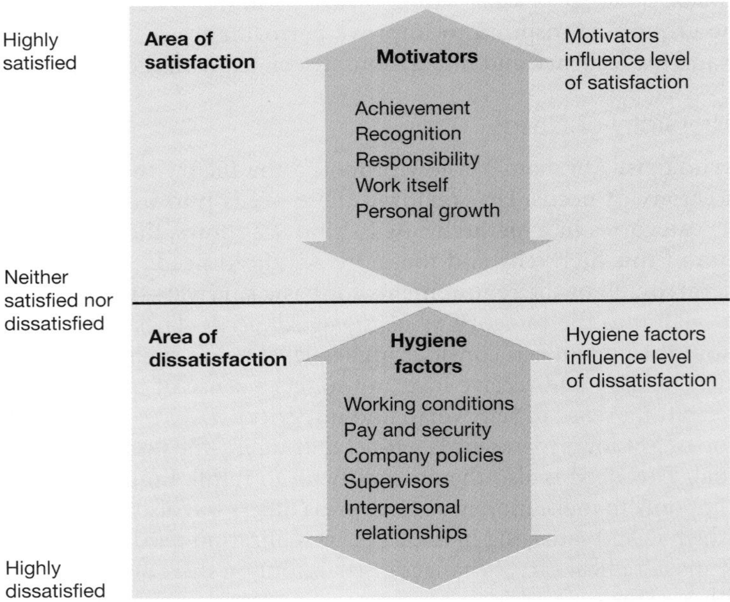

hygiene factors
Aspects of the work environment that are associated with dissatisfaction

motivators
Factors of human relations in business that may increase motivation

What Herzberg called **hygiene factors** are associated with *dissatisfying* experiences. The potential sources of dissatisfaction include working conditions, company policies, and job security. Management can lessen worker dissatisfaction by improving hygiene factors that concern employees, but such improvements seldom influence satisfaction. On the other hand, managers can help employees feel more motivated and, ultimately, more satisfied by paying attention to **motivators** such as achievement, recognition, responsibility, and other personally rewarding factors. Herzberg's theory is related to Maslow's hierarchy of needs: The motivators closely resemble the higher-level needs, and the hygiene factors resemble the lower-level needs.

Should managers concentrate on motivators or on hygiene factors? It depends. A skilled, well-paid, middle-class, middle-aged employee may be motivated to perform better if motivators are supplied. However, a young, unskilled worker who earns low wages or an employee who is insecure will probably still need the support of strong hygiene factors to reduce dissatisfaction before the motivators can be effective.

McGregor's Theory X and Theory Y

Theory X
Managerial assumption that employees are irresponsible, are not ambitious, and dislike work; therefore, managers must use force, control, or threats to motivate them

Theory Y
Managerial assumption that employees like work, are naturally committed to certain goals, are capable of creativity, and seek out responsibility under the right conditions

In the 1960s psychologist Douglas McGregor identified two radically different sets of assumptions that underlie most management thinking. He classified these sets of assumptions into two categories: *Theory X* and *Theory Y* (see Exhibit 9.4).

According to McGregor, **Theory X**-oriented managers believe that employees dislike work and can be motivated only by the fear of losing their jobs or by *extrinsic rewards* such as money, promotions, and tenure. This management style emphasizes physiological and safety needs and tends to ignore the higher-level needs in Maslow's hierarchy. In contrast, **Theory Y**-oriented managers believe that employees like work and can be motivated by working for goals that promote creativity or for causes they believe in. Thus, Theory Y-oriented managers seek to motivate employees through *intrinsic rewards.*

The assumptions behind Theory X emphasize authority; the assumptions behind Theory Y emphasize growth and self-direction. It was McGregor's belief that, although

Exhibit 9.4 Theory X and Theory Y

McGregor proposed two distinct views of human nature. The assumptions of Theory X are basically negative, whereas those of Theory Y are basically positive.

THEORY X	THEORY Y
1. Employees inherently dislike work and will avoid it whenever possible.	1. Employees like work and consider it as natural as play and rest.
2. Because employees dislike work, they must be threatened with punishment to achieve goals.	2. People naturally work toward goals they are committed to.
3. Employees will avoid responsibilities whenever possible.	3. The average person can learn to accept and even seek responsibility.
4. Employees value security above all other job factors.	4. The average person's intellectual potential is only partially realized.

some employees need the strong direction demanded by Theory X, those who are ready to realize their social, esteem, and self-actualization needs will not work well under Theory X assumptions.[9]

Ouchi's Theory Z

Another perspective on motivation was developed by William Ouchi, who studied Japanese and North American management practices. Ouchi's **Theory Z** assumes that employees are more motivated if you involve them in all aspects of company decision making and treat them like family. Managers who adopt these practices believe that employees with a sense of identity and belonging are more likely to perform their jobs conscientiously and will try more enthusiastically to achieve company goals. Embraced in one form or another by most Fortune 500 companies, Theory Z is the core of such practices as self-directed work teams, quality circles, and other forms of participative management that make employees more responsible for the outcome of their efforts.

Theory Z
Human relations approach that emphasizes involving employees at all levels and treating them like family

KEEPING PACE WITH TODAY'S WORKFORCE

Although motivational theories shed some light on what managers can do to motivate employees to work efficiently and effectively toward achieving the organization's goals, managers must also address the needs of today's workforce. They must manage a diverse group of individuals and recognize that all employees have interests and obligations outside of work, such as family, volunteer activities, and hobbies. Addressing employees' many needs becomes even more critical in a work environment plagued by a number of staffing challenges.

Staffing Challenges

L.O. 2

If you ask business leaders what their biggest challenges are today, you will most likely get the following answers: finding, attracting, and keeping talented people; rightsizing their workforces; and satisfying employees' desire for a work–life balance.[10] Finding and keeping good workers is especially difficult for small-company owners, who often trail bigger companies in salary, benefits, job security, and other criteria that lead workers to choose one company over another.

Shortage of Skilled Labour

A close look at Appendix D confirms that many of today's growing occupations require specialized skills or training, whereas the shrinking occupations involve activities that require fewer skills or ones that are increasingly being automated. In fact, nearly all jobs today require computer literacy. Machinists, for example, need computer skills to operate chip-controlled equipment. Even package delivery involves data entry. But finding technology-literate employees is difficult for most companies today.

Some companies are revamping rigid pay systems to make it easier for employees to move laterally and enhance their skills. Others are installing new career development programs to help employees plan their career moves. Managers at International Paper, for example, sit down with every employee once a year to discuss his or her career desires, separate from the annual performance review.[11] Still others are instituting educational programs to attract and keep skilled employees. Cisco Systems, a manufacturer of computer network routers, runs its own Networking Academy. This in-house vocational program teaches students how to build and manage the computer-server networks the company sells. Cisco hopes that eventually the students will return to the company for permanent jobs.[12] The problem is real and companies must learn to cope. For more information on this topic, see the box entitled "Too Many Workers? Not For Long."

UPS took a particularly creative approach with its staffing challenge when Louisville, Kentucky, could not supply the 6000 additional employees the company needed for its growing US$6 billion air-freight business. Rather than moving its main U.S. air hub from Louisville to another location, UPS partnered with the city of Louisville to attract new employees to the area. Together they built the "UPS University" and special dormitories so student-workers could sleep during the day, attend classes taught by professors from the University of Louisville at night, and then work the UPS graveyard shift (11:30 p.m. to 3:30 a.m.) and still have time to study.[13]

Downsizing and Rightsizing

The increasing demand for educated workers and the continuing conversion from a manufacturing-based economy to a service-based economy are forcing companies to pull apart their workforces and then piece them back together differently. Factors contributing to *downsizing* decisions include company reorganizations, business downturns, elimination of unprofitable product lines, outsourcing, mergers and acquisitions, and a general mismatch between employee job skills and job demands. Each week we see examples of companies shuffling to address concerns. Colgate-Palmolive recently announced that it was slashing 4400 jobs from its global workforce of 37 000. Because of this decision employees at a plant in Toronto and a warehouse in Moncton lost their jobs. The company's stock increased 8.2 percent that day.[14] During the same week Montreal-based Domtar, North America's third-largest manufacturer of commercial and office printing paper, decided to slash 800 jobs and shut a plant in Cornwall, Ontario. The company pointed to the increased value of the Canadian dollar as a source of rising costs.[15] Even though corporate downsizing continues today, what is puzzling is a concurrent trend toward "upsizing," or massive hiring—often within the same firm.[16]

Canadians have felt their share of grief over lost jobs due to restructuring and outsourcing but they have also benefited from such moves over the years. Union official John Drueke said his "heart just dropped" after learning about the closing of the Life Savers Michigan plant to shift production to a facility in Quebec. The company cited high U.S. sugar prices as the major factor behind the relocation.

This phenomenon can best be explained by the needs of companies to *rightsize,* or realign their workforces into business growth areas. For example, employees from Department A are let go while new hires are sought to keep up with the growth demands of Department B. Such was the case at Hewlett-Packard when the company shed marketing jobs but added new positions in consulting and sales. "In many cases, companies are trying to upgrade their talent," says one human resources expert.[17]

Employee Loyalty As you can imagine, rightsizing is a contributing factor to declining employee loyalty. Devastated by the lack of job security, employees quickly learn to "do what's best for me," as Exhibit 9.5 on page 230

Too Many Workers? Not for Long

Focused on today's labour problems, most companies aren't looking too far around the bend. But when they do, they're in for some big surprises. According to demographers and economists, labour shortages—especially of skilled employees—will become a central issue for companies looking to acquire and retain staff. Companies in Canada and the rest of the industrialized world will face an unprecedented problem. As the baby boomers (people born from 1947 to 1966) begin to retire, the labour pool will have trouble keeping up. In 2001, a report by the Conference Board of Canada indicated that the baby boom generation made up 47 percent of the labour force. By 2010 the projected retirements will create shortages especially in areas of technology, health care, and manufacturing. The problems become clearer when we examine specific scenarios. John Murphy, executive vice-president of human resources at Ontario Power Generation (OPG) faced the following issue: the average age of his workforce was 45 and he projected that the organization would need to replace more than a quarter of its 11 000 staff members within five years. Many of these individuals were top-level engineers and managers who would be taking valuable skill sets with them.[18]

Japan, with one-fifth of the population already over 65, has already begun to feel the effects of this demographic nightmare. The government is stepping up its campaign to maintain the workforce with initiatives to increase the retirement age from 60 to 65 and with programs to encourage more women to join the workforce or to stay home and have more babies. Improved maternity benefits and tax breaks for growing families appear to be just the beginning.[19]

While a labour shortage presents tremendous hurdles for employers, it brings opportunity for employees. A slower-growing workforce could indeed shift the balance of power to workers, forcing employers to hike wages, add daycare centres, increase flexible work hours, provide more training, and develop innovative ways to attract and retrain existing employees. RBC Financial Group accommodates its diverse employees by promoting growth initiatives; each year 12 000 members of the 70 000 workforce move to new positions they find through internal postings. Additionally, as the projected shortages become clearer, older workers could suddenly take on value as a skilled pool of labour. "At RBC Financial Group retirees can work part time for up to 30 months without incurring a penalty on their pension."[20]

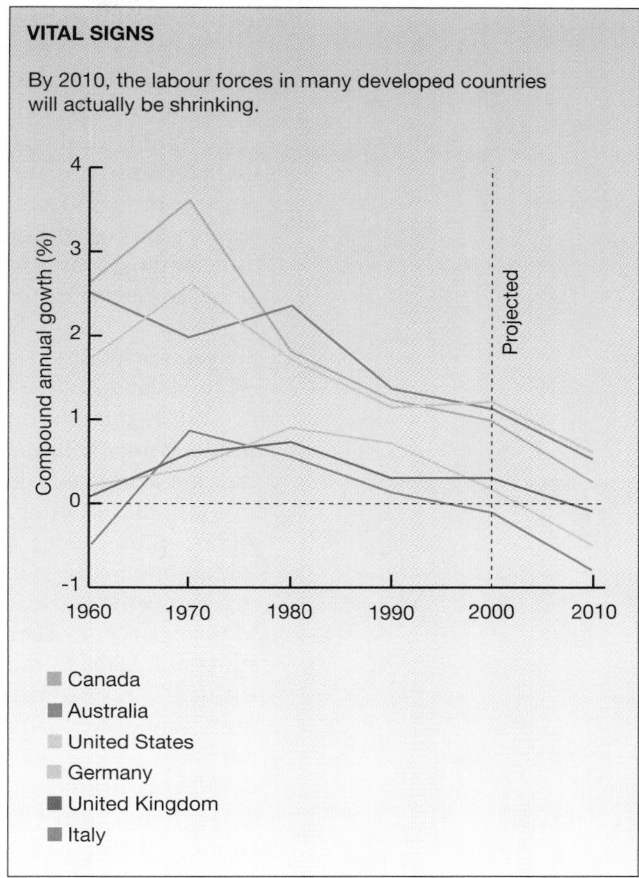

Source: Data taken from Watson Wyatt Worldwide.

In Canada, the problem is compounded when you consider that about 40 000 skilled individuals leave the country every year for other opportunities or better pay in the United States or abroad.[21] Bottom line: Employers that refit the work environment to appeal to both young and old, experienced and inexperienced, native and immigrant will end up in the best position. But they must begin making such changes now by training and recruiting valuable human resources.

Questions for Critical Thinking

1. Why do experts predict a skilled-labour shortage in the near future?
2. What can employers do to prepare for a future skilled-labour shortage?

shows. For some, that means putting job security and a long-term financial future ahead of finding challenging work. Public affairs specialist Yara Lizarraga didn't even consider looking for another job when her employer Agilent Technologies asked her to take a 10 percent pay cut. "If I said it didn't hurt, I'd be lying," says Lizarraga. "But I'm just so grateful to have a job."[22]

Today's employees have more realistic expectations. They recognize that the old idea of a paternal company taking care of employees has, for the most part, died. Despite these altered expectations, job uncertainty is a major source of stress and employees are challenged to deal with the ambiguities of the modern work environment.[23] They realize that companies are going to do whatever they have to do to succeed and survive. This may mean manufacturing in South America, eliminating three layers of management, closing down plants, or cutting salaries and perks.[24] Even the Japanese tradition of lifetime employment is under attack. After years of severe economic recession and intense global competition, the Japanese are realizing that unconditional loyalty is becoming too expensive to justify. To remain competitive, Japanese companies are chipping away at their seniority-based management system and are forcing executives to perform or go—bringing Japan a little closer to the North American model.[25]

While many individuals acknowledge the forces of the global economy, not all employees are willing to look at the company's bottom line and be understanding when they are losing a job that they worked hard to establish. As Bombardier continued to announce layoff after layoff, many remaining employees were looking at seniority lists and becoming concerned, frustrated, angry, or depressed. This sort of environment can lead to bizarre behaviour regardless of the business environment. For some individuals this can lead to a lessened sense of belonging and frequent surfing of job sites like Monster.ca. For others faced with uncertainty, employee loyalty crosses the lines of ethics and leads to minor criminal activity. Many people begin to believe that they are entitled to take something of value to compensate for their loss. The theft can range from minor office supplies to inventory to misappropriated funds.[26]

Employee Burnout Rightsizing is also putting pressure on remaining employees to work longer hours. When 3M spun off its data storage and medical imaging divisions, some employees began working 80-hour weeks. One 3M customer service consultant summed up the feelings of many employees when he said, "I always perceived work to be a means to an end, but not *the* end."[27] Others are working longer hours just to keep up. "It seems like you work, work, work," says one chemist.[28]

On average, workers are putting in 260 more hours a year than a decade ago—many without overtime pay.[29] Such long hours can lead to employee *burnout,* which is characterized by emotional exhaustion, depersonalization, and lower levels of achievement. Severe burnout or stress may even lead to clinical depression.[30] Other sources of employee burnout are job insecurity, technological advancements, and information overload:

Exhibit 9.5 The Committed Employee—Then and Now

Employee loyalty isn't what it used to be. A recent survey confirms that even today's most valuable committed workers often put career development and life and family issues ahead of company goals. This chart illustrates this shift in workforce commitment.

CHARACTERISTIC	THEN	NOW
Attachment to employer	Long-term	Near-term
Readiness to change jobs	Not interested	Not looking (but will listen)
Priorities on the job	The firm and its goals	Personal life and career
Devotion to employer goals	Follows orders	Buys in (usually)
Motto	Always faithful	Seize the day

- *Job insecurity.* Workers anxious about job security feel they have to give more or risk being seen as expendable. Practices that were once considered crises-mode workloads have now become business as usual. These extra hours, which don't always bring extra pay, can leave employees feeling burned out and resentful.[31]
- *Technological advancements.* New technology allows employees to work from home, but being wired to the office 24 hours a day can add extra pressure. Employees feel compelled to answer that voice mail or e-mail whatever the hour. "We have all these great tools to save our time," notes one career expert. "Instead, it just extends our week. We're never out of touch anymore."[32]
- *Information overload.* Managers claim they're unable to handle the vast amounts of information they now receive. In fact, more information has been produced in the last 30 years than in the previous 5000, and the total quantity of printed material is doubling every five years—and accelerating.[33]

How does burnout affect the ability of workers to do their jobs? "When you feel under stress, you find your mental wheels spinning and you work mechanically rather than creatively," says one human resources expert. "The tasks that normally would take a few minutes sit unfinished for days because you lose the capacity to prioritize and you put off larger, important projects that take more energy and concentration."[34]

Quality of Work Life

A recent survey found that 42 percent of all job seekers identified work-life issues as the most important consideration in their choice of a new job. For some employees the primary work-life issue is caring for an elderly parent; for others it is child care, rising college tuition costs, or a desire to return to school part time.[35] Regardless, achieving a work-life balance is especially difficult when both parents work or in situations where downsizing and restructuring have left remaining employees with heavier workloads than in the past.

To help employees balance the demands of work and family, businesses are offering child-care assistance, family leave, flexible work schedules, telecommuting, and other solutions that are explored later in this chapter and in Chapter 10. Many companies are also focusing on improving the **quality of work life (QWL)**, the environment created by work and job conditions. At Dofasco, the Hamilton-based steel manufacturer, the company is going the extra mile and providing mental wellness questionnaires to address work-related stress and improve QWL.[36] Hewlett-Packard is addressing the fundamental problems of how much time a job really demands and how to build a life beyond work by encouraging employees to set leisure goals and focus on developing their personal lives. As Hewlett-Packard knows, an improved QWL benefits both the individual and the organization. Employees gain the chance to use their specialized abilities, improve their skills, and balance their lives. The organization gains a more motivated and loyal employee.[37]

quality of work life (QWL)
Overall environment that results from job and work conditions

Two common ways of improving QWL are through **job enrichment**, which reduces specialization and makes work more meaningful by expanding each job's responsibilities, and **job redesign**, which restructures work to provide a better fit between employees' skills and their jobs. Quality of work life can be improved in other ways, too. Many organizations are providing their employees with a number of benefits designed to help them balance their work with personal responsibilities. Pepsi has an on-site dry cleaning drop-off at its New York headquarters, and Hewlett-Packard has sponsored schools at company sites that allow employees to visit their children during lunchtime and after school. All of these measures can improve employees' lives by freeing up their time and by making work a more enjoyable place to be.[38] See the box entitled "Chuckle While You Work."

job enrichment
Reducing work specialization and making work more meaningful by adding to the responsibilities of each job

job redesign
Designing a better fit between employees' skills and their work to increase job satisfaction

Demographic Challenges

The workforce is undergoing significant changes that require major alterations in how managers keep employees happy and productive. One of the most significant demographic trends facing companies today is increasing workforce diversity.

Chuckle While You Work

Lighten up. Let loose. Laugh a little. Experts are now advising managers to make company-sponsored fun a fundamental part of work. That's because after experiencing more than a decade of restructuring, downsizing, and re-engineering, employees could use a laugh or two. In fact, a recent survey of 1300 corporate managers showed that more than 60 percent disagreed with the statement "I have fun at work these days."

"Because we spend more of our waking hours working than doing anything else, fun should be a very fundamental part of work," notes one expert on human behaviour. In fact, workplace fun is increasingly important because today's jobs are more insecure and more competitive than they once were. Furthermore, camaraderie is diminishing as employees spend more and more time relating to machines than to each other, they often eat lunch at their desks, or they work from home.

Although traditional business wisdom says that people having fun on the job are probably slacking off, studies show that a happy workforce is also a productive one. For one thing, a little wisecracking and laughs can go a long way toward relieving stress. Moreover, fun can raise a company's bottom line by improving health, reducing absenteeism, boosting morale, building teamwork, releasing creativity, improving productivity, and increasing enthusiasm. So while the pursuit of fun may seem frivolous to the serious-minded, more and more companies are beginning to see the value of a good hearty laugh or a little giggle now and then.

Take Sprint, for example. Recent company-sponsored fun days encouraged employees to wear clothes backwards and to go on a photo safari with disposable cameras, taking candid photos of other employees. At Lands' End—voted as one of the best places to work—employees can participate in the company's "Cruise Room," where reps can enjoy calypso music and fruit punch on their breaks. Other companies have organized employee costume parties, hosted goofy birthday celebrations, and sponsored fun-filled weekends at hotels. Still others are lifting the workplace spirit by hanging funny signs and posters in offices, holding a messiest desk contest with prizes, and posting comic strips and snapshots on company bulletin boards. These companies and others recognize that if work is fun, people will want to come to work. "Our people are our most important assets," says one executive. "We try to make work a fun place where they can stay as long as they want and get excellent benefits."

Questions for Critical Thinking

1. Under which level of Maslow's hierarchy of needs would you place having fun at work?
2. Would a manager who promoted workplace fun be Theory X- or Theory Y-oriented?

L.O. 3

Workforce Diversity

The Canadian workforce is diverse in race, gender, age, culture, family structures, religion, and linguistic and educational backgrounds—and will become even more diverse in the years ahead. Managing this changing mixture in the labour force can be difficult. A diverse workforce brings with it a wide range of skills, traditions, backgrounds, experiences, outlooks, and attitudes toward work that can affect individuals' job performance. Moreover, a diverse workforce brings language and communication challenges. Two major trends contributing to the diversity of the workforce are the influx of new immigrants and the aging population.

New Immigrants Thirteen to fourteen percent of the Canadian population are visible minorities. This figure is expected to increase to about 20 percent by 2016. Approximately, 37 percent of Toronto and Vancouver citizens are visible minorities. Calgary is next on the list at 17 percent with Edmonton, Winnipeg, Ottawa, and Montreal in the 12 to 14 percent range. Seventy-three percent of new immigrants are visible minorities; therefore, it is easy to see the importance of these various groups in the continued growth of the nation. Many of these individuals come to Canada with tremendous academic and work experience but face an uphill battle to find employment equivalent to their skills.[39]

Aging Population As previously described, the population is aging; this situation creates new challenges and concerns for employers and employees alike. Experts predict that because of inadequate pensions and a general desire to stay active, many baby boomers will put off retirement until they are in their seventies. While this could help solve the problems of upcoming labour shortages, there are other issues to be considered. Older, more experienced employees command higher salaries. "For my salary, the company could hire two twenty-somethings," says a 41-year-old. "I'm good at what I do. But am I better than two people? Even I know that's not true." Not only do older employees earn more, but the costs of employee benefits such as medical insurance and pensions rise with age as well.[40] Furthermore, as the rate of change gets faster, it can be difficult for older employees to keep up unless they have the stamina of a 25-year-old.

On the other hand, older employees provide certain advantages to employers. They have more experience, and are usually more seasoned decision-makers. They are also more likely to show up on time and less likely to quit. But these traits pale by comparison with the highly desired traits characteristic of younger workers, who appear more flexible, more adaptable, more accepting of new technology, and better at learning new skills.[41]

As baby boomers reach retirement age the role of mature employees will grow in all aspects of the labour force from part-time positions as retail clerks to corporate career extensions.

Diversity Initiatives To cope with increasing workforce diversity, many companies offer employees sensitivity or awareness training to help them understand the various attitudes and beliefs that minorities and immigrants bring to their jobs. These classes also help managers become more sensitive to the behaviour and communication patterns of employees with diverse backgrounds.

Besides the immigrant populations, Aboriginal groups are an important segment to be considered. In Saskatchewan, Aboriginal people will account for 20 percent of the population by 2015.[42] The Canadian Imperial Bank of Commerce (CIBC) is supporting the creation of an employee-driven diversity network designed to support the 400 native staff members across the country. Procter & Gamble offers a two-day "diversity training" course to all its employees. "Their 2000 Canadian-based employees are actively encouraged to participate in a dozen or so cultural events produced each year for the employees." P&G also offers a prayer room to accommodate people of various faiths on-site.[43]

Although encouraging sensitivity to employee differences is important, a company stands to benefit most when it incorporates its employees' diverse perspectives into the organization's work. This enables the company to uncover new opportunities by rethinking primary tasks and redefining markets, products, strategies, missions, business practices, and even cultures. Western Union's Canadian marketing team is a prime example of a firm that has embraced diversity and gone well beyond inclusion. In fact, among the key members of this national marketing team are individuals from China, India, Columbia, Poland, the Philippines, and also one natural-born Canadian. These individuals bring valuable knowledge of their communities and support a network of 3000 "ethnic agents." Diversity can be an important asset, and one challenge of corporate human relations is to make the most of this asset. Companies are starting to get this message. For example, the Royal Bank of Canada has created a Diversity Leadership Council, led by the company's CEO, to move the issue forward.[44]

Gender-Related Issues

Another demographic challenge companies have been dealing with for years is the gender gap in compensation. Additionally, even though women have made tremendous advances, only seven heads of Fortune 500 companies are women.[45] In Canada, only 19 of the top 500 companies have female leaders and only 14.4 percent of corporate officer positions are occupied by women.[46] Some attribute this inequality to the *glass ceiling.*

glass ceiling
Invisible barrier attributable to subtle discrimination that keeps women (and minorities) out of the top positions in business

The Glass Ceiling An invisible barrier that keeps women and minorities from reaching the highest-level positions is referred to as the **glass ceiling**. One theory suggests that top management has long been dominated by white males who tend to hire and promote employees who look, act, and think as they do. Another theory holds that stereotyping by male middle managers leads them to believe that family life will interfere with a woman's work. As a result, women are relegated to less visible assignments in the company, so their work goes unnoticed by top executives and their careers stagnate.[47] Many women, like many men, decide to self-impose career limitations to address family concerns and quality of life. However, unlike men, the remaining female labour pool has been stereotyped into a company-wide limiting mindset.[48] Legislation such as the Employment Equity Act is placing legal parameters on companies to eliminate systematic discrimination.

sexism
Discrimination on the basis of gender

sexual harassment
Unwelcome sexual advance, request for sexual favours, or other verbal or physical conduct of a sexual nature within the workplace

At a recent summit to celebrate Canada's most powerful women, Rose Patten, senior executive vice-president of human resources and head of office strategic management at BMO, was honoured. In the banking sector, BMO leads the way in this regard with women now comprising 35 percent of the company's executives. This represents a dramatic change since 1990 when only 9 percent of these positions were held by women. But despite these gains the Canadian banking industry has yet to see its first female CEO.[49]

In recent years women have made significant strides toward overcoming **sexism**, or job discrimination on the basis of gender. These steps have been achieved thanks to a combination of changing societal attitudes and company commitments to workplace diversity. Such initiatives include long-term commitments to hiring more women, company-sponsored networking and career planning for women, diversity training and workshops, and mentoring programs designed to help female employees move more quickly through the ranks. Pitney Bowes' long-term commitment to diversity, for instance, has resulted in women holding 5 of the top 11 jobs at the company. The initial appointment of Carly Fiorina as CEO of Hewlett-Packard (HP) was hailed by many as a milestone for women. Despite her recent departure, women account for more than a quarter of HP's managers; it seems that the glass ceiling at this company has been shattered.[50]

Should women be allowed to wear whatever they want to work? For every Erin Brokovich, who can make gains by wearing low-cut tops and short skirts, it's more common for a women in such outfits not to be taken seriously. Workplace attire is an important element in moulding the culture of a firm. Regardless of the company's policies, this factor in no way excuses sexual harassment.

Sexual Harassment Another sensitive issue that women and men face in the workplace is **sexual harassment**, which takes two forms: the obvious request for sexual favours with an implicit reward or punishment related to work, and the more subtle creation of a sexist environment in which employees are made to feel uncomfortable by off-colour jokes, lewd remarks, and posturing. Even though male employees may also be targets of these practices and both male and female employees may experience same-sex harassment, sexual harassment of female employees by male colleagues continues to make up the majority of reported cases.

With all the focus on this issue in recent years, you might believe that the problem is diminishing. However, according to the Human Rights Commission of Canada the numbers of complaints are actually increasing.[51] Is this because more people are stepping forward? Is this a sign that many people still don't get the message? To put an end to sexual harassment, companies are now enforcing strict harassment policies. Recent court rulings explain how all employers—large and small—can protect themselves from potential sexual harassment lawsuits. In short, a company can defend itself successfully if it can prove that it had an effective policy against sexual harassment in place and that the employee alleging harassment failed to take advantage of this policy. To be effective, the policy must be in writing, must be communicated to all employees, and must be enforced.[52] This means that the company must train all employees on the policy, and the company must have clear procedures for reporting such behaviour—including allowing employees access to management beyond their supervisors. Without such policies, companies can be held indirectly responsible for a harasser's actions even when top managers had no idea that such practices were going on.[53]

Alternative Work Arrangements

L.O. 4

To meet today's staffing and demographic challenges, many companies are adopting alternative work arrangements. Three of the most popular arrangements are flextime, telecommuting, and job sharing. Many organizations find that a mix of these arrangements and other employee benefits works better than a one-size-fits-all approach.[54]

Flextime

flextime
Scheduling system in which employees are allowed certain options regarding time of arrival and departure

An increasingly important alternative work arrangement, **flextime** is a scheduling system that allows employees to choose their own hours within certain limits. For instance, a company may require everyone to be at work between 10:00 a.m. and 2:00 p.m., but employees may arrive or depart whenever they want as long as they work a total of eight hours every day. Another popular flextime schedule is to work four 10-hour days each week, taking one prearranged day off (see Exhibit 9.6). Of course, flextime is more feasible in white-collar businesses that do not have to maintain standard customer service hours. For this reason, it is not usually an option for employees on production teams, in retail stores, or in many offices where employees have to be on hand to wait on customers or answer calls.

The sense of control employees get from arranging their own work schedules is motivating for many. Companies have found that flextime reduces turnover, enables the company to adapt to business cycles, allows operation of a round-the-clock business, and helps maintain morale and performance after re-engineering or downsizing. Still, flextime is not without drawbacks. They include supervisors who feel uncomfortable and less in control when employees are coming and going, and co-workers who resent flextimers because they assume that people who work flexible hours don't take their jobs seriously enough.[55]

Telecommuting

telecommuting
Working from home and communicating with the company's main office via computer and communication devices

Related to flexible schedules is **telecommuting**—working from home or another location using computers and telecommunications equipment to stay in touch with the employer's offices. Depending on which study you read, between 20 and 58 percent of employers now offer telecommuting arrangements for their employees.

Companies such as AT&T, IBM, and Lucent Technologies provide employees with laptops, dedicated phone lines, software support, fax-printer units, help lines, and full technical backup at the nearest corporate facility. Some even provide employees who work at home

Exhibit 9.6 Nine-to-Five Is Not for Everyone

For many full-time employees and independent contractors, their degree of job satisfaction is closely linked to the availability of the following job conditions or attributes.

Full-time, permanent employees and independent contractors who say these are "extremely important" in job satisfaction

	Full-time	Independent
Ability to work from home	15%	44%
Flexible work schedule	40%	62%
Freedom from office politics	44%	60%
Believing in what they do	72%	83%
Making right amount of money	50%	46%
Work they find challenging	55%	59%

GeniusBabies.com, seller of educational toys, allows workers such as Michelle Donahue-Arpas to telecommute so she can spend more time with her daughter.

with a generous allowance for furnishings and equipment to be used at their discretion.[56] Still, some company operations clearly are not designed for telecommuting. For example, a printer who runs giant colour presses cannot run the presses from home. But for other jobs that can be performed from remote sites, telecommuting helps meet employees' needs for flexibility while boosting their productivity as much as 20 percent.[57]

Telecommuting offers many advantages. For one thing, it can save a company money by eliminating offices people don't need, consolidating others, and reducing related overhead costs.[58] Telecommuting also enables a company to hire talented people in distant areas without requiring them to relocate. This benefit expands the company's pool of potential job candidates because employees who have an employed spouse, children in school, or elderly parents to care for are reluctant to move.[59] Employees also like telecommuting because they can set their own hours, reduce job-related expenses such as commuting costs, and spend more time with their families.

Telecommuting does have its limitations. The challenges of managing the cultural changes required by telecommuting are substantial. In telecommuting situations, mid-level managers relinquish direct, visual employee supervision. Some find it scary to be in the position of managing people they can't see. Others are concerned that people working at home will slack off or that telecommuting could cause resentment among office-bound colleagues or weaken company loyalty.[60] Regardless, companies are learning that you can't just give people computers, send them home, and call them telecommuters. You have to teach an employee how to think like a telecommuter.

Merrill Lynch recognizes this fact. Prospective telecommuters must submit a detailed proposal that covers when and how they're going to work at home and even what their home office will look like. Next, they participate in a series of meetings. Finally, they spend two weeks in a simulation lab that lets employees and their managers experience the change. Once at home, telecommuters are required to document their at-home working hours and submit weekly progress reports.[61] But even for those companies that provide support, some telecommuters are finding that this "ideal setup" is not for everyone.

Job Sharing

job sharing
Splitting a single full-time job between two employees for their convenience

Job sharing, which lets two employees share a single full-time job and split the salary and benefits, has been slowly gaining acceptance as a way to work part-time in a full-time position. According to a survey by Hewitt Associates, a firm specializing in employee benefits, 37 percent of employers offer job-sharing arrangements to their employees.[62] But such arrangements are usually offered to people who already work for the company and who need to cut back their hours. Rather than lose a good employee or have to find and train someone new, the company finds a way to split responsibilities. The company benefits because the position is rarely left uncovered during times of vacation or illness and because two people, instead of just one person, bring their ideas and creativity to the job.[63]

L.O. 5

WORKING WITH LABOUR UNIONS

Today's employees want alternative work arrangements in addition to safe and comfortable working conditions and sufficient pay. At the same time, however, business owners must focus on using company resources to increase productivity and profits. In the best of times and in the most enlightened companies, these two sets of needs can often be met simultaneously. However, when the economy slows down and competition speeds up, balancing the needs of employees with those of management can be a challenge.

Because of this potential for conflict, many employees join **labour unions**, organizations that seek to protect employee interests by negotiating with employers for better wages and benefits, improved working conditions, and increased job security. Historically, labour unions have played an important role in Canadian employee-management relations and are largely responsible for the establishment of worker's compensation, child-labour laws, overtime rules, minimum-wage laws, severance pay, and more. Employees are most likely to turn to unions if they are deeply dissatisfied with their current job conditions, if they believe that unionization can be helpful in improving those conditions.

labour unions
Organizations of employees formed to protect and advance their members' interests

One advantage of joining labour unions is that it gives employees stronger bargaining power. By combining forces, union employees can put more pressure on management than they could as individuals. During the most prosperous years at Bombardier, unions were able to pressure the company into providing various wage- and work-related concessions. Still, not all employees support labour unions. Many believe that unions hurt employee initiative and are not necessary to ensure fair treatment from employers.

Many companies that have successfully resisted unionization seem to have adopted participative management styles and an enhanced sense of responsibility toward employees. Others have used every legally available tactic to avoid unionization (see the box entitled "Wal-Mart and the Dreaded U-Word"). Marriott International has recognized that the primary reasons employees consider unionizing is because they feel they are not treated well by management. To demonstrate to workers that they are valued, Marriott offers its employees stock options, social service referral networks, daycare, training classes, and opportunities for advancement. As a result, Marriott's employee turnover is well below that of most companies, and its employees' enthusiasm is high.[64] But even good working conditions are no guarantee that employees won't seek union representation. For instance, although Starbucks is renowned for its generous employee benefit programs and supportive work environment, employees of stores in Vancouver, British Columbia, organized and successfully bargained for higher wages.[65]

Wal-Mart and the Dreaded U-Word

Wal-Mart—the world's largest company—has long resisted unionization of its employees. Sam Walton, who founded the firm, believed that unions are divisive and unnecessary, especially in light of Wal-Mart's benefits and open-door policy. All Wal-Mart employees are encouraged to voice their complaints and recommendations to management. Additionally, Wal-Mart keeps on top of workplace issues by conducting regular surveys to measure employee contentment. To keep employees motivated, store managers are given authority to solve problems, stock clerks are promoted to managerial positions, and all workers are encouraged to participate in the company's stock ownership plan. Of course, this is the company's perspective.

On the other side of the debate, many would argue that Wal-Mart simply wants to control its employees and will do anything in its power to destroy union initiatives and keep wages at a low level. Canadian outlets are leading the fight to unionize the company in North America. A store in Jonquière, Quebec, was the first Wal-Mart outlet in North America to unionize. The company began negotiations on the first contract with the union, but Wal-Mart warned that the store was unprofitable and that an unfavourable deal would force the company to close it. A few months later, after some initial talks, Wal-Mart announced that it was closing the outlet.

In Weyburn, Saskatchewan, a drive to unionize an outlet has led to a lengthy fight in court and a promise by the company to take its appeal all the way to the Supreme Court of Canada if necessary. This after the Court of Appeal of Saskatchewan agreed with the province's Labour Board decision to force Wal-Mart to hand over certain documents that were used to squash union drives. Among the controversial papers was an internal managerial manual entitled "Toolbox to Remaining Union Free."[66]

Questions for Critical Thinking

1. Why are Wal-Mart executives so concerned about the potential unionization of a couple of stores in Canada?
2. What can employers do to help reduce the chances that their employees will unionize?

The Collective Bargaining Process

collective bargaining
Process used by unions and management to negotiate work contracts

As long as a union has been recognized as the exclusive bargaining agent for a group of employees, its main job is to negotiate employment contracts with management. In a process known as **collective bargaining**, union and management negotiators work together to create the human resources policies that will apply to the unionized employees—and other employees covered by the contract—for a certain period, usually three years.

Most labour contracts are a compromise between the desires of union members and those of management. The union pushes for the best possible deal for its members, and management tries to negotiate agreements that are best for the company (and the shareholders, if a corporation is publicly held). Exhibit 9.7 illustrates the collective bargaining process.

Meeting and Reaching an Agreement

When the negotiating teams, made up of representatives of the union and management, actually sit down together, they state their opening positions and each side discusses its position point by point. Labour usually wants additions to the current contract. In a cooperative atmosphere, the real issues behind the demands gradually come to light. For example, management may begin by demanding the right to determine the sizes of work crews when all it really wants is smaller work crews; the union, however, wants to protect the jobs of its members and keep crew sizes as large as possible but may agree to certain reductions in exchange for, say, higher pay. After many stages of bargaining, each party presents its package of terms, and any gaps between labour and management demands are then dealt with.

mediation
Process for resolving a labour contract dispute in which a neutral third party meets with both sides and attempts to steer them toward a solution

arbitration
Process for resolving a labour contract dispute in which an impartial third party studies the issues and makes a binding decision

If negotiations reach an impasse, outside help may be needed. The most common alternative is **mediation**—bringing in an impartial third party to study the situation and make recommendations for resolution of the differences. Mediators are generally well-respected community leaders whom both sides will listen to. However, mediators can only offer suggestions, and their solutions are not binding. When a legally binding settlement is needed, the negotiators may submit to **arbitration**—a process in which an impartial referee listens to both sides and then makes a judgment by accepting one side's view. In *compulsory arbitration,* the parties are required by a government agency to sub-

Exhibit 9.7 The Collective Bargaining Process

Contract negotiations go through the four basic steps shown here.

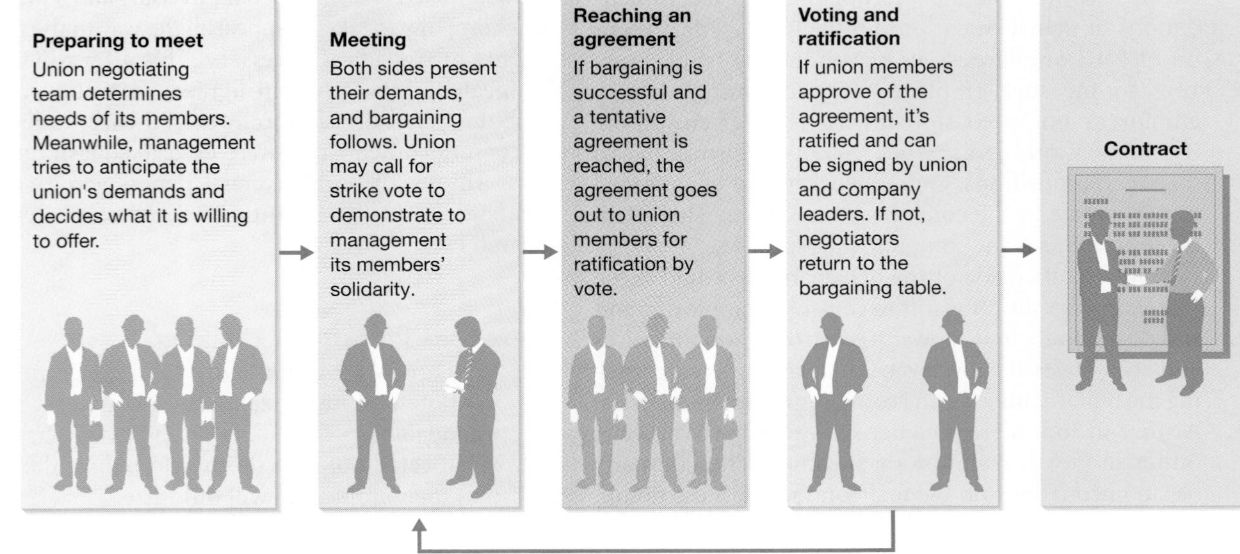

mit to arbitration; in *voluntary arbitration,* the parties agree on their own to use arbitration to settle their differences.

Exercising Options When Negotiations Break Down

L.O. 6

The vast majority of management-union negotiations are settled quickly, easily, and in a businesslike manner. Nevertheless, sometimes negotiations reach an impasse when neither side is willing to compromise. Both labour and management are able to draw on many powerful options when negotiations or mediation procedures break down.

Labour's Options Strikes and picket lines are perhaps labour's best-known tactics, but other options are also used.

- *Strike.* The most powerful weapon that organized labour can use, a **strike** refers to a temporary work stoppage aimed at forcing management to accept union demands. The basic idea behind the strike is that, in the long run, it costs management more in lost earnings to resist union demands than to give in. If the union has leverage, the tool can be effective. UPS's 3800 Canadian workers went on strike, effectively halting operations in the country and disrupting operations in the U.S. right before the holiday rush. Two days later the company and the Teamsters union reached an agreement.[67] However, strikes are a risky proposition and can lead to lengthy, costly disputes. Workers at a Quebec-based aluminum smelter refinery, jointly owned by Alcoa and Alcan, learned that lesson the hard way. The work stoppage lasted for more than five months even though the strike was costing employees valuable wages and the owners $21.5 million per month.[68] An essential part of any strike is **picketing**, in which union members positioned at entrances to company premises march back and forth with signs and leaflets, trying to persuade non-striking employees to join them and to persuade customers and others to stop doing business with the company.
- *Boycott.* A less direct union weapon is the **boycott**, in which union members and sympathizers refuse to buy or handle the product of a target company. Millions of union members form an enormous bloc of purchasing power, which may be able to pressure management into making concessions.
- *Publicity.* Increasingly, labour is pressing its case by launching publicity campaigns, often called *corporate campaigns,* against the target company and companies affiliated with it. These campaigns might include sending investors alerts that question the firm's solvency, staging rallies during peak business hours, sending letters to charitable groups questioning executives' motives, handing out leaflets that describe safety and health code violations, and stimulating negative stories in the press.

strike
Temporary work stoppage to pressure management to accept the union's demands

picketing
Strike activity in which union members march before company entrances to protest against an employer

boycott
Union activity in which members and sympathizers refuse to buy or handle the product of a target company

Labour's other options include *slowdowns,* in which employees continue to do their jobs but at a snail's pace, and *sickouts,* in which employees fake illness and stay home. Both can cripple a company. On one occasion, United Airlines was forced to cancel more than 20 000 flights during the peak summer travel months because company pilots refused to fly overtime hours and called in sick to protest the slow pace of contract negotiations.[69]

L.O. 7

Management's Options As powerful as the union's tactics are, companies are not helpless when it comes to fighting back. Management can use a number of legal methods to pressure unions when negotiations stall:

- *Strike-breakers.* In most jurisdictions, when union members walk off their jobs, management can legally replace them with **strike-breakers**, non-union workers hired to do the jobs of striking workers (union members brand them as "scabs"). British Columbia and Quebec are the only two jurisdictions in North America that make this practice illegal. Although management can take on the responsibilities of unionized workers, the firm cannot hire strike-breakers. A similar law was instituted in Ontario in the 1990s but was overturned two years later.[70]
- *Lockouts.* During a **lockout**, management prevents union employees from entering the workplace, in order to pressure the union to accept a contract proposal. A lock-

strike-breakers
Non-union workers hired to replace striking workers

lockouts
Management tactics in which union members are prevented from entering a business during a strike

out is management's counterpart to a strike. It is a pre-emptive measure designed to force a union to accept management's demands. Lockouts are legal only if the union and management have come to an impasse in negotiations and the employer is defending a legitimate bargaining position. Hockey fans know this tactic well. Despite billionaire owners and millionaire players the 2004–2005 NHL season was cancelled because of a lockout.[71]

injunction
Court order prohibiting certain actions by striking workers

- *Injunctions.* An **injunction** is a court order prohibiting union workers from taking certain actions. Management used this weapon without restriction in the early days of unionism, when companies typically sought injunctions to order striking employees back to work on the grounds that the strikers were interfering with business. Today, injunctions are legal only in certain cases. Union-government negotiations have often ended with court proceedings ordering workers back to work under threat of severe consequences such as lost seniority or dismissal.

The Labour Movement Today

Unions remain a significant force in employee-management relations in Canada. However, the shift from a manufacturing-based economy to one dominated by service industries has posed challenges for unions that have watched manufacturing jobs outsourced to other low-cost nations, thus weakening their traditional base. Women, young workers, and highly skilled workers have been harder to organize with traditional methods, as have workers in less hierarchical organizations.[72] Even though unions are sticking to their traditional causes—good wages, safe conditions, and benefits—some progressive, realistic labour leaders are pursuing new workplace issues such as job security, increasing health care costs, labour involvement in management decisions, child care, and more job training.[73]

Aliant workers demonstrate their displeasure with management by chanting and picketing in order to gain attention and rally support for their demands in a recent work dispute.

The current climate contains some interesting contrasts. According to the Conference Board of Canada, in the next few years we will see more collaboration between management and labour in the private sector. A case in point, at Bombardier unions have been forced to deal with labour cuts as the industry suffers. However, the unions are acting as important lobbyists to gain government aid for the new C Series line of planes. At the other extreme, public-sector negotiations between unions and governments are expected to be quite confrontational.[74] What does the future hold for employee-management relations? It is difficult to make predictions. But many experts agree that today's global economic conditions severely limit the ability of unions to regain the strength they once had. This is the case both in Canada and in other industrialized countries.

SUMMARY OF LEARNING OBJECTIVES

1 Identify and explain four important theories of employee motivation.

Maslow's hierarchy organizes individual needs into five categories and proposes that the individual must satisfy the most basic needs before being able to address higher-level needs. Herzberg's two-factor theory suggests that hygiene factors—such as working conditions, company policies, and job security—can influence employee dissatisfaction, but an improvement in these factors will not motivate employees. Only motivational factors such as recognition and responsibility can improve employee performance. McGregor's theory proposes two distinct views of individuals: Theory X-oriented managers believe that people dislike work and can be motivated only by fear, whereas Theory Y-oriented managers believe that people like work and are motivated by exposure to opportunities and challenges. Ouchi's Theory Z assumes that employees will be more motivated if you involve them in company decision making. This is the core thinking of companies that use teams in the workplace and adopt a more participative management style.

2 Discuss three staffing challenges employers are facing in today's workplace.

A shortage of skilled labour, rightsizing the workforce, and an increasing employee desire to balance work and life responsibilities are making it difficult for employers to find and keep talented people. The factors contributing to these staffing challenges are the increasing use of technology in the workplace, the conversion of a manufacturing-based economy to a service-based economy, a general mismatch between employee job skills and job demands, declining employee loyalty, and increasing employee burnout.

3 Highlight two trends contributing to the diversity of the Canadian workforce.

The influx of immigrants and the aging population are two trends contributing to the diversity of the Canadian workforce. The percentage of immigrant workers in the Canadian workforce is climbing as employers clamour to fill their critical labour shortages. The aging workforce is a result of the decline in the number of young people entering the workforce and the decision of baby boomers to delay retirement for a number of reasons.

4 Discuss three popular alternative work arrangements companies are offering their employees.

To meet today's staffing and demographic challenges, companies are offering their employees flextime (the ability to vary their work hours), telecommuting (the ability to work from home or another location), and job sharing (the ability to share a single full-time job with a co-worker).

5 Understand the role of unions and the challenges of reaching a collective bargaining agreement in the modern era.

After years of corporate downsizing, rightsizing, and outsourcing, the role of the modern union has changed even if some union leaders refuse to accept it. Competing in a global economy has forced many firms to abandon former practices and reduce cost structures with dramatic moves. Unions will still flex their muscles in times of prosperity but economic downturns and intense competition have forced many bargaining units to re-evaluate goals and negotiate under new terms.

6 Cite three options unions can exercise when negotiations with management break down.

Unions can conduct strikes, organize boycotts, and use publicity to pressure management into complying with union proposals. A strike is a temporary work stoppage, which the union hopes will cost management enough in lost earnings so that management will be forced to accept union demands. A boycott is a union tactic designed to pressure management into making concessions by convincing sympathizers to refuse to buy or handle the product of the target company. A negative publicity campaign against the target company is a pressure tactic designed to smear the reputation of the company in hopes of gaining management's attention.

7 Cite three options management can exercise when negotiations with a union break down.

To pressure a union into accepting its proposals, management may continue running the business with strike-breakers (non-union workers hired to do the jobs of striking workers), institute a lockout of union members by preventing union employees from entering the workplace, or seek an injunction against a strike or other union activity. Strike-breakers are not permitted by law in British Columbia and Quebec.

Behind the SCENES

Bombardier: Flying through Turbulent Skies

In 2005, Laurent Beaudoin took the reins of Bombardier after the sudden removal of Paul Tellier had raised eyebrows in the business community. Observers anxiously awaited a decision on the prospective C Series line of aircraft. Many experts believed that the choice was a make or break move for the firm. At stake was the company's ability to secure deals with airlines that were looking for an expanded roster beyond the 50-, 70-, and 90-seat planes that defined Bombardier's aerospace group. Inseparably linked to the outcome of this decision were the firm's long-term revenues and profits and, of course, the jobs of thousands of employees in Canada and beyond. The situation was further complicated by potential government subsidies, the competition's (Embraer's) stake in the expanding market, the "China factor," and union-management relations.

EMPLOYEE CUTS

Between 2003 and 2005, corporate downsizing was a harsh reality for Bombardier's employees. The bravado and knife-to-the-throat attitude of their unions was replaced by the realization that the good times were over, at least for a while. Union-management negotiations between Bombardier and the Canadian Auto Workers union (CAW) in 2003 concluded with no wage concessions but the acceptance of 500 layoffs in the Downsview, Ontario, plant. A few weeks earlier, employees at the Wichita, Kansas, plant accepted a contract that froze wages, suspended pension payments for a year, and required machinists to pay more for their health insurance. The string of announcements continued in 2003: 85 jobs cut in Wichita, Kansas; 1050 jobs cut in Belfast, Ireland; 150 jobs cut in Montreal; 300 rail jobs cut in Thunder Bay; 1150 aerospace jobs cut in Wichita and Quebec. In 2004 the story continued: 6600 jobs slashed in the rail division, mostly in Europe; 2000 aerospace jobs lost in Belfast and Montreal; 2200 rail jobs cut, primarily in Germany and Britain, with 500 in Canada. These announcements effectively meant that the workforce was trimmed from 75 000 in 2003 to 53 000 by the 2006 implementation date. Employees who survived the cuts were shell shocked. The effects of the extended downsizing practices were affecting employee morale and loyalty. However, the challenges were not complete: new threats lay ahead.

GROWING CHALLENGES

Bombardier's major direct competitor is Brazilian-owned Embraer. While Bombardier was still considering the C Series, Embraer had already introduced a new 100-seat plane that extended its product line beyond the 70- to 90-seat range that both companies traditionally offered to the marketplace. The Brazilian firm had announced more than $4 billion in sales that likely occurred directly at Bombardier's expense. In response, Bombardier was once again considering building the C Series 115- to 130-seat plane, but facing several problems. First, the company had looked at the idea prior to September 11, 2001, and concluded it did not make any financial sense. It lacked the estimated $2 billion to develop the project. Additionally, the construction of this plane would put it in the sights of Airbus and Boeing, the two giants in the industry. Both would have the resources to seize market share in the 100- to 130-seat category if they felt Bombardier was entering their turf.

The projected C Series line of planes will have a huge impact on Bombardier's long-term competitive position.

Further complicating issues was the emergence of the Chinese market, which represented a major growth opportunity in the coming years. Bombardier was actually in negotiations with the Chinese government, in 2001, to build a plant in China, but the deal was never completed. Embraer soon jumped in and created a joint-venture plant with the state-owned China Aviation Industry Corporation II to build 50-seat planes in China. Bombardier was clearly falling behind in the race to capture this vital business. Its relationship with the Chinese government was further damaged in November 2004 when a CRJ-200 airplane, flying from Baotou to Shanghai, crashed and killed 54 people. The Chinese government immediately grounded the entire fleet of CRJ-200 planes. Pressure was on the firm to address this market. Would Bombardier build a plant in China? What does the future hold for the current employees of Bombardier? Can it be long before a major portion of the assembly is outsourced to a location where wages are lower and skilled workers are available, such as China? (360 jobs were recently outsourced to a facility in Mexico; this is likely just the first step.)

THE GREAT SOCIAL EQUALIZER

Why haven't more aerospace jobs migrated to places like China? Answer: government money! Lots of it! The new C Series plane is no exception. Governments provide funds to keep jobs in the economy, boost the image of the nation, and help support sub-industries such as plane parts suppliers. Industry Minister David Emerson was clearly voicing support for Bombardier, and the C Series was initially projected to receive $380 million in funding. Among other perks, the federal government had already provided a fund for loan guarantees amounting to $1.5 billion. Bombardier was also looking to the Quebec government and potentially to the Ontario government to reach a figure of $700 million in public funding for this particular project. At the time, another ambitious plan that was floating around indicated that the government was considering a $50 billion long-term program to provide loan guarantees and grants over a 20-year period. This according to a cabinet document leaked to media. Regardless of the final numbers one thing is clear: these government funds come with the understanding that jobs will remain in Canada. With several governments in American states, Quebec, Ontario, and the U.K. trying to secure a deal, the ultimate choice will be heavily influenced by local government support.

DECISION TIME

Bombardier's decision to build the new C Series planes was a complicated one, with various stakeholders jockeying for position. In early 2005, the company's board of directors granted the company the authority to seek "launch customers." This announcement represented stage one, but many questions remained. Would the company choose to keep jobs in Canada? Would the Canadian government step up with more money? Would employees eventually price themselves out of the market? What would happen next time the company was on solid ground and employees began to make wage demands? Could Bombardier afford to do nothing and watch Embraer steal market share? Should the firm follow through and build the C Series, and risk the chance of engaging Boeing and Airbus? Would Bombardier return to its glory days?[75]

Critical Thinking Questions

1. In this chapter we have examined employee loyalty and burnout. How do these concepts apply to Bombardier's recent staffing policies?
2. Do you believe that it is inevitable that many or most of the assembly jobs will end up being outsourced to China or other locations abroad?
3. Bombardier's decision to build the C Series is a major issue for its workforce. As key stakeholders, what role can the firm's employees play in the process?
4. The Canadian government has provided many subsidies to Bombardier to help protect jobs and support the growth of the firm. Do you think the government should continue to fund companies in this manner? Explain.
5. Do you think Bombardier should proceed with the C Series project? List the pros and cons. How do you think Boeing and Airbus will respond if Bombardier moves forward with the C Series project?

Learn More Online

Log on to the Bombardier website at www.bombardier.com. How many employees does Bombardier currently employ? Have any additional cuts been made? How is the C Series project progressing? Have there been any recent employee-management issues? Has Bombardier engaged in any CBA discussions with its unions in the past year? What were the results? Has Bombardier's aerospace division expanded its assembly operations beyond North America? How much are Bombardier's shares worth today?

KEY TERMS

arbitration (238)
behaviour modification (223)
boycott (239)
collective bargaining (238)
flextime (235)
glass ceiling (234)
human relations (222)
hygiene factors (226)
injunction (240)
job enrichment (231)
job redesign (231)
job sharing (236)
labour unions (237)
lockouts (239)
management by objectives (MBO) (223)
mediation (238)
morale (222)
motivation (223)
motivators (226)
picketing (239)
quality of work life (QWL) (231)
scientific management (223)
sexism (234)
sexual harassment (234)
strike (239)
strike-breakers (239)
telecommuting (235)
Theory X (226)
Theory Y (226)
Theory Z (227)

TEST YOUR KNOWLEDGE

Questions for Review

1. What is the goal of human relations?
2. What is rightsizing?
3. What are the principal causes of employee burnout?
4. What is meant by the glass ceiling?
5. What is quality of work life, and how does it influence employee motivation?

Questions for Analysis

6. Why do managers often find it difficult to motivate employees who remain after downsizing?
7. How can diversity initiatives benefit a company?
8. What are some of the advantages and disadvantages of alternative work arrangements?
9. Why do employees choose to join labour unions? Why do they not join labour unions?
10. **Ethical Considerations.** You have a golf game scheduled for Sunday afternoon, and you've worked all weekend to write a proposal to be presented on Monday morning. The proposal is more or less finished, but a few more hours of work would make it polished and persuasive. Do you cancel the game?

Questions for Application

11. Some of your talented and hardworking employees come to you one day and say they do not feel challenged. They expected to be able to diversify their skills more and take on greater responsibility than they now have. How do you respond?

12. Assume you are the plant manager for a company that manufactures tires for cars and light trucks. To compete more economically in the global market, the company is seriously considering closing the plant within the next year and moving manufacturing operations to Southeast Asia. Upon hearing about the possible plant closing, the union votes to launch a strike in one week if its demands for job security aren't met. Because of a recent surge in orders, the company is not in a position to close the plant yet. What are your options as you continue to negotiate with union representatives? Which option would you choose and why?
13. **Integrated.** How do economic concepts such as profit motive and competitive advantage (see Chapter 1) affect today's workforce?
14. **Integrated.** Why is it difficult for small businesses to allow employees to telecommute, share jobs, and work flexible hours?

PRACTISE YOUR KNOWLEDGE

SHARPENING YOUR COMMUNICATION SKILLS

As the director of public relations for a major airline your job is to prepare news releases should the pilots decide to strike. This is a challenging task because many people will be affected by a strike. Being a good communicator, you know that one of the first things you must do before preparing a message is to analyze the audience. Think about an airline strike and answer these questions briefly to practise this important communication technique:

1. What groups of people do you think would be interested in the information about the airline strike?
2. What do you think each of these groups would want to know about most?
3. How might they react to the information you will provide? Summarize your answers to these three questions in a short memo to your instructor.

BUILDING YOUR TEAM SKILLS

Debate the pros and cons of telecommuting for an accounting, computer programming, or graphics design firm. Break into groups of four students, with two students taking the employees' pro side and the other two taking management's con side. As you prepare for this debate, consider the following factors: employee motivation, staffing challenges, quality of work life, costs, control, and feasibility.

During your team's debate, let one side present its arguments while the other side takes notes on the major points. After both sides have completed their presentations, discuss all of the supporting points and try to reach a consensus as to whether your firm will support telecommuting. Draft a one-page statement outlining your team's conclusion and reasoning, and then share it during a class discussion.

Compare your team's conclusion and reasoning with those of other teams. Do most teams believe telecommuting is a good or bad idea? What issues do most teams agree on? What issues do they disagree on?

EXPAND YOUR KNOWLEDGE

DISCOVERING CAREER OPPORTUNITIES

Is an alternative work arrangement such as flextime, job sharing, or telecommuting in your career future? This exercise will help you think about whether these work arrangements fit into your career plans.

1. Look at the list of possible business careers in Appendix D. Of the careers that interest you, which seem best suited to flextime? To job sharing? To telecommuting?
2. Select one of the careers that seems suited to telecommuting. What job functions do you think could be performed at home or from another remote location?
3. Thinking about the same career, do you think it would be possible to split the job's responsibilities with a co-worker under a job-sharing arrangement? What issues, if any, might you need to resolve first?

DEVELOPING YOUR RESEARCH SKILLS

Select one or two articles from recent issues of business journals or newspapers (print or online editions) that relate to employee motivation or morale.

1. What is the problem or trend discussed in the article(s) and how is it influencing employee attitudes or motivation?
2. Is this problem unique to this company, or does it have broader implications? Who is affected by it now, and who do you think might be affected by it in the future?
3. What challenges and opportunities does this situation present to the company or industry? The employees? Management?

See It on the **WEB**

URLs for all Internet exercises are provided at the website for this book, www.pearsoned.ca/bovee. When you log on to the text website, select Chapter 9, select Destinations, then click on the name of the featured website, and review the website to complete the following exercises.

Explore the following chapter-related websites, review their content, and answer the following questions for each website you visit:

1. What is the purpose of this website?
2. What kinds of information does this website contain? Please be specific.
3. How is the information provided at this website useful for business people? Consumers?
4. How did you expand your knowledge of motivation and employee-management relations by reviewing the material at this website? What new things did you learn about these topics?

WORKING HARD ON THE WEB

Frustrated workers and managers now have a place to go to voice their opinions, commiserate with others, and get advice on how to motivate employees. The place is Hard@Work, a website created "to reduce the oversupply of fear and alienation in the workplace by meeting the pent-up demand for constructive communication about what's happening on the job." Visitors can hang around the "Water Cooler" to chat with others about work issues and careers; play "Stump the Mentor," which offers suggestions for handling sticky work situations; or dig into the "Rock Pile," which features realistic case studies. Hard@Work offers something for workers and job seekers alike. www.hardatwork.com

TELECOMMUTING YOUR WAY TO SUCCESS

Does telecommuting reality match the hype? Follow the links at this website and decide for yourself. Read the guidelines and articles. Learn some telecommuting basics to find out if you possess the skills and qualifications required to succeed in telecommuting. Get some facts and figures so you can use them effectively in a telecommuting proposal to your boss. Then read some success stories. Finally, explore your flexible options by learning about other alternative working arrangements. Which ones are suited to you? www.telecommuting.about.com

Part 4
Managing Employees

Chapter 10
Managing Human Resources

LEARNING OBJECTIVES

After studying this chapter, you will be able to

1. List six main functions of human resources departments
2. Cite seven methods recruiters use to find job candidates
3. Identify the six stages in the hiring process
4. Discuss how companies incorporate objectivity into employee performance appraisals
5. Highlight five popular employee benefits
6. Describe four ways an employee's status may change and discuss why many employers like to fill job vacancies from within

Behind the SCENES

Brewing Up People Policies for Chainwide Success

By offering benefits to all employees (including part-timers), Starbucks attracts and keeps quality employees.

www.starbucks.com

Hiring, training, and compensating a diverse workforce of 90 000 employees in more than 8500 locations worldwide would be a difficult task for any company. Starbucks manages to serve 30 million customers each week. In Canada, there are 430 stores that employ 7000 employees. The company plans to add about 100 new stores in this market in 2005, and will continue its aggressive expansion worldwide in the upcoming years. Its current status aside, Starbucks faced tremendous challenges when it initially embarked on its expansion quest.

The human resources task was especially difficult in an industry whose annual employee turnover rate approached 300 percent. It was even more of a challenge for a company that was striving to open a new store every day, despite a tight labour market, an uncertain global economy, and increasingly intense competition. This was the high-pressure situation facing Starbucks Coffee Company in the 1990s, when CEO Howard Schultz set a torrid pace for global expansion. Starbucks wanted to perk past US$1 billion in yearly sales and spread its coffee cult across the continents. Its initial foreign expansion took place in Vancouver, a natural candidate for the Seattle-based icon. Soon, the rich aroma of fresh-brewed espresso was appearing throughout neighbourhoods all over North America, with new stores planned for the United Kingdom, Japan, and China. But Schultz and his management team knew that good locations and top-quality coffee were just part of the company's formula for success.

To keep up with this ambitious schedule of new store openings, Starbucks had to find, recruit, and train 700 new employees every month, no easy feat "when there is a shortage of labour and few people want to work behind a retail counter," as Schultz noted. Moreover, Starbucks' employees had to deliver consistently superior customer service in every store and every market. In other words, Starbucks' employees (known internally as partners) had to do more than simply pour coffee—they had to believe passionately in the product and pay attention to all of the details that can make or break the retail experience for the chain's 30 million weekly customers.

Schultz knew it would take more than good pay and company benefits to motivate and inspire employees. But what could he do? If you were a member of Schultz's management team, how would you attract, train, and compensate a diverse workforce? What human resources policies and practices would you implement to motivate employees to give topnotch service?[1]

UNDERSTANDING WHAT HUMAN RESOURCES MANAGERS DO

L.O. 1

Hiring the right people to help a company reach its goals and then overseeing their training and development, motivation, evaluation, and compensation is critical to a company's success. These activities are collectively known as **human resources management (HRM)**, which encompasses all tasks involved in acquiring, maintaining, and developing an organization's employees. Because of the accelerating rate at which today's workforce, economy, and corporate cultures are being transformed, the role of HRM is increasingly viewed as a strategic one.

human resources management (HRM)
Specialized function of planning that focuses on obtaining employees, overseeing their training, and evaluating and compensating them

Human resources (HR) managers must figure out how to attract qualified employees from a shrinking pool of entry-level candidates; how to train less-educated, poorly

Exhibit 10.1 The Functions of the Human Resources Department

Human resources departments are responsible for these six important functions.

skilled employees; how to keep experienced employees when they have few opportunities for advancement; and how to lay off employees equitably when downsizing is necessary. They must also retrain employees to cope with increasing automation and computerization, manage increasingly complex (and expensive) employee benefits programs, shape workplace policies to address changing workforce demographics and employee needs (as discussed in Chapter 9), and cope with the challenge of meeting government regulations in hiring practices and equal opportunity employment.

In short, human resources managers and staff members keep the organization running smoothly at every level by planning for a company's staffing needs, recruiting and hiring employees, training and developing employees and managers, and appraising employee performance. The HR staff also administers compensation and employee benefits and oversees changes in employment status (promotion, reassignment, termination or resignation, and retirement). This chapter explores each of these human resources responsibilities, beginning with planning (see Exhibit 10.1).

PLANNING FOR A COMPANY'S STAFFING NEEDS

Proper planning is critical because a miscalculation could leave a company without enough employees to keep up with demand, resulting in customer dissatisfaction and lost business. Yet if a company expands its staff too rapidly, profits may be eaten up by payroll or the firm may have to lay off people who were just recruited and trained at considerable expense. The planning function consists of two steps: (1) forecasting supply and demand, and (2) evaluating job requirements (see Exhibit 10.2).

Forecasting Supply and Demand

Planning begins with forecasting *demand*, the amount and type of employees that will be needed at various times. For example, suppose Starbucks is planning to open another store in Regina within six months. The HR department would forecast that the store will need a store manager and an assistant manager as well as part-time salespeople.

Exhibit 10.2 **Steps in Human Resources Planning**

Careful attention to each phase of this sequence helps ensure that a company will have the right human resources when it needs them.

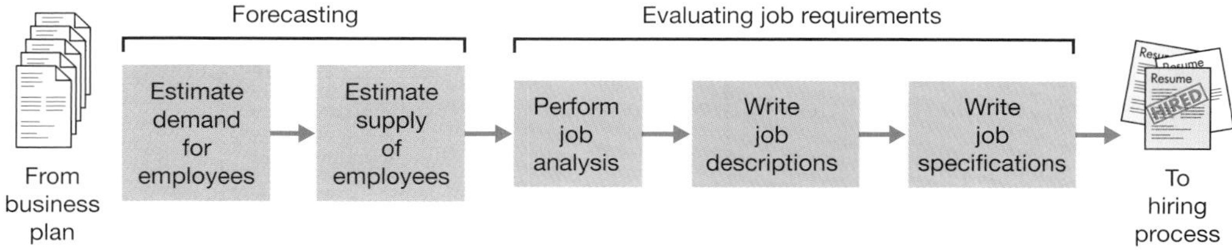

Although Starbucks might start looking immediately for someone as highly placed as the manager, hiring salespeople might be postponed until just before the store opens.

The next task is to estimate the *supply* of available employees. In many cases, that supply is within the company already—perhaps just needing training to fill future requirements. Starbucks may well find that the assistant manager at an existing store can be promoted to manage the new store and one of the current salespeople can be named assistant manager. If existing employees cannot be tapped for new positions, the human resources manager must determine how to find people outside the company who have the necessary skills. In some cases, managers will want to consider strategic staffing alternatives such as hiring part-time and temporary employees to avoid drastic overstaffing or understaffing.

Part-Time and Temporary Employees

More and more businesses try to save money and increase flexibility by building their workforces around part-time and temporary employees, or "temps," whose schedules can be rearranged to suit the company's needs. As a result, this segment of the labour force has increased by leaps and bounds in recent years. The temporary ranks include computer systems analysts, human resources directors, accountants, and doctors; technical fields make up the fastest-growing segment of temporary employment.

Companies are incorporating temporary workers in long-term plans, whereas 15 years ago they used temps to fill occasional vacancies. The use of temps is an excellent recruiting technique because it allows companies to try out employees before hiring them permanently. Thus, what often begins as a temp assignment can turn into multiyear employment. In fact, temps often do the same work as the company's permanent employees, but because they are temporary they do not qualify for the same benefits enjoyed by regular workers. However, some perma-temps have sued companies, saying that they are, in fact, full-time employees and as such deserve employee benefits.[2]

Retired workers are a great resource for HR managers looking for qualified temporary and part-time workers. This segment has historically been downplayed and ignored by some recruiters. However, with seniors living longer, healthier lives and with an unprecedented pool of potential baby boomer retirees on the horizon, attitudes are quickly changing. A recent *Globe and Mail* report unofficially named four companies (Merck Frosst Canada Inc., Royal Bank of Canada, Home Depot Canada, and Avis) as the "best employers of people over 50." These companies are actively pursuing this growing segment. For example, Doug Gerrard, age 62, started working at a Home Depot location in Mississauga, Ontario, as a part-time sales associate. He spends most of the week running his own computer business. He was quickly hired full time and promoted to a supervisor position. His computer business is now his part-time occupation.[3]

Outsourcing

Outsourcing is another way that companies fulfill their human resources needs without hiring permanent employees. Companies outsource some tasks or projects because the outside source can provide materials, parts, or services better, at a lower price, and more efficiently. Outsourcing is also used to take advantage of others' expertise and to increase flexibility. Outsourcing has many advantages: It gives companies access to new resources and world-class capabilities, it shares the risk of getting the work done, and it frees company resources for other purposes. Still, outsourcing has its share of risks, including loss of control, greater dependency on suppliers, and loss of in-house skills. Some companies have also experienced work delays, unhappy customers, and labour union battles as a result of outsourcing.[4]

Evaluating Job Requirements

The second step of the planning function is to evaluate job requirements. If you were the owner of a small business, you might have a good grasp of the requirements of all the jobs in your company. However, in large organizations where hundreds or thousands of employees are performing a wide variety of jobs, management needs a more formal and objective method of evaluating job requirements. That method is called **job analysis**.

job analysis
Process by which jobs are studied to determine the tasks and dynamics involved in performing them

job description
Statement of the tasks involved in a given job and the conditions under which the holder of the job will work

job specification
Statement describing the kind of person who would best fit the job—including skills, education, and previous experience

To obtain the information needed for a job analysis, the HR staff asks employees or supervisors several questions: What is the purpose of the job? What tasks are involved in the job? What qualifications and skills are needed to do the job effectively? In what kind of setting does the job take place? Is there much public contact involved? Does the job entail much time pressure? Sometimes they obtain job information by observing employees directly. Other times they ask employees to keep daily diaries describing exactly what they do during the workday.

Once a job analysis has been completed, the HR staff develops a **job description**, a formal statement summarizing the tasks involved in the job and the conditions under which the employee will work. In most cases, the staff will also develop a **job specification**, a statement describing the skills, education, and previous experience that the job requires.

L.O. 2

RECRUITING, HIRING, AND TRAINING NEW EMPLOYEES

Having forecast a company's supply and demand for employees and evaluated job requirements, the HR manager's next step is to match the job specification with an actual person or selection of people. This task is accomplished through **recruiting**, the process of attracting suitable candidates for an organization's jobs. One recent study shows that companies with excellent recruiting and retention policies provide a nearly 8 percent higher return to shareholders than those that do not have such policies.[5]

recruiting
Process of attracting appropriate applicants for an organization's jobs

Recruiters are specialists on the HR staff who are responsible for locating job candidates. They use a variety of methods and resources including internal searches, newspaper and Internet advertising, public and private employment agencies, campuses and career offices, trade shows, corporate "head-hunters" (people who try to attract people at other companies), and referrals from employees or colleagues in the industry (see Exhibit 10.3). One of the fastest-growing recruitment resources for both large and small businesses is the Internet. Today, many companies recruit online through their websites in addition to using popular online recruiting services, as the "E-Business in Action" feature at the end of this part discusses.

L.O. 3

The Hiring Process

After exploring at least one—but usually more—of the available recruitment channels to assemble a pool of applicants, the human resources department may spend weeks and sometimes months on the hiring process. Most companies go through the same basic stages as they sift through applications to come up with the person (or persons) they want.

The first stage is to select a small number of qualified candidates from all applications received. Finalists may be chosen on the basis of a standard application form that all

Exhibit 10.3 How Employers and Job-Seekers Approach the Recruiting Process

Studies show that employers prefer to fill job openings with people from within their organization or from an employee's recommendation. Placing want ads is often viewed as a last resort. In contrast, typical job seekers begin their job-search process from the opposite direction (starting with reading a newspaper or Internet ads).

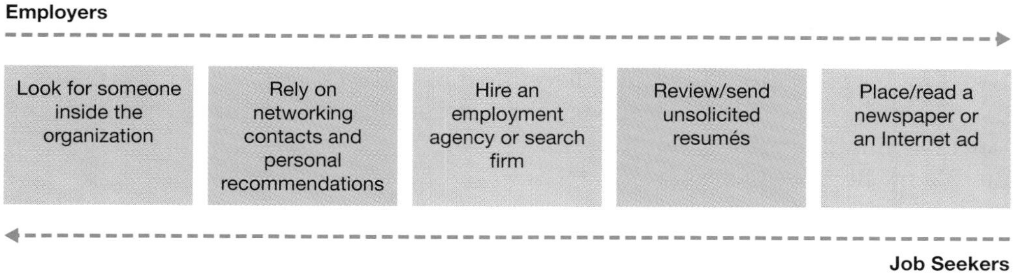

candidates fill out or on the basis of a resumé—a summary of education, experience, and personal data compiled by each applicant (see "Preparing Your Resumé" in Appendix D for further details). Sometimes both sources of information are used. Many organizations now use computer scanners to help them quickly sort through resumés and weed out those that don't match the requirements of the job. While it is good to stand out from the crowd it is important to use common sense in the process. A recent resumé stunt led to the evacuation of an office building and a hotel and a call to the bomb squad. The actual package delivered was harmless but it was designed to appear like a bomb. Needless to say, recruiters at Cossette Communications were not impressed with the candidate.[6]

The second stage in the hiring process is to interview each candidate to clarify qualifications and fill in any missing information (see "Interviewing with Potential Employers" in Appendix D for further details). Another goal of the interview is to get an idea of the applicant's personality and ability to work well with others. Depending on the type of job at stake, candidates may also be asked to take a test or a series of tests.

After the initial pre-screening interviews comes the third stage, when the best candidates may be asked to meet with someone in the HR department who will conduct a more probing interview. For higher-level positions, candidates may go through a series of interviews with managers, potential co-workers, and the employees who will make up the successful candidate's staff. Sometimes this process can take weeks. Consider Southwest Airlines. To fill 4200 job openings in one year, the company interviewed nearly 80 000 people. For many positions, candidates undergo a rigorous interview process that can take weeks before they are hired (see the box entitled "Radical Job Recruitment: Lights, Camera, Interview"). Southwest wants to make sure that new employees will fit in with the company's culture. The payback: low turnover and high customer satisfaction.[7]

After all interviews have been completed, the process moves to the final stages. In the fourth stage, the department supervisor evaluates the candidates, sometimes in consultation with a higher-level manager, the HR department, and staff. During the fifth stage, the employer checks the references of the top few candidates. The employer may also research the candidates' education, previous employment, and motor vehicle records. A growing number of employers are also checking candidates' credit histories, a practice that is drawing criticism as a violation of privacy.[8] In the sixth stage, the supervisor selects the most suitable person for the job. Now the search is over—provided the candidate accepts the offer.

Background Checks

Violence in the workplace is an increasing threat that can harm employees and customers, hurt productivity, and lead to expensive lawsuits and higher health care costs.

Radical Job Recruitment: Lights, Camera, Interview

The process of job recruitment has been commercialized and sold to television viewers in the form of an entertaining extended job interview process. *The Apprentice* pits aspiring "executives" against each other in team competitions based on various business tasks. "You're fired" has become a familiar phrase in popular culture. Donald Trump, the egomaniac real estate developer, and Mark Burnett, the godfather of reality TV, launched the HR process, or at least some distorted version of the process, into prime-time TV. Mark Cuban and Richard Branson soon followed. Can it be long before a Canadian version is launched? (Conrad Black might be occupied with other issues.)

On *The Apprentice* more than 1 million applications are reduced to just 18 candidates who battle in diverse assignments that range from selling lemonade on the street to creating advertisements for Fortune 500 companies. While this environment is artificial, it does parallel real-life practices in some ways. Many firms are employing unconventional techniques such as asking employees to perform improvisational skits to demonstrate their reactions to a fabricated situation. People will eventually get tired of these TV shows, but the task of identifying the best candidates will remain a challenge for recruiters.[10]

Questions for Critical Thinking

1. Why would a potential employer ask a candidate to perform an improvisational skit during an interview?
2. Do you believe that simulated interview tools are effective?
3. Do you believe that the format of *The Apprentice* helps the best candidate climb to the top and hear those famous words: "You're hired"?

More than 1 million physical assaults occur at work each year. If an employer fails to address "preventable violence," that employer can be found liable. This means that companies need to be especially careful about negligent hiring.[9]

As Exhibit 10.4 shows, employers conduct a variety of background checks on job applicants to ensure accuracy and combat fraud by verifying all educational credentials and previous jobs, accounting for any large time gaps between jobs, and checking references. Background checks are particularly important for jobs in which employees are in a position to possibly harm others. For example, a trucking company must check applicants' driving records to avoid hiring a new trucker with numerous violations.

Hiring and the Law

Laws and regulations govern many aspects of the hiring process. In particular, employers must be careful to avoid discrimination in the wording of their application forms, in interviewing, and in testing. Employers must also respect the privacy of applicants. Consider the dilemma this situation presents for employers.

On the one hand, asking questions about unrelated factors such as citizenship, marital status, age, and religion violates regulations because such questions may lead to discrimination. In addition, employers are not allowed to ask questions about whether a person has children, whether a person owns or rents a home, what caused a physical disability, whether a person belongs to a union, whether a person has ever been arrested, or when a person attended school. The exception is when such information is related to a bona fide occupational qualification for the specific job.

Employers must also be careful in their hiring practices to ensure that they are not found liable for illegal recruitment practices. For example, a judge in British Columbia recently awarded RBC Dominion Securities $2.25 million after Merrill Lynch Canada lured away a dozen investment advisers. The defection practically led to the collapse of

Exhibit 10.4 **Checking Out New Hires**

Today's employers are scrutinizing new employees more closely.

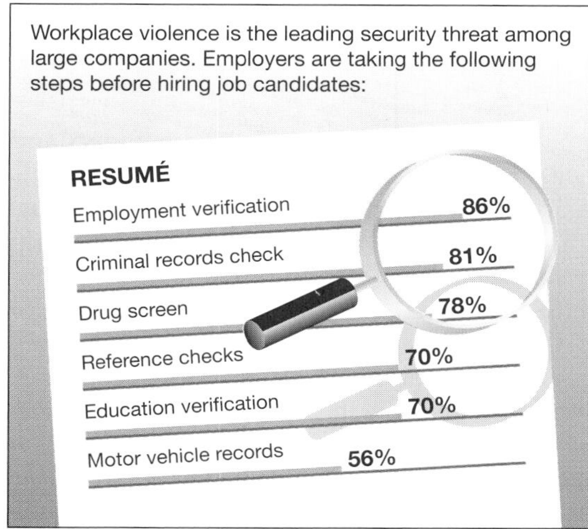

RBC's Cranbrook office and was challenged because of the manner in which the exodus took place. Individual brokers can switch organizations and bring their client lists to their new employer but the judge in this case ruled that the recruitment was deceitful, covert, and deliberately executed over a seven-month period.[11]

Testing

One much-debated aspect of the hiring process is testing—using not only the tests that prospective employers give job applicants but any devices that can evaluate employees when making job decisions. Tests are used to evaluate abilities, intelligence, interests, and sometimes even physical condition and personality.

Many companies rely on pre-employment testing to determine whether applicants are suited to the job and whether they'll be worth the expense of hiring and training. Companies use three main procedures: job-skills testing, psychological testing, and drug testing. Job-skills tests are the most common type, designed to assess competency or specific abilities needed to perform a job. Psychological tests usually take the form of questionnaires. These tests can be used to assess overall intellectual ability, attitudes toward work, interests, managerial potential, or personality characteristics—including dependability, commitment, and motivation. When Brigitte Catellier applied for the post of vice-president of legal affairs at Montreal-based Astral Media she was put to the test. She chuckled at one of the first questions that asked whether she would prefer to be an astronaut, an acrobat, or a research technician. But the test was no laughing matter. The gruelling eight tests in seven hours contained hundreds of questions and was a final hurdle in her job search. She also spent two hours with an industrial psychologist before a decision was made between her and another candidate.[12] People who favour psychological testing say that it can predict how well employees will actually perform on the job. However, critics say that such tests are ineffective and potentially discriminatory.

To avoid the increased costs and reduced productivity associated with drug abuse in the workplace (estimated to cost industry some US$100 billion a year), many employers require applicants to be tested for drug use. Studies show that substance abusers have two to four times as many workplace accidents as people who do not use drugs. Moreover, drug use can be linked to more than 40 percent of industry fatalities. Companies with mandatory testing have found real advantages, including lower acci-

Yasuko Ishikawa, a Delta Air Lines flight attendant, was fired after a random urine test showed her sample had been tampered with. So Ishikawa took her case to court. The jury found that the lab conducting the drug test was negligent and awarded Ishikawa US$400 000. Delta also offered to reinstate her.

dent rates, fewer disability claims, and decreased violence and absenteeism. Nevertheless, some employers prefer not to incur the extra expense to administer drug tests, while others consider such tests to be an invasion of privacy.[13] Critics of drug testing say the results can be inaccurate and produce false positives.

Training and Development

To make sure that all new employees understand the company's goals, policies, and procedures, most large organizations and many small ones have well-defined **orientation** programs. Although they vary, such programs usually include information about company background and structure, equal opportunity practices, safety regulations, standards of employee conduct, company culture, employee compensation and benefit plans, work times, and other topics that newly hired employees might have questions about.[14] Orientation programs help new employees understand their role in the organization and feel more comfortable.

At Intel, for instance, all new hires participate in a six-month "integration" curriculum. Day One begins when new hires receive a packet at home. The packet contains material about the company's culture and values, along with some forms to fill out. During the first month, all new hires attend a class called "Working at Intel," a formal eight-hour introduction to the company's corporate culture. At the end of the six-month period, each new hire participates in a two-hour structured question-and-answer session in which an executive reviews the employee's transition into Intel and then asks a final long-term question: "What do you think it will take to succeed at Intel?"[15]

orientation
Session or procedure to introduce a new employee to the organization and its procedures

In addition to orientation programs, most companies offer training (and retraining) because employee competence has a direct effect on productivity and profits. The Bank of Montreal takes employee development seriously; the commitment is evident when you examine the company's training and education initiatives. In the early 1990s the firm built the BMO Institute for Learning, a place where employees could receive standard instruction and dabble in experiential learning. The bank's "university" comes complete with 12 fully wired classrooms, 8 role-play rooms, 20 break-out rooms, and a 250-seat presentation hall. The institute is also geared toward experiential learning and includes an obstacle course that contains an eight-metre wall designed for employees to experience the challenge of rappelling and to test their physical limitations.[16] Although some employers worry that employees who develop new or improved skills might leave them for higher-paying jobs, studies show that the contrary is true. The more training given to employees, the more likely they will want to stay, because training gives them a sense that they are going somewhere in their careers, even if they're not getting a promotion.[17]

Janice Wismer, vice-president of human resources at Canadian Tire, was identified as one of Canada's most innovative executives by *Canadian Business.* When she assumed her position at HR, employee product knowledge was identified as a major problem. According to Wismer, "Many employees would walk away from customers instead of approaching them to provide advice." Her solution was to create an Internet-based e-learning initiative rather than a traditional training model. Just three years after the implementation of the program, 98 percent of Canadian Tire stores had adopted the e-learning tool and 948 000 interactive lessons had been completed. These figures are quite impressive considering the fact that Canadian Tire stores are independently owned and operated and that each dealer had to pay an up-front charge to join the program. The initiative is credited with boosting sales and improving customer satisfaction.[18]

In many companies, training takes place at the work site, where an experienced employee oversees the trainee's on-the-job efforts, or in a classroom, where an expert lectures groups of employees. Employee training may also involve a self-study component using training manuals, computers, tests, and interactive modules. Employees at Days Inn participate in interactive, self-paced, web-based training to learn reservation

The Bank of Montreal has made a commitment to its employees to address lifelong learning and corporate retraining. The BMO Institute for Learning is a venue for both traditional classrooms and experiential activities.

operations, housekeeping duties, supervision, and even ways to deal with surly guests.[19] For additional information and examples see the box entitled "Click and Learn: E-Training Today's Employees").

APPRAISING EMPLOYEE PERFORMANCE

L.O. 4

How do employees know whether they are doing a good job? How can they improve their performance? What new skills should they learn? Most HR managers attempt to answer these questions by developing **performance appraisal** systems to objectively evaluate employees according to set criteria. Such systems promote fairness because their standards are usually job-related.

performance appraisal Evaluation of an employee's work according to specific criteria

The ultimate goal of performance appraisals is not to judge employees but rather to improve their performance. Thus, experts recommend that performance reviews be an ongoing discipline—not just a once-a-year event linked to employee raises. Periodic evaluations are especially important in today's project-driven, results-oriented workplace. In order to turn a non-performer into an asset for the company, managers must clarify expectations, break the silence, and provide feedback with constructive advice.[20] In order to provide constructive advice the appraisal must clarify expectations. What does a rating of 3 out of a possible 5 on customer service mean to an employee? In many cases, the answer is absolutely nothing; the score must be accompanied by two-way communication for improved performance.[21]

Most companies require regular written evaluations of each employee's work. To ensure objectivity and consistency, firms generally use a standard company performance appraisal form to evaluate employees. The evaluation criteria are in writing so that both employee and supervisor understand what is expected and are therefore able to determine whether the work is being done adequately. Written evaluations also provide a record of the employee's performance, which may protect the company in cases of disputed terminations.

Many performance appraisal systems require the employee to be rated by several people (including more than one supervisor and perhaps several co-workers). This practice further promotes fairness by correcting for possible biases. One appraisal format that moves the review process from a one-dimensional perspective to a multidimensional format is the 360-degree review. Designed to provide employees with a broader range of perspectives, the *360-degree review* solicits feedback from colleagues above, below, and around the employee to provide observations of the person's performance in several skill and behavioural categories. This means that employees rate the performance of their superiors as well as their peers.[22]

One of the biggest problems with any employee appraisal system is finding a way to measure productivity. In a production job, the person who types the most pages of

Click and Learn: E-Training Today's Employees

According to the Conference Board of Canada, 77 percent of all Canadian employers now offer some form of e-training to their employees. At Rogers Communications, sales representatives can learn how to deal with routine inquiries and difficult customers with their interactive online role-play scenarios.[23] Employers from automakers and software firms to hospitals and pharmaceutical companies are turning to computers to train today's employees. Electronic training, or e-learning, uses computers and live or taped webcasts, web-based self-paced tutorials, and other forms of electronic media such as CD-ROMs to instruct employees on new products, customer service, sales techniques, and more. What makes e-learning possible are the technological advances in today's workplace—more desktop computers, increased Internet access, and more bandwidth.

Dell Computer expects 90 percent of its learning solutions to be totally or partially technology enabled. General Motors University uses interactive satellite broadcasts to teach salespeople the best way to highlight features on new cars. Pharmaceutical companies such as Merck use live interactive Internet classes to instruct sales reps on the latest product information rather than fly them to a conference centre. IBM has moved virtually all content of the first three phases of management training online, for its first-line managers—eliminating the need to send them to offsite locations over the course of a training period that stretches over six months.

As these companies have learned, e-training has many benefits:

- *Reduced costs.* Much of the cost savings comes from reduced travel expenses and time savings. Intel has saved more than US$1 million annually by using e-training programs. "If we save our 70 000 employees just 20 minutes a year, that alone is $1 million in savings," says one Intel training manager.
- *Increased productivity.* "Our sales force can't come in for three-day conferences anymore," says one Black & Decker vice-president. "But they still need to understand the company's new products and features." So the company has instituted online training courses—which means the company's 700-person sales force can spend a combined 12 000 more days a year with customers.
- *Individualized pace.* E-learning allows you to learn at your own pace—skipping over material you already know and spending more time learning material that meets your specific needs. Canadian Tire offers a very diverse product line. Through e-learning, employees are able to focus on specific areas where they lack knowledge.
- *Increased consistency.* Companies can create one set of instructional materials that is used consistently by everyone in the organization. Thus all employees are learning the same thing—regardless of their location.
- *Improved information sharing.* While still in its infancy, e-learning is effectively changing the way companies transfer knowledge and information to employees and customers.

Questions for Critical Thinking

1. Why is e-learning an increasingly popular training approach for companies?
2. How might an economic slowdown affect e-learning?

acceptable copy or who assembles the most defect-free microprocessors in a given amount of time is clearly the most productive. But how does an employer evaluate the productivity of the registration clerk at a hotel or the middle manager at a large television station? Although the organization's overall productivity can be measured (number of rooms booked per night, number of viewers per hour), often the employer can't directly relate the results to any one employee's efforts.

Evaluating productivity becomes an even greater challenge in organizations where employees work in teams. Some companies meet this challenge by having teams evaluate themselves. About every three months a neutral facilitator leads a discussion in which team members rate team performance on a scale of 1 to 5. The criteria can include customer satisfaction, the ability to meet goals, employee behaviour toward co-workers and customers, job knowledge, motivation, and skills. During the meetings, members discuss the team's performance. Individual performance is also discussed, but only in the context of the team. Each person creates two columns on a sheet of paper, labelled "strengths" and "something to work on." Team members self-assess and then pass the list around the room so other team members can add their comments.[24]

ADMINISTERING COMPENSATION AND EMPLOYEE BENEFITS

L.O. 5

On what basis should employees be paid? How much should they be paid? When should they be paid? What benefits should they receive? Every day, company leaders confront these types of decisions. Administering **compensation**—a combination of payments in the form of wages or salaries, incentive payments, employee benefits, and employer services—is another major responsibility of a company's HR department.

compensation
Money, benefits, and services paid to employees for their work

Wages and Salaries

Many blue-collar (production) and some white-collar (management and clerical) employees receive compensation in the form of **wages**, which are based on calculating the number of hours worked, the number of units produced, or a combination of both time and productivity. Wages provide a direct incentive to an employee: The more hours worked or the more pieces completed, the higher the employee's paycheque. Moreover, employers in Canada must comply with federal and provincial labour laws that determine issues such as minimum hourly wages and overtime pay for employees.

wages
Cash payment based on the number of hours the employee has worked or the number of units the employee has produced

Employees whose output is not always directly related to the number of hours worked or the number of pieces produced are paid **salaries**. As with wages, salaries base compensation on time, but the unit of time is a week, two weeks, a month, or a year. Salaried employees such as managers normally receive no pay for the extra hours they sometimes put in; overtime is simply part of their obligation. However, they do get a certain amount of flexibility in their schedules.

salaries
Fixed weekly, monthly, or yearly cash compensation for work

Both wages and salaries are, in principle, based on the contribution of a particular job to the company. Thus, a sales manager, who is responsible for bringing in sales revenue, is paid more than a secretary, who handles administrative tasks but doesn't sell or supervise. However, pay often varies widely by position, industry, and location. Among the best-paid employees in the world are chief executive officers of large corporations.

Incentive Programs

To encourage employees to be more productive, innovative, and committed to their work, many companies provide managers and employees with **incentives**, cash payments that are linked to specific individual, group, and companywide goals; overall productivity; and company success. In other words, achievements, not just activities, become the basis for payment. The success of these programs often depends on how closely incentives are linked to actions within the employee's control:

incentives
Cash payments to employees who produce at a desired level or whose unit (often the company as a whole) produces at a desired level

- *Bonuses.* For both salaried and wage-earning employees, one type of incentive compensation is the **bonus**, a payment in addition to the regular wage or salary. As an incentive to reduce turnover during the year, some firms pay an annual year-end bonus, amounting to a certain percentage of each employee's wages. Other cash bonuses are tied to company performance.
- *Commissions.* In contrast to bonuses, **commissions** are a form of compensation that pays employees a percentage of sales made. Used mainly for sales staff, they may be either the sole compensation or an incentive payment in addition to a regular salary.
- *Profit sharing.* Employees may be rewarded for staying with a company and encouraged to work harder through **profit sharing**, a system in which employees receive a portion of the company's profits. Depending on the company, profits may be distributed quarterly, semi-annually, or annually.

bonus
Cash payment, in addition to the regular wage or salary, that serves as a reward for achievement

commissions
Payments to employees equal to a certain percentage of sales made

profit sharing
System for distributing a portion of the company's profits to employees

These incentive programs are so popular in today's workplace that many employees consider their dollar value as part of their overall salary package.

Employee Benefits and Services

Companies also regularly provide **employee benefits**—financial benefits other than wages, salaries, and incentives. For example, Starbucks offers dental insurance, vaca-

employee benefits
Compensation other than wages, salaries, and incentive programs

tion and holiday pay, stock options, discounts on products, and a free pound of coffee every week. The benefits package is available to part-time as well as full-time employees, which helps the company attract and retain good people at every level.

Companies may offer employee benefits either as a preset package—that is, the employee gets whatever insurance, paid holidays, pension plan, and other benefits the company sets up—or as flexible benefits, recognizing that people have different priorities and needs at different stages of their lives. Flexible plans allow employees to pick their benefits—up to a certain dollar amount—to create a benefits package tailored to their individual needs. Moreover, they smooth out imbalances in benefits received by single employees and workers with families.[25] An employee with a young family might want extra life or health insurance, whereas a single employee might choose to "buy" an extra week or two of vacation time by giving up some other benefit.

The benefits most commonly provided by employers are insurance, retirement benefits, employee share-ownership plans, stock options, and family benefits. In the following sections, we will explore how these benefits and services are undergoing considerable change to meet the needs of today's workforce.

Insurance

Insurance is the most popular employee benefit. Many businesses offer substantial compensation in the form of life and health insurance, dental and vision plans, disability insurance, and long-term-care insurance. In the past, a company would negotiate a group insurance plan for employees and pay most of the premium costs. However, faced with exploding health expenses, many companies now require employees to pay part of their insurance premiums or more of the actual bills.[26] In addition, more companies are hiring part-time and temporary workers, who typically receive few company benefits. Nonetheless, some companies provide benefits because doing so discourages employee turnover. Howard Schultz figures that recruiting, interviewing, and training a new employee costs more than two years of medical coverage for an employee who stays with the company.[27]

Retirement Benefits

The Canada Pension Plan (QPP in Quebec), the Old Age Security plan, and the Guaranteed Income Supplement (GIS) were all created by governments to provide basic support to those who could not accumulate the retirement money they would need later in life. The Canada and Quebec Pension Plan is funded by employee contributions and matching employer contributions. If you are self-employed, you pay both portions. The Old Age Security program is funded by the government of Canada from general tax revenues.[28]

pension plan
Company-sponsored program for providing retirees with income

In addition to government pension plans, many employees receive company-sponsored retirement benefits. Studies show that 72 percent of workers at large firms (those with more than 500 employees) have some form of company-sponsored retirement coverage.[29] The most popular type of retirement coverage is the **pension plan**, which is funded by company contributions. Each year, enough money is theoretically set aside in a separate pension account to cover employees' future retirement benefits. However, a recent study conducted by the Certified General Accountants Association of Canada indicated that 59 percent of pension plans were running deficits that required $160 billion to cover the difference. This dangerous practice has led to some heart-wrenching results. For example, workers at the St. Anne Nacawick pulp mill in New Brunswick learned that all employees under the age of 55 were losing their pensions regardless of years of service. This news came to light after the company announced that it was going bankrupt. Workers over the age of 55 were also penalized 10 to 25 percent of their entitled amount.[30]

Defined Contribution Plans versus Defined Benefit Plans In *defined benefit plans* employers typically promise to pay their employees a fixed dollar amount, upon retirement, based on the employee's retirement age, final average salary, and years of service.[31]

For example, a formula could award 2.5 percent of a person's average salary (based on the five best years) to a maximum of 30 years. Based on this formula, an employee would be entitled to 75 percent of his or her salary at the end of 30 years.[32] *Defined contribution plans* are similar to savings plans that provide a future benefit based on annual employer contributions, voluntary employee matching contributions, and accumulated investment earnings. Since securities markets can be unpredictable, the pension amount is more uncertain than in a defined benefit plan. In this case, funds contributed on the employee's behalf along with investment gains are used to buy an annuity that pays the employee a fixed income upon retirement. In recent years, other defined contribution plans have been gaining popularity, such as group RRSPs and deferred profit sharing plans.[33]

Richard Tucker (left) of Renous, New Brunswick and Fred Gallant of St. Louis-de-Kent, New Brunswick walk to their car after protesting the closure of the St. Anne Nackawic pulp mill. Unfortunately, the mill's 400 employees lost their jobs; many were also shocked to find out that they had lost their pensions after the mill declared bankruptcy and revealed that the pension plan was in financial disarray.

Plans have evolved to accommodate a more mobile workforce. But the shift toward the increased use of defined contribution plans does have some drawbacks. First, they increase the burden on workers to set aside money for retirement and invest it wisely. Second, many employees fail to diversify and instead invest heavily in the employer's stock—subjecting their retirement savings to the fate of one company. Ask former Nortel employees about how millions on paper can dwindle to almost nothing in reality. There are many tales to be told. For example, when Enron's stock plummeted from US$85 a share to less than 60 cents, employees lost about US$1 billion in retirement savings. Roger Boyce, a 30-year employee who had accumulated more than US$900 000 in funds, watched the value of his account decline to less than US$10 000. After the collapse of the company Boyce is rethinking retirement—and suing his former employer.[34]

Registered Retirement Savings Plan The Registered Retirement Savings Plan (RRSP) was designed as an investment vehicle by the Canadian government to provide individuals added incentive to save their money. Under this plan, the contributor receives tax advantages upon making the purchase. RRSPs entitle investors to deduct their contributions from their taxable income. For example, if Phil earns $60 000 per year and he invests $7000 in an RRSP, he will pay the same amount of taxes as someone in an identical situation who earns $53 000 but does not invest in an RRSP. This investment tool also permits Phil, a 35-year-old man, to watch his savings grow tax free until retirement (likely in 30 years). RRSPs provide some of the same advantages as company pensions while providing flexibility for the employee.

Employee Share-Ownership Plans

Another employee benefit being offered by a number of companies is the **employee share-ownership plan (ESOP)**, under which a company places a certain amount of its stock in trust for some or all of its employees, with each employee entitled to a certain share. These plans allow employees to later purchase the shares at a fixed price. If the company does well, the ESOP may provide a substantial employee benefit. At Telus, employees are able to invest up to 6 percent of their salaries in company shares, which are then increased by employer contributions. Telus adds $2 for every $5 contributed by an employee. When phone stocks fall, employees feel the pinch, but regardless of the economic trends the goal remains the same: to earn increased equity for the firm and for these very important contributing members of the company.[35] Of course, linking the financial success of employees to the success of the company is indeed a worthy goal, but some say that in the long run ESOPs are not effective performance motivators.

employee share-ownership plan (ESOP)
Program enabling employees to become partial owners of a company

In the early 1990s, United Airlines' pilots made major wage concessions in exchange for a 55 percent equity stake in the company via an ESOP. As a result of those concessions, United's pilots trailed the industry in pay. Nevertheless, the pilots hoped to recover their lost wages and more through increased market value of their ESOP shares.

After United Airlines employees bought a majority stake in their company, managers began referring to employees as "owners" and the airline changed its motto to "fly our friendly skies." The company's ESOP was even trumpeted on the cover of Business Week. But the era of harmony flickered only briefly because the plan had several flaws.

The company hoped to gain enhanced employee morale and improved customer service by making the employees stockholders. Neither long-term benefit materialized. In the beginning, the ESOP helped streamline United's operations and cut costs. The company posted record profits for a short period, and employee owners watched as their stock soared.[36] But the era of harmony and enthusiasm flickered only briefly. United's stock soon began to fall because of competitive pressures, rising fuel costs, and internal battling among union members. By the turn of the century, funding of the United Airlines ESOP had expired and failed.[37]

Stock Options

A related method for tying employee compensation to company performance is the stock option plan. **Stock options** grant employees the right to purchase a set number of shares of the employer's stock at a specific price, called the *grant* or *exercise price*, during a certain time period. Options typically "vest" over five years, at a rate of 20 percent annually. This means that at the end of one year employees can purchase up to 20 percent of the shares in the original grant, at the end of two years up to 40 percent, and so on. If the stock's market price exceeds the exercise price, the option holder can exercise the option and sell the stock at a profit. If the stock's price falls below the exercise price, the options become worthless.

stock options
Contract allowing the holder to purchase or sell a certain number of shares of a particular stock at a given price by a certain date

Stock options can be a win-win situation for employers and employees. From the employer's perspective, stock options cost little, provide long-term incentives for good people to stay with the company, and encourage employees to work harder because they have a vested interest in the company doing well. For, example, CIBC World Markets is providing stocks and options to "young performers" in order to encourage employee loyalty.[38] From the employee's perspective, stock options can generate a handsome profit if the stock's market price exceeds the grant price. But stock options lose their appeal when the stock does not perform as expected. Employees could lose considerable profits if the stock's price falls below the option grant price.[39]

Family Benefits

Government programs have been designed to protect workers and provide mechanisms for meeting family obligations. In Canada, women are entitled to a maternity leave period of one year, whereas American women only receive 12 weeks.[40] In Quebec, this benefit is further supported by subsidized daycare that enables parents to have access to $7-a-day care centres. This model is being considered by other provinces, and a federal government program is not outside the realm of possibility. Regardless of the current government programs, companies have an important role to play in providing employees with family benefits. For example, the Ford Motor Company plans to open more than a dozen daycare centres providing employees with 24-hour child care—part of a sweeping plan to provide family-related services in more than 30 locations. "Not only will [the centres] attract and retain the best, but the workforce, when they're at work, don't have to worry about their children and where they are," says one company spokesperson.[41] Approximately 10 percent of companies provide daycare facilities on their premises, but 86 percent of companies surveyed by Hewitt & Associates offer some form of child-care assistance. Types of assistance include dependant-care spending accounts and resource and referral (R&R) services, which help employees find suitable child care. Firms estimate that they save anywhere from $2.00 to $6.75 in lost productivity and employee absenteeism for every $1.00 they spend on R&R programs.[42]

A related family issue is care for aging parents. An estimated 50 percent of employers offer some form of elder-care assistance, ranging from referral services that help find care providers to dependant-care allowances. Some companies will even agree to move elderly relatives when they transfer an employee to another location.[43]

CEO Jim Goodnight of SAS Institute (a software development firm) takes a snack break with children at the company's on-site daycare centre.

Other Employee Benefits

Although sometimes overlooked, paid holidays, sick pay, premium pay for working overtime or unusual hours, and paid vacations are important benefits. Companies handle holiday pay in various ways. To provide incentives for employee loyalty, most companies grant employees longer paid vacations after they've been with the organization for a prescribed number of years. Some companies let employees buy additional vacation time or sell unused days back to the employer. Sick-day allowances also vary from company to company and from industry to industry. Some companies have begun offering paid-time-off banks that combine vacation, personal use, and sick days into one package. Employees can then take a certain number of days off each year for whatever reason necessary, with no questions asked.[44]

Companies offer a variety of additional benefits, including sabbaticals, tuition loans and reimbursements, professional development opportunities, personal computers, financial counselling and legal services, assistance with buying a home, paid expenses for spouses who travel with employees, employee assistance programs, nap time, and wellness programs. Typical wellness programs include health screenings, wellness education programs, and fitness programs. Delta Hotels has received a gold trophy in the prestigious National Quality Institute Canada Excellence Awards for providing a healthy workplace as well as for its dedication to a companywide wellness program. M&M Meat Shops credits its formal wellness program with keeping employee turnover and absenteeism to a minimum.[45] Company rewards for implementing such programs include reduced absenteeism, health care costs, sickness, and work-related accidents.[46]

Employee assistance programs (EAPs) offer private and confidential counselling to employees. EAPs are designed to help with issues related to drugs, alcohol, finances, stress, family, and other personal problems. Studies show that the average annual cost for EAP services runs from $12 to $20 per employee. However, these services save between $5 and $16 for each dollar spent as a result of improved safety and productivity, as well as reduced employee turnover.[47] Magna Corporation offers an EAP to all employees in its family of companies. Its EAP is part of a portfolio of support programs that also includes an Employee Equity Program, a Profit Participation Program, as well as pension and RRSP plans.[48]

employee assistance programs (EAPs)
Company-sponsored counselling or referral plans for employees with personal problems

Benefits such as company cars, paid country club memberships, free parking, and expanded casual dress days are often referred to as perks. In a tight job market companies offer perks to attract the best managers.[49] "But recruitment perks only go so far," says one compensation expert. "Organizations must offer the total work experience to attract talent." To keep talent from leaving, they must offer workers challenging jobs and training, more family-related benefits, and better management supervision.[50]

OVERSEEING CHANGES IN EMPLOYMENT STATUS

L.O. 6

Of course, providing competitive compensation and good employee benefits is no guarantee that employees will stay with the company. Employees leave companies for a variety of reasons. Some may decide to retire. Others may resign voluntarily to pursue a better opportunity. Still others may make a change because they are promoted, reassigned, or terminated. When a vacancy occurs, companies must go to the trouble and expense of finding a replacement from inside or outside the company. Overseeing changes in employment status is another responsibility of the human resources department.

Promoting and Reassigning Employees

As Exhibit 10.3 shows, many companies prefer to look within the organization to fill job vacancies. In part, this "promote from within" policy allows a company to benefit from the training and experience of its own workforce. This policy also rewards employees who have worked hard and demonstrated the ability to handle more challenging tasks. In addition, morale is usually better when a company promotes from within because employees see that they can advance.

However, a potential pitfall of internal promotion is that a person may be given a job beyond his or her competence. A common practice is for someone who is good at one kind of job to be made a manager. Yet managing often requires a completely different set of skills. Someone who consistently racks up the most sales in the company, for example, is not necessarily a good candidate for sales manager. If the promotion is a mistake, the company not only loses its sales leader but also risks losing the employee altogether. People who can't perform well in a new job generally become demoralized and lose confidence in the abilities they do have. At the very least, support and training are needed to help promoted employees perform well.

Terminating Employees

termination
Act of removing an employee through layoff or firing

A company invests time, effort, and money in each new employee it recruits and trains. This investment is lost when an employee is removed by **termination**—permanently laying the employee off because of cutbacks or firing the employee for poor performance. Many companies facing a downturn in business have avoided large-scale layoffs by cutting administrative costs (curtailing travel, seminars, and so on), freezing wages, postponing new hiring, implementing job-sharing programs, or encouraging early retirement. However, sometimes a company has no alternative but to reduce the size of its workforce, leaving the human resources department to handle layoffs and their resulting effects on both the terminated and the remaining employees.

layoffs
Termination of employees for economic or business reasons

Layoffs are the termination of employees for economic or business reasons unrelated to employee performance. Companies are free to make layoffs in any manner they choose, just as long as certain demographic groups are not disproportionately affected. But as Michael Dell puts it, making cuts "is one of the hardest, most gut-wrenching decisions you can make as a leader." Layoffs are "an admission that we screwed up" by overhiring, admits Dell. If there's a lesson, says Dell, it's that "when things heat up quite a bit, we should take some pause."[51]

To help ease the pain of layoffs, many companies provide laid-off employees with job-hunting assistance. *Outplacement* aids such as resumé-writing courses, career counselling, office space, and secretarial help are offered to laid-off executives and blue-collar employees alike. Moreover, outplacement centres offer courses and tests to help employees decide what types of jobs are best suited for them.[52] When Levi Strauss & Co. decided to shut down their North American production plants, 1100 Canadian workers in Edmonton and at two Ontario plants, Stoney Creek and Brantford, were left without work. Despite the devastating decision the company made significant efforts to cushion the impact. Employees were given significant severance packages as well as a transitional payment for job retraining. The company donated $1 million to local educational institutions and community agencies to deal with the layoffs. Self-esteem workshops were heavily attended by both former workers and managers. In Edmonton, concerted organized efforts enabled 105 workers to find new jobs between the time the announcement was made and the day the plant closed. Another 137 were enrolled in retraining programs, 51 retired, 66 were actively seeking a job, and 129 were weighing their options. Despite the decision to move offshore to match its competitor's production costs, Levi acknowledged the contribution of its former employees and showed some compassion.[53]

Some companies adopt no-layoff, or guaranteed-employment, policies. This means that in an economic downturn, employees may be shifted to other types of jobs, perhaps at reduced pay, or given the chance to participate in work-sharing programs. Such no-layoff policies help promote employee loyalty and motivation, which benefit the company over the long run. (See the box entitled "Should Employees Pay to Keep Their Jobs?").

Retiring Employees

The population is aging rapidly. For the business community, an aging population presents two challenges. The first is to give job opportunities to people who are willing and able to work but who happen to be past the traditional retirement age. Many older citizens are concerned about their ability to live comfortably on fixed retirement incomes. Others simply prefer to work. The second challenge posed by an aging workforce is to find ways to encourage older employees to retire early. Older employees that want to work past 65 have the freedom to do so. Six provinces and three territories in Canada have abolished mandatory retirement age and pressure is mounting on the other provinces to follow.[54] One method a company may use to encourage retirement is to offer older employees financial incentives to resign, such as enhanced retirement benefits or one-time cash payments. Inducing employees to depart by offering them financial incentives is known as a **worker buyout**. This method can be a lot more expensive than firing or laying off employees. However, the method has several advantages: the morale of the remaining employees is preserved because they feel less threatened about their own security, younger employees see increased chances for promotion, and the risk of age-discrimination lawsuits is minimized.

worker buyout Distribution of financial incentives to employees who voluntarily depart; usually undertaken in order to reduce the payroll

Should Employees Pay to Keep Their Jobs?

At the height of the economic boom, managers handed out signing bonuses, stock options, and other perks like candy—doing whatever it took to recruit and retain employees. Then came the bust. With labour shortages still fresh in their minds, managers wrestled with a different issue: how to run their businesses, hang on to their workers, and maintain worker morale while still cutting labour costs.

Facing a weakened economy, some companies immediately laid off thousands of employees. Others recognized that human capital is their most important asset and tried to limit mass layoffs so they wouldn't have to hastily rehire when the economy recovered. Maintaining huge payroll costs, which can account for two-thirds of most companies' expenses, is a challenge during an economic downturn. So some companies froze wages or cut pay across the surviving workforce to distribute the pain more equitably.

Salary and benefit cuts "are the last thing you want to do in a down economy," warn some HR experts. "It's never good to take away from the people you want to keep." In fact, many companies who imposed widespread pay cuts in past recessions say they would never do it again. The cuts generated millions in savings. But worker morale—and productivity—plummeted. These experts argue that it would be better for companies to lay off their least-productive workers so they can afford to keep more-productive employees. Not so, say others, who maintain that you can't have good morale unless all employees have confidence that a company will treat them fairly, which for some employees means avoiding layoffs at all costs—even if they have to swallow a pay cut.

The debate continues over which approach is the lesser of two evils: massive layoffs or some layoffs combined with across-the-board pay and benefits cuts for those who survive. From a company perspective, hiring and firing and then rehiring is an exercise they'd rather not repeat. But maintaining high payroll costs in poor economic times is also something they can't afford. From an employee's perspective, finding a new job in a recession is extremely difficult, so some are willing to pay to keep their jobs. But here's the twist: If employees feel they are being exploited by companies who are using an economic downturn to take back some of their hard-earned gains in the past decade or so, they will be the first to bolt when the economy strengthens.

Questions for Critical Thinking

1. What are management's staffing options in a declining economy?
2. Debate the options you just identified. Which options do your classmates prefer? Why? Do you agree?

SUMMARY OF LEARNING OBJECTIVES

1 List six main functions of human resources departments.

Human resources departments plan for a company's staffing needs, recruit and hire new employees, train and develop employees, appraise employee performance, administer compensation and employee benefits, and oversee changes in employment status.

2 Cite seven methods recruiters use to find job candidates.

Recruiters find job candidates by (1) promoting internal candidates, (2) advertising in newspapers and on the Internet, (3) using public and private employment agencies, (4) recruiting at college campuses and career placement offices, (5) attending trade shows, (6) hiring corporate "head-hunters," and (7) soliciting referrals from employees or colleagues in the industry.

3 Identify the six stages in the hiring process.

The stages in the hiring process are (1) narrowing down the number of qualified candidates, (2) performing initial screening interviews, (3) administering a series of follow-up interviews, (4) evaluating candidates, (5) conducting reference checks, and (6) selecting the right candidate.

4 Discuss how companies incorporate objectivity into employee performance appraisals.

Employee performance appraisals are an effective way to inform employees whether they are doing a good job and how they can improve their performance. To ensure objectivity and fairness, most firms use a standard, companywide format, provide a written record of appraisals for future reference, and solicit several perspectives by engaging superiors, peers, and colleagues at different levels in the organization in the review process.

5 Highlight five popular employee benefits.

The two most popular employee benefits are insurance (health, life, disability, and long-term care) and retirement benefits, such as pension plans that help employees save for later years. Employee share-ownership plans and stock options, two additional benefits, allow employees to receive or purchase shares of the company's stock and thus obtain a stake in the company. Family benefits programs are also popular and include maternity and paternity leave, child-care assistance, and elder-care assistance.

6 Describe four ways an employee's status may change and discuss why many employers like to fill job vacancies from within.

An employee's status may change through promotion or through reassignment to a different position, through termination, through voluntary resignation, or through retirement. Employers like to fill vacancies created from such changes by promoting from within for these reasons: The employee has been trained by the company and knows the ropes, it boosts employee morale, and it sends a message to other employees that good performance will be rewarded.

Behind the SCENES

Perking Up the Perfect Blend at Starbucks

On the fast track toward global growth, the Starbucks chain helped transform the ordinary cup of coffee into a wide variety of taste choices for millions of coffee lovers. Along the way, the company's astonishing success encouraged competitors to join the fray. Now expansion-minded companies like Second Cup and Seattle's Best Coffee were turning up the heat in the upscale coffee category. To maintain growth, Starbucks managers had to ensure that their stores provided the best service along with superb coffee—which meant attracting, training, and compensating a diverse and dedicated workforce.

Guided by the company mission statement, CEO Howard Schultz and his managers designed a variety of human resources programs to motivate Starbucks partners (employees). First, they raised employees' base pay. Next management bucked the trend in the industry by offering full medical, dental, life insurance, and disability insurance benefits to every partner who worked at least 20 hours per week. These partners were also eligible for paid vacation days and retirement savings plans, benefits not commonly available to part-time workers. Finally, Starbucks invested in its workforce by providing new hires with 24 hours of training about the finer points of coffee brewing as well as the company's culture and values.

But the most innovative benefit brewed up by management was its Bean Stock, a program offering stock options not just to upper-echelon managers but to all partners who worked 20 or more hours per week. "We established Bean Stock in 1991 as a way of investing in our partners and creating ownership across the company," explained Bradley Honeycutt, vice-president of HR services. "It's been a key to retaining good people and building loyalty." For those who want to enlarge their financial stake in Starbucks, management devised a program that permitted partners to buy company stock at a discount. Owning a piece of the company motivated employees to take customer service to an even higher level of excellence. "We do everything we possibly can to get our customers to come back," says Schultz.

To help partners better balance their work and family obligations—another priority for Starbucks—the human resources department designed a comprehensive work-life program featuring flexible work schedules, access to employee assistance specialists, and referrals for child-care and elder-care support. The company also encouraged employees to become involved in their local communities, and honoured employees whose achievements exemplified the company's values. Finally, to encourage open communication and employee feedback, good or bad, management began holding a series of open forums in which company performance, results, and plans were openly discussed. Employees were encouraged to share ideas. "There is a tremendous amount of sharing in the company," notes Schultz. "It makes everybody think like an owner."

While most CEOs say that people are their most important asset, Starbucks lives that idea every day by giving people a stake in the outcome and treating them with respect and dignity. In all, putting employees first has helped Starbucks expand by attracting an energetic, committed workforce and keeping turnover lower than the industry average.[55]

Critical Thinking Questions

1. Why do Starbucks' human resources managers need to be kept informed about any changes in the number and timing of new store openings planned for the coming year?
2. Why does Starbucks offer benefits to its part-time labour force?
3. How does Starbucks' liberal employee-benefits program motivate its employees?

Learn More Online

Go to Chapter 10 of this text's website at www.pearsoned.ca/bovee, and click on the hotlink to get to the Starbucks website. Then visit the site's job section to see how Starbucks presents its HR policies to potential employees. Browse the pages that discuss working at Starbucks. Read about company culture, diversity, benefits, and learning and career development. Why would Starbucks post information about company culture in this section of the website? Why would job candidates be interested in learning about the culture as well as the employee benefits and training at Starbucks?

KEY TERMS

bonus (257)
commissions (257)
compensation (257)
employee assistance programs (EAPs) (261)
employee benefits (257)
employee share-ownership plan (ESOP) (259)
human resources management (HRM) (247)
incentives (257)
job analysis (250)
job description (250)
job specification (250)
layoffs (262)
orientation (254)
pension plan (258)
performance appraisal (255)
profit sharing (257)
recruiting (250)
salaries (257)
stock options (260)
termination (262)
wages (257)
worker buyout (263)

TEST YOUR KNOWLEDGE

Questions for Review

1. What do human resources managers do?
2. What are some strategic staffing alternatives that organizations use to avoid overstaffing and understaffing?
3. What is the purpose of conducting a job analysis? What are some of the techniques used for gathering information?
4. What are three types of pre-employment tests administered by companies, and how is each of these tests used to assist with the hiring decision?
5. What functions do orientation programs serve?

Questions for Analysis

6. How do incentive programs encourage employees to be more productive, innovative, and committed to their work?
7. Why do some employers offer comprehensive benefits even though the costs of doing so have risen significantly in recent years?
8. What are the advantages and disadvantages of Registered Retirement Savings Plans (RRSP) retirement plans?
9. **Ethical Considerations.** Corporate head-hunters have been known to raid other companies of their top talent to fill vacant or new positions for their clients. Is it ethical to contact the CEO of one company and lure him or her to join the management team of another company?

Questions for Application

10. If you were on the human resources staff at a large health care organization that was looking for a new manager of information systems, what recruiting method(s) would you use and why?
11. Assume you are the manager of human resources at a manufacturing company that employs about 500 people. A recent cyclical downturn in your industry has led to financial losses, and top management is talking about laying off workers. Several supervisors have come to you with creative ways of keeping employees on the payroll, such as exchanging workers with other local companies. Why might you want to consider this option? What other options exist besides layoffs?
12. **Integrated.** Of the five levels in Maslow's hierarchy of needs, which is satisfied by offering salary? By offering health care benefits? By offering training opportunities? By developing flexible job descriptions?
13. **Integrated.** What are some of the human resources issues managers are likely to encounter when two companies (in the same industry) merge?

PRACTISE YOUR KNOWLEDGE

SHARPENING YOUR COMMUNICATION SKILLS

Visit the HRSDC Website (Human Resources Skill Development Canada) at www.hrsdc.gc.ca/en/home.shtml to learn about youth employment programs. Begin by clicking onto the Human Resources link followed by the Hiring link. This will lead you to a page that includes access to Youth Employment Strategy (YES). Look through the site in detail and then use the information on this website to write a short memo to your instructor summarizing what you've learned.

BUILDING YOUR TEAM SKILLS

Team up with a classmate to practise your responses to interview questions. Use the list of common interview questions provided in Appendix D, and take turns posing and responding to those questions. Which questions did you find most difficult to answer? What insights did you gain about your strengths and weaknesses by answering those questions? Why is it a good idea to rehearse your answers before going to an interview?

EXPAND YOUR KNOWLEDGE

DISCOVERING CAREER OPPORTUNITIES

If you pursue a career in human resources, you'll be deeply involved in helping organizations find, select, train, evaluate, and retain employees. You have to like people and be a good communicator to succeed in HR. Is this field for you? Using your local Sunday newspaper, the *Globe and Mail*, the *National Post*, and online sources such as Monster (www.monster.ca), find ads seeking applicants for positions in the field of human resources.

1. What educational qualifications, technical knowledge, or specialized skills are applicants for these jobs expected to have? How do these requirements fit with your background and educational plans?
2. Next, look at the duties mentioned in the ad for each job. What do you think you would be doing on an average day in these jobs? Does the work in each job sound interesting and challenging?
3. Now think about how you might fit into one of these positions. Do you prefer to work alone, or do you enjoy teamwork? How much paperwork are you willing to do? Do you communicate better in person, on paper, or by phone? Considering your answers to these questions, which of the HR jobs seems to be the closest match for your personal style?

DEVELOPING YOUR RESEARCH SKILLS

Locate one or more articles in business journals or newspapers (print or online editions) that illustrate how a company or industry is adapting to changes in its workforce. (Examples include retraining, literacy or basic-skills training, flexible benefits, and benefits aimed at working parents or people who care for aging relatives.)

1. What changes in the workforce or employee needs caused the company to adapt? What did the company do to respond to these changes? Was the company's response voluntary or legally mandated?
2. Is the company alone in facing these changes, or is the entire industry trying to adapt? What are other companies in the industry doing to adapt to the changes?
3. What other changes in the workforce or in employee needs do you think this company is likely to face in the next few years? Why?

See It on the **WEB**

URLs for all Internet exercises are provided at the website for this book, www.pearsoned.ca/bovee. When you log on to the text website, select Chapter 10, then select Destinations. Click on the name of the featured website and review the website to complete the following exercises.

Explore the following chapter-related websites, review their content, and answer the following questions for each website you visit:

1. What is the purpose of this website?
2. What kinds of information does this website contain? Please be specific.
3. How is the information provided at this website useful for business people? Consumers?
4. How did you expand your knowledge of human resources management by reviewing the material at this website? What new things did you learn about this topic?

STAYING ON TOP OF THE HR WORLD

Like all areas of business, the world of human resources changes quickly. To stay informed about trends in recruiting, compensation, benefits, and employee satisfaction, turn to HR Live. Browse through some of the top recruiting markets for occupations that interest you. Read one of the recent layoff reports from your province. This comprehensive online resource provides HR professionals with information about employment markets and trends, labour statistics, recruiting methods, layoffs, and much more. The site also offers convenient links to job fairs and conventions in a variety of industries so recruiters (and job seekers) can plan ahead. www.hrlive.com

MAXIMIZING YOUR EARNING POTENTIAL

You know you should be making more money. So now what? Log on to salaryexpert.com to find out what people in your field are making across Canada. Sharpen your skills and knowledge so you can get the job, salary, and benefits you want.

LEARNING OBJECTIVES

The purpose of this video is to help you

1. Understand the various challenges facing today's workforce.
2. Recognize sources of stress and identify policies designed to relieve the mounting pressure on employees.
3. Identify sources of motivation in the workplace and factors that diminish employee morale.

SYNOPSIS

How many times have you heard a friend, colleague, or family member utter these words: "I am so stressed." This common bond can be linked to long hours, unreachable deadlines, unwritten rules, difficult bosses, overtime, downsizing, and rightsizing. One recent survey of 33 000 Canadians shed some light on the topic. The subject clearly struck a nerve, as after answering all of the detailed questions more than 10 000 people went a step further and added written comments. People are starting work early, working late, and coming in on the weekends. Fifty- to sixty-hour weeks are the norm for many workers; in some industries a 50-hour week is equated with "slacking off." This pressure to perform and to go above and beyond the standard workweek has created various side effects. Companies are paying millions in insurance claims for antidepressant drugs, and absenteeism is costing the Canadian economy $3 billion per year. Corporate Canada is opening its eyes to this problem; many companies have created flex hours, telecommuting, and other programs. However, many employees believe that their employers talk about quality of work life and family-friendly policies but don't actually encourage them.

Bob Howe heads up a small law firm in Toronto. In most big law firms, face time (time spent in the office between 8:00 am and 8:00 p.m.) is a vital element. Many lawyers work 12 or more hours per day regularly. At Davies-Howe employees have more flexible work hours and a more humane environment, yet they have not sacrificed their pay. How? The firm traded its fancy office for a lower-rent location and passes the savings on to lawyers in the form of more reasonable workloads. With more and more employees feeling overwhelmed by the pressure to perform it is clear that companies that can effectively deal with this problem will be in a better position to excel in the future.

Discussion Questions

1. *For analysis:* Why are so many workers raising the white flag and complaining about their working conditions? What has changed in the last decade or two?
2. *For analysis:* How does low employee morale affect worker productivity?
3. *For application:* Using Hertzberg's Two-Factor Theory explain the apparent satisfaction being experienced by the lawyers at the Davies-Howe law firm.
4. *For debate:* In many countries employees enjoy a shorter workweek. Should the Canadian government shorten the official workweek? Will this help reduce absenteeism and lead to a more motivated workforce? Would such a move lead to a lazier workforce?

ONLINE EXPLORATION

Visit the following Human Resources and Skills Development Canada (HRSDC) website at www.hrsdc.gc.ca/asp/gateway.asp?hr=en/lp/spila/wlb/01home.shtml&hs=wnc. Read Linda Duxbury's research findings under the heading "Voices of Canadians: Seeking Work Life Balance." Read another recent study on the topic of work-life balance. What are some of the key issues being addressed by the article? Does it support the claims that were made in the video?

On Location VIDEO CASE

Managing the Human Side of the Business: Park Place Entertainment (Caesar's)

LEARNING OBJECTIVES

The purpose of this video is to help you

1. Recognize how human resource management contributes to organizational performance.
2. Understand how and why HR managers make plans and decisions about staffing.
3. Identify some of the ways in which HR managers handle staff evaluation and development.

SYNOPSIS

Park Place (Caesar's) Entertainment owns and operates resorts and casinos around the world. Its human resources department is responsible for hiring, training, and managing a diverse group of more than 52 000 employees. HR managers have created specific job descriptions for each position, instituted training programs for employee and management development, and established incentive programs to reward good performance. Park Place's 360-degree evaluation method allows supervisors to get performance feedback from the employees they supervise. Because its customers come from many countries and speak many languages, the company seeks out employees from diverse backgrounds, varying the recruitment process for different properties in different areas.

Discussion Questions

1. *For analysis:* What are the advantages and disadvantages of centralizing the recruiting process at a company such as Park Place Entertainment?
2. *For analysis*: Why did Park Place begin the restructuring of its HR department by standardizing training for supervisors?
3. *For application*: What steps might Park Place's HR executives take to reduce turnover among the employees at particular resorts?
4. *For application*: How might Park Place encourage its employees to refer friends as candidates for open positions?
5. *For debate*: Rather than hiring employees when business booms and then laying some off when business falls off, should Park Place temporarily rehire some of its retired supervisors and employees during peak periods? Support your chosen position.

ONLINE EXPLORATION

Visit the Park Place (Caesar's) Entertainment website at www.caesars.com/Corporate/AboutUs/ and browse the home page to see the locations and names of the company's resorts and casinos. Then follow the company information link to look at career opportunities and company benefits. What kinds of jobs are being featured on the website? Why would Park Place arrange jobs by region? How does the firm make it convenient for applicants to submit resumés online? Why would Park Place put so much emphasis on Internet recruiting?

E-Business IN ACTION

Job Recruiting Moves to the Net

E-cruiting (recruiting over the Internet) has become an integral part of HR strategy for companies of all sizes. Companies have discovered that the Internet is a fast, convenient, and inexpensive way to find prospective job candidates. Job candidates are finding that the Internet is a convenient way to gather company information, search for job vacancies, and post resumés for large-volume distribution using career websites such as Monster.ca, Workopolis.com, Hotjobs.ca, and Jobpostings.ca (also know as job boards).

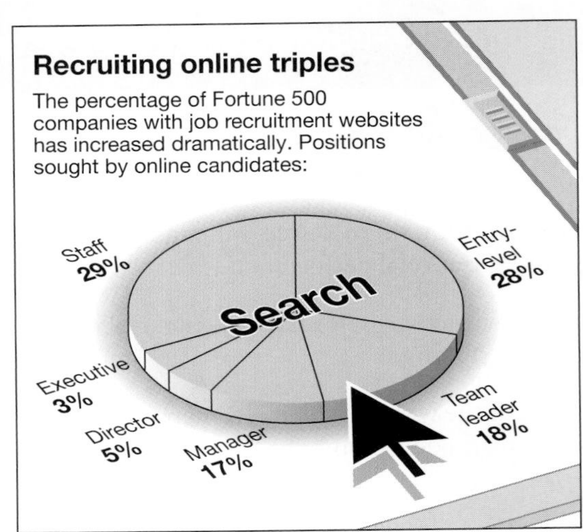

The Traditional Path versus E-Cruiting

Before the advent of the Internet, recruiting followed a traditional path: A company "announced" a job opening to the marketplace (through a classified ad, an executive recruiter, employee referral incentives, a job fair, or other medium), and recruiters made endless rounds of cold telephone calls to identify potential job candidates. Then, after a lengthy process of sorting through faxed and mailed resumés, someone from human resources called the most promising candidates and interviewed them.

This process, however, is expensive and inefficient. For one thing, communication by regular mail is slow. By the time a phone call is made or snail mail is received, a good candidate may have accepted another job. Plus, the cost of placing classified ads in newspapers is high, so most ads contain brief job descriptions and appear for only a few days or weeks. Furthermore, the traditional process operates mostly in one direction. Most applicants do not place ads announcing their availability—although some job seekers do send unsolicited letters with resumés.

Thanks to the Internet, however, the recruiting process is changing. Companies are using the Internet to search for resumés of promising candidates, take online applications, accept electronic resumés, conduct interviews, and administer tests. Recruiters at Amazon.com, for example, post ads on job boards and actively search the Web for resumés. "To be a recruiter at Amazon.com, you have to like the thrill of the hunt," says Amazon's manager of technical recruiting. Amazon's recruiters sort through hundreds of candidates they consider for every position by using a tool to pre-sort and categorize resumés. Like Amazon, many companies now advertise job vacancies on their company websites and on third-party job boards. From entry-level position to CEO, no job is outside the Internet's reach.

Benefits and Drawbacks of E-Cruiting

In comparison to traditional recruiting methods, the benefits of Internet recruiting are many:

- *Speed.* The Internet allows job seekers to search for jobs quickly, from any place and at any time, and to communicate via e-mail with potential employers. Companies can also save time in the hiring process by using the Internet to become a 24-hour, seven-days-a-week recruiter and give applicants quick responses to their queries. Determined nocturnal head-hunters can snap up hot resumés posted on the Internet before dawn and contact candidates immediately by e-mail. Some companies report receiving responses and resumés only minutes after posting a job opening.
- *Reach.* The Internet allows employers to contact a broader selection of applicants more quickly, target specific types of applicants more easily, and reach highly skilled applicants more efficiently. Some company websites bring in thousands of resumés in one week, a volume that would be far too cumbersome to manage through traditional means.
- *Cost savings.* Electronic ads typically cost much less than traditional print, career fairs, and open houses. Moreover, processing electronic application forms is more efficient than processing paper forms. Intelligent automated search agents can filter or pre-screen potential applicants and find resumés that match job descriptions and specific employer criteria.

Of course, e-cruiting is not without drawbacks. The biggest complaint voiced by companies is that the Internet produces more job applicants than ever before. The number of resumés one company received went from 6000 to 24 000 annually after going online. The increased volume of resumés makes it more difficult to separate promising candidates from unqualified ones. Companies get resumés from faraway places such as

Albania and Timbuktu. "People will send their resumé because it's very simple to cut and paste. But, they're in no way qualified for the position," notes one HR director. Another drawback is that not everyone has Internet access or uses the Internet to search for jobs.

The Future of E-Cruiting

In spite of these drawbacks, the future of e-cruiting looks promising. The transfer to e-cruiting will be more attractive as new screening and matching tools are developed to manage the volume of resumés and to weed out inappropriate ones. "There is still a large window of opportunity for companies to leverage the Internet and other technologies as part of their recruiting strategies," notes Gordon Bingham, senior vice-president at Olsten, a strategic staffing firm. But the e-cruiting bandwagon is rolling and picking up steam.[56]

Questions for Critical Thinking

1. How are job seekers and employers using the Internet in the recruiting process?
2. What are the benefits and drawbacks of Internet recruiting?
3. What steps would you take to make your resumé stand out among the thousands that are transmitted electronically? (Hint: Think of content.)

Business PlanPro **EXERCISES**

Managing Human Resources and Employee Relations

Review Appendix C, Your Business Plan (on pages 397–398), to learn how to use Business PlanPro Software so you can complete these exercises.

Think Like a Pro

Objective: By completing these exercises you will become acquainted with the sections of a business plan that address staffing the enterprise and managing employees. You will use the sample business plan for Sagebrush Sam's (listed as Restaurant-Steak Buffet in the Sample Plan Browser) in this exercise.

1. What do the mission statement and keys to success sections say about Sagebrush Sam's approach to employee relations? Why are good relations with employees so important to the success of this type of business?
2. What workforce challenges is Sagebrush Sam's likely to encounter as it grows?
3. What are the company's estimates for manager and employee compensation, and how do these estimates change over the years covered by the plan?
4. According to the business plan, Sagebrush Sam's will need a director of store operations when it has more than five units. How might the company recruit a manager with the appropriate experience and background for this position?

Create Your Own Business Plan

The success of your business depends on hiring, training, and motivating the right employees. Answer the following questions as you continue to develop your own business plan. How many employees will your business require? Of these, how many will be managers? How will you motivate your staff? Will you pay them a salary or a commission? Will you offer alternative work arrangements? If so, which ones? Will you use part-time and temporary employees? Will you provide your employees with benefits? Which ones?

Chapter 11
Developing Product and Pricing Strategies

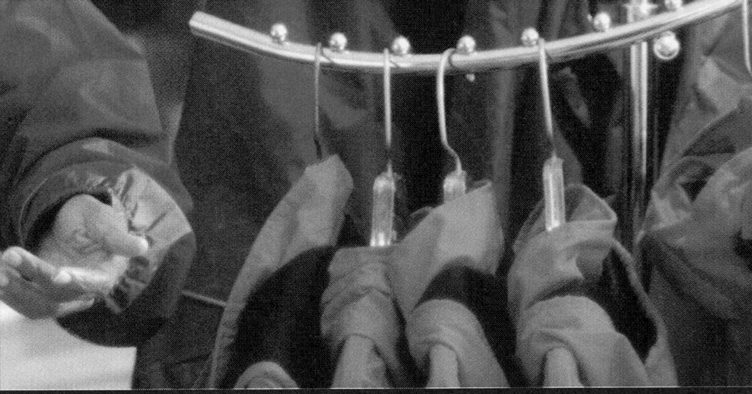

LEARNING OBJECTIVES

After studying this chapter, you will be able to

1. Explain what marketing is and describe the four utilities created by marketing
2. Explain why and how companies learn about their customers
3. Outline the three steps in the strategic marketing planning process
4. Define market segmentation and cite six factors used to identify segments
5. Highlight the four stages in the life cycle of a product and the marketing focus of each stage
6. Discuss the functions of packaging and labelling
7. Identify four ways of expanding a product line and discuss two risks that product line extensions pose
8. List seven factors that influence pricing decisions and cite five common pricing methods

Behind the SCENES

Flying High with Adobe's Acrobat

Adobe's Acrobat Reader is only a small part of a dynamic software package.

www.adobe.com

At a time when the World Wide Web, graphical Internet browsers, and e-mail were still works in progress, Adobe Systems Incorporated, a computer software company, was on the forefront of a technological breakthrough. Its Acrobat software program allowed a document created on one computer to be opened, read, annotated, saved, and printed by another computer—even if that computer used an entirely different operating system.

The key to Adobe's new product was its cross-platform Portable Document Format, or PDF. This format allows documents to retain their original layout, formatting, and design elements—such as typefaces, fonts, pictures, and so on—regardless of the computer's operating system. By contrast, Microsoft Word documents created and opened on different operating systems frequently have garbled fonts and design elements. Even worse, Word files can be easily transformed by an accidental keystroke or two. Adobe Acrobat, however, prevents such user corruption by separating the software into two components—one to create documents in PDF format and a Reader to view the PDF documents. Because computer users needed only the Reader to view newsletters, reports, manuals, and other formatted files, Acrobat became the ideal software for sharing documents over the Internet. Heralded as the "Most Significant Technology" at the computer-industry Comdex trade show, the software promised to change the way companies communicate.

But in spite of its potential, the product got off to a slow start. For one thing, the concept of electronic documents wasn't a high priority for most businesses in the early 1990s. For another, many companies were struggling to get existing—and widely disparate—computer networks to talk to each other. Thus, the idea of turning vast paper files into documents that could be shared electronically seemed, if not frivolous, at least premature. Moreover, publishers of electronic material had no way of knowing whether their target audiences would own a copy of the Acrobat Reader or would be willing to pay $50 for the software just to view electronic documents.

Adobe's software product faced many hurdles. Founded in 1982, Adobe Systems had relied mainly on trade shows and word-of-mouth in the graphic design community to promote its software programs. But now Acrobat needed a different marketing strategy—one that would tout its many benefits and capture the lion's share of the market before competitors caught on. If you were a member of Adobe's management team at that time, what marketing strategies would you develop to turn Acrobat's promise into profits?[1]

WHAT IS MARKETING?

L.O. 1

Even though you are just beginning a formal classroom study of business, you probably already know quite a bit about marketing. Companies like Adobe have been trying to sell you products for years, and you've learned something about their techniques—contests, advertisements, fancy displays of merchandise, price markdowns, and product giveaways, to name but a few. Molson has a tremendous variety of approaches to garner attention. These range from its interactive website to the "House of Blues" concert series to its sponsorship of the CFL and five of its teams: Saskatchewan Roughriders, Edmonton Eskimos, Calgary Stampeders, Ottawa Renegades, and Montreal Allouettes. However, marketing involves much more than a fancy display of merchandise, a clever commercial, or a special contest. In fact, a lot of planning and execution are needed to develop a new product, set its price, get it into stores, and convince people to buy it.

Think about all the decisions you would have to make if you worked at Adobe Systems, for example. How many software packages would you need to sell in order to be profitable? Which types of customers would purchase your software products? How would you attract new customers? How would you price and promote the software? What would you do if another software company offered an equally attractive product at a lower price? These are just a few of the many marketing decisions that all companies make in order to be successful.

marketing
Process of planning and executing the conception, pricing, promotion, and distribution of ideas, goods, and services to create and maintain relationships that satisfy individual and organizational objectives

customer service
Efforts a company makes to satisfy its customers to help them realize the greatest possible value from the products they are purchasing

The American Marketing Association (AMA) defines **marketing** as planning and executing the conception, pricing, promotion, and distribution of ideas, goods, and services to create exchanges that satisfy individual and organizational objectives.[2] With respect to products, marketing involves all decisions related to determining a product's characteristics, price, production specifications, market-entry date, distribution, promotion, and sales. With respect to customers, marketing involves understanding customers' needs and their buying behaviour, creating consumer awareness, providing **customer service**—which is everything a company does to satisfy its customers—and maintaining relationships with customers long after the sales transaction is complete (see Exhibit 11.1).

Most people, of course, think of marketing in connection with selling tangible goods for a profit (the term *product* refers to any "bundle of value" that can be exchanged in a marketing transaction). But marketing applies to services, non-profit organizations, peo-

Exhibit 11.1 What Is Marketing?

Each of the core marketing concepts—needs, wants, demands, products, services, value, satisfactions, quality, exchanges, transactions, relationships, and markets—builds on the ones before it.

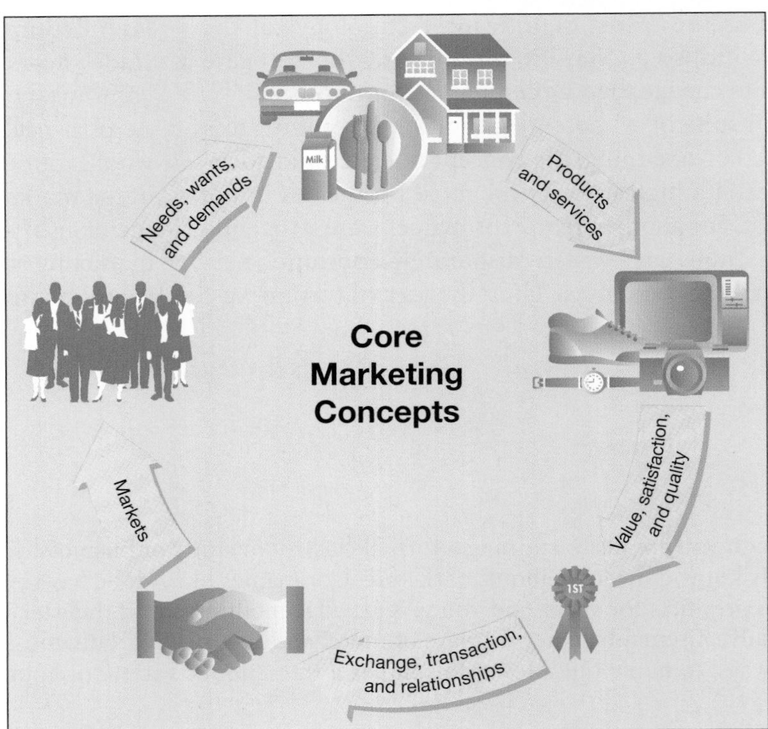

ple, places, and causes, too. Politicians always market themselves. In the 2004 federal election campaign the Liberal party downplayed the party name in favour of putting Paul Martin in the forefront. Since the Liberal party's brand equity had been hurt by the sponsorship scandal, the standard promotional cry, Vote Liberal, was replaced by billboards encouraging Canadians to vote for the "Martin team" or "equipe Martin." Martin's party won a very slim victory as a minority government. It was immediately put under pressure and soon was on life support when Martin's name became more closely linked to the scandal and new elections were demanded. Places (such as Paris, Poland, or a local municipality) that want to attract residents, tourists, and business investment also promote their respective strengths. **Place marketing** describes efforts to market geographical areas ranging from neighbourhoods to entire countries. **Cause-related marketing** promotes a cause or a social issue—such as physical fitness, cancer awareness, recycling, or highway safety. Special Olympics Canada urges support by reminding us of the athlete's oath: "Let me win, but if I cannot win, let me be brave in the attempt." The aim is to inspire financial support, volunteers, and fans to this very worthy cause.[3]

place marketing
Marketing efforts to attract people and organizations to a particular geographical area

cause-related marketing
Identification and marketing of a social issue, cause, or idea to selected target markets

The Role of Marketing in Society

Take another look at the AMA definition of marketing. Notice that marketing involves an exchange between two parties—the buyer and the selling organization—both of whom must obtain satisfaction from the transaction. This definition suggests that marketing plays an important role in society by helping people satisfy their needs and wants and by helping organizations determine what to produce.

Needs and Wants

To survive, people need food, water, air, shelter, and clothing. A **need** represents a difference between your actual state and your ideal state. You're hungry and you don't want to be hungry; you need to eat. Needs create the motivation to buy products and are therefore at the core of any discussion of marketing.

Your **wants** are based on your needs but are more specific. Producers do not create needs, but they do shape your wants by exposing you to alternatives. For instance, when you need some food, you may want a Snickers bar or an orange. A fundamental goal of marketing is to direct the customer's basic need for various products into the desire to purchase specific brands. Al Ries and Jack Trout, co-authors of *The 22 Immutable Laws of Marketing*, note that customers' wants are directed by changing people's perception of products.[4] After all, what's the real difference between Scott and Bounty paper towels? Is one actually more absorbent than the other, or do you only perceive it that way?

need
Difference between a person's actual state and his or her ideal state; provides the basic motivation to make a purchase

wants
Objects that are desirable in light of a person's experiences, culture, personality and perspective

exchange process
Act of obtaining a desired object from another party by offering something of value in return

transaction
Exchange between parties

Exchanges and Transactions

When you participate in the **exchange process**, you trade something of value (usually money) for something else of value, whether you're buying an airline ticket, a car, or a college education. When you make a purchase, you cast your vote for that item and encourage the producer of that item to make more of it. In this way, supply and demand are balanced, and society obtains the goods and services that are most satisfying.

When the exchange actually occurs, it takes the form of a **transaction**. Party A gives Party B $1.29 and gets a medium Coke in return. A trade of values takes place. Most transactions in today's society involve money, but money is not necessarily required. For example, when you were a child, you may have traded your peanut butter sandwich for a friend's bologna and cheese in a barter transaction that involved no money.

Special Olympics Canada advertisements provide an effective example of cause-related marketing. They are not selling a shiny new product but rather are looking to gain attention and inspire support for the games and the organization.

The Four Utilities

utility
Power of a good or service to satisfy a human need

form utility
Consumer value created by converting raw materials and other inputs into finished goods and services

time utility
Consumer value added by making a product available at a convenient time

place utility
Consumer value added by making a product available in a convenient location

possession utility
Consumer value created when someone takes ownership of a product

marketing concept
Approach to business management that stresses customer needs and wants, seeks long-term profitability, and integrates marketing with other functional units within the organization

To encourage the exchange process, marketers enhance the appeal of their products and services by adding **utility**, something of value to customers (see Exhibit 11.2). When organizations change raw materials into finished goods, they are creating **form utility** desired by consumers. For example, when Nokia combines plastic, computer chips, and other materials to make digital phones, the company is providing form utility. In other cases, marketers try to make their products available when and where customers want to buy them, creating **time utility** and **place utility**. Overnight couriers such as Purolator create time utility, whereas ATM machines in shopping malls create place utility. The final form of utility is **possession utility**—the satisfaction that buyers get when they actually possess a product, both legally and physically. The Royal Bank, for example, creates possession utility by offering loans that allow people to buy homes they could otherwise not afford.

The Marketing Concept

The underlying philosophy that guides all marketing decisions and activities is known as the **marketing concept**, the idea that companies should stress customers' needs and wants while seeking long-term profitability and coordinating their own marketing efforts to achieve the company's long-term goals. The Bay, Costco, Telus, Hyatt Hotels, and hundreds of well-known successful companies have adopted the marketing concept. These customer-focused companies modify their marketing strategies and product offerings to satisfy customers' changing needs and wants.

For example, at the Bay, sales associates can enhance their knowledge and improve their customer service through workshops, online learning, and the "HBC University." Employees can log onto the Online Personal Approach to Learning (OPAL) and access more than 200 online courses that range from health and safety issues to product knowledge. Additionally, OPAL keeps track of courses that associates have taken. "HBC University provides associates with a centralized resource and support for learning and development. All HBC associates become students of HBC's University."[5]

L.O. 2

Understanding Today's Customers

To implement the marketing concept, companies must have good information about what customers want. They must "know and understand the customer so well that the product or service fits him and sells itself," says management consultant and author Peter Drucker.[6] This is a challenge because today's customers are not very easy to understand. Customers are sophisticated, price sensitive, and demanding. They live time-compressed lifestyles and have little patience for retailers who do not understand them or will not adapt business practices to meet their needs. They expect products and services to be delivered faster and more conveniently. They have no qualms about switching to competitors if their demands are not met. Armed with facts, prices, data,

Exhibit 11.2 Examples of the Four Utilities

The utility of a good or service has four aspects, each of which enhances the product's value to the consumer.

UTILITY	EXAMPLE
Form utility	Gummy Bears appeal to youngsters because of their shapes and colours.
Time utility	LensCrafters has captured a big chunk of the market for eyeglasses by providing on-the-spot, one-hour service.
Place utility	Danier Leather offers convenient home delivery of the latest leather fashion apparel and accessories.
Possession utility	RealNetworks, producer of software for listening to music from the Internet, allows customers to download and install its programs directly from the company's website.

product reviews, advice, how-to guides, and databases, today's customers are informed, which places them in an unprecedented position of control.[7]

Home buyers, for example, use real estate websites to gain more control of the house-hunting process. Home descriptions, room dimensions, photographs, virtual tours, property tax information, and school and town information are all provided on websites—making it possible for customers to do their research online before setting foot in the real estate office.[8] The same is true for car buyers. They walk into car dealerships reading spec sheets obtained from websites that disclose the dealer's invoice cost, dealer rebates, and other purchasing incentives.[9] From travel agents to supermarkets to auto dealers to furniture stores to realtors—today's customers are indeed calling the shots, which is why it becomes increasingly important for businesses to understand how buyers think and what buyers want.

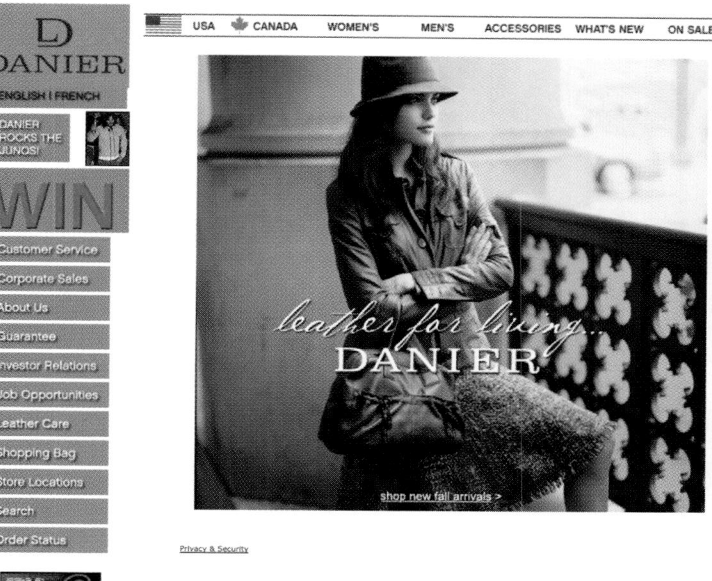

Danier offers its customers the convenience of purchasing its products from home. To facilitate the process, it has created interactive features on its site that allow customers to chat with customer service, get behind-the-scenes footage as well as an option to view a store live.

The Buyers' Decision Process Suppose you want to buy a car. Do you rush to the dealer and buy the first car you see? Of course not. Like most buyers, you go through a decision process, outlined in Exhibit 11.3, that begins with identifying a problem, which in this case is the need for a car. Your next step is to look for a solution to your problem. Possibilities occur to you on the basis of your experience (perhaps you recently drove a certain make or model) and on your exposure to marketing messages. If none of the obvious solutions seems satisfying, you gather additional information. The more complex the problem, the more information you are likely to seek from friends or relatives, magazines, salespeople, store displays, and sales literature.

Once you have all the information in hand, you are ready to make a choice. You may select one of the alternatives, such as a new Chevy Blazer or a used Ford Explorer. You might even postpone the decision or decide against making any purchase at all, depending on the magnitude of your desire, the outside pressure to buy, and your financial resources. If you decide to buy, you will evaluate the wisdom of your choice. If the item you bought is satisfying, you might buy the same product again under similar circumstances, thus developing a loyalty to the brand. If it is not satisfying, you will probably not repeat the purchase.

If the purchase was a major one, you will sometimes suffer from **cognitive dissonance**, commonly known as buyer's remorse. You will think about all the alternatives you rejected and wonder whether one of them might have been a better choice. At this stage, you're likely to seek reassurance that you have done the right thing. Realizing this tendency, many marketers try to reinforce their sales with guarantees, phone calls to check on the customer's satisfaction, user hotlines, follow-up letters, and so on. Such efforts help pave the way for repeat business.

cognitive dissonance
Anxiety following a purchase that prompts buyers to seek reassurance about the purchase; commonly known as buyer's remorse

Exhibit 11.3 The Consumer Decision Process

Consumers go through a decision-making process that can include up to five steps.

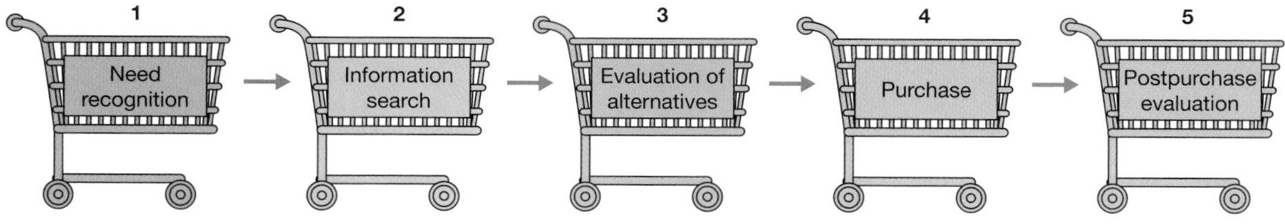

Saturn employees greet this new car buyer. This is all part of Saturn's personal touch. The purpose is to celebrate the important purchase decision and to introduce the client to the staff that will service the car in the future.

Saturn uses a "No-Hassle, No-Haggle" policy to help relieve the stress of negotiating for a new car. They also offer a 30-day return policy to their customers. Of course they do everything in their power to avoid such returns. The extended customer service is evident the moment the client picks up the car; customers are greeted by the staff and sent off to music and a drumbeat as they unveil their car and ride off. Phone calls to ensure satisfaction are also part of the Saturn touch.[10]

Factors That Influence the Buyer's Decision Process Throughout the buying process, various factors may influence a buyer's purchase decision. An awareness of the following factors and consumer preferences enables companies to appeal to the group most likely to respond to its products and services:

- *Culture.* The cultures and subcultures that people belong to shape their values, attitudes, and beliefs and influence the way they respond to the world around them. Understanding culture is therefore an increasingly important step in international business and in marketing to diverse populations within a country. Specifically the Canadian marketer must pay careful attention to the French-Canadian population across the nation while paying particular attention to Quebec and New Brunswick. Additionally, certain ethnic groups have a powerful identity that marketers may wish to access. Cleve Lu, founder of Era Integrated Marketing, helps AIM Trimark and other major companies tailor and adapt messages geared toward the unique Chinese-Canadian culture.[11]
- *Social class.* In addition to being members of a particular culture, people also belong to a certain social class—be it upper, middle, lower, or somewhere in between. In general, members of various classes pursue different activities, buy different goods, shop in different places, and react to different media.
- *Reference groups.* A reference group consists of people who have a good deal in common: family members, friends, co-workers, sports enthusiasts, music lovers, computer buffs. Individuals are members of many such reference groups, and they use the opinions of the appropriate group as a benchmark when they buy certain types of goods or services.
- *Self-image.* The tendency to believe that "you are what you buy" is especially prevalent among young people. Marketers capitalize on people's need to express their identity through their purchases by emphasizing the image value of goods and services. That's why professional athletes and musicians frequently appear as product endorsers—so that consumers will incorporate part of these celebrities' public image into their own self-image. Jarome Iginla, captain of the Calgary Flames, is a hockey hero who celebrates his birthday on Canada Day. He is becoming an increasingly appealing celebrity for endorsement contracts. His inspired run to the Stanley Cup finals in the 2004 playoffs, as well as his notable exploits in the Olympics and World Cup, has increased his equity as a promotional spokesperson.[12]
- *Situational factors.* These factors include events or circumstances in people's lives that are more circumstantial but that can influence buying patterns. Such factors might include having a coupon, being in a hurry, celebrating a holiday, being in a bad mood, and so on.

Marketing Research and Customer Databases

marketing research
The collection and analysis of information for making marketing decisions

Many companies obtain information about customers' changing needs by engaging in **marketing research**—the process of gathering and analyzing information about customers, markets, and related marketing issues. Popular marketing research tools include personal observations, customer surveys and questionnaires, experiments, telephone or personal interviews, studies of small samples of the consumer population, and focused interviews of 6 to 10 people (called *focus groups*).

Another way to learn about customer preferences is to gather and analyze all kinds of customer-related data. **Database marketing** is the process of recording and analyzing customer interactions, preferences, and buying behaviour for the purpose of contacting and transacting with customers (see the box entitled "Your Right to Privacy versus the Marketing Databases"). Companies gather information about customers by engaging in two-way, ongoing dialogues with customers through e-mail, web pages, fax machines, and toll-free telephone numbers.

Jarome Iginla's exploits on the ice, in the NHL and in international competitions, make him an attractive candidate to endorse products in the Canadian market.

Capital One, for example, has become a leading North American credit card company by collecting extensive records on millions of consumers and using that information to plan its marketing strategies. As Capital One's CEO Richard Fairbank knows, every credit card transaction, Internet sale, and frequent-buyer purchase leaves behind a trail of information that retailers can use to their advantage. Frequent-shopper card programs, good for a wealth of discounts at checkout, have convinced customers to share some of the most intimate details about their lives. For instance, customer grocery purchases reveal preferences for everything from hygiene products to junk food to magazines.

Once companies gather data about customers, they enter this information into customer databases to remember customer preferences and priorities and to make the customer's experience more personal and enjoyable. Allstate, for example, uses database marketing to collect huge amounts of data about applicants (credit reports, driving records, claims histories) in order to quickly price a customer's insurance policy.[13] Ritz Carlton records all customer requests, comments, and complaints in a worldwide database that now contains individual profiles of more than 500 000 guests. By accessing these profiles, employees at any Ritz Carlton hotel can accommodate the individual tastes of its customers from anywhere in the world.[14]

database marketing
Process of building, maintaining, and using customer databases for the purpose of contacting customers and transacting business

Building Relationships with Customers

Another way that companies remain customer-focused is by building long-term, satisfying relationships with key parties—customers, suppliers, distributors—to retain their long-term business. This practice, commonly referred to as **relationship marketing**, focuses on establishing a learning relationship with each customer. Thus, the relationship between customer and company does not end with the sales transaction; instead, it is viewed as an ongoing process.[15] Moreover, the relationship gets smarter with each customer interaction—you learn something about your customer and you change your product or service to meet the customer's needs.

relationship marketing
A focus on developing and maintaining long-term relationships with customers, suppliers, and distributors for mutual benefit

Maintaining long-term relationships with customers has many benefits:[16]

- Acquiring a new customer can cost up to five times as much as keeping an existing one.
- Long-term customers buy more, take less of a company's time, bring in new customers, and are less price-sensitive.
- Satisfied customers are the best advertisement for a product.
- Firms perceived to offer superior customer service find that they can charge as much as 10 percent more than their competitors.
- Research shows that dissatisfied customers may tell as many as 20 other people about their bad experiences.

But keeping customers satisfied in an environment where they have more product information available than ever before is a challenge. So some companies try to gain a

Your Right to Privacy versus the Marketing Databases

Are all the details of your personal life really private? Consider this: Your bank knows your account balance, your credit history, and your Social Insurance Number. Government agencies know how much money you made last year, the kind of car you own, and how many parking tickets you've had. Credit agencies know to whom you owe money, and how much you owe. This list goes on and on, from video stores to insurance companies. Every time you register online, or even click on a website, all sorts of data are being collected about you. By depositing "cookies" on your hard drive, web marketers can follow your path and track the sites you visit.

Of course, there's nothing unethical about collecting data or maintaining a database. The ethical problems arise when marketers buy, borrow, rent, or exchange information, usually without your knowledge or permission. Who should have the right to see your records? The answer depends on where you live. In Europe, strict privacy regulations prevent companies from using data about individuals without asking permission and explaining how the data will be used. But in Canada and most other countries, marketers can easily buy information about who you are, where you live, how much you earn, and what you buy—for as little as a nickel.

Many web marketers post privacy policies showing how they use personal data. Since January 1, 2001, the Personal Information Protection and Electronic Documents Act has applied to federal businesses. "It gives the individual control over personal information by requiring organizations to obtain consent to collect, use or disclose information." The law indicates the obligations of organizations, the rules of conduct, as well as the rights of individuals. If a person feels as though their rights have been violated and they are unable to resolve them directly they can submit a formal complaint to the Office of the Privacy Commissioner of Canada (1-800-282-1376).[17]

As you can imagine, the consumer's right to privacy is an ongoing debate—one that has intensified and taken on new dimensions since the September 11, 2001, terrorist attacks. Privacy advocates argue that people should have the right to be left alone, whereas marketers argue that they should have the right to freedom of speech—the right to inform customers about their offers. Thus, the ultimate dilemma: Do a marketer's needs and freedom of speech outweigh the consumer's right to privacy? What's your opinion?

Questions for Critical Thinking

1. Should a marketer selling long-distance telephone service be allowed to see your telephone records without your knowledge or permission?
2. Should web marketers be required to conspicuously post their privacy policies and ask consent before collecting and using visitors' personal data?

competitive edge by differentiating the customer experience—making it more personal and compelling.

One-to-one marketing involves individualizing a firm's marketing efforts for a single customer to accommodate the specific customer's needs. Capital One, for instance, attracts millions of customers by presenting itself a little differently to each customer. The company offers more than 7000 variations of its credit cards in the U.S. and up to 20 000 variations of other products, from phone cards to insurance.[18] The four key steps to putting an effective one-to-one marketing program in place are (1) identifying your customers, (2) differentiating among them, (3) interacting with them, and (4) customizing your product or service to fit each individual customer's needs.[19]

L.O. 3

PLANNING YOUR MARKETING STRATEGIES

By now you can see why successful marketing rarely happens without carefully analyzing and understanding your customers. Once you have learned about your customers, you're ready to begin planning your marketing strategies. *Strategic marketing planning* is a process that involves three steps: (1) examining your current marketing situation, (2) assessing your opportunities and setting your objectives, and (3) developing a marketing strategy to reach those objectives (see Exhibit 11.4). The purpose of strategic marketing planning is to help you identify and create a competitive advantage, something that sets you apart from your rivals and makes your product more appealing to customers.[20] Most companies record the results of

Exhibit 11.4 The Strategic Marketing Planning Process

Strategic marketing planning comprises three steps: (1) examining your current marketing situation, (2) assessing your opportunities and setting objectives, and (3) developing your marketing strategy.

their planning efforts in a document called the *marketing plan*. Here's a closer look at the three steps in the process.

Step 1: Examining Your Current Marketing Situation

Examining your current marketing situation includes reviewing your past performance (how well each product is doing in each market where you sell it), evaluating your competition, examining your internal strengths and weaknesses, and analyzing the external environment.

Reviewing Performance

Unless you're starting a new business, your company has a history of marketing performance. Maybe sales have slowed in the past year; maybe you've had to cut prices so much that you're barely earning a profit; or maybe sales are going quite well and you have money to invest in new marketing activities. Reviewing where you are and how you got there is critical, because you will want to repeat your successes and learn from your past mistakes.

Evaluating Competition

In addition to reviewing past performance, you must also evaluate your competition. If you own a Burger King franchise, for example, you need to watch what McDonald's, Harvey's and Wendy's are doing. You also have to keep an eye on Swiss Chalet, Subway, Pizza Hut, and other restaurants in addition to paying attention to any number of ways your customers might satisfy their hunger—including fixing a sandwich at home.

Furthermore, you need to watch the horizon for competitors that do not yet exist, such as the next big food trend. The recent "carb craze," created by low-carb diets like the Atkins Diet, has had a huge impact on consumer eating habits. Krispy Kreme has been severely hurt by the attention and the conscious efforts of individuals to reduce their carb intake.[21] Other firms like Subway embraced the opportunity and reached out to this large group of dieters by offering Atkins-friendly wraps and Atkins-friendly fresh salads.[22]

Subway jumped onto the "carb craze" and offered its clients products that met their needs and were endorsed by the Atkins name.

Examining Internal Strengths and Weaknesses

Successful marketers try to identify both sources of competitive advantage and areas that need improvement. They look at such things as management, financial resources, production capabilities, distribution networks, managerial expertise, and promotional capabilities. This step is important because you can't develop a successful marketing strategy if you don't know your strengths as well as your limitations. On the basis of your internal analysis, you will be able to decide whether your business should (1) limit itself to those opportunities for which it possesses the required strengths or (2) challenge itself to reach higher goals by acquiring and developing new strengths.

Understanding your strengths and weaknesses is especially important when evaluating the merits of global expansion. Selling products overseas requires not only managerial expertise and financial resources but also the ability to adjust your operation to different cultures, customs, legal requirements, and product specifications. Even selling on the Internet requires technological expertise and commitment as well as a thorough understanding of customer buying behaviour.

Analyzing the External Environment

Marketers must also analyze a number of external environment factors when planning their marketing strategies. These factors include:

- *Economic conditions.* The Bank of Canada's policies cannot be controlled by an organization. Marketers are greatly affected by trends in interest rates, inflation, unemployment, personal income, and savings rates. In tough times, consumers put off buying expensive items such as major appliances, cars, and homes. They cut back on travel, entertainment, and luxury goods. When the economy is good, consumers open their wallets and satisfy their demand for higher-priced goods and services.
- *Natural environment.* Changes in the natural environment can affect marketers, both positively and negatively. Interruptions in the supply of raw materials can upset even the most carefully conceived marketing plans. Floods, droughts, and cold weather can affect the price and availability of many products as well as the behaviour of target customers. For example, ski resorts are highly dependent on the weather. Extreme cold spells or a very mild winter can have a huge negative impact. The result can be devastating for a small ski operator; however, even major companies like Vancouver, British Columbia's Intrawest are not immune to the uncontrollable impact of Mother Nature. Each individual mountain has to face these challenges. In Intrawest's case the effects are lessened by the geographic dispersion of their locations. They have resorts spread out across North America; from Mt. Tremblant in Quebec to Whistler/Blackcomb in British Columbia to U.S. locations like Copper Mountain in Colorado.[23]
- *Social and cultural trends.* Planners also study the social and cultural environment to determine shifts in consumer values. If social trends are running against a product, the producer might need more advertising to educate consumers about the product's benefits or alter the product to make it more appealing. For example, when beef consumption fell out of favour, marketers used ads to educate consumers on the benefits of including more beef in their diet.
- *Laws and regulations.* Like every other function in business today, marketing is controlled by laws at the local, provincial, federal, and international levels. From product design to pricing to advertising, virtually every task you'll encounter in marketing is affected in some way by laws and regulations. For example, the Food and Drug Regulations force marketers to put standardized nutritional labels on food products. Although these regulations cost manufacturers millions of dollars, they have a huge positive impact for food-testing laboratories.[24]
- *Technology.* When technology changes, so must your marketing approaches. Look at *Encyclopaedia Britannica.* It didn't take long for new computer technology to almost wreck this 230-year-old publishing company. In 1990 the company reported record sales of US$650 million. But then the bottom fell out. With a set of books costing more than US$1500, weighing 53 kilograms, and taking 1.5 metres of shelf space, consumers soon opted for affordable CD-ROM and Internet reference works offered by competitors. Scrambling to survive, *Britannica* tried a number of electronic options. Today,

Encyclopaedia Britannica delivers information via the Internet and CD-ROMs, but only time will tell whether the company can thrive in the digital age.[25]

Marketers must not only keep on top of today's external environment, they must also think about tomorrow's changes. Car manufacturers, for example, are responding to increasing consumer and governmental pressure to clean up the environment by announcing plans to produce more hybrid gas-and-electric vehicles.

Ski resort operators have a tenuous relationship with Mother Nature, since uncontrollable weather patterns often reduce potential profits by driving skiers and snowboarders away.

Step 2: Assessing Your Opportunities and Setting Your Objectives

Once you've examined your current marketing situation, you're ready to assess your marketing opportunities and set your objectives. Successful companies are always on the lookout for new marketing opportunities, which can be classified into four options: selling more of your existing products in current markets (market penetration), creating new products for your current markets (new product development), selling your existing products in new markets (geographic expansion), and creating new products for new markets (diversification).[26] These four options are listed in order of increasing risk; trying new products in unfamiliar markets is usually the riskiest choice of all.

With opportunities in mind, you are ready to set your marketing objectives. A common marketing objective is to achieve a certain level of **market share**, which is a firm's portion of the total sales within a market. Objectives must be specific and measurable. Establishing a goal to "increase sales in the future" is not a good objective; it doesn't say by how much or by what date. On the other hand, a goal to "increase sales 25 percent by the end of next year" provides a clear target and a reference against which progress can be measured. Objectives should also be challenging enough to be motivating. Whatever objectives you set, be sure all employees know and understand what the organization wants to accomplish. Every Ritz Carlton employee, for example, attends a daily 15-minute meeting in which managers repeat the hotel chain's business goals and commitment to customer service.[27]

market share
A firm's portion of the total sales in a market

Step 3: Developing Your Marketing Strategy

Using your current marketing situation and your objectives as your guide, you're ready to move to the third step. This is where you develop your **marketing strategy**, which consists of dividing your market into *segments* and *niches,* choosing your *target markets* and the *position* you'd like to establish in those markets, and then developing a *marketing mix* to help you get there.

marketing strategy
Overall plan for marketing a product

Dividing Markets into Segments

L.O. 4

A **market** contains all the customers or businesses that might be interested in a product and can pay for it. Most companies subdivide the market in an economical and feasible manner by identifying *market segments,* or homogeneous groups of customers within a market that are significantly different from each other. This process is called **market segmentation**; its objective is to group customers with similar characteristics, behaviour, and needs. Each of these market segments can then be targeted by offering products that are priced, distributed, and promoted differently.

market
People or businesses that need or want a product and have the money to buy it

market segmentation
Division of total market into smaller, relatively homogeneous groups

The goal of market segmentation is to understand why certain customers buy what they buy so that you can sell them your products and services by targeting their needs. Here are six factors marketers frequently use to identify market segments:

- *Demographics.* When you segment a market using **demographics**, the statistical analysis of a population, you subdivide your customers according to characteristics such as age, gender, income, race, occupation, and ethnic group. Be aware, however,

demographics
Study of statistical characteristics of a population

Questionable Marketing Tactics on Campus

Alarmed by how quickly university and college students can bury themselves in debt and fed up with aggressive sales tactics, a growing number of universities are banning or restricting credit card marketing on campus.

Administrators complain that students are bombarded with credit card offers from the moment they step on campus. Marketers have shown up on campuses unannounced and without permission to hawk cards; they stuff applications into bags at campus bookstores and entice students to apply for cards and take on debt with free T-shirts, music CDs, and promises of an easy way to pay for spring break vacations. Some yell at students to get their attention and follow them through hallways to make a sale; they even get student organizations to work for them so that friends pressure friends.

Students are, of course, a prized target for the credit card industry because consumers tend to be loyal to their first credit card. Even though students often have little or no income, they are not considered high-risk borrowers because parents generally bail them out if they get into trouble. As a result, roughly 63 percent of full-time students now have a credit card in their own name. But only about half of those students pay their bills in full each month, and the number of students who usually make just the minimum payment is rising.

While some schools have banned credit card marketers from campus to protect students from their own potentially destructive credit practices, many students say it's unfair for schools to do so. After all, marketers don't give up. They just move across the street or to other locations frequented by students.

Questions for Critical Thinking

1. Should credit card companies be prohibited from soliciting on campuses? Why or why not?
2. Why do credit card companies target students even though they have little or no income?

that according to recent studies, demographic variables are poor predictors of behaviour. For instance, not all Canadian men aged 35 to 44 making $100 000 per year buy a Mercedes. In fact, some don't even buy a luxury car, and those who do may not purchase such cars for the same reasons.[28]

geographic segmentation Categorization of customers according to their geographical location

- *Geographics.* When differences in buying behaviour are influenced by where people live, it makes sense to use **geographic segmentation**. Segmenting the market into different geographical units such as regions, cities, towns, or neighbourhoods allows companies to customize and sell products that meet the needs of specific markets. For instance, car rental agencies stock more four-wheel-drive vehicles in mountainous regions. The Canadian market can be divided into various regions: Maritimes, Quebec, Ontario, Prairies, and Western Canada.[29]

psychographics Classification of customers on the basis of their psychological makeup

- *Psychographics.* Whereas demographic segmentation is the study of people from the outside, **psychographics** is the analysis of people from the inside, focusing on their psychological makeup, including attitudes, interests, opinions, and lifestyles. Psychographic analysis focuses on why people behave the way they do by examining such issues as brand preferences, media preferences, reading habits, values, and self-concept. It attempts to understand consumer habits by looking beyond simple statistical data profiles.

geodemographics Method of combining geographical data with demographic data to develop profiles of neighbourhood segments

- *Geodemographics.* Dividing markets into distinct neighbourhoods by combining geographical and demographic data is the goal of **geodemographics**. "Systems like PRIZM, developed by Claritas Corporation, and Compusearch's Psyte neighbourhood classification system can link census data with market potential at the level of postal codes and neighbourhoods."[30]

behavioural segmentation Categorization of customers according to their relationship with products or response to product characteristics

- *Behaviour.* Markets can also be segmented according to customers' knowledge of, attitude toward, use of, or response to products or product characteristics. This approach is known as **behavioural segmentation**. Many web-based companies ask first-time visitors to fill out a personal profile so they can gear product recommendations and even display customized web pages that appeal to certain behavioural segments.

- *Usage.* All customers are not created equal. That may sound like a controversial statement but in terms of marketing it is vital that firms identify and target individuals that are heavy users. Rewards, special financing, and focused promotions are common. It is estimated that for most firms 80 percent of sales come from 20 percent of the consumers (the 80/20 rule).[31] This also helps explain why it seems like every second commercial during a broadcast of *Hockey Night in Canada* is for beer whereas during a CBC drama airing at the same time on another night this is not the case.

An increasingly popular way to segment e-commerce customers is by Internet usage patterns. Companies are finding that categorizing web users by their session length, time per page, category concentration, and so on helps define the types of marketing that are best suited for each user type.[32]

When you segment your market, you end up with several customer groups, each representing a potentially productive focus for marketing efforts. However, keep in mind that marketers also segment customers using multiple variables in order to produce more narrowly defined target groups known as *micro-segments* or *niches.*[33]

Choosing Your Target Markets

Once you have segmented your market, the next step is to find appropriate target segments or **target markets** to focus your efforts on. Deciding exactly which segment to target—and when—is not an easy task. Sometimes the answer will be obvious, such as when you lack the necessary technological skills or financial power to enter a particular market segment. At other times, you'll have the resources to compete in several segments but not enough resources to compete in all of them. In general, marketers use a variety of criteria to narrow their focus to a few suitable market segments. These criteria can include size of segment, competition in the segment, sales and profit potential, compatibility with company resources and strengths, costs, growth potential, and risks.[34]

target markets
Specific customer groups or segments to whom a company wants to sell a particular product

Targeting is such a critical part of strategic marketing that missteps can be costly, as Motorola found out. The company stayed focused on the traditional cellphone market segment long after rivals Nokia and Ericsson had expanded into the digital phone segment. By the time Motorola began to work on digital phones, its competitors had grabbed market share and brand loyalty in that fast-growing segment.[35]

Reaching a specific target requires careful strategy and expertise. Even with their tremendous knowledge and resources Bell Mobility decided to team up with the British-based Virgin group in 2005 to launch a wireless no-contract service aimed at the under-25 crowd. Features geared toward this market include simplified e-mail as well as music content from MTV. Virgin made a similar successful deal in the U.S. in 2002 and has managed to sign up 1.75 million subscribers.[36]

Exhibit 11.5 diagrams three popular strategies for reaching target markets. Companies that practise *undifferentiated marketing* (or mass marketing) ignore differences among buyers and offer only one product or product line to satisfy the entire market. This strategy, which concludes that all buyers have similar needs that can be served with the same standardized product, was more popular in the past than it is today. Initially, Henry Ford sold only one car type (the Model T Ford) in one colour (black) to the entire market.

By contrast, companies that manufacture or sell a variety of products to several target customer groups practise *differentiated marketing.* General Motors, for instance, manufactures a car for every personality, and Nike produces a shoe for every athlete. Differentiated marketing is a popular approach, but it requires substantial resources because you have to tailor products, prices, promotional efforts, and distribution arrangements for each customer group.

When company resources are limited, *concentrated (niche) marketing* may be the best marketing strategy. You acknowledge that different market segments exist and choose to target just one. WestJet was created by four Calgary entrepreneurs who saw an opportunity to provide low-fare air travel across western Canada.[37] The biggest advantage of concentrated marketing is that it allows you to focus all your time and resources on a single type of customer. The strategy can be risky, however, because you've staked your com-

Exhibit 11.5 Market-Coverage Strategies

Three alternative market-coverage strategies are undifferentiated marketing, differentiated marketing, and concentrated marketing.

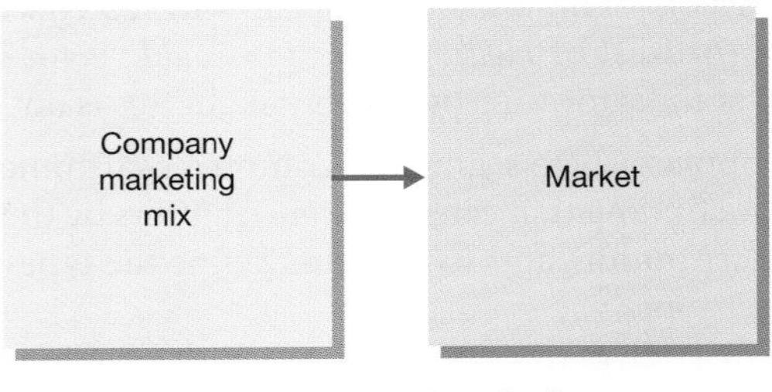

1. Undifferentiated marketing

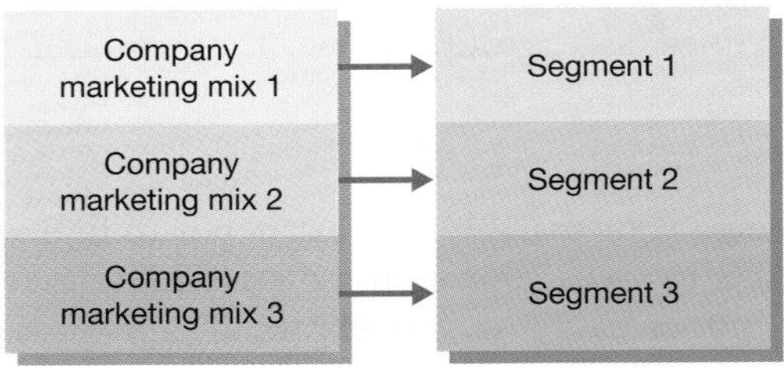

2. Differentiated marketing

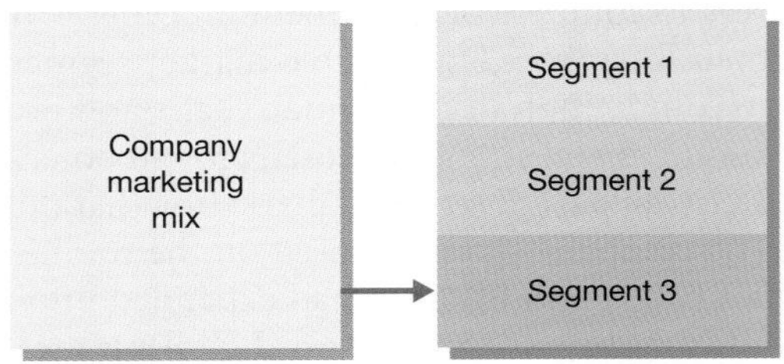

3. Concentrated marketing

pany's fortune on just one segment. For that reason many top firms turn to companies like Youthography, a Toronto-based youth marketing consultancy that provides expertise on people aged 13 to 29. Bell Mobility and the CIBC are among its key accounts.[38]

Positioning Your Product

positioning
Using promotion, product, distribution, and price to differentiate a good or service from those of competitors in the mind of the prospective buyer

Once a company has decided which segments of the market it will enter, it must then decide what position it wants to occupy in those segments. **Positioning** your product is the act of designing your company's offering and image so that it occupies a meaningful and distinct competitive position in your target customers' minds.

Even though consumers position products with or without the help of marketers, marketers do not want to leave their product's position to chance. Instead, they choose positions that will give their products the greatest advantage in selected target markets.[39] They can position their products on specific product features or attributes (such as size, ease of use, style, performance, quality, durability, or design), on the services that accompany the product (such as convenient delivery, lifetime customer support, or installation methods), on the product's image (such as reliability or sophistication), on price (such as low cost or premium), on category leadership (such as the leading online bookseller), and so forth. For example, BMW and Porsche associate their products with performance, Mercedes Benz with luxury, and Volvo with safety. Organizing products and services into categories based on the perceived position helps consumers simplify the buying process. Instead of test-driving all cars, for instance, they may focus on those they perceive to be high-performance vehicles.

Developing the Marketing Mix

After you've segmented your market, selected your target market, and positioned your product, your next task is to develop a marketing mix. A firm's **marketing mix** (often called the *four Ps*) consists of product, price, place (or distribution), and promotion (see Exhibit 11.6).

marketing mix
The four key elements of marketing strategy: product, price, distribution (place), and promotion

Products The most basic marketing mix element is *product,* which covers the product itself plus brand name, design, packaging, services, quality, and warranty. From a marketing standpoint, a **product** is anything offered for the purpose of satisfying a want or a need in a marketing exchange. If you were asked to name three popular products off the top of your head, you might think of Doritos tortilla chips, the Volkswagen Golf, and Gatorade drinks. You might not think of the Ottawa Senators, MarineLand, or *Hockey Night in Canada.* That's because we tend to think of products as *tangible* objects, or things that we can actually touch and possess. Hockey teams, amusement parks, and television programs provide an *intangible* service for our use or enjoyment, not for our ownership; nevertheless, these and other services are products just the same. In fact, broadly defined, products can be persons, places, physical objects, ideas, services, and organizations.

product
Good or service used as the basis of commerce

Pricing **Price**, the amount of money customers pay for the product (including any discounts) is the second major component of a firm's marketing mix. As Adobe Systems knows, developing a product's price is one of the most critical decisions a company must make, because price is the only element in a company's marketing mix that produces revenue—all other elements represent cost. Thus, setting a product's price not only determines the amount of income your company will generate from sales of that product but it can differentiate the product from competition. As you can imagine, determining the right price is not an easy task. If a company charges too much, it will generate fewer sales, as Adobe Systems discovered with its Acrobat product. If it charges too little, it will sacrifice potential profits.

price
The amount of money charged for a product or service

Exhibit 11.6 **Positioning and the Marketing Environment**

When positioning products for target markets, you need to consider the four marketing mix elements plus the external environment.

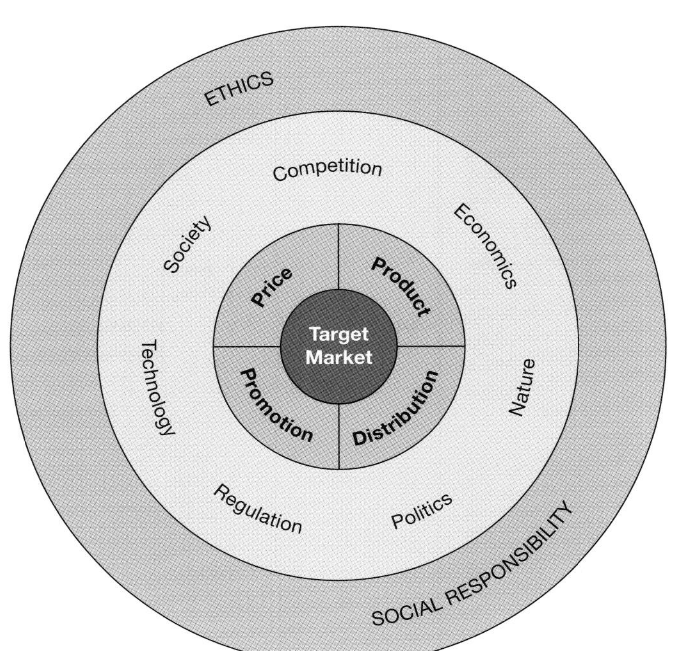

Distribution or Place *Place* (commonly referred to as *distribution*) is the third marketing mix element. It covers the organized network of firms that move goods and services from the producer to the consumer. This network is also known as *marketing channels* or **distribution channels**. A company's channel decisions directly affect all other marketing decisions. For instance, a company's pricing depends on whether it uses mass merchandisers or high-quality specialty stores. A firm's sales force and advertising decisions depend on how much training, motivation, and support the dealers need.[40]

distribution channels
Systems for moving goods and services from producers to customers; also known as marketing channels

promotion
Wide variety of persuasive techniques used by companies to communicate with their target markets and the general public

Promotion **Promotion**, the fourth marketing mix element, includes all activities the firm undertakes to communicate and promote its products to the target market. Among these activities are advertising, personal selling, public relations, and sales promotion. Promotion may take the form of direct, face-to-face communication or indirect communication through such media as television, radio, magazines, newspapers, direct mail, billboards, bus ads, the Internet, and other channels. Of the four components in a firm's marketing mix, promotion is perhaps the one most often associated with marketing. Although it is no guarantee of success, promotion does have a profound impact on a product's performance in the marketplace.

The remainder of this chapter takes a closer look at what's involved in developing product and pricing strategies. Then Chapter 12 discusses the steps involved in developing a firm's distribution and promotional strategies.

DEVELOPING PRODUCT STRATEGIES

Think about Adobe's Acrobat software, MarineLand, and your favourite music artist. You wouldn't market these products in the same way because buyer behaviour, product characteristics, market expectations, competition, and other elements of the equation are entirely different. Acknowledging these differences, marketers most commonly categorize products on the basis of tangibility and use.

Types of Products

Although some products are predominantly tangible and others are mostly intangible, most products fall somewhere between those two extremes. When you buy software such as Adobe's Acrobat, for example, you get service features along with the product—such as product updates, customer assistance, and so on. The *product continuum* indicates the relative amounts of tangible and intangible components in a product (see Exhibit 11.7). Education is a product at the intangible extreme, whereas salt and shoes are at the tangible extreme. Kelsey's bar and grill outlets fall in the middle because they involve both tangible (food) and intangible (service) components.

Service products have some special characteristics that affect the way they are marketed. As we have seen, *intangibility* is one fundamental characteristic. You can't usually show a service in an ad, demonstrate it before customers buy, mass-produce it, or give customers anything tangible to show for their purchase. Services marketers often compensate for intangibility by using tangible symbols or by adding tangible components to their products. Prudential Insurance, for example, uses the Rock of Gibraltar as a symbol of stability.

MarineLand ads are ever-present during the summer season; the catchy jingle and repeated ads place MarineLand on the minds of Canadians.

Exhibit 11.7 The Product Continuum

Products contain both tangible and intangible components; predominantly tangible products are categorized as goods, whereas predominantly intangible products are categorized as services.

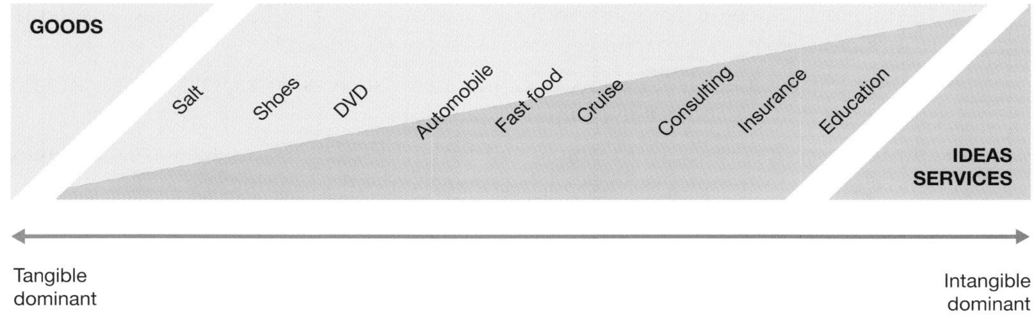

Another unique aspect of service products is *perishability.* Because services cannot usually be created in advance or held in storage until people are ready to buy, services are time-sensitive. For instance, if WestJet doesn't sell seats on a particular flight, once the flight takes off an unsold seat can never produce revenue. Hotel rooms, movie theatre seats, and restaurants are similar. For this reason, many services try to shift customer demand by offering discounts or promotions during slow periods.

Another way that marketers categorize products is by use. Both organizations and consumers use many of the same products, but they use them for different reasons and in different ways. Individual consumers or households generally purchase smaller quantities of goods and services for personal use. Products that are primarily sold to consumers are known as *consumer products.* Consumer products can be classified into four subgroups, depending on how people shop for them:

- *Convenience products* are the goods and services that people buy frequently, without much conscious thought, such as toothpaste, dry cleaning, film developing, and photocopying.
- *Shopping products* are fairly important goods and services that people buy less frequently: a stereo, a computer, a refrigerator, or a university education. Such purchases require more thought and comparison shopping to check on price, features, quality, and reputation.
- *Specialty products* include CK perfume, Armani suits; particular brands that the buyer especially wants and will seek out, regardless of location or price. Specialty products are not necessarily expensive, but they are products that customers go out of their way to buy and rarely accept substitutes for.
- *Unsought goods* are products that people do not normally think of buying, such as life insurance, cemetery plots, and new products they must be made aware of through promotion.[41]

By contrast, *organizational products,* or products sold to firms, are generally purchased in large quantities and are not for personal use. Two categories of organizational products are expense items and capital items. *Expense items* are relatively inexpensive goods and services that organizations generally use within a year of purchase. Examples are pencils and printer cartridges. *Capital items,* by contrast, are more expensive organizational products and have a longer useful life. Examples include desks, photocopiers, and computers.

Aside from dividing products into expense and capital items, organizational buyers and sellers often classify products according to their intended usage.

- Raw materials like iron ore, crude petroleum, lumber, and chemicals are used in the production of final products.

- Components like spark plugs and printer cartridges are similar to raw materials. They also become part of the manufacturer's final products.
- Supplies such as pencils, nails, and light bulbs that are used in a firm's daily operations are considered expense items.
- Installations such as factories, power plants, airports, production lines, and semiconductor fabrication machinery are major capital projects.
- Equipment includes less-expensive capital items such as desks, telephones, and fax machines that are shorter-lived than installations.
- Business services range from simple and fairly risk-free services such as landscaping and cleaning to complex services such as management consulting and auditing.

L.O. 5

The Product Life Cycle

product life cycle
Four basic stages through which a product progresses: introduction, growth, maturity, and decline

Regardless of a product's classification, few products last forever. Most products go through a **product life cycle**, passing through four distinct stages in sales and profits: introduction, growth, maturity, and decline (see Exhibit 11.8). As the product passes from stage to stage, various marketing approaches become appropriate.

The product life cycle can describe a product class (gasoline-powered automobiles), a product form (sports-utility vehicles), or a brand (Ford Explorer). Product classes and forms tend to have the longest life cycles, whereas specific brands tend to have shorter life cycles. The amount of time that a product remains in any one stage depends on customer needs and preferences, economic conditions, the nature of the product, and the marketer's strategy. Still, the proliferation of new products, changing technology, globalization, and the ability to quickly imitate competitors is hurtling product forms and brands through their life cycles much faster today.

Consider electronics, where product life is now a matter of months: Panasonic replaces its consumer electronic products with new models every 90 days.[42] Why? Smart companies know that if they don't keep innovating, competitors who do will capture the business. Such was the case with Polaroid, a company that failed to properly respond to digital technology. One by one, Polaroid customers defected to digital cameras or other technologies. Polaroid missed the opportunity to leverage its name and take advantage of new technologies.[43]

Introduction

The first stage in the product life cycle is the *introductory stage*, during which producers launch a new product and stimulate demand. In this stage, companies typically

Exhibit 11.8 **The Product Life Cycle**

Most products and product categories move through a life cycle similar to the one represented by the curve in this diagram. However, the duration of each stage varies widely from product to product.

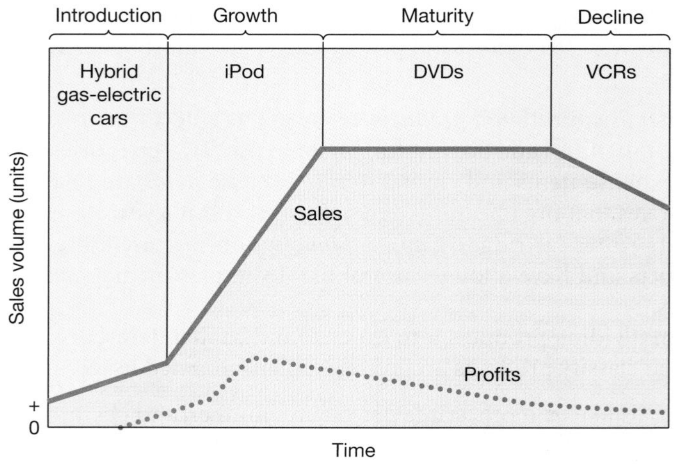

spend heavily on conducting research and development efforts to create the new product, on developing promotions to build awareness of the product, and on establishing the distribution system to get the product into the marketplace. Every product—from personal computers to digital cameras—gets its start in this stage. The producer makes little profit during the introduction; however, these start-up costs are a necessary investment if the new product is to succeed.

Toyota launched the Prius hybrid gas/electric car in 1997. In this day and age of high gas prices it would seem like a great consumer match; however, enthusiasm for gas savings was met with a high price tag because of a lack of scale economies and the high research and development costs. As the costs and price stabilize and decline, the Prius and its direct competitors will continue to capture a greater share of the market. Toyota moved into the second generation of its Prius vehicle in 2004 and is banking on capitalizing on any extra costs in the short term to establish itself in this growth market.[44]

Growth

After the introductory stage comes the *growth stage,* marked by a rapid jump in sales and, usually, an increase in the number of competitors and distribution outlets. As competition increases, so does the struggle for market share. This situation creates pressure to introduce new product features and to maintain large promotional budgets and competitive prices. In fact, marketing in this stage is so expensive that it can drive out smaller, weaker firms. With enough growth, however, a firm can often produce and deliver its products more economically than in the introduction phase. Thus, the growth stage can reap handsome profits for those who survive.

Maturity

During the *maturity stage,* the longest in the product life cycle, sales begin to level off or show a slight decline. Most products are in the maturity stage of the life cycle where competition increases and market share is maximized—making further expansion difficult. Because the costs of introduction and growth have diminished in this stage, most companies try to keep mature products alive so they can use the resulting profits to fund development of new products. Some companies extend the life of a mature product by modifying the product's characteristics to improve the product's quality and performance. Keebler, for instance, has extended the life of its popular cookies by selling them in convenient mini-versions. Packaged in resealable cans, the mini-cookies are sold at convenience stores to appeal to consumers on the run.[45]

brand
A name, term, sign, symbol, design, or combination of these used to identify the products of a firm and to differentiate them from competing products

Decline

Although maturity can be extended for many years, most products eventually enter the *decline stage,* when sales and profits slip and then fade away. Declines occur for several reasons: changing demographics, shifts in popular taste, product competition, and advances in technology. When a product reaches this point in the life cycle, the company must decide whether to keep it and reduce the product's costs to compensate for declining sales or discontinue it and focus on developing newer products. General Motors, for instance, recently decided to kill off the 103-year-old Oldsmobile brand. "The decision was long overdue," notes one marketing expert. Sales of Olds have been declining for more than a decade, and the brand has lost its identity.[46]

The Prius is a gas/electric hybrid alternative for those fed up with increasing gas prices and those who are environmentally friendly. With a consumption rating of 4.0 L/100 km in the city and 4.2 L/100 km on the highway, it lives up to its expectations.

Product Identities

Creating an identity for your products is an important part of developing effective product strategies. Companies create product identities by assigning their products a **brand** identity—a unique name or design that sets the product apart from those offered by competitors—and by designing and producing an attractive package and label for the product.

Branding

brand names
Portion of a brand that can be expressed orally, including letters, words, or numbers

brand mark Portion of a brand that cannot be expressed verbally

Jeep, Levi's 501 and Labatt are **brand names**, the portion of a brand that can be spoken, including letters, words, or numbers. McDonald's golden arches symbol is an example of a **brand mark**, the portion of a brand that cannot be expressed verbally. The choice of a brand name and any associated brand marks can be a critical success factor. A well-known brand name, for instance, can generate more sales than an unknown name. As a result, manufacturers aggressively protect their names.

trademark
Brand that has been given legal protection so that its owner has exclusive rights to its use

Brand names and brand symbols may be registered with the Trade-marks Office in Gatineau, Quebec.[47] As Appendix B explains, a **trademark** is a brand that has been given legal protection so that its owner has exclusive rights to its use. Keep in mind, however, that when a name becomes too widely used it no longer qualifies for protection under trademark laws. Cellophane, kerosene, linoleum, escalator, zipper, shredded wheat, and raisin bran are just a few of the many brand names that have passed into public domain, much to their creators' dismay.

Sometimes companies, such as Warner Brothers, *license* or sell the rights to specific well-known names and symbols—such as Looney Tunes cartoon characters—to manufacturers that use the licensed items to help sell products. In fact, 65 percent of Fortune 500 companies have licensing agreements. Licensing can be a terrific source of revenue. General Mills alone has more than 1200 licensing agreements that cover everything from clothes to cologne and generate annual revenues of US$1.1 billion.[48]

national brands
Brands owned by the manufacturers and distributed nationally

private brands
Brands that carry the label of a retailer or a wholesaler rather than a manufacturer

generic products
Products characterized by a plain label, with no advertising and no brand name

Brand names may be owned by manufacturers, retailers, wholesalers, and a variety of business types. Brands offered and promoted by a national manufacturer, such as Procter & Gamble's Tide detergent and Pampers disposable diapers, are called **national brands**. **Private brands** are not linked to a manufacturer but instead carry a wholesaler's or a retailer's brand. President's Choice and Motomaster are private brands sold by Loblaws and Canadian Tire stores, respectively. As an alternative to branded products, some retailers also offer **generic products**, which are packaged in plain containers that bear only the name of the product. Generic products can cost up to 40 percent less than brand-name products because of uneven quality, plain packaging, and lack of promotion. Yet generic goods have found a definite market niche, as a look at your local supermarket shelves will confirm.

co-branding
Partnership between two or more companies to closely link their brand names together for a single product

Co-branding is another way to strengthen brands and products. **Co-branding** occurs when two or more companies team up to closely link their names in a single product. Nabisco Cranberry Newtons filled with Ocean Spray cranberries is an example of successful co-branding. Co-branding can help companies reach new audiences and tap the equity of particularly strong brands.[49] Moreover, it can help change a product's image. In an attempt to associate the Kodak brand with the output side of digital photography, the company has been co-branding its name with all things digital. The Kodak name sits above Lexmark's logo on an inkjet printer (one of the first to print photographic inkjet paper), and it's all over the websites of companies that trumpet their use of Kodak processing and papers.[50]

brand equity
The extra value a brand name provides to a product beyond its functional benefits

Brand equity is a term used to describe the extra value a brand name provides to a product beyond its functional benefits.[51] It can be loosely compared to stock value. Stock price variations are usually based on economic performance and the company's future prospects. On the other hand, *brand equity* is based on reputation and perception among target groups. It is directly linked to issues like customer satisfaction, value, and long-term integrated marketing communication effects. It is established by the consumer's experiences and views of the brand name. Therefore, if a company launches a poorly manufactured product that fails miserably and leaves a lot of unhappy customers, brand equity may be damaged. Similarly, if a brand is associated with a crisis (e.g., food poisoning, unfair labour practices) all products carrying the brand name are affected. At the opposite extreme all positive coverage (e.g., corporate responsibility, good product reviews, positive word of mouth) are reflected on all products that carry a particular brand name. In practical terms, strong brand equity helps a company take advantage of consumer perceptions in order to maintain and increase market share, set or maintain premium prices, launch new readily acceptable products, and fight competitively for consumer business.

Packaging

L.O. 6

Another way that marketers create an identity for their products is through packaging. Most products need some form of packaging to protect the product from damage or tampering and to make it convenient for customers to purchase. In some cases, packaging is an essential part of the product itself, such as microwave popcorn or toothpaste in pump dispensers. Besides function, however, packaging plays an important role in a product's marketing strategy. Packaging makes products easier to display, facilitates the sale of smaller products, serves as a means of product differentiation, and enhances the product's overall appeal and convenience.

Companies spend a lot of money on packaging to attract consumer attention and to promote a product's benefits through the package's shape, composition, and design. Gatorade's ergonomically designed bottle, Quaker Oats cereal in bags, and Coca-Cola's 12-pack refrigerator dispenser are examples of innovative packaging with strong consumer appeal.

Labelling

Labelling is an integral part of packaging. Whether the label is a separate element attached to the package or a printed part of the container, it serves to identify a brand. Labels also provide grading information about the product and information about ingredients, operating procedures, shelf life, or risks. The labelling of foods, drugs, cosmetics, and many health products is regulated under various federal laws, which often require disclosures about potential dangers, benefits, and other issues consumers need to consider when making a buying decision.

Labels do more than communicate with consumers. They are also used by manufacturers and retailers as a tool for monitoring product performance and inventory. **Universal Product Codes (UPCs)**, those black stripes on packages, give companies a cost-effective method of tracking the movement of goods. Store checkout scanners read UPC codes and relay the identity, sales, and prices of all products to the retailer's computer system. Such data can help retailers and manufacturers measure the effectiveness of promotions such as coupons and in-store displays. They are also helpful for inventory control.

Universal Product Codes (UPCs)
A bar code on a product's package that provides information read by optical scanners

Product-Line and Product-Mix Strategies

L.O. 7

In addition to developing branding, packaging, and labelling strategies, a company must decide how many products it will offer. To stay competitive, most companies continually add and drop products to ensure that declining items will be replaced by growth products. A **product line** is a group of products that are similar in terms of use or characteristics. The General Mills Canada snack-food product line, for example, includes Bugles, Fruit Roll-Ups, Nature Valley Granola Bars, and Pop Secret popcorn. Within each product line, a company confronts decisions about the number of goods and services to offer.

product line
A series of related products offered by a firm

An organization with several product lines has a **product mix**, a collection of goods or services offered for sale. For example, the General Mills product mix consists of cereals, baking products, desserts, snack foods, main meals, and so on (see Exhibit 11.9). Three important dimensions of a company's product mix are *width, length,* and *depth.* A company's product mix is *wide* if it has several different product lines. General Mills Canada's product mix, for instance, is fairly wide with five or more product lines. A company's product mix is long if it carries several items in its product lines, as General Mills Canada does. A product mix is deep if it has a number of versions of *each* product in a product line. General Mills Canada, for example, produces several different versions of Cheerios—frosted, multigrain, and honey nut. The same is true for many other prod-

product mix
Complete list of all products that a company offers for sale

Exhibit 11.9 The Product Mix at General Mills Canada

Selected products from General Mills Canada show a product mix that is fairly wide but that varies in length and depth within each product line.[52]

	READY-TO-EAT CEREALS	MAIN MEALS AND SIDE DISHES	BAKING PRODUCTS AND DESSERTS	SNACKS	FROZEN SNACKS
PRODUCT LINES	Cheerios	Green Giant Create-a-Meal	Bisquick	Bugles	Pillsbury Pizza Minis
	Oatmeal Crisp	Hamburger Helper	Betty Crocker angel food cakes	Nature Valley Crunchy granola bars	Pillsbury Mini Pops
	Golden Grahams	Chicken Helper	Betty Crocker brownie mixes	Nature Valley Chewy Trail Mix bars	Pillsbury Pizza Pops
	Lucky Charms	Tuna Helper	Betty Crocker SuperMoist cake mixes	Pop Secret Popcorn	
	Count Chocula	Bowl Appetit	Betty Crocker Snackin' Cake mixes	Fruit Roll Ups	
	Chex	Green Giant canned vegetables	Betty Crocker frosting	Fruit by the Foot	
	Trix	Specialty potatoes (mashed and sliced)		Dunkaroos	
	Fibre 1	Old El Paso meals			

ucts in the company's other product lines. When deciding on the dimensions of a product mix, a company must weigh the risks and rewards associated with various approaches. Some companies limit the number of product offerings and focus on selling a few selected items to be economical: Doing so keeps the production costs per unit down and limits selling expenses to a single sales force. Other companies adopt a full-line strategy as a protection against shifts in technology, taste, and economic conditions.

As Exhibit 11.10 shows, you can expand your product line in a number of ways. You can introduce additional items in a given product category under the same brand name—such as new flavours, forms, colours, ingredients, or package sizes.[53] Coke's introduction of the Vanilla Coke brand extension fared much better than Pepsi's big product extension at the time: Pepsi Blue. Pepsi licked its wounds and quickly launched Pepsi Vanilla to match its main competitor. A new extension game soon followed between Coke and Pepsi as they both launched low-carb colas: Coca-Cola C2 and Pepsi Edge.

You can also expand your product line by adding new but similar products bearing the same product name. Kraft, for example, has extended its Jell-O product line with new products such as gelatine in a cup, pudding in a cup, and cheesecake snacks in a cup. These products build on the convenience-with-quality image of the Jell-O family brand.[54] Building on the name recognition of an existing brand cuts the costs and risks of introducing new products. However, there are limits to how far a brand name can be stretched to accommodate new products and still fit the buyer's perception of what the brand stands for. Snickers ice cream bars and Dr. Scholl's socks and shoes worked as brand extensions, but Bic perfume and Rubbermaid computer accessories did not.

L.O. 8

DEVELOPING PRICING STRATEGIES

A company's pricing decisions are determined by manufacturing and selling costs, competition, and the needs of wholesalers and retailers who distribute the product to

Exhibit 11.10 Expanding the Product Line

Knowing that no product or category has an unlimited life cycle, companies use one or more of these product-line expansion methods to keep sales strong.

METHOD OF EXPANSION	HOW IT WORKS	EXAMPLE
Line filling	Developing items to fill gaps in the market that have been overlooked by competitors or have emerged as consumers' tastes and needs shift	Alka-Seltzer Plus cold medicine
Line extension	Creating a new variation of a basic product	Oatmeal Crisp – Maple Nut
Brand extension	Putting the brand for an existing product category into a new category	Nestle Smarties Ice Cream
Line stretching	Adding higher- or lower-priced items at either end of the product line to extend its appeal to new economic groups	Volkswagen Phaeton; Mercedes C230 sport coupe

the final customer. In addition, pricing is influenced by a firm's marketing objectives, government regulations, consumer perceptions, and consumer demand.

- *Marketing objectives.* The first step in setting a price is to match it to the objectives you set in your strategic marketing plan. Is your goal to increase market share, increase sales, improve profits, project a particular image, or combat competition? For example, Rolex uses premium pricing along with other marketing mix elements to give its watches a luxury position. As this chapter's case study shows, Adobe Systems ultimately decided to price its Acrobat Reader for free. Adobe hoped to stimulate sales of the full Acrobat product by providing the general public with the necessary tools to read PDF documents.
- *Government regulations.* Government plays a big role in pricing in many countries. To protect consumers and encourage fair competition, government has enacted various price-related laws over the years. Three important classes of pricing are regulated: (1) *price fixing*—an agreement among two or more companies supplying the same type of products as to the prices they will charge; (2) *price discrimination*—the practice of unfairly offering attractive discounts to some customers but not to others; and (3) *deceptive pricing*—pricing schemes that are considered misleading.
- *Consumer perceptions.* Another consideration is the perception of quality that your price will elicit from your customers. When people shop, they usually have a rough price range in mind. An unexpectedly low price triggers fear that the item is of low quality. South Korean carmaker Hyundai, for example, decided not to cut prices when the dollar gained strength against the Korean won, because the company did not want to reinforce an image of shoddy goods.[55]
- *Consumer demand.* Whereas a company's costs establish a floor for prices, demand for a product establishes a ceiling. Theoretically, if the price for an item is too high, demand falls and the producers reduce their prices to stimulate demand. Conversely, if the price for an item is too low, demand increases and the producers are motivated to raise prices. As prices climb and profits improve, producers boost their output until supply and demand are in balance and prices stabilize. Nonetheless, the relationship between price and demand isn't always this perfect. Some goods and services are relatively insensitive to changes in price; others are highly responsive. Marketers refer to sensitivity as **price elasticity**—how responsive demand will be to a change in price.

When companies set their prices they take these factors—among others—into account before choosing a general pricing approach. Common

price elasticity
A measure of the sensitivity of demand to changes in price

How much extra will consumers pay for convenience? Marketers of bottled water have managed to convince people to pay a premium for a product that is available for free. Consumers perceive the water to be of higher quality; however, many popular brands are taken from public distribution systems.

pricing approaches include cost-based, price-based, skimming, penetration pricing, and discounting.

Cost-Based and Price-Based Pricing

Many companies simplify the pricing task by using *cost-based pricing* (also known as cost-plus pricing). They price by starting with the cost of producing a good or a service and then add a mark-up to the cost of the product. This form of pricing, while simple, makes little sense. First, any pricing that ignores demand and competitor prices is not likely to lead to the best price. Second, although cost-based pricing may ensure a certain profit, companies using this strategy tend to sacrifice profit opportunity.

Recent thinking holds that cost should be the last item analyzed in the pricing formula, not the first. Companies that use *price-based pricing* can maximize their profit by first establishing an optimal price for a product or service. The product's price is based on an analysis of a product's competitive advantages, the users' perception of the item, and the market being targeted. Once the desired price has been established, the firm focuses its energies on keeping costs at a level that will allow a healthy profit. Although few businesses fail from overpricing their products, many more will fail from underpricing them.[56]

Price Skimming

skimming
Charging a high price for a new product during the introductory stage and lowering the price later

A product's price seldom remains constant and will vary depending on the product's stage in its life cycle. During the introductory phase, for example, the objective might be to recover product development costs as quickly as possible. To achieve this goal, the manufacturer might charge a high initial price—a practice known as **skimming**—and then drop the price later, when the product is no longer a novelty and competition heats up. Products such as HDTV and flat-screen monitors are perfect examples of this practice. Price skimming makes sense under two conditions: (1) if the product's quality and image support a higher price, and (2) if competitors cannot easily enter the market with competing products and undercut the price.

Penetration Pricing

penetration pricing
Introducing a new product at a low price in hopes of building sales volume quickly

Rather than setting a high initial price to skim off a small but profitable market segment, a company might try to build sales volume by charging a low initial price, a practice known as **penetration pricing**. This approach has the added advantage of discouraging competition, because the low price (which competitors would be pressured to match) limits the profit potential for everyone.

Penetration pricing can also help expand the entire product category by attracting customers who wouldn't have purchased at higher, skim-pricing levels. Furthermore, if a company is new to a category pioneered by another company, this strategy can help take customers away from the pioneer.[57] Still, the strategy makes most sense when the market is highly price sensitive so that a low price generates additional sales and the company can maintain its low-price position long enough to keep out competition.

Price Discounts

discount pricing
Offering a reduction in price

Once a company has set a product's price, it may choose to adjust that price from time to time to account for changing market situations or changing customer preferences. When you use **discount pricing**, you offer various types of temporary price reductions, depending on the type of customer being targeted and the type of item being offered. You may decide to offer a trade discount to wholesalers or retailers as a way of encouraging orders, or you may offer cash discounts to reward customers who pay cash or pay promptly. You may offer a quantity discount to buyers who buy large volumes, or you may offer a seasonal discount to buyers who buy merchandise or services out of season.

Another way to discount products is by *value pricing* them, charging a fairly affordable price for a high-quality offering. Many restaurants offer value menus for certain times of the day or certain customer segments, such as seniors. This strategy builds loyalty among price-conscious customers without damaging a product's quality image.

Although discounts are a popular way to boost sales of a product, the downside is that they can touch off price wars among competitors. Price wars encourage customers to focus only on a product's pricing, and not on its value or benefits. Thus, they can hurt a business—even an entire industry—for years. Consider the price war that web-based Amazon.com started when it began selling *New York Times* bestselling books at a 50 percent discount in an effort to bring more customers to its site. Online rivals Barnesandnoble.com quickly matched Amazon.com's prices, and smaller bookstores were forced to lower their prices on bestsellers. To offset the loss of revenue, some small bookstores stocked their shelves with more profitable book categories, such as specialty books. Others could not compete and eventually closed up shop.[58]

SUMMARY OF LEARNING OBJECTIVES

1 Explain what marketing is and describe the four utilities created by marketing.

Marketing is the process of planning and executing the conception, pricing, promotion, and distribution of ideas, goods, and services to create exchanges that satisfy individual and organizational objectives. Marketers enhance the appeal of their products and services by adding utility. Form utility is created when companies turn raw materials into finished goods desired by consumers. Time utility is created by making the product available when the consumer wants to buy it. Place utility is created when a product is made available at a location that is convenient for the consumer. Possession utility is created by facilitating the transfer of ownership from seller to buyer.

2 Explain why and how companies learn about their customers.

Companies learn about their customers so they can stay in touch with their current needs and wants, deliver quality products, and provide good customer service. Such attention tends to keep customers satisfied and helps retain their long-term loyalty. Moreover, studies show that sales to repeat customers are more profitable. Most companies learn about their customers by studying consumer behaviour, conducting marketing research, and capturing and analyzing customer data.

3 Outline the three steps in the strategic marketing planning process.

The three steps in the strategic marketing planning process are (1) examining your current marketing situation, which includes reviewing your past performance, evaluating your competition, examining your internal strengths and weaknesses, and analyzing the external environment; (2) assessing your opportunities and setting your objectives; and (3) developing your marketing strategy, which covers segmenting your market, choosing your target markets, positioning your product, and creating a marketing mix to satisfy the target market.

4 Define market segmentation and cite six factors used to identify segments.

Market segmentation is the process of subdividing a market into homogeneous groups to identify potential customers and to devise marketing approaches geared to their needs and interests. The six most common factors used to identify segments are demographics, geographics, psychographics, geodemographics, behaviour, and usage.

5 Highlight the four stages in the life cycle of a product and the marketing focus of each stage.

Products start in the introductory stage where marketers focus on stimulating demand for the new product. As the product progresses through the growth stage, marketers focus on increasing the product's market share. During the maturity stage, marketers try to extend the life of the product by highlighting improvements or by repackaging the product in different sizes. Eventually, all products move to a decline stage, where the marketer must decide whether to keep the product and reduce its costs to compensate for declining sales or discontinue it.

6 Discuss the functions of packaging and labelling.

Packaging provides protection for the product, makes products easier to display, and attracts attention. In addition, packaging enhances the convenience of the product and communicates its attributes to the buyer. Labels help identify and distinguish the brand and product. They provide information about the product—including ingredients, risks, shelf life, and operating procedures. And they contain UPC codes, which are used for scanning sales information and monitoring inventory and pricing.

Identify four ways of expanding a product line and discuss two risks that product line extensions pose.

A product line can be expanded by filling gaps in the market, extending the line to include new varieties of existing products, extending the brand to new product categories, and stretching the line to include lower- or higher-priced items. Two of the biggest risks with product line extensions include a loss of brand identity (weakening of the brand's meaning) and cannibalization of sales of other products in the product line.

List seven factors that influence pricing decisions and cite five common pricing methods.

Pricing decisions are influenced by manufacturing and selling costs, competition, the needs of wholesalers and retailers who distribute the product to the final customer, a firm's marketing objectives, government regulations, consumer perceptions, and consumer demand. Five common pricing methods are cost-based, price-based, skimming, penetration pricing, and discounting.

Behind the SCENES

Turning a Profit by Giving Away the Product

Adobe Systems faced a difficult challenge. Its new Acrobat software turned somersaults over the competition by removing critical formatting barriers so that documents shared electronically retained their original appearance. But only a few companies recognized the software's benefits. Still, with the World Wide Web and graphical Internet browsers gaining popularity, Adobe knew that it had to move fast if Acrobat were to become the industry-wide standard for viewing electronic documents across the Web. It had to break through corporate barriers and convince consumers of the product's potential.

To create consumer awareness, Acrobat marketers designed a series of slick advertisements that highlighted the many benefits of the software, including improved communication, reduced paperwork, and increased productivity. The ads further explained that the Reader was only a small part of a much more dynamic software program and that users could purchase the product's components separately: the complete Acrobat software program for about US$250 or only the Reader for US$50.

But few people were willing to pay $50 to view documents—especially documents that constituted a tiny minority of those available on the Web. So Adobe shifted gears and decided to give away the Reader for free. Then, to expedite distribution, Adobe entered into an agreement with Netscape to bundle a copy of the Reader with its browser software and made similar deals with IBM and Macintosh to include a copy of Reader software with all new computers. Moreover, it encouraged consumers to download copies of the Reader through the Internet at no charge.

Adobe's marketing strategy soon paid off. With more than 320 million copies of Acrobat distributed worldwide, PDF has indeed become the industry standard. As the number of people using Adobe's Acrobat Reader skyrocketed, so did the demand for the full product required to create PDF documents. Soon businesses and government agencies were using Acrobat to convert documents into PDF files to share with employees and customers over computer networks on the Internet.

Thanks to smart marketing, Adobe is one of the world's largest software companies, employs more than 3700 people, and generates more than US$1.2 billion in annual sales.[59]

Critical Thinking Questions

1. Why was Adobe Acrobat a challenging product to market?
2. Why did Adobe decide to give away the Acrobat Reader software?
3. What pricing strategy does Adobe appear to be using by giving away the Reader?

Learn More Online

Go to Chapter 11 of this text's website at www.pearsoned.ca/bovee, and click on the hotlink to the Adobe Systems website. After reviewing the site, analyze Adobe's product line: How many software products does Adobe produce? Is the company's product mix wide or narrow? Which of the following consumer product classifications best describes Adobe's Reader: convenience product, shopping product, specialty product, or unsought good? From a company's perspective, would you consider the entire Adobe Acrobat software package to be an organizational expense or a capital item?

KEY TERMS

behavioural segmentation (284)
brand (291)
brand equity (292)
brand mark (292)
brand names (292)
cause-related marketing (275)
co-branding (292)
cognitive dissonance (277)
customer service (274)
database marketing (279)
demographics (283)
discount pricing (296)
distribution channels (288)
exchange process (275)
form utility (276)
generic products (292)
geodemographics (284)
geographic segmentation (284)
market (283)
market segmentation (283)
market share (283)
marketing (274)
marketing concept (276)
marketing mix (287)
marketing research (278)
marketing strategy (283)
national brands (292)
need (275)
penetration pricing (296)
place marketing (275)
place utility (276)
positioning (286)
possession utility (276)
price (287)
price elasticity (295)
private brands (292)
product (287)
product life cycle (290)
product line (293)
product mix (293)
promotion (288)
psychographics (284)
relationship marketing (279)
skimming (296)
target markets (285)
time utility (276)
trademark (292)
transaction (275)
utility (276)
Universal Product Codes (UPCs) (293)
wants (275)

TEST YOUR KNOWLEDGE

Questions for Review

1. What are some of the characteristics of today's customers?
2. What is strategic marketing planning, and what is its purpose?
3. What external environmental factors affect strategic marketing decisions?
4. What are the four basic components of the marketing mix?
5. What are the functions of packaging and labelling?

Questions for Analysis

6. How can marketing research and database marketing help companies improve their marketing efforts?
7. Why do companies segment markets?
8. How could a marketer confuse a consumer when developing a product's positioning strategies?
9. Why is it important to review the objectives of a strategic marketing plan before setting a product's price?
10. **Ethical Considerations.** Why might an employee with high personal ethical standards act less ethically when developing packaging, labelling, or pricing strategies?

Questions for Application

11. How do airlines deal with the intangibility and perishability of the service they provide?
12. Think of a shopping product you recently purchased and review your decision process. Why did you need or want that product? How did the product's marketing influence your purchase decision? How did you investigate the product before making your purchase decision? Did you experience cognitive dissonance after your decision?
13. **Integrated.** Why is it important to analyze a firm's marketing plan before designing the production process for a service or a good? What kinds of information are generally included in a marketing plan that might affect the design of the production process as discussed in Chapter 8?
14. **Integrated.** How might the following economic indicators discussed in Chapter 1 affect a company's marketing decisions: consumer price index, inflation, unemployment?

PRACTISE YOUR KNOWLEDGE

SHARPENING YOUR COMMUNICATION SKILLS

Collect some examples of mail communications you have received from companies trying to sell you something. How do these communications try to get your attention? Highlight all instances in which these communications use the word *you* or even your personal name. How is using the word *you* an effective way to communicate with customers? Does the communication appeal to your emotion or to your logic? How does the company highlight the benefits of its product or services? How does the company talk about price? Finally, how does the company motivate you to act? Bring your samples to class and be prepared to present your analysis of these factors to your classmates.

BUILDING YOUR TEAM SKILLS

In the course of planning a marketing strategy, marketers need to analyze the external environment to consider how forces outside the firm may create new opportunities and challenges. One important environmental factor for merchandise buyers at Canadian Tire is weather conditions. For example, when merchandise buyers for lawn and garden products think about the assortment and number of products to purchase for the chain's stores, they don't place any orders without first poring over long-range weather forecasts for each market.

In particular, temperature and precipitation predictions are critical to the company's marketing plan, because they offer clues to consumer demand for barbecues, lawn furniture, gardening tools, and other merchandise. What other products would benefit from examining weather forecasts? With your team, brainstorm to identify at least three types of products (in addition to lawn and garden items) for which Canadian Tire should examine the weather as part of its analysis of the external environment. Share your recommendations with the entire class. How many teams identified the same products your team did?

EXPAND YOUR KNOWLEDGE

DISCOVERING CAREER OPPORTUNITIES

Jobs in the four Ps of marketing cover a wide range of activities, including a variety of jobs such as personal selling, advertising, marketing research, product management, and public relations. You can get more information about various marketing positions by consulting your local job bank, as well as online job search websites such as Monster.ca.

1. Select a specific marketing job that interests you. Using one or more of the preceding resources, find out more about this chosen job. What specific duties and responsibilities do people in this position typically handle?
2. Search through help-wanted ads in newspapers, specialized magazines, or websites to find two openings in the field you are researching. What educational background and work experience are employers seeking in candidates for this position? What kind of work assignments are mentioned in these ads?
3. Now think about your talents, interests, and goals. How do your strengths fit with the requirements, duties, and responsibilities of this job? Do you think you would find this field enjoyable and rewarding? Why?

DEVELOPING YOUR RESEARCH SKILLS

From recent issues of business journals and newspapers (print or online editions), select an article that describes in some detail a particular company's attempt to build relationships with its customers (either in general or for a particular product or product line).

1. Describe the company's market. What geographic, demographic, behavioural, or psychographic segments of the market is the company targeting?
2. How does the company hold a dialogue with its customers? Does the company maintain a customer database? If so, what kinds of information does it gather?
3. According to the article, how successful has the company been in understanding its customers?

See It on the **WEB**

URLs for all Internet exercises are provided at the website for this book, www.pearsoned.ca/bovee. When you log on to the text website, select Chapter 11, then select Destinations. Click on the name of the featured website and review the website to complete the following exercises.

Explore the following chapter-related websites, review their content, and answer the following questions for each website you visit:

1. What is the purpose of this website?
2. What kinds of information does this website contain? Please be specific.
3. How is the information provided at this website useful for business people? Consumers?
4. How did you expand your knowledge of marketing, customers, products, or pricing by reviewing the material at this website? What new things did you learn about these topics?

PROTECT YOUR TRADEMARK

Got a winning idea for a new product? Don't forget to protect your idea trademark by registering it. Visit the Canadian Intellectual Property Office and learn the basic facts about registering a trademark, such as who is allowed to use the TM symbol and how a trademark differs from a service mark. Find out how the process works and how much it costs. In fact, why not search its database now to see whether anyone has already registered your trademark? http://cipo.gc.ca/

SIGN UP FOR ELECTRONIC COMMERCE 101

Think you may be interested in moving your business onto the Net but you don't know where to start? Study the basics at Electronic Commerce 101 before you plan your marketing strategies. Find out how to succeed in electronic commerce. Read the beginners' guide and the step-by-step process of becoming e-commerce enabled. Learn how to process payments, credit cards, and e-cash. Find out the top 10 ways websites lose customers. Still have a question? This site has free advice from more than 7000 experts. www.ecommerce.about.com/smallbusiness/ecommerce/library/bl101

Chapter 12
Developing Distribution and Promotional Strategies

LEARNING OBJECTIVES

After studying this chapter, you will be able to

1. Explain what marketing intermediaries do and list their seven primary functions
2. Explain how wholesalers and retailers function as intermediaries
3. Discuss the key factors that influence channel design and selection
4. Differentiate between intensive, selective, and exclusive distribution strategies
5. Discuss the Internet's effect on the distribution function
6. Identify the five basic categories of promotion
7. Distinguish between the two main types of sales promotions and give examples of each
8. Discuss the use of integrated marketing communications

Behind the SCENES

MEC: Two Million Members and Climbing

www.mec.ca

For more than three decades, Mountain Equipment Cooperative (MEC) has been serving the recreational outdoor needs of Canadians. Originally founded in 1971 by a group of students from the University of British Columbia, MEC has grown into Canada's largest retail cooperative by membership statistics. Expanding from its roots in Vancouver, MEC has established a retail footprint across the various regions of the country and also serves Canadians through catalogue and telephone sales.

MEC has demonstrated a pattern of socially responsible behaviour. The co-op sends a portion of its gross sales to environmental initiatives and has also incorporated the philosophy into the physical structure of its retail outlets. For example, the location in Montreal can boast to be the "most energy efficient retail building in the province, incorporating geothermal energy, radiant heating and cooling, and a natural ventilation system that reduces energy consumption by approximately 50 percent. Additionally, a roof water collection system reuses the roof water runoff for the landscape irrigation system."[1]

The retail outlets range in size from 10 000 to 45 000 square feet and offer a wide variety of outdoor equipment, including camping gear, hiking gear, cycling accessories, and equipment for snow sports. The shopping experience at MEC is accentuated by a customer-centred approach. From rock climbing walls to demo stations it is easy to see why more than 2 million people have said yes to MEC membership.

In spite of its successful climb during its first three decades of operation, MEC was aware that it could provide improved access to its products by entering the Internet age. It was servicing its customers with its retail outlets and supplementing that with catalogue and phone sales but it knew that the long-term growth of the company would require an efficient website. If MEC ignored this channel it could leave room for current and potential competitors to gain advantage. One problem with launching the site is that the Internet retail arm might replace sales from current retail channels. The careful coordination of the system was vital to ensure that the full potential was achieved. The official launch dates to May 2001. This decision was very important and required careful planning and implementation. Consider the following questions as if you were a member of MEC's management team at this important crossroad: What are some of the concerns faced by MEC in launching its site? Should the company keep the online business a separate entity or is it better off integrating the operations? What would you do? What can a company do to help reduce cannibalization of in-store sales?[2]

Mountain Equipment Cooperative has grown into a top supplier of specialty outdoor gear, selling through its retail outlets across Canada and by direct sales via the Internet, telephone and mail.

DEVELOPING DISTRIBUTION STRATEGIES

MEC is just one example of how producers use intermediaries to get their products to market. Getting products to consumers is the role of distribution, the third element of a firm's marketing mix—also known as *place.* As Chapter 11 points out, distribution channels or *marketing channels* are an organized network of firms that work together to get goods and services from producer to consumer. A company's **distribution strategy**, which is its overall plan for moving products to buyers, plays a major role in the firm's success.

distribution strategy
Firm's overall plan for moving products to intermediaries and final customers

marketing intermediaries
Business people and organizations that channel goods and services from producers to consumers

Think of all the products you buy: food, toiletries, clothing, sports equipment, train tickets, haircuts, gasoline, stationery, appliances, CDs, DVDs, books, and all the rest. How many of these products do you buy directly from the producer? For most people, the answer is not many. Most companies do not sell their goods directly to the final users, even though the Internet is making it easier to do so these days. Instead, producers in many industries work with **marketing intermediaries** (also called *middlemen*) to bring their products to market.

L.O. 1, 2

Understanding the Role of Marketing Intermediaries

wholesalers
Firms that sell products to other firms for resale or for organizational use

Two main types of marketing intermediaries are wholesalers and retailers. **Wholesalers** sell primarily to retailers, to other wholesalers, and to organizational users such as government agencies, institutions, and commercial operations. In turn, the customers of wholesalers either resell the products or use them to make products of their own. For example, fruit and vegetable wholesalers such as F.G. Lister and Canadawide help to increase efficiency, reduce transactions, and ensure that these perishable products reach a variety of locations. From small mom and pop fruit stores to large grocery chains and restaurants, the system needs to be efficient in order to ensure timely delivery and avoid produce loss.

retailers
Firms that sell goods and services to individuals for their own use rather than for resale

By contrast, **retailers** sell products to the final consumer for personal use. Retailers can operate out of a physical facility (supermarket, gas station, or kiosk), through vending equipment (soft-drink machine, newspaper box, or automated teller), or from a virtual store (via telephone, catalogue, or website). Most retailers today reach shoppers through a carefully balanced blend of store and non-store retail outlets. The major types of retailers are described in Exhibit 12.1.

Wholesalers and retailers are instrumental in creating three of the four forms of utility mentioned in Chapter 11: place utility, time utility, and possession utility. They provide an efficient process for transferring products from the producer to the customer, they reduce the number of transactions, and they ensure that goods and services

Exhibit 12.1 **Types of Retail Stores**

The definition of retailer covers many types of outlets. This table shows some of the most common types.

TYPE OF RETAILER	DESCRIPTION	EXAMPLES
Category killer	A specialty store that focuses on specific products on a giant scale and dominates retail sales in the product categories	Staples; Bureau En Gros; Toys "R" Us
Convenience store	Offers staple convenience goods, long service hours, quick checkouts	Couche Tarde; Mac's; Beckers
Department store	Offers a wide variety of merchandise, in departmentalized sections, with many customer services, all under one roof	The Bay; Sears
Discount store	Offers a wide variety of merchandise at low prices and few services	Wal-Mart
Factory/retail outlet	Large outlet store selling discontinued items, overruns, and factory seconds	Nike outlet store
Hypermarket	Giant store offering food and general merchandise at discount prices	Wal-Mart
Off-price store	Offers designer and brand-name merchandise at low prices and few services	Winners
Specialty store	Offers a complete selection in a narrow range of merchandise	Aldo shoes
Supermarket	Large, self-service store offering a wide selection of food and non-food merchandise	Loblaws; Sobeys
Warehouse club	Large, warehouse-style store that sells food and general merchandise at discount prices; some require club membership	Costco

are available at a convenient time and place for consumers. In short, wholesalers and retailers perform a number of specific distribution functions that make life easier for both producers and customers:

- *Match buyers and sellers.* By making sellers' products available to multiple buyers, intermediaries such as MEC reduce the number of transactions between producers and customers.
- *Provide market information.* Intermediaries such as MEC collect valuable data about customer purchases: who buys, how often, and how much. Collecting such data allows them to spot buying patterns and to share marketplace information with producers.
- *Provide promotional and sales support.* Many intermediaries, such as Pepsi distributors, create advertising, produce eye-catching displays, and use other promotional devices for some or all of the products they sell. Some employ a sales force, which can perform a number of selling functions.
- *Gather an assortment of goods.* MEC, Staples, and other intermediaries receive bulk shipments from producers and break them into more convenient units by sorting, standardizing, and dividing bulk quantities into smaller packages.
- *Transport and store the product.* Intermediaries such as Future Shop and The Brick retail stores maintain an inventory of merchandise that they acquire from producers so they can quickly fill customers' orders. In many cases, retailers purchase this merchandise from wholesalers who, in addition to breaking bulk, may also transport the goods from the producer to the retail outlets.
- *Assume risks.* When intermediaries accept goods from manufacturers, they take on the risks associated with damage, theft, product perishability, and obsolescence. For example, if products stocked or displayed at The Bay are stolen or become obsolete, The Bay assumes responsibility for the loss.
- *Provide financing.* Large intermediaries sometimes provide loans to smaller producers.

As Exhibit 12.2 shows, without marketing intermediaries, the buying and selling process would be expensive and time-consuming.

Exhibit 12.2 **How Intermediaries Simplify Commerce**

Intermediaries actually reduce the price customers pay for many goods and services, because they reduce the number of contacts between producers and consumers that would otherwise be necessary. They also create place, time, and possession utility.

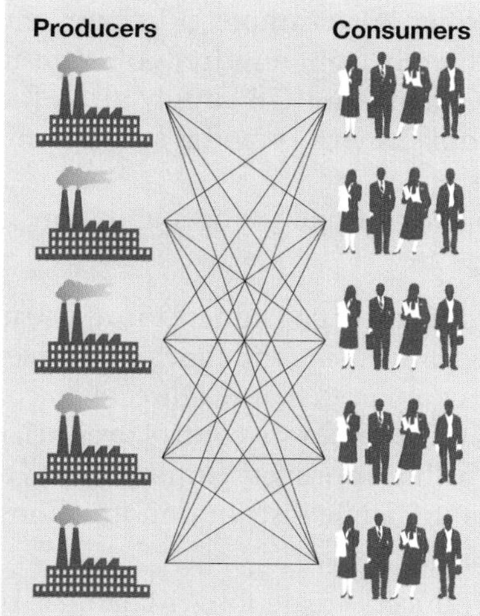

Number of transactions required when consumers buy directly from manufacturers

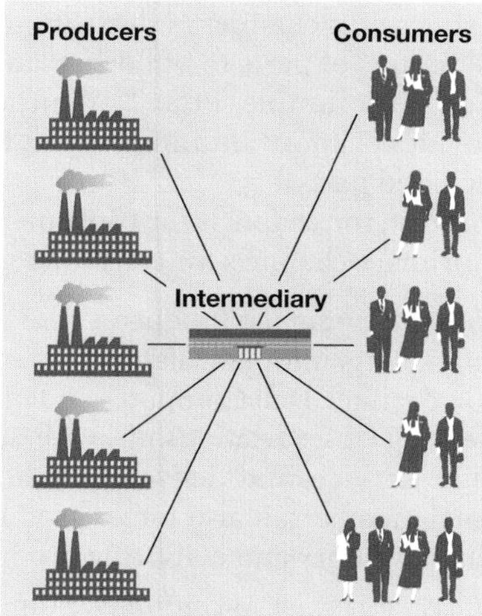

Number of transactions required when buying is conducted via intermediary

Exhibit 12.3 Alternative Channels of Distribution

Producers of consumer and business goods and services must analyze the alternative channels of distribution available for their products so they can select the channels that best meet their marketing objectives and their customers' needs.

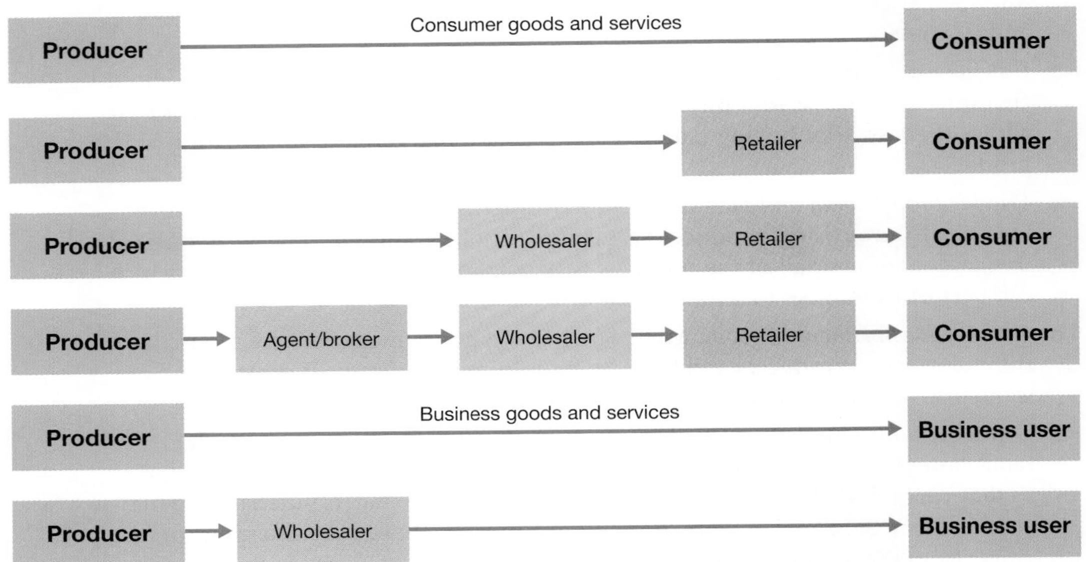

Selecting Your Marketing Channels

distribution mix
Combination of intermediaries and channels a producer uses to get a product to end-users

Distribution channels come in all shapes and sizes. Some channels are short and simple; others are complex and involve many people and organizations. A company's decision about the number and type of intermediaries to use—its **distribution mix**—depends on the kind of product being sold and the marketing practices of the industry. An arrangement that works well for a power tool and appliance manufacturer like Black & Decker or a book publisher like Pearson Canada would not necessarily work for an insurance company like Sun Life. In general, consumer products and business products tend to move through different channels (see Exhibit 12.3).

Length of Distribution Channels

Most businesses purchase goods they use in their operations directly from producers, so the distribution channel is short. Bombardier, for example, purchases more than 10 000 kilograms of parts to build airplanes directly from hundreds of large and small companies. For example, Pratt & Whitney Canada and GE supply aircraft engines, Alcoa provides primary aluminium, and Heroux-Devtek provides sub-assemblies and main machined parts.[3]

In contrast, the channels for consumer goods are usually longer and more complex. The four primary channels for consumer goods are

- *Producer to consumer.* Producers who sell directly to consumers through catalogues, telemarketing, infomercials, and the Internet are using the shortest, simplest distribution channel. Dell Computer and other companies that sell directly to consumers are seeking closer relationships with customers and more control over pricing, promotion, service, and delivery.[4] Although this approach eliminates payments to channel members, it also forces producers to handle distribution functions such as storing inventory and delivering products.
- *Producer to retailer to consumer.* Some producers create longer channels by selling their products to retailers such as Rona or Canadian Tire, which then resell them to consumers. Sico Paint, Scott's "Turf Builder" fertilizer, and GE light bulbs are examples of products distributed in this way.

- *Producer to wholesaler to retailer to consumer.* Most manufacturers of supermarket and drugstore items rely on even longer channels. They sell their products to wholesalers, who in turn sell to the retailers. This approach works particularly well for small producers who lack the resources to sell or deliver merchandise to individual retail sites.
- *Producer to agent/broker to wholesaler to retailer to consumer.* Additional channel levels are common in certain industries, such as agriculture, where specialists are required to negotiate transactions or to perform functions such as sorting, grading, or subdividing the goods.

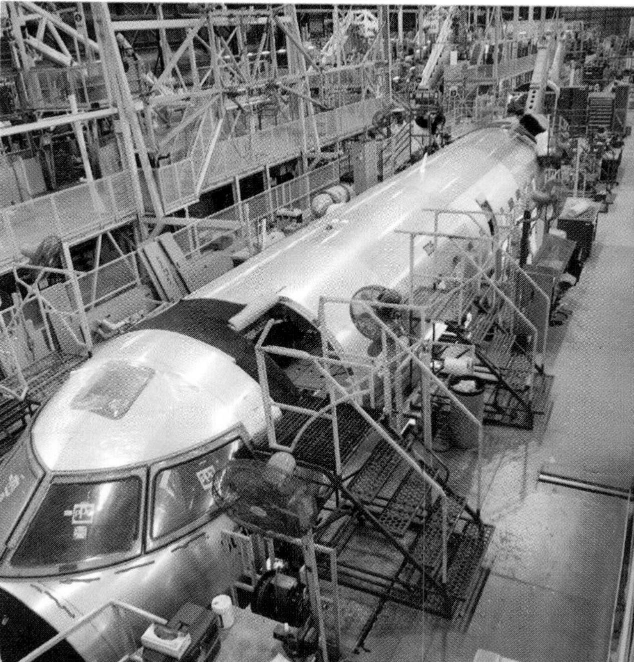

Each Bombardier airplane contains thousands of parts purchased directly from hundreds of small, medium and large sized suppliers.

Factors That Influence Channel Selection

L.O. 3

Should you sell directly to end-users or rely on intermediaries? Which intermediaries should you choose? Should you try to sell your product in every available outlet or limit distribution to a few exclusive outlets? Should you use more than one channel? These are some of the critical decisions that managers face when designing and selecting marketing channels for any product.

Building an effective channel system takes years and, like all marketing relationships, requires commitment. Thus, companies take extra care when establishing their initial marketing channels because changing distribution arrangements at a later date may prove difficult. As Chris DeNove, a channel expert, puts it, "It's much more difficult to modify an existing system than to start with a clean slate." Citing the automobile industry, for example, DeNove points out that "if an auto maker could start over now, none of them would create a franchise distribution system that looks like the existing one."[5]

When establishing marketing channels, companies must consider four key factors: market coverage, cost, control, and channel conflict.

L.O. 4

Market Coverage The appropriate *market coverage*—the number of wholesalers or retailers that will carry a product—varies by type of product. Inexpensive convenience goods or organizational supplies such as computer paper and pens sell best if they are available in as many outlets as possible. Such **intensive distribution** requires wholesalers and retailers of many types. In contrast, shopping goods (goods that require some thought before being purchased) such as Sub Zero refrigerators require different market coverage, because customers shop for such products by comparing features and prices. For these items, the best strategy is usually **selective distribution**, selling through a limited number of outlets that can give the product adequate sales and service support.

intensive distribution
Market coverage strategy that tries to place a product in as many outlets as possible

selective distribution
Market coverage strategy that uses a limited number of outlets to distribute products

exclusive distribution
Market coverage strategy that gives intermediaries exclusive rights to sell a product in a specific geographical area

If producers of expensive specialty or technical products do not sell directly to customers, they may choose **exclusive distribution**, offering products in only one outlet in each market area. High-end vehicle manufacturers have traditionally relied on exclusive distribution agreements to sell through one dealership in each local area. By contrast, other firms use multiple channels to increase their market coverage and reach several target markets. Apparel manufacturers such as Gildan Activewear frequently sell through a combination of channels, including department stores, specialty stores, the Internet, and catalogues.

Cost Costs play a major role in determining a firm's channel selection. It takes money to perform all of the functions that are handled by intermediaries. Small or new companies often cannot afford to hire a sales force large enough to sell directly to end-users or to call on a host of retail outlets. Neither can they afford to build large warehouses and distribution centres or to buy trucks to transport their goods. These firms need the help of intermediaries who can spread the cost of such activities across a number of non-competing products. With time and a larger sales base, a producer may build enough strength to take over some of these functions and reduce the length of the distribution channel.

Holt Renfrew is an upscale retail outlet that carries many high-end brand names like Burberry. Its nine outlets serve many major Canadian cities, including Vancouver, Edmonton, Calgary, Toronto, Ottawa, Montreal, and Quebec City.

Control A third issue to consider when selecting distribution channels is control of how, where, when, and for how much your product is sold. Longer distribution channels mean less control for producers, who become increasingly distant from sellers and buyers as the number of intermediaries multiplies. On the other hand, companies may not want to concentrate too many distribution functions in the hands of too few intermediaries. Control becomes critical when a firm's reputation is at stake. For instance, high-priced fashion brands, such as Burberry or Louis Vuitton, generally limit distribution to exclusive boutiques or high-end retail stores such as Holt Renfrew. Otherwise, their brands could lose some of their appeal if they were available at mid-priced retailers such as Sears Canada. Similarly, producers of complex technical products such as X-ray machines don't want their products handled by unqualified intermediaries that can't provide adequate customer service.

A brand's reputation is also linked to, and at times dependent on, the success of the retailers it selects. Consider the relationships forged by Zellers with fashion brands like Massimo. Does this relationship make economic sense for both parties? In recent years, Zellers has been attempting to move its image slightly above its traditional low-cost, no-frills image in order to distinguish itself from Wal-Mart, the powerful low-cost force in the retail market. Brand identity is a valid tool for this cause. On the other hand, Massimo increases its distribution with this deal but must also consider how this relationship affects consumer perception of their brand.

Channel Conflict Because the success of individual channel members depends on the overall channel success, ideally all channel members should work together smoothly. However, individual channel members must also run their own businesses profitably, which means that they often disagree on the roles each member should play. Such disagreements create *channel conflict*.[6]

Channel conflict may arise when suppliers provide inadequate product support, when markets are oversaturated with intermediaries, or when companies sell products via multiple channels, each of which is competing for the same customers. For instance, Hallmark's decision to sell cards to mass-market outlets such as discount stores, supermarkets, and drugstores angered its 8200 independent dealers, who were forced to compete with large chains.[7]

Similarly, when producers choose to sell direct to consumers via the Internet, they run the risk of damaging their existing relationships with other channel members. Such was the case when Avon decided to sell their cosmetics online. Avon has had a presence in Canada since 1914 and can boast an extensive network of more than 65 000 sales dealers across the country, and 3.5 million representatives worldwide. The heart and soul of Avon Canada and by extension Avon International are these loyal dealers. The introduction of the online distribution channel initially angered many representatives, who saw this as a threat to their existing sales markets. Many agents were also concerned that Avon's push into retail outlets would further hurt their businesses. Through a concerted effort by Avon headquarters, some reps now embrace the slightly more upscale retail "Becoming line" as an advertisement for the lower-end product lines they traditionally carry.[8]

Managing Physical Distribution

Developing a distribution strategy involves more than selecting the most effective channels for selling a product. Companies must also decide on the best way to move their products and services through the channels so that they are available to the customers at the right place, at the right time, and in the right amount. **Physical distribution** encompasses all activities required to move finished products from the producer to the consumer, including order processing, inventory control, warehousing, materials handling, and outbound transportation (see Exhibit 12.4).

physical distribution
All activities required to move finished products from the producer to the consumer

Exhibit 12.4 Steps in the Physical Distribution Process

The phases of a distribution system should mesh as smoothly as the cogs in a machine. Because the steps are interrelated, a change in one phase can affect the other phases. The objective of the process is to provide a target level of customer service at the lowest overall cost.

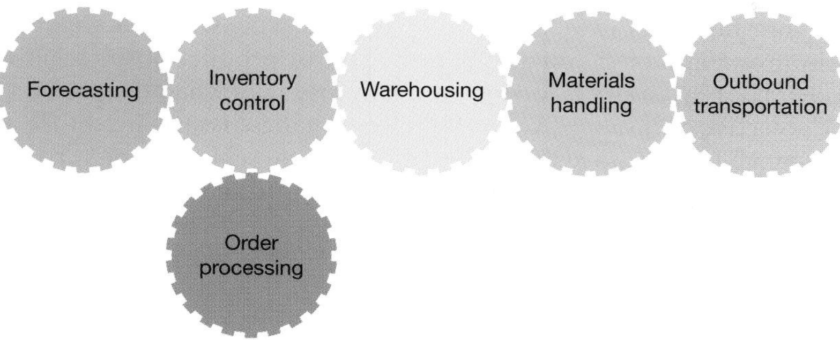

The physical movement of goods may not appear glamorous or exciting, but it is vital to a company's success. To illustrate the importance of physical distribution, consider this: A typical box of breakfast cereal can spend as long as 104 days getting from factory to supermarket, moving haltingly through a series of wholesalers and distributors, each of which has a warehouse. In fact, so many physical distribution systems are hurt by duplication and inefficiency that in industry after industry executives have been placing one item near the top of the corporate agenda: **logistics**—the planning and movement of goods and information throughout the supply chain.

logistics
The planning and movement of goods and related information throughout the supply chain

Hard pressed to knock out competitors on quality or price, companies are trying to gain an edge by streamlining processes that traverse companies and continents—no easy task, although the payback can be enormous.

In the past few years, Zara, a Spanish clothing retailer, has been expanding its operations; it now accounts for 741 locations around the world. It has begun to make an imprint on the Canadian clothing landscape with 13 stores in Montreal, Quebec City, Calgary, Toronto, and Vancouver. One of the secrets to its success is a lightning-fast distribution system that allows it to transform an idea or design into a product and have it on its shelves within three weeks. While this system required a substantial upfront cost it helped the firm to spot the latest trends and reduce inventory costs. Some of its competitors still plan and produce their goods as much as five months in advance. Zara's system produces at least 10 000 designs annually and creates a sense of urgency among its regular clientele since no style lasts more than four weeks.[9]

As the Zara example demonstrates, the key to success in managing physical distribution is to achieve a competitive level of customer service at the lowest total cost. Doing so requires trade-offs, because as the level of service improves, the cost of distribution increases. For instance, if you reduce the level of inventory to cut your storage costs, you run the risk of being unable to fill orders in a timely fashion. Or, if you use slower forms of transportation, you reduce your shipping costs, but you probably increase your storage costs. The trick is to optimize the *total* cost of achieving the desired level of service. This optimization requires a careful analysis of each step in the distribution process in relation to every other step. Let's take a closer look at each of these steps.

Order Processing

Order processing involves preparing orders for shipment and receiving orders when shipments arrive. It includes a number of activities, such as checking the customer's credit, recording the sale, making the appropriate accounting entries, arranging for the item to be shipped, adjusting the inventory records, and billing the customer. Because order processing involves direct interaction with the customer, it affects a company's reputation for customer service. Most companies establish standards for filling orders within a specific time period.

Inventory Control

As Chapter 8 discusses, in an ideal world a company would always have just the right amount of goods on hand to fill the orders it receives. In reality, however, inventory and sales are seldom in perfect balance. Most firms like to build a supply of finished goods so that they can fill orders in a timely fashion. But how much inventory is enough? If your inventory is too large, you pay extra expenses for storage space, handling, insurance, and taxes; you also run the risk of product obsolescence. On the other hand, if your inventory is too low, you may lose sales when the product is not in stock. The objective of *inventory control* is to resolve these issues. Inventory managers decide how much product to keep on hand and when to replenish the supply of goods in inventory. They also decide how to distribute products to customers if orders exceed supply.

Warehousing

warehouse
Facility for storing inventory

distribution centres
Warehouse facilities that specialize in collecting and shipping merchandise

Products held in inventory are physically stored in a **warehouse**, which may be owned by the manufacturer, by an intermediary, or by a private company that leases space to others. Some warehouses are almost purely holding facilities in which goods are stored for relatively long periods. Other warehouses, known as **distribution centres**, serve as command posts for moving products to customers. In a typical distribution centre, goods produced at a company's various locations are collected, sorted, coded, and redistributed to fill customer orders.

Some of today's most advanced physical distribution centres employ satellite navigation and communication, voice-input computers, machine vision, robots, onboard computer logbooks, and planning software that relies on artificial intelligence. FedEx, for instance, runs a fully automated distribution centre. The company's US$180 million small-package sorting system processes more than 400 000 packages an hour. Each parcel is scanned four times, weighed, and measured, and its digital image is recorded on computer. In addition, the company's world shipping software streamlines customer billing, reduces shipping paperwork, and allows customers to track their shipments on the Internet.[10]

materials handling
Movement of goods within a firm's warehouse terminal, factory, or store

Even the national carriers have come a long way from their traditional delivery systems. Canada Post has been serving Canadians for more than 150 years. As transportation and communications have evolved, so have their operating methods. Canada Post now processes approximately 11 billion articles of mail each year. It is increasingly moving into providing integrated solutions for business-to-business needs, such as its merchandise return service aimed particularly at retailers and e-tailers. Canada Post accomplishes this with 25 major plants and a sophisticated national control centre that oversees the system.[11]

Canada Post's national control centre serves to coordinate the mail/parcel distribution system and ensures prompt delivery. Along with regional centres it anticipates problems such as weather conditions and highway closures and sets contingency plans into action.

Materials Handling

An important part of warehousing activities is **materials handling**, the movement of goods within and between physical distribution facilities. One main area of concern is storage method—whether to keep supplies and finished goods in individual packages, in large boxes, or in sealed shipping containers. The choice of storage method depends on how the product is shipped, in what quantities, and to which locations. For example, a firm that typically sends small quantities of goods to widely scattered customers would not want to use large containers. Materials handling also involves keeping track of inventory so that the company knows where in the distribution process its goods are located and when they need to be moved.

Outbound Transportation

For any business, the cost of transportation is normally the largest single item in the overall cost of physical distribution.

Five common types of outbound transportation are rail, truck, water (ships), air (planes), and pipeline. When choosing among these five modes of transportation, managers weigh the advantages and disadvantages of each. In particular, they consider such factors as storage, financing, sales, inventory size, speed, product perishability, dependability, flexibility, and convenience—to name a few. The goal is to maximize the efficiency of the entire distribution process while minimizing overall cost.

Incorporating the Internet into Your Distribution Strategies

L.O. 5

The Internet's efficient and effective global reach is revolutionizing the way goods and services are sold and distributed. Amazon.com's Jeff Bezos was a pioneer in recognizing the Internet's potential for making goods and services available to buyers. He reasoned that, given a choice, many people would prefer the ease and convenience of online shopping to visiting a store every time they wanted to buy a book. He also believed that publishers would welcome Amazon.com as yet another way to get their books into the hands of readers. Today, a growing number of businesses sell a huge selection of goods and services online. For some, like Amazon, the Internet is their only marketing channel. But for others, like Future Shop, the Internet offers an additional way to sell to customers and provide product information.

An increasing number of businesses are using the Internet to improve the efficiency of their distribution systems and to expand their market reach. Some are using the Internet to eliminate the middleman, whereas others are incorporating Internet middlemen into their distribution system. For example, Kanetix bills itself as Canada's insurance marketplace. It allows shoppers to obtain multiple quotes from various insurance providers such as RBC Insurance and Standard Life. Consumers can purchase directly online or can be connected directly to the insurer of choice (see the box entitled "Kanetix—Canada's Insurance Marketplace").[12]

In short, the Internet is a powerful force that is changing the role of traditional intermediaries. The livelihoods of travel agents, retailers, real estate agents, and independent sales representatives are threatened as never before, as the Internet increasingly allows sellers and buyers to find each other and do business directly or differently.

PROMOTIONAL STRATEGIES

Although distribution is a critical element in the marketing mix, promotion is perhaps the one element you associate most with the marketing function. That's because promotion is highly visible to consumers. In Chapter 11 we defined promotion as a form of persuasive communication that motivates people to buy whatever an organization is selling—goods, services, or ideas. Promotion may take the form of direct, face-to-face communication or indirect communication through such media as television, radio, magazines, newspapers, direct mail, billboards, the Internet, floor ads, and other channels. How do you decide on which forms of promotion to use? Many firms develop a **promotional strategy**; that is, they define the direction and scope of the promotional activities their companies will take to meet their marketing objectives.

promotional strategy
Statement or document that defines the direction and scope of the promotional activities that a company will use to meet its marketing objectives

Developing a promotional strategy encompasses several steps. You begin by setting your promotional goals. Next you take several product variables into consideration and decide on the best market approach before selecting your promotional mix. Finally, you fine-tune your product mix to make sure that all of your promotional elements communicate the same message.

Setting Your Promotional Goals

You can use promotion to achieve three basic goals: to inform, to persuade, and to remind. *Informing* is the first promotional priority, because people cannot buy something until they are aware of it and know what it can do for them.

Potential customers need to know where the item can be purchased, how much it costs, and how to use it. *Persuading* is also an important priority, because most people

Kanetix—Canada's Insurance Marketplace

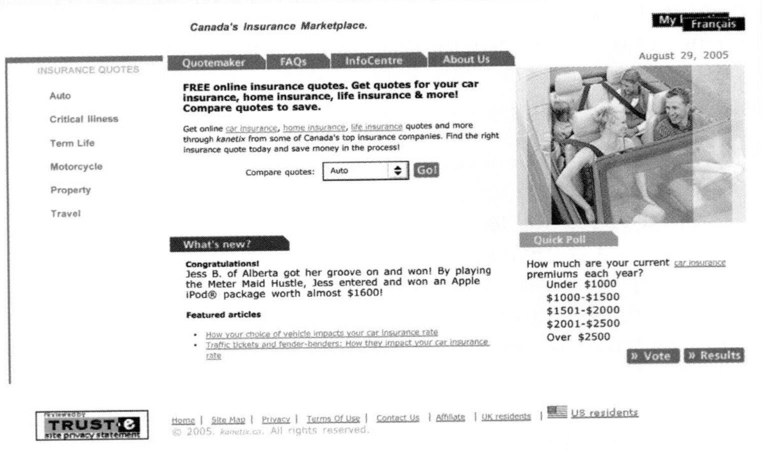

www.kanetix.ca

Since its launch in 1999, Kanetix has established itself as one of the most popular insurance destinations on the Web. Every day thousands of Canadians use this online quote comparison service to shop for car, home, life, and/or travel coverage. Unlike many of its fellow e-commerce ventures launched at that exciting time, Kanetix survived the Internet bubble. The site helps consumers compare quotes from more than 35 of Canada's top insurance providers and facilitates the connection to the insurance company of choice. Kanetix has managed to build its presence by providing cost efficiency and time efficiency to the marketplace.

THE VALUE PROPOSITION

Shopping for insurance the traditional way can be very time consuming. Detailed information must be registered with each company that the client approaches. Each company spends valuable time and the client ends up answering the same questions over and over again. Kanetix offers a win-win solution for customers and suppliers in a one-stop-shopping environment. In only minutes, consumers are able to locate a reputable insurance supplier with attractive rates. Conversely, insurance companies are able to target the consumers they want, based on the profile, driving habits, and insurance history of each shopper. It is possible that the quotes may not match the client's current insurance premiums because of discounts that insurance companies provide for loyal customers. Even in such cases Kanetix provides the peace of mind that the consumer's current price is a fair one.

GROWTH AND CHANGE

Kanetix has experienced significant growth since it expanded nationally in 2001. The number of users comparing quotes online more than doubled the following year, and increased by another 49 percent in 2003 to more than 1 million online quotes. Originally Kanetix targeted young male drivers in their twenties paying high insurance premiums; however, the average age of the Kanetix user is now over 35. The service has evolved and now caters to a diverse group of shoppers ranging from high-risk drivers to families with multiple drivers. Additionally, with the launch into the United States in 2005 the company has chartered a course for continued leadership and growth in this dynamic market.

PROTECTION OF PRIVACY

Internet security and privacy issues are a vital area of concern for all online providers. Kanetix protects the privacy of clients and allows them to shop anonymously, without fear of an insurance agent calling or e-mailing in the future. Personal information is only requested when the shopper is ready to purchase an insurance policy, and these data are collected and protected with the highest security standards.

INSURANCE FULFILLMENT ONLINE OR OFFLINE

Additionally, fulfillment of an insurance policy can be completed by applying for coverage online or by phone. Kanetix recognizes that not all consumers are comfortable completing an insurance transaction online. Its call centre is available to answer questions about the website or the insurance purchase process and can connect shoppers with a licensed insurance representative from any of the insurance suppliers featured on the site.[13]

Questions for Critical Thinking

1. From a consumer's perspective, what are the advantages of using the Kanetix service?
2. How does Kanetix address customer concerns with using the Internet for insurance quotes? How can it further reduce these concerns?

need to be encouraged to purchase something new or to switch brands. Advertising that meets this goal is classified as **persuasive advertising**. *Reminding* the customer of the product's availability and benefits is also important, because such reminders stimulate additional purchases. The term for such promotional efforts is **reminder advertising**.

Beyond these general objectives, your promotional strategy should accomplish specific objectives: It should attract new customers, increase usage among existing customers, aid distributors, stabilize sales, boost brand-name recognition, create sales leads, differentiate the product, and influence decision makers.

persuasive advertising
Advertising designed to encourage product sampling and brand switching

reminder advertising
Advertising intended to remind existing customers of a product's availability and benefits

Analyzing Product Variables

Before selecting your promotional mix, you must consider a number of product and market factors. To begin with, you must consider the nature of your product. Various types of products lend themselves to differing forms of promotion. Simple, familiar items like laundry detergent can be explained adequately through advertising, but personal selling is generally required to communicate the features of unfamiliar and sophisticated goods and services such as office-automation equipment or municipal waste-treatment facilities. Direct, personal contact is particularly important in promoting customized services such as interior design, financial advice, or legal counsel. In general, consumer and organizational goods usually require different promotional mixes.

The product's price is also a factor in the selection of the promotional mix. Inexpensive items such as shaving cream or breakfast cereal sold to a mass market are well suited to advertising and sales promotion, which have a relatively low per-unit cost. At the other extreme, products with a high unit price such as in-ground swimming pools lend themselves to personal selling because the high cost of a sales call is justified by the price of the product. Furthermore, the nature of the selling process often demands face-to-face interaction between the buyer and seller.

Another factor that influences both the level and mix of promotional activity is the product's position in its life cycle. Early on, when the seller is trying to inform the customer about the product and build the distribution network, promotional efforts are in high gear. Selective advertising, sales promotion, and public relations are used to build awareness and to encourage early adopters to try the product; personal selling is used to gain the cooperation of intermediaries. Gillette, for example, spent US$300 million to promote the launch of the Mach3 razor during its first year—on top of more than US$750 million in development costs—to accelerate the Mach3's transition from the costly introduction stage to the profitable growth stage faster than any previous Gillette razors. Just 18 months after the Mach3 was launched, sales for the product hit US$1 billion, making it the company's most successful new product ever.[14] As the Mach3 product moved along the product life cycle Gillette launched Mach3 Turbo, Mach3 Turbo champion, and M3 Power with similar support. The Mach3 line now accounts for approximately 27 percent of the global market share but Schick is aiming to reduce this figure with their Quattro four-bladed option.[15]

As the market expands during the growth phase, the seller broadens its advertising and sales promotion activities to reach a wider audience and continues to use personal selling to expand the distribution network. When the product reaches maturity and competition is at its peak, the seller's primary goal is to differentiate the product from rival brands. Advertising generally dominates the promotional mix during this phase, but sales promotion is an important supplemental tool, particularly for low-priced consumer products. As the product begins to decline, the level of promotion generally tapers off. Advertising and selling efforts are carefully targeted toward loyal, steady customers.

The goal of this advertisement is to inform or remind consumers of Vans' shoes and to stimulate them to buy the product by associating the product with fun times.

Deciding on Your Market Approach

The selection of your promotional mix also depends on whether you plan to focus your marketing effort on intermediaries or on final cus-

push strategy
Promotional approach designed to motivate wholesalers and retailers to push a producer's products to end users

pull strategy
Promotional strategy that stimulates consumer demand, which then exerts pressure on wholesalers and retailers to carry a product

tomers. If the focus is on intermediaries, the producer uses a **push strategy** to persuade wholesalers and retailers to carry the item. Producers may, for instance, offer wholesalers or retailers special discounts or incentives for purchasing larger quantities. You would expect to see personal selling and sales promotions to dominate the promotional mix aimed at intermediaries. If the marketing focus is on end-users, the producer uses a **pull strategy** to appeal directly to the ultimate customer, using advertising, direct mail, contests, discount coupons, and so on. With this approach, consumers learn of the product through promotion and request it from retailers, who respond by asking their wholesalers for it or by going directly to the producer (see Exhibit 12.5).

The power of the "pull strategy" is very evident around the Christmas holidays when Canadian shoppers flock to retail outlets like The Bay or Toys "R" Us and desperately search for that heavily promoted "hot toy" of the season. Retailers seize the opportunity and attempt to re-order large quantities when frenzied customers come to them in desperate need of satisfying their child's demands.

Most companies use both push and pull tactics to increase the impact of their promotional efforts. For example, when Schering-Plough introduced Claritin antihistamine, it used push tactics to educate physicians about the prescription drug's use and effectiveness, while it used pull tactics such as television and print advertising to increase market awareness and encourage consumers to ask for the new medication. This diverse, high-powered promotional mix helped Claritin capture a whopping 54 percent of the antihistamine drug market within a short time.[16]

The promotional mix is also influenced by the size and concentration of the market. In markets with many widely dispersed buyers, advertising is generally the most economical way of communicating the product's features. In markets with relatively few customers, particularly when they are clustered in a limited area, personal selling is a practical promotional alternative. Many marketers use a combination of methods, often relying on advertising and public relations to build awareness and interest, following up with personal selling to complete the sale.

Exhibit 12.5 **Push and Pull Strategies**

Push strategies "push" products through distribution channels to final consumers by persuading wholesalers and retailers to carry the product. Pull strategies use consumer promotions and advertising to induce consumers to buy the product and "pull" the product through the distribution channels.

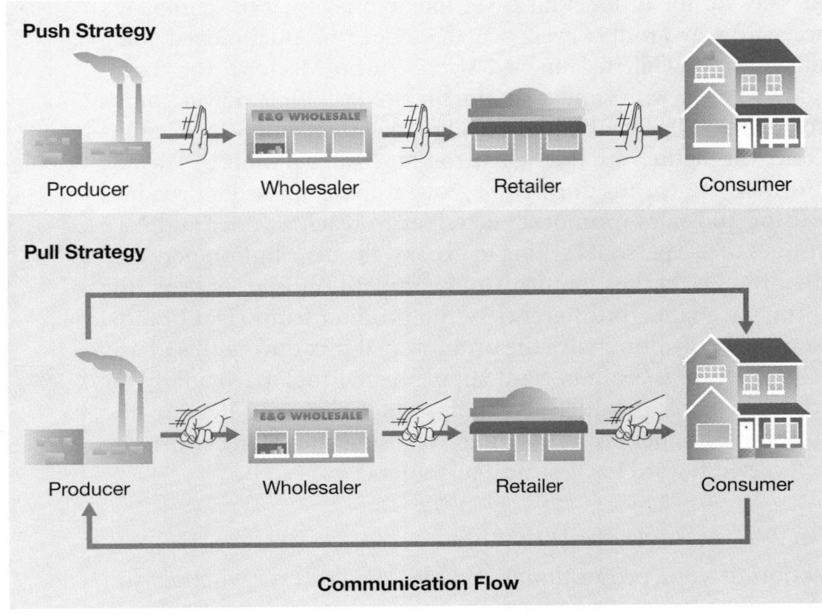

Exhibit 12.6 The Five Elements of Promotion

The promotional mix typically includes a blend of various elements. The most effective mix depends on the nature of the market and the characteristics of the good or service being marketed. Over time, the mix for a particular product may change.

ACTIVITY	REACH	TIMING	FLEXIBILITY	COST/ EXPOSURE
Personal Selling	Direct personal interaction with limited reach	Regular, recurrent contact	Message tailored to customer and adjusted to reflect feedback	Relatively high
Advertising	Indirect interaction with large reach	Regular, recurrent contact	Standard, unvarying message	Low to moderate
Direct Marketing	Direct personal interaction with large reach	Intermittent, based on short-term sales objectives	Customized, varying message	Relatively high
Sales Promotion	Indirect interaction with large reach	Intermittent, based on short-term sales objectives	Standard, unvarying message	Varies
Public Relations	Indirect interaction with large reach	Intermittent, as newsworthy events occur	Standard, unvarying message	No direct cost

Selecting Your Promotional Mix

L.O. 6

Within the framework of a company's promotional goods, product variables, and market approach, marketers use a mix of five activities to achieve their promotional objectives: personal selling, advertising, direct marketing, sales promotion, and public relations. These elements can be combined in various ways to create a **promotional mix** for a particular product or idea (see Exhibit 12.6).

promotional mix Particular blend of personal selling, advertising, direct marketing, sales promotion, and public relations that a company uses to reach potential customers

personal selling In-person communication between a seller and one or more potential buyers

Personal Selling

Personal selling is the interpersonal aspect of the promotional mix. It involves person-to-person presentation—face to face, by phone, or by interactive media such as Web TV's videoconferencing or customized websites—for the purpose of making sales and building customer relationships. Personal selling allows for immediate interaction between the buyer and seller. It also enables the seller to adjust the message to the specific needs, interests, and reactions of the individual customer. The chief disadvantage of face-to-face personal selling is its relatively high cost—about US$170 per sales call according to one recent study.[17]

Although it may look easy, personal selling is not a simple task. Some sales, of course, are made in a matter of minutes. However, other sales, particularly for large organizational purchases, can take months to complete. Many salespeople follow a carefully planned seven-step process from start to finish, as Exhibit 12.7 suggests.

- *Prospecting.* Finding and qualifying potential buyers of the product or service.
- *Preparing.* Considering various options for approaching the prospect and preparing for the sales call.

Exhibit 12.7 The Personal Selling Process

The personal selling process can involve up to seven steps, starting with prospecting for sales leads and ending with following up after the sale has been closed.

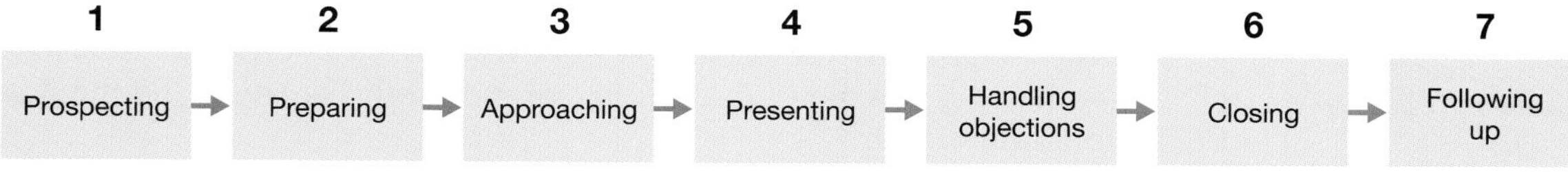

- *Approaching.* Contacting the prospect, getting his or her attention, and building interest in the product or service.
- *Presenting.* Communicating a message that persuades a prospect to buy.
- *Handling objections.* Countering the buyer's objections with convincing claims.
- *Closing.* Asking the prospect to buy the product.
- *Following up.* Checking customer satisfaction following the sale and building goodwill.

Technological advances are facilitating these steps and the entire selling process. Some companies are using custom software to provide online proposal-generation and order-management systems. The software relieves salespeople of non-productive tasks and allows sales reps to spend more time attending to customers' specific needs. Sales reps at Owens-Corning use laptops, the Internet, and a custom software package called Field Automation Sales Team system (FAST) to inquire about customers' backgrounds and sales histories, resolve customer service issues on the spot, modify pricing information as needed, print customized sales material, and more. Such technology empowers Owens-Corning reps. "They become the real managers of their own business and their own territories," says Owens-Corning's regional general manager.[18]

Advertising and Direct Marketing

advertising
Paid, non-personal communication to a target market from an identified sponsor using mass communications channels

direct marketing
Direct communication other than personal sales contacts designed to effect a measurable response

Advertising and direct marketing are the two elements of a firm's promotional mix with which consumers are most familiar. **Advertising** consists of messages paid for by an identified sponsor and transmitted through a mass communication medium such as television, radio, or newspapers. **Direct marketing** is defined by the Direct Marketing Association as distributing promotional materials directly to a consumer or business recipient for the purpose of generating (1) a response in the form of an order, (2) a request for further information, or (3) a visit to a store or other place of business for purchase of a specific product or service.[19]

All forms of advertising and direct marketing have three objectives: to create product awareness, to create and maintain the image of a product, and to stimulate consumer demand. Advertising and direct marketing are also the promotional approaches that best reach mass audiences quickly at a relatively low per-person cost. But, to be effective, your messages must be persuasive, stand out from the competition's, and motivate your target audience—a lofty goal considering the fact that Canadian consumers are bombarded by ads. As a recent article in *Marketing* magazine pointed out, Canadians are exposed to thousands of messages each day. When you include television, radio ads, bus and subway ads, billboards, and ads on varied objects from T-shirts to coffee mugs, this figure is put into context.[20] Basically, you can say whatever you want, just as long as you stay within the boundaries of the law and conform to the moral and ethical standards of the advertising medium and trade associations.

Events like the F1 Canadian Grand Prix and the Molson Indy races were threatened because of anti-tobacco legislation. As you can see from this photo of Paul Tracy's Indy car, such teams and events are heavily sponsored by the tobacco industry.

To limit promotional abuses, the Canadian Radio-television and Telecommunications Commission (CRTC) regulates broadcasted advertisements, while Advertising Standards Canada administers codes of practice that are voluntarily established.[21] Certain industries fall under additional authority; for example, pharmaceutical advertisements fall under the domain of Health Canada. Recently some groups have accused Health Canada of dropping the ball by relaxing regulations and allowing two types of ads: reminder ads (that focus on the drug but not the disease), and help-seeking ads (that discuss the disease but not the drug). Critics argue that drugs should not be promoted in the same way as cola. They point to the string of Viagra ads that focus solely on the end result: men are shown singing in the shower, skipping to work, and smiling from ear to ear. By giving the audience a wink and a nod these ads avoid the origins of the situation and the side effects of the drug.[22]

On the other hand, when governments step in they can sometimes create a politically dangerous backlash. Anti-tobacco legislation has been in the news because it puts the future of popular events in danger when the big tobacco dollars evaporate and promoters scramble to fill the void. Few people dispute the positive intention of the laws, but when large, well-attended events like the Canadian Grand Prix were put in danger, federal and provincial governments scrambled to save them.[23]

Direct-Marketing Vehicles

Direct marketing is an effective promotional tool for many companies because it enables them to more precisely target and personalize messages to specific consumer and business segments and build long-term customer relationships.[24] The most popular direct marketing vehicles are direct mail, targeted e-mail, telemarketing, and the Internet.

- *Direct mail.* The principal vehicle for direct marketing is **direct mail**, which includes catalogues, brochures, videotapes, disks, and other promotional materials delivered through Canada Post and private carriers.
- *Target e-mail.* Increasingly, companies are sending e-mails to highly targeted lists of prospects. This technique works much the same way as offline direct marketing campaigns. Companies build databases of e-mail addresses by enticing customers to register on a website in exchange for information or access to a special offer.[25]
- *Telemarketing.* Another popular form of direct marketing is **telemarketing**, or selling over the telephone. Telemarketing is a low-cost way to efficiently reach many people. Unfortunately, it has a spotted reputation because of some shady practitioners. "The Canadian Government has taken aim at telemarketers with the Competition Act (Bill C-20) and a further amendment, Bill C-51 that defines new offences as "enterprise crimes" and brings them within the scope of the Criminal Code scheme for seizure and forfeiture of proceeds."[26]
- *Internet.* As with targeted e-mail, marketers can use the Internet's interactive options to tailor a unique pitch to the individual. For example, companies can alert customers to special savings or remind them of past purchases based on their user profiles. The principal advantages of Internet direct marketing are timeliness, global reach, relatively low cost, and two-way communication using features such as chat and instant messaging.

Advertising Categories

Advertising is commonly classified by type. **Product advertising** is the most common type, designed to sell specific goods or services, such as Tim Hortons Timbits, Kellogg's cereals, or MAC cosmetics. Product advertising generally describes the product's features and may mention its price. **Institutional advertising** is designed to create goodwill and build a desired image for a company rather than to sell specific products. As discussed in Chapter 3, many companies are now spending large sums for institutional advertising that focuses on *green marketing*, creating an image of companies as corporate conservationists. Institutional advertisers point out their actions, contributions, and philosophies not only as supporting the environmental movement but as leading the way. When used as *corporate advertising*, institutional advertising often promotes an entire line of a company's products. Institutional ads can also be used to remind investors that the company is doing well.

Advertising can also be classified according to the sponsor. **National advertising** is sponsored by companies that sell trademarked products on a nationwide basis. The term *national* refers to the level of the advertiser,

direct mail
Advertising sent directly to potential customers

telemarketing
Selling or supporting the sales process over the telephone

product advertising
Advertising that tries to sell specific goods or services, generally by describing features, benefits, and, occasionally, price

institutional advertising
Advertising that seeks to create goodwill and to build a desired image for a company rather than to sell specific products

national advertising
Advertising sponsored by companies that sell products on a nationwide basis; refers to the geographic reach of the advertiser, not the geographic coverage of the ad

Advertisers pay a premium to be viewed at a major event such as the Grey Cup. While not taking in the $2.4 million per spot that the Super Bowl does, the Grey Cup is a significant event that has clients lining up to associate themselves with the game and the spectacle of artists like Timmins, Ontario, native Shania Twain.

not the geographic coverage of the ad. If a national manufacturer places an ad in only one city, the ad is still classified as a national ad. By contrast, **local advertising** is sponsored by a local merchant. Grocery store ads in the local newspaper are a good example. **Cooperative advertising** is a financial arrangement whereby companies with products sold nationally share the costs of local advertising with local merchants and wholesalers. As a result, it is a cross between local and national advertising. A national furniture manufacture like Palliser may share costs with local furniture shops.

local advertising
Advertising sponsored by a local merchant

cooperative advertising
Joint efforts between local and national advertisers, in which producers of nationally sold products share the costs of local advertising with local merchants and wholesalers

Regardless of which type of advertising you use, you must get your message to your target audience by using suitable **media**, or channels of communication. Advertising media fall into six major categories, each with its own strengths and weaknesses, as highlighted in Exhibit 12.8. Your goal, as a marketer, is to select a **media mix**—the combination of print, broadcast, and other media that maximizes the return of your advertising dollar. The box entitled "Zoom Media: A Good Place for an Ad" describes an unconventional but successful advertising approach.

media
Communications channels, such as newspapers, radio, and television

L.O. 7

media mix
Combination of various media options that a company uses in an advertising campaign

Sales Promotion

Sales promotion, which includes a wide range of events and activities designed to stimulate immediate interest in and encourage the purchase of your product or service, is the fourth element of the promotional mix. The impact of sales promotion activities is often short term; thus, sales promotions are not as effective as advertising or personal selling in building long-term brand preference.[27] Sales promotion consists of two basic categories: consumer promotion and trade promotion.

sales promotion
Wide range of events and activities (including coupons, rebates, contests, in-store demonstrations, free samples, trade shows, and point-of-purchase displays) designed to stimulate interest in a product

Consumer Promotion **Consumer promotion** is aimed directly at final users of the product. Companies use a variety of promotional tools and incentives to stimulate repeat purchases and to entice new users:

- *Coupons.* The biggest category of consumer promotion—and the most popular with consumers—is **coupons**, certificates that spur sales by giving buyers a discount when they purchase specified products. Customers redeem their coupons at the

consumer promotion
Sales promotion aimed at final consumers

Exhibit 12.8 Advantages and Disadvantages of Major Advertising Media

When selecting the media mix, companies attempt to match the characteristics of the media audiences with the characteristics of the customer segments being targeted. A typical advertising campaign involves the use of several media.

MEDIUM	ADVANTAGES	DISADVANTAGES
Newspapers	Extensive market coverage; low cost; short lead time for placing ads; good local market coverage; geographic selectivity	Poor graphic quality; short life span; cluttered pages; visual competition from other ads
Television	Great impact; broad reach; appealing to senses of sight, sound, and motion; creative opportunities for demonstration; high attention; entertainment carryover	High cost for production and air time; less audience selectivity; long preparation time; vulnerability to remote controls
Direct mail	Can deliver large amounts of information to narrowly selected audiences; excellent control over quality of message; personalization	High cost per contact; delivery delays; difficulty of obtaining desired mailing list; consumer resistance; generally poor image (junk mail)
Radio	Low cost; high frequency; immediacy; highly portable; high geographic and demographic selectivity	No visual possibilities; short life for message; commercial clutter; lower attention than television; easy to switch stations
Magazines	Good reproduction; long life; local and regional market selectivity; authority and credibility; multiple readers	Limited demonstration possibilities; long lead time between placing and publishing ads; high cost; less compelling than other major media
Internet	Fast-growing reach; low cost; ability to personalize; can appeal to senses of sight, sound, and motion	Difficulty in measuring audiences; consumer resistance; increasing clutter

Zoom Media: A Good Place for an Ad

Consumers are faced with an endless string of ads on television, in magazines, on the radio, and in other traditional media outlets. It is difficult for sponsors to get a message through to the current ad-weary generation. Once upon a time, a firm could advertise on a local station and feel confident that it would reach a significant portion of the targeted community. Today, satellite and digital cable are providing countless stations and fragmenting the market. Personal video recorders are reducing the ad impressions as consumers are able to skip ads like never before. Furthermore, traditional media are competing for our leisure time with alternatives like the Internet. What can a savvy marketer do? Zoom Media offers a solution by enabling sponsors to place strategically integrated messages into consumers' everyday work and play environments.

You may or may not be familiar with Zoom Media, but you have seen its ads. They are located in washrooms across the country, from your local school campus to the resto-bar you frequent to sports and medical complexes in your community. What began in 1991 as a university project to raise awareness and reduce the spread of sexually transmitted diseases eventually grew into Zoom Media. This company now boast 40 000 billboard locations in more than 5700 venues. Carl Grenier and his team pioneered this advertising approach; they began by acquiring the rights to display ads in restaurants and bars. The Zoom resto-bar division now serves 1922 different outlets. If a sponsor is targeting a specific youth segment it can reach them directly in their favourite bar or restaurant hangout. Zoom also serves 73 campuses, 329 sports clubs, 223 medical facilities, and 224 golf courses across Canada and the United States. According to research, consumers are at peace with the invasion of their washrooms: "80% of students appreciate the ads and 54% of students recall the advertisements."[28]

Zoom Media continues to expand its reach. With its recent acquisition of Parkad Media Ltd. it has branched out to serve parking lots. In addition to its extensive network of restaurants, Zoom Media has forged an alliance with McDonald's and serves 558 franchise locations. One thing is clear: washrooms across the nation have become a new permanent outlet to access your mind and influence your perception of products.[29]

Zoom Media pioneered the concept of bathroom ads; however, the idea spread quickly as marketers immediately identified the targeting possibilities offered by this approach.

Questions for Critical Thinking

1. One of the benefits of Zoom Media's approach is the opportunity for sponsors to target specific groups.
   a. Name a product/brand that would be a good candidate to promote in Zoom's golf network? Explain.
   b. Which products/brands would fit in better in Zoom's McDonald's network? Explain.
2. How do Zoom's washroom ads fulfill the three principle objectives of advertising?

time of purchase.[30] Companies offer coupons on packages, in print ads, in direct mail, at the checkout, and on the Internet to encourage trial of new products, reach out to non-users of mature products, encourage repeat buying, and temporarily lower a product's price.[31]

coupons
Certificates that offer discounts on particular items and are redeemed at the time of purchase

- *Rebates.* Similar to coupons, rebates are another popular promotional tool. Instead of receiving the discount at the time of purchase, buyers generally get reimbursement cheques from the manufacturer by submitting proofs of purchase along with a prepared manufacturer's rebate form. Because many buyers neglect to redeem the rebates, the costs of running such programs remain relatively low. Moreover, rebates allow the manufacturer to promote the reduced price even though customers pay the full price at checkout.[32]

point-of-purchase display
Advertising or other display materials set up at retail locations to promote products to potential customers as they are making their purchase decisions

- *Point-of-purchase.* Another widely used consumer promotion technique is the **point-of-purchase (POP) display**, a device for showing a product in a way that stimulates immediate sales. It may be simple, such as the end-of-aisle stacks of cola in a supermarket or the racks of gum and mints at checkout counters, or it may be more elaborate, such as ad decals strategically placed on floor aisles. Simple or elaborate, point-of-purchase displays really work: Studies show that in almost every instance, such displays significantly increase sales.[33]
- *Special-event sponsorship.* Sponsoring special events has become one of the most popular sales promotion tactics. Thousands of companies spend billions of dollars to sponsor events ranging from golf to opera. The 2002 Winter Olympic Games in Salt Lake City, Utah, drew more than 64 corporate sponsors, who contributed more than US$800 million in cash, goods, and services. Visa, Coca-Cola, and McDonald's were some of the games' largest sponsors.[34] The organizers of the upcoming 2010 Vancouver-Whistler Winter Games are banking on receiving about $600 million to help finance the games.[35] They are off to a good start; Bell Canada secured the rights as the official telecommunications sponsor in a $200 million deal.[36]

cross-promotion
Jointly advertising two or more non-competing brands

- *Cross-promotion.* Another popular sales promotion vehicle is **cross-promotion**, which involves using one brand to advertise another, non-competing brand. One of the most successful cross-promotion campaigns ever is "Intel Inside." Just two years following the campaign's inception, awareness of the Intel chip went from roughly 22 percent of PC buyers to more than 80 percent.[37]
- *Samples.* Samples are an effective way to introduce a new product, encourage non-users to try an existing product, encourage current buyers to use the product in a new way, or expand distribution into new areas. Butler and Procter & Gamble give dentists toothbrushes to pass on to their patients. Halls puts bins heaped with cough drops in theatre lobbies.[38] Despite its recent problems, Krispy Kreme has used extensive sampling to successfully create a buzz. For example, before opening its first outlet in Montreal the company intensively seeded the marketplace with free samples, most notably at college and university campuses. This approach led to line-ups and a tremendous word-of-mouth success. Similar campaigns were repeated across the country as Krispy Kreme moved into the market and attempted to make a minor dent in Tim Hortons market dominance.[39]

premiums
Free or bargain-priced items offered to encourage consumers to buy a product

specialty advertising
Advertising that appears on various items such as coffee mugs, pens, and calendars, designed to help keep a company's name in front of customers

Other popular consumer sales promotion techniques include in-store demonstrations, loyalty and frequency programs such as frequent-flyer miles, and **premiums**, which are free or bargain-priced items offered to encourage the consumer to buy a product. Contests, sweepstakes, and games are also quite popular in some industries and can generate a great deal of public attention, particularly when valuable or unusual prizes are offered. **Specialty advertising** (on pens, calendars, T-shirts, and so on) helps keep a company's name in front of customers for a long period of time.

trade promotions
Sales promotion efforts aimed at convincing distributors or retailers to push a producer's products

trade allowance
Discount offered by producers to wholesalers and retailers

Trade Promotion Although shoppers are more aware of consumer promotion, trade promotions actually account for the largest share of promotional spending. **Trade promotions** are aimed at convincing distributors or retailers to sell a company's products by offering them a discount on the product's price, or a **trade allowance**. The distributor or retailer can pocket the savings and increase company profits or can pass the savings on to the consumer to generate additional sales. Besides discounts, other popular trade allowance forms are display premiums, dealer contests or sweepstakes, and travel bonus programs. All are designed to motivate distributors or retailers to push particular merchandise.

Public Relations

Public relations encompasses all of the non-sales communications that businesses have with their many stakeholders—communities, investors, industry analysts, government agencies and officials, and the news media. Companies rely on public relations to build a favourable corporate image and foster positive relations with these groups.

public relations
Non-sales communication that businesses have with their various audiences (includes both communication with the general public and press relations)

In fact, successful companies recognize that a good reputation is one of a business's most important assets. A recent study shows that companies with a good public image have a big edge over less-respected companies. Consumers are more than twice as likely to buy new products from companies they admire, which is why smart companies work hard to build and protect their reputations. Sometimes companies hire public relations firms to help them maintain or restore their public image. For instance, tire maker Bridgestone/Firestone hired a public relations firm to help it restore its shattered reputation following the recall of 6.5 million Firestone tires that had been involved in more than 170 traffic deaths and 700 injuries.[40]

Public relations are not limited to corporate causes. After the SARS outbreak, Mike Myers provided the city of Toronto with some much-needed PR support. He went on major programs in the United States urging people to visit the city and educating them on the actual risks related to SARS.

Two standard public relations tools are the news release and the news conference. A **news release** is a short memo sent to the media covering topics that are of potential news interest; a *video news release* is a brief video clip sent to television stations. Companies use news releases to get favourable news coverage about themselves and their products. Richard Branson is a master at this game. During the initial Canadian launch of Virgin Mobile he swept through the country with spectacles that were covered by local and national papers.[41] When a business has significant news to announce, it will often arrange a **news conference**. Both tools are used when the company's news is of widespread interest, when products need to be demonstrated, or when company officials want to be available to answer questions from the media.

news release
Brief statement or video program released to the press announcing new products, management changes, sales performance, and other potential news items

news conference
Gathering of media representatives at which companies announce new information; also called a press briefing

Integrating Your Marketing Communications

L.O. 8

With five major promotional methods available—personal selling, advertising, direct marketing, sales promotion, and public relations—how do you decide on the right mix for your product? There are no easy answers, because you must take many factors into account. In fact, when you consider all the ways that audiences can receive marketing messages today, the potential for confusion is not all that surprising. Besides the traditional media—radio, television, billboards, print ads, and direct-mail promotions—marketers are using websites, e-mail, faxes, kiosks, sponsorships, and a number of clever vehicles to deliver messages to targeted audiences. Coordinating promotional and communication efforts is becoming vital if a company is to send a consistent effective message.

Integrated marketing communications (**IMC**) is a strategy of coordinating and integrating all one's communications and promotional efforts to provide customers with clarity, consistency, and maximum communications impact. "It's everything from running ads to developing new media, to creating custom media, licensing, promotion, sweepstakes—every aspect of communicating to consumers," says one media expert.[42] The basics of IMC are quite simple: communicating with one voice and one message to the marketplace, as Exhibit 12.9 suggests.

integrated marketing communications (**IMC**)
Strategy of coordinating and integrating communications and promotional efforts with customers to ensure greater efficiency and effectiveness

The need for communicating with one voice is even greater today. Consumers are exposed to a greater variety of marketing communications and don't necessarily distinguish among message sources the way that marketers do. In the consumer's mind, messages from different sources blur into one single message about the company. Thus,

Exhibit 12.9 **Integrated Marketing Communications**

Coordinating the five elements of promotion delivers a consistent message to the marketplace.

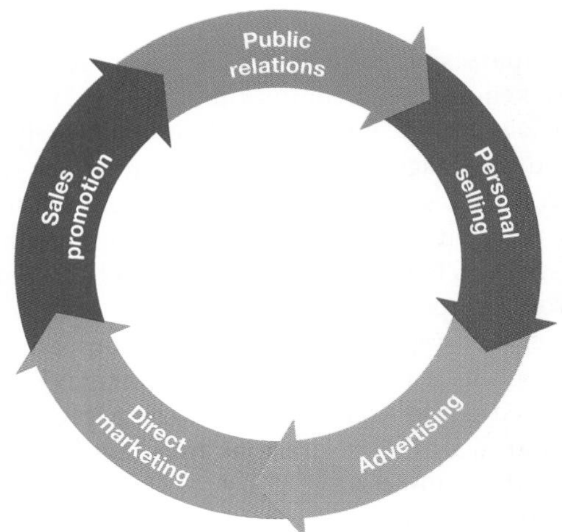

conflicting messages from different sources can result in confused company images and brand positions.[43]

Properly implemented, IMC increases marketing and promotional effectiveness. For example, Molson benefited from the tremendous exposure of its "I AM" campaign for years. The results were not a chance occurrence. Molson coordinated a deliberate message across media. Its ads captured the attention of the TV viewer, while the "I AM" website had interactive features for surfers to explore. Molson encouraged and actively pursued opportunities for product exposure, and this campaign managed to generate countless articles on the topic.[44] After Molson's merger with Coors the company moved away from this position. The first post-merger campaign had the following nationalistically generic slogan: "It Starts Here."

While integrating your communications and promotional efforts may seem logical and relatively simple, many organizations find IMC difficult to implement. They discover that over time their promotional mixes develop into collections of disconnected efforts. Organizational resistance is the primary cause for IMC failure. Many marketing departments are accustomed to autonomy and see IMC as a threat to their resources and decision-making power. Besides, moving to an IMC approach requires new ways of organizing, planning, and managing all marketing functions, and some marketing departments are not up to the task.[45]

SUMMARY OF LEARNING OBJECTIVES

1 Explain what marketing intermediaries do and list their seven primary functions.

Marketing intermediaries, or middlemen, bring producers' products to market and help ensure that the goods and services are available in the right time, place, and amount. More specifically, intermediaries match buyers and sellers; provide market information; provide promotional and sales support; sort, standardize, and divide merchandise; transport and store the product; assume risks; and provide financing.

2 Explain how wholesalers and retailers function as intermediaries.

Wholesalers buy from producers and sell to retailers, to other wholesalers, and to organizational customers such as businesses, government agencies, and institutions. Retailers buy from producers or wholesalers and sell the products to the final consumers.

3 Discuss the key factors that influence channel design and selection.

Channel design and selection are influenced by the type of product and industry practices. They are also influenced by a firm's desired market coverage (intense, selective, or exclusive), financial ability, desire for control, and potential for channel conflict.

4 Differentiate between intensive, selective, and exclusive distribution strategies.

With an intensive distribution strategy, a company attempts to saturate the market with its products by offering them in every available outlet. Companies that use a more selective approach to distribution choose a limited number of retailers that can adequately support the product. Firms that use exclusive distribution grant a single wholesaler or retailer the exclusive right to sell the product within a given geographic area.

5 Discuss the Internet's effect on the distribution function.

Companies are using the Internet to enhance their existing channel structures, expand their market reach, and add efficiencies to their channel structures. Some are eliminating layers of intermediaries from a marketing channel and transferring the eliminated intermediary functions to the Internet. In many cases, these changes—especially the bypassing of a channel—are causing channel conflict.

6 Identify the five basic categories of promotion.

The five basic categories of promotion are (1) personal selling, which involves contacting customers by phone, interactive media, or in person to make a sale; (2) advertising, which is a paid sponsored message transmitted by mass communication media; (3) direct marketing, which is the distribution of promotional material to consumers via direct mail, e-mail, telemarketing, or the Internet to generate an order or other consumer response; (4) sales promotion, which includes a number of consumer and promotional tools designed to stimulate consumer interest in a product and encourage a purchase; and (5) public relations, which includes non-sales communications between businesses and their stakeholders to foster positive relationships.

7 Distinguish between the two main types of sales promotion and give examples of each.

The two main types of sales promotion are consumer promotion and trade promotion. Consumer promotions are intended to motivate the final consumer to try new products or to experiment with the company's brands. Examples include coupons, cross-promotion, specialty advertising, premiums, point-of-purchase displays, and special events. Trade promotions are designed to induce wholesalers and retailers to stimulate sales of a producer's products. Examples include trade allowances, display premiums, dealer contests, and travel bonus programs.

8 Discuss the use of integrated marketing communications.

The likelihood of sending conflicting marketing messages to consumers increases when companies use a greater variety of marketing communications. Integrated marketing communications (IMC) is a process of coordinating all of a company's communications and promotional efforts so that they present only one consistent message to the marketplace. Properly implemented, IMC increases marketing and promotional effectiveness.

Behind the SCENES

MEC: Effectively Blending Retail and E-tail Channels

After carefully evaluating the advantages and disadvantages of establishing an online presence, MEC moved forward and launched its site in 2001. From the beginning, MEC concentrated on creating a "multi-channel" approach to its system that harmoniously blends its online and offline outlets. MEC built functionality into its operating methods to improve member services. For example, MEC offers in-store shipping pickup and store level stock checks. Additionally, it made an effort to integrate its marketing communication messages. MEC markets its "Hero products" with similar graphics in store, in catalogues, and online.

The company continues to mail approximately 750 000 English-language catalogues and 75 000 French-language catalogues twice a year (Fall/Winter, Spring/Summer). Most are sent out directly to members, who are encouraged to shop on the Internet. The website often serves an information gathering purpose that leads to online, telephone, or in-store sales. The basic idea is that the more product information available at the consumer's fingertips, the better.

Overall, MEC's blend of bricks and clicks has proven to be quite successful. The MEC website received nearly 5 million visits in 2003, up significantly from 3 million in the previous year. MEC's sales accounted for more than $169.6 million; web sales accounted for $7.1 million, or approximately 4.1 percent of overall sales. Additionally, 8 percent of online sales came from non-Canadian Internet users.

The multi-channel approach is an integral part of MEC's future growth; it creates purchase synergy because consumers have access to a variety of information sources that lead them to an MEC channel.[46]

Critical Thinking Questions

1. How did MEC blend its online and offline channels?
2. How has MEC's success as a traditional retailer benefited its online business?

Learn More Online

Go to Chapter 12 of this text's website at www.pearsoned.ca/bovee, and click on the hotlink to the MEC website. After reviewing the site, answer the following questions: What are MEC's return policies for online customers? How does MEC promote its physical stores?

KEY TERMS

advertising (316)
consumer promotion (318)
cooperative advertising (318)
coupons (318)
cross-promotion (320)
direct mail (317)
direct marketing (316)
distribution centres (310)
distribution mix (306)
distribution strategy (303)
exclusive distribution (307)
institutional advertising (317)
integrated marketing communications (IMC) (321)
intensive distribution (307)
local advertising (318)
logistics (309)
marketing intermediaries (304)
materials handling (310)
media (318)
media mix (318)
national advertising (317)
news conference (321)
news release (321)
personal selling (315)
persuasive advertising (313)
physical distribution (308)
point-of-purchase display (320)
premiums (320)
product advertising (317)
promotional mix (315)
promotional strategy (311)
public relations (321)
pull strategy (314)
push strategy (314)
reminder advertising (313)
retailers (304)
sales promotion (318)
selective distribution (307)
specialty advertising (320)
telemarketing (317)
trade allowance (320)
trade promotions (320)
warehouse (310)
wholesalers (304)

TEST YOUR KNOWLEDGE

Questions for Review

1. What is a distribution channel?
2. What forms of utility do intermediaries create?
3. What are the two main types of intermediaries and how do they differ?
4. What are the three basic goals of promotion?
5. What are some common types of consumer promotion?

Questions for Analysis

6. How does the presence of intermediaries in the distribution channel affect the price of products?
7. What trade-offs must you consider when adopting a physical distribution system?
8. If a manufacturer starts to sell its goods on its company website, why might this arouse channel conflict?
9. Why are public relations an important element of a firm's promotional mix?
10. **Ethical Considerations.** Direct-mail marketers often publish different prices in different catalogues targeted at different market segments. When you call to order, the sales representative first asks for your customer or catalogue number or postal code so that the rep knows which price to charge you. Is this practice ethical?

Questions for Application

11. Scan your local papers and highlight or clip ads that could possibly mislead the public. What do you find misleading about the ad? How would you improve it?
12. Find three newspaper or magazine ads that you think are particularly effective and three more that you think are ineffective. What do you like about the

effective ads? How might you improve the ineffective ads?

13. **Integrated.** In Chapter 8 we discussed the fact that supply chain management integrates all of the activities involved in the production of goods and services from suppliers to customers. What are the benefits of involving distributors in the design, manufacturing, or sale of a company's product or service?
14. **Integrated.** Which of the four basic functions of management discussed in Chapter 6 would be involved in decisions that establish or change a company's channels of distribution? Explain your answer.

PRACTISE YOUR KNOWLEDGE

SHARPENING YOUR COMMUNICATION SKILLS

Select a product you're familiar with and examine the strategies used to advertise and promote that product. Identify the media (website, print, television, radio, billboards, and so on) used to advertise the product. Consider the following:

- Where do the ads appear?
- Who is the target audience? Does the company attempt to appeal to a wide variety of people with differing ads?
- What creative theme or appeal is being used?
- Is the company taking advantage of any Internet technologies for promotion?

Prepare a brief summary of your findings as directed by your instructor. Compare your findings with those of other students, and note any differences or similarities in the promotion of your selected products.

BUILDING YOUR TEAM SKILLS

In small groups discuss three or four recent ads or consumer promotions that you think were particularly effective. Using the knowledge you've gained from this chapter, try to come to a consensus on what attributes contributed to the success of each ad or promotion. For instance, was it persuasive? Informative? Competitive? Creative? Did it stimulate you to buy the product? Why? Compare your results with those of other teams. Did you mention the same ads? Did you list the same attributes?

EXPAND YOUR KNOWLEDGE

DISCOVERING CAREER OPPORTUNITIES

Retailing is a dynamic, fast-paced field with many career opportunities in both store and non-store settings. In addition to hiring full-time employees when needed, retailers of all types often hire extra employees on a temporary basis for peak selling periods such as the year-end holidays. You can find out about seasonal and year-round job openings by checking newspaper classified ads, looking for signs in store windows, and browsing the websites of online retailers.

1. Select a major retailer, such as a chain store in your area or a retailer on the Internet. Is this a specialty store, discount store, department store, or another type of retailer?
2. Visit the website of the retailer you selected. Does the site discuss the company's hiring procedures? If so, what are they? What qualifications are required for a position with the company?
3. Research your chosen retailer using library sources or online resources. Is this retailer expanding? Is it profitable? Has it recently acquired or been acquired by another firm? What are the implications of this acquisition for job opportunities?

DEVELOPING YOUR RESEARCH SKILLS

Find an article in a business journal or newspaper (online or print editions) discussing changes a company is making to its distribution strategy or channels. For example, is a manufacturer selling products direct to consumers? Is a physical retailer offering goods via a company website? Is a company eliminating the intermediary? Has a non-store retailer decided to open a physical store? Is a category killer opening smaller stores? Has a major retail tenant closed its stores in a mall?

1. What changes in the company's distribution structure or strategy have taken place? What additional changes, if any, are planned?
2. What were the reasons for the changes? What role, if any, did electronic commerce play in the changes?
3. If you were a stockholder in this company, would you view these changes as positive or negative? What, if anything, might you do differently?

See It on the **WEB**

URLs for all Internet exercises are provided at the website for this book, www.pearsoned.ca/bovee. When you log on to the text website, select Chapter 12, then select Destinations. Click on the name of the featured website and review the website to complete the following exercises.

Explore the following website in detail and answer the following questions.

1. What is the purpose of this website?
2. What kinds of information does this website contain? Please be specific.
3. How is the information provided at this website useful for business people? Consumers?
4. How did you expand your knowledge of distribution and promotion by reviewing the material at this website? What new things did you learn about these topics?

LEARN THE CONSUMER MARKETING LAWS

Thinking about advertising or marketing your product? There are some laws you'll need to obey. Visit the Canadian Radio-television and Telecommunications Commission (CRTC) website to learn how this agency protects consumers against unfair and deceptive marketing practices. How many minutes of commercial time can a broadcaster have in an hour? How does the CRTC regulate advertisements of alcoholic beverages? How does the commission regulate advertising aimed at children? www.crtc.gc.ca

Advertising in Crisis: Zapping Those Ads

LEARNING OBJECTIVES

The purpose of this video is to help you

1. Identify the current challenges facing the advertising industry.
2. Determine the impact that the personal video recorder is having on traditional advertising.
3. Examine the various promotional responses being employed by companies and identify new alternatives in the marketplace.

SYNOPSIS

The advertising industry is in a transition period. The market is fragmenting; there are hundreds of options on network stations and specialty channels. With Internet outlets looming as a long-term threat, TV advertisers are being confronted by an important short-term challenge: the personal video recorder (PVR). PVRs allow customers to record programs efficiently, pause live television, and rewind a program while it is in progress. As well, PVRs allow viewers to skip over commercials. This device is a major threat to advertising firms and the TV networks that depend on advertising revenue. Some experts have predicted that the 30-second ad is on death row. Currently only 4.5 percent of Canadians possess PVRs, but that number is expected to grow to 22 percent by 2009.[47] According to Josh Bernhoff, the PVR is shifting viewing habits: it simplifies the recording process and puts the viewer in control. Bernhoff provides some eye opening figures to support these fears.

Networks and advertisers have responded with a new widespread emphasis on product placement within TV programs. However, companies are also looking at other options, including tapping into more unconventional advertising choices like airports and movie theatres. This new reality has also led to the introduction of an unfamiliar word in the advertising world: *accountability*. Companies are focusing on benchmarks and measurable results to justify fees. In addition, new ventures like etc.tv are pitching a new model in which advertising would be available on demand. Regardless of the adopted approach, one thing is clear: power is shifting from advertisers to viewers.

Discussion Questions

1. *For analysis:* What makes experts believe that the PVR could lead to the death of the 30-second ad? Do you believe this claim? (Experts made similar claims when the VCR was introduced.)
2. *For analysis:* In what way will the rise of the PVR affect how companies allocate their promotional mix?
3. *For application:* The concept behind etc.tv is in the developmental stage. How can etc.tv build awareness for the service once it is commercialized?
4. *For application:* What techniques can marketers use to ensure that minor impressions are made even if viewers reach for the PVR remote when an ad is aired?
5. *For debate:* A five-second product placement within a TV program is more effective than a traditional 30-second advertising spot. Provide support for this argument.

ONLINE EXPLORATION

Visit www.videotron.com for some additional information on etc.tv. Conduct an Internet search on the company. Has it signed any new deals? What is the current status of the deal with Videotron? Search for more recent press releases.

On Location VIDEO CASE

Revving Up Promotion: BMW Motorcycles

LEARNING OBJECTIVES

The purpose of this video is to help you

1. Describe the purpose of product promotion.
2. Understand how and why a company must coordinate all elements in its promotional mix.
3. Discuss how the message and the media work together in an effective advertising campaign.

SYNOPSIS

Car buyers are extremely familiar with the BMW brand; however, BMW has a lower awareness among motorcycle buyers. This is a major challenge for BMW Motorcycles, which has been producing high-end motorcycles for more than 80 years. The company's promotional goal is to attract serious riders who are looking for an exceptional riding experience. To do so, its marketers carefully coordinate every promotional detail to convey a unified brand message positioning the BMW motorcycle as "the ultimate riding machine," as its advertising slogan states. Using print and television advertising, personal selling in dealerships, sales promotion, and a virtual showroom on the Web, BMW is driving its brand message home to motorcycle enthusiasts.

Discussion Questions

1. *For analysis:* What are the advantages of using personal advertising copy and encouraging customers to become missionaries for BMW motorcycles?
2. *For analysis:* Why would BMW use its website as a virtual showroom rather than also selling online directly to consumers?
3. *For application:* What are some ways that BMW might use public relations to build brand awareness?
4. *For application:* How might BMW use direct mail to bring potential buyers into its motorcycle dealerships?
5. *For debate:* Should BMW develop and promote a new brand to differentiate its motorcycles from competing brands as well as from BMW cars? Support your chosen position.

ONLINE EXPLORATION

Visit the BMW Motorcycles site, www.bmwmotorcycles.com, and notice the links on the home page. Then look at the pages promoting new models and pre-owned motorcycles. Finally follow the link to look at the contact page. Which elements of the promotional mix are in evidence on this site? How does this site support the company's "ultimate riding machine" brand message? How does the site make it easy for customers to obtain more information and ask questions about BMW motorcycles and dealer services?

E-Business IN ACTION

Clicks and Bricks: Bridging the Physical and Virtual Worlds

In the mid-1990s, experts advised physical retail stores to keep their e-businesses separate from their traditional stores. The thinking was that the creation of separate e-businesses would allow the web entity to speed up decision making, be more flexible, be more entrepreneurial, act independently, and thus compete more effectively with pure-play e-businesses (those that exist only on the Internet, such as Amazon.com). While some retailers embraced this approach, others debated whether to sell online at all. They worried about spreading their human and financial resources too thin. They worried about competing with their existing distributors, their competitors, and themselves (because their e-sales could "cannibalize" or steal sales from their physical stores).

Mixing Clicks with Bricks

The experts were wrong. Separate e-businesses promised considerable shareholder potential; however, running separate online and offline operations did not work. Consider Barnes & Noble. To compete with Amazon.com, Barnes & Noble established a new independent division—Barnesandnoble.com—and later spun the division off as a stand-alone company. But unlike pure e-business companies, barnesandnoble.com lacked a sense of urgency about the Web and let Amazon capture the lion's share of initial e-business and publicity. Moreover, customers did not care that the two were separate entities. Web customers became confused and angry when they tried to return books purchased online to the physical Barnes & Noble bookstores, only to be turned away. Furthermore, the strategy forced the physical stores to compete with their online brother and prevented them from sharing management teams, combining marketing programs, or achieving economies of scale.

It didn't take long for Barnes & Noble to realize its decision to separate its online and physical stores was a mistake and decide to combine the two operations. This move made it possible for web customers to return purchases at a company's physical stores. Other companies have since followed Barnes & Noble's lead by reeling in their separate e-businesses or launching websites that are seamless additions to the company. Indigo Books and Music Inc. presents another example of the importance of mixing clicks and bricks. In a recent holiday season during a period when in-store sales were being hurt by severe winter storms, the online site managed to surpass expectations as shoppers turned to the company's website in greater numbers and helped make up for some of the lost business.

Creating the Perfect Blend

After much debate, experts now agree that integrating a retailer's physical store operation with its web operation is the most effective approach to e-commerce. Mixing clicks with bricks (also known as *clicks-and-bricks* or *clicks-and-mortar*) makes a store's physical and web operations transparent to the customer. A Sears customer, for instance, can gather product information from Sears.ca before heading to the outlet at the local mall. Salespeople can then add value by doing things the website can't—such as answering specific product questions and demonstrating products. At Future Shop customers who purchase online can only receive their shipment at home; however, the company plans to allow for in-store pick up in the near future. But online customers are able to return merchandise directly to a physical Future Shop location within 30 days of purchase.

A clicks-and-bricks strategy is beneficial for retailers. Multichannel customers who shop both online and in stores tend to be more loyal and spend more. Eddie Bauer (which sells products through catalogues, retail stores, and its website) reports that shoppers who use all three methods to purchase from the company spend five times more than those who shop only by catalogue. Moreover, clicks-and-bricks retailers can use their websites to advertise, test merchandise, suggest gifts, increase product awareness, cross-promote online and offline products, and drive traffic to their physical stores or vice versa. Some are even using their websites to provide specialty items not available in stores. "We don't have the same real estate issues," says one spokesperson for the Gap, which offers plus sizes for men and women exclusively online. "It's an easy, lower-cost way to get merchandise out there quickly."

But there are limitations to mixing clicks with bricks. Not all retailers, especially those that don't have a catalogue business, are able to offer their entire inventories online because of the expense of photographing and describing every item. This confuses customers. Delivery fees continue to be a barrier to online purchases, which is why so many companies offer free delivery when you spend, say, $100. Still, if you don't mix clicks with bricks, "you literally won't exist as a retailer," declares one e-commerce expert. The Web is where most consumers do their initial phases of shopping—whether it's as basic as price comparison or searching for store locations. However, unlike the early naive days of the Internet it is not enough to set up a site and hope for the best. According to one expert, companies need to focus on three basic elements: (1) have a goal, (2) design your site to be measurable, and (3) treat your site like an ongoing experiment (a work in progress). In short, sites need to be managed, maintained, and measured in order to offer the e-shopper an optimal experience.[48]

Questions for Critical Thinking

1. Why did retailers initially separate their physical and web stores?
2. Why did the strategy to separate online and offline stores fail?
3. What are the benefits of a clicks-and-bricks strategy?

Business PlanPro **EXERCISES**

Developing Marketing Strategies to Satisfy Customers

Review Appendix C, "Your Business Plan" (on pages 397–398), to learn how to use BusinessPlan Pro Software so you can complete these exercises.

Think Like a Pro

Objective: By completing these exercises you will become acquainted with the sections of a business plan that address a firm's product, pricing, promotion, and distribution strategies. You will use the sample business plan for Boulder Stop (listed as Sports Equipment-Cafe in the Sample Plan Browser) in this exercise.

1. Define the target market for Boulder Stop. How will the company differentiate its products and services from its competitors'?
2. Describe the company's pricing, promotion, sales, and distribution strategies. Which distribution channels will the company use to deliver its products?
3. Rank the company's three market segmentation categories according to their importance.
4. According to the Keys to Success section, what must Boulder Stop do to be successful?

Create Your Own Business Plan

Consider your own target market and customers as you continue working on the business plan you are creating. How will you segment your target market? Which customers are likely to buy your product or service? Describe your product, pricing, promotion, and distribution strategies. Now make some preliminary sales forecasts. Under which section headings will you present this information?

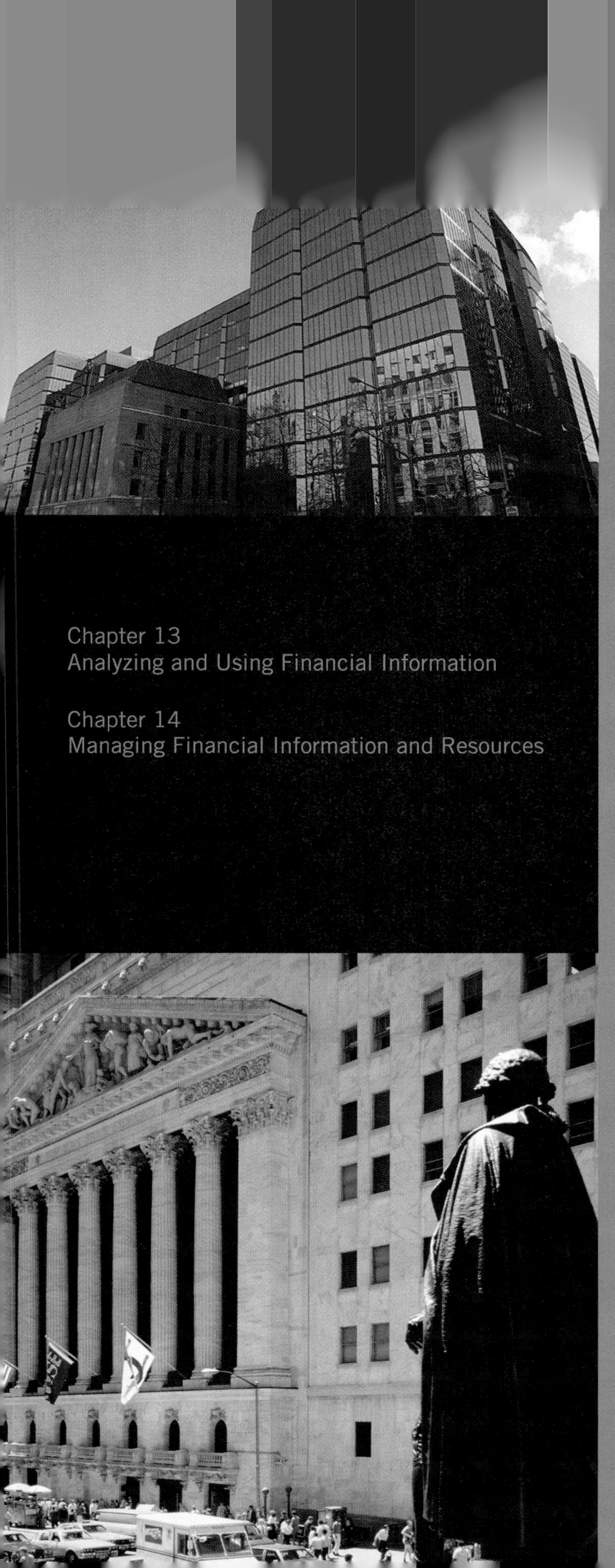

Chapter 13
Analyzing and Using Financial Information

LEARNING OBJECTIVES

After studying this chapter, you will be able to

1. Discuss how managers and outsiders use financial information
2. Describe what accountants do
3. State the basic accounting equation and explain the purpose of double-entry bookkeeping and the matching principle
4. Differentiate between cash basis and accrual basis accounting
5. Explain the purpose of the balance sheet and identify its three main sections
6. Explain the purpose of the income statement
7. Explain the purpose of the statement of cash flows
8. Explain the purpose of ratio analysis and list the four main categories of financial ratios
9. Identify the responsibilities of a financial manager

Behind the SCENES

Nortel Is in Trouble for Raiding the Cookie Jar

www.nortel.com

Nortel, one of Canada's best-known telecommunication companies, is currently experiencing problems for raiding the cookie jar. Unfortunately for the company's investors, the cookie jar was full of money that was used to prop up Nortel's revenue and turn losses into profits. As a result of this practice, the company will have to restate its net income and revenue for 2001 through to the first two quarters of 2004.

If Nortel is unable to provide accurate sales and revenue figures that adhere to generally accepted accounting principles (GAAP), they are in danger of being delisted from the Toronto (TSX) and New York (NYSE) stock exchanges.[1] This would be an amazing fall from grace for a company that in the 1990s gained a reputation as one of the key builders of the Internet.

During the Internet boom of the 1990s Nortel saw its revenue triple from an average of $10 billion a year to $30 billion and its share price peak on the TSX at $124.50. It seemed as if almost every person in Canada had some money invested in the company. Today, as the company struggles to provide accurate financial figures for the 2001 to 2004 periods, the stock consistently trades below $5.00.[2]

Nortel's current problem of inaccurate financial statements came to light when then CEO Frank Dunn informed the board of directors that the company would lose approximately $112 million in the first part of 2003. However, by March he reported a profit of $40 million based on an accounting manoeuvre known as cookie jar accounting. As a result, Nortel employees earned a bonus of 10 to 25 percent of their annual salary. When the board of directors realized the profit was a product of illusionary or false accounting, they terminated Dunn along with the company's chief financial officer and top controller.[3]

Raiding the cookie jar, or cookie jar accounting, is the process of establishing a pool of money that the company can use in the future to refund customers who may be unhappy due to a missed deadline, poor service, or product defects. For example, if Nortel sells a customer $10 million of goods it may put $1 million of this amount away to offset any future problems with that customer. The $1 million becomes an expense on the income statement for that year and reduces the company's net income.

In the 1990s, Nortel appeared to be putting more money away than it would ever need to pay unsatisfied customers, thus establishing a cookie jar full of money. When the market slowed, Nortel continuously raided this cookie jar, taking out money and counting it as revenue so investors would never know that sales were declining. This resulted in Nortel turning a potential $112 million loss into a $40 million profit. The company then proceeded to repeat this process for the remainder of the year and into the first half of 2004.[4,5]

Bill Owens, who replaced Dunn as Nortel's CEO, has been working diligently to repair investor confidence in the troubled company. But he has had to postpone the restatement of revenue and net profit several times, and customers are becoming concerned about the long-term viability of the company.

Do you think investors will trust Nortel's financial statements when it restates its earnings from 2001 to 2004? If you were a Nortel customer would you consider switching to another company because of these accounting problems? Do you think Nortel might be losing out on potential sales as a result of this accounting scandal?

L.O. 1

WHAT IS ACCOUNTING?

accounting
Measuring, interpreting, and communicating financial information to support internal and external decision making

As Bill Owens knows, it's difficult to manage a business today without accurate and up-to-date financial information. **Accounting** is the system a business uses to identify, measure, and communicate financial information to others inside and outside the organization. Financial information is important to businesses such as Nortel for two reasons: First, it helps managers and owners plan and control a company's operation and make informed business decisions. Second, it helps outsiders evaluate a business. Suppliers, banks, and other lenders want to know whether a business is creditworthy; investors and shareholders are concerned with a company's profit potential; government agencies are interested in a business's tax accounting.

Because outsiders and insiders use accounting information for different purposes, accounting has two distinct facets. **Financial accounting** is concerned with preparing financial statements and other information for outsiders such as *shareholders* and *creditors* (people or organizations that have loaned a company money or have extended it credit); **management accounting** is concerned with preparing cost analyses, profitability reports, budgets, and other information for insiders such as management and other company decision makers. To be useful, all accounting information must be accurate, objective, consistent over time, and comparable to information supplied by other companies.

financial accounting
Area of accounting concerned with preparing financial information for users outside the organization

management accounting
Area of accounting concerned with preparing data for use by managers within the organization

What Accountants Do

L.O. 2

Some people confuse the work accountants do with **bookkeeping**, which is the clerical function of recording the economic activities of a business. Although some accountants do perform bookkeeping functions, their work generally goes well beyond the scope of this activity. Accountants design accounting systems, prepare financial statements, analyze and interpret financial information, prepare financial forecasts and budgets, and prepare tax returns. Some accountants specialize in certain areas of accounting, such as **cost accounting** (computing and analyzing production costs), **tax accounting** (preparing tax returns and interpreting tax law), or **financial analysis** (evaluating a company's performance and the financial implications of strategic decisions such as product pricing, employee benefits, and business acquisitions).

In addition to traditional accounting work, accountants may also help clients improve business processes, plan for the future, evaluate product performance, analyze profitability by customer and product groups, design and install new computer systems, assist companies with decision making, and provide a variety of other management consulting services. Performing these functions requires a strong business background and a variety of business skills beyond accounting (see Exhibit 13.1).

bookkeeping
Record keeping, clerical aspect of accounting

cost accounting
Area of accounting focusing on the calculation of manufacturing and storage costs of products for use or sale in a business

tax accounting
Area of accounting focusing on tax preparation and tax planning

financial analysis
Process of evaluating a company's performance and analyzing the costs and benefits of a strategic action

Exhibit 13.1 Ten Most Important Skills for Accountants

Besides having a thorough knowledge of accounting, today's accountants need the right mix of personal and business skills to increase their chances for a successful career.

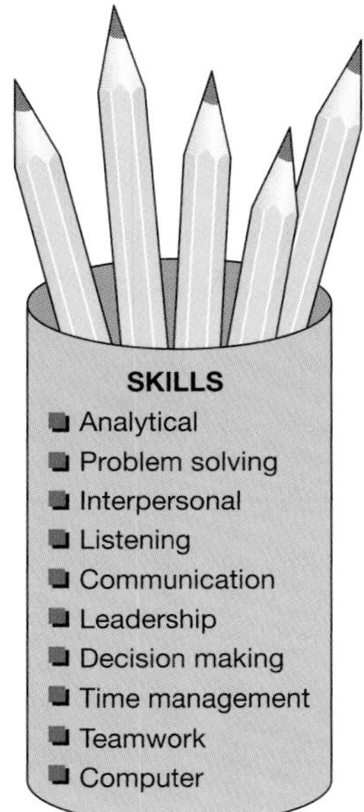

private accountants
In-house accountants employed by organizations and businesses other than a public accounting firm; also called *corporate accountants*

controller
Highest-ranking accountant in a company, responsible for overseeing all accounting functions

chartered accountants (CAs)
Professionally licensed accountants who meet certain requirements for education and experience and who pass a comprehensive examination

certified management accountants (CMAs)
Accountants who have fulfilled the requirements for certification as a specialist in management accounting

certified general accountants (CGAs)
Accountants who have fulfilled the requirements for certification as a general accountant

public accountants
Professionals who provide accounting services to other businesses and individuals for a fee

audit
Formal evaluation of the fairness and reliability of a client's financial statements

Most accountants are **private accountants** (sometimes called *corporate accountants*). Private accountants work for a business, a government agency (such as the Canadian Customs and Revenue Agency, a school, or a local police department), or a non-profit corporation (such as a church, charity, or hospital).[6] Private accountants generally work together as a team under the supervision of the organization's **controller**, who reports to the vice-president of finance. Exhibit 13.2 shows the typical finance department of a large company. In smaller organizations, the controller may be in charge of the company's entire finance operation and report directly to the president.

Although certification is not required of private accountants, many are licensed **chartered accounts (CAs)**, which means they have passed a rigorous licensing exam. To become eligible to sit for the exam, candidates must earn a university degree, complete prerequisite courses in accounting and information systems, and complete 24 to 30 months of training in a public accounting firm. A growing number of private accountants are becoming **certified management accountants (CMAs)**; to do so they must earn a university degree (except in British Columbia), complete prerequisite course work, pass an entrance exam prior to admission, complete a two-year professional component called Strategic Leadership, and complete 24 months of relevant work experience. People interested in another professional designation in Canada may opt for the **certified general accountant (CGAs)** designation, which requires a university degree, work experience, and the successful completion of an examination. The main difference between the three designations is the focus of their educational program and training: the CA educational program emphasizes auditing and is generally considered the most prestigious of the three designations, CMAs focus on combining management and accounting training, while CGAs learn about completing financial statements and taxes. The case study entitled "Will CAs and CMAs Merge" provides more information about accounting designations in Canada.

Public accountants, by contrast, are independent of the businesses, organizations, and individuals they serve. Most public accountants are employed by public accounting firms that provide a variety of accounting and consulting services for their clients. Members of the firm are generally CAs and must obtain the CA designation before they are eligible to conduct an **audit**—a formal evaluation of a company's accounting records and processes to ensure the integrity and reliability of a company's financial statements.

Exhibit 13.2 Typical Finance Department

Here is a typical finance department of a large company. In smaller companies, the controller may be the highest-ranking accountant and report directly to the president.

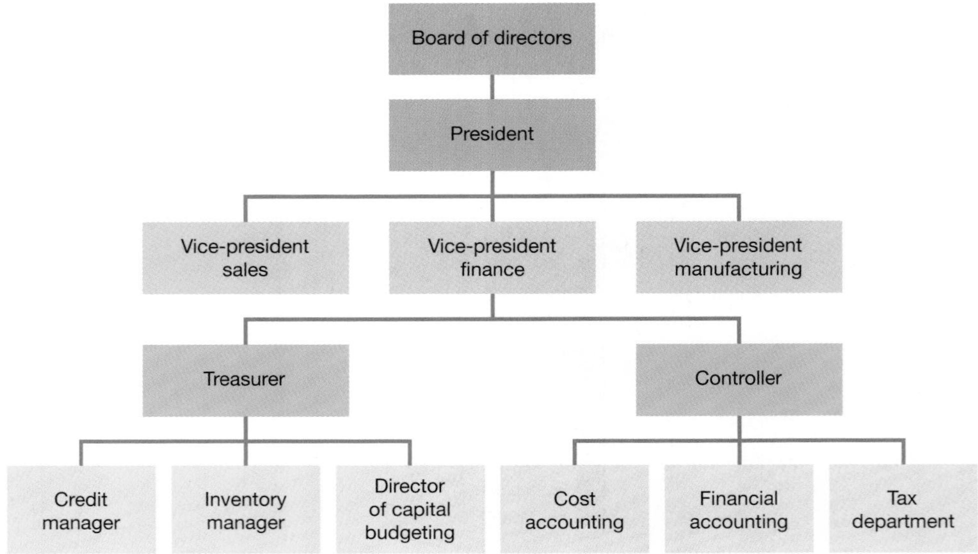

Case Study: Will CAs and CMAs Merge?

On May 11, 2004, the Canadian Institute of Chartered Accountants, which represents chartered accountants (CAs), and the Society of Management Accountants, which represents certified management accountants (CMAs), announced that both professional organizations had approved guiding principles for a merger. Members of the new professional organization would receive the designation of CA and a new educational program would be developed that combined the strengths of the current CA and CMA educational components. The final step in the merger would be a ratification process by provincial and territorial bodies that would result in a new organization in 2005.

The following is an excerpt from a discussion between some chartered accountants (CA) and certified management accountants (CMA) following the announcement.

> Rod (CA): I can't believe we are going to dilute our professional standard by merging with CMAs. All we will end up doing is lowering our designation standards, allowing people to gain access to the designation of CA without a business degree, flooding the job mark, and probably reduce our level of compensation. Furthermore, CMAs are not real accountants, they can't perform audits, they haven't passed the same rigorous examination process, and do not deserve the valuable CA designation.
>
> Amanda (CMA): First of all, let's get something straight: I do not want to be taken over by the CA profession. My designation is just as valuable, if not more so, as it includes complex management training, something that CAs don't have. I'll admit CAs are better at accounting, but CMAs are much better at management and I would much rather be in charge, managing a firm, than performing audits any day. In addition, while some CMAs do not have a degree, it has become a requirement in our training program. I would also like to remind Rod that not too long ago a university degree was not a requirement for the CA program.
>
> Marie (CA): I think you are both right and wrong. At first I did not like the idea of a merger. I was upset that 35 000 CMAs would be given the CA designation without completing the same level of training. But I am an accountant, and after looking at the numbers, this merger makes sense. There are over 68 000 CAs in Canada and when you combine them with 35 000 CMAs, we will have a larger, stronger, and more influential body. We will reduce confusion in the marketplace and broaden everyone's career choices.
>
> In addition, the two designations are quite complementary. Currently, the CA educational program puts an enhanced emphasis on accounting but lacks management training, while CMAs emphasize management and not as much accounting. Imagine the educational program that we can design when we combine the strengths of both. Our brand will only become stronger.
>
> Pierre (CA): I agree with Marie. I love the idea of a merger for many of the same reasons. But I also think there is another "numbers" issue that many CAs like Rod are ignoring. The majority of CAs are well on their way to retirement and not enough new students are enrolling in the CA program due to the lack of available training opportunities. Instead, many of the top students are opting for a MBA or a CMA. By 2008, the number of CAs in Canada will actually start to decline.
>
> Today CAs are in high demand for top accounting and financial jobs, but recruiters indicated that if CA numbers start to fall, they will look towards MBAs and CMAs to fill these positions. Eventually we lose market share to other designations. By merging, we will create more opportunities, increase our market share, and ensure that there will be enough CAs in the years to come.
>
> Brenda (CMA): I don't know what to think. I became a CMA because I didn't want to spend the three years required under the CA program learning how to perform audits or write the UFE [the CA exam]. But the CMA training program consisted of a four-year university degree, 18 courses in business, economics, law and accounting, a comprehensive entrance exam, a two-year professional component, and two years of work experience. It was quite rigorous and I am proud of my designation.
>
> Right now, I will admit that CAs are probably considered more prestigious than CMAs, but if their numbers continue to decline and

our numbers go up, I think this could change. In a couple of years, I can see CAs doing nothing but audits and CMAs holding most of the top management positions. After all, there are more middle managers enrolling in the CMA program because they can do so without changing their rate of pay. Most experienced managers would never consider registering in a CA program because they would be paid as a CA student, which is often much less than they are making.

Amanda (CMA): You have all made some interesting points. I would also like to add that CMAs who become CAs under the proposed merger would not be able to perform audits unless they have the knowledge and training.

But even after this discussion, I am not convinced. I don't want to give up my designation and be classified as a CA even if some think it's more prestigious. It seems like a takeover to me. After all, we would be adopting the CAs' professional standards . . . I just don't know.

Rod (CA): You have made some interesting points. In reality, I have the more prestigious designation of the two and am not interested in devaluing it by merging with CMAs. Oh, I almost forgot, of course CMAs would be adopting our standards as we are the leaders in the field.

Questions for Critical Thinking

1. After reading the discussion, what are your thoughts on Rod's arguments that CAs do not need to merge with CMAs?
2. Why would Amanda fear being "taken over" by the CA profession?
3. Will merging the two professional organizations increase the brand value of the designation or reduce its influence in the market?
4. On March 4, 2005, both sides agreed to end merger discussions since a satisfactory agreement could not be reached. One of the main sticking points was classifying all members under the CA designation. Do you think this is a good argument to make against the merger?
5. Do you think CMAs will ever merge with CAs? Why or why not? You may want to visit the CMA website at www.cma-canada.org or the CA website at www.cica.ca to learn more about the talks and the reasons why the merger failed.

Companies whose stock (ownership shares) is publicly traded in Canada are required to file audited financial statements with the stock exchange on which they trade. During an audit, CAs who work for an independent accounting firm (also known as *external* auditors) review a client's financial records to determine whether the statements that summarize these records have been prepared in accordance with **generally accepted accounting principles (GAAP)**, basic accounting standards and procedures that have been agreed on by regulators, auditors, and companies over decades. GAAP aims to give a fair and true picture of a company's financial position.

generally accepted accounting principles (GAAP)
Professionally approved Canadian standards and practices used by accountants in the preparation of financial statements

Once the auditors have completed an audit, they attach a report summarizing their findings to the client's published financial statements. Sometimes these reports disclose information that might materially affect the client's financial position, such as the bankruptcy of a major supplier, a large obsolete inventory, costly environmental problems, or questionable accounting practices. Most companies, however, receive a clean audit report, which means that to the best of the auditors' knowledge the company's financial statements are accurate.

internal auditors
Employees who analyze and evaluate a company's operations and data to determine their accuracy

To assist with the auditing process, many large organizations employ **internal auditors**—employees who investigate and evaluate the organization's internal operations and data to determine whether they are accurate and whether they comply with GAAP, federal laws, and industry regulations. Although this self-checking process is vital to an organization's financial health, an internal audit is not a substitute for having an independent auditor look things over and render an unbiased opinion. Many people, such as creditors, shareholders, investors, and government agencies, rely on the integrity of a company's financial statements and place great trust and confidence in the independence of auditors whose detached position allows them to be objective and, when necessary, critical.

The Rules of Accounting

L.O. 3

All Canadian public companies such as Nortel and Bombardier must publish their financial statements in accordance with GAAP. This requirement makes it possible for external users to compare the financial results of one company with those of another and to gain a general idea of a firm's relative effectiveness and its standing within a particular industry. In Canada, the Canadian Institute of Chartered Accountants (CICA) is responsible for developing and monitoring GAAP. Other countries, of course, have similar governing boards. In the United States, for example, the Financial Accounting Standards Board (FASB) establishes GAAP, which means that American companies such as Disney or GE report accounting data using rules that are different from those used in Canada. Since some Canadian companies report their earnings using both Canadian and American GAAP, their results can differ depending on which GAAP they use. Talisman Energy, a Canadian oil company, reported a net income of $906 million in 2000 using Canadian GAAP, but when it applied American GAAP its net income shrunk to $762 million.

Some large companies that list their securities on more than one stock exchange must, however, convert financial statements prepared under foreign accounting rules to the GAAP of the country in which the exchange is listed. So a company that trades on both the TSX and the NYSE exchange will have to produce two separate sets of financial statements. This requirement ensures that all companies listed on a stock exchange are on even ground. But it can also create problems for foreign companies. For instance, when Daimler-Benz listed its stock on the New York Stock Exchange in 1993, the company's $102 million profit changed to a $579 million loss for the same period because of a difference between German accounting rules and U.S. GAAP.[7]

Recent proposals to develop a uniform set of global accounting rules known as international accounting standards (IAS) could help eliminate such differences and simplify the bookkeeping process for multinational companies. But such global rules are meeting strong resistance from the U.S. Securities and Exchange Commission (SEC) and other regulators, which are concerned that many of the international accounting standards are not as strict as GAAP.[8]

How Strict Is GAAP?

GAAP sets forth the principles and guidelines that companies and accountants must follow when preparing financial reports or recording accounting transactions (which we will discuss later in this chapter). But, as with any rules, GAAP can be interpreted aggressively or conservatively. In other words, the rules give executives the freedom to use their judgment in areas that can dramatically affect the company's bottom line without breaking any rules. Unfortunately, some companies take advantage of this flexibility by resorting to a number of accounting tricks that overstate expenses, puff up income, and hide problems from the public. Canadian airplane maker Bombardier has long been criticized by investors for using programmed accounting that sees the company generously estimate the number of planes that will be sold and base production costs on this

Accountants perform a variety of services for their clients beyond tax preparation and auditing. Many serve on strategic planning teams and help companies plan for the future.

Companies bend and stretch accounting rules and "cook the books" to make their numbers prettier. It's not fraud—it can even be legal—but it is deceptive.

estimate. Financial analysts note that while this form of accounting is allowable under GAAP, it is quite aggressive and if the company fails to sell as many planes as it estimates, the profit per plane could change dramatically from what was recorded. For example, when Bombardier makes a new plane, it estimates how many it will sell over a 20-year period and base production costs on the economics of scale realized from producing that many planes. If, however, it fails to sell that number of plans, the cost structure could be much higher than previously recorded and profits would have to be changed.

Consider WorldCom. In June 2002, the SEC accused WorldCom of fraud after the telecommunications giant revealed that it had concealed US$3.8 billion in expenses, allowing the company to report a US$1.5 billion profit for a five-quarter period when, in fact, the company actually suffered a loss. Coming fast on the heels of the Enron scandal, WorldCom's disclosure further jolted the public's already shaken confidence in the reliability of corporate financial reporting and put pressure on regulators to clamp down on financial wrongdoings. In July 2002, WorldCom filed for bankruptcy court protection.

Of course, no one can calculate how many companies resort to accounting trickery, because such offences only are counted when companies get caught or when they restate their earnings. What is clear, however, is that in most cases "accounting irregularities don't start with dishonesty; rather they start with pressure for financial performance," says one financial expert.[9] Such pressure comes from employee shareholders whose life savings are invested in company stock, executives whose bonuses are tied to a company's bottom line, and financial managers who must meet Bay and Wall street estimates or pump up a company's stock price. For some examples of unethical accounting, see the box entitled "Where Were the Auditors?"

The Changes Ahead

Hoping to put an end to financial wrongdoings, the United States passed the Sarbanes-Oxley Act on July 30, 2002, hoping to restore confidence in corporate financial reporting. Among the changes were a move to take away the accounting industry's authority to set auditing standards and to give such authority to an independent oversight board, an SEC order requiring CEOs and financial chiefs at companies with more than US$1.2 billion in revenue to swear under oath and in writing that the numbers reported in company financials are indeed correct, tougher criminal penalties for corporate executives convicted of fraud, a ban on accounting firms being able to sell many forms of consulting services to their audit clients, and a time requirement for the rotation of company auditors.[10]

In Canada, where regulation is enforced by 13 provincial and territorial agencies, an independent task force was established to bolster investor confidence and develop rules to avoid accounting and corporate governance problems. The task force recommended that Canada adopt a single securities commission, CEOs and CFOs certify they have reviewed their company's financial statements, deadlines for filing financial reports be shortened, and companies disclose significant business transactions within 75 days and divulge executive compensation packages to shareholders. The recommendations were adopted by most provincial and territorial enforcement agencies on March 30, 2004.

L.O. 3

WHAT ARE THE FUNDAMENTAL ACCOUNTING CONCEPTS?

As pressure mounts for companies to produce cleaner financial statements and to disclose material information promptly, the need increases for all business people—not just accountants—to understand basic accounting concepts. In the next sections we discuss the fundamental accounting concepts, explore the key elements of financial

Where Were the Auditors?

Where were the auditors when nearly US$2 billion in revenue disappeared at Xerox Corp.; when Nortel engaged in an accounting scheme that allowed it to create a $40 million profit using accounting tricks; when Atlas Cold Storage hid losses and overstated revenue, costing shareholders $100 million in value on one single trading day; when more than US$3.8 billion in expenses were wiped out at WorldCom; and when more than US$1.2 billion in shareholder equity vaporized at Enron? That's a question that more and more people began asking at the beginning of the twenty-first century as one after another corporate accounting scandal hit the headlines. And it's a question that lawmakers, stakeholders, and accountants hope to resolve soon.

Auditors maintain that in many cases it's impossible to detect deliberately misleading bookkeeping, and it's unfair to hold them accountable when they fail to do so. An auditor "cannot provide 100 percent guarantee against fraud," says Chuck Landes, director of auditing for the American Institute of Certified Public Accountants (AICPA), although statistics show that auditors do a good job. Of more than 15 000 public companies examined by auditors every year, only 0.1 percent of audits fail. But the price of those few failures is high. According to one SEC spokesperson, from 1995 through 2001 investors lost about US$200 billion because of financial fraud and the accompanying earnings restatements.

Some link the rise in bad corporate bookkeeping to a change in review methods used by auditing firms. They claim that auditors aren't looking in the right places. In the past, auditors used a labour-intensive process of sifting through thousands of transactions to determine if bookkeeping entries were correct. Now, auditors focus on analyzing the computerized bookkeeping programs and internal controls that are supposed to prevent errors. The flaw in this approach is that while it prevents low-level employees from swiping petty cash, it doesn't catch the executives who shift millions or billions using creative and manipulative accounting schemes.

Others blame the recent parade of scandals on the conflict of interest that exists when an accounting firm earns millions performing consulting work for an audit client. "If you are auditing your own creations, it is very difficult to criticize them," says one accounting expert. The potential conflict indeed played a role in Enron's demise. The energy giant paid Andersen accountants US$27 million in consulting fees and US$25 million in audit fees in 2000, while the two companies maintained an unusually close relationship.

In 1998, the SEC turned up the heat on such potential conflicts of interest by requiring disclosure of consulting fees paid to auditors in company financial statements. Several accounting firms responded by selling their technology consulting operations. But some have retained their other consulting functions such as tax management, human resources, and merger and acquisition advice. They argue that providing these consulting services helps them learn more about their clients' operations, which makes it more likely they will spot fraud. Others disagree. The debate continues, but this much is certain: Auditing is a vital function upon which free enterprise and the health of the global economy depend. So expect to see some major changes ahead as lawmakers, regulators, and other stakeholders hammer out new ways to restore investor confidence in corporate financial reporting.

Questions for Critical Thinking

1. Should accounting firms be allowed to perform management consulting functions for their audit clients? Why or why not?
2. Why is the auditing function of such vital importance to the global economy? (*Hint:* Think of the outcome of the Enron scandal.)

statements, and explain how managers and investors analyze a company's financial statements to make decisions.

In their work with financial data, accountants are guided by three basic concepts: the *fundamental accounting equation, double-entry bookkeeping,* and the *matching principle.* Let's take a closer look at each of these concepts.

The Accounting Equation

For thousands of years, businesses and governments have kept records of their **assets**—valuable items they own or lease, such as equipment, cash, land, buildings, inventory, and investments. Claims against those assets are **liabilities**, or what the business owes to its creditors—such as banks and suppliers. For example, when a

assets
Any things of value owned or leased by a business

liabilities
Claims against a firm's assets by creditors

company borrows money to purchase a building, the lender or creditor has a claim against the company's assets. What remains after liabilities have been deducted from assets is **owners' equity**:

owners' equity
Portion of a company's assets that belongs to the owners after obligations to all creditors have been met

Assets – Liabilities = Owners' equity

Using the principles of algebra, this equation can be restated in a variety of formats. The most common is the simple **accounting equation**, which serves as the framework for the entire accounting process:

accounting equation
Basic accounting equation that assets equal liabilities plus owners' equity

Assets = Liabilities + Owners' equity

This equation suggests that either creditors or owners provide all of the assets in a corporation. Think of it this way: If you were starting a new business, you could contribute cash to the company to buy the assets you need to run your business or you could borrow money from a bank (the creditor) or you could do both. The company's liabilities are placed before owners' equity in the accounting equation because creditors are paid first. After liabilities have been paid, anything left over belongs to the owners or, in the case of a corporation, to the shareholders. As a business engages in economic activity, the dollar amounts and composition of its assets, liabilities, and owners' equity change. However, the equation must always be in balance; in other words, one side of the equation must always equal the other side.

L.O. 4

Double-Entry Bookkeeping and the Matching Principle

double-entry bookkeeping
Way of recording financial transactions that requires two entries for every transaction so that the accounting equation is always kept in balance

To keep the accounting equation in balance, companies use a **double-entry bookkeeping** system that records every transaction affecting assets, liabilities, or owners' equity. For example, if Domtar, a Quebec-based forestry company, purchased a $6000 computer system on credit, assets would increase by $6000 (the cost of the system) and liabilities would also increase by $6000 (the amount the company owes the vendor), keeping the accounting equation in balance. But if Domtar paid cash outright for the equipment (instead of arranging for credit), the company's total assets and total liabilities would not change, because the $6000 increase in equipment would be offset by an equal $6000 reduction in cash. In fact, the company would just be switching assets—cash for equipment.

matching principle
Fundamental principle requiring that expenses incurred in producing revenue be deducted from the revenues they generate during an accounting period

accrual basis
Accounting method in which revenue is recorded when a sale is made and an expense is recorded when it is incurred

The **matching principle** requires that expenses incurred in producing revenues be deducted from the revenue they generated during the same accounting period. This matching of expenses and revenue is necessary for the company's financial statements to present an accurate picture of the profitability of a business. Accountants match revenue to expenses by adopting the **accrual basis** of accounting, which states that revenue is recognized when you make a sale or provide a service, not when you are paid. Similarly, your expenses are recorded when you receive the benefit of a service or when you use an asset to produce revenue—not when you pay for it. Accrual accounting focuses on the economic substance of the event instead of on the movement of cash. It's a way of recognizing that revenue can be earned either before or after cash is received and that expenses can be incurred when you receive a benefit (such as a shipment of supplies) whether before or after you pay for it.

cash basis
Accounting method in which revenue is recorded when payment is received and an expense is recorded when cash is paid

If a business runs on a **cash basis**, the company records revenue only when money from the sale is actually received. Your chequebook is an easy-to-understand cash-based accounting system: You record cheques at the time of purchase and deposits at the time of receipt. Revenue thus equals cash received, and expenses equal cash paid. The trouble with cash-based accounting, however, is that it can be misleading. You can misrepresent expenses and income by the way you time payments. It's easy to inflate income, for example, by delaying the payment of bills. For that reason, public companies are required to keep their books on an accrual basis.

depreciation
Accounting procedure for systematically spreading the cost of a tangible asset over its estimated useful life

Depreciation, or the allocation of the cost of a tangible long-term asset over a period of time, is another way that companies match expenses with revenue. During the normal course of business, a company enters into many transactions that benefit more than one accounting period—such as the purchase of buildings, inventory, and equipment. When you buy a piece of real estate or equipment, instead of deducting the entire cost of the item at the time of purchase, you depreciate it, or spread its cost over the asset's useful life (because the asset will likely generate income for years to come). If the company were to expense long-term assets at the time of purchase, the financial performance of the company would be distorted in the year of purchase as well as in all future years when these assets generate revenue.

HOW ARE FINANCIAL STATEMENTS USED?

An accounting system is made up of thousands of individual transactions—debits and credits to be exact. During the accounting process, sales, purchases, and other transactions are recorded and classified into individual accounts. Once these individual transactions are recorded and then summarized, accountants must review the resulting transaction summaries and adjust or correct all errors or discrepancies before they can **close the books**, or transfer net revenue and expense items to retained earnings. Exhibit 13.3 presents the process for putting all of a company's financial data into standardized formats that can be used for decision making, analysis, and planning. To make sense of these individual transactions, accountants summarize them by preparing financial statements.

close the books
The act of transferring net revenue and expense account balances to retained earnings for the period

Understanding Financial Statements

L.O. 5

Financial statements consist of three separate yet interrelated reports: the *balance sheet,* the *income statement,* and the *statement of cash flows.* Together these statements provide information about an organization's financial strength and ability to meet current obligations, the effectiveness of its sales and collection efforts, and its effectiveness in managing its assets. Organizations and individuals use financial statements to spot opportunities and problems, to make business decisions, and to evaluate a company's past performance, present condition, and future prospects. In sum, they're indispensable.

In the following sections we will examine the financial statements of Computer Central, a company engaged in direct sales and distribution of brand-name personal

Exhibit 13.3 **The Accounting Process**

The traditional printed accounting forms are shown here. Today, nearly all companies use the computer equivalents of these forms.

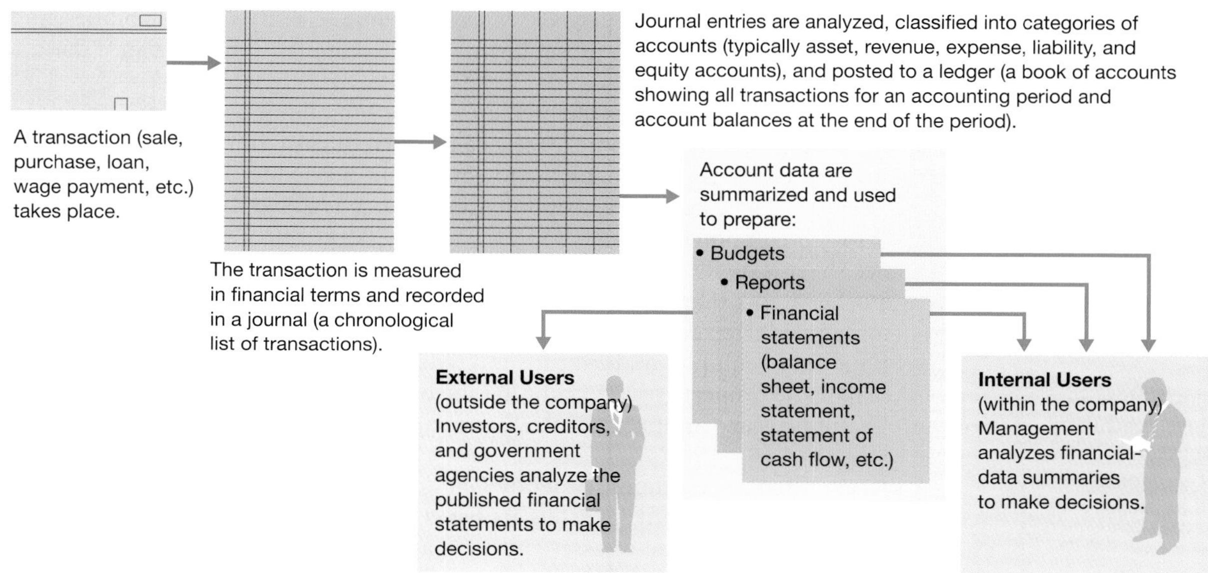

computers (such as H-P, Toshiba, and Macintosh) and related computer products (such as software, printer cartridges, and scanners). The company conducts its primary business from a combined telemarketing, corporate office, warehouse, and showroom facility in Halifax, Nova Scotia. There, Computer Central's 600-plus account executives service more than 634 000 customers annually. In 2002 the company shipped more than 2.3 million orders, amounting to more than $1.7 billion in sales—a 35 percent increase in sales from the prior year. The company's daily sales volume has grown exponentially over the last decade—from $232 000 to $6.8 million. Because of this tremendous growth and the increasing demand for new computer products, the company recently purchased a 84,125-square-metre building. Keep these points in mind as we discuss Computer Central's financial statements in the following sections.

Balance Sheet

balance sheet
Statement of a firm's financial position on a particular date; also known as a *statement of financial position*

The **balance sheet**, also known as the *statement of financial position,* is a snapshot of a company's financial position on a particular date, such as December 31, 2004. In effect, it freezes all business actions and provides a baseline from which a company can measure change. This statement is called a balance sheet because it includes all elements in the accounting equation and shows the balance between assets on one side of the equation and liabilities and owners' equity on the other side. In other words, as in the accounting equation, a change on one side of the balance sheet means changes elsewhere. Exhibit 13.4 is the balance sheet for Computer Central as of December 31, 2004.

In reality, however, no business can stand still while its financial condition is being examined. A business may make hundreds of transactions of various kinds every working day. Even during a holiday, office fixtures grow older and decrease in value and interest on savings accounts accumulates. Yet the accountant must set up a balance sheet so that managers and other interested parties can evaluate the business's financial position as if it were static, rather than ever-changing.

calendar year
Twelve-month accounting period that begins on January 1 and ends on December 31

fiscal year
Any 12 consecutive months used as an accounting period

Every company prepares a balance sheet at least once a year, most often at the end of the **calendar year**, covering January 1 to December 31. However, many business and government bodies use a **fiscal year**, which may be any 12 consecutive months. For example, a company may use a fiscal year of June 1 to May 31 because its peak selling season ends in May. Its fiscal year would then correspond to its full annual cycle of manufacturing and selling. Some companies prepare a balance sheet more often than once a year, perhaps at the end of each month or quarter. Thus, every balance sheet is dated to show the exact date when the financial snapshot was taken.

By reading a company's balance sheet you should be able to determine the size of the company, the major assets owned, any asset changes that occurred in recent periods, how the company's assets are financed, and any major changes that have occurred in the company's debt and equity in recent periods. Most companies classify assets, liabilities, and owners' equity into categories like those shown in the Computer Central balance sheet.

current assets
Cash and items that can be turned into cash within one year

fixed assets
Assets retained for long-term use, such as land, buildings, machinery, and equipment; also referred to as *property, plant, and equipment*

Assets As discussed earlier in this chapter, an asset is something owned by a company that will be used to generate income. Assets can consist of cash, things that can be converted into cash (such as investments), and equipment needed to make products or to provide services. For example, Computer Central needs a warehouse and a sizable inventory to sell computer products to its customers. Most often, the assets section of the balance sheet is divided into current assets and *fixed assets.* **Current assets** include cash and other items that will or can become cash within the following year. **Fixed assets** (sometimes referred to as *property, plant, and equipment*) are long-term investments in buildings, equipment, furniture and fixtures, transportation equipment, land, and other tangible property used in running the business. Fixed assets have a useful life of more than one year. Computer Central's principal fixed asset is the company's warehouse facility.

Assets are listed in descending order by *liquidity,* or the ease with which they can be converted into cash. Thus, current assets are listed before fixed assets. The balance sheet gives a subtotal for each type of asset and then a grand total for all assets. Computer Central's current assets consist primarily of cash, investments in short-term marketable

Exhibit 13.4 Balance Sheet for Computer Central

The categories used on Computer Central's year-end balance sheet are typical.

Current Assets
Cash and other items that will or can be converted to cash within one year.

Fixed Assets
Long-term investments in buildings, equipment, furniture, and any other tangible property expected to be used in running the business for a period longer than one year.

Current Liabilities
Amounts owed by the company that are to be repaid within one year.

Long-Term Liabilities
Debts that are due a year or more after the date of the balance.

Shareholders' Equity
Money contributed to the company for ownership interests, as well as the accumulation of profits that have not been paid out as dividends (retained earnings).

Computer Central Balance Sheet As of December 31, 2004 (in thousands)		
ASSETS		
Current Assets		
Cash	$4,230	
Marketable Securities	36,458	
Accounts Receivable	158,204	
Inventory	64,392	
Miscellaneous Prepaid and Deferred Items	6,504	
Total Current Assets		$269,788
Fixed Assets		
Property and Equipment	53,188	
Less: Accumulated Depreciation	–16,132	
Total Fixed Assets		37,056
Other Assets		4,977
Total Assets		**$311,821**
LIABILITIES AND SHAREHOLDERS' EQUITY		
Current Liabilities		
Accounts Payable	$41,358	
Accrued Expenses	29,700	
Total Current Liabilities		$71,058
Long-Term Liabilities		
Loans Payable	$15,000	
Total Long-Term Liabilities		15,000
Total Liabilities		86,058
Shareholders' Equity		
Common Stock		
(21,571 shares @ $.01 par value)	$216	
Less: Treasury Stock (50,000 shares)	–2,089	
Paid-in Capital	81,352	
Retained Earnings	146,284	
Total Shareholders' Equity		225,763
Total Liabilities and Shareholders' Equity		**$311,821**

securities such as money-market funds, accounts receivable (or amounts due from customers), and inventory (such as computers, software, and other items the company sells to customers).

Liabilities Liabilities come after assets because they represent claims against the company's assets, as shown in the basic accounting equation: Assets = Liabilities + Owners' equity. Liabilities may be current or long-term, and they are listed in the order in which they will come due. The balance sheet gives subtotals for **current liabilities** (obligations

current liabilities
Obligations that must be met within a year

long-term liabilities
Obligations that fall due more than a year from the date of the balance sheet

that will have to be met within one year of the date of the balance sheet) and **long-term liabilities** (obligations that are due one year or more after the date of the balance sheet), and then it gives a grand total for all liabilities.

Current liabilities include accounts payable, short-term financing, and accrued expenses. *Accounts payable* includes the money the company owes its suppliers (such as Hewlett-Packard and Toshiba) as well as money it owes vendors for miscellaneous services (such as electricity and telephone charges). *Short-term financing* consists of trade credit—the amount owed to suppliers for products purchased but not yet paid for—and commercial paper—short-term promissory notes of major corporations sold in denominations of $100 000 or more, with maturities of up to 270 days (the maximum allowed by law without registration). *Accrued expenses* are expenses that have been incurred but for which bills have not yet been received. For example, because Computer Central's account executives earn commissions on computer sales to customers, the company has a liability to its account executives once the sale is made—regardless of when a cheque is issued to the employee. Thus, the company must record this liability because it represents a claim against company assets. If such expenses and their associated liabilities were not recorded, the company's financial statements would be misleading and would violate the matching principle (because the commission expenses that were earned at the time of sale would not be matched to the revenue generated from the sale).

lease
Legal agreement that obligates the user of an asset to make payments to the owner of the asset in exchange for using it

retained earnings
The portion of shareholders' equity earned by the company but not distributed to its owners in the form of dividends

Long-term liabilities include loans, leases, and bonds. As Chapter 4 points out, bank loans may be secured or unsecured. The borrowing company makes principal and interest payments to the bank over the term of the loan, and its obligation is limited to these payments (see "Debt versus Equity Financing" on page 109). Leases are an alternative to loans. Rather than borrowing money to buy a piece of equipment, a firm may enter into a long-term **lease**, under which the owner of an item allows another party to use it in exchange for regular payments. Bonds are certificates that obligate the company to repay a certain sum, plus interest, to the bondholder on a specific date. Bonds are traded on organized securities exchanges and are discussed in detail in Chapter 14.

Computer Central's long-term liabilities are relatively small for a company its size. In 2004, the company purchased a new $30 million warehouse facility with $15 million in cash it had saved over many years and a five-year, $15 million bank loan. The company invests its excess cash in short-term marketable securities so it can earn interest on these funds until they are needed for future projects.

Businesses rely on bank loans as a chief source of long-term financing. Here bankers review a company's financial statements to determine whether the firm is creditworthy.

Owners' Equity The owners' investment in a business is listed on the balance sheet under owners' equity (or shareholders' equity for a corporation such as Computer Central). Sole proprietorships list owner's equity under the owner's name with the amount (assets minus liabilities). Small partnerships list each partner's share of the business separately, and large partnerships list the total of all partners' shares. Shareholders' equity for a corporation is presented in terms of the amount of common stock that is outstanding, meaning the amount that is in the hands of the shareholders. The combined amount of the assigned or par value of the common stock plus the amount paid over the par value (paid-in capital) represents the shareholders' total investment. Roughly $81 million was paid into the corporation by Computer Central shareholders at the time the company's shares were issued. In 2004, the company repurchased 50 000 shares of the company's own stock in the open market for $948 000. The company will use this *treasury stock* for its employee stock option plan and other general corporate purposes.

Shareholders' equity also includes a corporation's **retained earnings**—the portion of shareholders' equity that is not distributed to its owners in the form of dividends. Computer Central's retained earnings amount to $146 million. The company did not pay dividends. Instead, it is building its cash reserves for future asset purchases and to finance future growth.

Income Statement

L.O. 6

If the balance sheet is a snapshot, the income statement is a movie. The **income statement** shows an organization's profit performance over a specific period of time, typically one year. It summarizes all **revenues** (or sales), the amounts that have been or are to be received from customers for goods or services delivered to them, and all **expenses**, the costs that have arisen in generating revenues. Expenses and income taxes are then subtracted from revenues to show the actual profit or loss of a company, a figure known as **net income**—profit, or the *bottom line.* By briefly reviewing a company's income statements you should have a general sense of the company's size, its trend in sales, its major expenses, and the resulting net income or loss. Owners, creditors, and investors can evaluate the company's past performance and future prospects by comparing net income for one year with net income for previous years. Exhibit 13.5 is the 2004 income statement for Computer Central, showing net income of almost $66 million. This is a 32 percent increase over the company's net income of $50 million for the previous year.

Expenses, the costs of doing business, include both the direct costs associated with creating or purchasing products for sale and the indirect costs associated with operating the business. Whether a company manufactures or purchases its inventory, the cost of storing the product for sale (such as heating the warehouse, paying the rent, and buying insurance on the storage facility) is added to the difference between the cost of the beginning inventory and the cost of the ending inventory in order to compute the actual

income statement
Financial record of a company's revenues, expenses, and profits over a given period of time

revenues
Amount earned from sales of goods or services and inflow from miscellaneous sources such as interest, rent, and royalties

expenses
Costs created in the process of generating revenues

net income
Profit earned or loss incurred by a firm, determined by subtracting expenses from revenues; also called the *bottom line*

Exhibit 13.5 **Income Statement for Computer Central**

An income statement summarizes the company's financial operations over a particular accounting period, usually a year.

Revenues
Funds received from sales of goods and services to customers as well as other items such as rent, interest, and dividends. Net sales are gross sales less returns and allowances.

Cost of Goods Sold
Cost of merchandise or services that generate a company's income by adding purchases to beginning inventory and then subtracting ending inventory.

Operating Expenses
Generally classified as selling and general expenses. Selling expenses are those incurred through the marketing and distributing of the company's products. General expenses are operating expenses incurred in the overall administration of a business.

Net Income After Taxes
Profit or loss over a specific period determined by subtracting all expenses and taxes from revenues.

Computer Central
Income Statement
Year ended December 31, 2004
(in thousands)

Revenues		
Gross Sales	$1,991,489	
Less Sales Returns and Allowances	−258,000	
Net Sales		$1,733,489
Cost of Goods Sold		
Beginning Inventory	$61,941	
Add: Purchases During the Year	1,515,765	
Cost of Goods Available for Sale	−1,577,706	
Less: Ending Inventory	64,392	
Total Cost of Goods Sold		−1,513,314
Gross Profit		$220,175
Operating Expenses		
Selling Expenses	$75,523	
General Expenses	40,014	
Total Operating Expenses		115,537
Net Operating Income (Gross Profit Less Operating Expenses)		104,638
Other Income		4,373
Net Income Before Income Taxes		109,011
Less: Income Taxes		−43,170
Net Income After Taxes		**$65,841**

cost of goods sold
Cost of producing or acquiring a company's products for sale during a given period

gross profit
Amount remaining when the cost of goods sold is deducted from net sales; also known as *gross margin*

operating expenses
All costs of operation that are not included under cost of goods sold

selling expenses
All operating expenses associated with marketing goods or services

general expenses
Operating expenses, such as office and administrative expenses, not directly associated with creating or marketing a good or a service

cost of items that were sold during a period—or the **cost of goods sold**. The computation can be summarized as follows:

Cost of goods sold = Beginning inventory + Net purchases - Ending inventory

As shown in Exhibit 13.5, cost of goods sold is deducted from sales to obtain a company's **gross profit**—a key figure used in financial statement analysis. In addition to the costs directly associated with producing goods, companies deduct **operating expenses**, which include both *selling expenses* and *general expenses,* to compute a firm's *net operating income,* or the income that is generated from business operations. **Selling expenses** are operating expenses incurred through marketing and distributing the product (such as wages or salaries of salespeople, advertising, supplies, insurance for the sales operation, depreciation for the store and sales equipment, and other sales department expenses such as telephone charges). **General expenses** are operating expenses incurred in the overall administration of a business. They include professional services (accounting and legal fees), office salaries, depreciation of office equipment, insurance for office operations, supplies, and so on.

A firm's net operating income is then adjusted by the amount of any non-operating income or expense items such as the gain or loss on the sale of a building. The result is the firm's net income or loss before income taxes (losses are shown in parentheses), a key figure used in budgeting, cash-flow analysis, and a variety of other financial computations. Finally, income taxes are deducted to compute the company's net income or loss for the period.

L.O. 7

Statement of Cash Flows

statement of cash flows
Statement of a firm's cash receipts and cash payments that presents information on its sources and uses of cash

In addition to preparing a balance sheet and an income statement, all public companies and many privately owned companies prepare a **statement of cash flows** to show how much cash the company generated over time and where it went (see Exhibit 13.6). The statement of cash flows tracks the cash coming into and flowing out of a company's bank accounts. It reveals the increase or decrease in the company's cash for the period and summarizes (by category) the sources of that change. From a brief review of this statement you should have a general sense of the amount of cash created or consumed by daily operations, the amount of cash invested in fixed or other assets, the amount of debt borrowed or repaid, and the proceeds from the sale of stock or payments for dividends. In addition, an analysis of cash flows provides a good idea of a company's ability to pay its short-term obligations when they become due.

As Exhibit 13.6 shows, the cash-flow statement is organized into three parts. Computer Central's statement of cash flows shows that the company used $15 million of its cash reserves and the proceeds of a $15 million bank loan in 2004 to pay for its new facility.

Analyzing Financial Statements

Once financial statements have been prepared, managers and outsiders use these statements to evaluate the financial health of the organization, make business decisions, and spot opportunities for improvements by looking at the company's performance in relation to its past performance, the economy as a whole, and the performance of its competitors.

Trend Analysis

The process of comparing financial data from year to year in order to see how they have changed is known as *trend analysis.* You can use trend analysis to uncover shifts in the nature of the business over time. Most large companies provide data for trend analysis in their annual reports. Their balance sheets and income statements typically show three to five years or more of data (making comparative statement analysis possible). Changes in other key items—such as revenues, income, earnings per share, and dividends per share—are usually presented in tables and graphs.

Of course, when you are comparing one period with another, it's important to take into account the effects of extraordinary or unusual items such as the sale of major

Exhibit 13.6 **Statement of Cash Flows for Computer Central**

A statement of cash flows shows a firm's cash receipts and cash payments as a result of three main activities—operating, investing, and financing—for a period.

Cash flows from operations
How much cash a company's business generates or uses, contains clues to how healthy earnings are. Most companies start with net income from the income statement and detail items that cause income to differ from cash.

Cash flows from investments
Cash used to buy or received from selling stock, assets, and businesses, plus capital expenditures.

Cash flows from financing
Cash from or paid to outsiders—such as banks or stockholders. If positive, the company relied on outsiders for funds. If negative, the company may have paid down debt or bought back stock.

Computer Central Statement of Cash Flows Year ended December 31, 2004 (in thousands)		
Cash Flows from Operating Activities:*		
Net Income	$ 65,841	
Adjustments to Reconcile Net Income to Net Cash Provided by Operating Activities	–61,317	
Net Cash Provided by or Used in Operating Activities		$4,524
Cash Flows from Investing Activities:		
Purchase of Property and Equipment	–30,110	
Purchase of Securities	–114,932	
Redemptions of Securities	112,463	
Net Cash Provided by or Used in Operating Activities		–32,579
Cash Flows from Financing Activities		
Loan Proceeds	15,000	
Purchase of Treasury Stock	–2,089	
Proceeds from Exercise of Stock Options	1,141	
Net Cash Provided by or Used in Financing Activities		14,052
Net (Decrease) Increase in Cash		–14,003
Cash and Cash Equivalents at Beginning of Year		$18,233
Cash and Cash Equivalents at End of Year		$4,230

* Note: Numbers preceded by minus sign indicate cash outflows

assets, the purchase of a new line of products from another company, weather, or economic conditions that may have affected the company in one period but not the next. These extraordinary items are usually disclosed in the text portion of a company's annual report or in the notes to the financial statements. For example, CAE, a Canadian flight simulator company, has referred to the events of September 11, 2001, as an extraordinary event that made comparing trends problematic over sequential time periods. One problem for investors is determining whether an extraordinary event is going to become ordinary. Many companies in Canada and around the world, for example, are noting the spike in oil prices as an event that is affecting their income statements and making trend comparison difficult. These companies are saying that the downward pressure on their earnings caused by the high price of oil will ease off as oil returns to normal levels, so any trend downward should be discounted. Recently, however, financial analysts have stated they expect oil to stay highly priced and perhaps continue to rise dramatically, causing investors to wonder whether the so-called reversible trend downward in earnings is in fact reversible.

Ratio Analysis

L.O. 8

Managers and others compute financial ratios to facilitate the comparison of one company's financial results with those of competing firms and with industry averages. **Ratio analysis** compares two elements from the same year's financial figures. They are called *ratios* because they are computed by dividing one element of a financial statement by another. The advantage of using ratios is that it puts companies on the same footing; that is, it makes it possible to compare different-sized companies and changing dollar

ratio analysis
Use of quantitative measures to evaluate a firm's financial performance

amounts. For example, by using ratios, you can easily compare a large supermarket's ability to generate profit out of sales with a similar statistic for a small grocery store.

The benefit of converting numbers into ratios can be explained by the following example: Suppose you wanted to know how well your favourite baseball player is performing this year. To find out, you would check the player's statistics—batting average, runs batted in (RBIs), hits, and home runs. In other words, you would look at data that have been arranged into meaningful statistics that allow you to compare present performance with past performance and with the performance of other players in the league. Financial ratios do the same thing. They convert the raw numbers from the current and prior years' financial statements into ratios that highlight important relationships or measures of performance.[11]

Just as baseball statistics focus on various aspects of performance (such as hitting or pitching), financial ratios help companies understand their current operations and answer key questions: Is inventory too large? Are credit customers paying too slowly? Can the company pay its bills? Ratios also set standards and benchmarks for gauging future business by comparing a company's scores with industry averages that show the performance of competition. Every industry tends to have its own "normal" ratios, which act as yardsticks for individual companies. Dun and Bradstreet, a credit rating firm, and Robert Morris Associates publish both average financial figures and ratios for a variety of industries and company sizes.

Before reviewing specific ratios, consider two rules of thumb: First, avoid drawing too strong a conclusion from any one ratio. For instance, even with a low batting average, a baseball player's RBIs may prove valuable in the team's lineup. Second, once ratios have presented a general indication, refer back to the specific data involved to see whether the numbers confirm what the ratios suggest. In other words, do a little investigating, because statistics can be misleading. Remember, a baseball player who has been at bat only two times and has one hit has a batting average of .500.

Types of Financial Ratios

Financial ratios can be organized into the following groups, as Exhibit 13.7 shows: profitability, liquidity, activity, and leverage (or debt).

Profitability Ratios You can analyze how well a company is conducting its ongoing operations by computing **profitability ratios**, which show the state of the company's financial performance or how well it's generating profits. Three of the most common profitability ratios are **return on sales**, or profit margin (the net income a business makes per unit of sales); **return on investment (ROI)**, or return on equity (the income earned on the owner's investment); and **earnings per share** (the profit earned for each share of stock outstanding). Exhibit 13.7 shows how to compute these profitability ratios by using the financial information from Computer Central.

Liquidity Ratios **Liquidity ratios** measure the ability of the firm to pay its short-term obligations. As you might expect, lenders and creditors are keenly interested in liquidity measures. Liquidity can be judged on the basis of *working capital,* the *current ratio,* and the *quick ratio.* A company's **working capital** (current assets minus current liabilities) is an indicator of liquidity because it represents current assets remaining after the payment of all current liabilities. The dollar amount of working capital can be misleading, however. For example, it may include the value of slow-moving inventory items that cannot be used to help pay a company's short-term debts.

A different picture of the company's liquidity is provided by the **current ratio**—current assets divided by current liabilities. This figure compares the current debt owed with the current assets available to pay that debt. The **quick ratio**, also called the *acid-test ratio,* is computed by subtracting inventory from current assets and then dividing the result by current liabilities. This ratio is often a better indicator of a firm's ability to pay creditors than the current ratio because the quick ratio leaves out inventories—which at times can be difficult to sell. Analysts generally consider a quick ratio of 1.0 to be reasonable, whereas a current ratio of 2.0 is considered a safe risk for short-term

profitability ratios
Ratios that measure the overall financial performance of a firm

return on sales
Ratio between net income after taxes and net sales; also known as *profit margin*

return on investment (ROI)
Ratio between net income after taxes and total owners' equity; also known as *return on equity*

earnings per share
Measure of a firm's profitability for each share of outstanding stock, calculated by dividing net income after taxes by the average number of shares of common stock outstanding

liquidity ratios
Ratios that measure a firm's ability to meet its short-term obligations when they are due

working capital
Current assets minus current liabilities

current ratio
Measure of a firm's short-term liquidity, calculated by dividing current assets by current liabilities

quick ratio
Measure of a firm's short-term liquidity, calculated by adding cash, marketable securities, and receivables, then dividing that sum by current liabilities; also known as the *acid-test ratio*

Exhibit 13.7 How Well Does This Company Stack Up?

Nearly all companies use ratios to evaluate how well the company is performing in relation to prior performance, the economy as a whole, and the company's competitors.

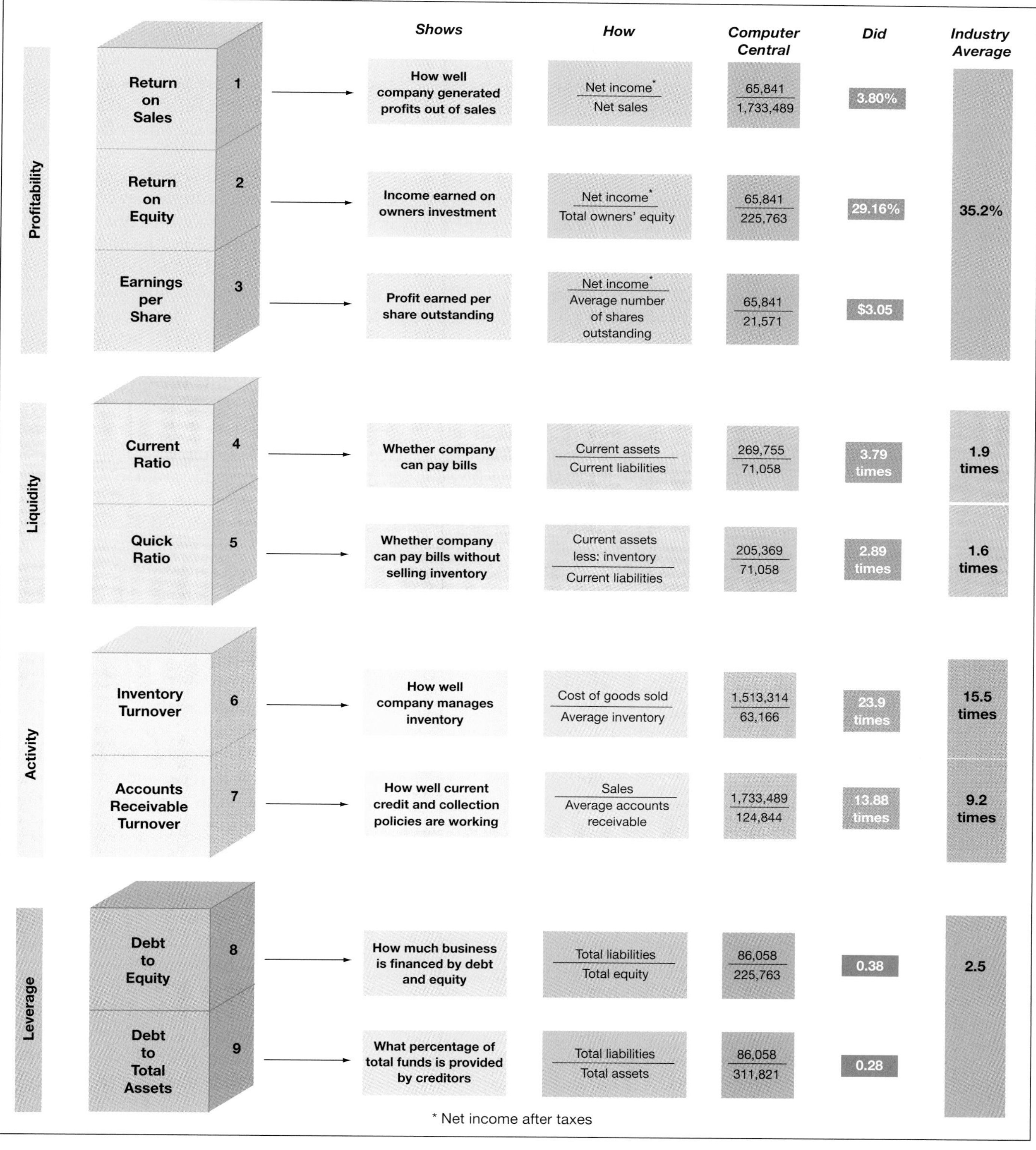

Category	Ratio	#	Shows	How	Computer Central	Did	Industry Average
Profitability	Return on Sales	1	How well company generated profits out of sales	Net income* / Net sales	65,841 / 1,733,489	3.80%	
Profitability	Return on Equity	2	Income earned on owners investment	Net income* / Total owners' equity	65,841 / 225,763	29.16%	35.2%
Profitability	Earnings per Share	3	Profit earned per share outstanding	Net income* / Average number of shares outstanding	65,841 / 21,571	$3.05	
Liquidity	Current Ratio	4	Whether company can pay bills	Current assets / Current liabilities	269,755 / 71,058	3.79 times	1.9 times
Liquidity	Quick Ratio	5	Whether company can pay bills without selling inventory	Current assets less: inventory / Current liabilities	205,369 / 71,058	2.89 times	1.6 times
Activity	Inventory Turnover	6	How well company manages inventory	Cost of goods sold / Average inventory	1,513,314 / 63,166	23.9 times	15.5 times
Activity	Accounts Receivable Turnover	7	How well current credit and collection policies are working	Sales / Average accounts receivable	1,733,489 / 124,844	13.88 times	9.2 times
Leverage	Debt to Equity	8	How much business is financed by debt and equity	Total liabilities / Total equity	86,058 / 225,763	0.38	2.5
Leverage	Debt to Total Assets	9	What percentage of total funds is provided by creditors	Total liabilities / Total assets	86,058 / 311,821	0.28	

* Net income after taxes

credit. Exhibit 13.7 shows that both the current and quick ratios of Computer Central are well above these benchmarks and industry averages.

activity ratios
Ratios that measure the effectiveness of the firm's use of its resources

inventory turnover ratio
Measure of the time a company takes to turn its inventory into sales, calculated by dividing cost of goods sold by the average value of inventory for a period

Activity Ratios A number of **activity ratios** may be used to analyze how well a company is managing its assets. The most common is the **inventory turnover ratio**, which measures how fast a company's inventory is turned into sales; in general, the quicker the better, because holding excess inventory can be expensive. When inventory sits on the shelf, money is tied up without earning interest; furthermore, the company incurs expenses for its storage, handling, insurance, and taxes. In addition, there is always a risk that the inventory will become obsolete before it can be converted into finished goods and sold. The firm's goal is to maintain enough inventory to fill orders in a timely fashion at the lowest cost.

Keep in mind that it's difficult to judge a company by its inventory level. For example, lower inventories might mean one of many things: you're running an efficient operation, the right inventory is not being stocked, or sales are booming and you need to increase your orders. Likewise, higher inventories could signal a decline in sales, careless ordering, or stocking up because of favourable pricing. The "ideal" turnover ratio varies with the type of operation. In 2004, Computer Central turned its inventory 23.9 times (see Exhibit 13.7). This rate is unusually high when compared with industry averages, and it suggests that the company stocks only enough inventory to fill current orders and cover a product's reorder time, as discussed in Chapter 8.

accounts receivable turnover ratio
Measure of time a company takes to turn its accounts receivable into cash, calculated by dividing sales by the average value of accounts receivable for a period

Another popular activity ratio is the **accounts receivable turnover ratio**, which measures how well a company's credit and collection policies are working by indicating how frequently accounts receivable are converted to cash. The volume of receivables outstanding depends on the financial manager's decisions regarding several issues, such as who qualifies for credit and who does not, how long customers are given to pay their bills, and how aggressive the firm is in collecting its debts. Be careful here as well. If the ratio is going up, you need to determine whether the company is doing a better job of collecting or sales are rising. If the ratio is going down, it may be because sales are decreasing or because collection efforts are sagging. In 2004, Computer Central turned its accounts receivable 13.88 times—considerably higher than the industry average (see Exhibit 13.7).

debt ratios
Ratios that measure a firm's reliance on debt financing of its operations (sometimes called *leverage ratios*)

debt-to-equity ratio
Measure of the extent to which a business is financed by debt as opposed to invested capital, calculated by dividing the company's total liabilities by owners' equity

Leverage, or Debt, Ratios You can measure a company's ability to pay its long-term debts by calculating its **debt ratios**, or leverage ratios. Lenders look at these ratios to determine whether the potential borrower has put enough money into the business to serve as a protective cushion for the loan. The **debt-to-equity ratio** (total liabilities divided by total equity) indicates the extent to which a business is financed by debt as opposed to invested capital (equity). From the lender's standpoint, the lower this ratio, the safer the company, because the company has less existing debt and may be able to repay additional money it wants to borrow. However, a company that is conservative in its long-term borrowing is not necessarily well managed; often a low level of debt is associated with a low growth rate. Computer Central's low debt-to-equity ratio of 38 percent (as shown in Exhibit 13.7) reflects the company's practice of financing its growth by using excess cash flow from operations and by selling shares of common stock to the public. Rogers Communications, owner of Rogers Cable, Rogers Wireless, and a host of other companies, takes a much more aggressive approach to debt management than Computer Central. Rogers Communications is pursuing a high-growth strategy and has financed the purchase of Microcell, a rival telecommunications company, almost entirely through the use of debt. As of March 2005, the company had a very high debt-to-equity ration of 2.8. Ted Rogers, owner of the company, hoped to quickly grow his business and his earnings to repay this debt. Companies that take an aggressive approach to acquiring debt will often face tough questions about their ability to make interest payments. While there is no ideal debt-to-equity ratio, anything above 2:1 is considered aggressive.

debt-to-total-assets ratio
Measure of a firm's ability to carry long-term debt, calculated by dividing total liabilities by total assets

The **debt-to-total-assets ratio** (total liabilities divided by total assets) also serves as a simple measure of a company's ability to carry long-term debt. As a rule of thumb, the amount of debt should not exceed 50 percent of the value of total assets. For Computer Central, this ratio is a very low 28 percent and again reflects the company's policy of using retained earnings to finance its growth (see Exhibit 13.7). However, this ratio, too, is not a magic formula. Like grades on a report card, ratios are clues to performance. Managers, creditors, lenders, and investors can use them to get a fairly accurate idea of how a company is doing. But remember, one ratio by itself doesn't tell the whole story.

WHAT DOES FINANCIAL MANAGEMENT INVOLVE?

L.O. 9

Planning for a firm's current and future money needs is the foundation of **financial management**, or finance. This area of concern involves making decisions about alternative sources and uses of funds with the goal of maximizing a company's value (see Exhibit 13.8). To achieve this goal, financial managers develop and implement a firm's financial plan, monitor a firm's cash flow and decide how to create or use excess funds, budget for current and future expenditures, recommend specific investments, develop a plan to finance the enterprise for future growth, and interact with banks and capital markets.

financial management
Effective acquisition and use of money

Developing and Implementing a Financial Plan

One way in which companies such as Domtar make sure they have enough money is by developing a *financial plan*. Normally in the form of a budget, a **financial plan** is a document that shows the funds a firm will need for a period of time as well as the sources and uses of those funds. When you prepare a financial plan for a company, you have two objectives: achieving a positive cash flow and efficiently investing excess cash flow to make your company grow. Financial planning requires looking beyond the four walls of the company to answer questions such as: Is the company introducing a new product in the near future or expanding its market? Is the industry growing? Is the national economy declining? Is inflation heating up? Would an investment in new technology improve productivity?[12] It should be noted that even small businesses depend on financial planning to assist them in moving the company forward. Michael Duck, owner of SureShot Dispensing, a small but growing Nova Scotia company that sells cream dispensers to McDonalds, Tim Hortons and Starbucks, has noted in speeches that his company's close attention to sound financial planning is one of the main reasons why it has been able to grow so quickly.

financial plan
A forecast of financial requirements and the financing sources to be used

Exhibit 13.8 **Sources and Uses of a Company's Funds**

Financial management involves finding suitable sources of funds and deciding on the most appropriate uses for those funds.

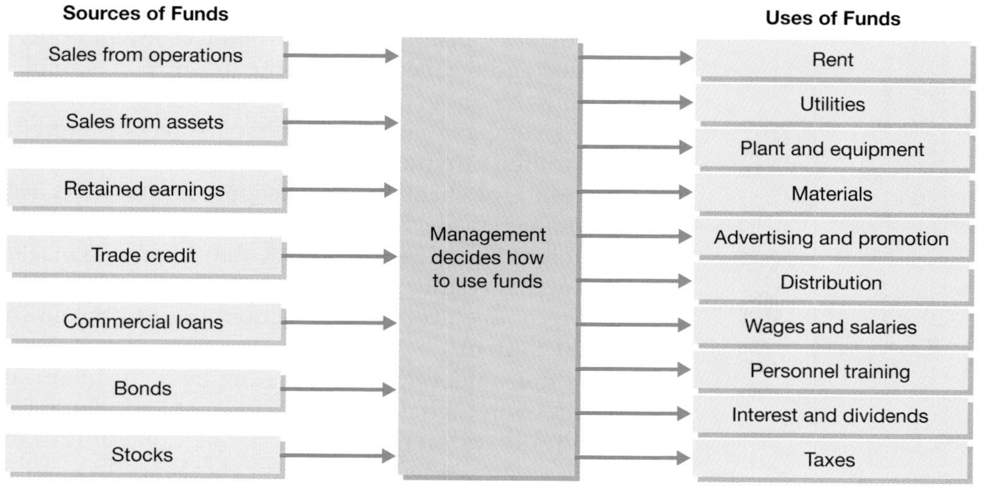

Monitoring Cash Flow

An underlying concept of any financial plan is that all money should be used productively. This concept is important because without cash a company cannot purchase the assets and supplies it needs to operate. In accounting, you prepare income statements to determine the net income of a firm. In finance, however, you focus on cash flows. Although the firm's income is important, cash flows are even more important because cash is necessary to purchase the assets required to continue operations and pay dividends to shareholders. Cash flows are generally related to net income; that is, companies with relatively high accounting profits generally have relatively high cash flows, but the relationship is not precise.

One way financial managers improve a company's cash flow is by monitoring its *working capital accounts:* cash, inventory, accounts receivable, and accounts payable. They use common sense procedures such as shrinking accounts receivable collection periods, dispatching bills on a timely basis without paying bills earlier than necessary, controlling the level of inventory, and investing excess cash so the company can earn as much interest as possible. Aggressive financial managers use electronic cash management (the ability to access bank account information online) to move cash between accounts and pay bills on a daily basis; they also invest excess cash on hand in short-term investments called **marketable securities**. These interest-bearing or dividend-paying investments include money-market funds or publicly traded stocks such as Bombardier or RBC. They are said to be "marketable" because they can be easily converted back to cash. Because marketable securities are generally used as contingency funds, however, most financial managers invest these funds in government securities or securities of solid companies—ones perceived to have the least amount of risk. (Securities are discussed in detail in Chapter 14.) To see the results of these decisions, you may want to read a company's annual report, which details all of the company's cash and non-cash activities for a year. For information on how to read an annual report, see the box entitled "How to Read an Annual Report."

marketable securities
Stocks, bonds, and other investments that can be turned into cash quickly

budget
Planning and control tool that reflects expected revenues, operating expenses, and cash receipts and outlays

financial control
The process of analyzing and adjusting the basic financial plan to correct for forecasted events that do not materialize

capital investments
Money paid to acquire something of permanent value in a business

Developing a Budget

In addition to developing a financial plan and monitoring cash flow, financial managers are responsible for developing a **budget**, a financial blueprint for a given period (often one year). Master (or operating) budgets help financial managers estimate the flow of money into and out of the business by structuring financial plans in a framework of a firm's total estimated revenues, expenses, and cash flows. Accountants provide much of the data required for budgets and are important members of the budget development team because they have a complete understanding of the company's operating costs.

Companies plan for construction projects such as this one years in advance and reflect the costs of such long-term projects in their capital budgets.

The master operating budget sets a standard for expenditures, provides guidelines for controlling costs, and offers an integrated and detailed plan for the future. For example, by reviewing the budget of any airline you can determine whether the company plans to increase its fleet of aircraft, add more routes, hire more employees, increase employees' pay, or continue or abandon any discounts for travellers. No wonder companies like to keep their budgets confidential. Once a budget has been developed, the finance manager compares actual results with projections to discover variances and recommends corrective action—a process known as **financial control**.

In addition to developing operating budgets, financial managers develop capital budgets to forecast and plan for a firm's **capital investments**, such as major expenditures in buildings or equipment. Capital investments generally cover a

How to Read an Annual Report

Whether you're thinking of investing in companies, becoming a supplier for them, or applying for a job with them, you'll need to know how to read annual reports in your career. Thus, it's worth your while to consider the advice of *Newsweek* columnist Jane Bryant Quinn, who provided the following pointers.

READ THE LETTERS

First, turn to the report of the certified public accountant. This third-party auditor will tell you right off the bat if the report conforms to generally accepted accounting principles. Now turn to the letter from the chairman. This letter should tell you how the company fared this year, but more important, the letter should tell you why. Keep an eye out for sentences that start with "Except for..." and "Despite the...." They're clues to problems. The chairman's letter should also give you insights into the company's future. For example, look for what's new in each line of business. Is management getting the company in good shape to weather the tough and competitive years ahead?

DIG INTO THE NUMBERS

Check out the trend in the company's working capital (the difference between current assets and current liabilities). If working capital is shrinking, it could mean trouble. One possibility: The company may not be able to keep dividends growing rapidly.

Another important number to analyze is earnings per share. Management can boost earnings by selling off a plant or by cutting the budget for research and advertising. See the footnotes; they often tell the whole story. If earnings are down only because of a change in accounting, maybe that's good! The company owes less tax and has more money in its pocket. If earnings are up, maybe that's bad. They may be up because of a special windfall that won't happen again next year. One good indicator is the trend in net sales. If sales increases are starting to slow, the company may be in trouble.

GET OUT YOUR CALCULATOR AND COMPARE

High and rising debt, relative to equity, may be no problem for a growing business. But it shows weakness in a company that's levelling out. So get out your calculator and divide long-term liabilities by shareholders' equity. That's the debt-to-equity ratio. A high ratio means the company borrows a lot of money to fund its growth. That's okay—if sales grow too, and if there's enough cash on hand to meet the payments. But if sales fall, watch out. The whole enterprise may slowly sink.

Remember, one ratio, one annual report, one chairman's letter won't tell you much. You have to compare. Is the company's debt-to-equity ratio better or worse than it used to be? Better or worse than the industry norms? In company watching, comparisons are everything. They tell you whether management is staying on top of things.

Questions for Critical Thinking

1. Why might a job seeker want to read a company's annual report before applying for a job with that company?
2. What types of valuable nonfinancial information might an annual report disclose to a potential supplier?

---

period of several years and help the company grow. Before investments can be made, however, a firm must decide on which of the many possible capital investments to make, how to finance those that are undertaken, and even whether to make any capital investments at all. This process is called **capital budgeting**.

capital budgeting
Process for evaluating proposed investments in select projects that provide the best long-term financial return

The process generally begins by having all divisions within a company submit their capital requests—essentially, "wish lists" of investments that would make the company more profitable and thus more valuable to its owners over time. Next, the financial manager decides which investments need evaluating and which don't. For example, the routine replacement of old equipment probably wouldn't need evaluating; however, the construction of a new manufacturing facility would. Finally, a financial evaluation is performed to determine whether the amount of money required for a particular investment will be greater than, equal to, or less than the amount of revenue it will generate. On the basis of this analysis, the financial manager can determine which projects to recommend to senior management for purchase approval. This process of capital budgeting is crucial to business, as the wrong investment can cost a company millions of dollars—not only in trying to recoup the investment dollars but in lost opportunity, as an investment in one project often means failing to invest in another project. For example, EnCanada, a Canadian oil and gas company, recently decided not to start drilling for natural gas off the coast of Nova Scotia after assessing the capital budgeting reports and determining that other drilling projects offered more potential. EnCanada, by forgoing drilling off Nova Scotia, is willing to bet that its investment dollars will be better spent on other projects.

SUMMARY OF LEARNING OBJECTIVES

Discuss how managers and outsiders use financial information.

Managers use financial information to control a company's operation and to make informed business decisions. Outsiders use financial information to evaluate whether a business is creditworthy or a good investment. Specifically, banks want to know if a business is able to pay back a loan, investors want to know if the company is earning a profit, and governments want to be assured that the company is paying the proper amount of taxes.

Describe what accountants do.

Accountants design and install accounting systems, prepare financial statements, analyze and interpret financial information, prepare financial forecasts and budgets, prepare tax returns, interpret tax law, compute and analyze production costs, evaluate a company's performance, and analyze the financial implications of business decisions. In addition to these functions, accountants help managers improve business procedures, plan for the future, evaluate product performance, analyze the firm's profitability, and design and install computer systems. Auditors are licensed certified public accountants who review accounting records and processes to assess whether they conform to generally accepted accounting principles (GAAP) and whether the company's financial statements fairly present the company's financial position and operating results.

State the basic accounting equation and explain the purpose of double-entry bookkeeping and the matching principle.

Assets = Liabilities + Owners' equity is the basic accounting equation. Double-entry bookkeeping is a system of recording financial transactions to keep the accounting equation in balance. The matching principle makes sure that expenses incurred in producing revenues are deducted from the revenue they generated during the same accounting period.

Differentiate between cash basis and accrual basis accounting.

Cash basis accounting recognizes revenue at the time payment is received, whereas accrual basis accounting recognizes revenue at the time of sale, even if payment is not made.

5

Explain the purpose of the balance sheet and identify its three main sections.

The balance sheet provides a snapshot of the business at a particular point in time. It shows the size of the company, the major assets owned, how the assets are financed, and the amount of owners' investment in the business. Its three main sections are assets, liabilities, and owners' equity.

6

Explain the purpose of the income statement.

The income statement reflects the results of operations over a period of time. It gives a general sense of a company's size and performance.

Explain the purpose of the statement of cash flows.

The statement of cash flows shows how a company's cash was received and spent in three areas: operations, investments, and financing. It gives a general sense of the amount of cash created or consumed by daily operations, fixed assets, investments, and debt over a period of time.

8

Explain the purpose of ratio analysis and list the four main categories of financial ratios.

Financial ratios provide information for analyzing the health and future prospects of a business. Ratios facilitate financial comparisons among different-sized companies and between a company and industry averages. Most of the important ratios fall into one of four categories: profitability ratios, which show how well the company generates profits; liquidity ratios, which measure the company's ability to pay its short-term obligations; activity ratios, which analyze how well a company is managing its assets; and debt ratios, which measure a company's ability to pay its long-term debt.

Identify the responsibilities of a financial manager.

The responsibilities of a financial manager include developing and implementing a firm's financial plan, monitoring a firm's cash flow and deciding how to create or use excess funds, budgeting for current and future expenditures, recommending specific investments, raising capital to finance the enterprise for future growth, and interacting with banks and capital markets.

Behind the SCENES

The Dark Clouds above Nortel Will Not Disappear with Restatement of Financials

On December 11, 2004, Nortel's CEO, Bill Owens, announced that in January 2005 the company would release restated net income and revenue for the period from 2001 through the first two quarters in 2004.[13] You would have to forgive investors if they remained skeptical of the announcement, as this was the fifth time the company had stated that results would be forthcoming. Still, many investors and customers greeted the news with relief, hoping that the company's fortunes would quickly turn positive when the accounting problems were put to rest.

Unfortunately for investors, the million-dollar, or perhaps billion-dollar, questions were: What was the impact of the accounting problems on sales? and What will the impact be going forward? Owens stated that he had heard competitors playing up the scandal, with customers using it as ammunition to question the long-term viability of Nortel. To counteract this, Owens travelled around the world visiting with large customers such as France Telecom and Deutsche Telekom, assuring them that Nortel was on firm financial footing. He reported that no orders had been cancelled because of the scandal. But what may be harder to measure is the loss of potential contracts; for example, the company failed to win a piece of the $1.5 billion high-speed wireless contract from Cingular, which many industry observers felt was Nortel's to lose.[14]

With a date for the restated earnings etched in stone or at least drawn in chalk, Nortel's managers tried to refocus investors on the opportunities that existed in the United States and China. Owens, a former U.S. admiral, pointed out that the annual $60 billion spent on telecommunications equipment in the United States had an obvious untapped market—China. Nortel had been operating in China for 30 years, was set to spend billions on wireless networks prior to the Olympics there in 2008, and was hoping to earn the majority of the contract work.[15]

Region watchers, however, noted that Nortel might not win as much business as it would have liked, as its reputation might be far from excellent in the region. Apparently, during the Internet craze of the 1990s, the company often let customer service fall by the wayside in China.[16]

China may also have proven to be the biggest obstacle that Owens had to hurdle, as the emergence of low-cost Chinese competitors such as Huawi Technologies and ZTE Corporation were forcing Nortel to significantly reduce expanses to 35 percent of revenue in 2005 and less than 30 percent of revenue in 2006. With Nortel shedding 60 000 jobs since 2000, closing numerous offices, and trimming research and development spending, insiders are left wondering where Owens would make cuts.

Critical Thinking Questions

1. Do you think Nortel's accounting problems hurt its business in 2004? Its current and future business? Why or why not?
2. Do you think Nortel was able to reach its cost cutting targets?
3. What impact would more layoffs and cuts have on staff?
4. Was it ethical for Nortel to lay off 60 000 people when its top managers earned millions of dollars in salary?

Learn More Online

Visit and review Nortel's website at www.nortel.com. Have there been any changes to upper management since this case? What are they? Search the site for the company's new releases and see what reasons they gave for these changes. Do you think Nortel will ever return to its former glory days?

KEY TERMS

accounting (332)
accounting equation (340)
accounts receivable turnover ratio (350)
accrual basis (340)
activity ratios (350)
assets (339)
audit (334)
balance sheet (342)
bookkeeping (333)
budget (352)
calendar year (342)
capital budgeting (353)
capital investments (352)
cash basis (340)
certified general accountants (CGAs) (334)
certified management accountants (CMAs) (334)
chartered accountants (CAs) (334)
close the books (341)
controller (334)
cost accounting (333)
cost of goods sold (346)
current assets (342)
current liabilities (343)
current ratio (348)
debt ratios (350)
debt-to-equity ratio (350)
debt-to-total-assets ratio (350)
depreciation (340)
double-entry bookkeeping (340)
earnings per share (348)
expenses (345)
financial accounting (333)
financial analysis (333)
financial control (352)
financial management (351)
financial plan (351)
fiscal year (342)
fixed assets (342)
general expenses (346)
generally accepted accounting principles (GAAP) (336)
gross profit (346)
income statement (345)
internal auditors (336)
inventory turnover ratio (350)
lease (344)
liabilities (339)
liquidity ratios (348)
long-term liabilities (344)
management accounting (333)
marketable securities (352)
matching principle (340)
net income (345)
operating expenses (346)
owners' equity (340)
private accountants (334)
profitability ratios (348)
public accountants (334)
quick ratio (348)
ratio analysis (347)
retained earnings (344)
return on investment (ROI) (348)
return on sales (348)
revenues (345)
selling expenses (346)
statement of cash flows (346)
tax accounting (333)
working capital (348)

TEST YOUR KNOWLEDGE

Questions for Review

1. What is GAAP?
2. What is an audit and why is it performed?
3. What is the matching principle?
4. What are the three main profitability ratios, and how is each calculated?
5. What is the primary goal of financial management?

Questions for Analysis

6. Why is accounting important to business?
7. Why do some companies resort to accounting tricks, and what steps are being taken to clamp down on such wrongdoings?
8. Why are the costs of fixed assets depreciated?
9. Why do companies prepare budgets?
10. **Ethical Considerations.** In the process of closing the company books, you encounter a problematic transaction. One of the company's customers was charged twice for the same project materials, resulting in a $1000 overcharge. You immediately notify the controller, whose response is, "Let it go, it happens often." What should you do now?

Questions for Application

11. The senior partner of an accounting firm is looking for ways to increase the firm's business. What other services besides traditional accounting can the firm offer to its clients? What new challenges might this additional work create?
12. Log on to the Toronto Stock Exchange website at www.tsx.com, and click on Listed Companies. Search for Royal Bank and Canadian Tire. Using these financials, compute the working capital, current ratio, and quick ratio for each company. Does one company appear to be more liquid than the other? Why?
13. **Integrated.** Review Chapter 3. Then review this chapter's discussion of Bombardier. Do you think the concept of program accounting is ethical even though it may be legal? Is it ethical for the Bombardier family to control so many voting shares but own very little common stock?

14. **Integrated.** Your appliance manufacturing company recently implemented a just-in-time inventory system for all parts used in the manufacturing process. How might you expect this move to affect the company's inventory turnover rate, current ratio, and quick ratio?

PRACTISE YOUR KNOWLEDGE

SHARPENING YOUR COMMUNICATION SKILLS

Obtain a copy of the annual report of a business and examine what the report shows about finances and current operations. In addition to other chapter material, use the information in the box entitled "How to Read an Annual Report" on page 353 as a guideline for understanding the annual report's content.

- Consider the statements made by the CEO regarding the past year: Did the company do well, or are changes in operations necessary to its future well-being? What are the projections for future growth in sales and profits?
- Examine the financial summaries for information about the fiscal condition of the company: Did the company show a profit?
- If possible, obtain a copy of the company's annual report from the previous year, and compare it with the current report to determine whether past projections were accurate.
- Prepare a brief written summary of your conclusions.

ALPINE MANUFACTURING INCOME STATEMENT YEAR ENDED DECEMBER 31, 2004	
Sales	$1 800
Less: Cost of Goods Sold	1 000
Gross Profit	$ 800
Less: Total Operating Expenses	450
Net Operating Income Before Income Taxes	350
Less: Income Taxes	50
NET INCOME AFTER INCOME TAXES	$ 300

BUILDING YOUR TEAM SKILLS

Divide into small groups and compute the following financial ratios for Alpine Manufacturing using the company's balance sheet and income statement. Compare your answers to those of your classmates:

- Profitability ratios: return on sales; return on equity; earning per share
- Liquidity ratios: current ratio; quick ratio
- Activity ratios: inventory turnover; accounts receivable turnover
- Leverage ratios: debt to equity; debt to total assets

ALPINE MANUFACTURING BALANCE SHEET DECEMBER 31, 2004	
ASSETS	
Cash	$ 100
Accounts Receivable (beginning balance $350)	300
Inventory (beginning balance $250)	300
Current Assets	$ 700
Fixed Assets	2 300
Total Assets	$3 000
LIABILITIES AND SHAREHOLDERS' EQUITY	
Current Liabilities (beginning balance $300)	$ 400
Long-Term Debts	1 600
Shareholders' Equity (100 common shares outstanding valued at $12 each)	1 000
Total Liabilities and Shareholders' Equity	$3 000

EXPAND YOUR KNOWLEDGE

DISCOVERING CAREER OPPORTUNITIES

People interested in entering the field of accounting can choose among a wide variety of careers with diverse responsibilities and challenges. Select one of the occupations mentioned in this chapter. Using library sources, Internet websites from one of the major accounting firms, or the websites for CICA (CAs), CMAs, or CGAs, dig deeper to learn more about your chosen occupation.

1. What are the day-to-day duties of this occupation? How would these duties contribute to the financial success of a company?

2. What skills and educational qualifications would you need to enter this occupation? How do these qualifications fit with your current plans, skills, and interests?
3. What kinds of employers hire people for this position? According to your research, does the number of employers seem to be increasing or decreasing? How do you think this trend will affect your employment possibilities if you choose this career?

DEVELOPING YOUR RESEARCH SKILLS

Select an article from a business journal or newspaper (print or online editions) that discusses the quarterly or year-end performance of a company that industry analysts consider notable for either positive or negative reasons.

1. Did the company report a profit or a loss for this accounting period? What other performance indicators were reported? Did the company's performance improve or decline over previous accounting periods?
2. Did the company's performance match industry analysts' expectations, or was it a surprise? How did analysts or other experts respond to the firm's actual quarterly or year-end results?
3. What reasons were given for the company's improvement or decline in performance?

See It on the **WEB**

URLs for all Internet exercises are provided at the website for this book, www.pearsoned.ca/bovee. When you log on to the text website, select Chapter 13, then select Destinations. Click on the name of the featured website and review the website to complete the following exercises.

Explore the following chapter-related websites, review their content, and answer the following questions for each website you visit:

1. What is the purpose of this website?
2. What kinds of information does this website contain? Please be specific.
3. How is the information provided at this website useful for business people? Consumers?
4. How did you expand your knowledge of accounting by reviewing the material at this website? What new things did you learn about accounting?

LINK YOUR WAY TO THE WORLD OF ACCOUNTING

Looking for one accounting supersite packed with information and links to financial resources? Check out the Electronic Accountant, an online launching point for accountants. This is the place to find answers to all kinds of questions about accounting, financial analysis, taxes, and more. Participate in one of the many focused discussion groups. Visit the niche sites for information on financial planning, practice management, technology consulting, or CPE requirements. Read the latest issues of *Accounting Technology* or the *Practical Accountant*. Don't leave without checking out the Career Center, where you'll find information on the latest accounting hot jobs and opportunities. www.electronicaccountant.com

SHARPEN YOUR PENCIL

You never know what you'll find at a gallery these days. How about annual reports—lots of them! Sharpen your pencil and start thinking like an accountant. Take a virtual field trip to the Report Gallery, where you can click to view the annual reports of Allstate, Boeing, and many other firms from around the world. Select an annual report for any company and examine the financial statements, chairman's letter, and auditor's report. Was it a good or bad year for the company? Who are the company's auditors? Did they issue a clean audit report? See www.reportgallery.com.

THINK LIKE AN ACCOUNTANT

Find out how the world of accounting is changing by exploring the valuable links at the CICA website. Learn about the many facets of accounting such as taxes, finance, auditing, and more. Follow the link to your provincial CICA society, and discover what it takes to become a CA or how to prepare for the CA exam. Learn how to read a financial report, and discover what financial statements say about your business. Check out the financial calculators. Increase your knowledge of accounting terms and accounting basics before participating in one of the site's discussion forums. Log on to www.cica.ca and find out more.

Chapter 14 Understanding Banking and Securities

LEARNING OBJECTIVES

After studying this chapter, you will be able to

1. Highlight the functions, characteristics, and common forms of money
2. Discuss the responsibilities and insurance methods of the Canadian Deposit Insurance Corporation (CDIC)
3. Discuss the Canadian banking industry
4. Differentiate among a share's par value, its market value, and its book value
5. Highlight the distinguishing features of common stock, preferred stock, bonds, and mutual funds
6. Differentiate among an auction exchange, dealer exchange, and electronic communication network (ECN)
7. Explain how government regulation of securities trading tries to protect investors

Behind the SCENES

Unfortunately, It Is the Wrong Royal Bank

www.rbs.co.uk
www.rbc.com

In 1990, the Royal Bank was considered a national bank and a small to mid-sized player in the global finance industry, ranking eighty-sixth in the world in asset size. Fast forward to 2005 and the Royal Bank is a source of national pride as it has grown into the seventh-largest financial institution in the world and is in the midst of a successful expansion into the American market. The catch here for Canadians is that it is the Royal Bank of Scotland (RBS), not the Royal Bank of Canada (RBC), that has jumped ahead of 79 banks in asset size over the past 14 years and has purchased the U.S. Charter One Financial bank for $10.5 billion, thus acquiring branches in Pittsburgh, Philadelphia, Vermont, Massachusetts, Michigan, Illinois, and other states.[1]

Meanwhile, the Royal Bank of Canada has slipped from thirty-eighth place in 1990 to fifty-first in 2004. How did the RBS jump 79 places in such a short period of time? By doing things that Canadian banks haven't been allowed to do. It participated in a series of mergers and acquisitions in its own country that was not only permitted but encouraged by the government. These mergers allowed RBS to grow in asset size and expand its investment pool, giving it the funds needed to successfully expand internationally.[2,3]

Bank analysts will argue that it did not have to be this way. In 1998, RBC announced that it was going to merge with the Bank of Montreal (BMO), and a short time later the Toronto Dominion Bank (TD) announced its plans to merge with Canadian Imperial Bank of Commerce (CIBC). But the Canadian government, led by then Prime Minister Jean Chrétien and Finance Minister Paul Martin, ended any merger talks by announcing it would not permit the banks to join forces. Chrétien and Martin's actions were fuelled by strong public sentiment that opposed bank mergers due to perceptions of dwindling customer service, less choice, and a reduction in the number of branches. Even after the RBC and BMO announced that a merged bank would cut service charges and expand the number of branches, the public remained firm in its opposition.

Shortly after denying the mergers, the Canadian government announced it would work with banking officials, businesses, and public interest groups to study the issue and establish clear guidelines concerning the question of bank mergers. As of 2005, Canadian chartered banks are still waiting for guidance from the government on whether they will be allowed to merge. Some financial analysts charge that it is too late, as Canadian banks, which were once mid-sized players on the world stage, have shrunk so much that any mergers might not even enable them to climb back to their previous status.[4]

Why do you think the Canadian public was so opposed to bank mergers? Why do you think government in the United Kingdom facilitated mergers? What are some of the benefits of such mergers? What are some of the potential concerns?

L.O. 1

MONEY AND FINANCIAL INSTITUTIONS

Businesses and individuals have an abundance of options when it comes to investing money. They can deposit it in a bank account, purchase company stocks or bonds, or acquire real estate, artwork, or other assets that they hope will appreciate over time. This chapter discusses two investment options: banking and securities markets. We begin by explaining some of the characteristics and types of money. Next, we look at common types of financial institutions, the services they provide, and the changing nature of the Canadian banking environment. In the second half of the chapter we explore three principal types of securities investments—stocks, bonds, and mutual funds—and discuss the types of securities markets in which such investments are traded. Finally, we conclude the chapter by looking at securities trading procedures, performance barometers, and regulations.

Characteristics and Types of Money

Money is anything generally accepted as a means of paying for goods and services. Before it was invented, people got what they needed by trading their services or possessions; in some societies, such as Russia, this system of trading, or bartering, still exists. However, barter is inconvenient and impractical in a global economy, where many of the things we want are intangible, come from places all over the world, and require the combined work of many people.

money
Anything generally accepted as a means of paying for goods and services

To be an effective medium of exchange, money must have these important characteristics: It must be divisible, portable (easy to carry), durable, and difficult to counterfeit, and it should have a stable value. In addition, money must perform three basic functions: First, it must serve as a medium of exchange—a tool for simplifying transactions between buyers and sellers. Second, it must serve as a measure of value so that you don't have to negotiate the relative worth of dissimilar items every time you buy something. Finally, money must serve as a temporary store of value—a way of accumulating your wealth until you need it.

Paper money and coins are the most visible types of money, but money exists in a variety of forms, including:

- **Currency**: Coins, bills, traveller's cheques, cashier's cheques, and money orders
- **Demand deposit**: Money available immediately on demand, such as from chequing accounts
- **Time deposits**: Accounts that pay interest and restrict the owner's right to withdraw funds on short notice, such as savings accounts, certificates of deposit, and money-market deposit accounts

currency
Bills and coins that make up a country's cash money

demand deposits
Money that can be used by the customer at any time, such as chequing accounts

time deposits
Bank accounts that pay interest and require advance notice before money can be withdrawn

Chequing and Savings Accounts

Money you put into your chequing account is a *demand deposit* or *near money*, available immediately (on demand) through the use of **cheques**, written orders that direct your bank to pay the stated amount of money to you or to someone else. Several types of chequing accounts exist, each offering benefits in exchange for monthly fees, minimum account balances, or other requirements. For example, high interest paying chequing accounts pay interest but limit the number of cheques customers can write and impose a fee if the account balance falls below a minimum level.

cheques
Written orders that tell the user's bank to pay a specific amount to a particular individual or business

You can also earn interest on the money you put in savings accounts. Originally, these accounts were known as *passbook savings accounts* because customers received a small passbook in which the bank recorded all deposits, withdrawals, and interest. Today, most banks send out statements instead of passbooks, so these accounts have become known as *statement savings accounts.* In general, money in savings accounts can be withdrawn at any time, but certain types of savings accounts may require advanced notice or impose withdrawal limits. For example, money in a *money-market deposit account* earns more interest, but you are allowed only a limited number of monthly withdrawals. Money held in a *Guaranteed Investment Certificate (GIC) account* earns an even higher interest rate, but you cannot withdraw the funds for a stated period, such as six months or more. If you want to make an early withdrawal from a GIC, you will lose some or all of the interest you've earned.

Credit, Debit, and Smart Cards

For everyday access to short-term credit, banks and other institutions issue **credit cards**, plastic cards that entitle customers to make purchases now and repay the

credit cards
Plastic cards that allow the user to buy now and repay the loaned amount at a future date

amount later. Credit cards are a popular substitute for currency and cheques. Many credit card issuers charge an annual fee for Visa and MasterCard credit cards, and all charge interest on any unpaid credit card balance. Credit cards have become immensely popular with consumers because they are convenient and allow people to postpone payment on purchases they make. They also help people manage their finances by either choosing to repay the full amount when they are billed or making small payments month by month until the debt has been repaid. Credit card companies make money by charging customers interest on their unpaid account balances and by charging businesses a processing fee, which can range from 2 to 5 percent of the value of each sales transaction paid by credit card. Nearly every store accepts credit cards, and mail-order merchants and Internet retailers are especially dependent on credit cards to facilitate purchases.

debit cards
Plastic cards that allow the bank to take money from the user's demand-deposit account and transfer it to a retailer's account

smart cards
Plastic cards with embedded computer chips that store money drawn from the user's demand-deposit account as well as information that can be used for purchases

In addition to credit cards, many banks offer **debit cards**, plastic cards that function like cheques in that the amount of a purchase is electronically deducted from the user's chequing account and transferred to the retailer's account at the time of the sale. Debit cards are ideal for customers who must control their spending or stick to a budget. Proportionately, Canada is the largest user of debit cards in the world. **Smart cards** are similar to debit cards; however, these plastic cards contain tiny computer chips that can store amounts of money (from the user's bank account) and selected data (such as shipping address, credit card information, frequent-flyer account numbers, health and insurance details, or other personal information). When a purchase is made, the store's equipment electronically deducts the amount from the value stored on the smart card and reads and verifies requisite customer information. Users reload money from their bank accounts to their smart cards as needed.

Although popular in Europe, smart cards have been slow to catch on in North America for two reasons: Low telephone rates (compared to those in European countries) make it affordable to verify credit card transactions over the phone, and it is not cost-effective for most North American businesses to replace current debit and credit card infrastructures with smart card readers and computer chip technology. Nevertheless, American Express has made inroads with its combination smart card and credit card, Blue. Designed to appeal to online shoppers, Blue comes with software and a small smart card reader that plugs into the user's serial port. Customers who purchase online simply insert Blue into the reader and type in a password, and the digital information stored on the smart card tells the vendor the customer's credit card number, expiration date, and shipping address.[5] See the box entitled "Surprise! You've Been Swiped" to learn about some of the current threats to various electronic payment systems.

Financial Institutions and Services

As a business person, you may or may not be responsible for writing company cheques or investing a firm's money, but you will be receiving a paycheque and you will need to deposit that cheque into a financial institution or cash it so that you can pay your bills. In fact, no matter where in the world you live, work, or travel, today's businesses and individuals require a wide range of financial services.

Deposit and Nondeposit Financial Institutions

The types of services provided by a financial institution are generally governed by whether it is a *deposit institution* or *nondeposit institution.* Deposit institutions accept deposits from customers or members and offer chequing and savings accounts, loans, and other banking services. Among the many deposit institutions are the following:

- *Chartered banks:* profit-oriented financial institutions that are federally regulated and chartered under the Bank Act. Chartered banks make money by charging customers fees and higher interest rates on loans than the interest rates they pay on customers' deposits.
- *Trust companies:* incorporated by either the federal or the provincial governments. Trust companies serve both individuals and businesses by acting as safeguards for

Surprise! You've Been Swiped

Skimming is the fastest-growing area of credit and debit card fraud. A skimmer is someone who steals customer account information by swiping a credit card through a handheld magnetic card reader—about the size of a pager. The reader copies the cardholder's name, account number, and even the card validation code—stored on the magnetic strip—giving the counterfeiter all the data needed to create a perfect clone of the credit card. Debit card skimming is almost identical to thieves cloning the debit card, but because of the need for the user's personal identification number (PIN) to gain access to funds, thieves have set up hidden cameras to record the PINs of unsuspecting users. Recently in Halifax, Nova Scotia, thieves took debit card skimming a step further by placing a clear plastic sleeve over the keypad on debit machines. The sleeve was linked to a computer and every time someone typed in his or her PIN the information was transferred directly to a PC. Card readers can be purchased for as little as US$100 over the Internet and are intended for legitimate use by banks, restaurants, retailers, and hotels. Unfortunately, some end up in the wrong hands.

Thieves and, increasingly, organized crime groups pay waiters and store clerks to steal information from credit cards using the concealed devices. By skimming 14 to 20 accounts, crooks can generate $50 000 to $60 000 worth of fraud that will probably go undiscovered until the victims get their bills—30 to 60 days after the crime. Moreover, skimmed data from, say, a customer in Quebec City or Ottawa can be e-mailed to Taiwan, Japan, or Europe and used for mail-order, telephone-order, or e-commerce overseas transactions within 24 to 48 hours of the theft. Professionals can even encode the stolen codes into a strip and use equipment to produce an electronically indistinguishable counterfeit card.

While credit and debit card issuers decline to say how much they are losing to skimmers—in part because they don't want to scare consumers out of using their plastic—industry analysts estimate skimmers reap more than US$125 million annually. To curb this fraud, major card issuers are cooperating with the RCMP to pool information about fraudulent transactions. For example, issuers can generate computer analyses that flag locations where numerous cards may have been skimmed. Or if someone in Hong Kong tries to buy something with a credit card that was used two hours earlier in Toronto, the computer will reject the transaction.

What can you do to prevent your cards from getting skimmed? Not much, say experts, besides covering up the keypad when entering your PIN, using PINs that are unrelated to personal characteristics and events, reading your bills closely, checking your accounts on the Web or by phone during the month to make sure there are no surprises, and reporting improper charges promptly. Although you're not liable for fraudulent credit card charges made to your accounts by skimmers or other scam artists, you do have to face the hassle of getting the unauthorized transactions removed from your bills. To date, banks have been willing to cover debit card losses, though some are now doing so only if the PIN is not easily detectable by knowing some of the user's personal information such as important birthdays or telephone numbers. Of course, you can always pay with old-fashioned cash. But if you carry a lot of that around, you may have to worry about the old-fashioned robber.

Questions for Critical Thinking

1. To curb the abuse, why don't credit or debit card issuers require customers to present additional personal validation data at the time of sale?
2. Why won't skimming increase the demand for smart cards?

funds and estates entrusted to them, serve as a trustee in bond sales, and often provide banking services.

- *Credit unions and caisses populaires:* non-profit member-owned organizations that take deposits only from members, such as one company's employees or one union's members or another designated group. The provinces and the Credit Union Central of Canada, which operates as the central finance facility for credit unions, regulate these organizations. Credit unions and caisses populaires offer the same services as chartered banks.

Nondeposit institutions offer specific financial services but do not accept deposits. Among the many nondeposit financial institutions are the following:

- *Insurance companies,* which provide insurance coverage for life, property, and other potential losses; they invest the payments they receive in real estate, in construction projects, and in other ways.
- *Pension funds,* which are set up by companies to provide retirement benefits for employees; money contributed by the company and its employees is put into securities and other investments.
- *Finance companies,* which lend money to consumers and businesses for home improvements, expansion, purchases, and other purposes.
- *Brokerage firms or security dealers,* which allow investors to buy and sell stocks, bonds, and other investments; many also offer chequing accounts, high-paying savings accounts, and loans to buy securities.

In the past, each financial institution focused on offering a particular set of financial services for specific customer groups. However, the competitive situation has evolved over the past 10 years as legislation has been passed allowing both deposit and nondeposit institutions to offer similar services. This blurring of the line between banks and other financial organizations has resulted in increased competition in the industry, which is designed to benefit consumers.

line of credit
Arrangement in which the financial institution makes money available for use at any time after a loan has been approved

automated teller machines (ATMs)
Electronic terminals that permit people to perform basic banking transactions 24 hours a day without a human teller

electronic funds transfer systems (EFTS)
Computerized systems for completing financial transactions

Loans

Loans are one of the most important services financial institutions provide. Individuals usually apply for mortgage loans when they want to buy a home. They also look to banks and financial services firms for auto loans, home improvement loans, student loans, and many other types of loans. Businesses rely on banks to provide loans for expansion, purchases of new equipment, construction or renovation of plants and facilities, or other large-scale projects. Some businesses obtain a working capital **line of credit**, which is an agreed-on maximum amount of money a bank is willing to lend to a business during a specific period of time, usually one year. Once a line of credit has been established, the business may obtain unsecured loans for any amount up to that limit, provided the bank has funds. The line of credit can be cancelled at any time, so companies that want to be sure to obtain credit when needed should arrange a revolving line of credit, which guarantees that the bank will honour the line of credit up to the stated amount.

Electronic Banking

Most deposit institutions offer electronic banking services that may be conducted from sites other than the bank's physical location. For instance, all over the world, customers rely on **automated teller machines (ATMs)** to withdraw money from their demand-deposit accounts at any hour. Look around: ATMs are everywhere, from banks, malls, and supermarkets to airports, resorts, and tourist attractions. Canada actually has the highest number of bank machines per capita in the world. By linking with regional, national, and international ATM networks, banks let customers withdraw cash far from home, make deposits, and handle other transactions. To compete, more banks are jazzing up their ATMs. The latest ATMs are wired to the Web and allow customers to pay insurance premiums and utility bills, print cashier's cheques, and purchase stamps, movie tickets, ski lift tickets, DVDs, and even foreign currency.

Although many banking transactions are conducted electronically these days, most business customers still require the personal services provided by community banks, such as cashier and certified cheques, loans, and account transaction inquiries.

Electronic funds transfer systems (EFTS) are another form of electronic banking. These computerized systems allow users to conduct financial transactions efficiently from remote locations. Today many employers are using EFTS to deposit employees' cheques directly into their bank accounts. This procedure saves employers and employees the worry and headache of handling large amounts of cash. Even the Canadian government uses EFTS for regular payments such as employment insurance benefits.

In addition to ATM and EFTS, banks and many insurance companies now offer Internet or online banking to accommodate the growing number of individuals and businesses that want to transfer money between accounts, check account balances, pay bills, apply for loans, and handle other transactions at any hour. Online banking is not only fast and easy for customers but also extremely cost-efficient for banks.[6] But as the "E-Business in Action" feature at the end of this chapter shows, online banking has been slow to take off (see pages 388–389).

Bank Safety

L.O. 2

The Canadian Deposit Insurance Corporation (CDIC) is a Crown corporation that was founded in 1967 to bring deposit insurance to the Canadian banking system. The insurance covers deposits at banks, trust companies, and loan companies up to $60 000, and reimburses clients when a member institution fails. As of April 2004, the CDIC insured $367 billion in deposits. Money deposited at credit unions and caisses populaires is protected by provincial insurance.

The Evolving Canadian Banking Environment

L.O. 3

Today's current banking system came about as a result of the Great Depression in the 1930s, when then Prime Minister Robert Bennett was facing criticism about the current financial structure, along with the lack of direct means for settling international accounts. Bennett appointed a Royal Commission to study Canada's monetary and financial system and it concluded that the country would benefit from a national bank. In 1935, the Bank Act was passed, officially bringing the Bank of Canada into existence. Originally, the bank was to be a private institution with shareholders but in 1938 the new prime minister, William Lyon Mackenzie King, nationalized the Bank of Canada. It immediately became the lone issuer of currency and manager of credit in the country. Today the Bank of Canada is in charge of setting interest rates; controlling the supply of money; administering the public debt, including the maintenance of records and making payments on the governments behalf; and providing a host central banking service, including setting regulations and acting as a bank for other Canadian financial institutions by accepting their deposits.

Canada's banking system was originally founded on the principles of branch banking, in which large national banks would open regional branches in rural communities. Since the population of Canada was quite small and spread out, this branch system enabled banks to open across the country with a limited amount of capital. For most of the twentieth century, Canada's finance industry was dominated by six unique participants: chartered banks, credit unions/caisses populaires, trust companies, insurance agencies, brokers, and other lending agencies. Each institution, with the exception of banks and credit unions/caisses populaires, operated in different markets offering Canadian diverse financial services. This began to change in the 1980s and 1990s when several amendments were made to the Bank Act to increase the amount of competition in the financial services industry. For example, banks were permitted to sell securities, insurance companies could compete in some areas with banks, and foreign banks were introduced to Canada.

As a result of these changes, Canadian banks became the dominant players in the financial service industry, holding more than 70 percent of domestic assets. The remaining 30 percent is spread out over credit unions/caisses populaires, trust companies, insurance companies, and other financial institutions. Of the 58 banks operating in Canada, the Big Six—Royal Bank of Canada, Bank of Montreal, Toronto Dominion Bank, Scotiabank, Canadian Imperial Bank of Commerce, and National Bank—account for 90 percent of the money controlled by banks and operate in excess of 8000 branches across the country. The Big Six banks are currently advocating bank mergers among themselves and with large insurance companies as an expansion strategy, but the Canadian government has blocked any merger activity to date due to public concern. The federal government is scheduled to announce guidelines for bank mergers sometime in 2005.

L.O. 4, 5

TYPES OF SECURITIES INVESTMENTS

With the line between banks and brokerage houses such as Schwab blurring, consumers now have more options as to where they can purchase **securities**—stocks, bonds, and other investments—to meet their investment goals. Securities are traded in organized markets. Corporations sell stocks or bonds to finance their operations or expansion, while governments and provinces issue bonds to raise money for building or public expenses—from national defence to road improvements. Here's a closer look at these three principal types of securities investments.

securities
Investments such as stocks, bonds, options, futures, and commodities

authorized stock
Maximum number of ownership shares into which a corporation's board of directors decides the business can be divided

issued stock
Portion of authorized stock sold to and held by shareholders

unissued stock
Portion of authorized stock not yet sold to shareholders

stock split
Increase in the number of shares of ownership that each stock certificate represents, at a proportionate drop in each share's value

par value
As shown on the stock certificate, a value assigned to a stock for use in bookkeeping and in calculating dividends

Stocks

As discussed in Chapter 5, a share of stock represents ownership in a corporation and is evidenced by a stock certificate. The number of shares a company sells depends on the amount of equity capital the company will require and on the price of each share it sells. A corporation's board of directors sets a maximum number of shares into which the business can be divided. In theory, all of these shares—called **authorized stock**—may be sold at once. In practice, however, the company sells only a part of its authorized stock. The part sold and held by shareholders is called **issued stock**; the unsold portion is called **unissued stock**. From time to time a company may announce a **stock split**, in which it increases the number of shares that each stock certificate represents while proportionately lowering the value of each share. Companies generally use a stock split to make the share price more affordable. So, if a company with 1 million shares outstanding and a stock price of $50 per share announces a two-for-one split, it is doubling the number of shares. After the split, the company will have 2 million shares outstanding, and each original share will become two shares worth $25 each. For example, Power Financial, a Montreal-based finance company that trades shares on the Toronto Stock Exchange (TSX) under the symbol POW.SV, completed a stock split in 2004, doubling the number of common shares from 197 million to more than 397 million and reducing the share price from approximately $52 to $26. Interestingly, while many companies willingly split their stock as a means of making it more attractive and to create more value for shareholders, Warren Buffet, who is regarded as the greatest investor over the past century, dislikes stock splits and has never split the stock of his company, Berkshire Hathaway. As a result of Buffet's stance on stock splits, the company's class "A" common shares recently traded in excess of US$85 000 per share on the New York Stock Exchange.

Branch bankers excel at personal service. They will meet with small-business owners and work with them on their business plan, and they will loan them money to help them grow their business to the next level.

When stock is first issued, the company assigns a **par value**, or dollar value, to the stock primarily for bookkeeping purposes. Par value is also used to calculate dividends (for certain kinds of stock). Keep in mind that par value is not the same as the stock's *market value,* the price at which a share currently sells, or its *book value,* the amount of net assets of a corporation represented by one share of common stock.

Common Stock

Most investors buy common stock, which represents an ownership interest in a publicly traded corporation. As

Chapter 5 points out, shareholders of this class of stock vote to elect the company's board of directors, vote on other important corporate issues, and receive dividend payments from the company's profits. But they have no say in day-to-day business activities. Still, common shareholders have the advantage of limited liability if the corporation gets into trouble, and as part owners they share in the fortunes of the business and are eligible to receive dividends as long as they hold the stock. In addition, common shareholders stand to make a profit if the stock price goes up and they sell their shares for more than the purchase price. The reverse is also true: Shareholders of common stock can lose money if the market price drops and they sell the stock for less than they paid for it.

Stock certificates represent a share of ownership of a company.

Preferred Stock

Investors who own preferred stock, the second major class of stock, enjoy higher dividends and a better claim (after creditors) on assets if the corporation fails. The amount of the dividend on preferred stock is printed on the stock certificate and set when the stock is first issued. If interest rates fluctuate, the market price of preferred stock will go up or down to adjust for the difference between the market interest rate and the stock's dividend.

Preferred stock often comes with special privileges. *Convertible preferred stock* can be exchanged, if the shareholder chooses, for a certain number of shares of common stock issued by the company. *Cumulative preferred stock* has an additional advantage: If the issuing company stops paying dividends for any reason, the dividends on these shares will be held (accumulate) until preferred shareholders have been paid in full—before common stockholders are paid.

Income Trusts

income trust
Legal entities that hold cash-generating businesses in trust and distribute the majority of income to unit holders in the form of dividends

Income trusts represent a unique type of company structure and investment opportunity that is growing substantially in Canada. In Canada, the number of trusts has doubled in the past few years, reaching approximately 175 in 2005. Eight of every ten dollars of new initial public offerings (IPOs) were trust companies in 2004, and their combined worth has risen from just over $20 billion in 2000 to approximately $110 billion in 2005. Trust companies closely resemble corporations in that they have investors who own shares of the company and these shares trade on stock exchanges (trust companies include .UN after their stock symbol to indicate they are trusts). Just like common stock, the shareholders in a trust vote at annual meetings and have rights to dividend. However, the shares are referred to as *units* and the owners are called trust holders. Where a trust differs most from traditional corporations is that it is a legal entity that holds cash-generating assets (a business) in a holding company, and the business does not reinvest any of its net income. Rather, it allows the majority of income to flow to the owners of the trust company, known as unit holders, through dividends. As a result, the income trust avoids paying tax and income is only taxed in the hands of the unit holders. Since income trusts pay out the majority of their net income to unit holders, their dividends are usually much higher than traditional common shares. For example, YellowPages income trust (YLO.UN) trades on the TSX and, as of March 2005, carried an approximate share price of $13 with a dividend yield of 7.32 percent. The only income that trusts do not pay to unit holders is used to cover expenses or to expand the business through the purchase of additional cash-generating assets.

Investors who purchase income trust units want to see their value or unit price appreciate while earning a high dividend yield. Part of the attractiveness of income trusts are the current low interest rates in Canada, which make it difficult for investors to earn interest from bonds. It is not uncommon to see trust companies pay dividend yields in excess of 7 percent, whereas most common shares pay dividends under 3 percent. Critics of trusts worry about their ability to sustain high dividend payout with little money being reinvested in the company; that some restaurant companies like the Keg and A&W which are income trusts, do not represent businesses with consistent cash flows; and that, if interest rates start to rise sharply, the price of the units may fall substantially, offsetting any income earned from the dividend.

Bonds

bond
Method of funding in which the issuer borrows from an investor and provides a written promise to make regular interest payments and repay the borrowed amount in the future

principal
Amount of money a corporation borrows from an investor through the sale of a bond

secured bonds
Bonds backed by specific assets that will be given to bondholders if the borrowed amount is not repaid

debentures
Corporate bonds backed only by the reputation of the issuer

convertible bonds
Corporate bonds that can be exchanged at the owner's discretion into common stock of the issuing company

Treasury bills
Short-term debt securities issued by the Bank of Canada; also referred to as *T-bills*

Unlike stock, which gives the investor an ownership stake in the corporation, bonds are debt financing. A **bond** is a method of raising money in which the issuing organization borrows from an investor and issues a written pledge to make regular interest payments and then repay the borrowed amount later. When you invest in this type of security, you are lending money to the company or government that issued the bond. Bonds are usually issued in multiples of $1000, such as $5000, $10 000, and $50 000. Also, like stocks, bonds are evidenced by a certificate, which shows the issuer's name, the amount borrowed (the **principal**), the date this principal amount will be repaid, and the annual interest rate investors receive.

The interest is stated in terms of an annual percentage rate but is usually paid at six-month intervals. For example, the holder of a $1000 bond that pays 8 percent interest due January 15 and July 15 could expect to receive $40 on each of those dates. A look at the financial section of any newspaper will show that some corporations sell new bonds at an interest rate two to three percentage points higher that that offered by other companies. Yet the terms of the bonds seem similar. Why? Because bonds are not guaranteed investments. The variations in interest rates reflect the degree of risk associated with the bond, which is closely tied to the financial stability of the issuing company. Agencies such as Standard & Poor's (S&P) and Moody's rate bonds on the basis of the issuers' financial strength. Exhibit 14.1 on page 369 shows that the safest corporate bonds are rated AAA (S&P) and Aaa (Moody's). Low-rated bonds, known as *junk bonds*, pay higher interest rates to compensate investors for the higher risk.

Corporate Bonds

Companies issue a variety of corporate bonds. **Secured bonds** are backed by company-owned property (such as airplanes or plant equipment) that will pass to the bondholders if the issuer does not repay the amount borrowed. *Mortgage bonds*, one type of secured bond, are backed by real property owned by the issuing corporation. **Debentures** are unsecured bonds, backed only by the corporation's promise to pay. Because debentures are riskier than other types of bonds, investors who buy these bonds receive higher interest rates. **Convertible bonds** can be exchanged at the investor's option for a certain number of shares of the corporation's common stock. Because of this feature, convertible bonds generally pay lower interest rates.

Bell South Telecommunications Bond Certificate
1. *Name of corporation issuing bond*
2. *Type of bond (debenture)*
3. *Face value of the bond*
4. *Annual interest rate (8.25%)*
5. *Maturity date (due 2032)*

Canadian Government Securities Bonds

Just as corporations raise money by issuing bonds, so too do municipal, provincial, and federal governments. As an investor, you can buy a variety of Canadian government securities, including Canada Savings Bonds, T-Bills, and bonds issued by various municipalities and provinces.

Treasury bills (also referred to as *T-bills*) are short-term debt obligations issued by the Bank of

Exhibit 14.1 Corporate Bond Ratings

Standard & Poor's (S&P) and Moody's Investors Service are two companies that rate the safety of corporate bonds. When its bonds receive a low rating, a company must pay a higher interest rate to compensate investors for the higher risk.

S&P	INTERPRETATION	MOODY'S	INTERPRETATION
AAA	Highest rating	Aaa	Prime quality
AA	Very strong capacity to pay	Aa	High grade
A	Strong capacity to pay; somewhat susceptible to changing business conditions	A	Upper-medium grade
BBB	More susceptible than A rated bonds	Baa	Medium grade
BB	Somewhat speculative	Ba	Somewhat speculative
B	Speculative	B	Speculative
CCC	Vulnerable to nonpayment	Caa	Poor standing; may be in default
CC	Highly vulnerable to nonpayment	Ca	Highly speculative; often in default
C	Bankruptcy petition filed or similar action taken	C	Lowest rated; extremely poor chance of ever attaining real investment standing
D	In default		

Canada that are repaid in less than one year. Treasury bills are sold at a discount and redeemed at face value. The difference between the purchase price and the redemption price is, in effect, the interest earned for the time periods.

Canada Savings Bonds are Canadian government bonds that investors can purchase and redeem at any time, although most are used as long-term investment devices. In general, Canadian government securities pay lower interest than corporate bonds because they are considered safer: There is very little risk that the government will fail to repay bondholders as promised. A traditional choice for many individual investors, Canada Savings Bonds are issued by the Canadian government in amounts ranging from $50 to $10 000.

Canada Savings Bonds
Debt securities issued by the Bank of Canada that are usually held in excess of one year

Mutual Funds

Mutual funds are financial organizations that pool money from many investors to buy a diversified mix of stocks, bonds, or other securities. The Canadian government made this type of investment popular by encouraging people to invest for their retirement by contributing to Registered Retirement Savings Plans (RRSPs). Canadians receive a tax credit for each dollar they invest in their RRSP to a maximum of $14 500 or 18.5 percent of their gross income per year. This type of investment also became fashionable during the bull market of the late 1990s and when banks started to offer investment advice as part of their regular services to customers. Mutual funds are particularly well suited for investors, like those saving for their retirement, who wish to spread a fixed amount of money over a variety of investments and do not have the time or experience to search out and manage investment opportunities. Investors hope to benefit from the purchase of mutual funds and other securities by receiving dividends, which are profits distributed to shareholders, and earning capital gains, which occur when an investor sells a security for a higher price than the purchase price. *No-load* funds charge no fee to buy or sell shares, whereas *load funds* charge investors a commission to buy or sell. The most common types of loads are front end (assessed when you purchase the fund) and back end (assessed when you sell the fund).

mutual funds
Financial organization pooling money to invest in diversified blends of stocks, bonds, or other securities

Investment companies offer two types of mutual funds. An *open-end fund* issues additional shares as new investors ask to buy them. In essence, the fund's books never close. The number of shares outstanding changes daily as investors buy new shares or redeem old ones. These shares aren't traded in a separate market. *Closed-end funds*, on the other hand, raise all of their money at once by distributing a fixed number of shares that trade much like stocks on major security exchanges. As soon as a certain number of shares are sold, the fund closes its books.

Various mutual funds have different investment priorities. Among the most popular mutual funds are **money-market funds**, which invest in short-term securities and other liquid investments. *Growth funds* invest in stocks of rapidly growing companies. *Income funds* invest in securities that pay high dividends and interest. *Balanced funds* invest in a carefully chosen mix of stocks and bonds. *Sector funds* (also known as *specialty* or *industry funds*) invest in companies within a particular industry. *Global funds* invest in foreign and Canadian securities, whereas *international funds* invest strictly in foreign securities. And *index funds* buy stocks in companies included in specific market averages, such as the S&P/TSE 300. You can buy shares in mutual funds through your broker or directly from the mutual fund company.

money-market funds
Mutual funds that invest in short-term securities and other liquid investments

primary market
Market where firms sell new securities issued publicly for the first time

secondary market
Market where subsequent owners trade previously issued shares of stocks and bonds

stock exchanges
Location where traders buy and sell stocks and bonds

L.O. 6

SECURITIES MARKETS

Where can you purchase bonds, stocks, and other securities? Stocks and bonds are bought and sold in two kinds of marketplaces: primary markets and secondary markets.

Newly issued shares or initial public offerings (IPOs) are sold in the **primary market**. Once these shares have been issued, subsequent investors can buy and sell them in the organized **secondary market** known as **stock exchanges** (or *securities exchanges*).

over-the-counter (OTC) market
Network of dealers who trade securities on computerized linkups rather than a trading floor

NASDAQ (National Association of Securities Dealers Automated Quotations)
National over-the-counter securities trading network

auction exchange
Centralized marketplace where securities are traded by specialists on behalf of investors

Securities Exchanges

The Toronto Stock Exchange (TSX) is the largest securities exchange in Canada, with more than 1300 companies trading approximately 240 million shares per day. The New York Stock Exchange (NYSE), also known as the "Big Board," is the world's largest securities exchange. The stocks and bonds of about 3000 companies, with a combined market value topping US$16 trillion, are traded on the exchange's floor.[7] After the NYSE, some of the largest stock exchanges are located in Tokyo, London, Frankfurt, and Paris. Many companies list their securities on more than one securities exchange. Thus, some TSX-listed stocks can also be bought and sold on the NYSE.

The New York Stock Exchange began under a buttonwood tree on Wall Street in 1792 as an agreement among a group of brokers to trade with one another. In 1817, the institution was established, with members taking seats in a room to trade stocks at designated times. For a long time, the floor was an important centre of power in brokerage firms. Then came the Internet and electronic communication networks (ECNs). Today, the NYSE is under competitive pressure to automate its trading systems.

The **over-the-counter (OTC) market** consists of a network of registered stock and bond representatives who are spread out across North America—and in some cases around the world. Most use a nationwide computer network owned by the National Association of Securities Dealers (NASD). This network is called **NASDAQ (National Association of Securities Dealers Automated Quotations)** and it is the second-largest stock market in the United States. In 1998 NASD (owners of NASDAQ) acquired the American Stock Exchange (the world's third-largest auction exchange), making NASDAQ an even stronger competitor to the New York Stock Exchange.[8] In Canada the OTC market is referred to as the Canadian Unlisted Board (CUB).

How to Buy and Sell Securities

The process for buying and selling securities varies according to the type of exchange. As Exhibit 14.2 depicts, in an **auction exchange**, such as the New York Stock Exchange, all buy and sell orders (and all information concerning companies traded on that exchange)

Exhibit 14.2 **Old and New Ways to Buy Stocks**

Some think that floor trading will become a thing of the past as electronic communication networks become increasingly popular.

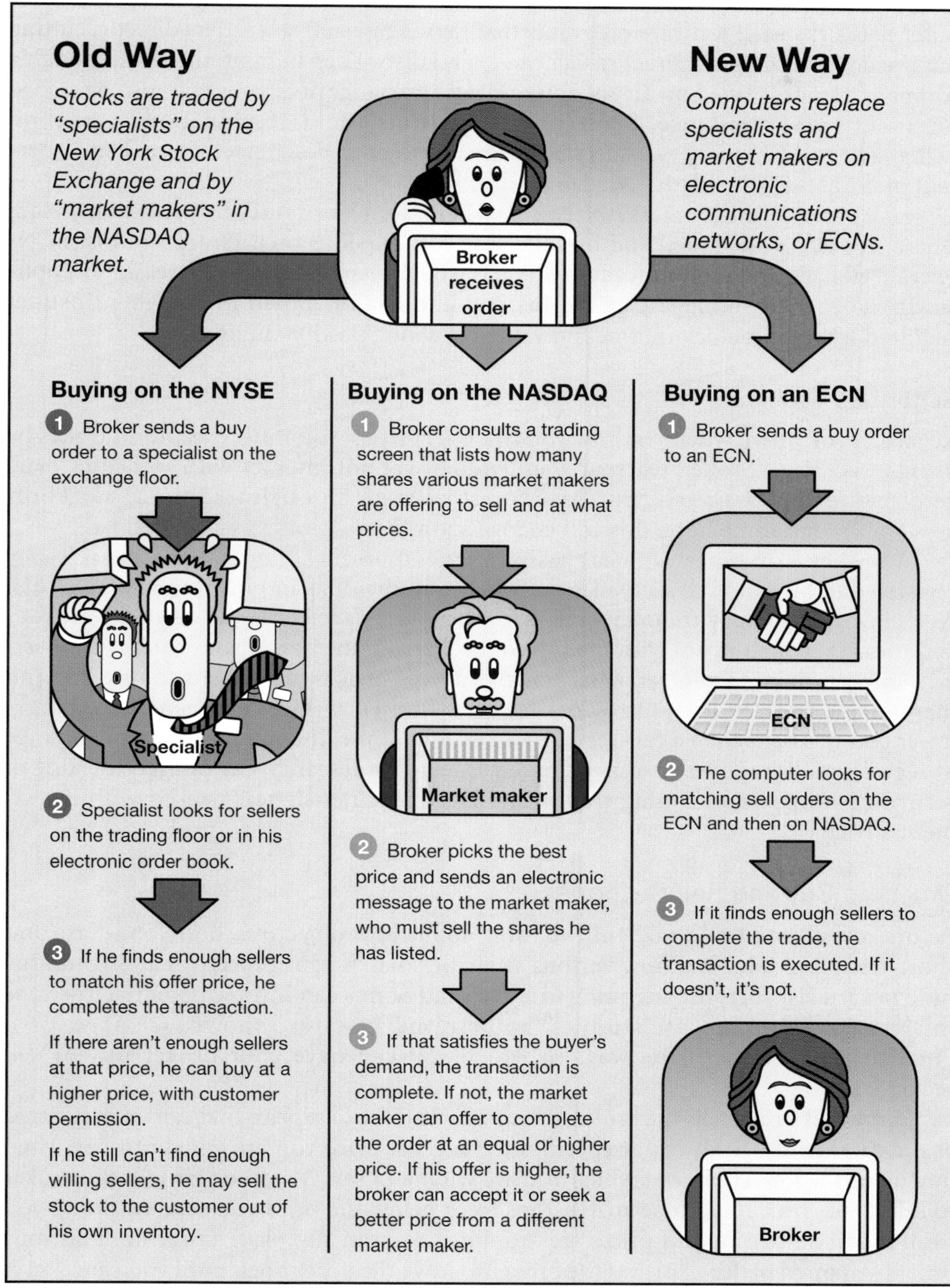

are funnelled onto an auction floor. There, buyers and sellers are matched by a **stock specialist**, a broker who occupies a post on the trading floor and conducts all trades in specific stocks via a central clearinghouse. If buying or selling imbalances occur in that stock, a specialist can halt trading to prevent the price from plunging without adequate cause. Specialists can also sell stock to customers out of their own inventory.[9] In Canada, the TSX and TSX Venture Exchanges buy and sell securities using an electronic trading system. While the NASDAQ is a **dealer exchange**, it has no central marketplace for making transactions. Instead, all buy and sell orders are executed through comput-

stock specialist
Intermediary who trades in a particular security on the floor of an auction exchange; "buyer of last resort"

dealer exchanges
Decentralized marketplaces where securities are bought and sold by dealers out of their own inventories

ers by **market makers**, registered stock and bond representatives who sell securities out of their own inventories.

market makers
Registered representatives who trade securities from their own inventories on dealer exchanges, making a ready market for buyers and sellers

electronic communication networks (ECNs)
Internet-based networks that match up buy and sell orders without using an intermediary

Electronic communication networks (ECNs) use the Internet to link buyers and sellers. Frequently referred to as a virtual stock market or cybermarket, ECNs have no exchange floors, specialists, or market makers. In fact, they are nothing more than computer networks with software programs that match buy and sell orders directly, cutting out the once-dominant market makers and specialists. Keep in mind that even though a company's stock is listed on an auction or dealer exchange, its shares may also be traded on an ECN. For instance, many brokerage firms use a combination of auction exchanges, dealer exchanges, and ECNs to execute their trades. In fact, more than 38 percent of NASDAQ shares are traded on ECNs.[10]

Like other securities marketplaces, ECNs aim to make money by providing a place where stocks can be traded and by collecting commissions on each trade. Most ECNs operate globally and economically—which is why they are becoming increasingly popular. In 2002, the two biggest ECNs, Instinet and Island, joined forces when Instinet acquired Island in a stock transaction valued at about US$508 million.[11]

Securities Brokers

Regardless of when, where, or how you trade securities, you must execute all trades by using a securities broker. Currently, individuals cannot interact with securities marketplaces or ECNs directly; purchases must be made through traditional stockbrokers—although some hope this will change soon.[12]

broker
An expert who has passed specific tests and is registered to trade securities for investors

A **broker** is an expert who has passed a series of formal examinations and is legally registered to buy and sell securities on behalf of individual and institutional investors. As an investor, you pay *transaction costs* for every buy or sell order, to cover the broker's commission, which varies with the type of broker and the size of your trade: A *full-service broker* provides financial management services such as investment counselling and planning; a *discount broker* provides fewer or limited services and generally charges lower commissions than a full-service broker. Still, some discount brokers offer a range of services and resources that include free or low-cost research, customized tracking of securities, e-mails confirming trades, and electronic newsletters packed with investment advice.

Orders to Buy and Sell Securities

market order
Authorization for a broker to buy or sell securities at the best price that can be negotiated at the moment

limit order
Market order that stipulates the highest or lowest price at which the customer is willing to trade securities

stop order
An order to sell a stock when its price falls to a particular point to limit an investor's losses

open order
Limit order that does not expire at the end of a trading day

day order
Any order to buy or sell a security that automatically expires if not executed on the day the order is placed

discretionary order
Market order that allows the broker to decide when to trade a security

Before you start to trade, take time to think about your objectives, both long-term and short-term. Next, look at how various securities match your objectives and your attitude toward risk, because investing in stocks and bonds can involve potential losses, as this chapter's special case study, "The Betrayed Investor," shows (see page 379). Finally, consider the many ways in which you can have your broker buy or sell securities.

A **market order** tells the broker to buy or sell at the best price that can be negotiated at the moment. A **limit order** specifies the highest price you are willing to pay when buying or the lowest price at which you are willing to sell. A **stop order** tells the broker to sell if the price of your security drops to or below the price you set, protecting you from losing more money if prices are dropping. You can also place a time limit on your orders. An **open order** instructs the broker to leave the order open until you cancel it. A **day order** is valid only on the day you place it and should not be confused with a *day trader*, a stock trader who holds positions for a very short time (minutes to hours) and closes out these positions within the same day.

If you have special confidence in your broker's ability, you may place a **discretionary order**, which gives the broker the right to buy or sell your securities at the broker's discretion. In some cases, discretionary orders can save you from taking a loss, because the broker may have a better sense of when to sell a stock. If the broker's judgment proves wrong, however, you cannot hold the broker legally responsible for the consequences, so investigate your broker's background and think carefully before you give anyone the right to trade your securities.

Investors sometimes borrow cash to buy stocks, a practice known as **margin trading**. Instead of paying for the stock in full, you borrow some of the money from your stockbroker, paying interest on the borrowed money and leaving the stock with the broker as collateral. Be aware, however, that margin trading increases risk. If the price of a stock you bought on margin goes down, you will have to give your broker more money or the broker will sell your stock. Such forced sales can cause prices to fall even further, triggering a vicious cycle of sales and margin calls.[13]

margin trading
Borrowing money from brokers to buy stock, paying interest on the borrowed money, and leaving the stock with the broker as collateral

If you believe that a stock's price is about to drop, you may choose a trading procedure known as **short selling.** With this procedure, you sell stock you borrow from a broker in the hope of buying it back later at a lower price. After you return the borrowed stock to the broker, you keep the price difference. For example, you might decide to borrow 25 shares that are selling for $30 per share and sell short because you think the share price is going to plummet. When the stock's price declines to $15, you buy 25 shares on the open market and make $15 profit on every share (minus transaction costs). Selling short is risky. If the stock had climbed to $32, you would have had to buy shares at that higher price, even though you would be losing money. For example, many investors thought shares of WestJet, a Canadian discount airline operator, were overvalued in the fall of 2004 and early winter of 2005 as the company faced increasing competition from Air Canada, CanJet and JetsGo. As a result, many investors sold their stock short hoping that the share price would drop. But when JetsGo unexpectedly went out of business, WestJet stock rose more than 20 percent in one day, causing many short sellers to lose significant amounts of money.

short selling
Selling stock borrowed from a broker with the intention of buying it back later at a lower price, repaying the broker, and keeping the profit

How to Analyze Financial News

Regardless of which trading procedures you use, you will want to monitor financial news sources to see how your investments are doing. Start with daily newspaper reports on securities markets. Other sources include newspapers aimed specifically at investors (such as the investment sections of the *Globe and Mail* and the *National Post*, *Investor's Business Daily*, and *Barron's*) and general-interest business publications that follow the the *Globe and Mail* and the *National Post*'s investment sections, as well as the corporate world, and give hints about investing (such as the *Wall Street Journal, Forbes, Fortune,* and *Canadian Business Week*). Standard & Poor's, Moody's Investor Service, and Value Line also publish newsletters and special reports on securities. Online sources include your brokerage firm's website plus a growing number of excellent financial websites listed in the box entitled "Put Your Money Where Your Mouse Is!"

What types of financial information should you be looking for? First, you want to determine the general direction of stock prices. If stock prices have been rising over a long period, the industry and the media will often describe this situation as a **bull market**. The reverse is a **bear market**, one characterized by a long-term trend of falling prices. You can see these broad market movements in Exhibit 14.3 on page 375. Once you have the general picture, look at the timing. Has a bull market lasted for too long, suggesting that stocks are overvalued and a *correction* (tumbling prices) might be imminent? Also watch the volume of shares traded each day. If the stock market is down on heavy volume (that is, if prices are moving downward and a lot of trading is going on), investors may be trying to sell before prices go down further—a bearish sign.

bull market
Rising stock market

bear market
Falling stock market

Watching Market Indexes and Averages

One way to determine whether the market is bullish or bearish is to watch **market indexes** and averages, which use the performance of a representative sampling of stocks, bonds, or commodities as a gauge of broader market activity. The most famous Canadian stock index is the S&P/TSX Composite Index, which measures the performance of the largest companies in the country; another well-known index is the TSX Venture Exchange that consists of smaller and/or new companies.

market indexes
Measures of market activity calculated from the prices of a selection of securities

The best-known American index is the Dow Jones Industrial Average (DJIA), which tracks the prices of 30 *blue-chip* or well-established stocks, each representing a particular sector of the U.S. economy. Critics say the Dow is too narrow and too susceptible to

Put Your Money Where Your Mouse Is!—Investment Information on the Internet

The Internet has been hailed as the great equalizer between individual investors and the experts on Bay and Wall streets. Today's investors have access to a staggering amount of valuable information and investment tools—many of which are used by professionals. But having access to information is one thing; using it wisely is another. So before you put a dollar (or a euro) into any investment, learn as much as possible about the market, the security, its issuer, and its potential. Here are some tips to point you in the right direction.

For "how-to" advice, try the Canadian Foundation for Investment Education (www.cfie.ca), Globe Investor (www.globeinvesetor.com), Globe Fund (www.globefund.com), *Report on Business* (www.robtv.com), the Motley Fool (www.fool.com), Quicken's financial site (www.quicken.com/investments), or *CNN/Money*'s website (http://money.cnn.com). For the latest online news and commentary about stocks, check out *Report on Business Television* (www.robtv.com), The Street (http://thestreet.com), CBS Market Watch (www.marketwatch.com), Jag Notes (www.jagnotes.com), and Wall Street Research Net (www.wsrn.com). Then research individual securities using Yahoo! (www.yahoo.com) or another Internet search tool. Plug in the company name and click to see the latest news. Go to Hoover's Online (www.hoovers.com) to read a little about the company's history and recent results. Be sure to stop by the company's website to read its press releases and financial statements. You can burrow even further into potential investments using the following websites:

- Corporate financial data filed for Canadian companies (www.sedar.com)
- Corporate financial data filed with the SEC (www.freeedgar.com)
- Toronto Stock Exchange (www.tsx.ca)

Construct a hypothetical portfolio on Quicken, Yahoo!, or another financial website and watch how your investments fare. Track your favourite market index on MSN MoneyCentral (http://moneycentral.msn.com) and compare it to your personal investment portfolio. Are your proposed investments meeting, missing, or beating the market index?

Now you're in a better position to buy securities, but your research shouldn't end here. Even after you start trading, you need to stay on top of the latest news and industry developments that can affect the securities in which you have invested. And if a potential investment seems too good to be true, point your web browser to the North American Securities Administrators Association (www.nasaa.org) and get some tips on investment fraud. Remember, when it comes to investments, your web surfing can really pay off.

Questions for Critical Thinking

1. Why is it important to learn about a company's financial results and background before buying its stock or bonds?
2. What are the disadvantages of searching for investment information on the Internet?

short-term swings, lacks the right stocks, and gives too much weight to higher-priced shares. But advocates say the Dow's 30 stocks serve as a general barometer of market conditions. Regardless, in 1999 the *Wall Street Journal* editors (guardians of the Dow) replaced time-honoured blue chips Chevron, Goodyear, Sears Roebuck, and Union Carbide with Microsoft, Intel, Home Depot, and SBC Communications.[14] These changes should make the DJIA more representative of the "new economy."

Another widely watched index in Canada is the TSX's 60 Index, which tracks the performances of 60 corporate stocks, fewer than the SP/TSX Index. This index is weighted by market value, not by stock price, so large companies carry far more weight than small ones.[15] A widely watched index in the United States is the Standard & Poor's 500 Stock Average (S&P 500), which tracks the performances of 500 corporate stocks, many more than the DJIA. The Wilshire 5000 Index, which actually covers some 7000 stocks, is the broadest index measuring U.S. market performance. To get a sense of how technology stocks are doing, check the NASDAQ Composite Index, covering more than 3000 over-the-counter stocks, including many high-tech firms. You can also look at indexes to learn about the performance of foreign markets, such as Japan's Nikkei 225 Index and the United Kingdom's FT-SE 100 Index.

Exhibit 14.3 **The Stock Market's Ups and Downs**

The peaks and valleys on this chart represent swings in the Dow Jones Industrial Average, the most widely used indicator of U.S. stock prices.

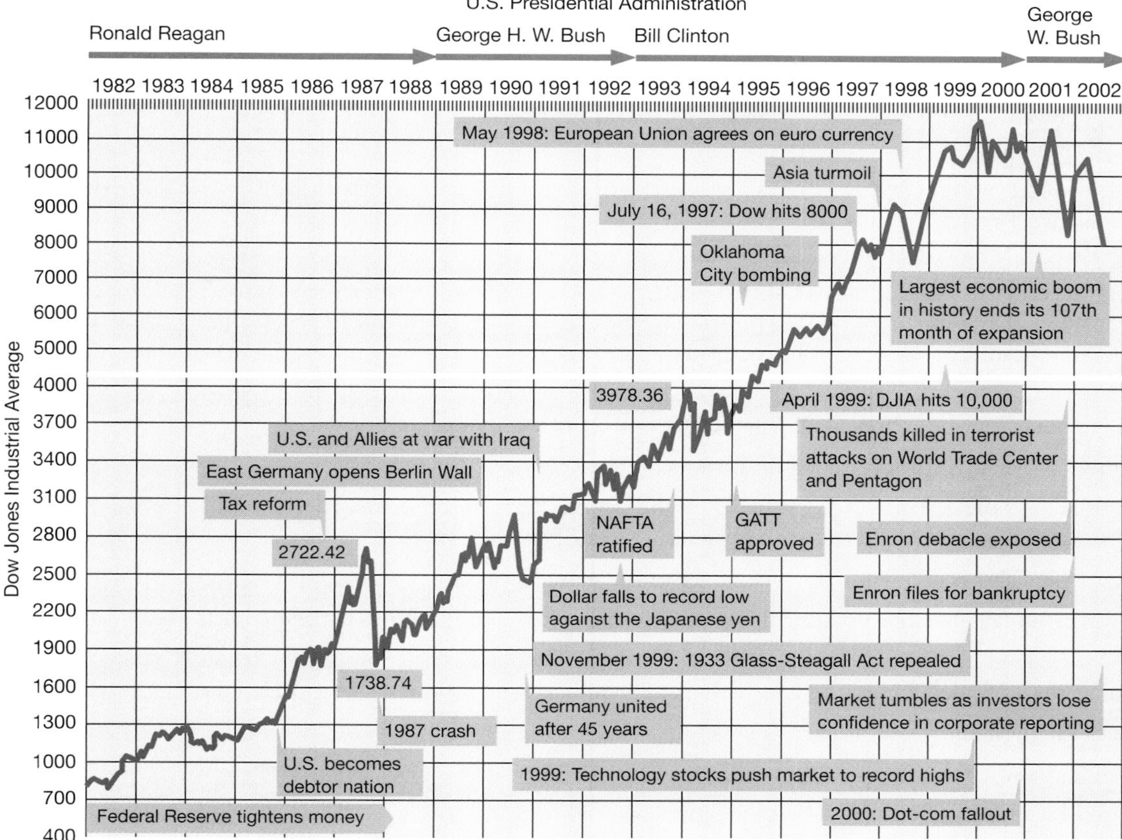

Interpreting the Financial News

In addition to watching market trends, you will want to follow the securities you own and others that look like promising investments. For stocks, you can turn to the stock exchange report in major daily newspapers. Exhibit 14.4 shows how to read this report, which includes high and low prices for the past 52 weeks, the number of shares traded (volume), and the change from the previous day's closing price. Canada started using decimals in 1996. Prior to that year, prices were quoted in fractions as small as 1/16. Using decimals in trading makes stock prices easier for many investors to understand. Moreover, quoting shares down to the penny permits stocks to be priced in smaller increments.[16]

price-earnings ratio
Ratio calculated by dividing a stock's market price by its prior year's earnings per share

Included in the stock exchange report is the **price-earnings ratio**, or *p/e ratio* (also known as the *price-earnings multiple*), which is computed by dividing a stock's market price by its *prior* year's earnings per share. Some investors also calculate a forward p/e ratio using *expected* year earnings in the ratio's denominator. Bear in mind that if a stock's p/e ratio is well below the industry norm, either the company is in trouble or it's an undiscovered gem with a relatively low stock price. For more detailed data on a stock, consult the company's annual reports or documents filed with the TSX in Canada or with the Securities and Exchange Commission (SEC) in the United States.

To follow specific bonds, check the bond quotation tables in major newspapers (see Exhibit 14.5 on page 377). When reading these tables, remember that the price is quoted as a percentage of the bond's value. For example, a $1000 bond shown closing at 65 actually sold at $650.

Exhibit 14.4 **How to Read a Newspaper Stock Quotation**

Even before you invest, you will want to follow the latest quotations for your stock. This table shows you how to read the newspaper stock quotation tables.

(1)		(2)	(3)	(4)	(5)	(6)	(7)	(8)		(9)	(10)
52-WEEK HIGH	52-WEEK LOW	STOCK	SYM	DIV	YLD %	PE	VOL 100S	HI	LOW	LAST	NET CHG
32.75	25.50	Power Corporation	POW.SV.58	1.89%	33.10	10917		30.90	29.25	30.42	+0.42
8.10	3.18	Nortel Networks	NT	-	-	16.3	364255	3.39	3.18	3.32	+0.02

1. **52-week high/low:** Indicates the highest and lowest trading price of the stock in the past 52 weeks plus the most recent week but not the most recent trading day (adjusted for splits). Stocks are quoted in dollars and cents. In most newspapers, boldfaced entries indicate stocks whose price changed by at least 4 percent, but only if the change was at least 75 cents a share.
2. **Stock:** The company's name may be abbreviated. A capital letter usually means a new word.
3. **Symbol:** Symbol under which this stock is traded on stock exchanges.
4. **Dividend:** Dividends are usually annual payments based on the last quarterly or semiannual declaration, although not all stocks pay dividends. Special or extra dividends or payments are identified in footnotes.
5. **Yield:** The percentage yield shows dividends as a percentage of the share price.
6. **PE:** Price-to-earnings ratio, calculated by dividing the stock's closing price by the earnings per share for the latest four quarters.
7. **Volume:** Daily total of shares traded, in hundreds. A listing of 888 indicates 88 800 shares were traded during that day.
8. **High/Low:** The stock's highest and lowest price for that day.
9. **Close:** Closing price of the stock that day.
10. **Net change:** Change in share price from the close of the previous trading day.

Common Stock Footnotes: d—new 52 week low; n—new; pf—preferred; s—stock split or stock dividend of 25 percent or more in previous 52 weeks; u—new 52 week high; v—trading halted on primary market; vi—in bankruptcy; x—ex dividend (the buyer won't receive a recently declared dividend, but the seller will)

Newspapers and business publications also include tables of price quotations for investments such as mutual funds, commodities, options, and government securities (see Exhibit 14.6). These same publications also carry news about current challenges the securities industry is facing, securities regulations, reported frauds, and proposals to improve investor protection.

L.O. 7

Industry Challenges

The Canadian markets are facing numerous challenges at the turn of the century. One of the largest complaints in Canada is the lack of a national securities regulator like the SEC in the United States. In Canada, the regulation of securities falls under the jurisdiction of the provinces, and laws can differ from province to province. The International Monetary Fund (IMF) has called on Canada to scrap the provincial system in favour of a national body. The Ontario Securities Commission (OSC) has emerged as the most powerful player of the 13 commissions and it regulates the largest markets in the country.

The push toward round-the-clock trading is another challenge securities markets are facing. Extending traditional trading hours of 9:30 a.m. to 4 p.m. (Eastern Canada time zone) by adding early morning and late night trading sessions is the next revolution

Exhibit 14.5 **How to Read a Newspaper Bond Quotation**

Newspapers often carry bond quotations in slightly different formats. As illustrated below they sometimes provide very basic information noting the issuer, the coupon rate (interest paid on the bonds), and the price yield (what interest rates the bonds are paying now). Other formats include much more detail, as illustrated below. Please note that newspapers show prices as a percentage of the bond's value, which is typically $1000.

			(1)		(2)			(3)	
ISSUER	COUPON	MATURITY	BID PRICE	ASK PRICE	BID YLD	ASK YLD	YLD	CHG	DATE
Royal Bank	5.000	2014-JAN-20	101.93		102.23	4.73	4.69	-0.042	
Bombardier	6.400	2006-DEC-22	101.15		101.88	5.67	5.22	-0.060	

1. **Company:** Name of company issuing the bond, such as Royal Bank, and bond description, such as 6 1/8 percent bond maturing in 2010.
2. **Coupon:** Interest the bond pays.
3. **Ask Yield:** Annual interest of $1000 bond divided by the closing price shown. The ask yield for the Royal Bank is approximately 4.75 percent.

Volume: Number of bonds traded (in thousands) that day.

Yield change: Change in bond price from the close of the previous trading day.

Exhibit 14.6 **How to Read a Newspaper Mutual Fund Quotation**

A mutual fund listing shows the new asset value of one share (the price at which one share is trading) and the change in trading price from one day to the next.

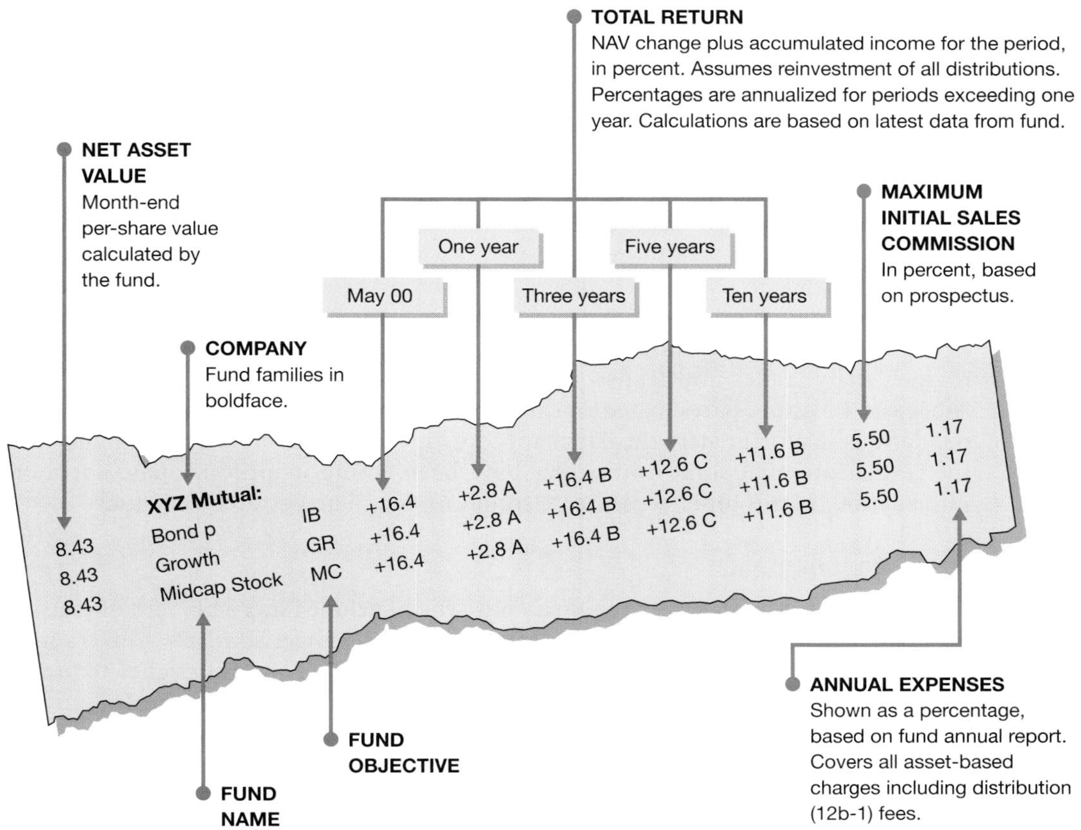

The online trading boom, which peaked along with the markets in March 2000, has been dropping ever since.

sweeping Bay and Wall streets. *After-hours trading* or *extended-hours trading* refers to the purchase and sale of publicly traded stocks after the major stock markets, such as the TSX, NYSE, and NASDAQ, close. Many securities exchanges now offer after-hours trading via ECNs that typically operate from 8:00 a.m. to 9:15 a.m. and 4:15 p.m. to 7 or 8 p.m., although some operate 24 hours a day. The biggest advantage to extended-hours trading is that it accommodates traders who live in regions outside the Eastern U.S. time zone. The biggest disadvantage, however, is lack of volume. Most institutional investors close up shop after the TSX and NYSE close. Nonetheless, to remain competitive, many traditional securities exchanges have already extended their traditional trading hours.[17]

Online trading is another phenomenon that has revolutionized the securities industry. When online trading first became popular in the 1990s, many full-service brokerages such as Merrill Lynch resisted offering such services because they worried about losing lucrative commissions. But now, most full-service firms and chartered banks offer some form of online trading to remain competitive in the marketplace. Investors who choose online trading execute their trades via a brokerage firm's website instead of by phoning a firm's brokers. Convenience, control, and lower commissions are the main advantages of online trading. Still, online trading is not for everyone. When you trade online, you trade alone, with no one to check for mistakes or offer advice. Moreover, online trading websites have had their share of problems. The top five consumer complaints filed with the SEC against online brokers are (1) failure to process orders or delays in executing orders, (2) difficulty in accessing one's account or contacting a broker, (3) errors in processing orders, (4) execution of orders at higher prices than posted on the website, and (5) errors and omissions in account records and documents.[18]

Regulation of Securities Markets

Whether you buy and sell securities online or use a traditional full-service house, your trades are governed by a network of provincial laws. Combined with industry self-regulation, these laws are designed to ensure that you and all investors receive accurate information and that no one artificially manipulates the market price of a given security. Trading in stocks and bonds is monitored by 13 provincial and territorial exchange commissions, although the OSC dictates policy for the largest Canadian markets. Each participating exchange is a member of the Canadian Securities Administrators, which seeks to harmonize and regulate Canadian capital markets. The actual equity trading is monitored by the market Regulations Services (RS), which reviews daily trades and transactions. For most of the twentieth century, North American investors participated in the market with a great deal of confidence in its regulations. Unfortunately this all changed with the stock market crash in 2000 and the revelations that some companies have been acting inappropriately. For more information on this topic, see the case study entitled "The Betrayed Investor."

Filing Requirements

Companies must meet certain requirements (which include filing a blizzard of registration papers and reports) to be listed on any stock exchange. Similarly, brokers must operate according to the rules of the exchanges, rules that are largely designed to protect investors. Overseeing all of these details keeps the TSX Group that runs the TSX and the Canadian Venture Exchange, along with the provincial exchange commissions and the RS very busy indeed. Every year it screens thousands of annual reports, handles investor complaints, and reviews prospectuses (a legal statement that describes the objectives of a specific investment) and proxy statements (a shareholder's written authorization giving

Case Study: The Betrayed Investor

High-profile companies go bust. Business leaders fall into disrepute. The stock market tumbles. Is North America's long infatuation with the stock market coming to an end?

FROM BOOM TO BUST

Owning stocks was simply a part of living in the 1990s. Expecting to see steady stock market gains, investors were given a fresh dose of reality when a stunning 113-month bull run ended in March 2000 and the turmoil began. "We were just riding the market, and we all felt like we were brilliant because our stocks were going up," says one accountant. But the dot-com crash, the September 11, 2001, terrorist attacks, and a wave of corporate scandals sent North America's financial markets into a tailspin, a chilling reminiscence of the 1930s. Some 100 million investors collectively lost more than US$5 trillion over a 24-month period starting in spring 2000. That's equal to the gross domestic product of Japan and France combined. It was money earmarked for retirement, university and college tuition, and medical bills.

DÉJÀ VU

The stock market tumble of the new millennium and the crash of the 1930s had some common elements. In both eras, self-dealing led to the misallocation of trillions of invested dollars and the ensuing collapse of investor confidence. Before the Great Crash of the 1930s, insiders used holding companies and other stock-watering schemes to bilk both investors and consumers. Banking houses combined brokerage, underwriting, and commercial banking to sell securities to the gullible. And more and more people invested "on margin."

The policy innovations of the 1930s were designed to block a repetition of such investor abuses by regulating securities markets, limiting margin investing, and so on. But back then no one imagined the investor abuses that brought today's stock market to its knees: auditors who had become servants of managers rather than of shareholders, brokers serving their own accounts rather than offering dispassionate advice to investors, bankers who put aside their fiduciary duties to cut deals with dubious investment partners, directors who were subservient to CEOs rather than vice versa, and executives who put their own short-term enrichment through stock options ahead of creating wealth for shareholders.

FED UP

Can Bay and Wall streets regain their golden image as the place for North Americans to invest money? "Not in this generation," says John Challenger, chief executive of outplacement firm Challenger, Gray & Christmas. There is a lot of anger out there. Investors assumed during the gold rush that they were going to become millionaires. But the rug has been pulled out, and it's been a very hard fall. Investors don't trust the word of their brokers and corporations. Consumers feel like dupes, and they are laying the blame on the investment communities.

"There is a loss of confidence in corporate North America," says one leading securities lawyer. Today's investors are angry and disillusioned. They are fed up with disappointing earnings, accounting scandals, the threat of terrorism, and global instability. The Investor Class has lost its appetite for risk and is parking its cash in unglamorous, low-yielding, money-market brokerage accounts. It simply doesn't want to make long-term commitments until it believes that the worst is over.

CHANGE IS INEVITABLE

The 2002 market meltdown could indeed be a historic turning point in North American business—similar to the wave of reform enacted during the 1930s. Proposals under current debate include making audits more strict, preventing executive and director abuses, restricting the use of stock options, and punishing offenders more severely. Hopes are that such reform will restore investor confidence in the stock market so that companies can get the funding they need to grow.

Still, with or without such reform, earnings aren't likely to boom and rekindle the force of the last bull market. "It's not that we can't get back to where we were," notes one corporate chief economist. "It's just that we were never really there to begin with."

Questions for Critical Thinking

1. Why is investor confidence important to the health of the North American economy?
2. After hearing about the stock market crash would you consider investing in large corporations upon graduation? Why or why not?

someone else the authority to cast his or her vote). The different regulatory bodies all maintain websites that contain mountains of public documents that investors can browse, download, or print to learn more about publicly traded companies.[19]

Regulation Fair Disclosure

Regulation Fair Disclosure (FD) is a principal that is supposed to create a level playing field for all investors. Specifically, the regulation mandates that any news with the potential to affect the price of a stock must be released to everyone simultaneously. In other words, the regulation prohibits companies from "selectively disclosing" important information (such as earnings estimates) to big institutional shareholders and market analysts ahead of regular investors. Otherwise, early news recipients would be able to "make a profit or avoid a loss at the expense of those kept in the dark."[20] In spite of its good intentions, the regulation could have unintended consequences, say critics. Some worry that instead of giving small and large investors equal access to market-sensitive information, the regulation could cut down on the amount of information received by everyone.

Securities Fraud

The combination of a "get-rich" mindset and the huge number of people now investing online has resulted in a rise in the number of Internet stock scams. Today, with just an e-mail address list and a chat-board alias or two, penny-stock promoters can dupe tens of thousands (if not millions) of investors by making false claims about a company, watching investors eager to make a fast profit pump up the company's stock price, then selling or dumping their penny shares at inflated prices and pocketing a handsome profit.

In fact, so pervasive has the problem become that the U.S. Department of Justice, the Federal Trade Commission, the U.S. Attorney's offices, and even the FBI have stepped up efforts to police such fraud. Even NASDAQ has developed an Internet search engine to find phrases such as "too good to be true," and it monitors securities chat forums for fraudulent or misleading information.[21] As an investor, your best defence against fraud is to carefully research securities before you buy and to steer clear of any investment that seems too good to be true (see Exhibit 14.7).

insider trading
Use of material nonpublic information to make an investment profit

Two particular forms of securities fraud making the headlines today are insider trading and accounting fraud. **Insider trading** occurs when people buy or sell a stock

Exhibit 14.7 **10 Questions to Ask Before You Invest**

You can avoid getting taken in an online stock scam by asking yourself the following 10 questions before you invest.

1. Is the investment registered with the SEC and your province's securities commission?
2. Have you read the company's audited financial statements?
3. Is the person recommending this investment a registered broker?
4. What does the person promoting the investment have to gain?
5. If the tip came from an online bulletin board or e-mail, is the author identifiable or using an alias? Is there any reason to trust that person?
6. Are you being pressured to act before you can evaluate the investment?
7. Does the investment promise you'll get rich quick, using words like "guaranteed," "high return," or "risk free"?
8. Does the investment match your objectives? Could you afford to lose all of the money you invest?
9. How easy would it be to sell the investment later? Remember, stocks with fewer shares are easy for promoters to manipulate and hard for investors to sell if the price starts falling.
10. Does the investment originate overseas? If yes, beware: It is tougher to track money sent abroad and harder for burned investors to have recourse to justice.

based on information that is not available to the general public, such as a company merger or new discovery. Insider trading can produce big profits for the unscrupulous, but it can also claim many victims. Acquisition companies, for example, are forced to pay higher-than-expected premiums to buy a target company when leaks trigger a run-up in the target's stock price. And shareholders who rely on the integrity of corporate executives can lose billions while friends of loose-lipped company insiders profit from the information. For example, in 2002 a congressional committee investigated Martha Stewart's personal sale of 4000 shares of ImClone Systems stock one day before the Food and Drug Administration rejected ImClone's application for approval of a cancer drug. The announcement sent ImClone's share tumbling. Stewart was a close friend of ImClone's former CEO, Samuel D. Waksal, who allegedly used the inside information to tip off his family members, who also sold their ImClone shares.[22]

Accounting trickery is another form of securities fraud, as Chapter 13 points out. In fact, the unusually high number of companies engaging in accounting tricks and fraud at the turn of this century has not only kept regulators busy but taken its toll on Canadian and U.S. securities markets and the global economy, as this chapter's special box, "Case Study: The Betrayed Investor," shows.

SUMMARY OF LEARNING OBJECTIVES

1 Highlight the functions, characteristics, and common forms of money.

Money functions as a medium of exchange, a measure of value, and a store of value. It must be divisible, portable, durable, stable, and difficult to counterfeit. Common forms of money include currency, such as coins, bills, traveller's cheques, cashier cheques, and money orders; demand deposits, such as chequing accounts; and time deposits, such as savings accounts, certificates of deposit, and money-market deposit accounts.

2 Discuss the responsibilities and insurance methods of the Canadian Deposit Insurance Corporation (CDIC).

The CDIC is a federal insurance program that protects deposits in member banks up to $60 000.

3 Discuss the Canadian banking industry.

The Canadian banking industry consists of large chartered banks operating small branches throughout the country with little influence from foreign competitors and trust companies. The Big Six banks are Royal Bank of Canada, Scotiabank, Canadian Imperial Bank of Commerce, Toronto Dominion Bank, Bank of Montreal, and National Bank. They control the majority of the nation's assets and are currently seeking a mandate from the government to merge with one another so they can compete on the world stage.

4 Differentiate among a stock's par value, its market value, and its book value.

Par value is the dollar value assigned to a stock for bookkeeping and for dividend calculations. Market value is the price at which a share of stock is currently selling. Book value is the portion of a corporation's net assets represented by a single share of common stock.

5 Highlight the distinguishing features of common stock, preferred stock, bonds, and mutual funds.

Common stock gives shareholders an ownership interest in the company, the right to elect directors and vote on important issues, and the chance to earn dividends and share in the fortunes of the company—while limiting the shareholder's liability to the price paid for the shares. Preferred stock gives shareholders a higher dividend than common stock and a preferred claim over creditors if the corporation fails. Special types of preferred stock have certain privileges. Bonds are long-term loans investors make to the issuing entity in return for a stated interest amount. The loan or principal is paid back to the bondholder over the life of the bond. Bonds may be secured, unsecured, or convertible. They may be issued by corporations or federal, provincial, and municipal agencies. Mutual funds are pools of money drawn from many investors to buy a variety of stocks, bonds, and other marketable securities. The primary benefit of this investment is diversification.

6 Differentiate among an auction exchange, dealer exchange, and electronic communication network (ECN).

Auction exchanges such as the Toronto Stock Exchange and the New York Stock Exchange funnel all buy and sell orders into one centralized location. Dealer exchanges such as NASDAQ are decentralized marketplaces in which dealers, known as market makers, are connected electronically to handle buy and sell orders without a single, centralized trading floor. Electronic computerized networks (ECNs) match buy and sell orders directly (cutting out the market makers and specialists); ECNs operate globally, and they operate economically.

Explain how government regulation of securities trading tries to protect investors.

The government tries to prevent fraud in the securities markets by requiring companies to file registration papers, fulfill certain requirements, and file periodic information reports so that investors receive accurate information. Government regulations also control the listing of companies on stock exchanges and prohibit such fraudulent acts as improper release of information, insider trading, stock scams, and other acts designed to deceive investors.

As illustrated in the opening vignette, the question of Canadian bank mergers has been before the Canadian government since 1998, when the Royal Bank of Canada (RBC) and the Bank of Montreal (BMO) announced merger plans, followed shortly by similar plans by the Toronto Dominion Bank (TD) and the Canadian Imperial Bank of Canada (CIBC). The government responded to public outrage over the deals by announcing that it would not allow any of the Big Six national banks to merge until it consulted with businesses both large and small, the public, consumer groups, and other parties with a vested interest, including insurance and mutual fund companies.

Unfortunately for the banks, the end result of this has been a government that has stated since 2001 that bank mergers, while not illegal, would have to meet strict public consultation prior to any acceptance. This law was followed with an announcement that clear guidelines would be established to clarify how many banks would be able to merge, list the demands that must be met for a merger to gain approval, and determine whether banks could merge with large insurance companies. The guidelines were expected to be announced in Spring 2004, but were pushed back by Prime Minister Paul Martin and Ralph Goodale until at least 2005.[23]

Proponents of bank mergers are starting to wonder why the government is dragging its feet on what should be an easy decision. They argue that banks should be allowed to merge, as this will enable them to access the necessary capital to grow, combine strengths, and offset weaknesses; make them less likely targets of foreign takeovers; increase their technology; and assist Canadian companies who are expanding internationally.

Other reasons include:

- Almost every Canadian owns shares in Canadian banks through pension plans or mutual funds. Banks have not been able to maximize shareholder value because of their inability to merge.
- Bank mergers will enable banks to cut costs and pass the savings onto consumers.
- As of 2001, the Big Six chartered banks earned 40 percent of their profits outside Canada but paid 80 percent of their taxes within Canada, and 90 percent of their employees worked in Canada.
- The inability of banks to merge or expand may be forcing them to increase profits by squeezing Canadian consumers.[24]
- Canadian banks are shrinking on the world stage. In 1984 all Canadian banks were among the world's top 40 by asset class. But by 1998 none of the banks were in the top 40, and they discussed the possibility of mergers in order to restore Canadian banks to previous status. If the rumoured mergers did occur, RBC and Sun Life would be ranked thirty-second, BMO and Scotiabank would move up to thirty-third position, and TD and Manulife would rank forty-fourth.[25]

Those opposed to the mergers also wonder why the government is taking its time with the guidelines, but for different reasons. Consumer groups and small businesses oppose the mergers, as they believe that merged banks will reduce expenses by cutting services, employees, and branches. Furthermore, they worry that in some small communities bank mergers will eliminate any consumer choice. Opponents argue that Canada is too small a country to host such large banks and the government should stop any mergers while forcing the banks to provide better services.

Critical Thinking Questions

1. Do you think the government was right to prevent the bank mergers? Why or why not?

2. Prior to reading this case, what did you know about bank mergers? Since public sentiment appears to be so important in gaining government approval, have the banks done enough to explain the positives of mergers since 1998?
3. The government seemed to be considering the rights of Canadian citizens as consumers when stopping the mergers. Do you think it gave equal thought to Canadian citizens as bank stakeholders? Why or why not?
4. Do you think consumers would trust the banks to pass savings onto consumers? Why or why not?

Learn More Online

Visit and review the website of the Canadian Bankers Association (www.cba.ca). What are the Association's views on the changes in the marketplace? How do these views differ from those expressed by the Canadian Federation of Independent Businesses (www.cfib.ca)? Conduct your own search online using various search engines. What additional information can you find?

KEY TERMS

auction exchange (370)
authorized stock (366)
automated teller machines (ATMs) (364)
bear market (373)
bond (368)
broker (372)
bull market (373)
Canada Savings Bonds (369)
cheques (361)
convertible bonds (368)
credit cards (361)
currency (361)
day order (372)
dealer exchanges (371)
debentures (368)
debit cards (362)
demand deposits (361)
discretionary order (372)
electronic communication networks (ECNs) (372)
electronic funds transfer systems (EFTS) (364)
income trust (367)
insider trading (380)
issued stock (366)
limit order (372)
line of credit (364)
margin trading (373)
market indexes (373)
market makers (372)
market order (372)
money (361)
money-market funds (370)
mutual funds (369)
NASDAQ (National Association of Securities Dealers Automated Quotations) (370)
open order (372)
over-the-counter (OTC) market (370)
par value (366)
price-earnings ratio (375)
primary market (370)
principal (368)
secondary market (370)
secured bonds (368)
securities (366)
short selling (373)
smart cards (362)
stock exchanges (370)
stock specialist (371)
stock split (366)
stop order (372)
time deposits (361)
Treasury bills (368)
unissued stock (366)

TEST YOUR KNOWLEDGE

Questions for Review

1. How do credit cards, debit cards, and smart cards work?
2. What are examples of deposit and nondeposit financial institutions?
3. What are the differences between a Treasury bill and a Canada Savings Bond?
4. What happens during a 2-for-1 stock split?
5. What is the function of the provincial securities commissions?

Questions for Analysis

6. What are some of the advantages of mutual funds?
7. Why did mutual funds become popular in Canada?
8. When might an investor sell a stock short? What risks are involved in selling short?
9. How are the Internet and e-commerce redefining the banking and investment industry?
10. **Ethical Considerations.** You work in the research and development department of a large corporation and have been involved in a discovery that could lead to a

new, profitable product. News of the discovery has not been made public. Is it legal for you to buy stock in the company? Now assume the same scenario but you talk to your friend about your discovery while dining at a restaurant. The person at the next table overhears the conversation. Is it legal for the eavesdropper to buy the company's stock before the public announcement of the news?

Questions for Application

11. What are the advantages and disadvantages of using cash, cheques, credit cards, and debit cards to pay for goods and services?
12. If you were thinking about buying shares of Bombardier, under what circumstances would you place a market order, a limit order, an open order, and a discretionary order?
13. **Integrated.** Besides watching market indexes, which economic statistics discussed in Chapter 1 might investors want to monitor? Why?
14. **Integrated.** Look back at Chapter 6 and review the discussion of mission statements. Suppose you were thinking about purchasing 100 shares of common stock in General Electric. Why might you want to first review the company's mission statement? What would you be looking for in the company's mission statement that could help you decide whether or not to invest?

PRACTISE YOUR KNOWLEDGE

SHARPENING YOUR COMMUNICATION SKILLS

Interviewing a broker is one of the most important steps you can take before hiring that broker to execute your trades or manage your funds and investment portfolio. Practise your communication skills by developing two sets of questions:

1. Questions you might ask a stockbroker to help you decide whether you would use his or her services.
2. Questions you might pose to that broker to help you evaluate the merits of purchasing a specific security.

BUILDING YOUR TEAM SKILLS

You and your team are going to pool your money and invest $5000. Before you plunge into any investments, how can you prepare yourselves to be good investors? First, consider your group's goals. What will you and your teammates do with any profits generated by your investments? Once you have agreed on a goal for your team's profits, think about how much money you will need to achieve this goal and how soon you want to achieve it.

Next, think about how much risk you personally are willing to take to achieve the goal. Bear in mind that safer investments generally offer lower returns than riskier investments—and certain investments, such as stocks, can lose money. Now hold a group discussion to find a level of risk that feels comfortable for everyone on your team.

Once your team has decided how much risk to take, consider which investments are best suited to your group's goals and chosen risk level. Will you choose stocks, bonds, a combination of both, or other securities? What are the advantages and disadvantages of each type of investment for your team's situation? Then come to a decision about specific investment opportunities—particular stocks, for example—that your group would like to investigate further.

Compare your group's goal, risk level, and investment possibilities with those of the other teams in your class and discuss the differences and similarities you see.

EXPAND YOUR KNOWLEDGE

DISCOVERING CAREER OPPORTUNITIES

Think you might be interested in a job in the securities and commodities industry? This industry has one of the most highly educated and skilled workforces of any industry. And the requirements for entry are high—most employees have a university degree and further training. Log on to the Investment Dealers Association at www.ida.ca and read up on educational and employment opportunities available in the field. Then answer the following questions:

1. What are the licensing and continuing education requirements for securities brokers?
2. What is the typical starting position for many people in the securities industry?
3. What factors are expected to contribute to the projected long-term growth of this industry?

DEVELOPING YOUR RESEARCH SKILLS

Since the turn of the century, the stocks of several high-profile companies, such as Tyco, Enron, and WorldCom, tumbled following the disclosures of negative company information. Use computer resources or business journals to find a company whose disclosure of negative information dramatically affected its securities. Then perform some research on that company so you can answer the following questions:

1. On what exchanges do the company's shares trade and under what ticker symbol?
2. What negative information did the company disclose? When? Did the company commit a fraudulent act? How did the information affect the company as a whole?
3. How did the negative information affect the company's securities? What was the company's stock price prior to the release of the negative information? Following the release of the information? What was the stock's 52-week high and low during the year the disclosure was made?

See It on the **WEB**

URLs for all Internet exercises are provided at the website for this book, www.pearsoned.ca/bovee. When you log on to the text website, select Chapter 14, select Destinations, then click on the name of the featured website, and review the website to complete the following exercises.

Explore the following chapter-related websites, review their content, and answer the following questions for each website you visit:

1. What is the purpose of this website?
2. What kinds of information does this website contain? Please be specific.
3. How is the information provided at this website useful for business people? Consumers?
4. How did you expand your knowledge of banking and securities markets by reviewing the material at this website? What new things did you learn about these topics?

VISIT THE BANK OF CANADA AND U.S. TREASURY

Visit the Bank of Canada's website at www.bankofcanada.ca and explore the sections on securities and monetary and financial policy. Then take a take a virtual tour of the U.S Treasury at www.ustreas.gov and click on Education to visit the Learning Vault. Once inside the vault, read about the duties and functions of the U.S Treasury, explore the fact sheets, and discover how money gets into circulation. Then explore this department from the inside out by clicking on the Site Index and following the links. Do you know how many notes a day the Bureau of Engraving and Printing (BEP) produces? Do you know how long $10 billion would last if you spent one dollar every second of every day? To find out, follow the link to the BEP governmental agency and brush up on your money facts. Don't leave this website without taking a peek at some new currency. Compare some of the differences in the sites, the content, and most importantly the policy statements.

STOCK UP AT THE TSX AND NYSE

Visit the Toronto Stock Exchange website at www.tsx.com, review some of the educational tools, read up on new regulations, and check out how some of Canada's companies are doing. Then take a tour the New York Stock Exchange at www.nyse.com. Visit the trading floor and learn about the hectic pace of trading. Find out why having a seat doesn't necessarily mean you'll have a chance to sit down. Listen in on a stock transaction and discover how a stock is bought and sold. Learn how investors are protected and how unusual stock transactions are spotted. Get the latest market information as well as a historical perspective of the exchange. Don't leave without checking out your favorite stock price. Maybe it's time to sell. Compare the differences between the exchanges. What similarities do you see?

INVEST WISELY, DON'T BE A FOOL

Here's a fun securities website (www.fool.com) you can fool around at for a while. Visit the Motley Fool and don't be afraid to ask a foolish investment question or two. Roll up your sleeves and do a little work on your own. Discover the strategies, ideas, and information needed to make investment decisions at Fool's School. Learn the steps to investing foolishly. Read the investing basics and learn how to value stocks, analyze stocks, or pick a stockbroker. Expand your knowledge of stocks, bonds, and mutual funds. Finally, discover the keys to successful investing.

LEARNING OBJECTIVES

The purpose of this video is to help you

1. Identify what measures shareholders can take to make corporate boards more accountable.
2. Define stock options.
3. Identify the pros and cons of stock options.
4. Examine how corporate governance and stock market returns can affect pension plans.

SYNOPSIS

The Carpenter's Union, which has over $3 billion dollars of their pension money invested in Canadian companies, represents a new trend of investors who are planning to hold companies liable for their decisions that affect shareholders. The group is initially focusing on the common corporate practice of companies not expensing stock options they provide to top management, a practice that the union claims distorts income statements and undervalues senior executive compensation plans. In order to do this, the union's members, traditional blue-collar workers, have to learn how corporate governance works, how to ask the proper questions at corporate annual general meetings, and how to conquer their fear of public speaking. If anything positive can be taken from the bursting of the stock market bubble and the corporate accounting scandals that followed, it's the increased interest shareholders have in the running of the companies that they invest in.

The practice of providing employees with stock options has been around for a considerable time. Most executives have a compensation package consisting of base pay and "stock options," which is the option to purchase an amount of stock in the future. Employees hope that the stock will be worth much more than the option price or the price that they can purchase them at, which will allow them to earn a substantial amount of money. These options are difficult to account for as they do not directly take cash out of a company. Instead they increase the number of shares outstanding when redeemed, which negatively impacts share price.

Critics of stock option compensation argue that stock options are a form of compensation and therefore are an expense. They also argue that stock options push managers to make decisions based on increasing the stock price in the short term rather than doing what's best for the company overall. One of the most consistent critics of stock options is world-famous investor Warren Buffet, who argues vehemently that companies are diluting shareholder value by not expensing stock options and that many companies actually repurchase shares with cash to prop up the share price after large amounts of options have been exercised.

Furthermore, stock options should not be accounted for as an expense on the balance sheet as they do not actually cost the company any money. The company does report the number of stock options granted in the annual report and if they are sold or exercised, as it is commonly referred to, the only negative impact on the company is an increase in the number of shares outstanding which dilutes the share price. Advocates also wonder how a company can expense an item when they have no idea what the item will actually be cashed in for or if it will be cashed in at all. Jack Welch, former CEO of GE, and commonly named as one of the best CEOs of the past century, argues that stock options enable companies to provide employees with a sense of ownership and a sense of belonging, which was a big part of GE's success.

Discussion Questions

1. *For analysis:* Do you think companies should expense stock options?
2. *For analysis:* Based on the video and the arguments in the case are you surprised that the Carpenter's Union has had some initial success with their call to expense stock options?
3. *For analysis:* If the stock market rises to and surpasses the levels it reached before the bubble crashed, do you think "expensing of options" will still be a cause for concern?

ONLINE EXPLORATION

Numerous articles have been written on the pros and cons of expensing stock option. Use Google or another Internet search engine to find additional arguments for or against the concept.

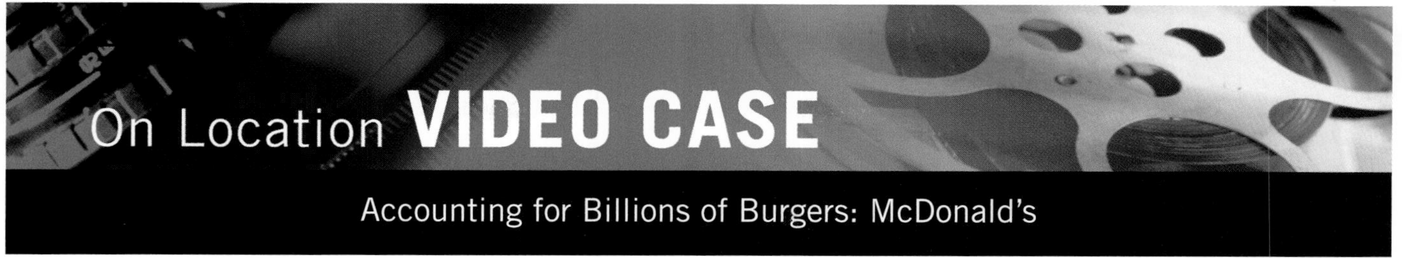

Accounting for Billions of Burgers: McDonald's

LEARNING OBJECTIVES

The purpose of this video is to help you

1. Understand the challenges a company may face in managing financial information from operations in multiple countries.
2. Consider how management and investors use the financial information reported by a public company.
3. Recognize how different laws and monetary systems can affect the accounting activities of a global corporation.

SYNOPSIS

Collecting, analyzing, and reporting financial data from more than 30 000 restaurants in 119 countries is no easy task, as the accounting experts at McDonald's know all too well. Every month, the individual restaurants send their sales figures to be consolidated with data from other restaurants at the local or country level. From there, the figures are sent to country-group offices and then to one of three major regional offices before going to their final destination at the McDonald's headquarters in Oak Brook, Illinois. In the past, financial information arrived in Illinois in bits and pieces, sent by courier, mail, or fax. Today, local and regional offices log on to a special secure website and enter their month-end figures, enabling the corporate controller to quickly produce financial statements and projections for internal and external use.

Discussion Questions

1. *For analysis:* Why does McDonald's use "constant currency" comparisons when reporting its financial results?
2. *For analysis:* What types of assets might McDonald's list for depreciation in its financial statements?
3. *For application:* What effect do the corporate income tax rates in the countries where McDonald's operates have on the income statements prepared in local offices?
4. *For application:* What problems might arise if individual McDonald's restaurants were required to enter sales data directly on the company's centralized accounting website, instead of following the current procedure of sending it through country and regional channels?
5. *For debate:* To help investors and analysts better assess the company's worldwide financial health, should McDonald's be required to disclose detailed financial results for every country and region? Support your chosen position.

ONLINE EXPLORATION

Visit the McDonald's corporate website at www.mcdonalds.com/corp.html, locate the most recent financial report (quarterly or annual), and examine both overall and regional results. What aspects of its results does McDonald's highlight in this report? What does McDonald's say about its use of constant currency reporting? Which regions are doing particularly well? Which are lagging? How does management explain any differences in performance? What does McDonald's say about its use of constant currency reporting?

E-Business IN ACTION

Cyberbanks Hit a Brick Wall

When cyberbanks (Internet-only banks) began popping up in the late 1990s, many believed they would revolutionize retail banking. Lower transactions costs, no physical building costs, and smaller staffs than physical banks meant that Internet banks could afford to offer customers higher interest rates on deposits, little or no transaction fees, and lower interest rates on loans. Furthermore, because they existed in cyberspace, customers could bank at home 24 hours a day, seven days a week. They could move money from a savings account to a chequing account—or even into the stock market—whenever they pleased. But the promise that banking customers would flock to cyberbanks and give traditional banks a run for their money never materialized.

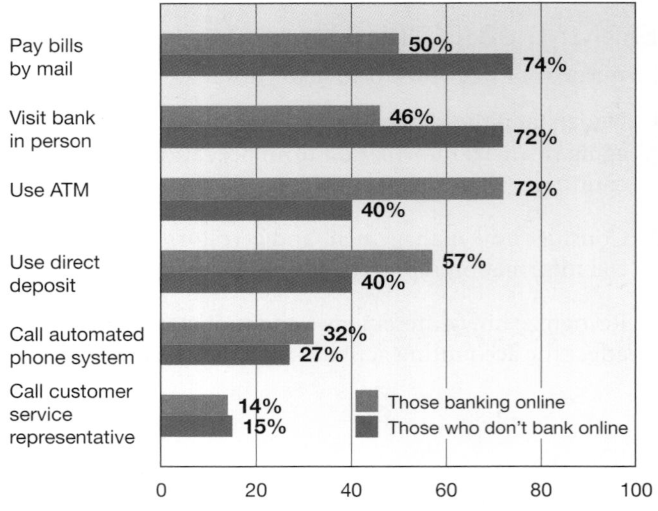

Tough Sell

Why didn't cyberbanks take off? Like most Internet-only start-ups, cyberbanks faced the following roadblocks:

- *Lack of name recognition.* To attract new customers, cyberbanks launched their e-businesses with expensive marketing campaigns, eliminating much of the Internet cost advantage.
- *No friendly banker.* Customers appreciated the cost advantages that cyberbanks offered, but without branches many online banks lacked a concrete place for customers to resolve problems. Customers wanted the assurance that someone was there (in person) if they needed help.
- *Limited services.* Customers still needed to venture into the physical world to get services cyberbanks did not offer: ATMs, safe deposit boxes, or business loans. Moreover, without a network of ATMs, cyber-customers faced hefty ATM fees and were required to deposit money into their cyberaccounts by mail.

To overcome these challenges, some cyberbanks got physical by opening service centres, setting up kiosks, and establishing ATM networks. Others offered rebates on ATM surcharges their customers paid to other banks. Still others, such as Juniper Financial in the U.S., formed alliances with stores like Mail Boxes Etc. so customers could deposit cheques nationwide. But these actions were not enough to fend off the awakening giants.

Bricks-and-Mortar Banks Wake Up

Rather than give traditional (bricks-and-mortar) banks a run for their money, cyberbanks gave them ideas. Some traditional banks established partnerships with key cyberbank players or swallowed them up altogether. Others, such as Bank One in the U.S., established their own virtual banks—keeping them separate entities. But in spite of their efforts, few traditional banks generated profits from their online banking ventures. Cyberbanking did not reach the mass appeal needed to justify the huge investment and operating costs involved.

From Competitive Edge to Commodity

The playing field has changed considerably since virtual banking first emerged. Online banking has moved from becoming a competitive edge to a commodity. Today, some 4 million Canadian households do at least some of their banking online, and online banking continues to grow rapidly. More than half of all banks offer some form of online banking services, such as transferring money, bill payments, loan applications, and account management. Some, such as TD, allow customers to set up a personal account and aggregate all the services they use into one webpage interface at www.TDbank.ca. But in spite of the rising use of online banking services, things look grim for the pure cyberbanks. Of the approximately 24 cyberbanks still in business at the turn of the century, fewer than five are expected to survive.[26]

Questions for Critical Thinking

1. What challenges did cyberbanks face in the competitive banking environment, and what steps did they take to overcome these challenges?
2. Why did most pure Internet banks close up or fold into their parent organizations?
3. What banking services, if any, do you perform online? What do you like and dislike about banking online?

Business PlanPro **EXERCISES**

Managing Financial Information and Resources Review Appendix C, Your Business Plan (on pages 397–398), to learn how to use Business PlanPro Software so you can complete these exercises.

Think Like a Pro

Objective: By completing these exercises you will become acquainted with the sections of a business plan that address a company's financial and operational projections. You will use the sample business plan for Fantastic Florals (listed as Import—Artificial Flowers in the Sample Plan Browser) in this exercise.

1. Identify the source(s) Fantastic Florals will use to fund its start-up costs. Why is it important to indicate how much start-up money will be used to fund assets versus expenses?
2. Review the financial assumptions, sales tables and graphs, and other financial information included in the Fantastic Florals plan. Assuming the financial projections are on target, would an investment of $75 000 for a 20 percent ownership stake in the company be prudent? Explain your answer. Which financial statement(s) did you use to make your decision?
3. Examine the company's projected gross margin for the years covered by the plan. How does Fantastic Florals' gross margin compare with the industry profile? How might a potential investor view this comparison?

Create Your Own Business Plan

Return to the plan you are developing for your own business. How will you categorize your revenue and expense items? Will you break down your sales by product type, by service, or by location? What general operating and product-related expenses will you incur? Set up your basic revenue and expense categories and build the framework for your profit and loss statement. How do the categories in your plan compare to those used by Fantastic Florals?

Appendix B
The Canadian Legal System

THE CANADIAN LEGAL SYSTEM

Throughout this textbook, we have discussed a number of regulatory agencies, such as the Ontario Securities Commission (OSC) or the Federal Trade Commission (FTC), whose function is to protect society from the potential abuses of business. In this appendix we explore how the Canadian government protects its citizens from corporate wrongdoing through its legal system. The law protects both businesses and individuals against those who threaten society. It also spells out accepted ways of performing many essential business functions—along with the penalties for failing to comply. In other words, like the average person, companies must obey the law or face the consequences.

As you read this material, keep in mind that many companies conduct business overseas. Thus, in addition to knowing Canadian laws, these companies must also be familiar with **international law**, the principles, customs, and rules that govern the relationships between sovereign states and international organizations and persons.[1] Successful global business requires an understanding of the domestic laws of trading partners as well as of established international trading standards and legal guidelines.

Global companies, such as Coca-Cola, must have a firm grasp of international law.

Sources of Law

A *law* is a rule developed by a society to govern the conduct of, and relationships among, its members. The Canadian constitution, including the Charter of Rights and Freedoms, is the foundation for Canadian laws and consists of two unique parts. The first part deals with the division of power and clarifies jurisdictions between federal and provincial government, while the second part is the Charter of Rights and Freedoms, which enshrines the fundamental rights and freedoms of Canadians. Because the constitution is a general document, laws offering specific answers to specific problems are constantly embellishing its basic principles. However, law is not static; it develops in response to changing conditions and social standards. Individual laws originate in various ways: through legislative action (*statutory law*), through administrative rulings (*administrative law*), and through customs and judicial precedents (*common law*). To one degree or another, all three forms of law affect businesses. Moreover, at times the three forms of law may overlap so that the differences between them become indistinguishable. Nonetheless, in cases where the three forms of law appear to conflict, statutory law generally prevails.

Statutory Law

Statutory law is law written by the federal or provincial governments. One very important part of statutory law affecting businesses is each province's **Sale of Goods Act**, which is based on the English Sale of Goods Act that was first enacted in 1893. The Act defines the legal framework for business transactions between producers and consumers and has remained virtually unchanged for the past century.

Administrative Law

Once laws have been passed by the federal or provincial government, an administrative agency or commission may take responsibility for enforcing them. That agency may be called on to clarify a regulation's intent, often by consulting representatives of the affected industry. The administrative agency may then write more specific regulations, which are considered **administrative law**. In Canada, many business activities, including employment standards and labour relations, fall under such regulatory bodies.

Common Law

Common law, the type of law that comes out of courtrooms and judge's decisions, began in England many centuries ago and was brought to Canada by colonists. It is applied in all provinces except Quebec, which has adopted a hybrid type of legal system. In Quebec, when dealing with criminal matters, they follow Canadian common law, but in non-criminal matters they follow a civil code. Common law is sometimes called the "unwritten law" to distinguish it from government Acts and administrative regulations, which are written documents. Instead, common law is established through customs and the precedents set in courtroom proceedings.

Despite its unwritten nature, common law has great continuity, which derives from the doctrine of ***stare decisis*** (Latin for "stand by decisions"). What the *stare decisis* doctrine means is that a judge's decisions establish a precedent for deciding future cases of a similar nature. Because common law is based on what has been decided before, the legal framework develops gradually.

In Canada, common law is applied and interpreted in the system of courts. Common law thus develops through the decisions in trial courts, special courts, and appellate courts. The **Supreme Court of Canada** sets precedents for the entire legal system. Lower courts must abide by these precedents as they pertain to similar cases.

Business Law

Although businesses must comply with the full body of laws that apply to individuals, a subset of laws can be defined more precisely as **business law**. This includes those elements of law that directly affect business activities. For example, laws pertaining to business licensing, employee safety, and corporate income taxes can all be considered business law. For the remainder of this appendix, we will examine some of the specific categories of laws affecting business, including torts; contracts; agency; property transactions; patents, trademarks, and copyrights; negotiable instruments; and bankruptcy.

Torts

A **tort** is a noncriminal act (other than breach of contract) that results in injury to a person or to property.[2] A tort can be either intentional or the result of negligence. The victim of a tort is legally entitled to some form of financial compensation, or **damages**, for his or her loss and suffering. This compensation is also known as a *compensatory damage award.* In some cases, the victim may also receive a *punitive damage award* to punish the wrongdoer and discourage repetition of the act if the misdeed was glaringly bad.

Intentional Torts An **intentional tort** is a wilful act that results in injury. For example, accidentally hitting a softball through someone's window is a tort, but purposely cutting down someone's tree because it obscures your view is an intentional tort. Note that *intent* in this case does not mean the intent to cause harm; it is the intent to commit a specific physical act. Some intentional torts involve communication of false statements that harm another's reputation. If the communication is in writing or on television, it is called *libel;* if it is spoken, it is *slander.*[3] For example, Jose Santos, the winning jockey in the 2003 Kentucky Derby, recently sued the *Miami Herald* for printing an article that accused him of using an electrical prod during the race. Although race officials subsequently cleared Santos of any improper behaviour, the outcome of his case will depend on whether he can prove that the paper knowingly published false information.[4]

In 2002, Enron executives testified before an administrative agency to defend the company's actions. Among other things, lawmakers had accused Enron of illegally manipulating California's energy market.

Negligence and Product Liability In contrast to intentional torts, torts of **negligence** involve a failure to use a reasonable amount of care necessary to protect others from unreasonable risk of injury.[5] Cases of alleged negligence often involve **product liability**, which is a product's capacity to cause damages or injury for which the producer or seller is held responsible. Product liability lawsuits cost business owners as much as US$150 billion every year.[6]

Consider American Home Products (AHP). In 1999, AHP agreed to pay about US$4 billion to thousands of individuals who contended they were injured by taking the company's popular diet pill combination fen-phen. The product, which had been hailed as a miracle weight-loss pill for the obese, was removed from the market at the request of the U.S. Food and Drug Administration (FDA) after studies linked the drugs to heart valve damage. More than 6 million people took fen-phen, but only those who developed problems were eligible to collect an injury award. Still, many of the injured turned down AHP's settlement offer, opting to pursue individual lawsuits in court.[7]

In the United States, a company may also be held liable for injury caused by a defective product even if the company used all reasonable care in the manufacture, distribution, or sale of its product. Such **strict product liability** makes it possible to assign liability without assigning fault. It must only be established that (1) the company is in the business of selling the product, (2) the product reached the customer or user without substantial change in its condition, (3) the product was defective, (4) the defective condition rendered the product unreasonably dangerous, and (5) the defective product caused the injury.[8] To date, Canadian companies are not held to such strict standards because product liability law does not exist in this form. However, many provinces are starting to consider the merits of such laws and they may come to fruition in the coming years.

Although few people would argue that individual victims of harmful products shouldn't be entitled to some sort of compensation, many people question whether such strict interpretation of product liability laws is good for society. Many individuals try to take advantage of the system by filing "frivolous" lawsuits. The large compensatory, and sometimes punitive, damages that plaintiffs are awarded make it difficult for many companies to obtain product liability insurance at a reasonable price. As a result, manufacturers have withheld products from the market that might otherwise benefit society.

Contracts

Broadly defined, a **contract** is an exchange of promises between two or more parties that is enforceable by law. Many business transactions—including buying and selling products, hiring employees, purchasing group insurance, and licensing technology—involve contracts. Contracts may be either express or implied. An **express contract** is derived from the words (either oral or written) of the parties; an **implied contract** stems from the actions or conduct of the parties.[9] Iris Kapustein learned the hard way how important written contracts can be in the business world. When she first started her trade show management and consulting firm, she operated on the principle of "my word is my bond." But after losing US$15 000 to clients who didn't pay, she adopted a new principle: All clients must sign contracts, and all contracts supplied by clients must be reviewed by her attorney.[10]

Facing the potential for product liability lawsuits, makers of cold and cough remedies removed products containing phenylpropanolamine (PPA) from drugstore shelves in 2000. The U.S. Food and Drug Administration banned the ingredient after reports showed that PPA could increase the risk of stroke in young women. Reformulated products using a safer ingredient soon appeared in their place.

Elements of a Contract The law of contracts deals largely with identifying the exchanges that can be classified as contracts. The following factors must usually be present for a contract to be valid and enforceable:

- *Both parties must intend to create a legal relationship.* The parties entering into the contract must intend for it to be a legal arrangement. Contracts start with an offer or a promise and the person making the promise must intend to be bound by that promise.
- *An offer must be made.* One party must propose that an agreement be entered into. The offer may be oral or written, but it must be firm, definite, and specific enough to make it clear that someone intends to be legally bound by the offer. Finally, the offer must be communicated to the intended party or parties.
- *An offer must be accepted.* For an offer to be accepted, there must be clear intent (spoken, written, or by action) to enter into the contract. An implied contract arises when a person requests or accepts something and the other party has indicated that payment is expected. If, for example, your car breaks down on the road and you call a mobile mechanic and ask him or her to repair it, you are obligated to pay the reasonable value for the services, even if you didn't agree to specific charges beforehand. However, when a specific offer is made, the acceptance must satisfy the terms of the offer. For example, if someone offers you a car for $18 000, and you say you would take it for $15 000, you have not accepted the offer. Your response is a *counteroffer,* which may or may not be accepted by the salesperson.
- *Both parties must give consideration.* A contract is legally binding only when the parties have bargained with each other and have exchanged something of value, which is called the **consideration**. The relative value of each party's consideration does not generally matter to the courts. In other words, if you make a deal with someone and later decide you didn't get enough in the deal, that result is not the court's concern. You entered into the deal with the original consideration in mind, and that fact is legally sufficient.[11]
- *Both parties must give genuine assent.* To have a legally enforceable contract, both parties must agree to it voluntarily. The contract must be free of fraud, duress, undue influence, and mutual mistake.[12] If only one party makes a mistake, it ordinarily does not affect the contract. On the other hand, if both parties made a mistake, the agreement would be void. For example, if both the buyer and the seller of a business believed the business was profitable, when in reality it was operating at a loss, their agreement would be void.

- *Both parties must be competent.* The law gives certain classes of people only a limited capacity to enter into contracts. Minors, people who are senile or insane, and in some cases those who are intoxicated cannot usually be bound by a contract for anything but the bare necessities: food, clothing, shelter, and medical care.
- *The contract must not involve an illegal act.* Courts will not enforce a promise that involves an illegal act. For example, a drug dealer cannot get help from the courts to enforce a contract to deliver illegal drugs at a prearranged price.
- *The contract must be in proper form.* Most contracts can be made orally, by an act, or by a casually written document; however, certain contracts are required by law to be in writing. For example, in some provinces under the Sales of Goods Act, the transfer of goods in amounts in excess of specific dollar figures, which vary by province, must be accompanied by a written document. The written form is also required for all real estate contracts.

A contract need not be long; all these elements of a contract may be contained in a simple document (see Exhibit B.1). In fact, a personal cheque is one type of simple contract.

Contract Performance Contracts normally expire when the agreed-to conditions have been met, called *performance* in legal terms. However, not all contracts run their expected course. Both parties involved can agree to back out of the contract, for instance. In other cases, one party fails to live up to the terms of the contract, a situation called **breach of contract**. The other party has several options at that point:

Exhibit B.1 **Elements of a Contract**

This simple document contains all of the essential elements of a valid contract.

The band titled XYZ agrees to provide entertainment at the Club de Hohenzollern on April 30, 2001, between 8:30 p.m. and midnight.

The band will be paid $500.00 for its performance.

Signed on the date of

February 19, 2001

Violetta Harvey

Violetta Harvey,
Manager,
Club de Hohenzollern
and

Ralph Perkins

Ralph Perkins,
Manager, XYZ

- *Discharge.* When one party violates the terms of the agreement, generally the other party is under no obligation to continue with his or her end of the contract. In other words, the second party is discharged from the contract.
- *Damages.* A party has the right to sue in court for damages that were foreseeable at the time the contract was entered into and that result from the other party's failure to fulfill the contract. The amount of damages awarded usually reflects the amount of profit lost and often includes court costs as well.
- *Specific performance.* A party can be compelled to live up to the terms of the contract if money damages would not be adequate.

Jeffrey Katzenberg, former Walt Disney studio chief, settled a bitter breach-of-contract lawsuit in 1999. Katzenberg, who left the company upon learning he would not be promoted to president, contended that he was owed as much as US$581 million. The amount was based on a unique contractual bonus arrangement whereby Katzenberg was to receive 2 percent of the projected future profits of films and television shows created during the 10 years he oversaw Disney's movie and television operations. The settlement figure was private, but analysts speculate that Katzenberg received about US$250 million.[13]

To control the increasing costs of litigation, more and more companies are now experimenting with alternatives to the courtroom. These include independent mediators, who sit down with the two parties and try to hammer out a satisfactory solution to contract problems, and mandatory arbitration, in which an impartial arbitrator or arbitration panel hears evidence from both sides and makes a legally binding decision. However, mandatory arbitration has come under fire by consumer groups because it can wipe out a customer's right to sue. For example, Gateway includes a clause in the purchase agreement documents it ships with every computer stating that any dispute or controversy arising from an agreement to purchase a Gateway product "shall be settled exclusively and finally by arbitration." Moreover, the courts have ruled that failure to read such documents constitutes acceptance of Gateway's terms. Although some consumers prefer to use alternative dispute resolution, those who do not wish to waive their right to sue are advised to read the fine print of all contracts and purchase agreements. The same advice applies to employment and service contracts.[14]

Warranties The Sales of Goods Act specifies that everyday sales transactions are a special kind of contract (although this provision applies only to tangible goods, not to services), even though they may not meet all of the exact requirements of regular contracts. Related to the sales contract is the notion of a **warranty**, which is a statement specifying what the producer of a product will do to compensate the buyer if the product is defective or if it malfunctions. Warranties come in several flavours. One important distinction is between *express warranties,* which are specific, written statements, and *implied warranties,* which are unwritten but involve certain protections under the law. Also, warranties are either *full* or *limited.* The former obligates the seller to repair or replace the product, without charge, in the event of any defect or malfunction, whereas the latter imposes restrictions on the defects or malfunctions that will be covered. Warranty laws also address a number of other details, including giving consumers instructions on how to exercise their rights under the warranty.[15]

Agency

These days it seems that nearly every celebrity has an agent. Hockey players hire agents to get them commercials and handle their contract negotiations; authors' agents sell manuscripts to the publishers that offer the largest advances; actors' agents try to find choice movie and television roles for their clients. These relationships illustrate a common legal association known as **agency**, which exists when one party, known as the *principal,* authorizes another party, known as the *agent,* to act on his or her behalf in contractual matters.[16]

All contractual obligations come into play in agency relationships. The principal usually creates this relationship by explicit authorization. In some cases—when a transfer of property is involved, for example—the authorization must be written in the form of a document called **power of attorney**, which states that one person may legally act for another (to the extent authorized).

Usually, an agency relationship is terminated when the objective of the relationship has been met or at the end of a period specified in the contract between agent and principal. It may also be ended by a change of circumstances, by the agent's breach of duty or loyalty, or by the death of either party.

Property Transactions

Anyone interested in business must know the basics of property law. Most people think of property as some object they own (a book, a car, a house). However, **property** is actually the relationship between the person having the rights to any tangible or intangible object and all other persons. The law recognizes two primary types of property: real and personal. **Real property** is land and everything permanently attached to it, such as trees, fences, or mineral deposits. **Personal property** is all property that is not real property; it may be tangible (cars, jewellery, or anything having a physical existence) or intangible (bank accounts, stocks, insurance policies, customer lists). A piece of marble in the earth is real property until it is cut and sold as a block, when it becomes personal property. Property rights are subject to various limitations and restrictions. For example, the government monitors the use of real property for the welfare of the public, to the point of explicitly prohibiting some property uses and abuses.[17]

Two types of documents are important in obtaining real property for factory, office, or store space: a deed and a lease. A **deed** is a legal document by which an owner transfers the *title,* or right of ownership, to real property to a new owner. A lease is used for a temporary transfer of interest in real property. The party that owns the property is commonly called the *landlord*; the party that occupies or gains the right to occupy the property is the *tenant.* The tenant pays the landlord, usually in periodic installments, for the use of the property. Generally, a lease may be granted for any length of time on which the two parties agree.

Patents, Trademarks, and Copyrights

If you invent a product, write a book, develop some new software, or simply come up with a unique name for your business, you probably want to prevent other people from using or prospering from your **intellectual property** without fairly compensating you. Several forms of legal protection are available for your creations. They include patents, trademarks, and copyrights. Which one you should use depends on what you have created. Having a patent, copyright, or trademark still doesn't guarantee that your idea or product will not be copied. However, they do provide you with legal recourse if your creations are infringed upon. It is important to note, however, that just because you protect your intellectual property in Canada does not provide it with protection in the United States or the rest of the world. To gain international protection you must register your property in each country separately, with the exception being copyright material that may be protected in some jurisdictions. For additional information visit the Canadian Intellectual Property Office's website at http://strategis.ic.gc.ca/sc_mrksv/cipo/welcome/welcom-e.html.

Patents A patent protects the invention or discovery of a new and useful process, an article of manufacture, a machine, a chemical substance, or an improvement on any of these. Issued by the Canadian Patent Office, a patent grants the owner the right to exclude others from making, using, or selling the invention for 20 years from the date the patent application is filed.[18] After that time, the patented item becomes available for common use. On the one hand, patent law guarantees the originator the right to use the discovery exclusively for a relatively long period of time, thus encouraging people to devise new machines, gadgets, and processes. On the other hand, it also ensures that rights to the new item will be released eventually, allowing other enterprises to discover even more innovative ways to use it.

Trademarks A trademark is any word, name, symbol, or device used to distinguish the product of one manufacturer from those made by others. In Canada, trademarks must be registered with the trademarks office and are renewable every 15 years. A service mark is the equivalent for services. McDonald's golden arches are one of the most visible of modern trademarks. Brand names such as Esso or Tim Hortons can also be registered as trademarks. Additionally, the distinct shape of a product or package (called *trade dress*) can also be registered. For example, if you manufacture candy in the shape of a giraffe, you could register this shape. In 1999, Apple Computer filed suit against Future Power for allegedly infringing on the iMac trade dress with its look-alike E-Power PC. Apple Computer asked the court to prohibit the sale of E-Power in addition to awarding actual and punitive damages. A U.S. District Court granted a preliminary injunction against Future Power from making, distributing, and selling a 15-inch all-in-one computer with a coloured plastic cover while the case was being heard. The two parties settled the lawsuit in 2001 when Future Power agreed to refrain from producing the look-alike until 2004.[19]

If properly registered and renewed every 15 years, a trademark generally belongs to its owner forever. Among the exceptions are popular brand names that have become generic terms, meaning that they describe a whole class of products. A brand-name trademark can become a generic term if the trademark has been allowed to expire, if it has been incorrectly used by its owner, or if the public comes to equate the name with the class of products, as was the case with zipper, linoleum, aspirin, and many other brand names.

Copyrights Copyrights protect the creators of literary, dramatic, musical, artistic, scientific, and other intellectual works. Any printed, filmed, or recorded material can be copyrighted. The copyright gives its owner the exclusive right to reproduce (copy), sell, or adapt the work he or she has created. Copyright law covers reproduction by photocopying, videotape, and magnetic storage.

The Copyright Office will issue a copyright to the creator or to whomever the creator has granted the right to reproduce the work. (A book, for example, may be copyrighted by the author or the publisher.) Copyrights issued through 1998 are good for 75 years from the date of publication. Copyrights issued after 1998 are valid for the lifetime of the creator plus 70 years.[20]

One of the most recognized trademarks in the world is the Nike Swoosh.

Napster became an Internet phenomenon by allowing its 32 million users to download virtually any popular music for free. But the courts eventually shut Napster down after major music labels sued the company for violating copyright laws. Napster filed for bankruptcy protection in 2002.

Copyright protection on the Internet has become an especially important topic as more businesses and individuals include original material on their websites. Technically, copyright protection exists from the moment material is created. Therefore, anything you post on a website is protected by copyright law. However, loose Internet standards and a history of sharing information via the Net has made it difficult for some users to accept this situation.

Negotiable Instruments

Whenever you write a personal cheque, you are creating a **negotiable instrument**, a transferable document that represents a promise to pay a specified amount. (*Negotiable* in this sense means that it can be sold or used as payment of a debt; an *instrument* is simply a written document that expresses a legal agreement.) In addition to cheques, negotiable instruments include certificates of deposit, promissory notes, and commercial paper. To be negotiable, an instrument must meet several criteria:[21]

- It must be in writing and signed by the person who created it.
- It must have an unconditional promise to pay a specified sum of money.
- It must be payable either on demand or at a specified date in the future.
- It must be payable either to some specified person or organization or to the person holding it (the bearer).

You can see how a personal cheque meets these criteria; when you write one, you are agreeing to pay the amount of the cheque to the person or organization to whom you're writing it.

Bankruptcy

Even though the Canadian legal system establishes rules of fair play and offers protection from the unscrupulous, it cannot prevent most businesses from taking on too much debt. The legal system does, however, provide help for businesses that find themselves in deep financial trouble. **Bankruptcy** is the legal means of relief for debtors (either individuals or businesses) who are unable to meet their financial obligations, and it is governed by the federal statute called the Bankruptcy and Insolvency Act.

Voluntary bankruptcy is initiated by the debtor. *Involuntary bankruptcy* is initiated by creditors. If a company emerges from bankruptcy as a leaner, healthier organization, creditors generally benefit. That's because once a company is back on its financial feet it can resume payments to creditors. Some companies such as Air Canada and Polaroid emerge from bankruptcy, but others such as Canada 3000 simply cease operations and sell all their assets. It is important to note that companies that are having trouble paying their debt do not always have to file for bankruptcy. Rather, they can try to work out arrangements with their creditors using either informal or formal negotiation. Informal negotiation involves contacting creditors and trying to work out arrangements in which creditors accept a lesser amount of money or receive payments over a longer period than originally stated in the contract. Unsecured creditors may agree to such negotiated terms because if the business were to file for bankruptcy, they often will receive nothing since secured creditors receive payment first. Secured creditors may be willing to accept different terms when the business does not have many assets and they would receive much less money than originally owed if the company went bankrupt. A formal proposal is one filed with a bankruptcy trustee, a specially trained chartered accountant appointed by the government through the Superintendent of Bankruptcies, and it falls under the Bankruptcy and Insolvency Act. In a formal proposal the trustee presents a plan to creditors asking them to accept different repayment terms than originally agreed upon. If the creditors accept the new terms, the company can keep operating as long as they meet these newly negotiated provisions. But if one secured creditor or the majority of unsecured creditors fail to agree to the formal proposal, the company is considered bankrupt.

As Exhibit B.2 shows, a number of bankruptcies of epic proportions by U.S. companies were filed in the first few years of the new millennium.

Exhibit B.2 **Largest U.S. Bankruptcies Since 1990**

Companies in banking, energy, and technology dominate the list of the largest U.S. corporate bankruptcies in recent years.

COMPANY	YEAR OF BANKRUPTCY	ASSETS PRIOR TO BANKRUPTCY (US$BILLIONS)
WorldCom, Inc.	2002	$103.9
Enron Corp.	2001	63.4
Conseco, Inc.	2002	61.4
Global Crossing Ltd.	2002	30.2
Pacific Gas and Electric Co.	2001	29.8
Adelphia Communications	2002	21.5
Mirant Corporation	2003	19.4
First Executive Corp.	1991	15.2
Gibraltar Financial Corp.	1990	15.0
Kmart Corp.	2002	14.6
FINOVA Group, Inc.	2001	14.1
HomeFed Corp.	1992	13.9
Southeast Banking Corp.	1991	13.4
NTL, Inc.	2002	13.0
Reliance Group Holdings, Inc.	2001	12.6
Imperial Corp. of America	1990	12.3
UAL Corp.	2002	12.2
Federal-Mogul Corp.	2001	10.2
First City Bankcorp of Texas	1992	9.9
First Capital Holdings	1991	9.7

Appendix C Your Business Plan

GETTING STARTED WITH BUSINESS PLANPRO SOFTWARE

Business PlanPro (BPP) software is a template for crafting a winning business plan. The software is designed to stimulate your thinking about the many tasks and decisions that go into planning and running a business. The software does not do your thinking for you. Instead, it leads you through a thought process by asking you to respond to questions about your business and to provide data for the preformatted tables and charts. Accompanying instructions, examples, and sample business plans provide you with a full range of assistance you can use to draft your own comprehensive business plan. By working through the exercises at the end of each text part, you will gain a practical skill for your business career.

When installing the software, be sure to install Adobe Acrobat Reader software so you can view the sample business plans included with the disk and downloadable from the Web. You can get an overview of the BPP software by clicking on the Help menu from the main screen, then selecting About Business PlanPro. Under the Help menu, you can click on contents and then Getting Help for operational instructions or to look up business terms in the software's Glossary. For quick answers to questions about using the software, look under the How Do I menu at the top right of the screen. An overview of the software's features is also on the Web at www.paloalto.com/prenticehall.

NAVIGATING THE SOFTWARE

One of the best ways to become familiar with the BPP software is by navigating one of the BPP sample business plans. Launch the BPP software, then click on Create a New Business Plan to reach the main screen. Now choose File from the menu and click Open Sample. This brings you to the Sample Plan Browser. An alternate way to get to this screen is by clicking on the Research It menu along the left of the screen, then selecting Sample Plan Browser.

The names of the sample plans are listed on the left, and the first page of plans bundled with the software can be seen on the right. To view a sample plan, double-click on the plan name. To page through a plan, simply click on the arrows on the bottom of the frame in which the plan pages appear. If you have an Internet connection, the software will download the latest version of the sample plan. You can also check the Web at www.bplans.com/sp to search through more than 60 sample plans created using BPP software. To see how a sample plan in the BPP software is organized or to move between sections in your order, click the Show/Hide Navigation icon to the right of the printer icon on the menu above the sample plan page. When you click on a section name, the plan displays that page.

As you will see when exploring the sample plans, the Executive Summary section provides a brief overview of the business plan. The Company Summary discusses company specifics such as the mission and ownership. The Products and Services section describes exactly what the company is selling. The Market Analysis examines the company's market, including competitors and customers. The Strategy and Implementation section indicates the company's broad course of action in the market, its sales goals, and how it will implement the plan. The Management Summary introduces the organizational structure and management personnel. Finally, the Financial Plan section presents profit-and-loss projections and other financial plans.

You may find it helpful to print out a full copy of the sample plan you have selected and review it as you navigate its contents on your screen. This way you can see how the software uses the information to construct a formal business plan. To print out the sample plan, click on the Printer icon and select Plan. You may also choose to print selected sections or the instructions or examples for a business plan. Once you've finished viewing or printing sample plans, click to close the frame and return to the main screen. You have multiple options for accessing the same information, as shown under the View menu. The Plan Manager option guides you through the process of researching a plan, building it, distributing and delivering it, and making it happen. The Plan Outline option allows you to develop the plan section by section in outline form. To access the text mode option, where you write your business plan's text, select Text Mode from the View menu. You can move between sections by selecting from topics in the Topic drop-down menu above the text screen or using the forward and backward arrows at the right of the Topic menu. To view related tables and charts, click the Table mode or the Chart mode under the View menu.

CREATING A WINNING BUSINESS PLAN

The exercises included at the end of each text part use the knowledge you've gained from reading that text part. Each exercise has two tasks: Think Like a Pro tasks require you to navigate the software, find and review information in the sample business plans, and evaluate and critique some of the thinking that went behind these plans. By reviewing these sample plans with a critical eye, you will begin to sharpen your own business planning skills. Create Your Own Business Plan tasks are an opportunity for you to apply your business planning skills to create your own winning business plan. So begin thinking now about the type of business you'd like to own or manage some day. Then develop and refine your business strategies as you work through the exercises.

Appendix D
Careers in Business and the Employment Search

THINKING ABOUT YOUR CAREER

Getting the job that's right for you takes more than sending out a few letters and signing up with the campus placement office. Planning and research are important if you want to find a company and a position that suits you. Before you limit your job search to a particular industry or functional specialty, analyze what you have to offer and what you hope to get from your work. Then you can identify employers who are likely to want you and vice versa.

What Do You Have to Offer?

Get started by jotting down 10 achievements you're proud of, such as learning to ski, taking a prize-winning photo, tutoring a child, or editing your school paper. Think carefully about what specific skills these achievements demanded. For example, leadership skills, speaking ability, and artistic talent may have helped you coordinate a winning presentation to your school's administration. As you analyze your achievements, you'll begin to recognize a pattern of skills. Which of them might be valuable to potential employers?

Next, look at your educational preparation, work experience, and extracurricular activities. What do your knowledge and experiences qualify you to do? What have you learned from volunteer work or class projects that could benefit you on the job? Have you held any offices, won any awards or scholarships, mastered a second or third language?

Take stock of your personal characteristics. Are you aggressive, a born leader? Or would you rather follow? Are you outgoing, articulate, great with people? Or do you prefer working alone? Make a list of what you believe are your four or five most important qualities. Ask a relative or friend to rate your traits as well.

If you're having trouble figuring out your interests, characteristics, or capabilities, consult your college placement office. Many campuses administer a variety of tests to help you identify interests, aptitudes, and personality traits. These tests won't reveal your "perfect" job, but they'll help you focus on the types of work best suited to your personality.

What Do You Want to Do?

Knowing what you can do is one thing. Knowing what you want to do is another. Don't lose sight of your own values. Discover the things that will bring you satisfaction and happiness on the job.

- *What would you like to do every day?* Talk to people in various occupations about their typical workday. You might consult relatives, local businesses, or former graduates (through your school's alumni relations office). Read about various occupations. Start with your campus library or placement office.
- *How would you like to work?* Consider how much independence you want on the job, how much variety you like, and whether you prefer to work with products, machines, people, ideas, figures, or some combination thereof. Do you like physical work, mental work, or a mix? Constant change or a predictable role?
- *What specific compensation do you expect*? What do you hope to earn in your first year? What kind of pay increase do you expect each year? What's your ultimate earnings goal? Would you be comfortable getting paid on commission, or do you prefer a steady paycheque? Are you willing to settle for less money in order to do something you really love?
- *Can you establish some general career goals*? Consider where you'd like to start, where you'd like to go from there, and the ultimate position you'd like to attain. How soon after joining the company would you like to receive your first promotion? Your next one? What additional training or preparation will you need to achieve them?
- *What size company would you prefer to work for?* Do you like the idea of working for a small, entrepreneurial operation? Or would you prefer a large corporation?
- *What type of operation is appealing to you?* Do you prefer to work for a profit-making company or a non-profit organization? Are you attracted to service businesses or manufacturing operations? Do you want regular, predictable hours, or do you thrive on flexible, varied hours? Would you enjoy a seasonally varied job such as education (which may give you summers off) or retailing (with its selling cycles)?

- *What location would you like?* Would you like to work in a city, a suburb, a small town, an industrial area, or an uptown setting? Do you favour a particular part of the country? A foreign country? Do you like working indoors or outdoors?
- *What facilities do you envision?* Is it important to you to work in an attractive place, or will simple, functional quarters be acceptable? Do you need a quiet office to work effectively, or can you concentrate in a noisy, open setting? Is access to public transportation or freeways important?
- *What sort of corporate culture are you most comfortable with?* Would you be happy in a formal hierarchy with clear reporting relationships? Or do you prefer less structure? Are you looking for a paternalistic firm or one that fosters individualism? Do you like a competitive environment? One that rewards teamwork? What qualities do you want in a boss?

SEEKING EMPLOYMENT OPPORTUNITIES AND INFORMATION

Whether your major is business, biology, or political science, once you know what you have to offer and what you want, you can start finding an employer to match your expectations. If you haven't already committed yourself to any particular career field, review the Human Resources and Skills Development Canada (HRSDC) website (www.hrsdc.gc.ca/en/home.shtml). Among the topics covered are career counselling, employment opportunities, wages, labour market trends, training, job descriptions, and prospects.[1]

Here is a brief overview of the future outlook for a number of careers in business:

- *Careers in Management.* Today's business environment requires the skills of effective managers to reduce costs, streamline operations, develop marketing strategies, and supervise workers. As discussed in Chapter 6, managers perform four basic functions: planning, organizing, leading, and controlling. Facing increased competition, many businesses are becoming more dependent on the expertise of outside management consultants—one of the fastest-growing occupations of all jobs. Outside management consultants perform many important tasks, but chief among them is evaluating operating conditions and making recommendations to improve effectiveness.
- *Careers in Human Resources.* As discussed in Chapters 9 and 10, human resource managers plan and direct human resource activities, including recruiting, training and development, compensation and benefits, employee and labour relations, and health and safety. Additionally, human resources managers develop and implement human resources systems and practices to accommodate a firm's strategy and to motivate and manage diverse workforces. Large numbers of job openings are expected in the human resources field in the near future. Efforts to recruit quality employees and to provide more employee training programs should create new human resources positions. With a vast supply of qualified workers and new graduates, however, the job market for human resources is likely to remain competitive.
- *Careers in Computers and Information Systems.* As competition and advanced technologies force companies to upgrade and improve their computer systems, the number of computer-related positions has increased. However, the recent technology bubble has severely affected the job market in the past few years. Two categories of jobs that have been hit the most are computer operators and data-entry clerks. More user-friendly computer software has greatly reduced the need for operators and data-entry processors, but displaced workers who keep up with changing technology should be capable of moving into growing areas of computer support.
- *Careers in Sales and Marketing.* Increasing competition in products and services should create greater needs for effective sales and marketing personnel in the future. Good job opportunities exist in the business-to-business sector. Effective salespeople are required and are well rewarded for making deals with retailers, manufacturers, and government. Jobs in the marketing communications fields of advertising and public relations are competitive options available as well. Employment opportunities for retail salespersons look good because of the need to replace the large number of workers who transfer to other occupations or leave the workforce each year. Opportunities for part-time work should be abundant. Employment for insurance and real estate agents, however, is expected to grow more slowly than average in the coming years. Computer technology will allow established agents to increase their sales volume and eliminate the need for additional marketing personnel in these fields. For additional information on the types of courses marketing majors take and what you can do with a degree in marketing, see Chapters 11 and 12.
- *Careers in Finance and Accounting.* As Chapter 13 points out, accountants and financial managers are needed in almost every industry. Most positions in finance and accounting are expected to grow as fast as the average for all occupations in the near future, as continued growth in the economy and population is expected to create more demand for trained financial personnel.
- *Careers in Economics.* As Chapter 1 discusses, economists study how society distributes scarce resources such as land, labour, raw materials, and machinery to produce goods and services. They conduct research, collect and analyze data, monitor economic trends, and develop forecasts. Economists are needed in many industries and spend time applying economic theory to

analyze issues that are important to their firms. For example, they might analyze the effects of global economic activity on the demand for the company's product, conduct a cost-benefit analysis of the projects the company is considering, or determine the effects of government regulations or taxes on the company. Employment of economists is expected to grow about as fast as the average for all occupations, with the best opportunities in private industry—especially research, testing, and consulting firms—as more companies contract out for economic research services.

- *Careers in Communications.* As businesses recognize the need for effective communications with their customers and the public, employment of communications personnel is expected to grow as fast as or faster than the average for all occupations in the near future. Recent graduates may face keen competition for entry positions in communications as the number of applicants is expected to exceed the number of job openings. Newly created jobs in the ever-expanding computer world—such as graphic designers for websites or technical writers for instruction manuals—are expected to improve the career outlook for new communications graduates.

Keep in mind that job growth varies widely by education and training requirements. Jobs that require university or college degrees, for example, are expected to grow substantially in the near future (see Exhibit D.1). Categories that do not require a degree are projected to grow slower than average in the future. Moreover, the hottest jobs in today's business world demand technological and computer skills. Even if you're interested in finance, human resources, or marketing positions, you'll need basic computer skills to snare the best jobs in your desired field of work.

Sources of Employment Information

One effective approach to the employment process is to gather as much information as you can, narrowing it as you go until you know precisely the companies you want to contact. Begin by finding out where the job opportunities are, which industries are strong, which parts of the country are booming, and which specific job categories offer the best prospects for the future.

From there you can investigate individual organizations, doing your best to learn as much about them as possible. Here are some good information sources:

- *Business and Financial News.* If you don't already do so, subscribe to a major newspaper (print or online editions) such as the *National Post* or *The Globe and Mail* and scan the business pages every day. Watch some of the television programs that focus on business, such as *Lunch Money* on Report on Business Television.
- *Networking.* You have any number of options for networking with people who work at the organizations you're interested in or who work in a field you would like to investigate. You may be able to network with executives in your field by joining or participating in student business organizations, especially those with ties to real-world organizations such as the Canadian Marketing Association. You might try visiting some organizations, contacting their personnel departments, and talking with key employees. Various avenues of networking should be explored in both formal and informal settings; it is a vital element of the job search and career advancement process.[2]
- *College and University Placement Offices.* Also known as career centres, these placement offices offer individual counselling, credential services, job fairs, on-campus interviews, and job listings. Advisers can give you advice on resumé writing and provide workshops in job-search techniques, interview techniques, and more.[3]

Employment Information on the Web

The Web offers an amazing amount of company and employment information, both general and specific:

- *Discussion Groups.* Using the Web, you can locate and communicate with potential employers through numerous types of discussion groups dedicated to your field. Usenet newsgroups provide an electronic bulletin board so that members can leave and retrieve messages whenever they visit. Listservs (Internet mailing lists) send each message to every member's e-mail address. Commercial systems (e.g., America Online) have their own discussion groups (and make a profit from the time users spend accessing their services). Once you locate a potential contact, you can use e-mail to request information about the company or inquire about job openings. These groups are also a valuable source for interview tips and stories of success and failure that can serve to educate novice employees.[4]

Cisco Systems participates in university and college job fairs as one way to recruit new employees.

Exhibit D.1 **The 25 Fastest-Growing Business Occupations**

According to government estimates, these 25 business occupations are expected to grow the fastest between 2002 and 2012. (The list does not include technical specialties such as engineering or computer programming.)

OCCUPATION	2002 EMPLOYMENT (THOUSANDS)	PROJECTED INCREASES BY 2012	
		NUMBER OF NEW JOBS (THOUSANDS)	% INCREASE
Computer and information systems managers	284	103	36.1
Personal financial advisers	126	44	34.6
Sales managers	343	105	30.5
Management analysts	577	176	30.4
Medical and health services managers	244	71	29.3
Agents and business managers of artists, performers, and athletes	15	4	27.8
Human resources, training and labour relations specialists	474	131	27,7
All other business operations specialists	1056	290	27.5
Advertising and promotion managers	85	21	25.0
Public relations managers	69	16	23.4
Marketing managers	203	43	21.3
Meeting and convention planners	37	8	21.3
Administrative services managers	321	63	19.8
Transportation, storage, and distribution managers	111	22	19.7
Accountants and auditors	1055	205	19.5
Human resources managers	202	39	19.4
Credit analysts	66	12	18.7
Financial analysts	172	32	18.7
Cost estimators	188	35	18.6
General and operation managers	2049	376	18.4
Financial managers	599	109	18.3
Appraisers and assessors of real estate	88	16	17.6
Chief executive	553	93	16.7
Claims adjusters, appraisers, examiners, and investigators	241	34	14.0
Budget analysts	62	9	14.0

- *Social Networking Sites.* Certain sites tailor directly to building networks with individuals who are working in a specific industry. LinkedIn.com is a site that is tailored to professionals and is a source for individuals in the employee marketplace to make career contacts.[5]
- *Career Counselling Websites.* You can also find job counselling online. You might begin your self-assessment, for example, with the Keirsey Temperament Sorter, an online personality test at www.keirsey.com. For excellent job-seeking tips and counselling, visit college- and university-run online career centres. Commercial career centres range from award winning to depressing, so seek out those whose advice is both useful and sensible.
- *Company Websites.* Find out whether a company you're interested in maintains a website. Those that do generally include a company profile, press releases, financial information, descriptive brochures, and information on employment opportunities. You'll also find information about an organization's mission, products, and employee benefits.

- *Job Boards.* An increasing number of large and small companies are posting job openings on Internet job boards such as the ones listed in Exhibit D.2. You can locate job board websites by knowing the URL (web address), using links from other sites, or using your favourite search engine. Job boards are an excellent place to post your resumé.

PREPARING YOUR RESUMÉ

A resumé is a structured, written summary of a person's education, employment background, and job qualifications. Although many people have misconceptions about resumés (see Exhibit D.3 on page 404), the fact is that a resumé is a form of advertising. It is intended to stimulate an employer's interest in you—in meeting you and learning more about you. A successful resumé inspires a prospective employer to invite you to interview with the company. Thus, your purpose in writing your resumé is to create interest—*not* to tell readers everything about you. In fact, it may be best only to hint at some things and leave the reader wanting more. The potential employer will then have even more reason to contact you.[7]

To write a successful resumé, you need to convey seven qualities that employers seek. You want to show that you (1) think in terms of results, (2) know how to get things done, (3) are well rounded, (4) show signs of progress, (5) have personal standards of excellence, (6) are flexible and willing to try new things, and (7) possess strong communication

Exhibit D.2 **Places to Start Your Online Job Search**

Begin your job search with these helpful online career resources.[6]

WEBSITE	DESCRIPTION AND FEATURES
Job Bank www.jobbank.gc.ca	A good place to begin. Offers an electronic listing of job openings across Canada. Provides information regarding education, knowledge, and skills requirements for most occupations. Includes links to multiple career resources including the specific details about the labour market for youths.
Federal Government Jobs www.jobs-emplois.gc.ca	A website for the Public Service Commission of Canada. It allows individuals to access more than 7000 federal jobs from one application for employment.
CareerBuilder www.careerbuilder.com	Offers a network of career services, job-search information, and tips on how to succeed once you're hired. Includes a database of 20 000 openings.
Workopolis Job Board www.workopolis.com	Provides prospective employees with a wealth of resources, including job postings by industry and tips on the following topics: resumé writing, interviewing, networking, and salary negotiations.
HotJobs.ca http://ca.hotjobs.yahoo.com/	A member-based website that charges companies a hefty fee to post openings or search through resumés. Job seekers can create a personal page to manage their search and collect statistics on how many companies have retrieved their resumé.
Net-Temps www.net-temps.ca	Maintained by career consultants; offers several thousand updated listings and real-time seminars. Network forums help you develop new contacts and job leads. Includes chat room for online interviews.
The Monster Board www.monster.ca	Posts more than 25 000 openings and 300 000 resumés. Heavily marketed, it brings a flood of employers (many with fewer than 500 employees).
Canadian Newspaper Help-Wanted Ads www.theworkplace.ca/page2.asp?sect=1	This website offers daily listings of job openings sorted by province and by local newspaper.

Exhibit D.3 **Fallacies and Facts about Resumés**

Many people incorrectly believe that a good resumé will get them the job they want.

FALLACY	FACT
✗ The purpose of a resumé is to list all your skills and abilities.	✓ The purpose of a resumé is to kindle employer interest and generate an interview.
✗ A good resumé will get you the job you want.	✓ All a resumé can do is get you in the door.
✗ Your resumé will be read carefully and thoroughly by an interested employer.	✓ Your resumé probably has less than 45 seconds to make an impression.
✗ The more good information you present about yourself in your resumé, the better.	✓ Too much information on a resumé may actually kill the reader's appetite to know more.
✗ If you want a really good resumé, have it prepared by a resumé service.	✓ Prepare your own resumé—unless the position is especially high-level or specialized. Even then, you should check carefully before using a service.

skills. As you organize and compose your resumé, think about how you can convey those seven qualities.

Controlling the Format and Style

With less than a minute to make a good impression, your resumé needs to look sharp and grab a recruiter's interest in the first few lines. A typical recruiter devotes 45 seconds to each resumé before tossing it into either the "maybe" or the "reject" pile.[8] Most recruiters scan a resumé rather than read it from top to bottom. If yours doesn't stand out, chances are the recruiter won't look at it long enough to judge your qualifications.

To give your printed resumé the best appearance possible, use a clean typeface on high-grade, letter-size bond paper (in white or some light earth tone). Your stationery and envelope should match. Leave ample margins all around, and make sure that any corrections are unnoticeable. Avoid italic typefaces, which are difficult to read, and use a quality printer.

Try to keep your resumé to one or two pages. If you have a great deal of experience and are applying for a higher-level position, you may need to prepare a somewhat longer resumé. The important thing is to have enough space to present a persuasive, but accurate, portrait of your skills and accomplishments.

Lay out your resumé so that the information is easy to grasp.[9] Break up the text with headings that call attention to various aspects of your background, such as work experience and education. Underline or boldface key points, or set them off in the left margin. Use indented lists to itemize your most important qualifications. Leave plenty of white space, even if you're forced to use two pages. Pay attention to mechanics and details. Make sure that headings and itemized lists are grammatically parallel and that grammar, spelling, and punctuation are correct.

Write in a simple and direct style to save your reader time. Use short, crisp phrases instead of whole sentences, and focus on what your reader needs to know. Absolutely avoid using the word *I*. You might say, "Coached a little league team to the provincial playoffs" or "Managed a fast-food restaurant and four employees."

Think about your resumé from the employer's perspective. Ask yourself: What key qualifications will an employer be looking for? Which of these are my greatest strengths? What will set me apart from other candidates? What are my greatest accomplishments, and what was produced as a result? Then tailor your resumé to appeal to the employer's needs.

Organizing Your Resumé around Your Strengths

As you compose your resumé, try to emphasize the information that has a bearing on your career objective, and minimize or exclude any that is irrelevant or counterproductive. To interest potential employers in your resumé, call attention to your best features and downplay your weaknesses—but be sure you do so without distorting or misrepresenting the facts.[10] Do you have something in your history that might trigger an employer's red flag? Some common problems and some quick suggestions for overcoming them are listed below.[11]

- *Frequent job changes.* Group all contract and temporary jobs under one heading if they're similar.
- *Gaps in work history.* Mention relevant experience and education gained during time gaps, such as volunteer or community work. If gaps are due to personal problems such as drug abuse, alcohol abuse, or mental illness, offer honest but general explanations about your absences ("I had serious health concerns and had to take time off to fully recover").
- *Inexperience.* Do related volunteer work. List relevant course work and internships. Offer hiring incentives such as "willing to work nights and weekends."

- *Overqualification.* Tone down your resumé, focusing exclusively on pertinent experience and skills.
- *Long-term employment with one company.* Itemize each position held at the firm to show "interior mobility" and increased responsibilities. Don't include obsolete skills and job titles.
- *Job termination for cause.* Be honest with interviewers. Show you're a hard-working employee and counter their concerns with proof such as recommendations and examples of completed projects.

To focus attention on your strongest points, adopt the appropriate organizational approach—make your resumé chronological, functional, or a combination of the two. The "right" choice depends on your background and your goals.

The Chronological Resumé

In a **chronological resumé**, the "Work Experience" section dominates and is placed in the most prominent slot, immediately after the name and address and the objective. You develop this section by listing your jobs sequentially in reverse order, beginning with the most recent position and working backwards toward earlier jobs. Under each listing, describe your responsibilities and accomplishments, giving the most space to the most recent positions. If you're just

Exhibit D.4 Chronological Resumé

Martin Rivas calls attention to his most recent achievements by setting them off in list form with bullets. The section titled "Intercultural and Technical Skills" emphasizes his international background, fluency in French and Spanish, and extensive computer skills—all of which are important qualifications for his target position.

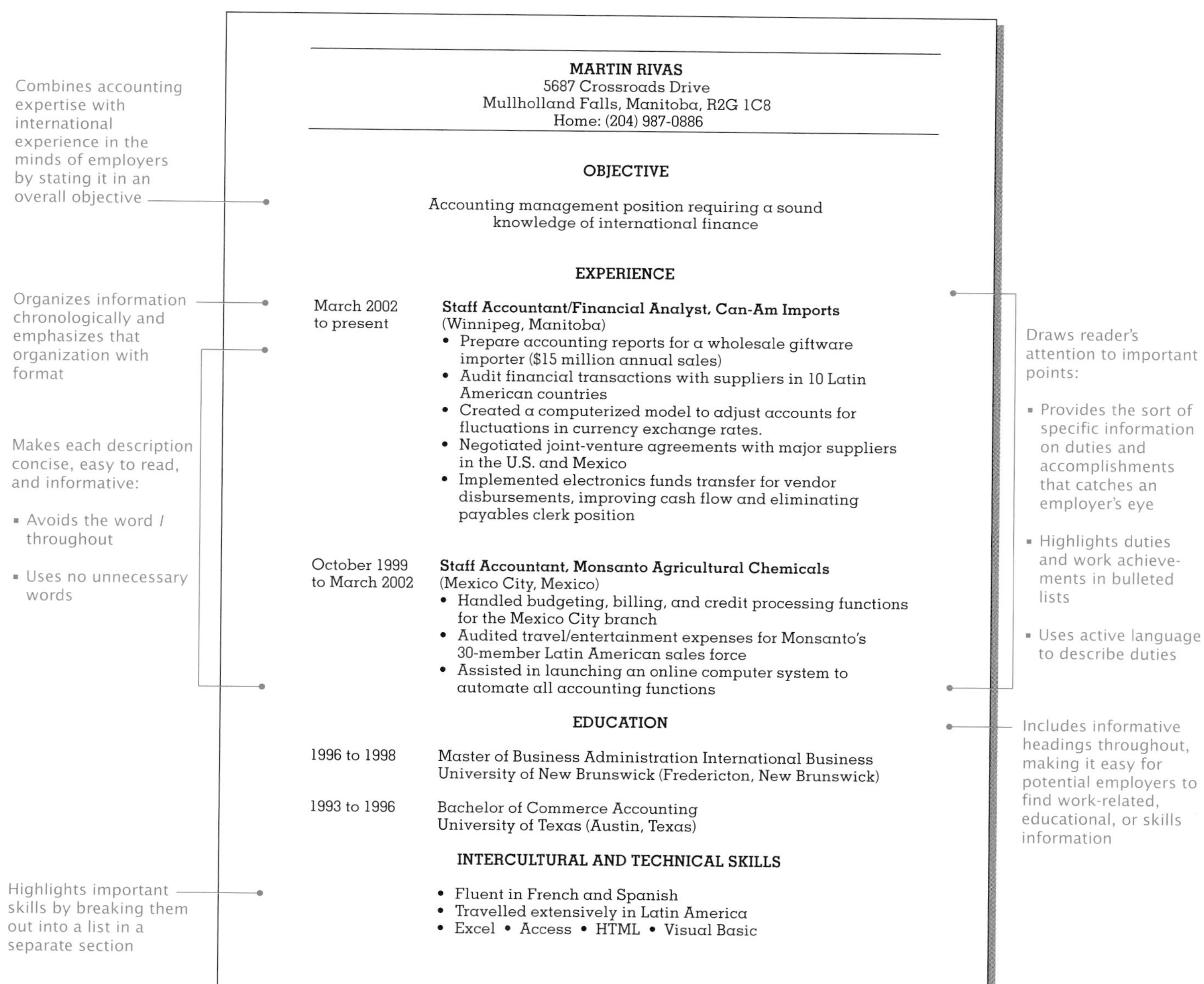

MARTIN RIVAS
5687 Crossroads Drive
Mullholland Falls, Manitoba, R2G 1C8
Home: (204) 987-0886

OBJECTIVE

Accounting management position requiring a sound knowledge of international finance

EXPERIENCE

March 2002 to present — **Staff Accountant/Financial Analyst, Can-Am Imports** (Winnipeg, Manitoba)
- Prepare accounting reports for a wholesale giftware importer ($15 million annual sales)
- Audit financial transactions with suppliers in 10 Latin American countries
- Created a computerized model to adjust accounts for fluctuations in currency exchange rates.
- Negotiated joint-venture agreements with major suppliers in the U.S. and Mexico
- Implemented electronics funds transfer for vendor disbursements, improving cash flow and eliminating payables clerk position

October 1999 to March 2002 — **Staff Accountant, Monsanto Agricultural Chemicals** (Mexico City, Mexico)
- Handled budgeting, billing, and credit processing functions for the Mexico City branch
- Audited travel/entertainment expenses for Monsanto's 30-member Latin American sales force
- Assisted in launching an online computer system to automate all accounting functions

EDUCATION

1996 to 1998 — Master of Business Administration International Business, University of New Brunswick (Fredericton, New Brunswick)

1993 to 1996 — Bachelor of Commerce Accounting, University of Texas (Austin, Texas)

INTERCULTURAL AND TECHNICAL SKILLS

- Fluent in French and Spanish
- Travelled extensively in Latin America
- Excel • Access • HTML • Visual Basic

graduating from college or university, you can vary this chronological approach by putting your educational qualifications before your experience, thereby focusing attention on your academic credentials.

The chronological approach is the most common way to organize a resumé, and many employers prefer it (see Exhibit D.4). This approach has three key advantages: (1) Employers are familiar with it and can easily find information, (2) it highlights growth and career progression, and (3) it highlights employment continuity and stability.[12] As vice-president of Korn/Ferry International, Robert Nesbit speaks for many recruiters: "Unless you have a really compelling reason, don't use any but the standard chronological format. Your resumé should not read like a treasure map, full of minute clues to the whereabouts of your jobs and experience. I want to be able to grasp quickly where a candidate has worked, how long, and in what capacities."[13]

The Functional Resumé

A **functional resumé** emphasizes a list of skills and accomplishments, identifying employers and academic experience in subordinate sections. This pattern stresses individual areas of competence, so it's useful for people who are just entering the job market, want to redirect their careers, or have little continuous career-related experience. The functional approach also has three advantages: (1) Without having to read through job descriptions, employers can see what you can do for them, (2) you can emphasize earlier job experience, and (3) you can de-emphasize any lack of career progress or lengthy unemployment. Bear in mind, however, that many seasoned employment professionals are suspect of this resumé style. They assume that candidates who use it are trying to hide something.[14]

The Combination Resumé

A **combination resumé** includes the best features of the chronological and functional approaches. Nevertheless, it is not commonly used because it has two major disadvantages: (1) it tends to be longer, and (2) it can be repetitious if you have to list your accomplishments and skills in both the functional section and the chronological job descriptions.[15]

Converting Your Traditional Resumé to a Scannable Format

You need to format your resumé in at least two and maybe three ways: (1) as a traditional printed document such as the one just discussed, (2) as a plain-text (or ASCII) document that can be scanned from a hard copy or submitted electronically, and (3) as an HTML-coded document that could be uploaded to the Internet to post on a web page (should you choose to).

Most companies encourage applicants to submit electronic or scannable resumés. By scanning these resumés into their electronic databases, companies can narrow down a pile of job applicants quickly. Scannable resumés should convey the same information as traditional resumés, but the format and style must be changed to one that is computer friendly because scannable resumés are not intended to be read by humans. To make your traditional resumé a scannable one, format it as plain text (ASCII) document, improve its look, and modify its content slightly by providing a list of key words and by balancing common language with current jargon (see Exhibit D.5).

Prepare Your Resumé in ASCII Format

ASCII is a common plain-text language that allows your resumé to be read by any scanner and accessed by any computer, regardless of the word processing software you used to prepare the document. All word processing programs allow you to save files as plain text. To convert your resumé to an ASCII plain-text file:

- Remove all formatting (boldfacing, underlining, italics, centring, bullets, graphic lines, etc.) and all formatting codes such as tab settings or tables.
- Remove shadows and reverse print (white letters on black background).
- Remove graphics and boxes.
- Use scannable typefaces (such as Helvetica, Univers, Times New Roman, Palatino, New Century Schoolbook, and Courier).
- Use a font size of 10 to 14 points.
- Remove multicolumn formats that resemble newspapers or newsletters.
- Save your document under a different name by using your word processor's "save as" option and selecting "text only with line breaks."

Improve the Look of Your Scannable Resumé

Resumés in ASCII format (without special formatting) look ugly in comparison to traditional resumés. Use the following formatting techniques (which are acceptable for scannable resumés) to enhance the resumé's overall look and effectiveness:

- Align text by adding some blank spaces (rather than tabs).
- Create headings and separate paragraphs by adding a few blank lines.
- Indicate bullets with an asterisk or the lowercase letter *o*.
- Use white space so that scanners and computers can tell when one topic ends and another begins.
- Do not condense the spacing between letters.
- Use all capital letters for section headings as long as the letters do not touch each other.
- Put your name at the top of each page on its own line (with no text appearing above or beside your name).
- Use the standard address format below your name.

Exhibit D.5 Electronic Resumé

Because some of his target employers will be scanning his resumé into a database, and because he wants to submit his resumé via e-mail or post it on the Internet, Martin Rivas created an electronic resumé by changing his formatting and adding a list of key words. However, the information remains essentially the same.

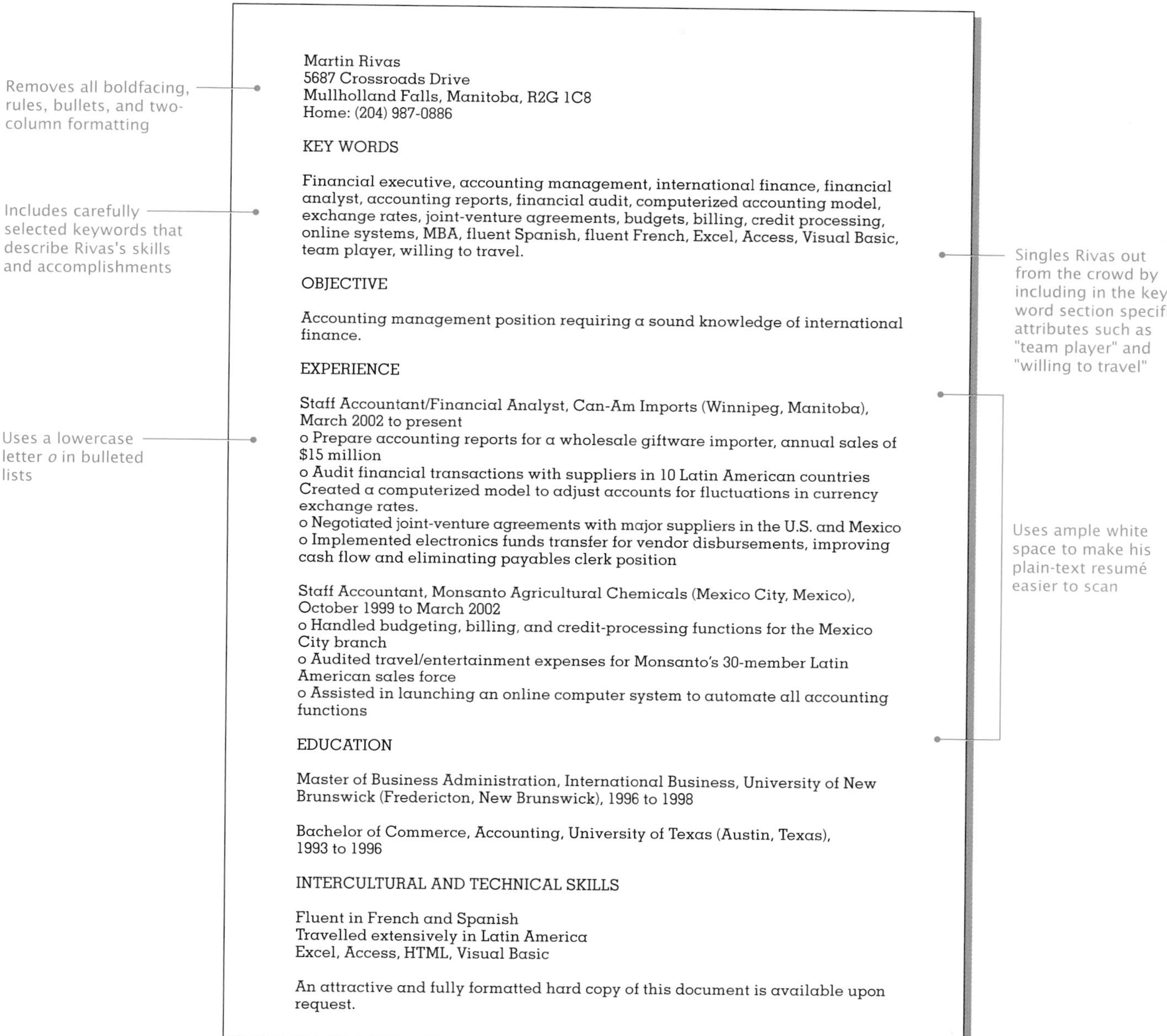

Martin Rivas
5687 Crossroads Drive
Mullholland Falls, Manitoba, R2G 1C8
Home: (204) 987-0886

KEY WORDS

Financial executive, accounting management, international finance, financial analyst, accounting reports, financial audit, computerized accounting model, exchange rates, joint-venture agreements, budgets, billing, credit processing, online systems, MBA, fluent Spanish, fluent French, Excel, Access, Visual Basic, team player, willing to travel.

OBJECTIVE

Accounting management position requiring a sound knowledge of international finance.

EXPERIENCE

Staff Accountant/Financial Analyst, Can-Am Imports (Winnipeg, Manitoba), March 2002 to present
o Prepare accounting reports for a wholesale giftware importer, annual sales of $15 million
o Audit financial transactions with suppliers in 10 Latin American countries Created a computerized model to adjust accounts for fluctuations in currency exchange rates.
o Negotiated joint-venture agreements with major suppliers in the U.S. and Mexico
o Implemented electronics funds transfer for vendor disbursements, improving cash flow and eliminating payables clerk position

Staff Accountant, Monsanto Agricultural Chemicals (Mexico City, Mexico), October 1999 to March 2002
o Handled budgeting, billing, and credit-processing functions for the Mexico City branch
o Audited travel/entertainment expenses for Monsanto's 30-member Latin American sales force
o Assisted in launching an online computer system to automate all accounting functions

EDUCATION

Master of Business Administration, International Business, University of New Brunswick (Fredericton, New Brunswick), 1996 to 1998

Bachelor of Commerce, Accounting, University of Texas (Austin, Texas), 1993 to 1996

INTERCULTURAL AND TECHNICAL SKILLS

Fluent in French and Spanish
Travelled extensively in Latin America
Excel, Access, HTML, Visual Basic

An attractive and fully formatted hard copy of this document is available upon request.

- List each phone number on its own line.
- Use white or light-coloured 8 1/2-by-11-inch paper, printing on one side only.

Keep in mind that scannable resumés are designed to be read by computers so it's fine to submit multiple pages, just don't get carried away. To increase your chances of a quality scan, do not fold or staple the resumé and do not send a photocopy. Provide a printed original, if possible.

Provide a List of Key Words

When converting your resumé to a scannable format, emphasize certain key words to help potential employers select your resumé from the thousands they scan. Employers generally search for nouns (because verbs tend to be generic rather than specific to a particular position or skill). To maximize the number of matches (or hits), include a key word summary of 20 to 30 words and phrases

Under Jeff Taylor's guidance, Monster.com now lists more than 10 million resumés on its recruitment website.

that define your skills, experience, education, professional affiliations, and so on. Place this list right after your name and address. A key word summary for an accountant, for example, might include the following terms: accountant, corporate controller, Fortune 1000, receivables, payables, inventory, cash flow, financial analysis, payroll experience, corporate taxes, activity-based accounting, problem solving, computer skills, Excel, Access, networks, HTML, Simply Accounting, ACCPAC, BA McMaster University—Accounting, CA, dean's list, articulate, team player, flexible, willing to travel, fluent French.

Balance Common Language with Current Jargon

Another way to maximize hits on your resumé is to use words that potential employers will understand (for example, say *keyboard,* not *input device*). Also, use abbreviations sparingly (except for common ones such as BA or MBA). At the same time, learn and use the important buzzwords in your field. Look for current jargon in the want ads of major newspapers such as *The Globe and Mail* and in other resumés in your field that are posted online. Be careful to check and recheck the spelling, capitalization, and punctuation of any jargon you include, and use only those words you see most often.

Submit Your Scannable Resumé

If an employer gives you an option of submitting a scannable resumé by mail, by fax, or by e-mail, choose e-mail. E-mail puts your resumé directly into the employer's database, bypassing the scanning process. If you send your resumé in a paper format by regular mail or by fax, you run the risk that an OCR scanning program will create an error when reading it. In fact, increasing numbers of job applicants are submitting both a traditional and a scannable resumé, explaining in their cover letter that the scannable resumé is for downloading into a database if the company desires.

If you're posting your scannable resumé to a resumé builder at a recruitment or company website, copy and paste the appropriate sections from your electronic file directly into the employer's form. This method avoids re-keying and eliminates errors.

If you fax your scannable resumé, set your machine to "fine" mode (to ensure a high-quality printout on the receiving end). If you're mailing your resumé, you may want to send both a well-designed traditional resumé and a scannable one. Simply attach Post-it Notes, labelling one "visual resumé" and the other "scannable resumé."

Building an Online Resumé

If you wish to post your resumé on your web page, provide employers with your URL; most recruiters won't take the time to use search engines to find your site. As you design your website resumé, think of important key words to use as hyperlinks—words that will grab an employer's attention and make the recruiter want to click on that hyperlink to learn more about you. You can make links to papers you've written, recommendations, and sound or video clips. Don't distract potential employers from your credentials by using hyperlinks to organizations or other websites.

Do not use photos and avoid providing information that reveals your age, sex, race, marital status, or religion. Because a website is a public access area, you should also leave out the names of references and previous employers. Either mention that references are available on request or say nothing. Also, instead of naming companies, simply refer to "a large accounting firm" or "a wholesale giftware importer." Finally, include an ASCII version of your resumé on your web page so that prospective employers can download it into their company's database.

Preparing Your Application Letter

Whenever you submit your resumé, accompany it with a cover, or application, letter to let readers know what you're sending, why you're sending it, and how they can benefit from reading it. Because your application letter is in your own style (rather than the choppy, shorthand style of your resumé), it gives you a chance to show your communication skills and some personality.

Always send your resumé(s) and application letter together, because each has a unique job to perform. The purpose of your resumé is to get employers interested enough to contact you for an interview. The purpose of your application letter is to get employers interested enough to read your resumé. Before drafting a letter, learn something about the organization you're applying to; then focus on your audience so that you can show you've done your homework. Imagine yourself in the recruiter's situation, and show how your background and talents will solve a particular problem or fill a specific need the company has. The more you can learn about the organization, the better you'll be able to capture the reader's attention and convey your interest in the company. During your research, find out the name, title, and department of the person you're writing to. Reaching and addressing the right person is the most effective way to gain attention. Avoid phrases such as "To Whom It May Concern" and "Dear Sir."

When putting yourself in your reader's shoes, remember that this person's in-box is probably overflowing with resumés and cover letters. So respect your reader's time. Steer clear of gimmicks, which almost never work, and include nothing in your cover letter that already appears in your resumé. Keep your letter straightforward, fact-based, short, upbeat, and professional (see Exhibit D.6).

Following Up on Your Application

If your application letter and resumé fail to bring a response within a month or so, follow up with a second letter to keep your file active. This follow-up letter also gives you a chance to update your original application with any recent job-related information. Even if you've received a letter acknowledging your application and saying that it

Exhibit D.6 Application Letter

In her unsolicited application letter, Glenda Johns manages to give a snapshot of her qualifications and skills without repeating what is said in her resumé.

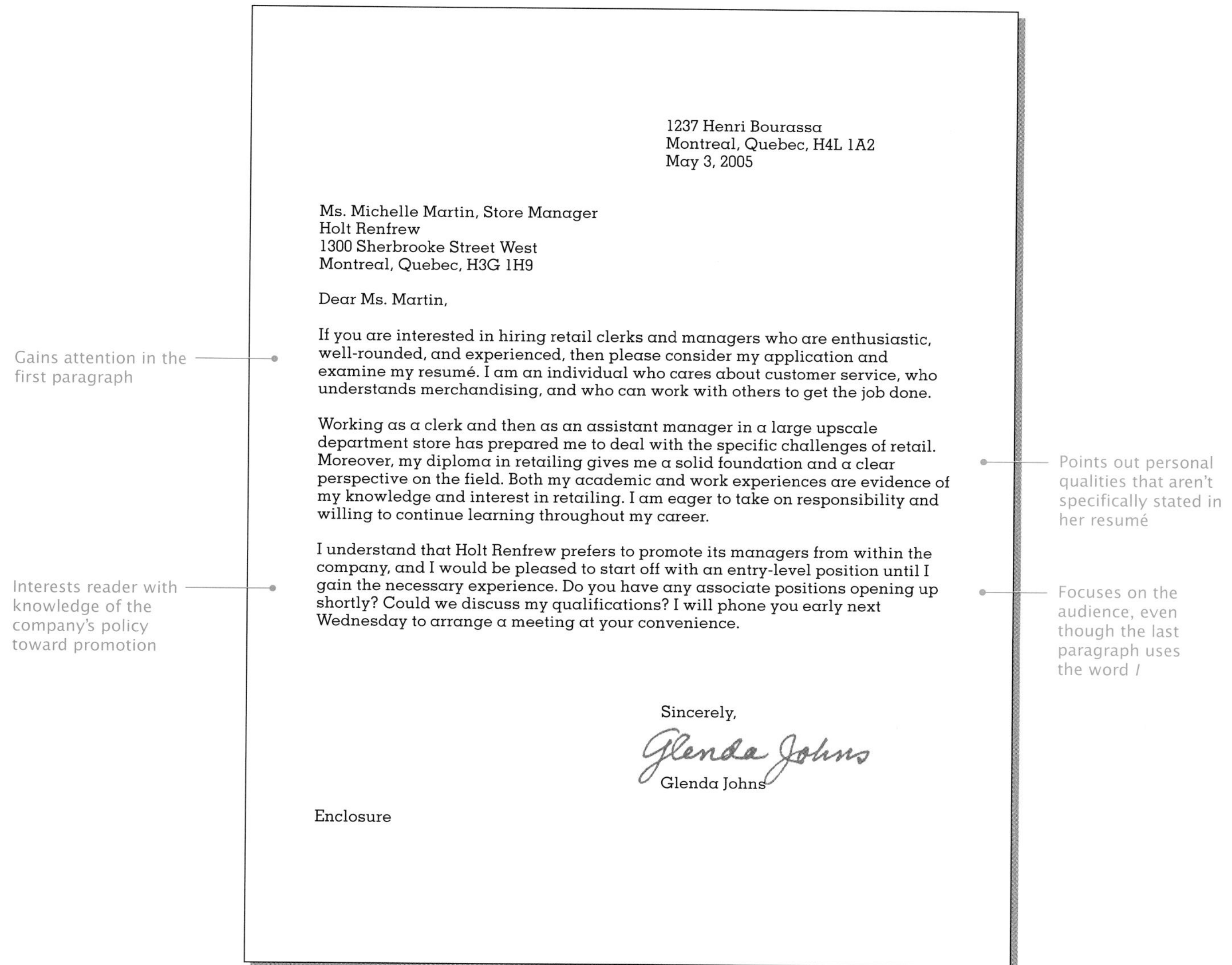

1237 Henri Bourassa
Montreal, Quebec, H4L 1A2
May 3, 2005

Ms. Michelle Martin, Store Manager
Holt Renfrew
1300 Sherbrooke Street West
Montreal, Quebec, H3G 1H9

Dear Ms. Martin,

If you are interested in hiring retail clerks and managers who are enthusiastic, well-rounded, and experienced, then please consider my application and examine my resumé. I am an individual who cares about customer service, who understands merchandising, and who can work with others to get the job done.

Working as a clerk and then as an assistant manager in a large upscale department store has prepared me to deal with the specific challenges of retail. Moreover, my diploma in retailing gives me a solid foundation and a clear perspective on the field. Both my academic and work experiences are evidence of my knowledge and interest in retailing. I am eager to take on responsibility and willing to continue learning throughout my career.

I understand that Holt Renfrew prefers to promote its managers from within the company, and I would be pleased to start off with an entry-level position until I gain the necessary experience. Do you have any associate positions opening up shortly? Could we discuss my qualifications? I will phone you early next Wednesday to arrange a meeting at your convenience.

Sincerely,

Glenda Johns

Glenda Johns

Enclosure

will be kept on file, don't hesitate to send a follow-up letter three months later to show that you are still interested. Such a letter can demonstrate that you're sincerely interested in working for the organization, that you're persistent in pursuing your goals, and that you're upgrading your skills to make yourself a better employee. It might just get you an interview.

INTERVIEWING WITH POTENTIAL EMPLOYERS

Approach job interviews with a sound appreciation of their dual purpose: The organization's main objective is to find the best person available for the job; the applicant's main objective is to find the job best suited to his or her goals and capabilities.

In general, the easiest way to connect with a big company is through your campus placement office; the most efficient way to approach a smaller business is by contacting the company directly. In either case, you move to the next stage and prepare to meet with a recruiter during an **employment interview**, a formal meeting during which an employer and an applicant ask questions and exchange information to see whether the applicant and the organization are a good match.

Most employers conduct two or three interviews before deciding whether to offer a person a job. The first interview, sometimes held on campus, is the **preliminary screening interview**, which helps employers eliminate unqualified applicants from the hiring process. Those candidates who best meet the organization's requirements are invited to visit company offices for further evaluation. Some organizations make a decision at that point, but many schedule a third interview to complete the evaluation process before extending a job offer.

Because the interview takes time, start seeking interviews well in advance of the date you want to start work. It takes an average of 10 interviews to get one job offer. If you hope to have several offers to choose from, you can expect to go through 20 or 30 interviews during your job search.[16] Some students start their job search as early as nine months before graduation. Early planning is even more crucial during downturns in the economy because many employers become more selective when times are tough.

What Employers Look For

Today's employers want candidates who are experienced, intelligent, good communicators, enthusiastic, creative, and motivated. In addition to these qualities, candidates must also fit in with the organization and meet the basic qualifications for the job.

To determine whether a candidate will be compatible with the other people in the organization, some interviewers may ask you questions about your interests, hobbies, awareness of world events, and so forth. Others may consider your personal style. You're likely to impress an employer by being open, enthusiastic, and interested. Still others may look for courtesy, sincerity, willingness to learn, and a style that is positive and self-confident. All of these qualities help a new employee adapt to a new workplace and new responsibilities.

When you're invited to interview for a position, the interviewer may already have some idea of whether you have the right qualifications, based on a review of your resumé. But during the interview, you'll be asked to describe your education and previous jobs in more depth so that the interviewer can determine how well your skills match the requirements. When describing your skills, be honest. Interviewers can be skeptical of candidates that have been overcoached and are too slick to be genuine. Talking around a topic, like a politician, can hurt your chances.[17] If you don't know how to do something, say so. In many cases, the interviewer will be seeking someone with the flexibility to apply diverse skills in several areas.

What Applicants Need to Find Out

What things should you find out about the prospective job and employer? By doing a little advance research and asking the right questions during the interview (see Exhibit D.7 on page 411), you can probably find answers to these questions and more:

- Are these my kind of people?
- Can I do this work?
- Will I enjoy the work?
- Is this job what I want?
- Does the job pay what I'm worth?
- What kind of person would I be working for?
- What sort of future can I look forward to with this organization?

How to Prepare for a Job Interview

It's perfectly normal to feel a little anxious before an interview. Don't worry too much, however; preparation will help you perform well. Learning about the organization and the job is important because it enables you to consider the employer's point of view. Here are some pointers to guide that preparation:

- *Think ahead about questions.* Most job interviews are essentially question-and-answer sessions: You answer the interviewer's questions about your background, and you ask questions of your own to determine whether the job and the organization are right for you. By planning for your interviews, you can handle these exchanges intelligently (see Exhibit D.8 on page 412). Of course, you don't want to memorize responses or sound overrehearsed.
- *Bolster your confidence.* By overcoming your tendencies to feel self-conscious or nervous during an interview, you can build your confidence and make a better

Exhibit D.7 **Fifteen Questions to Ask the Interviewer**

Learn as much as you can about potential employers by asking these questions.

QUESTIONS ABOUT THE JOB	QUESTIONS ABOUT THE ORGANIZATION
What are the job's major responsibilities?	What are the organization's major strengths? Weaknesses?
What qualities do you want in the person who fills this position?	Who are your organization's major competitors, and what are their strengths and weaknesses?
Do you want to know more about my related training?	What makes your organization different from others in the industry?
What is the first problem that needs the attention of the person you hire?	What are your organization's major markets?
Would relocation be required now or in the future?	Does the organization have any plans for new products? Acquisitions?
Why is this job now vacant?	How would you define your organization's managerial philosophy?
What can you tell me about the person I would report to?	What additional training does your organization provide?
	Do employees have an opportunity to continue their education with help from the organization?

impression. If some aspect of your background or appearance makes you uneasy, correct it or exercise positive traits to offset it, such as warmth, wit, intelligence, or charm. Instead of dwelling on your weaknesses, focus on your strengths so that you can emphasize them to an interviewer.

- *Polish your interview style.* Confidence helps you walk into an interview and give the interviewer an impression of poise, good manners, and good judgment. You're more likely to be invited back for a second interview or offered a job if you maintain eye contact, smile frequently, sit in an attentive position, and use frequent hand gestures. These nonverbal signals convince the interviewer that you're alert, assertive, dependable, confident, responsible, and energetic.[18] Work on eliminating speech mannerisms such as "you know," "like," and "um." Speak in your natural tone, and try to vary the pitch, rate, and volume of your voice to express enthusiasm and energy.
- *Plan to look good.* The best policy is to dress conservatively. Wear the best-quality businesslike clothing you can, preferably in a dark, solid colour. Avoid flamboyant styles, colours, and prints. Clean, unwrinkled clothes, well-shined shoes, neatly styled and combed hair, clean fingernails, and fresh breath help make a good first impression. Don't spoil the effect by smoking cigarettes before or during the interview. Finally, remember that one of the best ways to look good is to smile at appropriate moments.
- *Be ready when you arrive.* Be sure you know when and where the interview will be held. Take a small notebook, a pen, a list of your questions, a folder with two copies of your resumé, an outline of your research findings about the organization, and any correspondence about the position. You may also want to take a small calendar, a transcript of your grades, a list of references, and, if appropriate, samples of your work. After you arrive, relax. You may have to wait, so bring something to read or to occupy your time (the less frivolous or controversial, the better).

Additionally, research the current market and the employer extensively and impress everyone you encounter (including the receptionist).[19]

How to Follow Up After the Interview

Touching base with the prospective employer after the interview, either by phone or in writing, shows that you really want the job and are determined to get it. It also brings your name to the interviewer's attention again and reminds him or her that you're waiting to know the decision.

The two most common forms of follow up, the thank-you message and the inquiry, are generally handled by letter or e-mail. But a phone call can be just as effective, particularly if the employer favours a casual, personal style. Express your thanks within two days after the interview, even if you feel you have little chance for the job. In a brief message, acknowledge the interviewer's time and courtesy, convey your continued interest, and ask politely for a decision. If you're not advised of the interviewer's decision by the promised date or within two weeks, you might make an inquiry, particularly if you don't want to accept a job offer from a second firm before you have an answer from the first. Assume that a simple oversight is the reason for the delay, not outright rejection.

Exhibit D.8 **Twenty-Five Common Interview Questions**

Prepare for an interview in advance by thinking about your answers to these questions.

QUESTIONS ABOUT YOUR EDUCATION

1. What courses did you prefer? Why?
2. Do you think your extracurricular activities were worth the time spent on them? Why or why not?
3. When did you choose your major? Did you ever change your major? If so, why?
4. Do you feel you did the best scholastic work you are capable of?
5. Which of your college or university years was the toughest? Why?

QUESTIONS ABOUT EMPLOYERS AND JOBS

6. What jobs have you held? Why did you leave?
7. What percentage of your school expenses did you earn? How?
8. Why did you choose your particular field of work?
9. What are the disadvantages of your chosen field?
10. Have you served in the military? What rank did you achieve? What jobs did you perform?
11. What do you think about how this industry operates today?
12. Why do you think you would like this particular type of job?

QUESTIONS ABOUT PERSONAL ATTITUDES AND PREFERENCES

13. Do you prefer to work in any specific geographic location? If so, why?
14. How much money do you hope to be earning in five years? In 10 years?
15. What do you think determines a person's progress in a good organization?
16. What personal characteristics do you feel are necessary for success in your chosen field?
17. Tell me a story.
18. Do you like to travel?
19. Do you think grades should be considered by employers? Why or why not?

QUESTIONS ABOUT WORK HABITS

20. Do you prefer working with others or by yourself?
21. What type of boss do you prefer?
22. Have you ever had any difficulty getting along with colleagues or supervisors? With instructors? With other students?
23. Would you prefer to work in a large or a small organization? Why?
24. How do you feel about overtime work?
25. What have you done that shows initiative and willingness to work?

BUILDING YOUR CAREER

Having the right skills is one way to build toward a career. Employers seek people who are able and willing to adapt to diverse situations, who thrive in an ever-changing workplace, and who continue to learn throughout their careers. In addition, companies want team players with strong work records and leaders who are versatile. Many companies encourage managers to get varied job experience.[20] In some cases, your chances of being hired are better if you've studied abroad or learned another language. Many employers expect graduates to have a sound understanding of international affairs, and they're looking for employees with intercultural sensitivity and an ability to adapt in other cultures.[21]

Compile an employment portfolio. Get a three-ring notebook and a package of plastic sleeves that open at the top. Collect anything that shows your ability to perform, such as classroom or work evaluations, certificates, awards, and papers you've written. An employment portfolio serves as an excellent resource when writing your resumé and provides employers with tangible evidence of your professionalism.

As you search for a permanent job that fulfills your career goals, take interim job assignments, participate in an internship program, and consider temporary work or freelance jobs. Not only will these temporary assignments help you gain valuable experience and relevant contacts, but they will also provide you with important references and with items for your portfolio.[22] Employers will be more willing to find (or even to create) a position for someone they've learned to respect, and your temporary or freelance work gives them a chance to see what you can do.

If you're unable to find actual job experience, work on polishing and updating your skills. Network with professional colleagues and friends who can help you stay abreast of your occupation and industry. While you're waiting for responses to your resumé or your last interview, take a computer course or gain some other educational or life experience that would be difficult while working full time. Become familiar with the services offered by your campus career centre (or placement office). These centres offer individual placement counselling, credential services, job fairs, on-campus interviews, job listings, advice on computerized resumé-writing software, workshops in job-search techniques, resumé preparation, interview techniques, and more.[23]

Once an employer hires you and you're on the job, don't think you've reached the end of the process. The best thing you can do for your long-term career is to continue learning. Listen to and learn from those around you who have experience. Be ready and willing to take on new responsibilities, and actively pursue new or better skills. Employers appreciate applicants and employees with willingness and enthusiasm to learn, to listen, and to gain experience.

GLOSSARY

chronological resumé Most traditional type of resumé, listing employment history sequentially in reverse order so that the most recent experience is listed first

combination resumé A hybrid of a chronological and functional resumé that contains elements of both

employment interview Formal meeting during which an employer and an applicant ask questions and exchange information to see whether the applicant and the organization are a good match

functional resumé Organized around a list of skills and accomplishments, subordinating employers and academic experience in order to stress individual areas of competence

preliminary screening interview Meeting between an employer's representative and a candidate for the purpose of eliminating unqualified applicants from the hiring process

resumé Form of advertising that lists a person's education, employment background, and job qualifications in order to obtain an interview

References

Chapter 1

1 Amanda Lang, "Hockey Night in Forest Hill," *Report on Business Magazine*, April 2005, 15,16; Marina Strauss, "How HBC Swept Roots for the Games," *The Globe and Mail*, 4 March 2005, B2; Marina Strauss, "Roots Hopes to Get the Gold from Olympic Buzz," *The Globe and Mail*, 27 July 2004, B1, B21; Marina Strauss, "Budman Puts Down Roots in Europe," *The Globe and Mail*, 9 June 2004, B5; Melanie Wells, "Reach for the Sky," *Forbes Magazine*, 7 August 2000; Roots website [accessed 1 April 2005] www.roots.com/new_canada/html/pc_company_profile.shtml; Ian Austen, "Beaver Fever," *Canadian Business Magazine*, 4 April 2002; Yvonne Zacharias, "Roots Sets Its Sights on the 2010 Games," *Vancouver Sun*, 19 May 2004.

2 Canadian Red Cross website [accessed 30 March 2005] www.redcross.ca/cmslib/general/annual_report_2003_2004.pdf

3 Ken Stammen, "Where Big Planes Are Born," *Cincinnati Post*, 12 September 2000, 7C.

4 *IBM 1997 Annual Report*, Annual Report Gallery [accessed 21 April 1999] www.reportgallery.com.

5 *Bombardier Annual Report 2003–2004*, 53.

6 Statistics Canada website [accessed 22 June 22 2004] www.statscan.ca

7 U.S. Department of Commerce, Bureau of Economic Analysis website [accessed 24 September 1999] beadata.bea.doc.gov/bea/dn2/gpoc.htm; "Fortune 1000 Ranked within Industry," *Fortune*, 26 April 1999, F51–F73.

8 *Survey of Current Business* (Washington, DC: GPO, November 1997), Table B8, 132; *Infoplease Almanac*, Infoplease.com [accessed 22 September 1999] www.infoplease.com/ipa/A0302230.html

9 "Fortune 500: Largest Corporations," *Fortune Magazine*, 5 April 2004, B-1.

10 Michael R. Solomon et al., *Consumer Behaviour: Buying, Having, Being* (Toronto: Prentice Hall, 2005), 451.

11 Statistics Canada website [accessed 16 June16 2004] www.statscan.ca; *Statistical Abstract of the United States, 1996* (Washington, DC: GPO, 1996), 56–59, 394, 396.

12 Statistics Canada website [accessed 15 June 2004] www.statscan.ca, CANSIM Table 282-0008.

13 Bombardier website [accessed 31 March 2005] www.bombardier.com/index.jsp; Bombardier Financial Highlights.

14 MEC website [accessed 28 March 2004] www.mec.ca; company facts sheet, provided by Tim Southam, Communications Manager, MEC.

15 Cirque du Soleil website [accessed 19 June 2004] www.cirquedusoleil.com

16 Patrick Brethour, "WestJet Showing Strains of Spreading Its Wings," *The Globe and Mail*, 8 May 2004, B7; Westjet website [accessed 19 June 2004] www.westjet.ca

17 Robert L. Heilbroner and Lester C. Thurow, *Economics Explained* (New York: Simon & Schuster, 1994), 29–30.

18 Heilbroner and Thurow, *Economics Explained*, 250.

19 Heilbroner and Thurow, *Economics Explained*, 250.

20 Greg Steinmetz, "Her Majesty May Sell Part of London's Tube, Angering Some in U.K.," *Wall Street Journal*, 14 October 1999, A1, A12; Erik Eckholm, "Chinese Restate Goals to Reorganize State Companies," *New York Times*, 23 September 1999, A10; Dexter Roberts, "China's New Revolution," *Business Week*, 27 September 1999, 72–78.

21 Department of Finance website [accessed 30 March 2005] www.fin.gc.ca/news04/04-052e.html; Peter Verburg, "Fill'er up," *Canadian Business*, 29 March 2004; Keith Kalawsky, "Sell Low, Hold High," *Canadian Business*, 19 August 2004.

22 Air Canada website [accessed 1 April 2005] www.aircanada.com/en/about/media/facts/profile.html#fleet

23 Jeff Wise, "How Skiboarding Became the New Snowboarding," *New York Times Magazine*, 21 March 1999, 58–61.

24 LivePerson website [accessed 30 April 2005] www.liveperson.com/docs/casestudies/BellCanada_CaseStudy.pdf

25 Kathleen Madigan, "Keep Your Nest Egg Safe—Watch Housing Data," *Business Week*, 17 April 2000, 208–210.

26 Department of Justice Canada website [accessed 17 June 2004] http://laws.justice.gc.ca/en/C-34/35559.html

27 Adam Cohen, "No Split but Microsoft's a Monopolist," *Time*, 9 July 2001, 36–38; Ted Bridis and John R. Wilke, "Judge Orders Microsoft Broken in Two, Imposes Tough Restriction on Practices," *Wall Street Journal*, 8 June 2000, A3, A12; "Judge Suspends Restrictions on Microsoft," *Wall Street Journal*, 21 June 2000, A3; John R. Wilke and Rebecca Buckman, "Justices Decline Early Look at Microsoft," *Wall Street Journal*, 27 September 2000, A3, A17.

28 James Kanter, "Judge Seems Ready to Push Microsoft, EU Toward Deal," *The Globe and Mail*, 1 October 2004, B8.

29 Susan Monroe, "Canadian Bank Mergers Decision," 14 December 1998, Canada Online website [accessed 17 June 2004] http://canadaonline.about.com/library/weekly/aa121498.htm

30 *Merger Review Guidelines*, Department of Finance Canada website [accessed 17 June 2004] www.fin.gc.ca/news01/data/01-014_2e.html

31 Paul Waldie, "Central Bank Suggests Mergers No Threat," *The Globe and Mail*, 11 June 2004, B3.

32 "Privatizing BC Hydro Is Already Costing You Money," BC Citizens for Public Power website [accessed 22 June 2004] www.citizensforpublicpower.ca/articles/may04pluggedin.html

33 "Nortel Networks Provides Update on Status of Restatements and Related Matters and Business Performance," 2 June 2004, Nortel Networks website [accessed 22 June 2004] www.nortelnetworks.com

34 Government of Canada website [accessed 15 June 2004] www.gc.ca/depts/major//depind_e.html

35 Bank of Canada website [accessed 15 June 2004] www.bankofcanada.ca; Jeannine Aversa, "Fed Ends String of Rate Cuts," *Journal-Gazette*, 31 January 2001, 7B.

36 Bank of Canada website [accessed 17 June 2004] www.bankofcanada.ca/en/faq.htm

37 Budget 2004, Department of Finance Canada website [accessed 21 June 2004] www.fin.gc.ca/budget04/bp/bpc3e.htm

38 Tim Richardon, "Build a Better Mouse Trap," *Canadian Business,* 7 July 2004, 74.
39 Grant Buckler, "On-line Bill Paying Seen Gaining Currency Thanks to Merger," *The Globe and Mail,* 30 September 2004, B11.
40 Tavia Grant, "More Turning to E-Business Transactions," *The Globe and Mail,* 21 April 2005, B4.
41 Robert D. Hof, Gary McWilliams, and Gabrielle Saveri, "The Click Here Economy," *Business Week,* 22 June 1998, 122–128; Tim McCollum, "End Your Internet Anxieties Now," *Nation's Business,* April 1999, 19–26.
42 Efraim Turban and David King, *Introduction to E-Commerce* (Upper Saddle River, NJ: Pearson Education, 2003), 292–294; Michael Taylor, "Intranets—A New Technology Changes All the Rules," *Telecommunication,* January 1997, 39–40.
43 "Calling All Workers," Chief Information Officer website [accessed 3 May 2005] www.cio.com/archive/120101/rule_ford.html
44 Efraim Turban and David King, *Introduction to E-Commerce* (Upper Saddle River, NJ: Pearson Education, 2003), 292–294; Stephanie Armour, "Workers Just Click to Enroll for Benefits," *USA Today,* 8 November 2000, B1; Charlene Marmer Solomon, "Sharing Information across Borders and Time Zones," *Global Workforce,* March 1998, 13–18; Eryn Brown, "9 Ways to Win on the Web," *Fortune,* 24 May 1999, 112.
45 Material for this section was taken from Courtland L. Bovée and John V. Thill, *Business Communication Today,* 6th ed. (Upper Saddle River, NJ: Prentice Hall, 1999), 348–352.
46 Efraim Turban and David King, *Introduction to E-Commerce* (Upper Saddle River, NJ: Pearson Education, 2003), 237–238; John R. L. Rizza, "Extranets: The Internet Gets Down to Business," *Entrepreneurial Edge, 3,* 1998, 76–78; Samuel Greengard, "Extranets Linking Employees with Your Vendors," *Workforce,* November 1997, 28–34.
47 Andy Reinhardt, "The Paperless Manual," *Business Week e.Biz,* 18 September 2000, EB92.
48 Trevor Marshall, "Cashing Out," *Backbone Magazine,* January/February 2005, 27.
49 "Electronic Commerce and Technology," Statistics Canada website [accessed 5 May 2005] www.statcan.ca/Daily/English/050420/d050420b.htm
50 Steffano Korper and Juanita Ellis, *The E-Commerce Book: Building the E-Empire* (San Diego, CA: Academic Press, 2000), 80; Rodes Fishburne, Alex Frankel, Michelle Jeffers, Scott Lajoie, and Lee Patterson, "Voices of the Revolution," *Forbes ASAP,* 21 February 2000, 80–86.
51 Efraim Turban, Jae Lee, David King, and H. Michael Chung, *Electronic Commerce, A Managerial Perspective* (Upper Saddle River, NJ: Prentice Hall, 2000), 15–16.
52 Dell website [accessed 1 April 2005] www.dell.com/; Laurie Windham, *Dead Ahead* (New York: Allworth Press, 1999), 31–32.
53 Michelle Halpern, "Putting Best Deals Online," *Marketing,* 25 October 2004, 6; Walid Mougayar, *Opening Digital Markets* (New York: McGraw-Hill, 1998), 29–35.
54 Turban et al., *Electronic Commerce, A Managerial Perspective,* 15–16.
55 Korper and Ellis, *The E-Commerce Book: Building the E-Empire,* 4.
56 Kalakota and Robinson, *E-Business Roadmap for Success,* 22–23.
57 Peter Wolchack, "Racing to Catch Up," *Backbone,* November/December 2004, 35.
58 Paul Lima, "Entrepreneurs Tap Virtual Success on eBay," *The Globe and Mail,* 2 December 2004, B11.
59 Jim Middlemiss, "Message Mines," *Backbone,* March/April 2005, 14–18.
60 Brent Janh, "E-Sleuths Dissect WestJet Hard Drives," *The Globe and Mail, 29* November 2004, B1.
61 Sinclair Stewart, "Exodus at CIBC Unabated by Suit," *The Globe and Mail,* 7 January 2005, B1, B4; Shirley Won, "ATI E-mails May Be Used in Hearing, OSC Rules," *The Globe and Mail,* 14 April 2005, B6.
62 Christa Degnan, "Firings Renew Debate over E-Mail Policies," *PC Week Online,* 6 December 1999, www.zdnet.com.
63 Get Net Wise website [accessed 1 April 2005] www.getnetwise.org/glossary.php#S
64 Simon Avery, "Hacker Alert: Report Finds Surge in On-Line Attacks," *The Globe and Mail,* 21 March 2005, B1.
65 About Internet2 website [accessed 1 April 2005] www.internet2.edu/about/; Scott Thurm, "New and Improved," *Wall Street Journal,* 11 February 2002, R13.
66 Samuel Greengard, "How Secure Is Your Data?" *Workforce,* May 1998, 52–60; Nikhil Hutheesing and Philip E. Ross, "Hackerphobia," *Forbes,* 23 March 1998, 150–154.
67 Simon Avery, "Hacker Alert: Report Finds Surge in On-Line Attacks," *The Globe and Mail,* 21 March 2005, B1.
68 Mark Blanchford, "A Day in the Life of Superhighway Cops," *The Globe and Mail,* 7 October 2004, B15.
69 George Butters, "Cyberspace Confidential: Protecting Your Words," *The Globe and Mail,* 7 October 2004, B17; "Corporate Security Gets Urgent: 10 Tips for Creating a Network Security Policy," *Interactive Week,* 23 October 2001, techupdate.zdnet.com/techupdate/stories/main/0,14179,2819412-9,00.html.
70 Mark Blanchford, "A Day in the Life of Superhighway Cops," *The Globe and Mail,* 7 October 2004, B15; Richard Behar, "Fear along the Firewall," *Fortune,* 15 October 2001, 145–148; Brian Fonseca, "Study: Viruses Cost $12B in '99, *InfoWorld.com,* 17 January 2000 [cited 5 November 2001] www.computerworld.com.
71 David S. Bernstein, "We've Been Hacked," *Inc. Tech 2000,* no. 3, 1061.
72 Amanda Lang, "Hockey Night in Forest Hill"; Marina Strauss, "How HBC Swept Roots for the Games"; Marina Strauss, "Roots Hopes to Get the Gold from Olympic Buzz"; Marina Strauss, "Budman Puts Down Roots in Europe"; Melanie Wells, "Reach for the Sky"; Roots website [accessed 1 April 2005] www.roots.com/new_canada/html/pc_company_profile.shtml; Ian Austen, "Beaver Fever"; Yvonne Zacharias, "Roots Sets Its Sights on the 2010 Games".

Appendix A

1 Small Business Information Canada, "Top Level Domain" [accessed 23 December 2004] http://sbinfocanada.about.com/library/glossary/bldef-topdomain.htm
2 Paul Lima, "Hit Me!" *Backbone Magazine,* November/December 2004, 24; Jason Zien, "Measuring the Internet," About.com, 13 July 1999 [accessed 17 July 1999] internet.about.com/library/weekly/1999/aa071399a.htm; "FAST Aims for Largest Index," Search Engine Watch, 4 May 1999 [accessed 17 July 1999] searchenginewatch.internet.com/sere-port/99/05-fast.htm
3 Peter Wolchack, *Backbone Magazine,* November/December 2004, 16.
4 Paul Lima, "Hit Me!" *Backbone Magazine,* November/December 2004, 24.
5 Colussus Search Engine [accessed 23 December 2004] www.searchengine colossus.com/Canada.html; Ernest L. Maier, Anthony J. Faria, Peter Kaatrude, and Elizabeth Wood, *The Business Library and How to Use It* (Detroit: Omnigraphics, 1996), 84–97; Matt Lake, "Desperately Seeking Susan OR Suzie NOT Sushi," *New York Times,* 3 September 1998, D1, D7.

Chapter 2

1 Adapted from Regina Fazio Maruca, "The Right Way to Go Global," *Harvard Business Review,* March–April 1994, 135–145; Deborah Duarte and Nancy Snyder, "From Experience: Facilitating Global Organizational Learning in Product Development at Whirlpool Corporation," *Journal of Product Innovation Management, 14*(1) (January 1997): 48–55; Joe Jancsurak, "Whirlpool: U.S. Leader Pursues Global Blueprint," *Appliance Manufacturer, 45*(2) (February 1997): G21; Carl Quintanilla, "Despite Setbacks, Whirlpool Pursues Overseas Markets," *Wall Street Journal,* 9 December 1997, B4; Ian Katz, "Whirlpool: In the Wringer," *Business Week,* 14 December 1998, 831; Gale Cutler, "Asia Challenges Whirlpool Technology," *Research Technology Management,* September–October 1998, 4–6; "Whirlpool Europe and Tupperware Europe Announce Strategic Alliance," *Whirlpool*

Investor Relations, 28 April 1999, Whirlpool website [accessed 2 April 2005], www.whirlpoolcorp.com; Whirlpool Canada website [accessed 25 June 2004] www.whirlpoolcanada.com

2 Denis Seguin, "The Battle for Hollywood North," *Canadian Business*, 15 September 2003, 55–62.

3 UPS website [accessed 4 March 2005] www.shareholder.com/ups/downloads/factsheet.pdf, www.shareholder.com/ups/downloads/2003_Annual_Report.pdf; John Alden, "What in the World Drives UPS?" *International Business*, March/April 1998, 6–7;

4 "Getting It Right in Japan," *International Business*, May–June 1997, 19.

5 Peter Wonacott, Joseph B. White, and Norihiko Shirouz, "3 Billion Investment by GM Revs Up China's Car Industry," *The Globe and Mail* (original source WSJ.com), 8 June 2004, B13.

6 Corruption of Foreign Public Officials website [accessed 7 July 2004] www.bbnglobal.com/cpfpo_act.html

7 "Officially Supported Export Credits," OECD website [accessed 6 July 2004] www.oecd.com

8 James Wilfong and Toni Seger, *Taking Your Business Global* (Franklin Lakes, NJ: Career Press, 1997), 289.

9 Export Development Canada website [accessed 2 July 2004] www.edc.ca

10 Jules Abend, "Jockey Colors Its World," *Bobbin*, February 1999, 50–54.

11 Ricky W. Griffin and Michael W. Pustay, *International Business* (Reading, MA: Addison-Wesley, 1999), 415.

12 "Padgett Surveys Franchise/Small Business Sectors," *Franchising World*, March–April 1995, 46; John Stansworth, "Penetrating the Myths Surrounding Franchise Failure Rates—Some Old Lessons for New Business," *International Small Business Journal*, January–March 1995, 59–63; Laura Koss-Feder, "Building Better Franchise Relations," *Hotel & Motel Management*, 6 March 1995, 18; Carol Steinberg, "Franchise Fever," *World Trade*, July 1992, 86, 88, 90–91; John O'Dell, "Franchising America," *Los Angeles Times*, 25 June 1989, sec. IV, 1.

13 Dori Jones Yang, "An American (Coffee) in Paris—and Rome," *U.S. News and World Report*, 19 February 2001, 47.

14 Star Alliance website [accessed 28 June 2004] www.staralliance.com

15 "GM to Build new SUV at Ontario Plant," *Reuters*, 4 September 2002.

16 Lewis M. Simons, "High-Tech Jobs for Sale," *Time*, 22 July 1996, 59.

17 John Partridge, "Bombardier Holding off on China Plant," *The Globe and Mail*, 29 June 2004, B9.

18 Bertrand Marotte, "Couche-Tard's Head Store Clerk Corners Market by Adaptation," 2 April 2005, B4; Bertrand Marotte, "Clearing a Direct Path to the Cooler," 2 April 2005, B4; Couche-Tard website [accessed 7 July 2004] www.couche-tard.ca

19 Alden, "What in the World Drives UPS?" 6–7.

20 Ernest Beck and Emily Nelson, "As Wal-Mart Invades Europe, Rivals Rush to Match Its Formula," *Wall Street Journal*, 6 October 1999, A1, A6.

21 Rob Ferguson, "Canada Losing Ground in Foreign Investment," *Toronto Star*, Fall 2003; Press Release, 17 September 2003, A.T. Kearney website [accessed 27 April 2004] www.atkearney.com

22 Paulo Prado and Bruce Orwall, "A Certain 'Je Ne Sais Quoi' at Disney's New Park." *Wall Street Journal*, 12 March 2002, B1, B4.

23 Brian O'Keefe, "Global Brands," *Fortune*, 26 November 2001, 102–110.

24 Tara Parket-Pope, "Custom-Made," *Wall Street Journal*, 26 September 1996, R22–R23.

25 CBC videos, "Field of Seeds," 2002; Spitz Sales Inc. website [accessed 28 June 2004] www.spitzsales.com

26 Holley H. Ulbrich and Mellie L. Warner, *Managerial Economics* (New York: Barron's Educational Series, 1990), 190.

27 Strategis website [accessed 5 April 2005] http://strategis.gc.ca/sc_mrkti/tdst/tdo/tdo.php#tag; Jeff Sanford, "How to Cash in on Global Trade," *Canadian Business*, 7–20 June, 69.

28 "Balance of Payments," Government of Canada website [accessed 2 April 2005], http://canadianeconomy.gc.ca/english/economy/balance_payment.html

29 Robert J. Samuelson, "Trading with the Enemy," *Newsweek*, 1 April 1996, 41; Amy Borrus, Pete Engardio, and Dexter Roberts, "The New Trade Superpower," *Business Week*, 16 October 1995, 56–57; David A. Andelman, "Marco Polo Revisited," *American Management Journal*, August 1995, 10–12; John Greenwald, "Get Asia Now, Pay Later," *Time*, 10 October 1994, 61; Simons, "High-Tech Jobs for Sale," 59.

30 Thomas Watson, "Trade Wars: The U.S. Often Preaches Free Trade—but Often Practices Protectionism," *Canadian Business*, 29 December–18 January 2004, 38, 39.

31 Sandra Cordon, "Beef Dispute with U.S. Could Hurt Liberals," *The Globe and Mail*, 9 June 2004, A7; "Where's the Beef?" *Canadian Business*, 29 March–11 April, 9.

32 Eric Schmitt, "U.S. Backs Off Sanctions, Seeing Poor Effect Abroad," *New York Times*, 31 July 1998, A1, A6; Robert T. Gray, "Book Review," *Nation's Business*, January 1999, 47.

33 "Saudi Arabia Hopes to Join WTO by 2002," *Reuters Business Report*, 3 August 1997.

34 Matthew McClearn, "I Can't Believe It's Not Better," *Canadian Business*, 29 December–18 January 2004, 31–36.

35 Greg Keenan, "NAFTA 'Unreasonable, Toyota Says," *The Globe and Mail*, 28 June 2004, B17.

36 Barrie McKenna, "Canada Hails U.S. Decision to Relent on Lumber Duties," *The Globe and Mail*, 4 June 2004, B10.

37 Stephen Mertl, "New Faces at Softwood Lumber Talks Won't Mask Long-Standing Differences," *Canadian Press*, 28 March 2005, CBC website [accessed 2 April 2005].

38 James Cox, "Tariffs Shield Some U.S. Products," *USA Today*, 6 May 1999, 1B, 2B.

39 IMF website [accessed 28 June 2004] www.imf.org

40 Michael M. Phillips, "One by One," *Wall Street Journal*, 26 April 1999, R4, R7.

41 Christopher Koch. "It's a Wired, Wired World," *Webmaster*, March 1997, 50–55.

42 APEC website [accessed 5 April 2005] www.apecsec.org.sg/apec/about_apec.html; "APEC Ministers Commit to Sustainable Development," *Xinhau News Agency*, 11 June 1997; Fred C. Bergsten, "An Asian Push for World-Wide Free Trade: The Case For APEC," *The Economist*, 6 January 1996, 62; "U.S. Must Press to Reduce Trade Barriers in Asia, Pacific, Congress Told," *Gannett News Service*, 1995.

43 Masaaki Kotabe and Maria Cecilia Coutinho de Arruda, "South America's Free Trade Gambit," *Marketing Management*, Spring 1998, 3936.

44 "Grand Illusions," *The Economist*, 4 March 1995, 87; Bob Davis, "Global Paradox: Growth of Trade Binds Nations, But It Also Can Spur Separatism," *Wall Street Journal*, 20 June 1994, A1, A6; Barbara Rudolph, "Megamarket," *Time*, 10 August 1992, 43–44; Peter Truell, "Free Trade May Suffer from Regional Blocs," *Wall Street Journal*, 1 July 1991, A1.

45 Patrice M. Jones, "Leaving Trade Pact's Woes Behind," *Chicago Tribune*, 10 May 2000, sec. 3, 42.

46 Rafael A. Lecuona, "Economic Integration: NAFTA and MERCOSUR, A Comparative Analysis," *International Journal on World Peace*, December 1999, 27–49.

47 Emeric Lepourte, "Europe's Challenge to the U.S. in South America's Biggest Market," *Christian Science Monitor*, 8 April 1997, 19; Mario Osava, "Mercosur: Free Trade with Europe More Advantageous Than FTAA," *Inter Press English News Wire*, 6 May 1997; Robert Maynard, "At a Crossroads in Latin America," *Nation's Business*, April 1996, 38–39; Gregory L. Miles and Loubna Freih, "Join the Caribbean Revolution," *International Business*, September 1994, 42–54; Matt Moffett, "Spreading the Gospel," *Wall Street Journal*, 28 October 1994, R12.

48 Europa website [accessed 6 July 2004] http://europa.eu.int/abc/print_index_en.htm

49 Mitchener, "Increasingly Rules of Global Economy Are Set in Brussels," A1, A10.

50 Thomas Kamm, "EU Certifies Participants for Euro," *Wall Street Journal*, 26 March 1998, A14; Mitchener, "Increasingly Rules of Global Economy Are Set in Brussels," A1, A10.
51 Europa website [accessed 6 April 2005] http://europa.eu.int/abc/12lessons/index7_en.htm#
52 CNN Website, "Sweden: Euro Fallout Feared," 15 September 2003, http://edition.cnn.com/2003/WORLD/europe/09/15/sweden.euro/, [accessed: 6 April 2005].
53 Thane Peterson, "The Euro," *Business Week*, 27 April 1998, 90–94; Joan Warner, "The Great Money Bazaar," *Business Week*, 27 April 1998, 96–98; Gail Edmondson, "Industrial Evolution," *Business Week*, 27 April 1998, 100–101.
54 Doug Sanders, "Budget Crisis Threatens EU," *The Globe and Mail*, 16 June 2005, B1, B17; Barrie McKenna, "Euro Plunges as Continental Drift Widens," *The Globe and Mail*, 2 June 2005, B18.
55 Lecuona, "Economic Integration: NAFTA and MERCOSUR, A Comparative Analysis."
56 Anthony DePalma, "With the U.S. Economy Slumping, Canada and Mexico Are Reeling," *New York Times*, 17 December 2001, C13.
57 Geri Smith, "Betting on Free Trade," *Business Week*, 23 April 2001, 60–62.
58 Roy MacGregor, "A Small World Grows Ever Smaller, and Checking Out Isn't an Option," *The Globe and Mail*, 8 July 2005, A2.
59 KFC Fact Sheet, Hoovers website [accessed 6 April 2005] www.hoovers.com/kfc/—ID__56325—/free-co-factsheet.xhtml; Brian O'Keefe, "Global Brands," *Fortune*, 26 November 2001, 102–110.
60 See Note 1.
61 Simon Tuck, "Canada Must Axe Duties on Steel, Tribunal Sides with Foreign Firms," *The Globe and Mail*, 6 July 2004, B6.

Chapter 3

1 *Corporate Knights*, *3*(1), July 2004, 24–25; Telus website [accessed 10 April 2005] http://about.telus.com/downloads/investor-factsheet.pdf; 2003 Corporate Social Responsibility Report, Telus website [accessed 7 July 2004].
2 Karin Kovalsky, "Spy vs. Spy," *Canadian Business*, 13 February 2005, 33–43; Brent Jang, "Airline Says Trash Data a Treasure," *The Globe and Mail*, 25 November 2004, B1; John Partridge, "Air Canada Had WestJet Executive's Trash Digitally Reconstructed," *The Globe and Mail*, 30 June 2004, B1; "Air Canada Tries to Implicate WestJet CEO," *The Globe and Mail*, 6 July 2004, B3; John Partridge, "WestJet Says Air Canada Grandstanding in Dispute," *The Globe and Mail*, 7 July 2004, B5.
3 Michael McCarthy, "Recent Crop of Sneaky Ads Backfires," *USA Today*, 17 July 2001, 3B; "Publishers Clearing House Strikes Deceptive-Practices Accord," *New York Times*, 23 August 2000, A16.
4 Aaron Bernstein, Brian Grow, Darnell Little, Stanley Holmes, and Diane Brady, "Bracing for a Backlash," *Business Week*, 4 February 2002, 32–36.
5 Suzanne Wooley, "The Hustlers Queue Up on the Net," *Business Week*, 20 November 1995, 146–148.
6 Claudia Cattaneo, "Judge Orders Release of Secret Bre-X Report," *The Financial Post*, 8 January 1998.
7 National Fraud Information Center website [accessed 12 July 2004] media@nclnet.org
8 John S. McClenahen, "Your Employees Know Better," *Industry Week*, 1 March 1999, 12–14.
9 Betsy Stevens, "Communicating Ethical Values: A Study of Employee Perceptions," *Journal of Business Ethics*, June 1999, 113–120.
10 Petro-Canada website (Corporate Governance section) [accessed 4 July 2004] www.petro-canada.ca
11 Milton Bordwin, "The Three R's of Ethics," *Management Review*, June 1998, 59–61.
12 Code of Business Conduct, Bell Canada website [accessed 9 April 2005] www.bce.ca
13 Luma Muhtadie, "Canadians Want Whistle-Blowers Protected," *The Globe and Mail*, 28 October 2003.
14 Bank of Montreal website (Code of Conduct) [accessed 12 July 2004] www.bmo.ca
15 Bethany Mclean, "Why Enron Went Bust," *Fortune*, 24 December 2001, 59–68.
16 Kurt Eichenwald, "Canadian Bank Agrees to Pay Fine and Drop Unit in Enron Case," 23 December 2003, *New York Times* website [accessed 1 June 2004] www.nytimes.com/2003/12/23/business/23enron.html
17 Michael Tackett, "Enron's Fall Piques Congress' Interest in 401(k) Rules," *Chicago Tribune*, 25 January 2002, sec. 1, 1, 12.
18 Fred Tam, "Proper Controls Needed After Enron Debacle," *Business Times*, 14 February 2002, 18.
19 Bethany McLean, "Monster Mess," *Fortune*, 4 February 2002, 93–96.
20 Daniel Kadlec, "Who's Accountable?" *Time*, 21 January 2002, 28–34.
21 E.A. Torriero and Robert Manor, "Jury Finds Andersen Guilty," *Chicago Tribune*, 16 June 2002, sec. 1, 1, 12.
22 Environmental Protection Review Canada website [accessed 9 July 2004] www.eprc-rpec.gc.ca
23 Government of Canada (North American Agreement on Environmental Cooperation) website [accessed 6 April 2005] www.naaec.gc.ca/eng/agreement/agreement_e.htm
24 Zena Olijnyk, "Smells Like Victory," *Canadian Business Magazine*, August 17, 2001.
25 Eric Reguly, "Without U.S., Kyoto Is Wishful Thinking," *The Globe and Mail*, 5 July 2005, B2.
26 Eric Reguly, "Stop Whining, Kyoto's Here to Stay, So Learn to Love Emissions Trading," *The Globe and Mail*, 15 July 2004, B2.
27 Government of Canada website [accessed 6 April 2005] www.climatechange.gc.ca/cop/cop6_hague/english/overview_e.html; Eric Reguly, "Russia Puts Canada in a Kyoto Bind," *The Globe and Mail*, 5 October 2004, B2; Bill Kaufman, "Canada: Harper Will Kill Kyoto Protocol," *Calgary Sun*, 10 June 2004; The United Nations Framework Convention on Climate Change website [accessed 23 July 2004] http://int/resource/convkp.html; Joe Paraskevas, "Chretien Signs Kyoto Agreement," *Calgary Herald*, 17 December 2002.
28 Steven Chase and Greg Keenan, "Ottawa Gets Auto Emissions Deal," *The Globe and Mail*, 23 March 2005, B1; Patrick Brethour, "Canada's Big Emitters Brace for Investment Climate Change," *The Globe and Mail*, 19 February 2005, B4.
29 Cascades corporate newspaper release, May 2004, 8.
30 "Business of Social Responsibility," *Businessline*, 3 August 1999, 1.
31 "Does It Pay to Be Ethical?" *Business Ethics*, March-April 1997, 14–16; Don L. Boroughs, "The Bottom Line on Ethics," *U.S. News &; World Report*, 20 March 1995, 61–66.
32 Edward O. Welles, "Ben's Big Flop," *Inc.*, September 1998, 401; Constance L. Hays, "Getting Serious at Ben & Jerry's," *New York Times*, 22 May 1998, C1, C3.
33 Canadian Standards website [accessed 11 April 2005] www.csa.ca
34 Consumer Packaging and Labelling Act, Department of Justice Canada website [accessed 21 July 2004] http://laws.justice.gc.ca/en/c-38/36740.html
35 Patrick Bethour and Janet McFarland, "Forzani Agrees to Pay Record Settlement," *The Globe and Mail*, 7 July 2004, B1, B22.
36 Marina Strauss and Simon Tuck, "Tribunal Rules Sears Broke Law by Inflating Tire Savings," *The Globe and Mail*, 25 January 2005, B1, B8.
37 "New Cigarette Pack Warning Labels Appear," 22 December 2000, Health Canada website [accessed 22 July 2004] www.hc-sc.gc.ca/english/media/releases/2000/2000_21_tob-label.htm
38 Wendy Stueck, "Natives Hope for Big Gains from Inco's Nickel Riches," *The Globe and Mail*, 17 June 2004, B5; Wendy Stueck, "Voisey's Bay at Last Getting Off the Ground," *The Globe and Mail*, 17 June 2004, B1, B4; Peter Kennedy, "Inco Advances

Voisey's Startup by Six Months," *The Globe and Mail,* 21 July 2004, B4; Inco website (Voisey's Bay) [accessed 10 April 2005] www.inco.com/about/development/voisey/
39 Thomas A. Fogarty, "Corporations Use Causes for Effect," *USA Today*, 10 November 1997, 7B; Peaceworks website [accessed 22 June 1999] www.peaceworks.net; Florence Fabricant, "A Young Entrepreneur Makes Food, Not War," *New York Times*, 30 November 1996, sec. International Business, 21.
40 Laura Bogolmy, "The Bar Is Set-High," *Canadian Business,* 19 July–15 August 2004, 44–45.
41 Matthew McClearn, "Reformation: Alliance Atlantis Communications Inc.," *Canadian Business Magazine,* 5–18 August 2003, 55.
42 Employment Equity Act, Department of Justice website [accessed 8 July 2004] http://laws.justice.gc.ca/en/E-5.401/50057.html
43 Valerie Merchant, "The New Face of Work," 29 March 2004, *Canadian Business* website [accessed 22 July 2004] www.canadianbusiness.com/shared/print.jsp?content=20040329 5914859148
44 Canadian Centre for Occupational Health and Safety website [accessed 22 July 2004] www.ccohs.ca/ccohs.html
45 Sustainability Report Ranking, *Corporate Knights, 3*(1), 30.
46 See Note 1.
47 Tavia Grant, "More Turning to E-Business Transactions," *The Globe and Mail*, 21 April 2005, B4; Statistics Canada, "Electronic Commerce and Technology [accessed 9 May 2005] www.statcan.ca/Daily/English/050420/d050420b.htm; Sarah Lacy, "America: Still the High-Speed Laggard," *Business Week Online*, 6 April 2005; Dave Ebner, "The World's Most Connected Place," *The Globe and Mail*, 14 September 2004, I6; Diedre McMurdy, "Joys of Online Shopping," *Montreal Gazette*, 11 December 2003; Neal E. Boudette, "In Europe, Surfing a Web of Red Tape," *Wall Street Journal*, 29 October 1999, B1; Mark Landler, "Asia-Pacific: In China, Malaysia, and Singapore, Freedom and Control Dance a Digital Minute," *Strategy & Business*, First Quarter 2000, 72–75; Terry McCarthy, "China's Internet Gold Rush," *Time*, 28 February 2000, 50–51; James Cox, "E-Opportunity Abounds in China," *USA Today*, 27 April 2000, 3B; Martin Vander Weyer, "Globalism vs. Nationalism vs. E-business The World Debates," *Strategy & Business*, First Quarter 2000, 63–72; Walid Mougayar, *Opening Digital Markets* (New York: McGraw-Hill, 1998), 39–41; Stephanie Gruner, "Late to the Party," *Wall Street Journal*, 12 July 1999, R25; Andersen Consulting, "Europe Poised for Take-Off," Andersen Consulting website [accessed 2 May 2000] www.ac.com/ecommerce/ecom_efuture.html; David H. Freedman, "The Maybe Restoration," *Forbes ASAP*, 21 February 2000, 55–62; Peter Landers, "Electronics E-Commerce in Japan Is Held Back by Retail Traditions," *Wall Street Journal*, 30 March 2000, A22; Mohanbir Sawhney and Sumant Mandal, "Go Global," *Business 2.0*, May 2000, 178–215; Julie Schmitt, "Tech Tripping on Tradition," *USA Today*, 25 March 1999, 3B; Jim Rohwer, "Japan's Quiet Corporate Revolution," *Fortune*, 30 March 1998, 82–92; Irene M. Kunii and Brian Bremner, "Will Technology Leave Japan Behind?" *Business Week*, 31 August 1998, 124–126; Julie Schmit, "Asia's Culture Hampers Internet Commerce," *USA Today*, 16 February 1999, 6B; "On the Continent, On the Cusp," *New York Times*, 14 May 2000, sec. 3, 1, 18–19; Julie Schmit, "Japan Undergoes E-Makeover," *USA Today*, 19 April 2000, 1B, 2B; Justin Fox, "Surprise! Europe Has Web Fever," *Fortune*, 12 June 2000, 219–224.

Chapter 4

1 Diedre McMurdy, "Opportunity Knocks—Hard," *Canadian Business,* 10 December 2001; Randy Burns, Mission-Itech VP of marketing [3 August 2004]; Mission-Itech website [accessed 13 April 2005] www.itech.com; "Mission Hockey Merges with Itech," SkateLog.com website [accessed 30 June 2004] www.skatelog.com/skates/mission/2004-05-itech-merger.htm
2 Small Business Statistics, Industry Canada website [accessed 13 April 2005] http://strategis.ic.gc.ca/epic/internet/insbrp-rppe.nsf/en/rd00999e.html
3 Industry Canada website [accessed 14 April 2005] www.ic.gc.ca
4 Jim Hopkins, "Entrepreneur 101: Supervising Employees," *USA Today*, 12 September 2001, 9B; Claudia H. Deutsch, "When a Big Company Hatches a Lot of Little Ideas," *New York Times*, 23 September 1998, D4.
5 Industry Canada website [accessed 28 July 2004] http://strategis.ic.gc.ca/ssg/me000053.html
6 Small Business Statistics, Industry Canada website [accessed 27 July 2004] www.strategis.gc.ca/sbstatistics, 37.
7 Annabelle King, "Hang 'em High," *The Gazette* (Montreal), 2 July 2004, B1.
8 LeapFrog website [accessed 20 March 2002] www.leapfrogtoys.com
9 Adapted by Robert Soroka, Aux Soins Communicare website [accessed 10 April 2005] www.auxsoinscommunicare.com; Canadian Homecare Association/Canadienne de Soins a Domicile website [accessed 30 March 2005] www.cdnhome-care.on.ca; Statistics Canada, Community Profile: Montreal, www.hc-sc.gc.ca/seniors-aines/pubs/factoids/2001/pdf/1-30_f.pdf
10 "Matters of Fact," *Inc.*, April 1985, 32.
11 Annual Report 2004, Magna website [accessed 14 April 2005] http://library.corporate-ir.net/library/86/863/86334/items/144107/fullar.pdf
12 Brian O'Reilly, "The New Face of Small Business," *Fortune*, 2 May 1994, 82–88.
13 Michael Moeller, Steve Hamm, and Timothy J. Mullaney, "Remaking Microsoft," *Business Week*, 17 May 1999, 106–116.
14 Timothy D. Schelhardt, "David in Goliath," *Wall Street Journal*, 23 May 1996, R14; Deutsch, "When a Big Company Hatches a Lot of Little Ideas."
15 Angela Pacienza, "Job Website Serves Retired Workers," *The Globe and Mail,* 9 June 2004, C10.
16 *Inc. Special Edition—The State of Small Business 1997*, 20 May 1997, 112; James Wilfong and Toni Seger, *Taking Your Business Global* (Franklin Lakes, NJ: Career Press, 1997), 84
17 Rob Shaw, "Small Business Driving Growth, and Women Are in Control," *The Globe and Mail,* 29 June 2005, B3.
18 Small Business Statistics, Industry Canada [accessed 27 July 2004] www.strategis.gc.ca/sbstatistics, 33.
19 CIBC World Markets, "Start Me Up: A Look at New Entrepreneurs in Canada," *Canadaone Magazine* website [accessed 26 July 2004] www.canadaone.com/ezine/july04/small_business_startups.html
20 Michael Ryval, "Making a Statement On-Line," *The Globe and Mail,* 17 March 2005, B8.
21 Tony Martin, "Home-Business Operator Learns Her Lessons," *The Globe and Mail,* 17 July 2004, B8.
22 CIBC World Markets, "Start Me Up: A Look at New Entrepreneurs in Canada," *Canadaone Magazine* website [accessed 26 July 2004] www.canadaone.com/ezine/july04/small_business_startups.html
23 Wilfong and Seger, *Taking Your Business Global*, 78–80; Kelly J. Andrews, "Born or Bred?" *Entrepreneurial Edge, 3* (1998), 24–28.
24 Jane Applegate, *Succeeding in Small Business* (New York: Plume/Penguin, 1992), 1.
25 Jill Mahoney, "How Running Room's Founder Stays on Track," *The Globe and Mail,* 14 July 2004, B1; Running Room website [accessed 14 April 2005] www.runningroom.com/content/?id=124
26 Richard Bloom, "How to Sell Your Idea to the Money Men," *The Globe and Mail*, 20 October 2004, E5.
27 Norm Brodsky, "Caveat Emptor," *Inc.*, August 1998, 31–32; "Why Buy a Business?" CCH Toolkit website [accessed 20 May 1999] aol.toolkit.cch.com/text/PO1_0820.asp
28 *Montreal Entrepreneur's Guidebook*, 2nd edition (Youth Employment Services

Publication, 1999) 3-58, 3-59; Canadian Franchise Association website [accessed 29 July 2004] www.cfa.ca
29 International Franchise Association website [accessed 29 July 2004] www.franchise.org/intl/cprof/n-america.asp
30 Roberta Maynard, "Choosing a Franchise," *Nation's Business*, October 1996, 56–63.
31 Jeffrey A. Tannenbaum, "Taking a Bath," *Wall Street Journal*, 22 June 1998, 27.
32 World Franchising website [accessed 29 July 2004] www.worldfranchising.com/profiles/harveysrest.htm
33 Cara Operations Limited website [accessed 13 April 2005] www.cara.com/divisions.html
34 Michael Hopkins, "Zen and the Art of the Self-Managed Company," *Inc.*, November 2000, 54–63.
35 Joseph W. Duncan, "The True Failure Rate of Start-Ups," *D&B Reports*, January–February 1994; Maggie Jones, "Smart Cookies," *Working Woman*, April 1995, 50–52; Janice Maloney, "Failure May Not Be So Bad After All," *New York Times*, 23 September 1998, 12.
36 Marina Strauss, "Roots Hopes to Get the Gold from Olympic Buzz," *The Globe and Mail*, 27 July 2004, B1, B21; Marina Strauss, "Budman Puts Down Roots in Europe," *The Globe and Mail*, 9 June 2004, B5; Melanie Wells, "Reach for the Sky," *Forbes Magazine*, 7 August 2000.
37 Jerry Useem, "The Secret of My Success," *Inc.*, May 1998, 67–80
38 Maloney, "Failure May Not Be So Bad After All."
39 Loren Fox, "Hatching New Companies," *Upside*, February 2000, 144–152.
40 AgriTECH website [accessed 29 July 2004] www.agritechpark.com/services.html; CEIM website [accessed 29 July 2004] www.ceim.org/english.html; Toronto Fashion Incubator [accessed 29 July 2004] www.fasionincubator.ca/
41 Dale Buss, "Bringing New Firms out of Their Shell," *Nation's Business*, March 1997, 48–50; Fox, "Hatching New Companies."
42 Jonathan Katz, "Hatching Ideas," *Industry Week*, 18 September 2000, 63–65.
43 McGarvey, "Peak Performance."
44 Andrew Willis, "Scaled-Down Brick IPO Not a Bad Omen," *The Globe and Mail*, 20 July 2004, B16; Hoovers website [accessed 3 August 2004] www.hoovers.com
45 Jim Hopkins, "Corporate Giants Bankroll Start-Ups," *USA Today*, 29 March 2001, B1.
46 Bob Zider, "How Venture Capital Works," *Harvard Business Review*, November/December 1998, 131–139.
47 Shirley Won, "Wooing the Money Men," *The Globe and Mail*, 17 March 2005, C1.
48 Dori Jones Yang, "Venture Capitalists Seek Less Adventure," *U.S. News & World Report*, 4 June 2001, 39.
49 Charles B. Crawford, *Montreal Entrepreneur's Guidebook*, 1999, 7–33.
50 CBC video; *Crazy Plates* website [accessed 3 August 2004) www.crazyplates.com
51 Rodney Ho, "Banking on Plastic," *Wall Street Journal*, 9 March 1998, A1, A8.
52 Joel Russell, "Credit Card Capitalism," *Hispanic Business*, March 1998, 40.
53 Small Business Statistics, Industry Canada website [accessed 27 July 2004] www.strategis.gc.ca/sbstatistics, 11.
54 See Note 1.

Chapter 5
1 Konrad Yakabuski, "The Builder," *Report on Business Magazine*, October 2004, 85–96; Peter Shawn Taylor, "Home Fires Burning," *Canadian Business*, 11–24 October, 77–83; Haris Anwar, "Rona Eyes Continued Canadian Expansion," *The Globe and Mail*, 26 March 2005, B6; Patrick Brethour, "Rona Builds Up Alberta Business," *The Globe and Mail*, 22 December 2004, B1; Allan Swift, "Expansion Helps Power Rona Profit 77% in 2004," *The Globe and Mail*, 24 February 2005, B5; Zena Olijnyk, "Handy Woman," *Canadian Business*, 9 November 2003, 33–36; Rona website [accessed 11 November 2004] www.rona.ca/webapp/wcs/stores/servlet/rona/rona_corpo.jsp?sectionId=218&storeId=10001&langId=-1&catalogId=10051&parent_category_rn=0&invest=1; Home Hardware website [accessed 11 November 2004] www.homehardware.ca/index.htm
2 Norman M. Scarborough and Thomas W. Zimmerer, *Effective Small Business Management* (Upper Saddle River, NJ: Prentice Hall, 2000), 84.
3 "LLP Legislation Proclaimed in Manitoba," *CA Folio Newsletter, 121*, March/April 2003 [accessed 25 November 2004] www.icam.mb.ca/pdf/Folio121.pdf; McGill Legal Information Clinic Hotline [accessed 12 November 2005]; Scott A. Cambell, "Extra-Provincial Limited Liability Partnerships," *Business Beat, 11*(2), May 2001 [accessed 14 November 2004] www.mcleankerr.com/pdfs/LLP.PDF
4 James W. Cortada, "Do You Take This Partner," *Total Quality Review*, November–December 1995, 11.
5 Keith McArthur, "Court Approves Molson-Coors Merger After Last Minute Complaint Over Voting," *The Globe and Mail*, 3 February 2005, B1; Keith McArthur, Bertrand Marotte, and Derek DeCloet, "Merger Golden with Molson Shareholders," *The Globe and Mail*, 29 January 2005, B1; Keith McArthur, "Molson Deal Clears Key Hurdle," *The Globe and Mail*, 11 November 2004, B1.
6 RIM website (Investors Relations) [accessed 17 April 2005] www.rim.com
7 Bob Simon, "Inside Cirque du Soleil," *60 Minutes*, 13 December 1999; "Fab Four du Soleil," [accessed 25 November 2004] www.cbsnews.com/stories/2004/10/14/entertainment/printable649299.shtml
8 Laurence Zuckerman, "UPS Hears Market's Song, and Plans to Sell Some Stock," *New York Times*, 22 July 1999, A1, C23.
9 Konrad Yakabuski, "The Builder," *Report on Business Magazine*, October 2004, 85–96.
10 Vivien Kellerman, "A Growing Business Takes the Corporate Plunge," *New York Times*, 23 July 1994, Your Money, 31.
11 "200 Biggest Companies by Market Cap," *Report on Business Magazine*, July/August 2004, 91.
12 Wal-Mart website [accessed 27 November 2004] www.walmart.com; "30 Canadian Metropolitan Areas" [accessed 27 November 2004] www.canadainfolink.ca/cities.htm
13 Data for 31 July 2004, Globe Investor website [accessed 27 November 2004] http://investdb.theglobeandmail.com/invest/investSQL/gx.company_prof?company_id=181455&symbol_in=
14 Rana Dogar, "Crony Baloney," *Working Woman*, January 1997; Richard H. Koppes, "Institutional Investors, Now in Control of More Than Half the Shares of U.S. Corporations, Demand More Accountability," *National Law Journal*, 14 April 1997, B5; John A. Byrne, "The Best & Worst Boards," *Business Week*, 25 November 1996, 82–84; Anthony Bianco, John Byrne, Richard Melcher, and Mark Maremont, "The Rush to Quality on Corporate Boards," *Business Week*, 3 March 1997, 34–35.
15 "Independence Makes Big Gains in the Boardroom," *The Globe and Mail*, 12 October 2004, B1.
16 Elizabeth Church, "Boards Recruit New Faces, New Visions," *The Globe and Mail*, 13 October 2004, B1.
17 Virginia Citrano, "Politicians on Board," *Forbes* website, 11 August, 2004 [accessed 29 November 2004] www.forbes.com/business/2004/08/11/cx_vc_0811directors.html; *Forbes* website [accessed 9 September 2004] www.forbes.com
18 Gary Strauss, "From Public Service to Private Payday," *USA Today*, 17 April 2000, 1B, 2B.
19 "Cleaning Up the Boardroom," *New York Times*, 8 March 2002, A20.
20 Elizabeth Church, "Inside Canada's Best Boards," *The Globe and Mail*, 12 October 2004, B9; "Independence Makes Big Gains in the Boardroom," *The Globe and Mail*, 12 October 2004, B1.
21 Canada Business Services Centre website [accessed 28 November 2004] www.cbsc.org/english/search/display.cfm?code=4000&Coll=FE_FEDSBIS_E
22 "Revenue Ranking by Industry" (Financial Co-ops and Credit Unions), *Report on Business Magazine*, July/August 2004, 73.
23 Canada Business Services Centre website [accessed 28 November 2004] www.cbsc.org/

english/search/display.cfm?code=4000&Coll=FE_FEDSBIS_E
24 Canada Business Services Centre website [accessed 28 November 2004] http://www.cbsc.org/english/search/display.cfm?code=4000&Coll=FE_FEDSBIS_E
25 Alison MacGregor, "Reebok Scores with Acquisition of Hockey Co.," *The Gazette* (Montreal), 9 April 2004, B1.
26 Randy Burns, Mission-Itech VP of Marketing [3 August 2004]; Mission-Itech website [accessed 30 June 2004] www.itech.com; "Mission Hockey Merges with Itech," SkateLog.com website [accessed 30 June 2004] www.skatelog.com/skates/mission/2004-05-itech-merger.htm
27 Alison MacGregor, "Reebok Scores with Acquisition of Hockey Co."
28 David A. Nadler, "10 Steps to a Happy Merger," *New York Times*, 15 March 1998, BU14.
29 Peter Passell, "Do Mergers Really Yield Big Benefits?" *New York Times*, 14 May 1998, C1, C2.
30 Alex Taylor III, "More Mergers. Dumb Idea," *Fortune*, 15 February 1999, 26–27.
31 Matthew McClearn, "Merger Lessons," *Canadian Business*, 23 November 2003, 125.
32 Bertrand Marotte, "Bain Snaps Up Discount Chain Dollarama," *The Globe and Mail*, 26 November 2004, B5.
33 Marina Strauss, "Best Buy Courting Its Best Customers," *The Globe and Mail*, 13 August 2004, B3; Emily Church, "Best Buy Buying Canadian Retailer," 14 August 2001 [accessed 30 November 2004] www.cbs.marketwatch.com
34 Steven Chase, Paul Waldie, and Simon Tuck, "Bank Merger Rules Back on Track," *The Globe and Mail*, 7 July 2004, B1.
35 Bertrand Marotte, "Coutu Takes on Fortress Retail, USA," *The Globe and Mail*, 4 September 2004, B5.
36 Martin Peers, Nick Wingfield, and Laura Landro, "AOL, Time Warner Set Plan to Link in Mammoth Merger," *Wall Street Journal*, 11 January 2000, A1, A6; Thomas E. Weber, Martin Peers, and Nick Wingfield, "Two Titans in a Strategic Bind Bet on a Futuristic Megadeal," *Wall Street Journal*, 11 January 2000, B1, B12; "AOL and Time Warner Will Merge to Create World's First Internet-Age Media and Communications Company," America Online website [accessed 11 January 2000] media.web.aol.com/media/press.cfm.
37 Barrie McKenna and Virginia Galt, "P&G Cuts Mega-Deal with Gillette," *The Globe and Mail*, 29 January 2005, B4; Shawn McCarthy, "Investment Bankers Win Big in P&G Pact," *The Globe and Mail*, 29 January 2005, B4.
38 Merrill Goozner and John Schmeltzer, "Mass Exodus Hits Corporate Names," *Chicago Tribune*, 12 May 1998, sec. 3, 1, 3; Bill Vlasic, "The First Global Car Colossus," *Business Week*, 18 May 1998, 40–43; Abid Aslam, "Exxon-Mobil Merger Could Poison the Well," *Inter Press Service English News Wire*, 2 December 1998, Electric Library [accessed 2 June 1999]; Agis Salpukas, "Do Oil and Bigger Oil Mix?" *New York Times*, 2 December 1998, C1, C4.
39 Steve Lipen, "Concentration: Corporations' Dreams Converge in One Idea: It's Time to Do a Deal," *Wall Street Journal*, 26 February 1997, A1, A8.
40 Matthew McLearn, "Fido's New Master," *Canadian Business*, 27 September–10 October 2004, 43; Richard Blackwell, "Mr. Rogers Bets the Neighborhood," *The Globe and Mail*, 9 October 2004, B1, B4.
41 Matthew McClearn, "Aluminum Foil," *Canadian Business*, 29 September 2003, 29.
42 "Canada 3000 Bids $84 million for Royal Airlines," 29 January 2001, CBC News website [accessed 29 November 2004] http://cbc.ca/cgi-bin/templates/view.cgi?/news/2001/01/29/canada3000_royal010129
43 Gordon Pitts, "The Fall of Carly Fiorina," *The Globe and Mail*, 10 February 2005, A1; Simon Avery, "HP to Stay Carly's Course—Without Her at the Helm," *The Globe and Mail*, 10 February 2005, B1.
44 Joann S. Lublin, "'Poison Pills' Are Giving Shareholders a Big Headache, Union Proposals Assert," *Wall Street Journal*, 23 May 1997, C1.
45 Martha Groves and Stuart Silverstein, "Levi Strauss Offers Year's Pay as Incentive Bonus," *Los Angeles Times*, 13 June 2006, A1.
46 Michael Hickins, "Searching for Allies," *Management Review*, January 2000, 54–58.
47 Gary Dessler, *Management*, 2nd ed. (Upper Saddle River, NJ: Prentice Hall, 2001), 45.
48 BCE website [accessed 29 November 2004] www.bce.ca/en/news/releases/bc/2004/03/30/71061.html
49 See Note 1.
50 Charles Mandel, "In the World of B2B, You Can File This Under Oeno-Line," *The Globe and Mail*, 10 February 2005, C1, C18; adapted from Paulette Thomas, "The Morning After," *Wall Street Journal*, 27 March 2002, R12; "The Internet's Bust Became a Boom (Who Ever Doubted It?)," New York Metro.com website [accessed 23 December 2004] www.newyorkmetro.com/nymetro/news/yearinreview/2004/10673/; Michael Totty and Ann Grimes, "If at First You Don't Succeed," *Wall Street Journal*, 11 February 2002, R6–R7; J. William Gurley, "Startups, Beware: Obey the Law of Supply and Demand," *Fortune*, 29 May 2000, 278; William M. Bulkeley and Jim Carlton, "E-Tail Gets Derailed: How Web Upstarts Misjudged the Game," *Wall Street Journal*, 5 April 2000, A1, A6; Leslie Kaufman, "After Taking a Beating, Dot-Coms Now Seek Financial Saviors," *New York Times*, 18 April 2000, C1, C18; Kevin Maney, "Net Start-Ups Pull Out of the Garage," *USA Today*, 1 October 1999, 1B, 2B; Matt Krantz, "E-Retailers Run Low on Fuel," *USA Today*, 26 April 2000, 1B, 2B; "Survival of the Fastest," *Inc. Tech*, 16 November 1999, 44–58; Darnell Little, "Peapod Is in a Pickle," *Business Week*, 3 April 2000, 41; Heather Green, Nanette Byrnes, Norm Alster, and Arlene Weintraub, "The Dot.Coms Are Falling to Earth," *Business Week*, 17 April 2000, 48–49; John A. Byrne, "The Fall of a Dot-Com," *Business Week*, 1 May 2000, 150–160; Stephanie N. Mehta, "As Investors Play VC, It's Dot-Com Doomsday," *Fortune*, 1 May 2000, 40–41; David P. Hamilton and Mylene Mangalindan, "Angels of Death," *Wall Street Journal*, 25 May 2000, A1, A8; Luisa Kroll, "When the Music Stops," *Forbes*, 15 May 2000, 182; Chris Farrell, "Death of the Dot-Coms?" *Business Week*, 22 May 2000, 104E6; John Steele Gordon, "The Golden Spike," *Forbes ASAP*, 21 February 2000, 118–122; Eric W. Pfeiffer, "Where Are We in the Revolution?" *Forbes ASAP*, 21 February 2000, 68–70; James Lardner and Paul Sloan, "The Anatomy of Sickly IPOs," *U.S. News and World Report*, 29 May 2000, 42; Hillary Stout, "Crunch Time," *Wall Street Journal*, 7 June 2000, B1; Jerry Useem, "Dot-Coms—What Have We Learned?" *Fortune*, 30 October 2000, 82–104; Heather Green and Norm Alster, "Guess What—Venture Capitalists Aren't Geniuses," *Business Week*, 10 July 2000, 98; Thomas E. Weber, "What Were We Thinking?" *Wall Street Journal*, 18 July 2000, B1, B4; Greg Ip, Susan Pulliam, Scott Thurm, and Ruth Simon, "The Color Green," *Wall Street Journal*, 14 July 2000, A1, A8; "Business Brief—Value America: Bankruptcy-Code Filing Is Made by the Company," *Wall Street Journal*, 14 August 2000, B2.

Chapter 6

1 Annual Report, Nokia website [accessed 18 April 2005] www.nokia.com; Roma Luciw, "Nokia Market Share Slides as Firm Hit Hard by Rivals," *The Gazette* (Montreal), 9 July 2004; Janet Guyon, "Nokia Rocks Its Rivals," *Fortune*, 4 March 2002, 115–118; Dan Steinbock, *The Nokia Revolution* (New York: American Management Association, 2001); Kerry Capell, William Echikson, and Peter Elstrom, "Surprise! Nokia Doesn't Walk on Water," *Business Week*, 25 June 2001, 49; John S. McClenahen, "CEO of the Year: Nokia's Jorma Ollila Wants to Unwire the World," *Industry Week*, 20 November 2000, 38–44; "Nokia: A Finnish Fable," *The Economist*, 14 October 2000, 83–85; Stephen Baker with Inka Resch and Roger O. Crockett, "Nokia's Costly Stumble," *Business Week*, 14 August 2000, 42; "Business: Star Turn," *The Economist*, 5 August 2000, 60; Maryanne Murry Buechner, "Making the Call," *Time*, 29 May 2000, 64–65; Justin Fox,

"Nokia's Secret Code," *Fortune*, 1 May 2000, 160–174; Adrian Wooldridge, "Survey: Telecommunications: To the Finland Base Station," *The Economist*, 9 October 1999, S23–S27; Stephen Baker and Robert McNatt, "Now Nokia Is Net Crazy," *Business Week*, 5 April 1999, 6; "Jorma Ollila: Finn Fatale," *Business Week*, 11 January 1999, 78; Stephen Baker with Roger O. Crockett and Neil Gross, "Nokia," *Business Week*, 10 August 1998, 54.
2 Richard L. Daft, *Management*, 4th ed. (Fort Worth, TX: Dryden Press, 1997), 8.
3 Courtland L. Bovée, John V. Thill, Marian Burk Wood, and George P. Dovel, *Management* (New York: McGraw-Hill, 1993), 220; David H. Holt, *Management: Principles and Practices*, 2nd ed. (Upper Saddle River, NJ: Prentice Hall, 1990), 10–12; James A. F. Stoner, *Management*, 4th ed. (Upper Saddle River, NJ: Prentice Hall, 1989), 15–18.
4 Gillian Flynn, "A Flight Plan for Success," *Workforce*, July 1997, 72–128.
5 Stephen P. Robbins, *Managing Today* (Upper Saddle River, NJ: Prentice Hall, 1997), 452.
6 Leonard Goodstein, Timothy Nolan, and J. William Pfeiffer, *Applied Strategic Planning* (New York: McGraw-Hill, 1993), 169–192.
7 Norman M. Scarborough and Thomas W. Zimmerer, *Effective Small Business Management* (Upper Saddle River, NJ: Prentice Hall, 2000), 50.
8 Daft, *Management*, 221–223, 260–262.
9 Shoppers Drug Mart website [accessed 17 April 2005] www.shoppersdrugmart.ca; Marina Strauss, "Shoppers Sees Gold in Private Labels," *The Globe and Mail*, 3 January 2005, B1, B2; Rasha Mourtada, "Face Lift: Shoppers CEO Glenn Murphy Has Injected New Life into an Old Brand," *Canadian Business*, 9 November 2003, 91–95; Sheila McGovern, "We Won't Get Distracted: Coutu," *The Gazette* (Montreal), 27 October 2004, B1, B10.
10 Judy A. Smith, "Crisis Communications: The War on Two Fronts," *Industry Week*, 20 May 1996, 136; John F. Reukus, "Hazard Communication," *Occupational Hazards*, February 1998, 39; Kim M. Gibson and Steven H. Smith, "Do We Understand Each Other?" *Journal of Accountancy*, January 1998, 53.
11 Canadian Press, "Royal Bank Computer Glitch Affects Millions," CTV website [accessed 28 October 2004] www.ctv.ca/servlet/ArticleNews/story/CTVNews/1086207075506_81616275?s_name=&no_ads=
12 Michael Moeller, Steve Hamm, and Timothy J. Mullaney, "Remaking Microsoft," *Business Week*, 17 May 1999, 106–116.
13 Stephanie Armour, "Once Plagued by Pink Slips, Now They're in Driver's Seat," *USA Today*, 14 May 1998, 1B–2B.
14 Daft, *Management*, 219–221.
15 Gary A. Yukl, *Leadership in Organizations*, 2d ed. (Upper Saddle River, N.J.: Prentice Hall, 1989), 9, 175–176.
16 Daniel Goleman, "What Makes a Leader?" *Harvard Business Review*, November–December 1998, 92–102; Shari Caudron, "The Hard Case for Soft Skills," *Workforce*, July 1999, 60–66.
17 Daft, *Management*, 498–499.
18 Danny King, Bloomberg News, "EBay Chief Whitman Named Most Powerful Businesswoman," *The Gazette* (Montreal), 5 October 2004.
19 Jenny Anderson, "Al Gets the Chainsaw," *Institutional Investor*, October 1999, 224.
20 David Dotlich, James Noel, and Norman Walker, "Failure Breeds Successful Leaders, *The Globe and Mail*, 28 January 2005, C1.
21 Stratford Sherman, "Secrets of HP's 'Muddled' Team," *Fortune*, 18 March 1996, 116–120.
22 Daniel Goleman, "Leadership That Gets Results," *Harvard Business Review*, March–April 2000, 78–90.
23 Stephen P. Robbins and David A. De Cenzo, *Fundamentals of Management*, 2nd ed. (Upper Saddle River, NJ: Prentice Hall, 1998), 55–56; James Waldroop and Timothy Butler, "The Executive as Coach," *Harvard Business Review*, November–December 1996, 113.
24 "The Advantage of Female Mentoring," *Working Woman*, October 1991, 104.
25 Ram Charan and Geoffrey Colvin, "Why CEOs Fail," *Fortune*, 21 June 1999, 69–78.
26 James A. Belasco and Ralph C. Stayer, *Flight of the Buffalo* (New York: Warner Books, 1993), 138.
27 Eric Reguly, "Latest Ski-Doo Numbers Show Bombardier Didn't Get Best Price," *The Globe and Mail*, 28 October 2004, B2; Sean Silcoff, "Tellier's Decision Caused Rift: Book," *The Globe and Mail*, 19 October 2004, B6.
28 Michael Been and Nitin Nohria, "Cracking the Code of Change," *Harvard Business Review*, May–June 2000, 133–141
29 Barb Sawyers, "Ten Tips to Help Managers Communicate in Times of Change," *The Globe and Mail*, 15 September 2004, C3; Michael Barrier, "Managing Workers in Times of Change," *Nation's Business*, May 1998, 31–32.
30 John A. Byrne, Mike France, and Wendy Zellner, "Enron and Beyond," *Business Week*, 25 February 2002, 118–120.
31 Paul Waldie, "De Zen Cuts Deal, Gives Up Control of Royal Group," *The Globe and Mail*, 25 March 2005, B1; John Gray, "Royal Mess," *Canadian Business*, 25 October–7 November, 49.
32 Kostas N. Dervitsiotis, "The Challenge of Managing Organizational Change," *Total Quality Management*, February 1998, 109–122.
33 George Taninecz, "Borg-Warner Automotive," *Industry Week*, 19 October 1998, 44–46.
34 Bovée et al., *Management*, 680.
35 James R. Lackritz, "TQM within Fortune 500 Corporations," *Quality Progress*, February 1997, 69–72.
36 David Sirota, Brian Usilaner, and Michelle S. Weber, "Sustaining Quality Improvement," *Total Quality Review*, March–April 1994, 23; Joe Batten, "A Total Quality Culture," *Management Review*, May 1994, 61; Rahul Jacon, "More Than a Dying Fad?" *Fortune*, 18 October 1993, 66–72.
37 Lackritz, "TQM within Fortune 500 Corporations."
38 Robert L. Katz, "Skills of an Effective Administrator," *Harvard Business Review*, September–October 1974. Reprinted in *Paths toward Personal Progress: Leaders Are Made, Not Born* (Boston: Harvard Business Review, 1983), 23–35; Mike Dawson, "Leaders versus Managers," *Systems Management*, March 1995, 32; R. S. Dreyer, "Do Good Bosses Make Lousy Leaders?" *Supervision*, March 1995, 19–20; Michael Maccoby, "Teams Need Open Leaders," *Research-Technology Management*, January–February 1995, 57–59.
39 Courtland L. Bovée and John V. Thill, *Business Communication Today*, 6th ed. (Upper Saddle River, NJ: Prentice Hall, 2000), 4.
40 Daft, *Management*, 128; Kathryn M. Bartol and David C. Martin, *Management* (New York: McGraw-Hill, 1991), 268–272.
41 Bartol and Martin, *Management*, 268–272; Ricky W. Griffin, *Management*, 3rd ed. (Boston: Houghton Mifflin, 1990), 131–137.
42 Robbins, *Managing Today*, 72.
43 See Note 1.

Chapter 7

1 Best Manufacturing Practices, Wainwright Industries [accessed 7 May 2005] www.bmpcoe.org/bestpractices/internal/wainw/summary.html; Michael Barrier, "Creating a Violence Free Company Culture," *Nation's Business*, 1 February 1995, 22; Michael A. Verespej, "Wainwright Industries," *Industry Week*, 21 October 1996; "CEO of Baldridge-Winner Wainwright Industries Shares Learning on Leadership and Change," Center for Quality of Management [accessed 6 March 1999] www.cqm.org/whats_new/wainwright.htm; Arthur D. Wainwright, "People First Strategies Get Implemented," *Strategy and Leadership*, January–February 1997, 134–145.
2 Richard L. Daft, *Management*, 4th ed. (Fort Worth, TX: Dryden Press, 1997), 358.
3 Rob Goffee and Gareth Jones, "What Holds the Modern Company Together?" *Harvard Business Review*, November–December 1996, 134–145.

4 Peter F. Drucker, "Management's New Paradigms," *Forbes*, 5 October 1998, 152–176.
5 Stephen P. Robbins, *Managing Today!* (Upper Saddle River, NJ: Prentice Hall, 1997), 193; Daft, *Management*, 320.
6 Stephen P. Robbins and David A. De Cenzo, *Fundamentals of Management*, 2nd ed. (Upper Saddle River, NJ: Prentice Hall, 1998), 201; Daft, *Management*, 321.
7 BP website [accessed 6 December 2004] www.bp.com/sectiongenericarticle.do?categoryId=3&contentId=2006926; "Sharing Knowledge Through BP's Virtual Team Network," *Harvard Business Review*, September–October 1997, 152–153; British Petroleum website [accessed 20 April 2002] www.bp.com.
8 Alan Webber, "The Best Organization Is No Organization," *USA Today*, 13A; Eve Tahmincioglu, "How GM's Team Approach Works," *Gannett News Service*, 24 April 1996, S11.
9 Fred R. David, *Strategic Management*, 6th ed. (Upper Saddle River, NJ: Prentice Hall, 1997), 225; Kathryn M. Bartol and David C. Martin, *Management* (New York: McGraw-Hill, 1991), 352.
10 GE website [accessed 19 April 2005] www.ge.com/ar2004/om.jsp; Jeanne Dugan, Alison Rea, and Joseph Weber, "The BW 50: Business Week's Performance Rankings of the S&P 500 Best Performers," *Business Week*, 24 March 1997, 80.
11 Magna website [accessed 2 December 2004] www.magna.ca/magnaWeb.nsf/webpages/Magna+Worldwide+-+Global+Structure?OpenDocument#
12 Daft, *Management*, 325.
13 Bartol and Martin, *Management*, 345.
14 Courtland L. Bovée, John V. Thill, Marian Wood, and George Dovel, *Management* (New York: McGraw-Hill, 1993), 285.
15 Bartol and Martin, *Management*, 370–371.
16 Gary Izumo, "Teamwork Holds Key to Organization Success," *Los Angeles Times*, 20 August 1996, D9; Daft, *Management*, 328–329; David, *Strategic Management*, 223.
17 Rogers website [accessed 18 April 2005] www.rogers.com/english/investorrelations/index.html, www.rogers.com/english/investorrelations/edward_rogers.html
18 Steven Burke, "Acer Restructures into Six Divisions," *Computer Reseller News*, 13 July 1998, 10; Acer America website [accessed 20 July 2000] www.acer.com/aac/about/profile.htm.
19 Sobeys website [accessed 19 April 2005] www.sobeys.com/English/Annual_Reports/2004/r3.asp
20 Daft, *Management*, 332, 328–329; David, *Strategic Management*, 223; Bartol and Martin, *Management*, 376.
21 Dan Dimancescu and Kemp Dwenger, "Smoothing the Product Development Path," *Management Review*, 1 January 1996, 36.
22 Dimancescu and Dwenger, "Smoothing the Product Development Path."
23 Gary Dessler and Frederick A. Starke, *Management: Principles and Practices for Tomorrow's Leaders* (Toronto: Pearson/Prentice Hall, 2004), 246; Robbins, *Managing Today!* 209; Daft, *Management*, 333–336.
24 Daft, *Management*, 340–343; Robbins, *Managing Today!* 213–214.
25 Daft, *Management*, 340–343; Robbins, *Managing Today!* 213–214.
26 "The Horizontal Organization," *Soundview Executive Book Summaries, 21*(3) (March 1999): 1–8.
27 "The Horizontal Organization."
28 Daft, *Management*, 352–353; Richards, *Strategic Management*, 217; Bartol and Martin, *Management*, 357–358.
29 Stephen P. Robbins, *Essentials of Organizational Behavior*, 6th ed. (Upper Saddle River, NJ: Prentice Hall, 2000), 105.
30 Daft, *Management*, 591; Robbins, *Managing Today!* 295.
31 "Canadian Businesses Failing to Meet the Information Sharing Needs of Employees, Finds Ipsos-Reid Poll," Microsoft Canada website [accessed 4 December 2004] www.microsoft.com/canada/media/releases/2003_10_21_1.mspx
32 "Top Ranking in Study Boosts Microsoft's College Recruiting Efforts," 25 August 2004, Microsoft website [accessed 4 December 2004] www.microsoft.com/presspass/features/2004/aug04/08-25college.asp; "Microsoft Teamwork," *Executive Excellence*, 6 July 1996, 6–7.
33 Daft, *Management*, 594–595; Robbins and De Cenzo, *Fundamentals of Management*, 336; Robbins, *Managing Today!* 309.
34 Jeffrey Pfeffer, "When It Comes to 'Best Practices.'—Why Do Smart Organizations Occasionally Do Dumb Things?" *Organizational Dynamics*, 1 June 1996, 33.
35 Nicolas Van Praet, "Team Players," *The Gazette* (Montreal), 24 September 2004, B1; Jim Clemmer, "Team Spirit Built from the Top," *The Globe and Mail*, 26 November 2004, C1; Mountain Quest website [accessed 5 December 2004] www.mountainquest.ca/; Outward Bound Canada website [accessed 5 December 2004] www.outwardbound.ca/default.asp
36 SEI Canada website [accessed 4 December 2004] www.seic.com/company/default.asp?page=SEIoverview&menu=SEI overview; Scott Kirsner, "Total Teamwork: SEI Investments," *Fast Company, 14* (April 1998), 130.
37 Daft, *Management*, 594; Robbins and De Cenzo, *Fundamentals of Management*, 336.
38 Daft, *Management*, 594; Robbins and De Cenzo, *Fundamentals of Management*, 338; Robbins, *Managing Today!* 310–311.
39 Seth Lubove, "Destroying the Old Hierarchies," *Forbes*, 3 June 1996, 62–64.
40 Dantar Oosterwal, "Harley Davidson's Formula for NPD," Product Development and Management Association website [accessed 4 December 2004] www.pdma.org/visions/jan04/harley.html; Clyde Fessler, "Rotating Leadership at Harley-Davidson: From Hierarchy to Interdependence," *Strategy & Leadership*, July–August 1997, 42–43; Mark A. Brunelli, "How Harley-Davidson Uses Cross-Functional Teams," *Purchasing*, 4 November 1999, 148.
41 Ellen Neuborne, "Companies Save, but Workers Pay," *USA Today*, 25 February 1997, B1; Daft, *Management*, 594; Robbins and De Cenzo, *Fundamentals of Management*, 338; Robbins, *Managing Today!* 310.
42 "Canada-U.S. Task Force Presents Final Report on Blackout of August 2003," Natural Resources Canada website [accessed 4 December 2004] www.nrcan-rncan.gc.ca/media/newsreleases/2004/200414_e.htm
43 Daft, *Management*, 594.
44 Robbins, *Essentials of Organizational Behaviour*, 109.
45 Deborah L. Duarte and Nancy Tennant Snyder, *Mastering Virtual Teams* (San Francisco: Jossey-Bass Publishers, 1999), 23.
46 Alan Price, *Human Resources Management in a Business Context*, HRM Guide website [accessed 4 December 2004] http://hrmguide.net/hrm/chap4/ch4-links5.htm
47 "Sharing Knowledge through BP's Virtual Team Network," *Harvard Business Review*, September–October 1997, 152–153.
48 Daft, *Management*, 612–615.
49 Robbins, *Essentials of Organizational Behavior*, 98.
50 Ross Sherwood, "The Boss's Open Door Means More Time for Employees," *Reuters Business Report*, 30 September 1996.
51 "Customer Focused Empowerment Pays at Ritz-Carlton" [accessed 5 December 2004] www.serviceexcellence.co.uk/ritz.shtm; Neuborne, "Companies Save, but Workers Pay," B2; Charles L. Parnell, "Teamwork: Not a New Idea, But It's Transforming the Workplace," *Vital Speeches of the Day*, 1 November 1996, 46.
52 Robbins and De Cenzo, *Fundamentals of Management*, 151.
53 Jared Sandberg, "Teamwork: When It's a Bad Idea," *The Globe and Mail*, 1 October 2004, C7.
54 Larry Cole and Michael Cole, "Why Is the Teamwork Buzz Word Not Working?" *Communication World*, February/March 1999, 29; Patricia Buhler, "Managing in the 90s: Creating Flexibility in Today's Workplace," *Supervision*, January 1997, 241; Allison W. Amason, Allen C. Hochwarter, Wayne A. Thompson, and Kenneth R. Harrison, "Conflict: An Important Dimension in Successful Management

Teams," *Organizational Dynamics*, Autumn 1995, 201.
55 "The Saturn Difference," GM Canada website [accessed 5 December 2004] www.gmcanada.com/ssi/static/english_lw/vehicles/2005/saturn/difference/promise.html ; "Team Players," *Executive Excellence*, May 1999, 18.
56 Stephen P. Robbins, David A. Decenzo, and Robin Stuart-Kotze, *Fundamentals of Management*, 3rd Canadian ed. (Toronto: Pearson Canada/Prentice Hall, 2002), 218; Daft, *Management*, 602–603.
57 Robbins, *Managing Today!* 297–298; Daft, *Management*, 604–607.
58 Thomas K. Capozzoli, "Conflict Resolution—A Key Ingredient in Successful Teams," *Supervision*, November 1999, 14–16.
59 Daft, *Management*, 609–612.
60 Steven Crom and Herbert France, "Teamwork Brings Breakthrough Improvements in Quality and Climate," *Quality Progress*, March 1996, 39–41.
61 Karine Daisy, "Workplace Bullying: It Dismantles Teamwork, Hobbles Productivity—and Costs Money," *Canadian Business*, 13–26 September 2004, 87–88.
62 David, *Strategic Management*, 221.
63 See Note 1.

Chapter 8
1 Annual Report, Harley-Davidson website [accessed 23 April 2005] www.harley-davidson.com/co/en/company.asp?locale=en_CA&bmLocale=en_CA; Alan Ohnsman, "Harley Roars Past Sick GM in Market Value," *The Globe and Mail*, 17 March 2005, B3; Haris Anwar, "Harley Warns, Stock Hits Pothole," *The Globe and Mail*, 14 April 2005, B16; Jonathan Fahey, "Love into Money," *Forbes*, 7 January 2002, 60–65; Vincent J. Orange and David E. Robinson, "The Role of Certification in the Buyer/Planner Position: A Case Study at Harley-Davidson Motor Company," *Hospital/Materiel Management Quarterly*, February 1999, 28–36; Leslie P. Norton, "Potholes Ahead?" *Barron's*, 1 February 1999, 16–17; Bruce Caldwell, "Harley-Davidson Revs Up IT Horsepower," *Internetweek*, 7 December 1998, 63; Peter Bradley, "Harley-Davidson Keeps Its Eyes on the Road," *Logistics Management and Distribution Report*, August 1998, 68–73; "Harley-Davidson History" [accessed 23 April 1999] www.harley-davidson.com/company/history/history.asp; Harley-Davidson 1998 Annual Report [accessed 23 April 1999] www.harley-davidson.com/company/investor/ar/1998/growing/supply.asp
2 Roberta A. Russell and Bernard W. Taylor III, *Operations Management: Focusing on Quality and Competitiveness*, 2nd ed. (Upper Saddle River, NJ: Prentice Hall, 1998), 21.
3 Anderson Windows website [accessed 20 December 2004] www.andersenwindows.com/; Justin Martin, "Creating Greater Customer Value May Require a Lot of Changes," *Organizational Dynamics*, Summer 1998, 26.
4 Nike ID website [accessed 3 January 2005] http://nikeid.nike.com/nikeid/index.jhtml?_requestid=303930
5 John Greenwald, "Cruise Lines Go Overboard," *Time*, 11 May 1998, 42–45.
6 Joseph G. Monks, *Operations Management, Theory and Problems* (New York: McGraw-Hill, 1987), 7–8.
7 Bret Jang and Bertrand Marotte, "Air Canada Bets $6 Billion on Future," *The Globe and Mail*, 26 April 2005, B1.
8 Bertrand Marotte, "Gildan Takes T-Shirt Manufacturing to the Cutting Edge of Casual Apparel," *The Globe and Mail*, 3 July 2004, B1.
9 Mark M. Davis, Nicholas J. Aquilano, and Richard B. Chase, *Fundamentals of Operations Management* (Boston: Irwin McGraw-Hill, 1999), 241–242.
10 Jae K. Shim and Joel G. Siegel, *Operations Management* (Hauppauge, NY: Barron's Educational Series, 1999), 206.
11 Monks, *Operations Management, Theory and Problems*, 2–3.
12 Shim and Siegel, *Operations Management*, 206.
13 Monks, *Operations Management, Theory and Problems*, 125.
14 Davis, Aquilano, and Chase, *Fundamentals of Operations Management*, 254; Richard L. Daft, *Management*, 4th ed. (Fort Worth, TX: Dryden Press, 1997), 718.
15 Kathryn M. Bartol and David C. Martin, *Management* (New York: McGraw-Hill, 1991), 307–308.
16 Larry E. Long and Nancy Long, *Introduction to Computers and Information Systems*, 5th ed. (Upper Saddle River, NJ: Prentice Hall, 1997), 84.
17 Stuart F. Brown, "Giving More Jobs to Electronic Eyes," *Fortune*, 16 February 1998, 104B–104D.
18 "IBM and Dassault Awarded Boeing CATIA Contract," *CAD/CAM Update*, 1 January 1997, 1–8.
19 Russell and Taylor, *Operations Management*, 211.
20 2004 Ford F150 Special Features, Ford Truck Spec website [accessed 22 January 2005] www.ford-trucks.com/specs/2004/2004_f150_5.html; "CAD/CAM Industry Embracing Intranet-Based Technologies," *Computer Dealer News, 12* (28 November 1996): 21.
21 Drew Winter, "C3P: New Acronym Signals Big Change at Ford," *Ward's Auto World, 32* (1 August 1996): 34; Thomas Hoffman, "Ford to Cut Its Prototype Costs," *Computerworld*, 30 September 1996, 65; Drew Winter, "Massive Changes Coming in Computer Engineering," *Ward's Auto World, 32* (1 April 1996): 34.
22 Davis, Aquilano, and Chase, *Fundamentals of Operations Management*, 64; Russell and Taylor, *Operations Management*, 257–258.
23 Brian S. Moskal, "Born to Be Real," *Industry Week*, 2 August 1993, 14–18.
24 Russell and Taylor, *Operations Management*, 255–256.
25 John H. Sheridan, "Agile Manufacturing: Stepping Beyond Lean Production," *Industry Week*, 19 April 1993, 30–46.
26 Porche website [accessed 21 December 2004] www2.porche.com/; Robyn Meredith, "Porsche Goes Soccer Mom," *Forbes*, 4 February 2000, 54.
27 Simon Tuck and Greg Keenan, "GM Ups Ante in Bid for Federal Cash," *The Globe and Mail*, 20 December 2004, B1; Greg Keenan, "Ford's Chicago Plant Gets Flexible as Firm Chooses a Different Road for Survival," *The Globe and Mail*, 19 August 2004, B1; Steve Erwin, "Automakers Seek Production Flexibility," *The Gazette* (Montreal), 21 September 2004, E7.
28 John H. Sheridan, "Lessons from the Best," *Industry Week*, 19 February 1996, 16.
29 Greg Ip, "Risky Business," *Wall Street Journal* 24 October 2001, A1, A4.
30 Jon E. Hilsenrath, "Parts Shortages Hamper Electronics Makers: Surging Demand Shows Flaw in Just-in-Time Chains," *Wall Street Journal*, 7 July 2000, B5.
31 Shim and Siegel, *Operations Management*, 326.
32 Russell and Taylor, *Operations Management*, 712–733.
33 Greg Keenan, "Steel Firm Forges Strategy for Good and Bad Times," *The Globe and Mail*, 24 July 2004, B1.
34 Allen-Edmonds website [accessed 21 December 2004] www.allenedmonds.com; Patricia W. Hamilton, "Getting a Grip on Inventory," *D&B Reports*, March–April 1994, 32.
35 Russell and Taylor, *Operations Management*, 652–653.
36 Karl Ritzler, "A Mercedes Made from Scratch," *Atlanta Journal and Constitution*, 30 May 1997, S1.
37 Del Jones, "Training and Service at Top of Winners' List," *USA Today*, 17 October 1996, 5B.
38 John A. Byrne, "Never Mind the Buzzwords. Roll up Your Sleeves," *Business Week*, 22 January 1996, 84.
39 Davis, Aquilano, and Chase, *Fundamentals of Operations Management*, 177–179; Russell and Taylor, *Operations Management*, 131.
40 William M. Carley, "Charging Ahead: To Keep GE's Profits Rising, Welch Pushes Quality-Control Plan," *Wall Street Journal*, 13 January 1997, A1, A6.
41 Russell and Taylor, *Operations Management*, 131.
42 Gillian Babicz, "ISO 9004: The Other Half of the Consistent Pair," *Quality*, June 2001, 50–53; David Drickhemer, "Standards

Shake-Up," *Industry Week*, 5 March 2001, 37–40.
43 ISO website [accessed 18 April 2005] www.iso.org/iso/en/iso9000-14000/index.html; Hugh D. Menzies, "Global Guide: Quality Counts When Wooing Overseas Clients," *Your Company*, 1 June 1997, 64; Michael E. Raynor, "Worldwide Winners," *Total Quality Management*, July–August 1993, 43–48; Greg Bounds, Lyle Yorks, Mel Adams, and Gipsie Ranney, *Beyond Total Quality Management: Toward the Emerging Paradigm* (New York: McGraw-Hill, 1994), 212; Russell and Taylor, *Operations Management*, 115–116.
44 Ronald Henkoff, "Boeing's Big Problem," *Fortune*, 12 January 1998, 96–103; James Wallace, "How Boeing Blew It," *Sales and Marketing Management*, February 1998, 52–57; John Greenwald, "Is Boeing out of Its Spin?" *Time*, 13 July 1998, 67–69; John T. Landry, "Supply Chain Management: The Case for Alliances," *Harvard Business Review*, November–December 1998, 24–25.
45 Davis, Aquilano, and Chase, *Fundamentals of Operations Management*, 382.
46 Russell and Taylor, *Operations Management*, 440.
47 Landry, "Supply Chain Management."
48 Timothy M. Laseter, "Balanced Sourcing the Honda Way," *Strategy and Business*, Fourth Quarter 1998, 24–31.
49 George Taninecz, "Forging the Chain," *Industry Week*, 15 May 2000, 40–46.
50 Gail Edmunston, "Look Who's Building Bimmers," *Business Week Online*, 1 December 2003 [accessed 22 December 2004] http://yahoo.businessweek.com/magazine/content/03_48/b3860094.htm
51 Solectron website [accessed 22 December 2004] www.solectron.com/about/loc_americas.htm#CANADA; Gene Bylinsky, "For Sale Japanese Plants in the U.S.," *Fortune*, 21 February 2000, 240B–240D.
52 Solectron website [accessed 22 December 2004] www.solectron.com/about/loc_americas.htm#CANADA; Hansell, "Is This the Factory of the Future?"; Peter Engardio, "Souping Up the Supply Chain," *Business Week*, 31 August 1998, 110–112.
53 Alice Rangel de Paiva Abreu, Huw Beynon, and Jose Ricardo Ramalho, "The Dream Factory: VW's Modular Production System in Resende, Brazil," Sage Publications website [accessed 22 December 2004] http://wes.sagepub.com/cgi/content/abstract/14/2/265; David Woodruff, Ian Katz, and Keith Naughton, "VW's Factory of the Future," *Business Week*, 7 October 1996, 52, 56.
54 Greg Keenan, "Tiny Mercedes-Benz Rolls In," *The Globe and Mail*, 5 October 2004, B5; Tony Van Alphen, "Smart Sells Out in Canada" [accessed 23 April 2005] www.zapworld.com/about/news/watch_smart-canada.asp; Auto Intelligence website [accessed 22 December 2004] www.autointell.net/nao_companies/daimlerchrysler/smart/thesmart1.htm; Paul Williams, "Smart Cars Ready to Roll," *Backbone Magazine*, September–October 2004, 46–48; Francois Shalom, "Smart Car Is a Go in Canada," *The Gazette* (Montreal), 17 September 2004, B1; Paul Williams, "Driving Smart," *The Gazette* (Montreal), 13 October 2004, E3; Philip Siekman, "The Smart Car Is Looking More So," *Fortune*, 15 April 2002, 310(I)–310(P).
55 See Note 1.
56 "Electronic Commerce and Technology," Statistic Canada website, 20 April 2005 [accessed 7 May 2005] www.statcan.ca/Daily/English/050420/d050420b.htm; Peter Loftus, "E-Commerce: Business to Business Exchanges—Making It Work," *Wall Street Journal*, 11 February 2002, R16; "Compuware Covisint Continues to Lower the Cost of Doing Business in the Automotive Industry with Two New Services," 30 August 2004, Covisint website [accessed 23 December 2004] http://covisint.com/about/pressroom/pr/2004/2004.AUG.30.shtml; "B2B Exchanges 2.0: Not All E-markets Are Dot-bombs," ISI website [accessed 23 December 2004] www.researchandmarkets.com/reportinfo.asp?cat_id=41&report_id=228028; Covisint website [accessed 23 December 2004] http://covisint.com/about/members/; The Markets.com website [accessed 23 December 2004] www.themarkets.com/public/index.asp; Ralph Kisiel, "Automakers Saving by Using Covisint," *Crain's Detroit Business*, 21 January 2002, 12; Eric Young, "Web Marketplaces That Really Work," *Fortune Tech Review*, Winter 2002, 10; J. William Gurley, "Big Company.com: Should You Start a B2B Exchange?" *Fortune*, 3 April 2000, 2601; Peter D. Henig, "Revenge of the Bricks," *Red Herring*, August 2000, 121–134; Daniel Lyons, "B2Bluster," *Forbes*, 1 May 2000, 122–126; Steven Kaplan and Mohanbir Sawhney, "E-hubs: The New B2B Marketplaces," *Harvard Business Review*, May–June 2000, 97–100; Robert D. Hof, "Who Will Profit from the Internet Agora?" *Business Week E.Biz*, 5 June 2000, EB56–EB62; Joseph B. White, "Getting into Gear," *Wall Street Journal*, 17 April 2000, R65; Douglas A. Blackmon, "Where the Money Is," *Wall Street Journal*, 17 April 2000, R30–R32; Edward Iwata, "Despite the Hype, B2B Marketplaces Struggle," *USA Today*, 10 May 2000, 1B–2B; Jack Trout, "Stupid Net Tricks," *Business 2.0*, May 2000, 76–77; John W. Verity, "Invoice? What's an Invoice?" *Business Week*, 10 June 1996, 110–112; Christina Binkley, "Hyatt Plans Internet Firm with Marriott," *Wall Street Journal*, 2 May 2000, A3, A6; Clint Willis, "B2B... to Be? *Forbes ASAP*, 21 August 2000, 125–130; Jason Anders, "Yesterday's Darling," *Wall Street Journal*, 23 October 2000, R8.

Chapter 9

1 Bertrand Marotte, "New Jet Cleared for Business Takeoff," *The Globe and Mail*, 16 March 2005, B1; Allan Swift, "Bombardier, Union Reach Deal," *The Gazette* (Montreal), 3 March 2005, B1; Bombardier website [accessed 23 April 2005] www.bombardier.com; Simon Tuck, "Ottawa Eyes National Aerospace Plan," *The Globe and Mail*, 15 December 2004, B1; Brent Jang, "Next Stop: Make-or-Break Decision on Jets," *The Globe and Mail*, 14 December 2004, B7; Paul Waldie, "As Tellier and 2 Directors Leave, a Family Comes Full Circle," *The Globe and Mail*, 14 December 2004, B7; Bertrand Marotte, "Will Follow Through on Plan: Beaudoin," *The Globe and Mail*, 14 December 2004, B6; Gordon Pitts, "In the End, Even Tellier Couldn't Pull Miracles Out of the Bag," *The Globe and Mail*, 14 December 2004, B6; Simon Tuck and Rheal Seguin, "Tellier Resigns, Ottawa Plans Aid for Firm" *The Globe and Mail*, 14 December 2004, A1; Bertrand Marotte, "Bombardier Thrown into Turmoil Over Tellier's Sudden Departure," *The Globe and Mail*, 14 December 2004, B1; Derek DeCloet, "Beaudoin Has a Major Call to Make," *The Globe and Mail*, 14 December 2004, B6; John Saunders, "Bombardier Debt Rating Reduced to Junk Satus," *The Globe and Mail*, 12 November 2004, B3; Bertrand Marotte, "Bombardier Stock Dips After Crash in China," *The Globe and Mail*, 23 November 2004, B4; Bertrand Marotte, "Bombardier Turnaround Still On Track, Tellier Insists," *The Globe and Mail*, 2 December 2004, B1; Peter Shawn Tailor, "A Sweet Deal: Bombardier's Corporate Welfare," *Canadian Business*, 22 November–5 December 2004, 113; Sean Silcoff, "Tellier's Decision Caused Rift: Book," *The Gazette* (Montreal), 19 October 2004, B6; Elizabeth Thompson, "Canada Can't Afford to Lose Production of New Airliner, Lapierre Says," *The Gazette* (Montreal), 9 October 2004, A1, A4; "Bombardier Cuts 2,000 Jobs; Most in Montreal Area," CBC Business News website [accessed 7 October 2004] www.cbcnews.ca; Jerry Siebenmark, "Bombardier's Toronto Union Approves Agreement, Layoffs," *Wichita Business Journal*, 17 March 2003; "Pressure Mounts on CAW for Concessions at Bombardier, Air Canada," *Canadian Press*, 11 March 2003; Bertrand Marotte and Simon Tuck, "Kansas Vying for Assembly of New Bombardier Jet," *The Globe and Mail*, 16 October 2004, B5; Bertrand Marotte, "Bombardier Axes 2000, Warns More Jobs May Go," *The Globe and Mail*, 8 October, B1; Francois Shalom, "We'll Cut 2,000," *The Gazette* (Montreal), 8 October 2004, A1; Eric Reguly, "Lobbyists Facing a Tough Fight with New Minority Government," *The Globe and Mail*, 6 July 2004, B1; Conrad Yakabuski,

"Ottawa Should Help Bombardier" *The Globe and Mail*, 6 October 2004, B1; Simon Tuck and Bertrand Marotte, "Canada, Brazil to Resume Subsidy Talks," *The Globe and Mail*, 30 September 2004, B3; Bertrand Marotte, "Bombardier Rival Strikes Regional Jet Deal with China, *The Globe and Mail*, 13 September 2004, B3.
2 Dennis C. Kinlaw, "What Employees See Is What Organizations Get," *Management Solutions*, March 1988, 38–41.
3 Michael A. Verespej, "Balancing Act," *Industry Week*, 15 May 2000, 81–85.
4 John McMorrow, "Future Trends in Human Resources," *HR Focus*, September 1999, 8–9.
5 Robert B. Reich, "The Company of the Future," *Fast Company*, November 1998, 124–150.
6 Liberal Party of Canada website [accessed 7 December 2004] www.liberal.ca/bio_e.aspx?&id=35045
7 "Stronach Says She's Committed to Politics," CBC News website, 9 April 2004.
8 "Western Electric Hawthorne Studies Collection," Harvard Business School website [accessed 23 April 2005] www.library.hbs.edu/hc/wes/collections/labor/other/content/1001955886/; Barry L. Reece and Rhonda Brandt, *Effective Human Relations in Organizations*, (Boston: Houghton Mifflin, 1999), 17.
9 Douglas McGregor, *The Human Side of Enterprise* (New York: McGraw-Hill, 1960).
10 Reich, "The Company of the Future."
11 Aaron Bernstein, "We Want You to Stay. Really," *Business Week*, 22 June 1998, 67–72; Carol Kleiman, "The New Loyalty: A Work in Progress," *Chicago Tribune*, 15 August 1999, sec. 6, 1.
12 Kelly Barron and Ann Marsch, "The Skills Gap," *Forbes*, 23 February 1998, 44–45.
13 Greg Jaffe and Douglas A. Blackmon, "Just in Time. When UPS Demanded Workers, Louisville Did the Delivering," *Wall Street Journal*, 24 April 1998, A1, A10; James Ott, "UPS Hub 2000 at Louisville Marks New Airport Era," 20 July 1998, 471.
14 Anne D'Innocenzio, "Colgate-Palmolive to Cut 4,400 Jobs," *The Globe and Mail*, 8 December 2004, B12.
15 Bertrand Marotte, "Domtar Set to Slash 800 Jobs as Rising Dollar Boosts Costs," *The Globe and Mail*, 10 December 2004, B1.
16 Jennifer Laabs, "Has Downsizing Missed Its Mark?" *Workforce*, April 1999, 31–38.
17 Stephanie Armour, "Companies Hire Even as They Lay Off," *USA Today*, 15 May 2001, A1.
18 Andrew Wahl, "Leaders Wanted," *Canadian Business*, 1–14 March 2004, 31–35.
19 Laura Bogomolny, "Lessons from an Ancient Land," *Canadian Business*, 1–14 March 2004, 33.
20 Andrew Wahl, "Leaders Wanted," *Canadian Business*, 1–14 March 2004, 31–35.
21 Kamal Dib, "Diversity Works," *Canadian Business*, 29 March–11 April 2004, 53.
22 Michelle Kessler, "Days of BMW Signing Bonuses Long Gone," *USA Today*, 14 April 2002, 3B.
23 Barbara Moses, "How to Survive the Great Unknowns," *The Globe and Mail*, 15 September 2004, C3.
24 Jennifer Laabs, "The New Loyalty: Grasp It. Earn It. Keep It," *Workforce*, November 1998, 35–39.
25 Emily Thornton, "No Room at the Top," *Business Week*, 9 August 1999, 50; Michael A. Lev, "Lifetime Jobs May Be at Death's Door as Japan Tradition," *Chicago Tribune*, 11 October 1998, sec. 5, 1, 18.
26 Randy Ray, "Workplace Theft Takes a Big Toll," *The Globe and Mail*, 4 August 2004, C1.
27 John Greenwald, "Spinning Away," *Time*, 26 August 1996, 30–31.
28 Stephanie Armour, "Blame It on Downsizing, E-Mail, Laptops, and Dual-Career Families," *USA Today*, 13 March 1998, B1; Jennifer Laabs, "Workforce Overload," *Workforce*, January 1999, 30–37.
29 Michelle Conlin, Peter Coy, Ann Therese, and Gabrielle Saveri, "The Wild New Workforce," *Business Week*, 6 December 1999, 39–44.
30 Richard L. Daft, *Management*, 4th ed. (Fort Worth, TX: Dryden Press, 1997).
31 Stephanie Armour, "Workplace Demands Taking Up More Weekends," *USA Today*, 24 April 1998, B1; Laabs, "*Workforce Overload*."
32 Armour, "Workplace Demands Taking Up More Weekends."
33 Laabs, "Workforce Overload."
34 Michael A. Verespej, "Stressed Out," *Industry Week*, 21 February 2000, 30–34.
35 Verespej, "Balancing Act."
36 Wallace Immen, "Job Stress, Home Stress Linked," *The Globe and Mail*, 14 July 2004, C3.
37 Joanne Cole, "De-Stressing the Workplace," *HR Focus*, October 1999, 1, 10.
38 Jennifer Bresnehan, "The Elusive Muse," *CIO Enterprise*, 15 October 1997, 52; Kerry A. Dolan, "When Money Isn't Enough," *Forbes*, 18 November 1996, 164–170.
39 Kamal Dib, "Diversity Works," *Canadian Business*, 29 March–11 April 2004, 53.
40 Nina Munk, "Finished at Forty," *Fortune*, 1 February 1999, 50–66.
41 Munk, "Finished at Forty."
42 Valerie Marchant, "The New Face of Work," *Canadian Business*, March 29–April 11 2004.
43 Sherry Noik-Bent, "By Being Visible: How to Manage Multicultural Maze," *The Globe and Mail*, 24 November 2004, C1.
44 Virginia Galt, "Western Union Remakes 'Canadian' Image," *The Globe and Mail*, 23 November 2004, B1.
45 Amy Charmichael, "Female Executives Talk Shop and Share Know How," *The Globe and Mail*, 12 July 2004, B13.
46 Virginia Galt, "Glass Ceiling Still Tough to Crack," *The Globe and Mail*, 4 May 2005, C1.
47 Daft, *Management*, 462–463.
48 E. Armstrong, "My Glass Ceiling is Self-Imposed," *The Globe and Mail*, 15 December 2004, B15.
49 Shirley Won, "Women Climbing the Ranks at Banks," *The Globe and Mail*, 8 November 2004, B15.
50 Joseph White and Carol Hymowitz, "Broken Glass: Watershed Generation of Women Executives Is Rising to the Top," *Wall Street Journal*, 10 February 1997, A1, 6; Andrea Adelson, "Casual, Worker-Friendly, and a Moneymaker, Too: At Patagonia, Glass Ceiling Is Sky-High," *New York Times*, 30 June 1996, sec. Earning It, 8; Reed Abelson, "A Push from the Top Shatters a Glass Ceiling," *New York Times*, 22 August 1999, Y21, Y23.
51 Wallace Immen, "The Plague That Haunts Us Still," *The Globe and Mail*, 8 September 2004, C1.
52 Michael Barrier, "Sexual Harassment," *Nation's Business*, December 1998, 15–19.
53 Marianne Lavelle, "The New Rules of Sexual Harassment," *U.S. News & World Report*, 6 July 1998, 30–31.
54 Mahlon Apgar IV, "The Alternative Workplace: Changing Where and How People Work," *Harvard Business Review*, May–June 1998, 121–136.
55 Charlene Marmer Solomon, "Flexibility Comes Out of Flux," *Personnel Journal*, June 1996, 38–40.
56 Apgar, "The Alternative Workplace."
57 Carol Leonetti Dannhauser, "Who's in the Home Office?" *American Demographics*, June 1999, 50–56.
58 Apgar, "The Alternative Workplace."
59 Melanie Warner, "Working at Home—The Right Way to Be a Star in Your Bunny Slippers," *Fortune*, 3 March 1997, 166; Lin Grensing-Pophal, "Employing the Best People—From Afar," *Workforce*, March 1997, 30–32.
60 Kemba J. Dunham, "Telecommuters' Lament," *Wall Street Journal*, 31 October 2000, B1, B8.
61 Lisa Chadderdon, "Merrill Lynch Works—At Home," *Fast Company*, April–May 1998, 70–72.
62 Caudron, "Workers' Ideas for Improving Alternative Work Situations."
63 Caudron, "Workers' Ideas for Improving Alternative Work Situations."
64 Catherine Yang et al., "Low-Wage Lessons," *Business Week*, 11 November 1996, 108–110.
65 Martha Irvine, "Organizing Twentysomethings," *Los Angeles Times*, 7 September 1997, D5.
66 Konrad Yakabulski, "Wal-Mart Faces Battle of Quebec," *The Globe and Mail*, 16 February 2005, F16; Bertrand Marotte, "Union Weighs Public Boycott of Wal-Mart,"

The Globe and Mail, 12 February 2005, A11; Virginia Galt, "Wal-Mart Loses Labour Appeal in Sask. Court," *The Globe and Mail,* 24 November 2004, A1; Barrie McKenna, "Unions Starting to Make Inroads at Wal-Mart," *The Globe and Mail,* 23 August 2004, B1; Tu Thanh Ha, "Wal-Mart Employees in Quebec Win Union Approval," *The Globe and Mail,* 3 August 2004, A1; Patrick Brethour, "Wal-Mart Hails Saskatchewan Court Ruling on Rights in Union Drives," *The Globe and Mail,* 28 July 2004, B1.
67 "UPS Workers End Two Day Strike," *The Globe and Mail,* 24 November 2004, B12.
68 Nicholas Van Praet, "Alcoa Will Let Strike Roll On," *The Gazette* (Montreal), 8 October 2004, B3; Alcoa website [accessed 19 December 2004] www.alcoa.com/locations/becancour/en/home.asp
69 Susan Carey, "United Grapples with Summer of Widespread Discontent," *Wall Street Journal,* 8 August 2000, A2; Laurence Zuckerman and Matthew L. Wald, "Crisis for Air Traffic System: More Passengers, More Delays," *New York Times,* 5 September 2000, A1, C12.
70 Norma Kozhaya, "Striking Study: Quebec's Anti-Scab Law Increases the Number and Duration of Walkouts," *The Gazette* (Montreal), 3 September 2002, B3.
71 Bill Beacon, "World Stars Wake Up to Pay Cut," *The Globe and Mail,* 11 December 2004, S5.
72 International Labour Organization, *World Labour Report,* 4 November 1997 [accessed 7 November 1997] www.ilo.org.
73 Virginia Galt, "Their Backs against the Wall, Unions Are Opting for Compromise," *The Globe and Mail,* 5 July 2004, B1; Lloyd G. Reynolds, Stanley H. Masters, and Colletta H. Moser, *Labor Economics and Labor Relations,* 11th ed. (Upper Saddle River, NJ: Prentice Hall, 1998), 497; Indiana University News Bureau, "Trends in U.S. Labor Movement," *Futurist,* January–February 1996, 44; Barbara Presley Noble, "Reinventing Labor: An Interview with Union President Lynn Williams," *Harvard Business Review,* July–August 1993, 115–125.
74 Virginia Galt, "More Strife in Public Sector Collective Bargaining," *The Globe and Mail,* 17 December 2004, B5.
75 See Note 1.

Chapter 10
1 Peter Kennedy, "Starbucks Brewing Canadian Expansion," *The Globe and Mail,* 4 November 2004, B24; Abrahm Lustgarten, "A Hot, Steamy Cup of Customer Awareness," *Fortune,* 15 November 2004, 192; adapted from "Mr. Coffee," *Context,* August–September 2001, 20–25; Jennifer Ordonez, "Starbucks' Schultz to Leave Top Post, Lead Global Effort," *Wall Street Journal,* 7 April 2000, B3; Karyn Strauss, "Howard Schultz: Starbucks' CEO Serves a Blend of Community, Employee Commitment," *Nation's Restaurant News,* January 2000, 162–163; Carla Joinson, "The Cost of Doing Business?" *HR Magazine,* December 1999, 86–92; "Interview with Howard Schultz: Sharing Success," *Executive Excellence,* November 1999, 16–17; Kelly Barron, "The Cappuccino Conundrum," *Forbes,* 22 February 1999, 54–55; Naomi Weiss, "How Starbucks Impassions Workers to Drive Growth," *Workforce,* August 1998, 60–64; Scott S. Smith, "Grounds for Success," *Entrepreneur,* May 1998, 120–126; "Face Value: Perky People," *The Economist,* 30 May 1998, 66; Howard Schultz and Dori Jones Yang, "Starbucks: Making Values Pay," *Fortune,* 29 September 1997, 261–272.
2 Steven Greenhouse, "Equal Work, Less-Equal Perks," *New York Times,* 30 March 1998, C1, C6; Aaron Bernstein, "When Is a Temp Not a Temp?" *Business Week,* 7 December 1998, 90–92.
3 Virginia Galt, "Firms See Value in Putting Retirees Back to Work," *The Globe and Mail,* 8 September 2004, B7; Karin Rives, "Older Workers the Employees of Choice for Many Recruiters," *The Globe and Mail,* 12 July 2004, B13.
4 William J. Stevenson, *Production Operations Management,* 6th ed. (Boston: Irwin McGraw-Hill, 1999), 698; Laurie Edwards, "When Outsourcing Is Appropriate," *Wall Street and Technology,* July 1998, 96–98.
5 Stephanie Armour, "Some Companies Choose No-Layoff Policy," *USA Today,* 17 December 2001, 1B.
6 Wallace Immen, "Resume Stunts Can Count You Out, Rather Than Make You Stand Out," *The Globe and Mail,* 6 November 2004, B11.
7 George Donnelly, "Recruiting, Retention, and Returns," *CFO Magazine,* March 2000 [accessed 10 April 2000] www.cfonet.com/html/Articles/CFO/2000/00MArecr.html
8 Audrey Arthur, "How Much Should Employers Know?" *Black Enterprise,* October 1997, 56; Anthony Ramirez, "Name, Résumé, References. And How's Your Credit?" *New York Times,* 31 August 1997, F8.
9 Jonathan Segal, "When Norman Bates and Baby Jane Act Out at Work," *HR Magazine, 41* (1 February 1996): 31; Jenny C. McCune, "Companies Grapple with Workplace Violence," *Management Review,* March 1994, 52–57.
10 Wallace Immen, "Reality TV Reveals Real-Life Leaders' Flaws," *The Globe and Mail,* 3 December 2004, C3; Raizel Robin, "Dreams of the Donald," *Canadian Business,* 12–15 April 2004, 47–49.
11 Kirk Makin, "RBC Dominion Awarded $2.25-Million After Merrill Lures Brokers," *The Globe and Mail,* 12 November 2004, B4.
12 Wallace Immen, "Prospective Hires Put to the Test," *The Globe and Mail,* 26 January 2005, C1.
13 "Substance Abuse in the Workplace," *HR Focus,* February 1997, 1, 41; Tyler D. Hartwell, Paul D. Steele, and Nathaniel F. Rodman, "Workplace Alcohol-Testing Programs: Prevalence and Trends," *Monthly Labor Review,* June 1998, 27–34.
14 Randall S. Schuler, *Managing Human Resources* (Cincinnati, OH: South-Western College Publishing, 1998), 386.
15 Katharine Mieszkowski, "Report from the Future," *Fast Company,* February–March 1998, 28–30.
16 "Bank of Montreal Institute for Learning: Case Study," Moriyama & Teshima website [accessed 9 December 2004] www.mtarch.com/bofmcasestudy.html
17 Michael Barrier, "Develop Workers and Your Business," *Nation's Business,* December 1998, 25–27.
18 Laura Bogomolny, "Janice Wismer: Most Innovative Exec," *Canadian Business,* April 26–May 9 2004, 52.
19 Bill Roberts, "Training via the Desktop" *HR Magazine,* August 1998, 98–104.
20 Kathleen Redmond, "Confront Non-Performers without Feeling Angst," *The Globe and Mail,* 8 October 2004, C1.
21 Virginia Galt, "Making Performance Reviews Painless," *The Globe and Mail,* 6 January 2005, B11.
22 Kate Ludeman, "How to Conduct Self-Directed 360," *Training and Development,* July 2000, 44–47; Cassandra Hayes, "To Tell the Truth," *Black Enterprise,* December 1998, 55.
23 Virginia Galt, "Employers Jumping on E-Learning Bandwagon," *The Globe and Mail,* 12 June 2004, B10.
24 Gina Imperato, "How to Give Good Feedback," *Fast Company,* September 1998, 144–156.
25 Fiona Jebb, "Flex Appeal," *Management Today* (London), July 1998, 66–69; Milton Zall, "Implementing a Flexible Benefits Plan," *Fleet Equipment,* May 1999, B4–B8.
26 Julie Appleby, "Workers Pay More for Care," *USA Today,* 5 April 2001, 1B.
27 Don L. Boroughs, "The Bottom Line on Ethics," *U.S. News & World Report,* 20 March 1995, 63–54.
28 Luis R. Gomez-Mejia, David B. Balkin et al., *Managing Human Resources,* 3rd Canadian ed. (Toronto: Pearson/Prentice Hall, 2004), 332; "Canada and Quebec Pension Plan," [accessed 9 December 2004] http://benefits.org/interface/benefit/cpp.htm; HRSDC website [accessed 9 December 2004] www.hrsdc.gc.ca
29 Richard D. Pearce, "The Small Employer Retirement Plan Void," *Compensation and Benefits Management,* Winter 1999, 51–55.
30 "Unemployed New Brunswick Mill Workers Lose Their Pensions," CTV News [accessed 9 December 2004] www.ctv.ca/servlet/ArticleNews/story/CTV News/1102462269443_97871469

31 James H. Dulebohn, Brian Murray, and Minghe Sun, "Selection among Employer-Sponsored Pension Plans: The Role of Individual Differences," *Personal Psychology*, Summer 2000, 405–432.
32 Luis R. Gomez-Mejia, David B. Balkin et al., *Managing Human Resources,* 346–347.
33 Luis R. Gomez-Mejia, David B. Balkin et al., *Managing Human Resources,* 346–347.
34 Paul J. Lim and Matthew Benjamin, "The 401(k) Stumbles," *U.S. News & World Report*, 24 December 2001, 30–32.
35 "Notes to Consolidated Financial Statements," *Telus Annual Report 2003*, 70.
36 Suzanne I. Cohen, "United Airlines' ESOP Woes," *Risk Management*, June 2001, 9; Laurence Zuckerman, "Divided, an Airline Stumbles," *New York Times*, 14 March 2001, C1.
37 Michael Arndt, "Will United's Woes Spread?" *Business Week*, 13 November 2000, 180–192.
38 Andrew Willis, "CIBC Finds a Way to Reward a Job Well Done and Thwart Deserters at the Same Time," *The Globe and Mail*, 10 December 2004, B1.
39 Del Jones, "More Workers Get Options, Too," *USA Today*, 7 April 1999, 3B
40 Real Women of Canada website [accessed 10 December 2004] www.realwomenca.com/newsletter/2003_jan_feb/article_8.html
41 Stephanie Armour, "Ford Plans Ambitious Child-Care Program for Workers," *USA Today*, 22 November 2000, B1.
42 "Workplace Briefs," Gannett News Service, 24 April 1997; Julia Lawlor, "The Bottom Line," *Working Woman*, July–August 1996, 54–58, 74–76.
43 Stephanie Armour, "Employers Stepping Up in Elder Care," *USA Today*, 3 August 2000, 3B.
44 Del Jones, "Firms Take New Look at Sick Days," *USA Today*, 8 October 1996, 8B.
45 National Quality Institute website [accessed 24 April 2005] www.nqi.ca/caeawards/profiles/profiles2004.aspx#mmm Canada%20Awards%20For%20Excellence%202004
46 Atkinson, "Wellness, Employee Assistance Programs."
47 Atkinson, "Wellness, Employee Assistance Programs"; Kevin Dobbs, Jack Gordon, and David Stamps, "EAPs Cheap but Popular Perk," *Training*, February 2000, 26.
48 Magna Corporation website [accessed 11 December 2004] www.magna.com
49 "50 Benefits and Perks That Make Employees Want to Stay Forever," *HR Focus*, July 2000, S2–S3.
50 Edward Iwata, "Staff-Hungry Tech Firms Cast Exotic Lures," *USA Today*, 1 February 2000, B1.
51 Adam Cohen and Cathy Booth Thomas, "Inside a Layoff," *Time*, 16 April 2001, 38–40.
52 Rodney Ho, "AT&T's Offer of $10,000 May Test Entrepreneurship of Laid-Off Workers," *Wall Street Journal*, 12 March 1997; David Fischer and Kevin Whitelaw, "A New Way to Shine Up Corporate Profits," *U.S. News & World Report*, 15 April 1996, 55.
53 Virginia Galt, "Jeans Workers Helped to Face Life after Levi," *The Globe and Mail*, 11 October 2004, B1, B12.
54 Wallace Immen, "Post-65 Workers Productive and Engaged," *The Globe and Mail*, 18 March 2005, C1.
55 See Note 1.
56 Virginia Galt, "Job Seekers Can Get Free Advice On-Line," *The Globe and Mail*, 21 August 2004, B8; Efraim Turban and David King, *Introduction to E-Commerce* (Upper Saddle River, NJ: Pearson Education, 2003), 107–111; Marlene Piturro, "The Power of E-Cruiting," *Management Review*, January 2000, 33–38; "Online Recruiting: What Works, What Doesn't," *HR Focus*, March 2000, 11–15; "More Pros and Cons to Internet Recruiting," *HR Focus*, May 2000, 8; Christopher Caggiano, "The Truth about Internet Recruiting," *Inc.*, December 1999, 156; Peter Buxbaum, "Where's Dilbert?" *Chief Executive* [accessed 2 March 2000] www.chiefexecutive.net/mag/150tech/part1c.htm; James R. Borck, "Recruiting Systems Control Résumé Chaos," *InfoWorld*, 24 July 2000, 47-48; Bill Leonard, "Online and Overwhelmed," *HR Magazine*, August 2000, 36–42; Milton Zall, "Internet Recruiting," *Strategic Finance*, June 2000, 66–72; "Why Your Web Site Is More Important Than Ever to New Hires," *HR Focus*, June 2000, 9; Rachel Emma Silverman, "Recruiters' Hunt for Résumés Is Nocturnal Game," *Wall Street Journal*, 20 September 2000, B1–B4.

Chapter 11

1 Adobe website [accessed 27 April 2005] www.adobe.com/aboutadobe/main.html; "Adobe Named by Fortune as One of the 100 Best Companies to Work for in America," *Business Wire*, 24 January 2002, 1; Mylene Mangalindan, "Adobe Cuts Revenue and Profit Targets, Reduces Staff 5%, Blaming Economy," *Wall Street Journal*, 31 October 2001, B6; Melinda Patterson Grenier, "Turning Popularity into Profitability: Adobe Had a Popular Product; Making It Profitable Took Some Work," *Wall Street Journal*, 15 October 2001, R18; Karen Southwick, "How Far Can Serendipity Carry Adobe?" *Upside*, September 1995, 46; Kennedy Grey, "Rekindling an Old Spirit," *MC Technology Marketing Intelligence*, August 2000, 64–70; Paul Andrews, "Microsoft Can't Topple Adobe Acrobat," *Seattle Times*, 1 April 2002, C1.
2 "AMA Board Approves New Marketing Definition," *Marketing News*, 1 March 1985, 1.
3 www.cso.on.ca/CanadianSpecialOlympics/newsletters.html [accessed 7 April 2005]
4 Al Ries and Jack Trout, *The Immutable Laws of Marketing* (New York: HarperCollins, 1994), 19–25.
5 Hudson's Bay Company website [accessed 27 April 2005] www.hbc.com/hbc/careers/why/development/
6 Terry G. Vavra, "The Database Marketing Imperative," *Marketing Management, 2*(1) (1993): 47–57.
7 Peter Fingar, Harsha Kumar, and Tarun Sharma, *Enterprise E-Commerce* (Tampa, FL.: Meghan-Kiffer Press, 2000), 24, 109.
8 Barbara Whitaker, "House Hunting with Cursor and Click," *New York Times*, 24 September 1998, D1, D5.
9 Pierre M. Loewe and Mark S. Bonchek, "The Retail Revolution," *Management Review*, April 1999, 38–44.
10 Saturn Canada website [accessed 7 June 2004] www.saturncanada.com/ssi/english/vehicles/saturn/different/experience.html
11 John Gray, "Tailoring the Message: In a Multicultural Society All Ads Are Not Alike," *Canadian Business*, 29 March–11 April 2004, 65.
12 www.theglobeandmail.com/servlet/story/RTGAM.20040531.wrigin131/BNStory/spec [accessed 7 June 2004]
13 Janet Novack, "The Data Miners," *Forbes*, 12 February 1996, 96–97; Don Peppers and Martha Rogers, *Enterprise One to One* (New York: Doubleday, 1997), 120–121.
14 Louisa Wah, "The Almighty Customer," *Management Review*, February 1999, 16-22; James Lardner, "Your Every Command," *U.S. News & World Report*, 5 July 1999, 44–46.
15 Hal Lancaster, "Managing Your Career: Giving Good Service, Never an Easy Task, Is Getting a Lot Harder," *Wall Street Journal*, 9 June 1998, B1.
16 Janet Willen, "The Customer Is Wrong," *Business97*, October–November 1997, 40–42; William H. Davidow and Bro Uttal, *Total Customer Service: The Ultimate Weapon* (New York: Harper & Row, 1989), 8; Valarie A. Zeithaml, A. Parasuraman, and Leonard L. Berry, *Delivering Quality Service* (NewYork: Free Press, 1990), 9; George J. Castellese, "Customer Service... Building a Winning Team," *Supervision*, January 1995, 9–13; Erica G. Sorohan and Catherine M. Petrini, "Dumpsters, Ducks, and Customer Service," *Training and Development*, January 1995, 9.
17 Canada's Personal Information and Electronic Documents Act [accessed 2 June 2004] www.privcom.gc.ca/information/02_05_d_08_e.asp
18 Diane Brady, "Why Service Stinks," *Business Week*, 23 October 2000, 118–128.
19 Don Peppers, Martha Rogers, and Bob Dorf, "Is Your Company Ready for One-to-One Marketing?" *Harvard Business Review*, January–February 1999.

20 Malcolm H. B. McDonald, "Ten Barriers to Marketing Planning," *Journal of Product and Brand Management*, Fall 1992, 51–64.
21 John Saunders, "Krispy Kreme Hit by Carb Craze," *The Globe and Mail*, 8 May 2004, B4.
22 www.subway.com/subwayroot/index.aspx [accessed 2 June 2004]; www.usatoday.com/money/industries/food/2003-12-25-subway-atkins_x.htm [accessed 7 June 2004].
23 www.intrawest.net/ [accessed 3 June 2004]
24 Gordon S. Jepson and M. Susana Diaz, "New Canadian Food Labelling Regulations," www.com/articles/new_canadian_food_labeling_regulations.pdf [accessed 8 June 2004].
25 Leslie Kaufman, "Playing Catch-Up at the On-Line Mall," *New York Times*, 21 February 1999, sec. 3, 1, 6; Gary Samuels, "CD-ROMs First Big Victim," *Forbes*, 28 February 1994, 42–44; Richard A. Melcher, "Dusting off the Britannica," *Business Week*, 20 October 1997, 143–146.
26 Malcolm McDonald and John W. Leppard, *Marketing by Matrix* (Lincolnwood, IL: NTC, 1993), 10; H. Igor Ansoff, "Strategies for Diversification," *Harvard Business Review*, November–December 1957, 113–124; H. Igor Ansoff, *Corporate Strategy* (New York: McGraw-Hill, 1965).
27 Scott Hays, "Exceptional Customer Service Takes the 'Ritz' Touch," *Workforce*, January 1999, 99–102.
28 Jennifer Barron and Jill Hollingshead, "Making Segmentation Work," *MM*, January–February 2002, 24–28.
29 Keith J. Tuckwell, *Canadian Marketing in Action,* 6th ed. (Toronto: Prentice Hall, 2004), 149.
30 Philip Kotler, Gary Armstrong, and Peggy Cunningham, *Principles of Marketing*, 6th ed. (Toronto: Prentice Hall, 2005), 341.
31 M. Dale Beckman and John M. Rigby, *Foundations of Marketing*, 8th ed., (Toronto: Nelson, 2003), 61.
32 Horacio D. Rozanski, Gerry Bollman, and Martin Lipman, "Seize the Occasion," *Strategy and Business*, Third Quarter 2001, 42–51.
33 David Shani and Sujana Chalasani, "Exploring Niches Using Relationship Marketing," *Journal of Business and Industrial Marketing*, no. 4 (1993): 58–66.
34 Courtland L. Bovée, Michael J. Houston, and John V. Thill, *Marketing*, 2nd ed. (New York: McGraw-Hill, 1994), 224.
35 Daniel Roth, "First: From Poster Boy to Whipping Boy," *Fortune*, 6 July 1998, 28–29.
36 Sarah Dougherty, "Bell Mobility, Virgin Target Youth Market," *The Gazette* (Montreal), 30 March 2004.
37 Gary Armstrong and Philip Kotler, *Marketing: An Introduction*, 5th ed. (Upper Saddle River, NJ: Prentice Hall, 2000), 201–204.; http://c2dsp.westjet.com/internet/sky/about/index.jsp [accessed 9 June 2004]
38 Jim McElguinn, "Child's Play; Max Valiquette Makes Youth Marketing Look Easy," *Canadian Business*, 15–28 March 2004, 42.
39 Armstrong and Kotler, *Marketing: An Introduction*, 206.
40 Armstrong and Kotler, *Marketing: An Introduction*, 329.
41 Philip Kotler and Gary Armstrong, *Principles of Marketing*, 9th ed. (Upper Saddle River, NJ: Prentice Hall, 2001), 296.
42 "Preparing for a Point to Point World," *Marketing Management, 3*(4) (Spring 1995): 30–40.
43 Claudia H. Deutsch, "Deep in Debt Since 1988, Polaroid Files for Bankruptcy," *New York Times*, 13 October 2001, C1, C14.
44 Dan Proudfoot, "Three Detours on the Long, Winding Road to a Cleaner Fuel Conscience," *The Globe and Mail*, 3 June 2004, G6; www.toyota.com/about/news/product/2003/04/16-1-prius.html [accessed 9 June 2004].
45 Bruce Horovitz, "Cookie Makers Bake Up New Twists," *USA Today*, 27 March 2001, 3B.
46 Michael McCarthy, "Brands That Lose Their Punch Get Yanked," *USA Today*, 13 December 2000, 3B.
47 Canadian Intellectual Property Office website [accessed 9 June 2004] http://strategis.ic.gc.ca/sc_mrksv/cipo/help/faq_tm-e.html#1
48 Thomas K. Grose, "Brand New Goods," *Time.com*, 1 November 1999 [accessed 17 February 2001] www.time.com/time/magazine/article/0,9171,33124-1,00.html
49 Jagdish N. Sheth and Rajendra S. Sisodia, "Feeling the Heat," *Marketing Management, 4*(2) (Fall 1995): 9–23.
50 Claudia H. Deutsch, "Will That Be Paper or Pixel?" *New York Times*, 4 August 2000, C1, C4.
51 Eric N. Berkowitz, Frederick G. Crane et al., *Marketing*, 5th Canadian ed. (Toronto: McGraw-Hill, 2003), 307.
52 General Mills Canada, provided by Denise Nelson, Communications Department, 14 June 2004.
53 Armstrong and Kotler, *Marketing: An Introduction*, 234.
54 Nina Munk, "Gap Gets It," *Fortune*, 3 August 1998, 68–82.
55 Terril Yue Jones, "Fearing the Old Shoddy Image," *Forbes*, 12 January 1998 [accessed 16 June 1999] www.forbes.com/forbes/98/0112/6101064a.htm
56 Thomas T. Nagle, "Managing Price Competition," *Marketing Management, 2*(1) (1993): 38–45; Sheth and Sisodia, "Feeling the Heat," 21.
57 Gurumurthy Kalyanaram and Ragu Gurumurthy, "Market Entry Strategies: Pioneers versus Late Arrivals," *Strategy & Business*, Third quarter 1998 [accessed 16 June 1999] www.strategy-business.com
58 Tim Klass, "Web Bookstores Discount Bestsellers," *Associated Press Online*, 17 May 1999 [accessed 21 May 1999]. www.cbsmarketwatch.com.
59 See Note 1.

Chapter 12

1 Mountain Equipment Cooperative website [accessed 27 March 2004] www.mec.ca/Main/content_text.jsp?CONTENT%3C%eCNT_ID=615519&folder%3C%3EFOLDER_ID=652217&BMuid=1089928614906
2 Mountain Equipment Cooperative website [accessed 1 May 2005] www.mec.ca; *Computer World Canada*, 18 May 2001; *Canadian Retailer* (May/June 2001); MEC Facts, press release, Tim Southam, MEC Communications Specialist [29 April 2004].
3 Mona Aubin, Bombardier Communications; Matthew McClearn, "Bombardier's Bank," *Canadian Business*, 29 March 2004, 20.
4 Lisa Chadderdon, "How Dell Sells on the Web," *Fast Company*, September 1998, 58, 60.
5 Gregory L. White, "GM Is Forming Unit to Buy Dealerships," *Wall Street Journal*, 24 September 1999, A3; Joann Muller, "Meet Your Local GM Dealer: GM," *Business Week*, 11 October 1999, 48.
6 Philip Kotler and Gary Armstrong, *Principles of Marketing*, 9th ed. (Upper Saddle River, NJ: Prentice Hall, 2001), 435.
7 "Hallmark, a New Name in Mass Retailing," *Supermarket Business*, March 1997, 84; Daniel Roth, "Card Sharks," *Forbes*, 7 October 1996, 14; Julie Rygh, "Hallmark Cards Find Success with New Expressions Brand," *Knight-Ridder/Tribune Business News*, 31 August 1997, 831B0958.
8 Katarzyna Moreno, "UnbeComing," *Forbes*, 10 June 2002, 151–152; www.avon.ca.
9 Inditex (Zara) website [accessed 1 May 2005] www.inditex.com/en/who_we_are/stores; Richard Heller, "Galician Beauty," *Forbes*, 28 May 2001.
10 Colleen Gourley, "Retail Logistics in Cyberspace," *Distribution*, December 1996, 29; Dave Hirschman, "FedEx Starts Up Package Sorting System at Memphis Tenn. Airport," *Knight-Ridder/Tribune Business News*, 28 September 1997, 928B0953; "FedEx and Technology—Maintaining a Competitive Edge," PresWIRE, 2 December 1996.
11 *Annual Report 2004*, Canada Post website [accessed 1 May 2005] www.canadapost.ca.
12 Gregory Ellis, Kanetix co-founder [accessed 24 March 2004] www.kanetix.ca.
13 Adapted from information provided by Gregory Ellis, co-founder of Kanetix [8 April 2004]; Rob Carrick, *The Globe and Mail*, 23 March 2004; Kanetix website [accessed 1 May 2005] www.kanetix.ca.

14 Mark Maremont, "How Gillette Brought Its Mach3 to Market," *Wall Street Journal*, 15 April 1998, B1, B4; Jeremy Kahn, "Gillette Loses Face," *Fortune*, 8 November 1999, 147–148.
15 Brad Dorfman, "Gillette Profits Rise on Battery, Razor Sales," *Forbes*, 4 November 2003.
16 David J. Morrow, "From Lab to Patient, by Way of Your Den," *New York Times*, 7 June 1998, sec. 3, 1, 10.
17 Michele Marchetti, "What a Sales Call Costs," *Sales and Marketing Management*, September 2000, 80–82.
18 David Prater, "The Third Time's the Charm," *Sales and Marketing Management*, September 2000, 100–104; Gary Armstrong and Philip Kotler, *Marketing: An Introduction* (Upper Saddle River, NJ: Prentice Hall, 2000), 454.
19 Direct Marketing Association website [accessed 23 November 1997] www.the-dma.org/services1/libres-home1b.shtml
20 Karl Moore, "Gotta Get That Buzz," *Marketing*, 28 June–5 July 2004, 9.
21 Keith J. Tuckwell, *Canadian Advertising in Action*, 6th ed. (Toronto: Prentice Hall, 2003), 28; www.crtc.gc.ca/; www.adstandards.com/
22 John Heinzl, "Drug Makers Said to Skirt Canadian Restrictions on Ads," *The Globe and Mail*, 12 February 2002, B1.
23 David Leeder, GlobeandMail.com, 15 October 2003.
24 "Direct Hit," *The Economist*, 9 January 1999, 55–57.
25 Sarah Lorge, "Banner Ads vs. E-Mail Marketing," *Sales and Marketing Management*, August 1999, 15.
26 Canadian Fraud Laws [accessed 25 March 2004] www.canadianlawsite.com/fraud.htm
27 Armstrong and Kotler, *Marketing: An Introduction*, 409.
28 Zoom Media website [accessed 29 March 2004] www.zoom-media.com; additional information provided by Chantal Goncalves, Communications and Marketing Manager [30 April 2004].
29 Zoom Media press release, 4 December 2003; "Zoom Media Acquires Toronto Billboard Firm" [accessed 29 March 2004] www.globeandmail.com
30 "Coupons, Samples Drive Consumer Shopping Decisions," Cox Direct, 8 September 1998 [accessed 24 May 1999] www.justdelivered.com/itm/pressreleases/pr-090898-2.htm.
31 Paulette Thomas, "'e-Clicking' Coupons On-Line Has a Cost: Privacy," *Wall Street Journal*, 18 June 1998, B1, B8.
32 William M. Bulkeley, "Rebates' Secret Appeal to Manufacturers: Few Customers Actually Redeem Them," *Wall Street Journal*, 10 February 1998, B1, B8.
33 Lisa Z. Eccles, "Point of Purchase Advertising," *Advertising Age Supplement*, 26 September 1994, 1–6.
34 Grace Shim, "Sponsorship of the Rings," *Omaha World-Herald*, 7 February 2002, 1D.
35 Raizel Robin, "Let the Games Begin," *Canadian Business*, 5 August 2003, 17.
36 Keith McArthur, "Bell Beats Out Telus to Sponsor B.C.'s 2010 Olympics, *The Globe and Mail*, 19 October 2004, B1, B22.
37 Betsy Morris, "The Brand's the Thing," *Fortune*, 4 March 1996, 72–86.
38 "Effective Sampling Strategies," *Sales Marketing Network* [accessed 7 November 2000] www.info-now.com/html/1022dir1.asp
39 Krispy Kreme website [accessed 26 March 2004] www.krispykreme/can.html; Alex Mlynek, "Live and Learn: Ron Joyce," *Canadian Business*, 23 June 2003 [accessed 26 March 2004] www.canadianbusiness.com
40 Kathryn Kranhold and Stephen Power, "Bridgestone Turns to Ketchum to Redo Image after Tire Recall," *Wall Street Journal*, 12 September 2000, A4.
41 Catherine McLean, "Virgin's Sir Richard Makes Wireless Pitch," *The Globe and Mail*, 2 March 2005, B4; Catherine McLean, "Virgin Mobile Set to Ring up Canada," *The Globe and Mail*, 17 February 2005, B1, B8.
42 Verne Gay, "Milk, the Magazine," *American Demographics*, February 2000, 32–33.
43 Armstrong and Kotler, *Marketing: An Introduction*, 405.
44 Molson's "I AM" website [accessed 2 April 2004] www.iam.ca
45 Mountain Equipment Cooperative website, www.mec.ca; *Computer World Canada*, 18 May 2001; *Canadian Retailer* (May/June 2001); MEC Facts press release, source: Tim Southam, MEC Communications Specialist.
46 See Note 2.
47 Keith McArthur, "Is It the Death of the 30 Second Spot?" *The Globe and Mail*, 9 July 2005, B4.
48 Peter Wolchack, "E-Tail Success: Watch the Pennies," *Backbone Magazine*, January/February 2005, 6; Richard Bloom, "On-Line Shoppers Click Up Sales," *The Globe and Mail*, 28 December 2004, B1; Kevin Bartus, "Measuring What Works Online," 27 September 2004, 15, 16; Allison Kaplan, "Retailers Taking New Approach to Internet," *Knight Ridder Tribune News Service*, 11 June 2002, 1; Gerry Khermouch and Nanette Byrnes, "Come Back to Papa," *Business Week*, 19 February 2001, 42; Rebecca Quick, "Returns to Sender," *Wall Street Journal*, 17 July 2000, R8; Greg Farrell, "Clicks-and Mortar World Values Brands," *USA Today*, 5 October 1999, B1, B2; Ranjay Gulati and Jason Garino, "Get the Right Mix of Bricks and Clicks," *Harvard Business Review*, May–June 2000, 107–114; Anne Stuart, "Clicks & Bricks," *CIO*, 15 March 2000, 76–84; Jason Anders, "Sibling Rivalry," *Wall Street Journal*, 17 July 2000, R16; William M. Bulkeley, "Clicks and Mortar," *Wall* Street Journal, 17 July 2000, R4; Allanna Sullivan, "From a Call to a Click," *Wall Street Journal*, 17 July 2000, R30; Suein L. Hwang, "Clicks and Bricks," *Wall Street Journal*, 17 April 2000, R8, R10; Jeffrey Rothfeder, "Toys 'R' Us Battles Back," *Strategy and Business*, Quarter 2, 2000; Dennis K. Berman and Heather Green, "Cliff Hanger Christmas," *Business Week E.Biz*, 23 October 2000, EB30–EB38; Jerry Useem, "Dot-Coms What Have We Learned?" *Fortune*, 30 October 2000, 82–104.

Chapter 13

1 Mark Evans, "Nortel to begin results update on Jan. 10," *National Post*, National Edition, 9 December 2004, FP4.
2 Mark Evans, "Nortel wins US $1B order from Sprint," *National Post*, National Edition, 8 December 2004, FP4.
3 Simon Avery, "Nortel accounting woes 'an embarrassment,'" *The Globe and Mail*, 30 November 2004.
4 Kevin Restivo, "Nortel CEO says he's red-faced by financial report delay," *National Post*, National Edition 30 November 2004, FP3.
5 See note 3.
6 Robert Stuart, "Accountants in Management—A Globally Changing Role," *CMA Magazine*, 1 February 1997, 5.
7 Steve Zwick, "The Price of Transparency," *Time*, 19 February 2001, B8–B11.
8 Jeffrey E. Garten, "Global Accounting Rules? Not So Fast," *Business Week*, 5 April 1999, 26; Elizabeth Macdonald, "U.S. Accounting Board Faults Global Rules," *Wall Street Journal*, 18 October 1999, A1.
9 Matt Krantz and Gregg Farrell, "Fuzzy Accounting Raises Flags," *USA Today*, 22 June 2001, 1B.
10 Jeanne Cummings, "Bush to Seek Tougher Penalties In Assault on Corporate Fraud," *Wall Street Journal*, 9 July 2002, A1, A4; Paul Beckett, "SEC Order Forces Executive to Swear by Their Numbers," *Wall Street Journal*, 5 July 2002, A1, A6; Scot J. Paltrow, "Accounting-Overhaul Plans Draw Skepticism, "*Wall Street Journal*, 8 July 2002, C1, C16.
11 Frank Evans, "A Road Map to Your Financial Report," *Management Review*, October 1993, 39–47.
12 David H. Bangs, Jr., "Financial Troubleshooting," *Soundview Executive Book Summaries* 15, No. 5 (May 1993).
13 See note 1.
14 See note 2.
15 Andrew Wahl, "A slowpoke in China?" *Canadian Business*, online, October 25, 2004.
16 See note 15.

Chapter 14

1 Terence Corcoran, "Regulations stifle Canadian banks' growth," *The Windsor Star*, Final Edition, 10 May 2004, A6.

2 David Crane, "Good bank merger policy is worth waiting for," *Toronto Star*, Ontario Edition, 2 October 2004, D2.

3 Eric Beauchesne, "Most smaller firms oppose bank mergers," *Times-Colonist*, Final Edition, 8 October 2003, B5.

4 Rob Ferguson, "Bank mergers 'unlikely' before 2005; Issue remains hot potato for consumers, analyst says RBC; Centura plans to open 60 more branches in U.S.," *Toronto Star*, Ontario Edition, 10 Sept. 2003, C1.

5 Mandy Andress, "Smart Is Not Enough: Cards Must Also Be Easy and Useful," *InfoWorld*, 16 October 2000, 94; Mary Shacklett, "American Express' Blue is Setting the Pace in U.S. Smart Card Market," *Credit Union Magazine*, September 2000, 16A–17A.

6 Scott Woolley, "Virtual Banker," *Forbes*, 15 June 1998 [accessed 28 July 1999] www.forbes.com/forbes/98/0615/6112127a.htm; Dean Foust, "Will Online Banking Replace the ATM?" *Yahoo! Internet Life*, November 1998, 114–118.

7 New York Stock Exchange website [accessed 23 July 2002] www.nyse.com.

8 James K. Glassman, "Manager's Journal: Who Needs Stock Exchanges? Not Investors," *Wall Street Journal*, 8 May 2000, A42.

9 Julie Bort, "Trading Places," *Computerworld*, 27 May 1996, 1051.

10 Neil Weinberg, "The Big Board Comes Back from the Brink," Forbes, 13 November 2000, 274–281.

11 Gaston F. Ceron, "Instinet to Acquire Island ECN In a $508 Million Stock Deal," *Wall Street Journal*, 11 June 2002, C5.

12 Lee Copeland, "After-Hours Trading," *Computerworld*, 27 March 2000, 57.

13 John R. Dorfman, "Crash Courses," *Wall Street Journal*, 28 May 1996, R12–R13.

14 Katrina Brooker, "Could the Dow Become Extnict?" *Fortune*, 15 February 1999, 194–195; Anita Raghavan and Nancy Ann Jeffrey, "What, How, Why—So What Is the Dow Jones Industrial Average, Anyway?" *Wall Street Journal*, 28 May 1996, R30; E.S. Browning, "New Economy Stocks Join Industrials," *Wall Street Journal*, 27 October 1999, C1, C15.

15 Jeffrey M. Laderman, "Why It's So Tough to Beat the S&P," *Business Week*, 24 March 1997, 82–83.

16 E.S. Browning, "Journal Goes 'Decimal' With Nasdaq Tables," *Wall Street Journal*, 2 August 2000, C1; "SEC Orders Decimal Stock Prices," *Chicago Tribune*, 29 January 2000, sec. 2, 2.

17 See note 12.

18 SEC website [accessed 21 December 2000] www.sec.gov/consumer/jdatacom.htm.

19 David Diamond, "The Web's Most Wanted," *Business 2.0*, August 1999, 120–128.

20 Thor Valdmanis and Tom Lowry, "Wall Street's New Breed Revives Inside Trading," *USA Today*, 4 November 1999, 1B.

21 Rebecca Buckman, "NASD Maps War on Claims on Internet," *Wall Street Journal*, 24 March 1997, B98W.

22 Andrew Pollack, "Some Records of Stewart's Broker Subpoenaed," *New York Times*, 9 July 2002, C11; Constance L. Hays and Andrew Pollack, "Stewart Image and Company Built Upon It Take Battering," *New York Times*, 4 July 2002, C1.

23 See note 1.

24 See note 3.

25 See note 4.

26 Mark Sievewright, "Traditional vs. Virtual Service," *Credit Union Magazine*, February 2002, 26; Eileen Colkin, "Citibank," *Information Week*, 27 August 2001, 30; Andrew Ross Sorkin, "Put Your Money Where Your Modem Is," *New York Times*, 30 May 2002, G1; Erica Garcia, "What's Left of the Online Banks," *Money*, October 2001, 167; Jathon Sapsford, "Consumers Take Notice of Online Banks," *Wall Street Journal*, 28 November 2000, C1, C19; Lauren Bielski, "Online Banking Yet to Deliver," *American Bankers Association, ABA Banking Journal*, September 2000, 6, 12+; Heather Timmons, "online Banks Can't Go It Alone," *Business Week*, 31 July 2000, 86–87; Mark Skousen, "Online Banking's Goodies," *Forbes*, 12 June 2000, P366+; Tony Stanco, "Internet Banking—Some Big Players, But Little Returns So Far," *Boardwatch*, March 2000, 86–90; Carrick Mollenkamp, "Old-Line Banks Advance in Bricks-vs.-Clicks Battle," *Wall Street Journal*, 21 January 2000, C1.

Appendix B

1 Bill Shaw and Art Wolfe, *The Structure of the Legal Environment: Law, Ethics, and Business*, 2d ed. (Boston: PWS-Kent, 1991), 635.

2 Thomas W. Dunfee, Frank F. Gibson, John D. Blackburn, Douglas Whitman, F. William McCarty, and Bartley A. Brennan, *Modern Business Law* (New York: Random House, 1989), 164.

3 Bartley A. Brennan and Nancy K. Kubasek, *The Legal Environment of Business* (New York: McGraw-Hill, 1990), 183.

4 "'03 Derby Controversy: Santos Seeks $48M in Damages for Libel," *Newsday*, 10 May 2004 [accessed 16 May 2004] www.highbeam.com.

5 Brennan and Kubasek, *The Legal Environment of Business*, 184.

6 "Reasonable Product-Liability Reform," *Nation's Business*, 1 September 1997, 88.

7 Rick Schmitt and Scott Hensley, "Woman Wins $56.6 Million in AHP Case," *Wall Street Journal*, 9 April 2001, B7; David J. Morrow, "Maker of Diet Pill Agrees to Pay $3.75 Billion to Settle Liability Case," *New York Times* website [accessed 8 October 1999] www.nytimes.com.

8 Dunfee et al., *Modern Business Law*, 569.

9 Dunfee et al., *Modern Business Law*, 236.

10 Ethan A. Blumen, "Legal Land Mines," *Business 96*, June/July 1996, 53.

11 Dunfee et al., *Modern Business Law*, 284–297; Brennan and Kubasek, *The Legal Environment of Business*, 125–127; Douglas Whitman and John William Gergacz, *The Legal Environment of Business*, 2d ed. (New York: Random House, 1988), 196–197; *The Lawyer's Almanac* (Englewood Cliffs, N.J.: Prentice Hall Law & Business, 1991), 888.

12 Brennan and Kubasek, *The Legal Environment of Business*, 128.

13 James Bates, "Disney Settles Up with Its Former Studio Boss," *Los Angeles Times*, 8 July 1999, 1; Bruce Orwall, "Katzenberg Wins Round in Lawsuit with Walt Disney," *Wall Street Journal*, 20 May 1999, B161.

14 Roy Furchgott, "Opposition Builds to Mandatory Arbitration at Work," *New York Times*, 20 July 1997, F11; Barry Meier, "In Fine Print, Customers Lose Ability to Sue," *New York Times*, 10 March 1997, A1, C7.

15 Richard M. Steuer, *A Guide to Marketing Law: What Every Seller Should Know* (New York: Harcourt Brace Jovanovich, 1986), 151–152.

16 Dunfee et al., *Modern Business Law*, 745, 749.

17 Brennan and Kubasek, *The Legal Environment of Business*, 160; Whitman and Gergacz, *The Legal Environment of Business*, 260.

18 Henry R. Cheeseman, *Business Law*, (Upper Saddle River, N.J.: Prentice Hall, 2001), 324.

19 James Connell, "Tech Brief: Apple Look-Alike Suit Settled," *International Herald Tribune*, 7 June 2001, 17; David P. Hamilton, "Apples Sues Future Power and Daewood, Alleging They Copied Design of iMac," *Wall Street Journal*, 2 July 1999, B4; "Injunction Is Issued Against Makers of iMac Look Alikes," *Wall Street Journal*, 9 November 1999, B25.

20 Cheeseman, *Business Law*, 330.

21 Jerry M. Rosenberg, *Dictionary of Business and Management* (New York: Wiley, 1983), 340.

Exhibit B.2 adapted from BankruptcyData.com [accessed 16 May 2004] www.bankruptcydata.com.

Appendix D

1 Human Resources and Skills Development Canada website [accessed 27 April 2005] www.hrsdc.gc.ca/en/cs/comm/hrsd/about_us.shtml

2 Virginia Galt, "It's Who You Know Knows You," *The Globe and Mail*, 15 September 2004, C1.

3 Cheryl L. Noll, "Collaborating with the Career Planning and Placement Center in

the Job-Search Project," *Business Communication Quarterly, 58*(3) (1995): 53–55.
4 Virginia Galt, "Job Seekers Can Get Free Advice On-Line," *The Globe and Mail,* 21 August 2004, C1.
5 Jeanette Borzoby, "On-Line Networking Turns Friendship into Jobs," *The Globe and Mail,* 8 December 2004, C8.
6 Jobset.ca website [accessed 12 December 2004] www.jobsetc.ca/category_drilldown.jsp?category_id=113&crumb=1&crumb=16
7 Rockport Institute, "How to Write a Masterpiece of a Résumé" [accessed 12 December 2004] www.rockportinstitute.com/resumes.html
8 Beverly Culwell-Block and Jean Anna Sellers, "Résumé Content and Format—Do the Authorities Agree?" *Bulletin of the Association for Business Communication, 57*(4) (1994): 27–30.
9 Janice Tovey, "Using Visual Theory in the Creation of Résumés: A Bibliography," *The Bulletin of the Association for Business Communication, 54*(3) (September 1991): 97–99.
10 Pam Stanley-Weigand, "Organizing the Writing of Your Resume," *Bulletin of the Association for Business Communication, 54*(3) (September 1991): 11–12.
11 Susan Vaughn, "Answer the Hard Questions Before Asked," *Los Angeles Times,* 29 July 2001, W1–W2.
12 Richard H. Beatty and Nicholas C. Burkholder, *The Executive Career Guide for MBAs* (New York: Wiley, 1996), 133.
13 Adapted from Burdette E. Bostwick, *How to Find the Job You've Always Wanted* (New York: Wiley, 1982), 69–70.
14 Beatty and Burkholder, *The Executive Career Guide for MBAs,* 151.
15 Rockport Institute, "How to Write a Masterpiece of a Résumé."
16 William J. Banis, "The Art of Writing Job-Search Letters," *CPC Annual,* 36th ed., 2 (1992): 42–50.
17 Virginia Galt, "Some Job Candidates Getting Too Slick for Interviewers," *The Globe and Mail,* 7 February 2005, B1.
18 Robert Gifford, Cheuk Fan Ng, and Margaret Wilkinson, "Nonverbal Cues in the Employment Interview: Links between Applicant Qualities and Interviewer Judgments," *Journal of Applied Psychology, 70*(4) (1985): 729.
19 Wallace Immen, "How the Executive Job Interview Has Changed," *The Globe and Mail,* 28 August 2004, B9.
20 Amanda Bennett, "GE Redesigns Rungs of Career Ladder," *Wall Street Journal,* 15 March 1993, B1, B3.
21 Robin White Goode, "International and Foreign Language Skills Have an Edge," *Black Enterprise,* May 1995, 53.
22 Nancy M. Somerick, "Managing a Communication Internship Program," *Bulletin of the Association for Business Communication, 56*(3) (1993): 10–20.
23 Cheryl L. Noll, "Collaborating with the Career Planning and Placement Center in the Job-Search Project," *Business Communication Quarterly, 58*(3) (1995): 53–55.

Exhibit D.1 adapted from Daniel E. Hecker, "Occupational Employment Projections to 2012," *Monthly Labor Review,* February 2004, 80-105.

Exhibit D.7 adapted from Marilyn Sherman, "Questions R Us: What to Ask at a Job Interview," *Career World,* January 2004, 20; H. Lee Rust, *Job Search: The Complete Manual for Jobseekers* (New York: American Management Association, 1979), 56.

Glossary

absolute advantage A nation's ability to produce a particular product with fewer resources per unit of output than any other nation.

accountability Obligation to report results to supervisors or team members and to justify outcomes that fall below expectations.

accounting equation Basic accounting equation that assets equal liabilities plus owners' equity.

accounting Measuring, interpreting, and communicating financial information to support internal and external decision making.

accounts receivable turnover ratio Measure of time a company takes to turn its accounts receivable into cash, calculated by dividing sales by the average value of accounts receivable for a period.

accrual basis Accounting method in which revenue is recorded when a sale is made and an expense is recorded when it is incurred.

acquisition Form of business combination in which one company buys another company's voting stock.

activity ratios Ratios that measure the effectiveness of the firm's use of its resources.

administrative skills Technical skills in information gathering, data analysis, planning, organizing, and other aspects of managerial work.

advertising Paid, non-personal communication to a target market from an identified sponsor using mass communications channels.

analytic system Production process that breaks incoming materials into various component products and divisional patterns simultaneously.

arbitration Process for resolving a labour contract dispute in which an impartial third party studies the issues and makes a binding decision.

assets Any things of value owned or leased by a business.

auction exchange Centralized marketplace where securities are traded by specialists on behalf of investors.

audit Formal evaluation of the fairness and reliability of a client's financial statements.

authority Power granted by the organization to make decisions, take actions, and allocate resources to accomplish goals.

authorized stock Maximum number of ownership shares into which a corporation's board of directors decides the business can be divided.

autocratic leaders Leaders who do not involve others in decision making.

automated teller machines (ATMs) Electronic terminals that permit people to perform basic banking transactions 24 hours a day without a human teller.

balance of payments Sum of all payments one nation receives from other nations minus the sum of all payments it makes to other nations, over some specified period of time.

balance of trade Total value of the products a nation exports minus the total value of the products it imports, over some period of time.

balance sheet Statement of a firm's financial position on a particular date; also known as a *statement of financial position.*

barriers to entry Factors that make it difficult to launch a business in a particular industry.

bear market Falling stock market.

behaviour modification Systematic use of rewards and punishments to change human behaviour.

behavioural segmentation Categorization of customers according to their relationship with products or response to product characteristics.

board of directors Group of people, elected by the shareholders, who have the ultimate authority in guiding the affairs of a corporation.

bond Method of funding in which the issuer borrows from an investor and provides a written promise to make regular interest payments and repay the borrowed amount in the future.

bonus Cash payment, in addition to the regular wage or salary, that serves as a reward for achievement.

bookkeeping Record keeping, clerical aspect of accounting.

boycott Union activity in which members and sympathizers refuse to buy or handle the product of a target company.

brainstorming A preliminary technique often used in group situations to generate and develop ideas in a non-threatening environment.

brand equity The extra value a brand name provides to a product beyond its functional benefits.

brand mark Portion of a brand that cannot be expressed verbally.

brand names Portion of a brand that can be expressed orally, including letters, words, or numbers.

brand A name, term, sign, symbol, design, or combination of these used to identify the products of a firm and to differentiate them from competing products.

broker An expert who has passed specific tests and is registered to trade securities for investors.

budget Planning and control tool that reflects expected revenues, operating expenses, and cash receipts and outlays.

bull market Rising stock market.

business cycle Fluctuations in the rate of growth that an economy experiences over a period of several years.

business plan A written document that provides an orderly statement of a company's goals and how it intends to achieve those goals.

business Activity and enterprise that provides goods and services a society needs.

business-to-business e-commerce Electronic commerce that involves transactions between companies and their suppliers, manufacturers, or other companies.

business-to-consumer e-commerce Electronic commerce that involves transactions between businesses and the end user or consumer.

calendar year Twelve-month accounting period that begins on January 1 and ends on December 31.

Canada Savings Bonds Debt securities issued by the Bank of Canada that are usually held in excess of one year.

capacity planning A long-term strategic decision that determines the level of resources available to an organization to meet customer demand.

capital budgeting Process for evaluating proposed investments in select projects that provide the best long-term financial return.

capital investments Money paid to acquire something of permanent value in a business.

capital The physical, human-made elements used to produce goods and services, such as factories and computers; can also refer to the funds that finance the operations of a business.

capital-intensive businesses Businesses that require large investments in capital assets.

capitalism Economic system based on economic freedom and competition.

cash basis Accounting method in which revenue is recorded when payment is received and an expense is recorded when cash is paid.

cause-related marketing Identification and marketing of a social issue, cause, or idea to selected target markets.

cellular layout Method of arranging a facility so that parts with similar shapes or processing requirements are processed together in work centres.

centralization Concentration of decision-making authority at the top of the organization.

certified general accountants (CGAs) Accountants who have fulfilled the requirements for certification as a general accountant.

certified management accountants (CMAs) Accountants who have fulfilled the requirements for certification as a specialist in management accounting.

chain of command Pathway for the flow of authority from one management level to the next.

chartered accountants (CAs) Professionally licensed accountants who meet certain requirements for education and experience and who pass a comprehensive examination.

cheques Written orders that tell the user's bank to pay a specific amount to a particular individual or business.

chief executive officer (CEO) Person appointed by a corporation's board of directors to carry out the board's policies and supervise the activities of the corporation.

close the books The act of transferring net revenue and expense account balances to retained earnings for the period.

coaching Helping employees reach their highest potential by meeting with them, discussing problems that hinder their ability to work effectively, and offering suggestions and encouragement to overcome these problems.

co-branding Partnership between two or more companies to closely link their brand names together for a single product.

code of ethics Written statement setting forth the principles that guide an organization's decisions.

cognitive dissonance Anxiety following a purchase that prompts buyers to seek reassurance about the purchase; commonly known as buyer's remorse.

cohesiveness A measure of how committed the team members are to their team's goals.

collective bargaining Process used by unions and management to negotiate work contracts.

commissions Payments to employees equal to a certain percentage of sales made.

committee Team that may become a permanent part of the organization and is designed to deal with regularly recurring tasks.

common stock Shares whose owners have voting rights and have the last claim on distributed profits and assets.

communism Economic system in which all productive resources are owned and operated by the government, to the elimination of private property.

comparative advantage theory Theory that states that a country should produce and sell to other countries those items it produces most efficiently.

compensation Money, benefits, and services paid to employees for their work.

competition Rivalry among businesses for the same customer.

competitive advantage Ability to perform in one or more ways that competitor cannot match.

computer-aided design (CAD) Use of computer graphics and mathematical modelling in the development of products.

computer-aided engineering (CAE) Use of computers to test products without building an actual model.

computer-aided manufacturing (CAM) Use of computers to control production equipment.

computer-integrated manufacturing (CIM) Computer-based systems, including CAD and CAM, that coordinate and control all elements of design and production.

conceptual skills Ability to understand the relationship of parts to the whole.

conflict of interest Situation in which a business decision may be influenced by the potential for personal gain.

consumer price index (CPI) Monthly statistic that measures changes in the prices of about 400 goods and services that consumers buy.

consumer promotion Sales promotion aimed at final consumers.

consumerism Movement that pressures businesses to consider consumer needs and interests.

consumer-to-consumer e-commerce Electronic commerce that involves transactions between consumers.

contingency leadership Adapting the leadership style to what is most appropriate, given current business conditions.

controller Highest-ranking accountant in a company, responsible for overseeing all accounting functions.

controlling Process of measuring progress against goals and objectives and correcting deviations if results are not as expected.

convertible bonds Corporate bonds that can be exchanged at the owner's discretion into common stock of the issuing company.

cooperative advertising Joint efforts between local and national advertisers, in which producers of nationally sold products share the costs of local advertising with local merchants and wholesalers.

corporate culture A set of shared values and norms that support the management system and that guide management and employee behaviour.

corporation Legally chartered enterprise having most of the legal rights of a person, including the right to conduct business, to own and sell property, to borrow money, and to sue or be sued; owners of the corporation enjoy limited liability.

cost accounting Area of accounting focusing on the calculation of manufacturing and storage costs of products for use or sale in a business.

cost of goods sold Cost of producing or acquiring a company's products for sale during a given period.

coupons Certificates that offer discounts on particular items and are redeemed at the time of purchase.

cracking Entering a computer network for non-destructive reasons, such as to play a prank.

credit cards Plastic cards that allow the user to buy now and repay the loaned amount at a future date.

crisis management System for minimizing the harm that might result from some unusually threatening situations.

critical path In a PERT network diagram, the sequence of operations that requires the longest time to complete.

cross-functional teams Teams that draw together employees from different functional areas.

cross-promotion Jointly advertising two or more non-competing brands.

currency Bills and coins that make up a country's cash money.

current assets Cash and items that can be turned into cash within one year.

current liabilities Obligations that must be met within a year.

current ratio Measure of a firm's short-term liquidity, calculated by dividing current assets by current liabilities.

customer divisions Divisional structure that focuses on customers or clients.

customer service Efforts a company makes to satisfy its customers to help them realize the greatest possible value from the products they are purchasing.

database marketing Process of building, maintaining, and using customer databases for the purpose of contacting customers and transacting business.

day order Any order to buy or sell a security that automatically expires if not executed on the day the order is placed.

dealer exchanges Decentralized marketplaces where securities are bought and sold by dealers out of their own inventories.

debentures Corporate bonds backed only by the reputation of the issuer.

debit cards Plastic cards that allow the bank to take money from the user's demand-deposit account and transfer it to a retailer's account.

debt ratios Ratios that measure a firm's reliance on debt financing of its operations (sometimes called *leverage ratios*).

debt-to-equity ratio Measure of the extent to which a business is financed by debt as opposed to invested capital, calculated by dividing the company's total liabilities by owners' equity.

debt-to-total-assets ratio Measure of a firm's ability to carry long-term debt, calculated by dividing total liabilities by total assets.

decentralization Delegation of decision-making authority to employees in lower-level positions.

decision making Process of identifying a decision situation, analyzing the problem, weighing the alternatives, choosing an alternative and implementing it, and evaluating the results.

deflation Economic condition in which prices fall steadily throughout the economy.

delegation Assignment of work and the authority and responsibility required to complete it.

demand deposits Money that can be used by the customer at any time, such as chequing accounts.

demand Buyers' willingness and ability to purchase products.

democratic leaders Leaders who delegate authority and involve employees in decision making.

demographics Study of statistical characteristics of a population.

departmentalization by division Grouping departments according to similarities in product, process, customer, or geography.

departmentalization by function Grouping workers according to their similar skills, resource use, and expertise.

departmentalization by matrix Assigning employees to both a functional group and a project team (thus using functional and divisional patterns simultaneously).

departmentalization by network Electronically connecting separate companies that perform selected tasks for a small headquarters organization.

departmentalization Grouping people within an organization according to function, division, matrix, or network.

depreciation Accounting procedure for systematically spreading the cost of a tangible asset over its estimated useful life.

direct mail Advertising sent directly to potential customers.

direct marketing Direct communication other than personal sales contacts designed to effect a measurable response.

discount pricing Offering a reduction in price.

discretionary order Market order that allows the broker to decide when to trade a security.

discrimination In a social and economic sense, denial of opportunities to individuals on the basis of some characteristic that has no bearing on their ability to perform in a job.

dispatching Issuing work orders and schedules to department heads and supervisors.

distribution centres Warehouse facilities that specialize in collecting and shipping merchandise.

distribution channels Systems for moving goods and services from producers to customers; also known as marketing channels.

distribution mix Combination of intermediaries and channels a producer uses to get a product to end-users.

distribution strategy Firm's overall plan for moving products to intermediaries and final customers.

diversity initiatives Company policies designed to enhance opportunities for minorities and to promote understanding of diverse cultures, customs, and talents.

dividends Distributions of corporate assets to shareholders in the form of cash or other assets.

double-entry bookkeeping Way of recording financial transactions that requires two entries for every transaction so that the accounting equation is always kept in balance.

dumping Charging less than the actual cost or less than the home country's price for goods sold in other countries.

earnings per share Measure of a firm's profitability for each share of outstanding stock, calculated by dividing net income after taxes by the average number of shares of common stock outstanding.

ecology Study of the relationships among living things in the water, air, and soil, their environments, and the nutrients that support them.

economic indicators Statistics that measure variables in the economy.

economic system Means by which a society distributes its resources to satisfy its people's needs.

economics The study of how society uses scarce resources to produce and distribute goods and services.

economies of scale Savings from manufacturing, marketing, or buying in large quantities.

electronic business (e-business) A company that has transformed its key business processes to incorporate Internet technology into every phase of the operation.

electronic commerce (e-commerce) The general term for the buying and selling of goods and services on the Internet.

electronic communication networks (ECNs) Internet-based networks that match up buy and sell orders without using an intermediary.

electronic data interchange (EDI) Information systems that transmit documents such as invoices and purchase orders between computers, thereby lowering ordering costs and paperwork.

electronic funds transfer systems (EFTS) Computerized systems for completing financial transactions.

embargo Total ban on trade with a particular nation (a sanction) or of a particular product.

employee assistance programs (EAPs) Company-sponsored counselling or referral plans for employees with personal problems.

employee benefits Compensation other than wages, salaries, and incentive programs.

employee share-ownership plan (ESOP) Program enabling employees to become partial owners of a company.

enterprise resource planning (ERP) A comprehensive database system that includes information about the firm's suppliers and customers as well as data generated internally.

entrepreneurs People who accept the risk of failure in the private enterprise system.

equilibrium price Point at which quantity supplied equals quantity demanded.

ethical dilemma Situation in which both sides of an issue can be supported with valid arguments.

ethical lapse Situation in which an individual makes a decision that is morally wrong, illegal, or unethical.

ethics The rules or standards governing the conduct of a person or group.

euro The currency used by 12 European nations.

exchange process Act of obtaining a desired object from another party by offering something of value in return.

exchange rate Rate at which the money of one country is traded for the money of another.

exclusive distribution Market coverage strategy that gives intermediaries exclusive rights to sell a product in a specific geographical area.

expenses Costs created in the process of generating revenues.

exporting Selling and shipping goods or services to another country.

extranet Similar to an intranet, but extending the network to select people outside the organization.

factors of production Basic inputs that a society uses to produce goods and services, including natural resources, labour, capital, entrepreneurship, and knowledge.

financial accounting Area of accounting concerned with preparing financial information for users outside the organization.

financial analysis Process of evaluating a company's performance and analyzing the costs and benefits of a strategic action.

financial control The process of analyzing and adjusting the basic financial plan to correct for forecasted events that do not materialize.

financial management Effective acquisition and use of money.

financial plan A forecast of financial requirements and the financing sources to be used.

firewall Computer hardware and software that protects part or all of a private computer network attached to the Internet by preventing public users from accessing it.

first-line managers Those at the lowest level of the management hierarchy; they supervise the operating employees and implement the plans set at the higher management levels; also called supervisory managers.

fiscal policy Use of government revenue collection and spending to influence the business cycle.

fiscal year Any 12 consecutive months used as an accounting period.

fixed assets Assets retained for long-term use, such as land, buildings, machinery, and equipment; also referred to as *property, plant, and equipment.*

fixed-position layout Method of arranging a facility so that the product is stationary and equipment and personnel come to it.

flat organizations Organizations with a wide span of management and few hierarchical levels.

flexible manufacturing system (FMS) Production system using computer-controlled machines that can adapt to various versions of the same operation.

flextime Scheduling system in which employees are allowed certain options regarding time of arrival and departure.

foreign direct investment (FDI) Investment of money by foreign companies in domestic business enterprises.

form utility Consumer value created by converting raw materials and other inputs into finished goods and services.

formal organization A framework officially established by managers for accomplishing tasks that lead to achieving the organization's goals.

franchise Business arrangement in which a small business obtains the rights to sell the goods or services of the supplier (franchisor).

franchisee Small business owner who contracts for the right to sell goods or services of the supplier (franchisor) in exchange for some payment.

franchisor Supplier that grants a franchise to an individual or group (franchisee) in exchange for payments.

free riders Team members who do not contribute sufficiently to the group's activities because members are not being held individually accountable for their work.

free trade International trade without restrictive measures.

free-market system Economic system in which decisions about what to produce and in what quantities are decided by the market's buyers and sellers.

functional teams Teams whose members come from a single functional department and that are based on the organization's vertical structure.

Gantt chart Bar chart used to control schedules by showing how long each part of a production process should take and when it should take place.

general expenses Operating expenses, such as office and administrative expenses, not directly associated with creating or marketing a good or a service.

general partnership Partnership in which all partners have the right to participate as co-owners and are individually liable for the business's debts.

generally accepted accounting principles (GAAP) Professionally approved Canadian standards and practices used by accountants in the preparation of financial statements.

generic products Products characterized by a plain label, with no advertising and no brand name.

geodemographics Method of combining geographical data with demographic data to develop profiles of neighbourhood segments.

geographic divisions Divisional structure based on location of operations.

geographic segmentation Categorization of customers according to their geographical location.

glass ceiling Invisible barrier attributable to subtle discrimination that keeps women (and minorities) out of the top positions in business.

globalization Tendency of the world's economies to act as a single interdependent economy.

goal Broad, long-range target or aim.

goods-producing businesses Businesses that produce tangible products.

gross domestic product (GDP) Dollar value of all the final goods and services produced by businesses located within a nation's borders; excludes receipts from overseas operations of domestic companies.

gross national product (GNP) Dollar value of all the final goods and services produced by domestic businesses that includes receipts from overseas operations and excludes receipts from foreign-owned businesses within a nation's borders.

gross profit Amount remaining when the cost of goods sold is deducted from net sales; also known as *gross margin.*

hacking Breaking into a computer network to steal, delete, or change data.

hostile takeovers Situations in which an outside party buys enough stock in a corporation to take control against the wishes of the board of directors and corporate officers.

human relations Interaction among people within an organization for the purpose of achieving organizational and personal goals.

human resources management (HRM) Specialized function of planning that focuses on obtaining employees, overseeing their training, and evaluating and compensating them.

human resources All of the people who work for an organization.

hygiene factors Aspects of the work environment that are associated with dissatisfaction.

importing Purchasing goods or services from another country and bringing them into one's own country.

incentives Cash payments to employees who produce at a desired level or whose unit (often the company as a whole) produces at a desired level.

income statement Financial record of a company's revenues, expenses, and profits over a given period of time.

income trust Legal entities that hold cash-generating businesses in trust and distribute the majority of income to unit holders in the form of dividends.

incubators Facilities that house small businesses during their early growth phase.

inflation Economic condition in which prices rise steadily throughout the economy.

informal organization Network of informal employee interactions that are not defined by the formal structure.

initial public offering (IPO) Corporation's first offering of stock to the public.

injunction Court order prohibiting certain actions by striking workers.

insider trading The use of unpublicized information that an individual gains from the course of his or her job to benefit from fluctuations in the stock market.

insider trading Use of material nonpublic information to make an investment profit.

institutional advertising Advertising that seeks to create goodwill and to build a desired image for a company rather than to sell specific products.

integrated marketing communications (IMC) Strategy of coordinating and integrating communications and promotional efforts with customers to ensure greater efficiency and effectiveness.

intensive distribution Market coverage strategy that tries to place a product in as many outlets as possible.

internal auditors Employees who analyze and evaluate a company's operations and data to determine their accuracy.

interpersonal skills Skills required to understand other people and to interact effectively with them.

intranet A private network, set up within a corporation or organization, that operates over the Internet and may be used to link geographically remote sites.

inventory control System for determining the right quantity of various items to have on hand and keeping track of their location, use, and condition.

inventory turnover ratio Measure of the time a company takes to turn its inventory into sales, calculated by dividing cost of goods sold by the average value of inventory for a period.

inventory Goods kept in stock for the production process or for sales to final customers.

ISO 9000 Global standards set by the International Organization for Standardization establishing a minimum level of acceptable quality.

issued stock Portion of authorized stock sold to and held by shareholders.

job analysis Process by which jobs are studied to determine the tasks and dynamics involved in performing them.

job description Statement of the tasks involved in a given job and the conditions under which the holder of the job will work.

job enrichment Reducing work specialization and making work more meaningful by adding to the responsibilities of each job.

job redesign Designing a better fit between employees' skills and their work to increase job satisfaction.

job sharing Splitting a single full-time job between two employees for their convenience.

job specification Statement describing the kind of person who would best fit the job—including skills, education, and previous experience.

joint venture Cooperative partnership in which organizations share investment costs, risks, management, and profits in the development, production, or selling of products.

just-in-time (JIT) system Continuous system that pulls materials through the production process, making sure that all materials arrive just when they are needed with minimal inventory and waste.

knowledge Expertise gained through experience or association.

labour unions Organizations of employees formed to protect and advance their members' interests.

labour-intensive businesses Businesses in which labour costs are more significant than capital costs.

laissez-faire leaders Leaders who leave the actual decision making up to employees.

layoffs Termination of employees for economic or business reasons.

lead time Period that elapses between the ordering of materials and their arrival from the supplier.

leading Process of guiding and motivating people to work toward organizational goals.

lease Legal agreement that obligates the user of an asset to make payments to the owner of the asset in exchange for using it.

leveraged buyout (LBO) Situation in which individuals or a group of investors purchase a company primarily with debt secured by the company's assets.

liabilities Claims against a firm's assets by creditors.

licensing Agreement to produce and market another company's product in exchange for a royalty or fee.

limit order Market order that stipulates the highest or lowest price at which the customer is willing to trade securities.

limited partnership Partnership composed of one or more general partners and one or more partners whose liability is usually limited to the amount of their capital investment.

line of credit Arrangement in which the financial institution makes money available for use at any time after a loan has been approved.

line organization Chain-of-command system that establishes a clear line of authority flowing from the top down.

line-and-staff organization Organization system that has a clear chain of command but that also includes functional groups of people who provide advice and specialized services.

liquidity ratios Ratios that measure a firm's ability to meet its short-term obligations when they are due.

liquidity The level of ease with which an asset can be converted to cash.

local advertising Advertising sponsored by a local merchant.

lockouts Management tactics in which union members are prevented from entering a business during a strike.

logistics The planning and movement of goods and related information throughout the supply chain.

long-term liabilities Obligations that fall due more than a year from the date of the balance sheet.

management accounting Area of accounting concerned with preparing data for use by managers within the organization.

management by objectives (MBO) A motivational tool whereby managers and employees work together to structure personal goals and objectives for every individual, department, and project to mesh with the organization's goals.

management pyramid Organizational structure comprising top, middle, and lower management.

management Process of coordinating resources to meet organizational goals.

manufacturing resource planning (MRP II) Computer-based system that integrates data from all departments to manage inventory and production planning and control.

margin trading Borrowing money from brokers to buy stock, paying interest on the borrowed money, and leaving the stock with the broker as collateral.

market indexes Measures of market activity calculated from the prices of a selection of securities.

market makers Registered representatives who trade securities from their own inventories on dealer exchanges, making a ready market for buyers and sellers.

market order Authorization for a broker to buy or sell securities at the best price that can be negotiated at the moment.

market segmentation Division of total market into smaller, relatively homogeneous groups.

market share A firm's portion of the total sales in a market.

market People or businesses that need or want a product and have the money to buy it.

marketable securities Stocks, bonds, and other investments that can be turned into cash quickly.

marketing concept Approach to business management that stresses customer needs and wants, seeks long-term profitability, and integrates marketing with other functional units within the organization.

marketing intermediaries Business people and organizations that channel goods and services from producers to consumers.

marketing mix The four key elements of marketing strategy: product, price, distribution (place), and promotion.

marketing research The collection and analysis of information for making marketing decisions.

marketing strategy Overall plan for marketing a product.

marketing Process of planning and executing the conception, pricing, promotion, and distribution of ideas, goods, and services to create and maintain relationships that satisfy individual and organizational objectives.

mass customization Producing customized goods and services through mass production techniques.

mass production Manufacturing uniform products in great quantities.

matching principle Fundamental principle requiring that expenses incurred in producing revenue be deducted from the revenues they generate during an accounting period.

material requirements planning (MRP) Method of getting the correct materials where they are needed, on time, and without carrying unnecessary inventory.

materials handling Movement of goods within a firm's warehouse terminal, factory, or store.

media mix Combination of various media options that a company uses in an advertising campaign.

media Communications channels, such as newspapers, radio, and television.

mediation Process for resolving a labour contract dispute in which a neutral third party meets with both sides and attempts to steer them toward a solution.

mentor Experienced manager or employee with a wide network of industry colleagues who can explain office politics, serve as a role model for appropriate business behaviour, and help other employees negotiate the corporate structure.

merger Form of business combination in which two companies combine forces to create a new single entity.

middle managers Those in the middle of the management hierarchy; they develop plans to implement the goals of top managers and coordinate the work of first-line managers.

mission statement A statement of the organization's purpose, basic goals, and philosophies.

mobile commerce Transaction of electronic commerce using wireless devices and wireless Internet access instead of PC-based technology..

monetary policy Government policy and actions taken by the Bank of Canada to regulate the nation's money supply.

money Anything generally accepted as a means of paying for goods and services.

money-market funds Mutual funds that invest in short-term securities and other liquid investments.

monopolistic competition Situation in which many sellers differentiate their products from those of competitors in at least some small way.

monopoly Market in which there are no direct competitors so that one company dominates.

morale Attitude an individual has toward his or her job and employer.

motivation Inner force that moves someone to take action.

motivators Factors of human relations in business that may increase motivation.

multinational corporations (MNCs) Companies with operations in more than one country.

mutual funds Financial organization pooling money to invest in diversified blends of stocks, bonds, or other securities.

NASDAQ (National Association of Securities Dealers Automated Quotations) National over-the-counter securities trading network.

national advertising Advertising sponsored by companies that sell products on a nationwide basis; refers to the geographic reach of the advertiser, not the geographic coverage of the ad.

national brands Brands owned by the manufacturers and distributed nationally.

natural resources Land, forests, minerals, water, and other tangible assets usable in their natural state.

need Difference between a person's actual state and his or her ideal state; provides the basic motivation to make a purchase.

net income Profit earned or loss incurred by a firm, determined by subtracting expenses from revenues; also called the *bottom line.*

news conference Gathering of media representatives at which companies announce new information; also called a press briefing.

news release Brief statement or video program released to the press announcing new products, management changes, sales performance, and other potential news items.

non-profit organizations Firms whose primary objective is something other than returning a profit to their owners.

norms Informal standards of conduct that guide team behaviour.

objective Specific, short-range target or aim.

oligopoly Market dominated by a few producers.

open order Limit order that does not expire at the end of a trading day.

operating expenses All costs of operation that are not included under cost of goods sold.

operational plans Plans that lay out the actions and the resource allocation needed to achieve operational objectives and to support tactical plans; usually defined for less than one year and developed by first-line managers.

organization chart Diagram showing how employees and tasks are grouped and where the lines of communication and authority flow.

organization structure Framework enabling managers to divide responsibilities, ensure employee accountability, and distribute decision-making authority.

organizing Process of arranging resources to carry out the organization's plans.

orientation Session or procedure to introduce a new employee to the organization and its procedures.

outsource Subcontract work to outside companies (often in other countries).

over-the-counter (OTC) market Network of dealers who trade securities on computerized linkups rather than a trading floor.

owners' equity Portion of a company's assets that belongs to the owners after obligations to all creditors have been met.

par value As shown on the stock certificate, a value assigned to a stock for use in bookkeeping and in calculating dividends.

parent company Company that owns most, if not all, of another company's stock and takes an active part in managing that other company.

participative management Sharing information with employees and involving them in decision making.

partnership Unincorporated business owned and operated by two or more people under a voluntary legal association.

penetration pricing Introducing a new product at a low price in hopes of building sales volume quickly.

pension plan Company-sponsored program for providing retirees with income.

performance appraisal Evaluation of an employee's work according to specific criteria.

perpetual inventory System that uses computers to monitor inventory levels and automatically generate purchase orders when supplies are needed.

personal selling In-person communication between a seller and one or more potential buyers.

persuasive advertising Advertising designed to encourage product sampling and brand switching.

philanthropic Descriptive term for altruistic actions such as donating money, time, goods, or services to charitable, humanitarian, or educational institutions.

physical distribution All activities required to move finished products from the producer to the consumer.

picketing Strike activity in which union members march before company entrances to protest against an employer.

place marketing Marketing efforts to attract people and organizations to a particular geographical area.

place utility Consumer value added by making a product available in a convenient location.

planned system Economic system in which the government controls most of the factors of production and regulates their allocation.

planning Establishing objectives and goals for an organization and determining the best ways to accomplish them.

point-of-purchase display Advertising or other display materials set up at retail locations to promote products to potential customers as they are making their purchase decisions.

pollution Damage to or destruction of the natural environment caused by the discharge of harmful substances.

positioning Using promotion, product, distribution, and price to differentiate a good or service from those of competitors in the mind of the prospective buyer.

possession utility Consumer value created when someone takes ownership of a product.

preferred stock Shares that give their owners first claim on a company's dividends and assets after paying all debts.

premiums Free or bargain-priced items offered to encourage consumers to buy a product.

price elasticity A measure of the sensitivity of demand to changes in price.

price The amount of money charged for a product or service.

price-earnings ratio Ratio calculated by dividing a stock's market price by its prior year's earnings per share.

primary market Market where firms sell new securities issued publicly for the first time.

prime interest rate Lowest interest rate banks offer on short-term loans to preferred borrowers.

principal Amount of money a corporation borrows from an investor through the sale of a bond.

private accountants In-house accountants employed by organizations and businesses other than a public accounting firm; also called *corporate accountants*.

private brands Brands that carry the label of a retailer or a wholesaler rather than a manufacturer.

private corporation Company owned by private individuals or companies.

privatizing The conversion of public ownership to private ownership.

problem-solving team Informal team of 5 to 12 employees from the same department who meet voluntarily to find ways of improving quality, efficiency, and the work environment.

process divisions Divisional structure based on the major steps of a production process.

process layout Method of arranging a facility so that production tasks are carried out in separate departments containing specialized equipment and personnel.

product advertising Advertising that tries to sell specific goods or services, generally by describing features, benefits, and, occasionally, price.

product divisions Divisional structure based on the products that are produced by the firm.

product layout Method of arranging a facility so that production proceeds along a line of workstations.

product life cycle Four basic stages through which a product progresses: introduction, growth, maturity, and decline.

product line A series of related products offered by a firm.

product mix Complete list of all products that a company offers for sale.

product Good or service used as the basis of commerce.

production and operations management (POM) Coordination of an organization's resources in manufacturing goods or delivering services.

production forecasts Estimates of how much of a company's goods and services must be produced in order to meet future demand.

production Transformation of resources into goods or services that people need or want.

profit sharing System for distributing a portion of the company's profits to employees.

profit Money that remains after expenses and taxes have been deducted from revenue generated by selling goods and services.

profitability ratios Ratios that measure the overall financial performance of a firm.

program evaluation and review technique (PERT) A planning tool that managers of complex projects use to determine the optimal order of activities, the expected time for project completion, and the best use of resources.

promotion Wide variety of persuasive techniques used by companies to communicate with their target markets and the general public.

promotional mix Particular blend of personal selling, advertising, direct marketing, sales promotion, and public relations that a company uses to reach potential customers.

promotional strategy Statement or document that defines the direction and scope of the promotional activities that a company will use to meet its marketing objectives.

protectionism Government policies aimed at shielding a country's industries from foreign competition.

proxy Document authorizing another person to vote on behalf of a shareholder in a corporation.

psychographics Classification of customers on the basis of their psychological makeup.

public accountants Professionals who provide accounting services to other businesses and individuals for a fee.

public corporation Corporation that actively sells stock on the open market.

public relations Non-sales communication that businesses have with their various audiences (includes both communication with the general public and press relations).

pull strategy Promotional strategy that stimulates consumer demand, which then exerts pressure on wholesalers and retailers to carry a product.

purchasing Acquiring the raw materials, parts, components, supplies, and finished products needed to produce goods and services.

pure competition Situation in which so many buyers and sellers exist that no single buyer or seller can individually influence market prices.

push strategy Promotional approach designed to motivate wholesalers and retailers to push a producer's products to end users.

quality assurance System of policies, practices, and procedures implemented throughout a company to create and produce quality goods and services.

quality control Routine checking and testing of a finished product for quality against an established standard.

quality of work life (QWL) Overall environment that results from job and work conditions.

quality A measure of how closely a product conforms to predetermined standards and customer expectations.

quick ratio Measure of a firm's short-term liquidity, calculated by adding cash, marketable securities, and receivables, then dividing that sum by current liabilities; also known as the *acid-test ratio.*

quotas Fixed limits on the quantity of imports a nation will allow for a specific product.

ratio analysis Use of quantitative measures to evaluate a firm's financial performance.

recession Period during which national income, employment, and production all fall.

recruiting Process of attracting appropriate applicants for an organization's jobs.

relationship marketing A focus on developing and maintaining long-term relationships with customers, suppliers, and distributors for mutual benefit.

reminder advertising Advertising intended to remind existing customers of a product's availability and benefits.

responsibility Obligation to perform the duties and achieve the goals and objectives associated with a particular position.

retailers Firms that sell goods and services to individuals for their own use rather than for resale.

retained earnings The portion of shareholders' equity earned by the company but not distributed to its owners in the form of dividends.

return on investment (ROI) Ratio between net income after taxes and total owners' equity; also known as *return on equity.*

return on sales Ratio between net income after taxes and net sales; also known as *profit margin.*

revenues Amount earned from sales of goods or services and inflow from miscellaneous sources such as interest, rent, and royalties.

robots Programmable machines that can complete a variety of tasks by working with tools and materials.

roles Behavioural patterns associated with or expected of certain positions.

routing Specifying the sequence of operations and the path the work will take through the production facility.

salaries Fixed weekly, monthly, or yearly cash compensation for work.

sales promotion Wide range of events and activities (including coupons, rebates, contests, in-store demonstrations, free samples, trade shows, and point-of-purchase displays) designed to stimulate interest in a product.

scheduling Process of determining how long each production operation takes and then setting a starting and ending time for each.

scientific management Management approach designed to improve employees' efficiency by scientifically studying their work.

secondary market Market where subsequent owners trade previously issued shares of stocks and bonds.

secured bonds Bonds backed by specific assets that will be given to bondholders if the borrowed amount is not repaid.

secured loans Loans backed up with something of value that the lender can claim in case of default, such as a piece of property.

securities Investments such as stocks, bonds, options, futures, and commodities.

selective distribution Market coverage strategy that uses a limited number of outlets to distribute products.

self-managed teams Teams in which members are responsible for an entire process or operation.

selling expenses All operating expenses associated with marketing goods or services.

service businesses Businesses that provide intangible products or perform useful labour on behalf of another.

setup costs Expenses incurred each time a producer organizes resources to begin producing goods or services.

sexism Discrimination on the basis of gender.

sexual harassment Unwelcome sexual advance, request for sexual favours, or other verbal or physical conduct of a sexual nature within the workplace.

shareholders Proportionate owners of a corporation; based on the number of shares held.

short selling Selling stock borrowed from a broker with the intention of buying it back later at a lower price, repaying the broker, and keeping the profit.

skimming Charging a high price for a new product during the introductory stage and lowering the price later.

small business Company that is independently owned and operated, is not dominant in its field, and meets certain criteria for the number of employees and annual sales revenue.

smart cards Plastic cards with embedded computer chips that store money drawn from the user's demand-deposit account as well as information that can be used for purchases.

social audit Assessment of a company's performance in the area of social responsibility.

social responsibility The concern of businesses for the welfare of society as a whole.

socialism Economic system characterized by public ownership and operation of key industries combined with private ownership and operation of less vital industries.

sole proprietorship Business owned by a single individual.

spam Unsolicited "junk" e-mail sent to large numbers of people to promote products or services.

span of management Number of people under one manager's control; also known as span of control.

special-purpose teams Temporary teams that exist outside the formal organization hierarchy and are created to achieve a specific goal.

specialty advertising Advertising that appears on various items such as coffee mugs, pens, and calendars, designed to help keep a company's name in front of customers.

stakeholders Individuals or groups to whom business has a responsibility.

standards Criteria against which performance is measured.

start-up companies New ventures.

statement of cash flows Statement of a firm's cash receipts and cash payments that presents information on its sources and uses of cash.

statistical process control (SPC) Use of random sampling and control charts to monitor the production process.

statistical quality control (SQC) Monitoring all aspects of the production process to see whether the process is operating as it should.

stock certificate Document that proves stock ownership.

stock exchanges Location where traders buy and sell stocks and bonds.

stock options Contract allowing the holder to purchase or sell a certain number of shares of a particular stock at a given price by a certain date.

stock specialist Intermediary who trades in a particular security on the floor of an auction exchange; "buyer of last resort".

stock split Increase in the number of shares of ownership that each stock certificate represents, at a proportionate drop in each share's value.

stock Shares of ownership in a corporation.

stop order An order to sell a stock when its price falls to a particular point to limit an investor's losses.

strategic alliance Long-term relationship in which two or more companies share ideas, resources, and technologies in order to establish competitive advantages.

strategic plans Plans that establish the actions and the resource allocation required to accomplish goals; usually defined for periods of two to five years and developed by top managers.

strike Temporary work stoppage to pressure management to accept the union's demands.

strike-breakers Non-union workers hired to replace striking workers.

subsidiary corporations Corporations whose stock is owned entirely or almost entirely by another corporation.

subsidies Government support provided to businesses in the form of money, tax breaks, or low rate/interest-free loans.

supply Specific quantity of a product that the seller is able and willing to provide.

supply-chain management Integrating all of the facilities, functions, and processes associated with the production of goods and services, from suppliers to customers.

synthetic system Production process that combines two or more materials or components to create finished products; the reverse of an analytic system.

tactical plans Plans that define the actions and the resource allocation necessary to achieve tactical objectives and to support strategic plans; usually defined for a period of one to three years and developed by middle managers.

tall organizations Organizations with a narrow span of management and many hierarchical levels.

target for the overnight rate The midpoint rate the Bank of Canada wants to see in the marketplace for overnight loans.

target markets Specific customer groups or segments to whom a company wants to sell a particular product.

tariffs Taxes levied on imports.

task force Team of people from several departments who are temporarily brought together to address a specific issue.

tax accounting Area of accounting focusing on tax preparation and tax planning.

team A unit of two or more people who share a mission and collective responsibility as they work together to achieve a goal.

technical skills Ability and knowledge to perform the mechanics of a particular job.

telecommute To work from home and communicate with the company's main office via computer and communication devices..

telecommuting Working from home and communicating with the company's main office via computer and communication devices.

telemarketing Selling or supporting the sales process over the telephone.

termination Act of removing an employee through layoff or firing.

Theory X Managerial assumption that employees are irresponsible, are not ambitious, and dislike work; therefore, managers must use force, control, or threats to motivate them.

Theory Y Managerial assumption that employees like work, are naturally committed to certain goals, are capable of creativity, and seek out responsibility under the right conditions.

Theory Z Human relations approach that emphasizes involving employees at all levels and treating them like family.

time deposits Bank accounts that pay interest and require advance notice before money can be withdrawn.

time utility Consumer value added by making a product available at a convenient time.

top managers Those at the highest level of the organization's management hierarchy; they are responsible for setting strategic goals, and they have the most power and responsibility in the organization.

total quality management (TQM) Comprehensive, strategic management approach that builds quality into every organizational process as a way of improving customer satisfaction.

trade allowance Discount offered by producers to wholesalers and retailers.

trade deficit Unfavourable trade balance created when a country imports more than it exports.

trade promotions Sales promotion efforts aimed at convincing distributors or retailers to push a producer's products.

trade surplus Favourable trade balance created when a country exports more than it imports.

trademark Brand that has been given legal protection so that its owner has exclusive rights to its use.

trading blocs Organizations of nations that remove barriers to trade among their members and that establish uniform barriers to trade with non-member nations.

transaction Exchange between parties.

Treasury bills Short-term debt securities issued by the Bank of Canada; also referred to as *T-bills.*

unissued stock Portion of authorized stock not yet sold to shareholders.

Universal Product Codes (UPCs) A bar code on a product's package that provides information read by optical scanners.

unlimited liability Legal condition under which any damages or debts attributable to the business can also be attached to the owner because the two have no separate legal existence.

unsecured loans Loans requiring no collateral but a good credit rating.

utility Power of a good or service to satisfy a human need.

venture capitalists Investment specialists who provide money to finance new businesses or turnarounds in exchange for a portion of the ownership, with the objective of making a considerable profit on the investment; also called VCs.

vertical organization Structure linking activities at the top of the organization with those at the middle and lower levels.

virtual team Team that uses communication technology to bring geographically distant employees together to achieve goals.

viruses Form of computer sabotage embedded in software or passed from one computer to the next that changes or deletes computer files or programs.

vision A viable view of the future that is rooted in but improves on the present.

wages Cash payment based on the number of hours the employee has worked or the number of units the employee has produced.

wants Objects that are desirable in light of a person's experiences, culture, personality and perspective.

warehouse Facility for storing inventory.

wholesalers Firms that sell products to other firms for resale or for organizational use.

work specialization Specialization in or responsibility for some portion of an organization's overall work tasks; also called division of labour.

worker buyout Distribution of financial incentives to employees who voluntarily depart; usually undertaken in order to reduce the payroll.

working capital Current assets minus current liabilities.

worms Form of computer sabotage sent by e-mail that reproduces—taking up network space and snarling connections.

Company/Brand/ Organization Index

Subject Index

Photo Credits

Chapter 1

Page 1, Corbis; pages 2 and 29, CP Archives; page 4, Dakota Studios/Getty Images, Inc. – Liaison; page 9, courtesy of Petro Canada; page 10, CP Archives; page 15 (top), Erik Freeland/Corbis/SABA Press Photos, Inc.; page 15 (bottom), Dennis Brack/Black Star; page 22, Chris Stewart/Black Star

Chapter 2

Page 39 (top), Adrian Brown/CP Archives; page 39 (bottom), © E.R. Degginger/Color Pic, Inc.; pages 40 and 60, Kraipit Phavut/SIPA Press; page 41, Miramax/Imaging/Parkway Productions/The Kobal Collection/Kraychyk, George; page 46 (top), AP/World Wide Photos; page 46 (bottom), www.star alliance.com; page 47, Paul Saneya/CP Archives; page 48, Greg Girard/Contact Press Images Inc.; page 53, courtesy of Coast Forest and Lumber Association; page 54, AP/World Wide Photos; page 58, Horacio Paone/The New York Times

Chapter 3

Page 38 (top), Black Star; page 38 (bottom), Nature Conservancy of Canada; pages 65 and 85, 2003 TELUS Corporate Social Responsibility Report; page 67, CP Archives; page 73, James Estrin/The New York Times; page 75, courtesy of Ethical Funds; page 80, © Basel Action Network (www.ban.org); page 81, © Alene M. McNeill

Chapter 4

Page 93, Corbis; pages 94 and 113, courtesy of Mission ITECH Hockey; page 95, Philip Saltonstall; page 96, © Aux Soins Communicaire 2004; page 98, Sheryl Nadler/CP Archives; page 104, courtesy of Danvin Inc.; page 105, Subway; page 107, courtesy of BDC, Business Development Bank of Canada; page 111, courtesy of Grante Publishing

Chapter 5

Page 117, courtesy of John Krygsman Renovations; pages 118 and 135, CP Archives; page 122, Ryan Remiorz/CP Archives; page 123, captured by Jodi Jacobson; page 124 (top), Jonathan Hayward/CP Archives; page 124 (bottom), CP Archives; page 125, Giboux/Getty Images, Inc. – Liaison; page 127, CP Archives; page 128, Gary I. Rothstein/Corbis/Sygma; page 133, AP/World Wide Photos; page 138, Courtesy of Industry Canada

Chapter 6

Page 145, Corbis; pages 146 and 163, © Suomen Kuvapalveluoy/Corbis Sygma; page 147, CP Archives 66-7; page 151, © Registered trademark of Royal Bank of Canada. Used with permission; page 154, AP/World Wide Photos; page 159, photo courtesy of Harry Rosen Inc.; page 161, William Mercer McLeod

Chapter 7

Page 167, Masterfile Corporation; pages 168 and 186, Wainwright Industries Inc.; page 170, Ryan Remiorz/CP Archives; page 176, Brian Bahr/Getty Images; page 178, © courtesy of Outward Bound; page 180, Barbel Schmidt Photography; page 185, Any Freeberg Photography

Chapter 8

Page 190, Corbis; pages 191 and 212, Eric Butler; page 193, courtesy of Vantage Furniture; page 194, courtesy of Nike Canada; page 195, Jonathan Atkin; page 201, AP/World Wide Photos; page 202, © 2001 Dennis Kleiman; page 206, Reuters/Larry Chan/Hulton/Archive; page 207, Jim West; page 210 (left), © Martyn Goddard/CORBIS; page 210 (right) © Gerard Ceries/Getty Editorial Images; page 215, courtesy of CAE

Chapter 9

Page 220, Lee Snider/The Image Works; pages 221 and 241, Jacques Boisinot/CP Archives; page 225, Tom Hanson/CP Archives; page 228, John Kringas/The Chicago Tribune; page 233, Bill Sikes/AP/World Wide Photos; page 234, Bob Marshak/Photofest; page 236, Nancy Pierce for The New York Times; page 240, Andrew Vaughan/CP Archives; page 242, Ryan Remiorz/CP Archives

Chapter 10

Page 246, Corbis; pages 247 and 264, Michael Newman/PhotoEdit; page 254, John Klicker; page 255, Bank of Montreal Institute for Learning-Management & Teshima

Architects; page 259, CP/Fredericton Daily Gleaner/Kate Leblanc; page 260, Don Hogan Charles/The New York Times; page 261, SAS Institute Inc.

Chapter 11

Page 272, Jose Luis Pelaez, Inc./Corbis; pages 273 and 298 – © 2001 Adobe Systems Incorporated. Used with express permission. All rights reserved. Adobe, Acrobat and Reader is/are [a] registered trademark[s] of Adobe Systems Incorporated in the United States and/or other countries; page 275, Special Olympics Canada; page 277, Danier Leather Inc.; page 278, courtesy of Saturn; page 279, Richard Lam/CP Archives; page 280, © Tim Boyle/Getty Images; page 283, Chuck Stoody/CPArchives; page 288, photo appears courtesy of Marineland, Niagara Falls, Canada; page 291, CP Archives; page 295, David Young-Wolff/Getty Images Inc.-Stone

Chapter 12

Page 302 (top), Getty Images Inc.-Liaison; page 302 (bottom), courtesy of Mazda & Doner Canada; pages 303 and 323, courtesy of Mountain Equipment; page 307, Paul Chiasson/CP Archives; page 308, courtesy of Holt Renfrew; page 310, courtesy of Canada Post; page 312, www.kanetix.ca; page 313, Vans, Inc.; page 316, Paul Chiasson/CP Archives; page 317, CP Archives; page 319, courtesy of Chantal Goncalves Communications

Chapter 13

Page 331 (top), CP Archives; page 331 (bottom), Getty Images, Inc.-Liaison; page 337, SuperStock, Inc.; page 338, Douglas Jones c/o Theispot-Showcase; page 344, Terry Vine/Getty Images Inc.-Stone; page 352, Bob Firth Photography/ImageState/International Stock Photography Ltd.

Chapter 14

Page 359, Masterfile Corporation; pages 360 and 382, © Registered trademark of Royal Bank of Canada. Used with permission; page 364, Michael Krasowitz/Getty Images, Inc.-Taxi; page 366, Ron Sherman, Photographer; pages 367 and 368, BellSouth Advertising & Publishing; page 370, Jeffrey MacMillian, U.S. News & World Report; page 378, Pat Sullivan/AP/World Wide Photos

Appendix B

Page 391, Panos Pictures; page 392, Panos Pictures; page 396, Chris Hondros/Newsmakers/Getty Images, Inc.—Liaison

Appendix D

Page 403, Mark Richards/PhotoEdit; page 411, Mark Wilson Photographer